Routledge International Handbook of the Sociology of Art and Culture

The *Routledge International Handbook of the Sociology of Art and Culture* offers a comprehensive overview of the sociology of art and culture, focusing especially – though not exclusively – on the visual arts, literature, music, and digital culture. Extending, and critiquing, Bourdieu's influential analysis of cultural capital, the distinguished international contributors explore the extent to which cultural omnivorousness has eclipsed highbrow culture, the role of age, gender and class on cultural practices, the character of aesthetic preferences, the contemporary significance of screen culture, and the restructuring of popular culture. The handbook critiques modes of sociological determinism in which cultural engagement is seen as the simple product of the educated middle classes. The contributions explore the critique of Eurocentrism and the global and cosmopolitan dimensions of cultural life. The book focuses particularly on bringing cutting edge 'relational' research methodologies, both qualitative and quantitative, to bear on these debates. This handbook not only describes the field, but also proposes an agenda for its development which will command major international interest.

Laurie Hanquinet is a Lecturer in the Department of Sociology at the University of York. Her main fields of interest are the sociology of culture and art as well as social sciences methodology. She has undertaken research on the visitors of modern and contemporary art museums, on the role of artists in society and on different dimensions of cultural participation. She is the author of *Du musée aux pratiques culturelles. Enquête sur les publics de musées d'art moderne et contemporain* (Éditions de l'Université de Bruxelles 2014).

Mike Savage became Professor of Sociology at the London School of Economics and Political Science (LSE) in September 2012, where he is also Head of Department and Co-Director of the International Inequalities Institute which began in 2015. Previously he was Professor at the University of Manchester, where he had been Director of the ESRC Centre for Research on Socio-Cultural Change (CRESC) from 2004 to 2010, and Professor at the University of York, where he founded the European Centre for Cultural Exploration from 2010 to 2012. His recent books include the co-authored *Social Class in the 21st century* (Penguin 2015) and *Identities and Social Change in Britain since 1940: The politics of method* (Oxford 2010).

Routledge International Handbook of the Sociology of Art and Culture

Edited by Laurie Hanquinet and Mike Savage

LONDON AND NEW YORK

First published 2016
by Routledge
2 Park Square, Milton Park, Abingdon, Oxon OX14 4RN

and by Routledge
711 Third Avenue, New York, NY 10017

First issued in paperback 2018

Routledge is an imprint of the Taylor & Francis Group, an informa business.

© 2016 Laurie Hanquinet and Mike Savage

The right of the editors to be identified as the authors of the editorial material, and of the authors for their individual chapters, has been asserted in accordance with sections 77 and 78 of the Copyright, Designs and Patents Act 1988.

All rights reserved. No part of this book may be reprinted or reproduced or utilised in any form or by any electronic, mechanical, or other means, now known or hereafter invented, including photocopying and recording, or in any information storage or retrieval system, without permission in writing from the publishers.

Trademark notice: Product or corporate names may be trademarks or registered trademarks, and are used only for identification and explanation without intent to infringe.

British Library Cataloguing-in-Publication Data
A catalogue record for this book is available from the British Library

Library of Congress Cataloging in Publication Data
Routledge international handbook of the sociology of art and culture / edited by Laurie Hanquinet and Mike Savage. – 1 Edition.
pages cm
1. Arts and society. I. Hanquinet, Laurie, editor.
NX180.S6R686 2015
701'.03–dc23
2015004366

ISBN 13: 978-1-138-59639-9 (pbk)
ISBN 13: 978-0-415-85511-2 (hbk)

Typeset in Bembo
by Cenveo Publisher Services

Contents

List of illustrations ix
Notes on contributors xi
Preface xvii

Contemporary challenges for the sociology of art and culture:
An introductory essay 1
Laurie Hanquinet and Mike Savage

PART I
Bourdieu's legacy and new perspectives for the sociology of art and culture 19

Introduction to Part I 21
Bourdieu: International influence and criticisms

1 The sociology of cultural participation in France thirty years
  after *Distinction* 26
  Philippe Coulangeon

2 A post-Bourdieusian sociology of valuation and evaluation for
  the field of cultural production 38
  Stefan Beljean, Phillipa Chong and Michèle Lamont

3 Contesting culture: Bourdieu and the strong program
  in cultural sociology 49
  Marco Santoro and Marco Solaroli

The omnivore debate

4 The cultural omnivore thesis: Methodological aspects of the debate 77
  Irmak Karademir Hazır and Alan Warde

5 After omnivorousness: Is Bourdieu still relevant? 90
Omar Lizardo and Sara Skiles

6 A critique of the omnivore: From the origin of the idea
of omnivorousness to the Latin American experience 104
Modesto Gayo

7 Age-period-cohort and cultural engagement 116
Aaron Reeves

Relational approaches to the sociology of art and culture

8 A social aesthetics as a general cultural sociology? 132
John Levi Martin and Ben Merriman

9 Genre: Relational approaches to the sociology of music 149
Jennifer C. Lena

10 Networks and culture 161
Alix Rule and Peter Bearman

11 Getting beyond the surface: Using geometric data analysis
in cultural sociology 174
Henk Roose

PART II
The fabric of aesthetics 191

Introduction to Part II 193
Production and mediation of aesthetics

12 From sociology of culture to sociology of artistic producers:
How to become a contemporary artist 199
Nathalie Heinich

13 Avant-garde artworks, artists and mediators: A state
of relationships 207
Nuria Peist

14 Learning how to think, and feel, about contemporary art:
An object relational aesthetic for sociology 219
Sophia Krzys Acord

15 Museum sociology 232
    Volker Kirchberg

Role of trans(national) contexts and globalization

16 Adjusting field theory: The dynamics of settler-colonial art fields 247
    Tony Bennett

17 The world market of translation in the globalization era:
    Symbolic capital and cultural diversity in the publishing field 262
    Gisèle Sapiro

18 The biennalization of art worlds: The culture of
    cultural events 277
    Monica Sassatelli

19 Aesthetic capital 290
    Sylvia Holla and Giselinde Kuipers

PART III
The complexity of cultural classifications 305

Introduction to Part III 307
Rethinking the oppositions between high and low culture

20 Cultural dissonances: The social in the singular 312
    Bernard Lahire

21 The multiplicity of highbrow culture: Taste boundaries among
    the new upper middle class 324
    Guy Bellavance

22 'There's something fundamental about what makes you laugh.'
    Comedy as an aesthetic experience 337
    Sam Friedman

23 Middlebrow book culture 351
    David Carter

Digital and screen culture

24 Digital sociology in the field of devices 367
    *Adrian Mackenzie, Richard Mills, Stuart Sharples,
    Matthew Fuller and Andrew Goffey*

25	Researching social analytics: Cultural sociology in the face of algorithmic power *Nick Couldry*	383
26	The rising power of screens: Changing cultural practices in France from 1973 to 2008 *Olivier Donnat*	396

Culture and place

27	Contesting the highbrow and lowbrow distinction: How Latin American scholars engage in cross-cultural debates *María Luisa Méndez*	409
28	The structuration of lifestyles in the city of Porto: A relational approach *Virgílio Borges Pereira*	421
29	When the artistic field meets the art worlds: Based on the case study of occupational painters in Shanghai *Chao Zhang*	437
30	Institutionalizing neo-bohemia *Richard Lloyd*	455

Index   *471*

Illustrations

Tables

3.1	The 'deep antinomies' in cultural theory according to Alexander and Smith	52
4.1	Articles on omnivorousness 1992–2013, by type of content	81
4.2	Measurement of omnivorousness in empirical articles	81
4.3	Distribution of the empirical articles: Field(s) of consumption chosen to measure omnivorousness	82
4.4	Distribution of empirical articles by countries studied	84
4.5	Methodological approaches to measuring omnivorousness in empirical articles	84
11.1	Relative contributions of variables and modalities to the orientation of axis two (in per cent)	177
11.2	Coordinates of mean points and variances of age categories on the first three axes (breakdown of variance along axes and age)	179
11.3	Contributions of modalities (in per cent) for first two axes in sub-cloud '14–25 years'	184
11.4	Contributions of modalities (in per cent) for first two axes in sub-cloud '55–85 years'	186
11.A1	Relative frequencies for participation variables ($n = 2{,}849$)	189
11.A2	Relative frequencies for dispositional variables ($n = 2{,}849$)	190
26.1	Cultural participation by generation, social background and gender	401
26.A1	Changing cultural and media practices, 1973–2008	407
27.1	Santiago: European aura of the city centre versus American dream of suburbia	417
28.1	Information used to elaborate the space of lifestyles based on MCA	426
28.2	Eigenvalues, percentage of explained variance, modified rates and cumulated modified rates	427
28.3	Contributions of modalities from each domain of practice to the variations on each axis, multiple correspondence analysis	427

Figures

3.1	The fractalization of cultural theory	63
7.1	Hypothetical examples of age, period, and cohort effects by decade of birth	120
7.2	The number of arts activities respondents participated in within the last 12 months in the UK, 2006–2008	122

7.3 The likelihood of consuming a broad range of cultural activities in the UK across cohorts, 1996–2008 — 123
11.1 Modalities contributing more than average to axis two in plane 1–2 and supplementary variables in plane 1–2 — 178
11.2 Three sub-clouds scoring high on axis three after hierarchical clustering in plane 1–3 — 180
11.3 Sub-clouds of two age segments in principal plane 1–2 with mean points and concentration ellipses — 182
11.4 CSA of sub-cloud '14–25 years' with modalities contributing more than average to sub-plane 1–2 — 183
11.5 CSA of sub-cloud '55–85 years' with modalities contributing more than average to sub-plane 1–2 — 185
15.1 Museum sociology as an interface between culture, museum and sociology — 237
15.2 Museum sociology in epistemic space — 241
16.1 Myth of the western man (white man's burden), Gordon Bennett, 1992 — 249
16.2 The field of modern art from art review 1990s — 253
24.1 Events on the Github.com timeline — 370
24.2 Top contributors to Linux on Github — 372
24.3 Patterns of repository events on Github — 375
28.1 Porto's space of lifestyles. Multiple correspondence analysis: Axes 1 and 2, indicating variables contributing to axis 1 — 428
28.2 Porto's space of lifestyles. Multiple correspondence analysis: Axes 1 and 2, indicating variables contributing to axis 2 — 429
28.3 Porto's space of lifestyles. Supplementary variables: Respondent's gender, age, cultural capital (measured in years of education), individual class fraction, and father's cultural capital (measured in years of education), axes 1 and 2 — 430
29.1 The view from inside Building 5 to the Lane 210 in TZF — 443
29.2 The first floor of Building 5 where Weiguang's studio was located — 445
29.3 Weiguang's painting of the city of Shanghai — 447
29.4 Weiguang's studio in TZF — 448
29.5 The label of a painting by Weiguang in his solo exhibition in 2014 — 449

Map

28.1 Correspondence between the major divisions of the city of Porto, the *PARISHES* and the approximate location of the observatories — 425

Notes on contributors

Sophia Krzys Acord is Associate Director of the Center for the Humanities and the Public Sphere, and Lecturer in Sociology, at the University of Florida. Her research examines the production of knowledge in the arts and humanities disciplines. She is founding editor of the journal *Music and Arts in Action*.

Peter Bearman is the Cole Professor of the Social Sciences at Columbia University. His current research focuses on networks and time.

Stefan Beljean is a graduate student in the Department of Sociology at Harvard University. His research interests lie at the intersection of cultural sociology, organizational research and the sociology of knowledge.

Guy Bellavance is a Professor at the *Urbanisation Culture Société* research centre of the *Institut national de la recherche scientifique* (INRS), Montréal, Canada. His areas of expertise are the sociology of the arts and cultural practices. His recent research has focused on the working conditions of artists, cultural consumption and taste, urban cultural life, cultural policies and the economics of culture.

Tony Bennett is Research Professor in Social and Cultural Theory in the Institute for Culture and Society at the University of Western Sydney. His main books include *Formalism and Marxism* (1979), *Bond and Beyond: The Political Career of a Popular Hero* (1987, with Janet Woollacott), *Outside Literature* (1991), *The Birth of the Museum* (1995), *Culture: A Reformer's Science* (1998), *Pasts Beyond Memory: Evolution, Museums, Colonialism* (2004) and *Making Culture, Changing Society* (2013). He is also a co-author of *Accounting for Tastes: Australian Everyday Cultures* (1999) and *Culture, Class, Distinction* (2009).

David Carter is Professor of Australian Literature and Cultural History at the University of Queensland. His books include *Always Almost Modern: Australian Print Culture and Modernity* (2013) and *Dispossession, Dreams and Diversity: Issues in Australian Studies* (2006), and, as editor, *Making Books: Contemporary Australian Publishing* (2007), *The Ideas Market: An Alternative Take on Australia's Intellectual Life* (2004) and, with Tony Bennett, *Culture in Australia: Policies, Publics and Programs* (2001).

Phillipa K. Chong is an Assistant Professor of Sociology at McMaster University and previously a Postdoctoral fellow in the Department of Sociology at Harvard University. Having published several articles related to evaluation and legitimacy in the cultural field, she is currently writing a book titled *How Reviewing Works: Book Reviewing in an Age when Everyone is a Critic*.

Notes on contributors

Philippe Coulangeon is Senior Researcher at the the French National Center for Scientific Research (CNRS). His areas of interest include sociology of culture, lifestyles and consumption, social stratification and class relations. He has published several papers and books in French and English, mainly about change and continuity in cultural inequalities in journals. His work appears in journals such as *Poetics* (2013), *Revue Française de Sociologie* (2009), *Actes de la recherche en Sciences sociales* (2008), and *Journal of Cultural Economy* (2008) and with Y. Lemel in the edited volumes *Social Status and Cultural Consumption* (Chan, ed., Cambridge University Press 2010) and *Quantifying Theory: Pierre Bourdieu* (Robson and Sanders, eds., Springer 2008).

Nick Couldry is a sociologist of media and culture. He is Professor of Media, Communications and Social Theory and Head of the Department of Media and Communications at the London School of Economics and was previously Professor of Media and Communications at Goldsmiths, University of London. He is the author or editor of eleven books including *Ethics of Media* (Palgrave MacMillan 2013), *Media, Society, World* (Polity 2012) and *Why Voice Matters* (Sage 2010). He is currently working with Andreas Hepp (University of Bremen) on a new book: *The Mediated Construction of Reality* (Polity Press forthcoming 2016).

Olivier Donnat is a Research Fellow in Sociology at the Studies Department of the French Ministry of Culture and Communication. He works on cultural participation and cultural policy since the 1980s, and he is the author of *Les Français et la culture. De l'exclusion à l'éclectisme* (La Découverte 1994), *Les publics de la culture* (Presses de Sciences Po 2003) and *Les pratiques culturelles des Français à l'ère numérique* (La Découverte 2009).

Sam Friedman is Assistant Professor in Sociology at the London School of Economics. He is the author of *Comedy and Distinction; The Cultural Currency of a 'Good' Sense of Humour* (Routledge 2014) and has published widely on class, culture and social mobility. He is also the Consulting Editor of *Fest*, the biggest magazine covering the Edinburgh Festivals.

Matthew Fuller's books include *Media Ecologies, Materialist Energies in Art and Technoculture* (MIT); *Behind the Blip, Essays on the Culture of Software* and *Elephant and Castle* (both Autonomedia) and with Andrew Goffey *Evil Media* (MIT). Editor of *Software Studies, a Lexicon* (MIT) and co-editor of the journal *Computational Culture*, he is involved in a number of projects in art, media and software. He is Professor of Cultural Studies and Director of the Centre for Cultural Studies, Goldsmiths, University of London.

Modesto Gayo is currently Associate Professor at Universidad Diego Portales, Santiago, Chile. He was a Research Fellow at the Centre for Research on Socio-Cultural Change (CRESC) and the Department of Sociology at the University of Manchester while working on the Cultural Capital and Social Exclusion project (2003–2006). His areas of interest are cultural inequalities and social reproduction, middle class theories and theories on nationalism. He has researched extensively about cultural capital in the United Kingdom, South America (particularly in Chile) and recently in Australia. He is a joint author of *Culture, Class, Distinction* (Routledge 2009) with Tony Bennett, Mike Savage, Elizabeth Silva, Alan Warde and David Wright.

Andrew Goffey, Associate Professor, Faculty of Arts, University of Nottingham, researches micropolitics of contemporary software culture and the work of Félix Guattari. He has several collaborative projects that explore the role of digital technology and associated practices in other areas of social and cultural life. These include a project looking at the 'information revolution' in the NHS, a project looking at the globalization of the mundane aesthetics of the creative and cultural industries and an Economic and Social Research Council–funded project on the digital commons.

Nathalie Heinich, a sociologist, is a Research Director at CNRS; she works within the *Ecole des Hautes Etudes en Sciences Sociales* (EHESS). Besides numerous articles, she has published many books dealing with the status of the artist and the notion of the author, contemporary art, the question of identity, the history of sociology and values. She is, for instance, the author of *La Gloire de Van Gogh* (Minuit 1991) [The Glory of Van Gogh, Princeton University Press 1996], *L'Épreuve de la grandeur* (La Découverte 1999), *Pourquoi Bourdieu* (Gallimard 2007), *De la visibilité* (Gallimard 2012) and *Le Paradigme de l'art contemporain* (Gallimard 2014).

Sylvia Holla is a PhD candidate in Cultural Sociology at the University of Amsterdam. She received her MA degree in social sciences (with distinction) from the same university in 2010. Her doctoral dissertation, which she expects to defend in 2015, explores how notions of beauty come into being in European fashion modeling industries, with a focus on bodily practices of male and female fashion models. She is a member of the editorial board of the Dutch journal *Sociologie* and the editor (with Laurens Buijs and Ingrid Geesink) of *The Sex Paradox: The Netherlands after the Sexual Revolution* (Amsterdam 2013).

Irmak Karademir Hazır is an Assistant Professor in the Department of Sociology at Middle East Technical University, Turkey. She earned her PhD degree in Sociology at the University of Manchester. Her areas of interest are sociology of consumption and taste, class identity and symbolic boundaries, class embodiment, sociology of body and socio-cultural change in Turkey.

Volker Kirchberg is Professor of Arts Organization and Arts Communication at the Institute of Sociology and Cultural Organization, Leuphana University of Lueneburg, Germany. His research and teaching areas are sociology of the arts, urban sociology, organizational sociology of arts and culture and the significance of arts and culture for sustainable development. He is author of *Gesellschaftliche Funktionen von Museen* [Social Functions of Museums] (2005) and co-editor of *Music City: Musical Approaches to the 'Creative City'* (2014).

Giselinde Kuipers is Professor of Cultural Sociology at the University of Amsterdam. She is the author of *Good Humor, Bad Taste: A Sociology of the Joke* (Berlin/New York 2006, second edition 2015) and has published widely on the sociology of humor, popular culture and taste, as well as the cultural industries and cultural globalization, often from a cross-national comparative perspective. From 2010–12 she was Norbert Elias Professor at Erasmus University Rotterdam. She is the principal investigator of the ERC project 'Towards a comparative sociology of beauty: The transnational modeling industry and the social shaping of beauty standards in six European countries' (2010–15).

Bernard Lahire is Full Professor of Sociology at the École Normale Supérieure de Lyon. He has recently published *La Culture des individus. Dissonances culturelles et distinction de soi* (La Découverte 2004), *The Plural Actor* (Cambridge, UK: Polity Press 2010) and *Dans les plis* *singuliers du social. Individus, institutions, socialisations* (La Découverte 2013). He was awarded the CNRS silver medal 2012 for the human and social sciences.

Michèle Lamont is Professor of Sociology and African and African American Studies and Robert I. Goldman Professor of European Studies at Harvard University. She is director of the Weatherhead Center for International Studies at Harvard University. She is also fellow of the Canadian Institute for Advanced Research, where she co-directs the program Successful Societies. A leading cultural sociologist, her research concerns the construction of worth across classes and ethnoracial groups, in peer review, and in stigmatization and discrimination.

Jennifer C. Lena is Associate Professor of Arts Administration at Columbia University Teachers College, with a courtesy appointment in Sociology. She also holds an appointment as Senior Research Scholar for the Strategic National Arts Alumni Project (SNAAP) at Indiana University. Her research focuses on understanding processes of classification, particularly the organizational and institutional conditions for the creation, modification or elimination of cultural categories like genres. She is the author of *Banding Together: How Communities Create Genres in Popular Music* (Princeton University Press 2012).

Omar Lizardo is an Associate Professor in the Department of Sociology at the University of Notre Dame. His research deals with various topics in sociological theory, cultural sociology, social stratification, social psychology, network theory and cognitive science. His work has appeared in such venues as *American Sociological Review, Theory and Society, Sociological Theory, Cultural Sociology* and *Poetics*.

Richard Lloyd is Associate Professor of Sociology at Vanderbilt University and author of *Neo-Bohemia: Art and Commerce in the Postindustrial City*. He writes for academic and public outlets on topics including cities in the Southern United States, conservative politics, art and music and urban design. His current research is focused on Nashville's music industry.

Adrian Mackenzie, Professor in Technological Cultures, Department of Sociology, Lancaster University, has published work on technology: *Transductions: Bodies and Machines at Speed* (2002; 2006), *Cutting Code: Software and Sociality* (2006), *Wirelessness: Radical Empiricism in Network Cultures* (2010) and *Into the Data: Learning from Machine Learning* (2015). He is currently working on the circulation of data intensive methods across science, government and business in network media. He co-directs the Centre for Science Studies, Lancaster University, UK.

John Levi Martin is a Professor of Sociology at the University of Chicago. He is the author of *Social Structures, The Explanation of Social Action* and *Thinking Through Theory*. He is currently working on Kant's theory of judgment and its role in the history of the social theory of action.

María Luisa Méndez is an Associate Professor of Sociology at *Universidad Diego Portales* and Principal Investigator at the Center for Social Conflict and Cohesion Studies, COES. Her research focuses on the study of the middle classes in Latin America from the perspective of urban and cultural sociology, and particularly explores processes of inequality reproduction and social conflict.

Notes on contributors

Ben Merriman is a doctoral candidate in Sociology at the University of Chicago. Ben's cultural research examines the sociology of literary production, including work on editorial judgment, gender inequality in publishing and the history of the novel.

Richard Mills is a Computational Social Scientist currently working in the Psychometrics Centre at the University of Cambridge on an FP7 project (Wikirate - Crowdsource better companies). Richard completed his PhD in Applied Social Statistics in 2013 with a thesis that concerned distributed moderation voting systems as used by websites like Reddit and Stack Overflow. Previously, he studied Psychology and conducted research on face recognition and spatial-numerical cognition.

Nuria Peist is a Professor of Art History at the *Universitat de Barcelona*. Her research focuses on the sociology of art and, in particular, the processes of recognition of modern and contemporary artists. She is a regular speaker at art history and sociology conferences and publishes articles in journals such as *Cultural Sociology*. She has published the book, *El éxito en el arte moderno: Trayectorias artísticas y procesos de reconocimiento* [Success in Modern Art: Artistic Careers and Recognition Processes] (Ábada Editores 2012).

Virgílio Borges Pereira is an Associate Professor of Sociology at the University of Porto, a Researcher at the Institute of Sociology and an Associate Researcher at the Centre for Studies in Architecture and Urbanism of the same university. His research combines sociological, historical and ethnographic approaches and focuses on the production of social and cultural inequalities in different spatial contexts of Northern Portugal, with a special interest in the study of the sociological legacy of Bourdieu's work. Among other publications, he is the author of *Classes e Culturas de Classe das Famílias Portuenses* [Classes and Class Cultures of Porto's Families], Porto, Afrontamento, 2005.

Aaron Reeves is a Senior Research Fellow in the Department of Sociology and a research fellow with Nuffield College at the University of Oxford. His work examines the causes and consequences of social, economic and cultural inequality in Europe and North America.

Henk Roose received his PhD in Sociology at Ghent University (Belgium). He is currently working there as Associate Professor (within the research teams CuDOS en POS+) teaching Methodology, Social Inequality and Cultural Sociology. His research focuses on the link between cultural participation and social stratification using Geometric Data Analysis, the empirical analysis of aesthetic dispositions and survey methods.

Alix Rule is a PhD candidate in Sociology at Columbia University, where she is an INCITE Graduate Fellow. She is a grantee of the Creative Capital | Warhol Foundation Arts Writers Grant Program.

Marco Santoro is Associate Professor of Sociology at the *Università degli Studi di Bologna, Dipartimento di Filosofia e Comunicazione* and a member of the CSE (*Centre de sociologie européenne*). A founding editor of *Sociologica: Italian Journal of Sociology online*, he is in the editorial board of the journals *Poetics, Cultural Sociology* and *American Journal of Cultural Sociology*. He works on cultural production and consumption, historical sociology of the social sciences, class cultures and mafias.

Notes on contributors

Gisèle Sapiro is Professor of Sociology at the *Ecole des Hautes Etudes en Sciences Sociales* and Research director at the CNRS. Her interests include the sociology of intellectuals, of literature and of translation. The author of *La Guerre des écrivains, 1940–1953* (1999; English transl.: *French Writers' War*, 2014) and *La Responsabilité de l'écrivain* (2011), she has (co-)edited *Pierre Bourdieu, sociologue* (2004), *Translatio* (2008), *Les Contradictions de la globalisation éditoriale* (2009), *L'Espace intellectuel en Europe* (2009), *Traduire la littérature et les sciences humaines* (2012), *Sciences humaines en traduction* (2014) and *Dictionnaire Bourdieu* (forthcoming).

Monica Sassatelli is Lecturer in the Department of Sociology at Goldsmiths, University of London. She has published in the sociology of culture, Europe and classical and contemporary social theory. She is the author of *Becoming Europeans: Cultural Identity and Cultural Policies* (Palgrave 2009) and co-editor of *Festivals and the Cultural Public Sphere* (with L. Giorgi and G. Delanty, Routledge 2011).

Stuart Sharples is a Lecturer in the Department of Mathematics and Statistics, Lancaster University. His work focuses on statistical modelling in the broader frame of data science.

Sara Skiles is a Senior Researcher Associate in the Department of Sociology at the University of Notre Dame. Her dissertation examines the relationship between aesthetic taste and symbolic boundaries. Her current research investigates the various influences of religious belief and behavior in the lives of adolescents and emerging adults. Her work has appeared in such venues as *Sociological Theory*, *Poetics* and *Sociology Compass*.

Marco Solaroli is a Research Fellow in the Department of Philosophy and Communication at the University of Bologna. His research interests are on Bourdieu, cultural sociology, cultural production, sociology of media and journalism, digital culture, photography and visual culture. Most recently he published *Iconicity: A Category for Social and Cultural Theory* in *Sociologica* n.1/2015.

Alan Warde is Professor of Sociology in the School of Social Sciences, University of Manchester, a Professorial Fellow of Manchester's Sustainable Consumption Institute (SCI), and Guest Professor at Universities of Uppsala and Aalborg. Research interests are wide but recently have concerned the sociology of consumption, the sociology of culture and the sociology of food and eating in the context of issues of sustainability. Recent publications include: Bennett T., Savage M., Silva E., Warde A., Gayo-Cal M. and Wright D., *Culture, Class, Distinction*, (London: Routledge 2009) and several journal articles about omnivorousness in *Cultural Sociology* and *Poetics*.

Chao Zhang is a Lecturer in the department of Sociology, Tongji University, Shanghai, China. She received her doctorate in sociology from the University of Manchester, focusing on gentrification and social relations in downtown Shanghai. Her research interests include urban sociology, cultural sociology and sociology of consumption. She also writes essays and columns, providing her observations and experiences with intellectual reflections.

Preface

The sociology of art and culture is one of the oldest and most distinguished fields of sociological endeavour. Yet in the current period it is highly ambivalent: fractured between competing qualitative and quantitative methodologies; beset by those seeing art and culture as a distinctive arena of inquiry against those who see it as all embracing; and with fundamental theoretical arguments between those interested in Bourdieu, Foucault, feminism, post-colonialism, pragmatism, science studies and more.

This handbook in no way attempts a comprehensive survey of this complicated terrain. It would, indeed, be hard to do this given the variety of contributions which could be elicited. We have instead edited this handbook to give more shape to the field and to provide students and researchers with reference points that we think offer a productive and exciting future. Our own theoretical orientations will be clear. Bringing together authors from across the globe, and with varying theoretical and methodological positions, we argue for an emergent mode of relational and aesthetic cultural sociology. Rather than deploying a diffuse interest in culture, we instead focus on the sociological analysis of artworks and cultural production and consumption, and we prioritize innovative methodological as much as theoretical repertoires for this purpose.

Rather than pitching an anthropological conception of 'everyday ordinary cultures' against a sociology of highbrow culture adorned with consecrated artworks, we instead render the aesthetic and relational components of art as a means of developing a distinctive perspective on the social itself. This approach, we believe, offers an exciting opportunity to place sociology of culture on a terrain where its interests can inform numerous domains of social inquiry.

In putting this book together, we had three major aims. First, we position our intervention as an elaboration of, and a defence of, a broadly Bourdieusian approach to cultural sociology. We see Bourdieu as a key reference point in debates about the relationship between the cultural and the social. However, we openly acknowledge that he is also a controversial figure who animates numerous kinds of opponents, including many who see themselves as cultural sociologists. We are not seeking to defend his specific arguments about the nature of cultural capital but rather to embrace his broader project of explicating the relational approach he elaborates through his interest in the 'field' metaphor. Many chapters of our handbook explore, from different perspectives, the potential of this post-Bourdieusian agenda. Readers will see there is no consensus amongst our contributors with respect to the value of his work, and we include critics as well as supporters of this thinking, but we expect readers will come away from this volume with a good sense of the nature of the contemporary debate inspired by Bourdieu's work.

Second, we champion a 'relational' perspective as central to the vision of sociology of art and culture we develop here. Rather than seeking to define the subject in terms of the interaction between pre-defined 'variables' or domains (such as 'art', or 'society' or 'social class'), this explores the interaction between diverse and heterogeneous practices and how specific cultural forms emerge from such dynamic flows. It places the focus on the immanence and emergence of cultural forms out of the webbed interactions and dynamics of social life. We see this relational perspective as breaking from linear conceptions of sociology and permitting a more developed way of linking theory and method – one which sees the aesthetic itself as crucial to explicating relationships themselves. In practical terms, we take this relational perspective to endorse an approach to art and culture which insists on examining processes of production, consumption and mediation.

Finally, we endorse methodological capacities that are both quantitative and qualitative. In cultural sociology the division between quantitative and qualitative is more entrenched, and more highly policed, than in many other branches of sociology. Qualitative perspectives remain dominant in numerous countries – such as in the UK – because they are seen as more appropriate for the kind of hermeneutical perspective which cultural sociology might appear to embrace. On the other hand, there is worldwide a large quantitative research community, which is especially strong in the United States and the Netherlands and which currently has little overlap with qualitative research. A central feature of our book is to insist on the need for both quantitative and qualitative analyses, especially as they can be deployed to elaborate the relational perspective we champion here. This allows us to move sociology of culture away from being simply a chance to reiterate the value of a hermeneutic sociology towards a more relational focus.

In pursuing these three overarching themes, our papers cover many parts of the world, where we deliberately seek to bring different styles of work from American and European traditions, as well as from other areas of the world. Substantively, the case studies range across artistic production and consumption, urban experience, design and intermediation, and political processes. We cover music, reading, TV, the visual arts, new media and urban culture. We hope these all give fascinating glimpses into the contemporary cultural scene, and more specifically into how sociological perspectives can give distinctive and powerful tools to examine them.

The handbook is composed of three main parts. The first part will discuss Bourdieu's heritage for the empirical sociology of culture and introduce new theoretical and methodological perspectives for the sub-discipline. We start by considering Bourdieu's influence in France and then tracing how his work has been influential – not without any criticisms – in the US and in other (supra)national contexts. We will reflect on the way that Bourdieu's work – its concepts, its innovative character but also its limitations – has generated powerful and distinctive paradigms in sociology of art and culture.

A particular focus, which recurs at several points in the book, is the 'omnivore' debate that first emerged in the work of the American sociologist Peterson. This attests that Bourdieu's key distinction which underlies his concept of cultural capital (which might crudely be characterized as 'snob versus slob') has been losing power in favour of a distinction between 'omnivores versus univores' (where the former have wide ranging tastes across numerous genres whilst the latter are characterised by unitary tastes). This handbook will showcase how this substantive debate on omnivorousness has pervaded all the sociology of culture and will critically reflect upon the consequences of this influence. We explore how this debate has provided a platform for engagement between different (quantitative and qualitative) traditions of cultural analysis which has facilitated unusually productive but also limited interventions. We will see how the debate on distinction has cross-fertilized with important methodological developments, including longitudinal and mixed methods.

We seek to move this debate onto more fertile terrain by focusing on research that champions in various ways one central aspect of Bourdieu's theory: its relational dimension. We will show how the relational approach is an emerging area of convergence across several traditions of work. This includes the increasing interest in the notion of 'field' but also includes those concerned with categorization and classification and also proponents of social network analysis and multiple correspondence analysis.

The second part will focus on the fabric of aesthetics by discussing the role of artists, cultural intermediaries and cultural institutions in the making of artworks and aesthetic principles, and the way these are embedded within different networks and circles. It will consider how aesthetic criteria, norms and contents emerged and spread out. This discussion will outline areas that would deserve further research – such as the study of contemporary art actors or the sociology of museums – and show the importance of socio-historical approaches.

It will also assess the impact of national and transnational contexts on cultural evaluation. The interest of the notion of field will be assessed in light of challenges raised by non-European contexts and globalization. These challenges will also be examined through a focus on specific art events that crystallize many tensions characterizing the art worlds and also on the evaluation of physical beauty.

The third part will return to the themes introduced by Bourdieu in the light of the issues raised under the fabric of aesthetics to provide a series of contemporary reflections on the state of the art in the sociology of art and culture. It begins with an investigation of the current significance of the opposition between high and low culture which lies at the heart of Bourdieu's thinking. New light will be shed on this now classical subject of research by changing the scale of analysis (e.g. the individual level), by considering other classificatory schemes (e.g. old versus new forms of artworks) and by examining new cultural domains (e.g. comedy). We will also reflect on how the overriding character of this tension between high and low might be rethought in the context of the neglected intermediate category of the middlebrow.

The second theme is the rise of the digital culture. The Internet, the World Wide Web and associated social networking sites and other blogs have reconfigured many aspects of people's everyday life. This section discusses the importance of analysing the field of devices and the practices of its players in order to better understand the specificities of digital culture and its objects. People's reflexive interactions with tools to measure online presence will also be investigated before assessing the impact of this 'new screen culture' on other forms of cultural engagement.

Our final theme concerns the link between place and culture. The complexity of cultural classifications and their interrelations with social stratification and spatial divisions will be outlined. By exploring the link between lifestyle, social position and spatial divisions, it will become clear that symbolic boundaries drawing on a diversity of cultural referents are embedded within a complex web of territorial boundaries. We will also show how specific lifestyles related to the development of a 'neo-bohemia' have been associated to urban restructurings and progressively used in neoliberal regeneration initiatives in post-industrial cities. We thus throw open the potential for the sociology of art and culture to inform analyses of urban and global change more effectively.

Before moving on to these different parts, we will first establish the underpinnings of this handbook by reflecting on the main current challenges for the sociology of art and culture.

Preface

In order to do so we will provide our own introductory account of the relationships between the art and the social within sociology. Here we position our handbook against those who seek to collapse the artwork into its social context and instead emphasise how an aesthetic and relational approach offers insights not only for the sub-discipline but for social science more broadly.

This handbook has been three years in the making and draws on extensive collaborations between ourselves as well as with numerous contributors. The idea for this book came originally from Laurie Hanquinet who, before coming to the UK, studied in Brussels at the crossroads of different theoretical and methodological traditions in the sociology of culture. The main ambition of this handbook was to reflect upon ways to cross-fertilize these traditions. Mike Savage enthusiastically agreed to collaborate in order to develop research interests in the aesthetic and relational perspectives in cultural sociology.

We would like to publically acknowledge the way that many of the ideas for this book arise out of the exciting and productive work within the ESRC Centre for Research on Socio-Cultural Change (CRESC) at the University of Manchester between 2004 and 2014 (and of which Mike Savage was a Director between 2004 and 2010). More broadly, the Department of Sociology at the University of Manchester, where Mike Savage was Professor between 1995 and 2010, was a vibrant location for research on the sociology of culture and stratification, with several of the contributors to this handbook having an association with this Department.

We would also like to thank the University of York for its support of the York Centre for Cultural Exploration, where Laurie and Mike worked together for two years and where the plans for this handbook were hatched. More recently, the Culture and Stratification network co-ordinated by Laurie and Mike, as well as Sam Friedman (LSE) and Andrew Miles (Manchester), has been an important platform for the approach to the sociology of art and culture which we champion here.

Finally we are very grateful to Cristiana Olcese (LSE) whose help has been essential to the preparation of this handbook and who worked tirelessly to bring this project to completion.

Contemporary challenges for the sociology of art and culture
An introductory essay

Laurie Hanquinet and Mike Savage

Throughout the world, cultural sociology has been one of the most rapidly growing and dynamic areas of the discipline[1]. In the USA, the section on culture of the American Sociological Association is one of the largest. In the UK, cultural sociology has been identified as one of the strongest and most vibrant areas of the discipline, and the British Sociological Association sponsors a specialist journal in the area: *Cultural Sociology*. In many European nations – notably the Netherlands and France – there are strong sociological communities conducting researching on people's consumption patterns, cultural tastes and leisure activities[2], whilst the significance of art and culture has long been an emphasis within post-colonial sociology which insists on the cultural stakes by which non-Western nations are subordinated to the Euro-American metropolises. This prominence of cultural sociology is, however, beset by a fundamental uncertainty over the object of the discipline, sometimes considered as the tension between a 'sociology of culture' and 'cultural sociology'. Should the discipline focus on culture as forms of art practice or art works, or should it broaden its reach to look at practices more generally and ways of life in an anthropological sense?

In the first 'camp' lies a focus on activities, such as the visual arts, music, film or literature, which have conventionally been consecrated as 'artistic'. There are certainly a number of canonical sociologists who have conducted research precisely on these areas, notably including Georg Simmel, Max Weber, Howard Becker and Pierre Bourdieu. All of these have explored how the artistic is illuminated through understanding its intersection with the social. And this distinctive sociological tradition of studies of art, literature and music remains powerful today through proponents such as Richard Peterson, Janet Wolff, Tia DeNora, Georgina Born and Paul Gilroy.

In the second 'camp' lies an insistence on the 'ordinariness' of culture, as routinely implicated in all aspects of social life, and it sees a cultural perspective as informing analyses of the social more generally. Here, drawing on anthropological perspectives, as well as that promoted in cultural and media studies, the cultural is powerfully omnipresent. For Jeffrey Alexander, the major proponent of what he terms the 'Strong Program in Cultural Sociology', 'to believe in the possibility of a "cultural sociology" is to subscribe to the idea that every action, no matter how instrumental, reflexive or coerced *vis-a-vis* its external environments ... is embedded to some extent in a horizon of affect and meaning' (Alexander and Smith 2001: 1).

In practice, these two perspectives are not in as much tension as might be anticipated. A sociological perspective on the 'arts' (readers should note that we include music, literature and other artistic forms within this term) typically decomposes them into ordinary activities, for instance rebutting the idea that 'great art' is the product of individual creativity of genii, and focusing on the specific institutional forces and everyday practices which serve to canonize, consecrate and marginalize. On the other hand, an emphasis on culture as embedded in ordinary everyday life tends to prioritize more specifically symbolic practices, thus directing attention to the media and the textual, oral and visual forms which embody them. This can therefore lead, willy-nilly, back to an interest in the art work as a materialization of the symbolic. For these reasons, whilst this tension between cultural sociology and the sociology of culture is long-standing, at the same time they bleed into one another.

We need to recognize at the outset the dangers of Anglophone framings here. In French, as Heinich (2010) recognizes, there is only difference between these broadly defined perspectives: the sociology of culture in France usually encompasses a wider range of practices (such as watching television) that are not necessarily recognized as belonging to the artistic realm. The differentiation is greater in English where the notion of 'culture' is not spontaneously associated with 'arts' as it is in France. The handbook seeks to make the bridge between art (or arts to account for the plurality of its forms of expression) and culture clear. It doesn't seek to reinstate art as one of the dimensions of culture which can include daily life activities that are not traditionally seen as artistic. On the contrary, it sees art and culture as related to each other in the way they both are defined and classified.

Whilst recognizing these variabilities, there is a broader issue that the social sciences have always struggled with knowing how to handle culture. Whereas there are disciplines which claim to exercise jurisdiction over the social (sociology, social anthropology, social policy, social studies), political (politics, political science) and the economy (economics, political economy), there is no discipline – apart from cultural studies, which is much less strongly institutionalized and is also often associated with the humanities – which claims jurisdiction over the 'cultural' in quite such direct terms[3].

Our handbook is animated by a belief that the relationship between these two meanings of cultural sociology needs to be re-oriented in favour of a greater attention to the forms of art and the aesthetics itself than is currently the case. We take the tension between broad and narrow definitions of culture as inevitable and do not seek to champion one over the other. Indeed, we see the recursive move by which the social environment helps explicate the arts, and the cultural helps unravel the social as one of the key dynamics of this area of inquiry. Nonetheless, our contention is that in recent decades too much energy has been spent on pursuing the broader contextual and social critique of culture with the result that cultural activities have tended to be seen only in terms of power struggles and not enough sociological focus has been placed on the specificities of the different arenas of cultural activity more narrowly defined or on their dialectic relations with the social, which are key constituents of both. We seek, in this handbook, to offer up-to-date resources – theoretical, substantive and methodological – to permit a more fertile and productive approach to an enriched sociology of culture and the arts which we will argue here are informed by concerns with the 'aesthetic' and the 'relational'.

It follows that in this handbook we specifically seek to avoid conflating culture with the social more generally. This is not because we think that 'culture' can be differentiated from the 'social' in any hard and fast way, but rather that since this is the routine practice of anthropologists, cultural studies experts as well as sociologists, there is no great need to edit a handbook in this area – and indeed such a handbook would be nigh on impossible to put together[4]. But we also want to avoid the opposite approach of the sociology of culture and the arts becoming a specialist sub-field concentrating on music, literature and visual arts etc., which does not necessarily speak to wider sociological concerns. And we also wish to resist a recent tendency to instate the 'art work' as an 'agent' in and of itself (e.g. Strandvad 2012). Instead, we deliberately seek to recognize this tension between the sociology of culture and cultural sociology – or more specifically between the definition of culture that is commonly attached to them – as productive and exciting, but we seek here to rebalance the relationship towards the 'arts'.

We use the rest of this introduction to review different key historical moments in the development of social scientific engagement with culture and the arts. Fundamentally, we show that there has always been instability in how the cultural and social are seen to interconnect, and such engagements are exciting and productive. At their most effective, they demonstrate the power of 'contextualist' approaches which have debunked art from its sacred status and shown how placing art forms within a wider social context both explicates the art form itself and also illuminates social relations more generally.

We trace four successive moments in this encounter, each of which develops at a particular time point and then continues to enjoy an afterlife. This historical account is not exhaustive. Our historical argument will be that as we move forward in time, the contextual movement of placing forms of art in a wider social environment is understood in an increasingly 'externalized' fashion so that the aesthetic and relational become cloaked and subsidiary to the social environment in which they are located. We seek, therefore, to return to rebalance this relationship in what we see as a more fluid and dynamic way.

Firstly, we examine the formation of the distinct realm of 'culture' itself. We briefly explore the classical Enlightenment tradition associated with the humanities disciplines which emphasizes the cultural value of art works, and we see how concerns with the nurturing of cultural excellence, notably associated with the concept of '*Bildung*', came to place emphasis not simply on the qualities of art works themselves but also the wider communities and practices which embraced them. These developed a concern with hermeneutics and hence saw the act of interpretation as placing the art work into a wider context; this tradition, enshrined in the practice of humanities disciplines, thereby opened itself up to the need to place culture and art in broader terms.

Secondly, and taking focus increasingly in the early twentieth century, we can see the power of modes of romantic social theory which deployed arguments about the role of culture as a means of resisting what were seen as instrumentalizing and 'massifying' trends within capitalist development. In this perspective, strident defences of 'culture' were seen to be essential to wider critique of capitalism more generally. Associated especially with the Frankfurt School, this perspective was also significant within social theory with the result that the 'truly' aesthetic was seen to be 'under threat' and needed to be pitched against its opposite – often defined as 'low' or 'mass' culture.

The third moment is one which we associate with the 'social critique of culture' which has become increasingly powerful, indeed highly routinized, during the second half of the twentieth century. In contrast to the romantic-inspired theorists who came before, and who focused their critique on mass or low culture, the focus now turned on contextualizing all cultural forms, including the social values underlying 'high' culture itself. The writings of Pierre Bourdieu – although he was actually ambivalent about the superiority of high culture – crystallized this perspective and have come to define the most visible and direct exemplification of this approach. In this movement, the 'aesthetic' was itself subject to external critique because it was deemed to champion privileged interests.

Finally, we turn to the more recent formalization of the contextual perspective through the increasing deployment of social scientific expertise involving formal methods allowing forms of art to be subject to external evaluation and critique in the name of a 'social'. This last current, which has held sway until recent times, takes several forms but notably includes the quantification of cultural activity as well as the deployment of a methodologically elaborated ethnographic turn. It is implicated in a thoroughgoing neo-liberal polity in which audit and accountability is extended to all arenas, so leading to the 'instrumentalization' of forms of art themselves (Yudice 2004). In all these cases, the art work is appraised fundamentally through the lens of social scientific methods, so allowing the external and contextual critique to take on new power and pervasiveness.

All four of these moments recognize tensions between art works and their context, and all define valuable ways of examining the interplay between culture and art on the one hand and the social on the other. Our overarching contention, however, is that in the last two moments, both of which have been fundamental to the development of the sociology of art and culture, the emphasis has shifted too far towards an external, 'social' critique, with the result that the arts are left as too passive in this complex inter-relationship. We argue in this introduction that whilst this familiar move to subjecting art and culture to 'external' evaluation in the name of the social is necessary, it runs the risk of stripping out the aesthetic. We think that embracing a relational perspective allows us to re-introduce the aesthetic in ways which provides a more balanced perspective.

In developing this argument, we see Bourdieu's thinking as the key platform on which to build. In fact, these ambivalences about the social and aesthetic are central to his own work. He did not simply embrace a relativist position in which cultural value could be defined in terms of its social context (Bennett 2005). We challenge the appropriation of his work which has tended to read him as offering a social critique of culture, rather than as also interested in the aesthetic itself (see further Hanquinet et al. 2014). And in seeking to champion this more fluid reading of Bourdieu's ongoing importance, we hope to show the value of his work for readers who may not feel intuitively drawn to his arguments. We do this in the context of mapping out the importance of the aesthetic and the relational as key areas of recent work whose concerns need to be placed at the heart of the sociology of art and culture.

The formation of 'high culture'

Raymond Williams provided the foundational account of the separation of 'culture' from 'society', a process which he traces to the development of eighteenth and nineteenth century capitalism (Williams 1956; 1985). Before this period, the original use of the word culture was associated with nurturing crops – as in agriculture. However, there was a steady trend to define more autonomy to the sphere of art, starting in the seventeenth century and culminating with the emergence of aesthetic modernism and the associated sacred status of arts from the later nineteenth century. Williams saw this elevation of 'culture' as a response to the challenges of industrialization and urbanization in which the idea of an autonomous arena of art could be held out as a counterbalance.

Culture as arts, and as enshrined by humanities disciplines, was defined as disconnected from the rest of the society. As Williams traces, this narrow concept of culture became strongly marked during the early phases of industrial capitalism when the quasi-sacred realm of art and culture was developed as a critical response to capitalist expansion and the proliferation of market principles. This helped generate the development of an autonomous sphere of high culture which was promoted for long as naturally superior to other forms of culture.

Unsurprisingly, it is at the end of the nineteenth century that the word 'Highbrow' emerged. Initially used in phrenology, the adjective quickly started to signify a capacity to aesthetic refinement, capacity for long assumed to be a gift given to the well-educated but not others (Levine 1990). Then art was the area of geniuses and only appreciable by highly educated people who had a natural inclination towards aesthetics.

Associated with this trend, forms of high culture became increasingly institutionalized during this period, in educational provision as well as in galleries and museums. As Genard (2011) reminded us, culture as *'Bildung'* – the German word referring to human elevation – implies education as well. This current became particularly visible in the development of major national cultural institutions, such as museums, in the eighteenth but mainly in the nineteenth centuries. Developed in great part for civilizing and educative purposes, cultural institutions played a crucial role in the institutionalization of highbrow or 'legitimate' arts in modern society (DiMaggio 1982; Levine 1990). These pretensions of universality initially connoted what was established as high culture.

However, it would be erroneous to see this consecration of high culture as uncontested. During the nineteenth century, there was a parallel increase of interest in the culture of the 'People', for instance, through interests in folklore, which could be interestingly associated with the idea of *'Kultur'*. As Charles Taylor (1992) has argued, the embrace of the ordinary and the everyday, and their mundane cultural articulation, has a long history. In response to the elaboration of highbrow culture, other modes of culture which appeared 'authentic' became subject to greater interest, and we can trace a range of nineteenth century commentators who also began to use a more anthropological vision. This was famously articulated by Tylor as 'Culture, or civilization, taken in its broad, ethnographic sense, is that complex whole which includes knowledge, belief, art, morals, law, custom, and any other capabilities and habits acquired by man as a member of society' (Tylor 1871: 1).

Here we see the emergence of the oscillation between narrow and broad definitions of culture which we have already introduced above. And in fact, the growing cultural apparatus did not simply separate culture from its context. We can see this most clearly by reflecting on *'Bildung'* (and different from the word for culture, *'Kultur'*). Originating in theological thinking such as that of Liebniz, *'Bildung'* was taken up by German critics and philosophers from the later eighteenth century to identify the role of human growth and development. Rather than positing human qualities transcendentally, as given, the focus was on processes of human and cultural 'maturation'. This framing became strongly enshrined in the burgeoning educational apparatus from the eighteenth century where the arts and humanities – history, theology, literature, philosophy, geography and languages – historically commanded a decisive presence through their institutionalization within the developing university system.

The important point here is that the process of *'Bildung'* also recognized the power of critique and challenge, where individuals had to work out for themselves cultural excellence through evaluation and experience. It hence admitted a certain fluidity in the definition of 'high culture' which prevented it from being neatly separated out from its context. It is in this sense that Matthew Arnold famously articulated in 1869 his view of culture not as a transcendental set of canonical art works (or as 'connoisseurship'), but as something to be striven for:

> There is a view in which all the love of our neighbour, the impulses towards action, help, and beneficence, the desire for removing human error, clearing human confusion, and diminishing human misery, the noble aspiration to leave the world better and happier than we found it,—motives eminently such as are called social,—come in as part of the grounds of culture, and the main and pre-eminent part.
>
> *(Arnold 1961: 91)*

Within this perspective, the common focus was on culture as the locus of, and arena for, excellence growth, and progress. It was implicated, thereby, to evolutionary conceptions of culture, and the social, and a concern with the qualities of the art work itself as embedded within a wider network. Through this way of thinking, the study of art works switched between the particular and the general, the art work and its context. We see here the development of a contextual way of thinking which enshrined a hermeneutic perspective in which cultural analysis required specific art works to be placed in the context which could thereby unravel their key features through forms of interpretation.

Our point here is that the elaboration of conceptions of the 'high culture' went hand in hand with endemic instability around definitions of the cultural itself. This reflects the oscillation between culture being restricted to prized and valued activities as opposed to those which are seen to be forms of mass behaviour wherein the cultural inheres in everyday life. The former might be exemplified as the literary or humanities based perspective, the latter as the anthropological. Both narrow and broad definitions of the cultural emerged together and need to be placed in relationship to each other: they have no meaning except with respect to each other. This is why our *Routledge International Handbook of the Sociology of Art and Culture* acknowledges this tension and sees it as fruitful rather than seeks to privilege one over the other.

The romantic-inspired critique and the moment of cultural studies

We have seen that the Enlightenment humanities project embodied, from its inception, a concern to relate art to a wider context, and this contextual approach was taken further by the development of the social sciences from the later nineteenth century. However, initially this 'sociological' moment was slow to crystallize. The social science infrastructure of the early twentieth century was locked into a 'gentlemanly embrace' in which evolutionary perspectives premised on the cultural and moral supremacy of the imperial nations were the unquestioned platform from which social scientific analysis was framed (Savage 2010). Works of social investigation were thus necessarily conducted by 'educated' and morally cultivated observers – philanthropists, missionaries, reformers, mappers and surveyors (e.g. Dirks 2002; Mitchell 2001) – and were seen to embody a concern with progress and cultural advance. Evolutionary concerns were central to these early social sciences (for instance, as articulated in the progressive politics of the Chicago school or the Fabian underpinnings of the London School of Economics).

This early social science was, therefore, complicit with underwriting and even formalizing the differentiation between 'high' and 'popular' culture which had become marked during the nineteenth century. Strongly influenced by romantic criticisms of a rapidly expanding capitalist society, sociological theorists ranging from Weber to Simmel and the Frankfurt School became increasingly bound up with reflecting on the differentiation of different spheres of cultural activity. Up to the mid-twentieth century, critiques of 'mass culture', which continued to embrace the superior values of 'high culture', abounded.

The Frankfurt School's thinking helped bridge currents from the humanities with those in the emerging social sciences. They identified the power of capitalism as central to the 'massification' of culture which thereby posed fundamental questions about the role of cultural critique. This approach, articulated most forcefully by Horkheimer and Adorno (2002), further established a negative view of popular culture when assimilated to low and mass culture, and this approach was taken up by social scientists as Adorno and became associated with research programmes analyzing radio listening along with Lazarfeld (Morrison 1978).

While Horkheimer and Adorno gave little value to low culture, defined as part of mass culture, because they are the products of structures of domination, contrary voices did also raise themselves, as a critical reaction against this very sharp differentiation. One of the most influential figures here was Walter Benjamin, who was to become the most celebrated cultural theorist of the later twentieth and early twenty-first century, and was yet emphatic that the art work could only be placed within a social environment which instrumentalized not only 'mass' culture, but even more so the cultural beacons themselves. His famous claim that 'there is no document of civilization that is not also a document of barbarism' (Benjamin 1969: 256) was his powerful statement that the most valued and venerated cultural artefacts were thereby those whose prominence was due to their association with the victors of history. Through this move, Benjamin placed the art work within an external environment which defined it and which gave it a profoundly tragic quality. Central to Benjamin's argument, therefore, was the association between the art work, tradition and power. The very maturation of culture involved defining it as a tradition, necessarily invoking a linear historical account affiliated with visions of progress and hence of those at the forefront of history – the ruling classes.

Through these intellectual moves, the tide turned progressively against the prized qualities of 'high culture'. Art and the definition of good taste were progressively criticized as less universal and the territory of the aesthetics was increasingly seen as in interaction with that of the social. What was thought of as 'pure' was revealed to be actually subject to social forces. In the 1960s, for instance, the museums were in crisis, being denounced as legitimacy instruments of the ruling classes. In addition the assumptions of universalism, aesthetic autonomy and neutrality on which museums had relied were reassessed in the light of ethnographic works (on this see Chaumier 2010) but also growing postcolonial critique. The narratives presented in museums could be considered as paternalistic and hegemonic while a diversity of cultural views and practices were unravelled and, we will see, soon embraced as a principle to live by (see Hooper-Greenhill 2000).

The notion of popular culture was, as a result, reconsidered, and treated in a more positive way, by being detached from the negative perception of it as associated with low culture. It should however be noted on this issue that for Adorno mass culture is not 'a culture that arises spontaneously from the masses themselves, the contemporary form of popular art' (Adorno and Rabinbach 1975: 12). Similarly Baudrillard also saw a great difference in the sense that popular culture never had the overriding characteristic that mass culture can have (see Célestin 1997). Still, at the end of the 50s and early 60s, Richard Hoggart (2009), one of the 'fathers' of the British Cultural Studies, felt the need to reaffirm the difference between mass and popular culture. Concerned by the omni-presence and 'emptiness' of the former, he wanted to show what was specific to the latter, as the culture of the working class. Stuart Hall (1981), his successor at the head of the Birmingham Centre for Contemporary Cultural Studies, deconstructed the very notion of 'popular'. He moved away from approaches that saw popular culture produced either for the masses, passive receptacles, or by the masses through their ways of life. Instead, going beyond this tension between production and consumption, he saw popular culture as historically and constantly conditioned by class struggles over culture and by their different related operating mechanisms between resistance and consent.

In addition, overtly imperialist visions of culture which had previously held sway were increasingly subject to critique. This was linked to the concern to render such cultures in ways which did not presuppose the superior values of the imperial powers and which sought to render these cultures 'in their own terms'. Politically, large scale de-colonization from the middle decades of the twentieth century came to challenge the assumptions of metropolitan dominance and led to a new interest in 'subaltern' cultures. A further argument too was the influential recognition that modern nationalism was, amongst other things, a cultural process in which modern nations deployed literary and media devices to construct images of an imagined community (Anderson 1983). By the later twentieth century, then, culture was seen to be diffused through all kinds of national formation.

Our argument is that both within the conception of arts and culture as associated with the formation of 'high culture' and in the romantic-inspired critique that informed early social science, there was a productive tension between narrow and broader definitions of culture. These tensions generated wide ranging debates regarding the moral and political stakes associated with the cultural. But these tensions have become less apparent as we move onto our final two 'moments'. We introduce this argument through a focus on the pivotal contribution of Bourdieu, who established the contextual critique of culture in a new, sociological, form. He provided one of the most consistent and elaborated versions of the 'social critique of culture' which became influential in the second half of the twentieth century, whereas important Marxist theoretical interventions failed to generate a comparable body of sustained research. Given the role of Bourdieu's thinking – some of which remains under-appreciated – as a platform for our own position in this handbook, we need to lay out his fundamental contribution in some depth.

The social critique of culture: Bourdieu and beyond

The views of Bourdieu can most profitably be understood as those of the last 'modern' sociologist, in that his sociology was a fundamental meditation on the transition from rural to urban society, from an economy of agrarian production to that marked by the dominance of symbolic exchange. His reflections cannot be separated from his own life history: brought up in rural south-west France in the 1930s and 1940s, and having spent his early adult years in the imperial colony of Algeria, his academic career was nonetheless nurtured in metropolitan Paris, the cultural capital not only of France, but of the world itself (Casanova 2000). This encounter led Bourdieu to delineate a fundamental opposition between these two worlds and to recognize the moralizing and condescending gaze of the educated observer based in the bastions of institutional power. However, rather than accepting the cultural authority of the intellectual, and its stated concerns with '*Bildung*', enlightenment and cultural value, he instead saw it as a socially and politically produced edifice which reproduced power and privilege.

In his most famous book, *Distinction* (1984), he thereby elaborated a 'social critique of the judgement of taste'. Through this turn, therefore, cultural sociology becomes a social critique of art itself through seeking to excavate the opaque and latent social characteristics of art, music, literature and culture more generally, which might be at odds with its declared intentions. A crucial part of his argument was that the claim to disinterestedness and canonical universalism evoked by the cultural authorities was actually central to their success through rendering cultural forms as modes of opaque domination. This can be seen as an extension of, but also a critique of, Marx's famous claims that the dominant ideas of any society are those of the ruling class. Marx's emphasis here was on how certain beliefs, embodied for instance in religion, emphasised the supremacy of the status quo. But Bourdieu's move was more radical in insisting that the most powerful and effective cultural motifs are those which claim to be disinterested and 'above' the nitty-gritty world of lobbying, manoeuvring and power play.

Various chapters of this handbook explore aspects of Bourdieu's arguments, and we do not need to dwell here on the numerous specific areas where his work has informed debate. It is clear from the composition of our textbook that we regard Bourdieu's contribution as fundamental. In the context of our introduction, our broader point is that the significance of Bourdieu's thinking lies in its particularly stark and direct way of posing the critique of humanities as central to the self-conception of sociology itself. He is representative of the rise of a social science apparatus (Savage 2010) which renders the social world through the methods and tools of the post war social sciences: notably through the tools of surveys and interviews. Through such mechanisms, the cultural can be collapsed into the judgements and practices of its participants and the aesthetic itself rendered opaque.

In Bourdieu's work, a social critique of the judgement of taste thus involves placing art and culture within a social world whereby it embodies forms of power and privilege. He was key to the development of the discipline of sociology of art in the way Zolberg describes the role of sociologists in that field:

> Because [sociologists] assume that, like other social phenomena, art cannot be fully understood divorced from its social context, and because […] an art work has monetary value, they accept that the value attached to it derives, not solely from aesthetic qualities intrinsic to the work, but from external conditions as well.
>
> *(1990: 9)*

Bourdieu's most famous contribution here, one of the pivotal concepts in cultural sociology, is that of 'cultural capital'. This simple notion instrumentalizes culture, seeing it as a mode of currency which can be exchanged, reproduced and accumulated. It also places culture alongside other kinds of capitals – such as economic, social or symbolic – thus putting the cultural within a wider social panorama.

Bourdieu's thinking captured a certain moment. It is during the years after 1950 that the proliferation of middle- and lowbrow cultural forms became more marked to the extent that the highbrow could less easily be mobilized as coterminous with culture tout court. A fundamental shift here lay, from the 1960s, with the emergence of what were identified as cultures of affluence. Historically, people's daily lives were characterized by those in authority as forms of pragmatic 'getting by' with only those with leisure having a claim to culture by virtue of being able to stand aside from the necessities of life. However, dramatic economic growth from the 1950s, initially in Europe, North America and Australasia, but then accelerating in many regions of the world from the 1980s, challenged this assumption. Increasingly, cultural motifs of numerous repertoires could be identified across all swathes of social activity.

In this context, therefore, the assumption that the cultural was necessarily tied up with 'high culture' came under increasing strain. Cultural forms were necessarily embedded within a wider range of circuits involved in cultural consumption and production, in ways which made differentiation between these realms even more difficult than previously. One possibility which this opened up was to see the site of popular culture as the site of projects of heroism, resistance and refusal which placed them on the same footing as high culture. Within this framing, the ontological differentiation between the social and cultural collapses but can be rescued through being associated with projects of consecration and boundary drawing. It is in this spirit that Tony Bennett (2007) has explored how the cultural can be mobilized, second hand, through the power of devices and orderings. The cultural here is not a distinctive ontological realm but rather an inscribed sector of the social.

However, it is also clear that such critical concerns are far from distinctive to cultural sociology, or indeed to Bourdieu alone. For, over the past half century, these contextualizing arguments form a staple repertoire within philosophy, anthropology and history, as well as to recent currents within the arts and humanities themselves. High culture and its institutions came under attack from the mid-twentieth century and came to be regarded as the culture of specific social groups by many who pleaded for 'cultural democracy' – through the recognition of the value of many different forms of culture – rather than 'simply' for 'cultural democratization' (Chaumier 2010). Sociology had a major role to play in this, but by deconstructing the social character of art it has also questioned its very aesthetic value. We will come back to that in a minute. This critical perception became further articulated through the artistic avant-garde which defined cultural advance through critique of previous art forms. As these currents expanded, we might see the latter decades of the twentieth century as seeing the radical extension of this instability within the art world so that wide ranging critique becomes endemic and inherently subjects the artistic canon to ubiquitous critique in which no form of art and culture holds canonical status. By the 1970s all branches of the arts and humanities were dominated by this turn. For instance, within art history, it is possible to distinguish 'the social history of art' which in the arguments of T.J. Clark (1999) allowed impressionist art to be understood as part of the 'painting of modern life'. Within literature, the last serious attempt to defend a canonical project was F.R. Leavis in the 1950s and 1960s, from which moment deconstructionism, structuralism and more general post-modern currents have become the wellspring of literary studies.

The result is that in recent decades all modes of cultural expression – textual, visual and aural – are subjected to extensive external review and critique, which tends to relativize their value. This is the world of 'the expediency of culture' (Yudice 2004), through Boltanski and Chiapello's *The New Spirit of Capitalism* (2005) and Nigel Thrift's *Knowing Capitalism* (2005). Nothing remains outside circuits of review and critique. To this extent, Bourdieu's arguments – or correlates of them – are now utterly mundane, and have become institutionalized as the core common sense of our time.

This contextual move has had profound implications for the analysis of art and culture. The most important of these was to hive off the study of cultural production from reception and consumption. Cultural sociology took up the study of the audiences for music, art and literature, but these studies for long took the art work itself as a given, often relying simply on audience taste for broad genre labels (such as classical music). On the other hand, analyses of cultural industries and production rarely engaged with these debates about the audiences for art. To put this in another way, supply and demand became separated out in ways which stripped out the art work itself from the focus of attention.

We need to make it clear that these tendencies were contested. Critical theory in particular, and Marxism more generally, strongly resisted these moves. Within the sociology of literature into the 1970s, most notably, questions of the aesthetic, production and consumption were closely inter-related. Such interests became focused in the trailblazing work of the Birmingham Centre for Cultural Studies, where questions of style jostled with analyses of class, gender and racial inequality. From this platform, these more critical concerns became sequestered into cultural studies and cultural theory more broadly and less frequently cross-fertilised with much of the research being conducted within the sociology of culture. The reasons for this lie – we think – with the formalization of the contextual critique associated with the increasing use of mainstream social science methods.

The formalization of the contextual critique

Although the social critique embraced the project of cultural democratization, it has transpired that it has not been very effective in extending the popular audiences for art. It is true that it contributed to the relativization of the sacred status given to what was traditionally considered as high but also to the promotion of new values in culture, such as leisure, entertainment, fun and play (Featherstone 1991). It would not be too far-fetched to assume that the massification of culture and its McDonaldization, to use Ritzer's terms, have helped to destabilize high culture's hegemony, not necessarily by overriding it but also by challenging its social status and importance (Michaud 1997).

However, most cultural institutions have remained over the years the privilege of a selected few. We have not arrived at an often feared and proclaimed situation in which anything goes. The power of high culture appears to continue in marked ways. And here we introduce our last moment, in which the increasing use of formal social scientific methods has permitted the social critique to grow in range and scope. Surveys, both qualitative and quantitative, have kept showing the relation between stratification and culture, even if they have started to investigate a more varied set of dimensions of social stratification. Therefore the partial relativization of culture went along with the growing formalization of sociological analysis of art and culture.

Over the past two decades the trend to use social scientific methods to render and delineate the social dynamics of diverse cultural worlds – art, literature, music and so forth – has become more marked. As we have seen, elements of this approach are evident in Bourdieu's sociology, notably in his use of formal quantitative methods, as well as case study analysis to analyse the patterns of cultural taste and participation and their relationship to social groups. Bourdieu's framing, however, was within field analysis, rather than through the more linear methods which became increasingly prominent in the last decades of the twentieth century. This concern to use standard multivariate models to analyse culture in the arenas of visual arts, music and leisure more generally became especially strong in American sociology, led originally by Lazarfeld from the later 1930s in his influential radio research programme funded by the Rockefeller foundation. These studies examined how audiences reacted to radio programmes and laid the platform for the development of survey methods in cultural analysis. Scholars such as Paul DiMaggio and Peterson proved highly influential here in the elaboration of this approach, and their joint 1975 paper examining the genesis of country music was one of the first of this kind. Oriented especially towards the quantitative expertise of American and some European nations, this championed mainstream social scientific methods. This was seen to permit sociologists to conduct the kind of analyses of culture that have long been conducted of the social structure and the economy.

Bourdieu's work was influential for the quantitative turn in setting a foil which others could dispute. His argument that there was a distinctive or high form of cultural capital, which embraces a Kantian aesthetic of disinterestedness and celebrates classical music, canonical literary forms and modes of modernist culture, proved an effective argument to test. A particular focus was whether in fact there was an association between the educated elites and such cultural forms. This mode of cultural sociology began to expand with the development of survey sources which systematically ask questions on cultural practices and tastes. Such surveys began in a significant form in the 1960s, sometimes in association with market research, which indeed constitute a major feature of Bourdieu's work. In France, the survey *'L'enquête sur les pratiques culturelles des Français'* started in the early 1970s. In the United States we can trace the way that the General Social Survey included questions on cultural taste and participation from the 1980s, and several European nations also developed cultural surveys during that period (e.g. the Amenities and Social Services Utilization Survey – AVO – in the Netherlands). Quite often influenced by American models, these data sources proved highly important as regression and other modelling methods were applied to them. The key intervention here was the arguments for the rise of the cultural omnivore originating with the American cultural sociologist Richard Peterson (e.g. Peterson and Simkus 1992). Here, survey data were used to test the idea that people were becoming more omnivorous, that is to say, happy to consume cultural forms which spanned high, middle and low brow formats. This issue is taken up in several chapters of this handbook. Note that Olivier Donnat (1994) also started to refer to the growing importance of eclecticism in the early 1990s.

Bourdieu's work hence generated a profusion of research on the audience of cultural institutions, surveys of cultural participation and so on, which all had Bourdieu's theory as a starting point even if sometimes the idea was to depart from it. Yet, the institutionalization of both sub-disciplines, sociology of art and sociology of culture, has also been marked by a focus on the link between stratification and culture in a quite repetitive and uncritical way. Following a certain interpretation of Bourdieu's work (1979), sociological accounts have often privileged what Woodward and Emmison call 'studies of objectified tastes' that relate people's cultural preferences to their socio-economic characteristics in a quite systematic way. As these authors put it, these studies 'emphasise that patterns of cultural taste are enmeshed within complexly interacting forms of social and cultural power, by means of which differences in tastes and cultural preferences are used as markers of social position.' (2001: 296).

These approaches shouldn't be dismissed. On the contrary, they have been extremely important in helping people to grasp the social importance of tastes and, more generally, culture in the understanding of social inequalities. They have shown how socially determined tastes could be through deconstructing the idea that tastes are just natural. However these studies have concentrated on a few indicators of culture, allegedly representative of high and low culture, but have lost sight of what high and low mean or, more accurately, how they should be traced back to how people do culture and make sense out of it. This neglects Bourdieu's own insistence that high and low cultures could only be seen as relational and could only be defined in the light of the constellation of co-existent lifestyles in which cultural practices and tastes were inserted. By emphasizing the links between lifestyles or ways of life and the definitions of high and low culture, he thus can be said to give warrant to a view that might conflate cultural analysis with social analysis more generally. Sometimes identified as the 'aestheticisation of everyday life' (Featherstone 1991), lifestyles are increasingly visually evocative – aesthetic in the plain sense of the terms – but also draw on aesthetic values and norms which are socio-historically built but still can't be reduced to their social implications (notably in terms of social stratification). Aesthetic and social structures – including moral values – co-construct each other in a relational way and can't simply be reduced to one another. It is precisely because of this that our handbook covers both sociology of culture and sociology of art. Both share many aspects, especially once one also wants to consider the aesthetic dimensions of culture and its social repercussions.

Towards a relational and aesthetic sociology of art and culture

Having elaborated our four 'moments', let us conclude by suggesting that we should now be championing a further phase, a critique which changes the stakes involved in understanding the boundaries between art and culture and the social and sees in the aesthetic and relational qualities of art itself the social being enacted, contested and refined. Within our third and fourth moments – the social critique, and its formalization – it was the categories of the economic, social and political which held sway over the cultural. However in recent sociological thinking there is a new focus on the aesthetic and the relational, and with this sensibility, we contend that the balance is shifting back towards the art work. A main aim of this handbook is to collect together a varied set of engagements with these twin interests so that readers might judge for themselves the potential of this new body of thinking.

This new perspective needs to be placed in contrast to what now constitutes mainstream approaches. We are surrounded by indicators of high and low tastes and genres. We have numerous ways – often very sophisticated – of linking them to social positionings. If this approach can be partly explained by the techniques of analysis employed (indeed some don't accommodate well with complex conceptualizations and operationalizations), it is worth noting that even key works in sociology of art, which could hardly be defined as positivist, have also focused on the social construction of arts and avoided any consideration of aesthetics (Howard Becker's *Art Worlds* [1982] being the perfect example). This handbook aims to show that cultural sociology as an external social critique *only* – focusing on the social patterning of specific tastes and practices or the social construction of the arts – has now reached its limit and that we today need to rethink the sub-discipline, its tools and theories.

This involves rendering a distinction between an instrumental and an aesthetic critique. We thus need to keep some distance from approaches which see the cultural as rendered through serving the purpose of diverse social groups, so that its significance depends on how it is an effective tool. Such perspectives lie at the heart of Karl Marx's famous emphasis on how the ruling ideas of society serve the interests of the ruling class. They have also been alleged to inform Bourdieu's insistence on the role of cultural capital, in which valued artistic and cultural forms permit the reproduction of the educated middle classes. Thus, to say that certain cultural modes advance the interests of specific groups, or exclude others, is most likely true but does not exhaust the meaning and significance of the cultural.

We can see the alternative mode of thinking as also having a long lineage – though one which is less powerful and more interrupted. It might include, for instance, the work of Walter Benjamin and the Frankfurt School, through the Birmingham Centre for Contemporary Cultural Studies – for instance Hebdige's insistence on style – through the thinking of Deleuze and Guattari. For contemporary purposes we see two major banners which can usefully update and renew this more fluid and dynamic way of appreciating art and culture: 1) aesthetics and 2) a relational approach.

1) *A focus on aesthetics.* This has taken place in different ways depending on whether the research has been looking into aesthetic experiences or aesthetic contents, norms and values. With regard to the first trend, the work of sociologists like Antoine Hennion and Tia DeNora has been influential. Their research focuses on the interactions between the object and the subject and how both are produced and transformed by these interactions. If we take the example of music, it is shaped through the meanings listeners 'attach' to it when they experience it at given moments (Hennion 2007). The distinction between music listener and creator as well as that between the object and the subject become blurred: first, the meaning attached to music is not a given but results from a mutually constitutive relationship (or 'reflexive activity,' Hennion would say) that attaches together an individual keen to experience and an object ready to surprise; second, music contributes to the development of the self (DeNora 1999). These approaches are most certainly valuable because they take the art work seriously. DeNora's perspective shows most interestingly how music has aesthetic properties that act in people's everyday life. For instance, some music pieces are capable of generating specific emotions (2001).

Most recently this interest on aesthetic experience has been widened with the idea that aesthetics or an aesthetic approach of sociology should not only focus on a specific range of goods, the arts. Instead, it would focus on the structures of experience, i.e. 'how actors respond to the qualitative properties of experience' to quote Martin in this volume. This perspective therefore takes very seriously the social organization of perceptions. This is a separate current to the micro-sociological approaches discussed in the previous paragraph which might be said to really seek to re-connect with the macro-social implications (see the critique of Born [2010] on this).

In addition, the growing interest in aesthetics can also lead researchers to reflect upon aesthetic norms and contents that underline the concepts and indicators we traditionally use. Arguably in line with Dewey's conception of aesthetic experience (Strandvad 2012), Hennion's theory of attachment (Hennion 2001), for instance, tells us little about how and why specific aesthetic properties and structures of art works, but also more general goods, become activated in the transformative encounter between the subject and the object. It does not explain much about how aesthetic boundaries evolve over time alongside with changes in aesthetic and social theory[5] and that these boundaries act as socially and historically situated structures for the development of people's tastes. We can see the value of this approach focusing on aesthetic boundaries by reflecting on how it can enrich key sociological discussions, such as the debates about omnivorousness, and about the boundaries between high and low but also the role of new media and of cities – and their symbolic power – in people's lifestyle. These issues are all discussed in this handbook, which probes a more aesthetically attuned approach to the sociology of culture and art.

We see this in keeping with our own work. For instance, we have recently shown with our colleague Henk Roose (also a contributor to this handbook) that the very content of highbrow culture might have changed reflecting now both classical and 'emerging' aesthetic values, such as the playful (Hanquinet, Roose and Savage 2014). This means that the very conceptualization of cultural capital – for those keen to employ the concept – should now take into consideration the plurality of aesthetic paradigms at play in its formation. According to this perspective, aesthetics doesn't only refer to the emotional and experiential encounter with objects but also to the ways in which our perceptions are influenced by values, images, codes and habits which can be traced back to the evolutions of the artistic and cultural fields. For instance the tension between high and low culture is still underlined by an opposition between art and money which served well the modernist myth of the artist as a sacred genius. Still today if an artist is making money (for instance, pop stars), there will always be the suspicion that she or he is not a real gifted person. In line with a current of sociology seeking to grasp values at stake in people's judgements (Heinich 2006), aesthetics is here seen as an important register of action whose complexity and origins must be unravelled in order to understand how people organize lifestyles in an aestheticized everyday life. These toolkits – to use Swidler's word – of values, images, codes and habits, which are then socio-historically developed, are essential to understand how people make sense of their environment and they will do so in a relational fashion as recent works in sociology have shown.

2) *A relational approach.* We see interests in relational sociology as also enriching the repertoire of the sociology of arts and culture. Interests in the 'relational' were formalized in the 1990s in the US through the development of arguments from the New York School (Mische 2011). Yet the ideas it promotes have a much longer history (Emirbayer [1997] argued that it could be traced back to the Pre-Socratics).

Relational perspectives are varied but have a certain 'style of thought'. Rather than attributing agency to objects, variables or attributes, they see the processes of interaction as central.

Bourdieu's conception of the 'field' has attracted considerable attention here. This sees the cultural as akin to a sporting game, with different contestants pitching for position. This metaphor therefore leads to a more fluid understanding of cultural process and also directs us to think about the aesthetic qualities arising from these interactions (in the same way that sporting encounters may have an aesthetic dimension arising from the game being more than the sum of its parts).

Martin (2003) has shown that this interest in field dynamics has a broader intellectual provenance than Bourdieu's sociology alone and associates it with the analysis of force and attraction within the natural sciences. In the context of the sociology of art and culture, we can see the appeal of this move: it takes the focus away from the individual artists and their 'intentionality', and it also focuses on the game itself rather than collapse it into the social context. Moretti has argued that this can allow a distinct perspective on the analysis of literary form, taken to mean 'a diagram of forces'. And this move has also allowed Moretti to use novel methods, ranging from maps, graphs and various kinds of quantitative analysis to open up literature to readings which extend well beyond authorial intention (Moretti 2005, 2014, and see also Bennett 2010).

As we will see in the handbook, field theory *à la Bourdieu* has been used in various ways but still has reaffirmed a large and encompassing definition of culture (as lifestyles articulated around diverse values, artistic—but not only) and enabled a certain widening of the meaning of aesthetics which can become a logic of action (see, for instance, Martin in this volume). Approaches that see the links between the social and the cultural in relational terms are attracted to modes of social theory which emphasize the importance of 'emergent properties' whereby certain processes cannot be reduced to the components which might make it up. Thus, we should resist reducing 'classical music' for instance, to being the taste of educated middle class people and should see it as embodying aesthetic forms which exceed the interests and conceptions of its enthusiasts (see for example, Benzecry 2011).

This argument can be affiliated to forms of complexity theory and to attempts to bridge the separation between structure and agency, and macro and micro, which abound in sociological theory. More radically still they embrace the possibility that the arts and the aesthetic have certain features which cannot readily be reduced to the social. Yet, this position against a certain form of reductionism shouldn't prevent us from seeing cultural and social logics as co-constructing each other.

The relational therefore allows us to see the aesthetic as emerging from encounters between diverse agents, giving us a way of moving beyond the tension between the art work and the social context. And for our purposes, it is also exciting that this idea permits the use of a range of heterodox quantitative methods such as social network analysis, cluster analysis and multiple correspondence analysis to formally describe patterns of interaction and differentiation. Here we methodologically move beyond the view that cultural analysis necessitates qualitative methods alone. By criticizing the reduction of social and cultural relations to attributes (or variables), links are also made to the pragmatist emphasis discussed as part of the aesthetic turn. Relational methods offer powerful resources for the mapping of associations and ties. This is a powerful approach which several chapters in this handbook explore in depth.

To sum up, taking together these two new currents offers powerful resources for re-charging the sociology of art and culture. Taking the aesthetics seriously here does not entail defining this term through a conventional perspective from the vantage point of the artistic canon. It makes us think in a more useful way about the relations between the cultural and the social and also about the important mediating role of aesthetic values, contents and norms.

This approach through aesthetics might also be seen as a way to render the social as relational, and through this move, cultural sociology offers a more powerful tool for conducting social analysis more generally.

Conclusion

We seek, in this book, to find a way of retaining the passions and intensities which attach to sociology of culture by not reducing it to a simply bounded or demarcated field with a clear object or mode of analysis. However, we also wish to find some way of establishing an intellectual coherence to the project of sociology of culture itself. We have put this handbook together in the view that the social critique, allied to the formalization of the contextual critique, has pulled too far away from the aesthetic aspects of inquiry, and we seek here to reach greater balance. We therefore argue for an aesthetically attuned and relational sociology of culture which we think can re-energise the discipline as a whole whilst also permitting a clear focus on the cultural, art and the aesthetics. The latter define values that are crucial in the formation of lifestyle which follows relational principles.

Our broad argument here is that we can most profitably develop a sociology of art and culture focusing on the aesthetic as implicated in, and emerging out of, interactions between diverse social agents. We find Bourdieu's conception of the field a useful way of understanding this, but there are other ways of elaborating this approach. We contend that this approach permits us to endorse the 'classic' move which criticizes a focus on the individual artist and their intentions without collapsing the study of art into the context. This is because aesthetic forms arise from the interaction between agents in the way that a beautiful game of tennis, for instance, emerges from encounter between players as they improvise and compete.

It follows from our argument that we do not seek to establish the sociology of art and culture as a closed specialism or paradigm. We are not seeking to define the field as some kind of parallel set of inquiries to that found in cultural and media studies. Rather, we see its fluidity and relative openness as a virtue to celebrate. One of the advantages of our perspective is that it elaborates the excitement of sociology of culture in terms of the contested definitions and stakes which the discipline conveys, recognizing how they have developed agonistically and in relationship to dominant intellectual currents of their day. It is through understanding oppositions with which cultural sociology is engaged that we can best define a productive future for this area of work. It is in this spirit that the chapters of this handbook have been written.

Notes

1. We would like to thank Tony Bennett and Sharon Macdonald for their astute comments on a draft of this introduction.
2. There are three different European Sociological Association Research Networks working on these areas (Sociology of Culture, of the Arts and of Consumption).
3. Cultural anthropology has a long history of seeking jurisdiction over the 'cultural' (especially in the United States) but has always been in contest with more 'social' approaches to anthropology which have been important in Europe.
4. Indeed, this is where we would differentiate the aims of our handbook from others which have a less focused approach, such as Hall, Gridstaff and Ming-Cheng's *Handbook of Cultural Sociology* (2012) and *The Oxford Handbook of Cultural Sociology* (Alexander, Jacobs and Smith 2013).
5. See Witkin (1997).

References

Adorno, T. and A. Rabinbach (1975) 'Culture industry reconsidered', *New German Critique*, 6(6): 12–19.
Alexander, J., R. Jacobs and P. Smith (2013) *The Oxford handbook of cultural sociology*, Oxford: Oxford University Press.
Alexander, J. and P. Smith (2001) 'The strong program in cultural sociology', in J. Turner, *The handbook of sociological theory*, New York: Kluwer, pp. 1–19.
Anderson, B. (1983) *Imagined community*, London: Verso.
Arnold, M. (1961) *Culture and anarchy*, Cambridge: Cambridge University Press.
Becker, H. (1982) *Art worlds*, Berkeley: University of California Press.
Benjamin, W. (1969) in *Illuminations*, trans. Harry Zohn, New York: Schocken Books, pp. 253–264 ('Theses on the philosophy of history').
Bennett, T. (2005) 'The historical universal: the role of cultural value in the historical sociology of Pierre Bourdieu', *British Journal of Sociology*, 56 (1): 141–164.
—— (2007) 'The work of culture', *Cultural Sociology*: 1: 31–47.
—— (2010) 'Sociology, aesthetics, expertise', *New Literary History*, 41: 253–276.
Benzecry, C. (2011) *The opera fanatic: ethnography of an obsession*, Chicago: University of Chicago Press.
Boltanski, L. and E. Chiapello (2005) *The new spirit of capitalism*, London: Verso.
Born, G. (2010) 'The social and the aesthetic: for a post-Bourdieuian theory of cultural production', *Cultural Sociology*, 4(2): 171–208.
Bourdieu, P. (1984) *Distinction: a social critique of the judgement of taste*, translated by Richard Nice, Cambridge, MA: Harvard University Press.
Casanova, P. (2000) *The world republic of letters*, London: Verso.
Célestin, R. (1997) 'Interview with Jean Baudrillard: from popular culture to mass culture', *The Journal of Twentieth-Century/Contemporary French Studies revue d'études français*, 1(1): 5–15.
Chaumier, S. (2010) *L'inculture pour tous. La nouvelle utopie des politiques culturelles*, Paris: L'Harmattan.
Clark, T.J. (1999) *The painting of modern life*, Princeton, NJ: Princeton University Press.
DeNora, T. (1999) 'Music as a technology of the self', *Poetics*, 27: 31–56.
—— (2001) *Music in everyday life*, Cambridge: Cambridge University Press.
DiMaggio, P. (1982) 'Cultural entrepreneurship in nineteenth-century Boston', *Media, Culture & Society*, (4): 33–50.
DiMaggio, P. and R. Peterson (1975) 'From region to class, the changing locus of country music: a test of the massification hypothesis', *Social Forces*, 53(3): 497–506.
Dirks, N. (2002) *Castes of mind*, Princeton, NJ: Princeton University Press.
Donnat, O. (1994) *Les Français face à la culture. De l'exclusion à l'éclectisme*, Paris: La découverte.
Emirbayer, M. (1997) 'Manifesto for a relational sociology', *American Journal of Sociology*, 103: 281–317.
Featherstone, M. (1991) *Consumer culture and postmodernism. Theory, culture and society*, ed., London: Sage.
Genard J.-L. (2011) *Démocratisation de la culture et/ou démocratie culturelle? Comment repenser aujourd'hui une politique de démocratisation de la culture?* At the conference 'Cinquante ans d'action publique en matière de culture au Québec' (4 et 5 avril: l'Université de Montréal). Available online at www.gestiondesarts.com/media/wysiwyg/documents/Genard.pdf (Accessed 15 January 2015).
Hall, J.R., L. Gridstaff and L. Ming-Cheng (eds.) (2012) *Handbook of cultural sociology*, London: Routledge.
Hall, S. (1981) 'Notes on deconstructing "the popular"', in Samuel R. (ed.) *People's history and socialist theory*, London: Routledge, pp. 227–240.
Hanquinet, L., H. Roose and M. Savage (2014) 'The eyes of the beholder: aesthetic preferences and the remaking of cultural capital', *Sociology*, 48(1): 111–132.
Heinich, N. (2006) 'La sociologie à l'épreuve des valeurs', *Cahiers internationaux de sociologie*, 121(2): 287–315.
—— (2010) 'What does "sociology of culture" mean? Notes on a few trans-cultural misunderstandings', *Cultural Sociology*, 4: 257–265.
Hennion, A. (2001) 'Music lovers: taste as performance', *Theory, Culture and Society*, 18(5): 1–22.
—— (2007) 'Those things that hold us together: taste and sociology', *Cultural Sociology*, 1(1): 97–114.
Hoggart, R. (2009) *The uses of literacy. Aspects of working-class life*, London: Penguin Books.
Hooper-Greenhill, E. (2000) *Museums and the interpretation of visual culture*, London: Routledge.
Horkheimer, M. and T.W. Adorno (2002) *Dialectic of enlightenment: philosophical fragments*, Stanford, CA: Stanford University Press, pp. 94–136.

Levine, L. (1990) *Highbrow/lowbrow. The emergence of cultural hierarchy in America*, Cambridge, MA: Harvard University Press.
Martin, J.L. (2003) 'What is field theory', *American Journal of Sociology*.
Michaud, Y. (1997) *La crise de l'art contemporain*, Paris: Presses Universitaires de France.
Mische, A. (2011) 'Relational sociology, culture, and agency', in J. Scott and P. Carrington (eds.), *The Sage handbook of social network analysis*, London: Sage, pp. 80–97.
Mitchell, T. (2001) *The rule of experts*, Berkeley, CA: University of California Press.
Moretti, F. (2005) *Graphs, Maps, Trees*, London: Verso.
—— (2014) *The bourgeois: between history and literature*, London: Verso.
Morrison, D.E. (1978) 'Kultur and culture: the case of Theodor W. Adorno and Paul F. Lazarsfeld', *Social Research*, 45(2): 331–355.
Peterson, R. and A. Simkus (1992) 'How musical tastes mark occupational status groups', in M. Fournier and M. Lamont (eds.), *Cultivating differences. Symbolic boundaries and the making of inequality*, Chicago: The University of Chicago Press, pp. 152–187.
Savage, M. (2010) *Identities and social change in Britain since 1940: the politics of method*, Oxford: Oxford University Press.
Strandvad, S.M. (2012) 'Attached by the product: a socio-material direction in the sociology of art', *Cultural Sociology*, 6(2): 163–176.
Taylor, C. (1992) *Sources of the self: the making of modern identity*, Cambridge, MA: Harvard University Press.
Thrift, N.J. (2005) *Knowing capitalism*, London: Sage.
Tylor, E. (1871) *Primitive culture*, London: Putnams.
Williams, R. (1956) *Culture and society*, Harmondsworth: Penguin.
—— (1985), *Keywords*, Oxford: Oxford University Press.
Witkin, R. (1997) 'Constructing a sociology for an icon of aesthetic modernity: Olympia revisited', *Sociological Theory*, 15(2): 101–125.
Woodward, I. and M. Emmison (2001) 'From aesthetic principles to collective sentiments: the logics of everyday judgements of taste', *Poetics*, 29(6): 295–316.
Yudice, G. (2004) *The expediency of culture*, Durham, NC: Duke University Press.
Zolberg, V.L. (1990) *Constructing a sociology of the arts*. Cambridge: Cambridge University Press.

Part I
Bourdieu's legacy and new perspectives for the sociology of art and culture

Introduction to Part I

One of the main themes of this handbook is to explore the implications of Bourdieu's work to the sociology of art and culture and to position his thinking against rival approaches. In some respects, Bourdieu's importance hardly needs emphasis. His account of French lifestyles and cultural taste in *Distinction* (1984) is one of the single most important monographs written in post-war sociology anywhere in the world. In emphasizing what he terms 'the social critique of the judgement of taste', Bourdieu fundamentally affirmed the ways in which art was implicated in the making and contesting of social relationships more widely. His fundamental move was to take the 'pure' aesthetic judgement not on its own terms – as a claim about universal standards of taste and value – but as embodying forms of privilege which precisely through lifting value out of its context thus empowers those with the capacity to be distant from the world of everyday necessity. Through this deft manoeuvre, the work of artists (and intellectuals more generally) is seen as exhibiting forms of cultural capital which are complicit with privilege and power. His arguments can thus be deeply unsettling to those working in the cultural sector, as well as to those schooled in the humanities disciplines, which can from within this purview, be seen to be implicated in cultural capital itself.

It is not the aim of any of our chapters to provide introductions to the way in which Bourdieu extends this thinking in the numerous fields in which he was interested. We assume that many readers will have some acquaintanceship with his ideas, and those who wish to find a good recent account may want to read the first chapter of Bennett *et al.*'s *Culture, Class, Distinction* (2009), or refer to the edited collections by Silva and Warde (2012) or Coulangeon and Duval (2014). Our main concern in this handbook is to unpack the Bourdieusian legacy so that readers can identify the relational and aesthetic potential of his thinking more directly. It should be noted at the outset that Bourdieu is a figure who excites both negative and positive passions which can lead to his thought being simplified and made more unitary than it actually is. Thus, the concept of cultural capital has been extensively reviled by those seeing it as reductive, simplistic or as denying agency and creativity. There is certainly no doubt – as we shall see shortly – that the concept can be used in a rather simplistic way – for instance by identifying it as coterminous with particular 'highbrow' tastes such as for the opera; however, our intention is to encourage a realization that there is much more to Bourdieu's thinking than this.

Our approach in this handbook is therefore not to pigeonhole a 'true' Bourdieu (to either criticize or praise), but to use his thinking as a resource to advance the research agenda today – and in a context which is very different to that in which he conducted his own research for *Distinction* fifty years ago. Rather than seeking to exemplify the arguments which Bourdieu made in *Distinction* through arguing that 'nothing has changed', it is ultimately more in keeping with his own historically oriented way of thinking to see how his approach can allow new insights to be generated.

Bourdieu and cultural sociology

The first section focuses directly on the significance of Bourdieu's thinking, originally in the French context but also more widely in terms of his role within cultural sociology. We start by reflecting on how Bourdieu has influenced French debate, both within the academy and beyond. Coulangeon's chapter offers a systematic account of how, in his native context, Bourdieu's thinking fed into cultural policy and politics through providing a distinctive account of the cleavages in cultural engagement. By bringing out the significance of politics in the French context, we can immediately identify a difference from his reception elsewhere, for the obvious reason that Bourdieu and his followers were not the kind of highly visible political agents elsewhere that they were in France. But Coulangeon also explores how Bourdieu's concept of cultural capital has always been contested even within France, notably through the work of Bernard Lahire who disputed the extent to which individuals had coherent cultural practices as one might expect if there were cohesive forms of 'highbrow' culture[1]. The irony, therefore, is that in his own French heartland, Bourdieu's conception of cultural capital, as it applies to the organization of taste, practices and lifestyles, is highly contested and little pursued in research in this area.

Within the French tradition, Bourdieu's work on production figures at least as strongly as that on consumption, but this is completely different to his reception in the Anglophone world. In the UK, as well as in Australia, Bourdieu's work was mainly appropriated through academics working in cultural studies, especially those influenced by debates about cultural consumption. Thus, from the 1980s, Mike Featherstone (1985), Scott Lash and John Urry (1987), Alan Warde (1997) and others all used Bourdieu to elaborate new concepts of lifestyle and consumption as part of their endeavours to show these areas of sociological exploration had previously been under-developed. The result here is that Bourdieu's interest in production and in intermediation was relatively little used, whereas his accounts of lifestyle and consumption – which were highly contested within France, as Coulangeon discusses – proved much more influential. This is the reason why in the second part of this handbook we deliberately introduce reflections on production and mediation to redress this imbalance and show recent changes in the Anglophone reception of Bourdieu's work.

The other contributions to this section are important for situating Bourdieu's contribution more broadly in global perspective so that its potential advantages and disadvantages become clear. Santoro and Solaroli offer the most engaged critique of the thinking of the American cultural sociologist Jeffrey Alexander that is currently available. This is an important paper since Alexander is one of Bourdieu's most vociferous critics and is responsible for the elaboration of the 'strong programme' of cultural sociology which might be seen as intellectual rival. Santoro and Solaroli demonstrate powerfully the weakness of Alexander's criticism of Bourdieu (as well as of the wider 'strong program') and argue that the two intellectual projects – Bourdieusian sociology and the so called 'strong program' – might be reframed as reciprocally reinforcing perspectives towards a more comprehensive and effective (and thus truly 'stronger') platform for the sociology of art and culture. We see this paper as a vital underpinning for the broader arguments of this handbook.

Beljean, Chong and Lamont also show the potential of Bourdieu's thinking to inform new areas of research even though his specific claims — about valuation in their case — may be criticized. They show how his specific, possibly reductive, approach towards valuation, which he elaborates in the French context, can be opened out to provide a wider ranging perspective, incorporating insights from intellectual traditions — such as pragmatism, science studies, and organisational sociology — which may appear to be alien to Bourdieu's thinking in his specific French context.

This first set of papers thus both situates Bourdieu's original contribution in his French context and also considers how it relates to cultural sociology more broadly. We see (from Beljean, Chong and Lamont) how Bourdieu's thinking can be adapted for broader projects around questions of valuation and (from Santoro and Solaroli) how it compares favourably with Alexander's strong programme.

The omnivore debate

The second section turns directly to the 'omnivore debate'. This may appear a rather narrow argument, exploring whether the better educated and more privileged classes are attracted towards plural rather than 'highbrow' tastes, but these chapters show that this seemingly specialized interest has actually become the lightning conductor for a number of orienting concerns in the sociology of art and culture. This is due to the way that the omnivore concept has lent itself to strategies for quantification as researchers measure the range and character of people's tastes using survey data. The omnivore debate was originated in the early 1990s by Richard Peterson, one of the most important American quantitative sociologists examining culture, almost as an aside, but has become a major research industry in its own right. The debate thus allowed Bourdieu's thinking to be introduced into 'mainstream' American sociology, and as Karademir Hazır and Warde show, the popularization of the concept of the cultural omnivore has come to have huge provenance in debates across the world.

Peterson's work is important because the omnivore concept allowed the quantification of cultural taste using data from numerous national surveys. Unlike the very rich and complex material on cultural taste used in Bourdieu's studies in France, most national surveys, especially those in the US, tended to contain only a few questions asking about preferential taste for specific genres of (mainly) music. The relative paucity of questions on cultural and aesthetic tastes made it challenging to say much of sociological interest by analyzing them. Peterson's important innovation here was to examine the extent to which people's tastes crossed the boundaries between what could be deemed to be 'highbrow' (for instance, classical music), 'middlebrow' (for instance, gospel music) and 'lowbrow' (for instance, rock music). Using this quite simple but deft approach, quantification becomes possible, and Bourdieu could be used as an intellectual foil that provided the 'null hypothesis' against which the omnivore thesis could launch itself. Thus, by showing that large numbers of well-educated people do not appear to have cohesive highbrow tastes as Bourdieu might think, but that they in fact range across a set of high, medium and low brow genres, the apparently banal finding that people have complex tastes was seen as a matter of interest because it was taken to refute the view that a distinctive kind of cultural capital existed.

Karademir Hazır and Warde show, sympathetically, how the omnivore debate has been so influential within the sociology of art and culture by extending methodological approaches and developing more sophisticated ways of thinking. Gayo's analysis of the omnivore concept, on the other hand, reviews how it has been received, especially within the South American context, in order to point to some of its limitations which become even more apparent when translated outside their native context.

However, Karademir and Warde show that the concept of the omnivore can be used productively to examine important issues, and it would be much too crude to dismiss it. We can see examples of this more creative approach in chapters from this handbook, such as those by Lizardo and Skiles and by Reeves, which show also how the omnivore itself can become a foil around which more sophisticated forms of thinking can be mounted, including those more sympathetic to Bourdieu's thinking. Here, rather than the omnivore being reified as a distinctive social 'type', the concept is seen to pose issues about the wider dynamics of cultural taste and participation. Both of these explore what has become one of the central issues, the role of age, generation and time more generally, in shaping the consumption of art and culture. This is an area where Bourdieu said relatively little, though research in the recent past has come to recognize this as a major divide, with younger generations having distinctive cultural profiles compared to older ones. Lizardo and Skiles, Reeves and Reeves in different ways, point to the prospects that more sophisticated strategies for quantification will allow the omnivore concept to be broken down into more telling and discrete categories, especially in ways which are more sensitive to questions of temporality.

Relational approaches to the sociology of art and culture

The final section opens up this discussion still further to reflect on the potential of 'relational approaches' within the sociology of art and culture. The argument that sociology needs to be relational has now been in existence for twenty years, being elaborated with particular force by Emirbayer (1997). We have discussed in the introduction to our book why we see this as a powerful mode for animating current debates in the area. A growing current of relational modes of thinking can be traced especially in American sociology, and we see these as very exciting and having great potential. This is partly because of the way that they articulate theoretical, substantive and methodological debates.

A feature of 'relationalism' is its potential to be associated to wider theoretical perspectives which resist positivist and linear perspectives, and Lévi-Martin and Merriman explore the nature of field analysis itself. They bring out how Bourdieu's use of field analysis goes beyond invoking the aesthetic simply as a particular part of the field and extends to the very organization of the field itself. In this respect, we can see how one of our main aims of this handbook is exemplified within this current of post-Bourdieusian thinking. The power of the field concept also comes out in numerous other papers in this handbook (and see also Savage and Silva 2013).

Our interest in relationality is also associated with important methodological arguments within sociology. Much of the analysis within the 'omnivore' literature uses conventional linear quantitative methods, such as regression models. There are, however, forms of quantitative analysis which do not seek to model discrete 'dependent variables' (such as the 'omnivore') but instead are interested in exploring the nature of relationships within a complex data set so that pattern of relationships can be delineated within it. Such approaches avoid one of the main criticisms of quantitative analyses of art and culture: that they seek to reduce measures of culture to simple or discrete variables that are thereby bound to be too crude to be meaningful.

Lena's paper is an important intervention which points to the limits of using 'genre' questions in cultural sociology. Her argument is crucial since genre questions are nearly invariably the focus of attention within the omnivore debate. Lena shows the problems of relying on genre questions and shows the power of using structural studies from anthropology and sociology to do more justice to the meaning of cultural works, and in particular to bring out their relational qualities.

Lena's analysis links to the paper by Rule and Bearman, who further reflect on the role of network thinking for developing relational research strategies. In the recent past, social network analysis has had an increasingly high profile but has rarely engaged with Bourdieu's thinking, yet in their important contribution Rule and Bearman show how thinking influenced by network analysis can cross-fertilize with broader relational perspectives to inform the sociology of art and culture.

Finally, we should remember that Bourdieu himself was a key figure in the use of quantitative relational methods, notably with his use of multiple correspondence analysis in *Distinction*, though surprisingly this technique was rarely used outside his native France for several decades after he completed this book. However, over the past decade, this picture has changed considerably, as research centred in Europe, but increasingly influential across the globe, has shown how MCA can be a powerful tool of analysis. The paper by Roose offers a clear introduction to this method. (Papers in other parts of this handbook, notably by Pereira, offer applications of this method). It is important to note that many of the contributors to this handbook, including Alan Warde, Irmak Karademir Hazır, Modesto Gayo, Tony Bennett, Gisèle Sapiro, Sam Friedman, as well as ourselves, have used the method of MCA extensively, and the intellectual underpinnings of our thinking can be seen as linked to our interest and excitement with the method.

The chapters in this first part are in some ways diverse in content matter and theoretical orientation, but together they all point to a strong platform for a relational sociology of art and culture. Only a few are written by scholars who avowedly see themselves as Bourdieusians first and foremost. Martin, by contrast, is informed by Chicago School pragmatism; Bearman by social network structuralism; Lamont by science studies and the sociology of symbolic boundaries; and Warde by debates on class and consumption. Nonetheless, what emerges from these papers taken together is the potential of Bourdieu's interest in relationality, fields, boundaries and forms of distinction to inform new currents of research across the globe.

Note

1 We might note that this interest in the French provenance of Bourdieu's empirical work is taken up in contributions from other parts of this handbook, namely Donnat on screen culture and Sapiro on translation.

References

Bennett T., M. Savage, E.B. Silva, A. Warde, M. Gayo-Cal and D. Wright (2009) *Culture, class, distinction*, London: Routledge.
Bourdieu, P. (1984) *Distinction: a social critique of the judgement of taste*, translated by Richard Nice, Cambridge, MA: Harvard University Press.
Coulangeon, P. and J. Duval (eds.), (2014) *The Routledge companion to Distinction*, London: Routledge.
Emirbayer, M. (1997) 'Manifesto for a relational sociology', *American Journal of Sociology*, 103(2): 281–317.
Featherstone, M. (1985) 'Lifestyle and consumer culture', *Theory, Culture and Society*, 4(1): 55–70.
Lash, S. and J. Urry (1987) *The end of organised capitalism*, Cambridge: Polity.
Savage, M. and E.B. Silva (2013) 'Special issue on field analysis in cultural sociology', *Cultural Sociology*, 7(2).
Silva, E.B. and A. Warde (eds.) (2012) *Cultural analysis and Bourdieu's legacy*, London: Routledge.
Warde, A. (1997) *Consumption, food and taste*, London: Sage.

1
The sociology of cultural participation in France thirty years after *Distinction*

Philippe Coulangeon

Bourdieu's lasting influence in France as regards the sociology of art and culture is threefold. First, more than thirty years after the publication of *Distinction* and ten years after the author's death, references to Bourdieu remain central for French sociologists studying art and culture. For many scholars, post-*Distinction* cultural sociology was inescapably shaped by the book's bold theoretical proposals, which required sociologists to take sides with respect to its arguments. Ironically, positions on Bourdieu's sociology of culture became themselves a matter of 'distinction' among academic circles, as they were subjected to the kind of relational analysis promoted by Bourdieu himself. As a result, *Distinction* has not only been a landmark in cultural sociology, but it has also contributed to in-depth changes in the rules of French cultural sociology which, since 1980, has appeared highly structured and has distanced itself from *Distinction*'s theoretical framework.

But *Distinction*'s impact was not limited to academics. It also influenced cultural policies during this period, in a country where public funding for art and culture has long been driven by a concern for democratization. Although Bourdieu's academic legacy in cultural sociology obviously reaches well beyond French borders, as the chapters of this volume attest, the political dimension of Bourdieu's legacy is more specifically restricted to France.

Finally, *Distinction*'s public impact is not limited to its influence on cultural policy making. In France, as seen elsewhere (Coulangeon and Duval 2014), *Distinction* was not originally read by academic circles only. It has also been extensively critiqued in the media by French conservatives who tend to consider his conceptualization of cultural production and reception as both reductionist and relativist. This criticism was notably developed by young French essayists of this time, in reaction to what they called the '68 thinking', which was associated with the May 1968 protests in France (Ferry and Renaut 1985). References to *Distinction* have also been implicit in many criticisms addressed to what were seen as the harmful influence assigned to Bourdieu in cultural and educational matters (Finkielkraut 1987). More broadly, French conservatives used to read Bourdieu as a mere variant of Marxism, at a time when French intellectuals remained highly influenced by post-Marxist leading authors, such as Louis Althusser, about whom Bourdieu was fiercely critical (Bourdieu 1975).

Interestingly enough, these three dimensions of Bourdieu's legacy often intertwine. In particular, some academic criticisms of Bourdieu echo those coming from the public sphere. For example, a significant amount of sociological controversy surrounding the diffusion of Bourdieu's theses about art and culture address the sociological reductionism with which he is also often credited by cultural production and mediation professionals. Similarly, some current debates on the democratization of culture also match questions being raised in cultural sociology regarding issues such as cultural legitimacy, cultural eclecticism and so on. Nonetheless, in what follows, these dimensions are by and large addressed separately. Additionally, as cultural sociology can be wide ranging, this chapter will mainly focus on cultural participation and the social stratification of cultural practices and tastes, which of course does not mean that Bourdieu's impact in cultural sociology is restricted to these topics.

The first part of this chapter reviews the current state of post-*Distinction* French cultural sociology, dealing more specifically with the fate of some of Bourdieu's main concepts in the sociology of cultural practices. The second part addresses more explicitly Bourdieu's legacy in the sociology of cultural participation by examining Bourdieu's direct and indirect influence on French cultural policy making and expertise. Finally, the last part of the text gives insight on contemporary cultural French divisions in relation to the theoretical and political issues raised by Bourdieu's legacy.

French cultural sociology after *Distinction*

The persisting impact of *Distinction* in French cultural sociology has been both theoretical and methodological. On the theoretical side, the book introduced concepts such as cultural capital, habitus, field and homology, which helped sociologists to rethink the relationships between social classes and tastes, attitudes and lifestyles in a way that is familiar today to almost every social scientist working in the cultural domain. It also introduced some methodological innovations that profoundly influenced social science practices in this area. That said, until recent years (Lebaron and Le Roux 2014), there has been no real debate among Bourdieu and his followers on the issues posed directly in *Distinction*. After this work, Bourdieu's main publications focused on topics such as academics, higher education, the State, the literary field, journalism and economics. He also published several theoretical and political books. Of course, some of those works led him to reinvestigate certain aspects of *Distinction*. However, he did not revisit cultural practices, and thus *Distinction* should be considered his definitive contribution to the topic (Coulangeon and Duval 2014).

As regards to the methodological aspects of *Distinction*, the combination of quantitative and qualitative materials on which the book relies is probably one of its main legacies. Then as now, many French sociologists' approach to cultural topics has mixed a comprehensive analysis of ethnographic material and a statistical analysis of survey data, as Bourdieu did. But the most significant and influential methodological innovation introduced by *Distinction* was undoubtedly the use of Multiple Correspondence Analysis (MCA), which was developed in the 1960s by a team of French mathematicians headed by Jean-Paul Benzécri. Breaking with the variable-oriented statistics that had been dominant in statistical sociology since the 1950s, MCA gave substance to the concept of homology in the realms of tastes, lifestyles and social positions (Rouanet, Ackermann and Le Roux 2000).

More generally, this methodology is inseparable from the relational approach linked to the notions of field and social space developed by Bourdieu in the 1970s. In this regard, tastes, attitudes and practices are not considered as substantial properties of individuals, nor even of the social groups to which they belong. In that sense, many of the current debates inspired by *Distinction*, especially those regarding 'omnivorousness', are couched within a more orthodox neo-positivist perspective. This is particularly the case in the 'omnivore' debate, where the highbrow/lowbrow boundary tends to be artificially rigidified, whereas in Bourdieu's perspective the border between cultural repertoires was considered fluid, continuously redefined due to the dynamics of the field (see chapters by Karademir Hazır and Warde and by Gayo-Cal in this volume). This is probably one of the reasons why Bourdieu, and his closest colleagues at the *Centre de sociologie européenne*, took very little part in these debates. Another benefit of this relational approach is its two-sided nature. Indeed, unlike more conventional approaches, it allows art and culture production and consumption to be simultaneously related together. This perspective was abundantly illustrated by Bourdieu himself, in relation to literature (Bourdieu 1996) and fine arts (Bourdieu 2013), in particular, and by some of his followers (cf. Sapiro 2002 and Sapiro 2003 on literature; and Duval 2006 and Duval 2011 on cinema). However, with the exception of some works on reading practices (Mauger and Fossé-Poliak 1998; Mauger, Fossé-Poliak and Pudal 1999) and recent methodological development in the geometric data analysis applied to cultural practices (Lebaron and Le Roux 2014), the sociology of cultural practice as such was not developed very much by Bourdieu's direct collaborators.

Nonetheless, the sociology of cultural practices has greatly expanded in France since the eighties, with growing numbers of PhD thesis, articles and books. Much research that has flourished in this area has often been preceded by a partial refutation or recasting of some of the book's core hypotheses, such as the homology thesis or the notion of cultural legitimacy. In 1989, two formerly close associates of Bourdieu, Claude Grignon and Jean-Claude Passeron, published a book, *Le savant et le populaire,* in which they argued there was a legitimist bias in Bourdieu's approach of popular culture. In their view, Bourdieu's analysis of popular culture in terms of its distance from dominant culture was overly exclusive and failed to properly appreciate its relative autonomy (Grignon and Passeron 1989). They also distance themselves from the pessimistic mass culture theorists (Marcuse 1964; Horkheimer and Adorno 2002), whose views on popular culture as structurally alienated they rejected. But according to them, taking the autonomy and dignity of popular culture into account does not mean that they deny its cultural domination. Finally, their book can be read as an attempt to combine Bourdieu's approach with the theoretical contributions of cultural studies. In fact, in the 1970s, Bourdieu himself heavily contributed to the introduction to France of authors such as Raymond Williams, E.P. Thompson, Richard Hoggart and Paul Willis.

Others criticized the social determinism and fatalism of Bourdieu's theses. Jacques Rancière, among others, argued that Bourdieu overstated the kind of cultural alienation that doomed the dominated to passively suffer from their domination due to the ignorance of the origin of their domination. On the contrary, he insisted on the relative clear-sightedness of the dominated and on the opportunities of cultural and political emancipation that exist as far as people are not locked in the culture of their class (1991; 2012).

In another vein, the cultural studies tradition inspired a more radical criticism of *Distinction* in France, mainly rooted in the field of media studies. During recent years, several French scholars (Macé and Maigret 2005; Glévarec and Pinet 2012) have called into question the very notion of cultural legitimacy in this era of mass and media culture where the boundaries between popular and high arts are becoming increasingly fuzzy. The blurring of the symbolic boundaries at work is strengthened, they argue, by the fact that these industries structurally stimulate diversity, continuously supporting the renewal of cultural norms and fashions. Finally, they advocate a sociology of individuality and diversity rather than a sociology of distinction and symbolic domination (Glévarec and Pinet 2013).

Other authors insist on the declining power of school education, where cultural norms increasingly compete with mass culture and creative industry prescriptions, so much so that teenagers, in particular, may experience a kind of 'inverted' domination of mass over legitimate culture (Pasquier 2005). Cultural domination, if any, is much more difficult to exert in a society where the cultural norms of the prescribers are manifold than it is in a society where the dominant can quietly rely upon the school cultural monopoly, like in France in the 1960s at the time when the raw empirical data used in *Distinction* was collected.

In a quite different register, and more inspired by Boltanski and Thévenot's theoretical model of justification logics (2006), Nathalie Heinich investigated the diversity of the axiological repertoires of taste judgements that ordinary people employ when exposed to contemporary art, insisting on the mix of ethical and aesthetic registers displayed by ordinary taste judgements (Heinich 1998). In a related vein, the pragmatist approach to taste has also been investigated by Antoine Hennion and his colleagues since the 1990s. This approach can be seen as another productive break from Bourdieu's theoretical framework in French cultural sociology (Hennion, Maisonneuve and Gomart 2000; Hennion and Fauquet 2001). They developed a constructivist conception of taste built on the idea of the amateur, which draws on specific skills developed by music lovers. At odds with the notion of *habitus*, they particularly stress the idiosyncratic nature of the field-related amateurs' competences. In their view, the skills developed by amateurs in relation to their commitment in one cultural field or genre are not systematically transposable from one domain to another.

The relationship between tastes and skills is also at the core of Bernard Lahire's 'dispositionnalist' sociology (2011). Lahire's analysis of the socio-genesis of taste relies on the sociology of *habitus*, but Lahire strays from Bourdieu's notion of *habitus* on two points. First, somewhat like Hennion and his co-authors, Lahire insists on the non-transferability of dispositions that he intrinsically considers domain-specific (Lahire 2014). People may be highly skilled in one artistic or cultural domain or genre and not in others, even when they are similar. As a result, he argues that people are very likely to display more dissonant cultural profiles than those postulated by theories of *habitus* (Lahire 2008).

But Lahire does not challenge the relevance of the very notion of *habitus*. Rather, he merely questions its postulated unity, which is also affected by the plurality of the social and cultural environments that people get involved in during their life, which most often result in a set of heterogeneous dispositions (Lahire 2003; Lahire 2004). Consequently, Lahire argues that people's practices, when considered in a wide variety of fields, are seldom as coherent as the theory of *habitus* suggests. The plurality of dispositions and *habitus* fragmentation were acknowledged in some of Bourdieu's later works (Bourdieu 2004; Bennett 2007). The plurality – and plasticity – of *habitus* can thus be seen as a promising extension rather than a refutation of Bourdieu's theses.

Finally, a great deal of research in France, like in other Western countries, pits the theoretical framework inherited from Bourdieu against the hypotheses drawn from Richard Peterson's thesis regarding the growing cultural eclecticism of the culturally and socially well-to-do (Peterson 1992, and see more generally, Karademir Hazır and Warde in this volume). Whereas some authors consider Peterson's findings to be a radical invalidation of Bourdieu's thesis (Glévarec 2013; Glévarec and Pinet 2013), others tend to combine the two theories (Coulangeon 2004; Coulangeon and Lemel 2007), and consider eclecticism to be a particular expression of the distinctive aesthetic disposition in a changing cultural context, as is the case in other countries (Lizardo and Skiles 2012). As a result, the rather extensive critiques made upon Bourdieu's arguments by French scholars do not mean that the posterity of *Distinction* is due to the fact that it constitutes a convenient foil for the critics that indirectly help to sustain it. The persisting influence of *Distinction* in the field of cultural sociology is rather predominantly due to the fact that it is still a stimulating framework to work with when considering the cultural dimension of class and social inequalities. As a generic process, distinction remains a structuring force of social relations, even if its actual manifestations are constantly renewed.

Bourdieu's legacy, from cultural sociology to cultural policies

Cultural sociology is certainly one of the areas where research orientations are the most closely defined by non-academic interests. This is especially the case for the sociology of cultural participation, which has been tightly shaped in France by the close collaboration between policy makers and social scientists that began immediately after World War II. Joffre Dumazedier, the leading French sociologist of leisure, was recruited by the French planning agency soon after the war ended, where he promoted the concept of cultural development that has been the cornerstone of French cultural policy since the 1950s (Dubois and Georgakakis 1993). A few years later, in 1963, Augustin Girard founded the research unit of the Ministry for Cultural Affairs, which became a meeting place for scholars – mainly social scientists – and policy makers (Girard and Gentil 1983). Sociology of culture and cultural policy studies' expertise has long been used together, especially during the implementation of repeated surveys on cultural participation commissioned by the Ministry's research unit. These largely quantitative surveys provided social scientists and policy makers with the statistical data that allowed them to measure and analyse the social determinants of cultural practices in a context where, since Malraux's nomination to the ministry of cultural affairs in 1959, cultural policies were mainly aimed at democratizing access to arts and culture. As noted by Vincent Dubois, this use of scientific expertise was certainly part of a strategy aimed at promoting the idea of culture as a legitimate policy domain (Dubois 2011).

Dubois highlighted the paradoxical influence Bourdieu had on the development of French cultural policy since the early 1970s (Dubois 2011). According to Dubois, while Bourdieu had a sizeable impact on the intellectual background of cultural policy makers and experts, his impact on the actual orientations of cultural policies was very limited. He collaborated on some occasions with the Ministry's research unit, such as on the survey of the European museum-going public, which Bourdieu used for his book *The Love of Art* (Bourdieu, Darbel and Schnapper 1990). This can be seen as the prototype for a series of surveys on French cultural practices commissioned by the Ministry starting in 1973 that are still the source of a large amount of research on cultural participation. In addition, the interest in the social determinants of inequalities in access to culture featured in Bourdieu and Darbel's book also has enabled some intellectual agreement with the promoters of a cultural policy principally aimed at reducing these inequalities (Donnat 2003). However, Bourdieu's sociology included critical arguments that profoundly challenged the beliefs and practices of cultural policy makers. These arguments were twofold. First, Bourdieu's notion of cultural capital profoundly challenged the received wisdom of the diffusion of arts and culture as a result of an 'elective shock' with no need for specific and systematic mediation, an idea that was at the core of Malraux's conception of democratization. In contrast, Bourdieu and his colleagues' analyses highlighted the crucial impact of family and education on the unequal access to art and culture. As a result, these analyses emphasized the limitations of the democratization strategy and suggested, by contrast, the outline of an efficient policy focused on the distribution of educational resources and cultural capital. However, as demonstrated by Dubois, such a recommendation was particularly unacceptable to the cultural policy makers of the time who were imbued with an anti-pedagogical conception of cultural policy that contravened the principles of popular education and socio-cultural animation that had characterized the cultural policy of the Third and Fourth Republics (from 1870 to 1940 and from 1946 to 1958) (Dubois 1999; Dubois and Laborier 2003).

The second critical argument provided by Bourdieu relates to the notion of the 'cultural arbitrary' (Bourdieu and Passeron 1977; Bourdieu and Passeron 1979, 1964) that calls into question the aim of the cultural democratization policy and not just the limitations of the means by which it was implemented. What was principally at stake in that critique was the legitimist orientation endorsed by a policy that aimed to democratize access to highbrow culture without any consideration for the underlying process of arbitrary symbolic domination that separated the highbrow from the lowbrow and thus reproduced class privilege (Ahearne 2006). It is in that context that an alternative conception arose in the late 1960s in response to the obvious limitations of cultural democratization and the theoretical criticisms that had been addressed to it.

By insisting on individual autonomy and creativity, this emerging conception argued that 'true' cultural democracy implied a wider recognition of cultural diversity. Hence, whereas cultural democratization, through its focus on the diffusion of high culture (such as opera and classical music), resulted in a clear rejection of popular education, amateur practices and the products of cultural industries outside the cultural policy area, cultural democracy was rooted in a much more relativist conception of cultural norms, according to which cultural policy might primarily support people's own cultural flourishing in a plurality of ways, whether artistic, recreational or educational (Santerre 2000). In other words, cultural democracy was aimed at breaking with the rather paternalistic approach of cultural 'enlightenment' that prevailed in the cultural democratization doctrine (Bjørnsen 2012). Culminating in the 1980s, when Jack Lang was the Minister of Culture, the assimilation of these pluralistic and relativist concepts was associated with some extension of the cultural policy domains that contributed to eroding the symbolic barrier between culture and leisure, highbrow and lowbrow arts, arts and entertainment, among other things. It also revived the popular education movement and has been progressively integrated in the elaboration and practice of cultural policy since the mid-1970s.

That being said, the influence that Bourdieu's argument of 'cultural arbitrary' might have exerted on the conception of cultural policy is quite uncertain and rather ambiguous. It is not at all sure that Bourdieu would have totally adhered to the 'cultural democracy' doctrine. As he stated in *Pascalian Meditations*,

> 'cultural policies' directed towards the most deprived are condemned to oscillate between two forms of hypocrisy.... On the one hand, in the name of a respect that is at once condescending and without consequences for cultural particularities and particularisms that are largely imposed and suffered, and which are thereby redefined as choices ... one encloses the dispossessed in their condition by failing to offer them real means of realizing their restricted possibilities. On the other hand, as the educational system now does, one universally imposes the same demands without any concern for equally universally distributing the means of satisfying them, thus helping to legitimate the inequality that one merely records and ratifies, while additionally exercising (first of all in the educational system) the symbolic violence associated with the effects of real inequality within formal equality.
>
> *(2000: 76)*

As demonstrated in this quote, which most likely illustrates a slight shift in Bourdieu's opinion between his writing from the 1960s and that of the 1970s, sociological criticism has not been exclusively addressed to the cultural arbitrary of cultural democratization universalism.

Bourdieu also demonstrated his scepticism regarding the cultural relativism associated with the cultural democracy doctrine. The influence that cultural sociology has had on the French conception and implementation of cultural policies cannot be reduced to this rather pessimistic conclusion, however. Many cultural policy actors and advisers, well aware of the limits of cultural democratization, are much more positively convinced of the virtues of cultural democracy. Indeed, the doctrinal controversy in cultural policies not only mirrors the influence Bourdieu had in the field in the 1960s and 1970s, but since it is an ongoing controversy, it also parallels more recent debates on cultural inequalities in social sciences (Coulangeon 2013), such as the 'highbrow/lowbrow' vs. 'omnivore/univore' debate.

The traditional 'highbrow/lowbrow' divide has long prevailed in the sociology of culture, ranking practices and tastes along a mass/elite spectrum. Not reducible to Bourdieu's legacy (Levine 1988; Gans 1999), it was particularly well-adapted to the underlying approach towards cultural inequalities that inspired the cultural democratization doctrine. The emergence of the so-called 'omnivore/univore' research agenda in the mid-1990s profoundly challenged this traditional perspective to the extent that the remaining class gradient henceforth became predominantly defined in reference to the amount and diversity of cultural repertoires people practiced (Peterson 1992; Peterson and Simkus 1992). It is worth noting that when this research agenda arose in the United States in the wake of Peterson's work, the idea that the spectrum of diversity in cultural practices and tastes could become a social marker in and of itself had already been proposed in France by Olivier Donnat, a French researcher who had been in charge of the design and implementation of the surveys of cultural practices at the Ministry of Culture since the late 1980s. In a book published in 1994, Donnat reformulated the issue of cultural inequalities, still central in the definition of cultural policies, in terms of exclusion rather than in terms of distinction, contrasting people enjoying access to a large amount and a wide diversity of cultural goods and practices to people almost entirely excluded from the cultural domain (Donnat 1994). Since then, the growing popularity of these issues has most likely contributed to the expansion of the scope of cultural policy beyond the field of legitimate culture, since cultural inequalities are no longer exclusively defined in terms of a privileged access to high arts and culture. In that sense, cultural sociology not only informs cultural policies, it also enlightens the changing nature of the cultural divisions that affect French society.

Contemporary French cultural divisions in the light of Bourdieu's sociology of culture

Recent empirical findings suggest increasingly unequal access to most cultural goods and amenities since the 1980s in France, regardless of the level of cultural consecration (Coulangeon 2013). In other words, the social space of cultural practices is persistently and chiefly structured in France by the same underlying principle which distinguishes those who appear more or less culturally engaged that has also been identified in other countries (Le Roux et al. 2008). At first glance, this may appear as consistently supportive of the omnivorous argument, if not convergent with the thesis of a decreasingly qualitative differentiation of class cultures and an increasingly quantitative distinction in access to a rather homogeneous mass culture (Wilensky 1964; Gartman 1991).

But this prevailing factor of the differentiation of cultural attitudes and practices is perhaps not just an issue of 'size', given that it does not indefinitely contrast the availability of all cultural goods and practices with their unavailability. In particular, both in the early 1980s and currently, the level of cultural engagement remains strikingly and negatively correlated with TV watching. People who spend a lot of time watching TV systematically display a weak commitment to other cultural practices. On the other hand, those highly involved in a variety of cultural practices generally spend very little time watching TV. This observation would certainly be strengthened by taking into account the different kinds of TV programs people watch. In addition, it is worth noting that TV watching is deeply rooted in contemporary working class culture (Schwartz 1990; Morley 1992). TV watching is indeed one of the rare cultural practices that is more intense among working classes than in any other social group and the television set in contemporary France is the only household good for which ownership is greater at the bottom than at the top of the social structure (INSEE 2011). Conversely, the cultural disqualification of and distance from television in France is nowhere greater than it is among upper classes (Boullier 1988; Lahire 2004). Accordingly, even when compounded with some scale of cultural diversity and eclecticism, the ranking of cultural repertoires is still relevant and certainly remains a matter of class (Coulangeon 2013).

Other research also suggests that illegitimate leisure practices in France, such as hunting, that are predominantly practised by the working class and in the rural areas are also strongly correlated with TV watching and negatively correlated with all other cultural activities (Coulangeon and Lemel 2009). Thus, this cultural engagement factor is often misleadingly interpreted as an indication of weakening cultural boundaries. This deceptive interpretation is frequent since a lot of available survey data on cultural practices relies on a disproportionate number of indicators tied to highbrow and middlebrow cultural practices and a symmetrically low number of indicators on the most common or illegitimate cultural practices. Including a more balanced number of legitimate and illegitimate items in survey questionnaires would make the highbrow/lowbrow divide more salient.

A second dimension of the differentiation of cultural practices and attitudes that emerges from empirical observation relates to the contrast between unequally established repertoires. In France, as in other contemporary contexts, the contrast between the 'established' and 'emergent' repertoires (Le Roux et al. 2008) is strongly related to age. Age is certainly a structuring variable that other contemporary French cultural sociologists have explored more than Bourdieu did (Pasquier 2005; Glévarec 2010). At the time when Bourdieu wrote *Distinction*, cultural attitudes, tastes and practices were already heavily structured by age (Herpin 1980; De Saint-Martin 2014). However, observed differences in cultural practices among age groups are quite ambiguous. First, all differences related to age measured in cross-sectional surveys unavoidably blend the life-cycle position with the birth cohort. In addition, it is by no means self-evident that age differences should always be interpreted in terms of cultural domination, to the extent that emergent repertoires are not systematically subordinated to established repertoires.

Therefore, these differences might be better interpreted in terms of temporal change and integrated in the underlying dynamics of fields, which was theorized by Bourdieu himself (Bourdieu 1983). These dynamics suggest that cultural divisions change over time but that some of the underlying factors of distinction remain. Nonetheless, a retrospective analysis of French data shows that today's individual disparities in terms of emergent and established practices, attitudes and tastes are perhaps no longer as distinctive as they were in the early 1980s (Coulangeon 2013). In other words, the kind of cultural legitimacy that is attached to the historical canon is probably weaker today than it was thirty years ago. This declining power of the canon might be partially related to the economic transformation of the cultural sector, increasingly based on the saturation of cultural markets by an oversupply of constantly renewing products. But this changing economic regime does not fundamentally alter the process of distinction, in which expressions are just becoming more versatile and less immediately visible.

Conclusion: Emerging cultural divisions and the question of mass culture

I have shown that Bourdieu's legacy in France is complex and ambivalent. In one respect, his legacy is very powerful. Thirty years after *Distinction*, cultural practices are still essentially seen in France as a matter of class competition and class boundaries. Of course, the social structure of cultural attitudes and tastes has been substantially and continuously renewed. In France as in other Western countries, the focus is increasingly, and probably will continue to be, on emergent cultural divisions and resources (Prieur and Savage 2013). As for emergent divisions, recent research tends to focus less on class and more on alternative principles of stratification, such as gender (Octobre 2011), ethnicity (Voisin 2013) and age and generation (Donnat 2011).

Among the emergent cultural resources that are of growing sociological concern, special attention should be paid to the impact of cosmopolitan cultural resources, which are of rising importance in a globalized world (Calhoun 2002, 2007; Prieur and Savage 2013). Multicultural capital is an increasingly valued form of cultural capital among the French upper class (Wagner 1998, 2010). Cosmopolitanism is particularly encouraged among the upper class in various ways, including the early promotion of the virtues of travelling during childhood and the transmission of cosmopolitan skills in education (Weenink 2008). This is especially the case in many elite French schools such as Sciences Po and the most prestigious business schools (Wagner 2007). It should be noted, however, that most of these cosmopolitan resources, and especially their linguistic components, cannot be acquired and transmitted only at school. Indeed, foreign language fluency has more to do with diffusion and repeated exposure to informal interactions than with scholastic training. Consequently, the symbolic and cultural inequalities that come hand in hand with unequal access to these resources cannot easily be compensated for by the education system. One can then conclude that the social value attached to cultural and symbolic resources that are imperfectly accessible through educational achievement strongly reinforces the non-egalitarian structure of class relationships in a way which suggests that the principles Bourdieu elaborates in *Distinction* remain valid.

The sociology of cultural practices has also been characterized in recent years by a growing focus on mass and media culture (Macé and Maigret 2005). This rising concern for mass culture should make it possible to dispel some of the ambiguities that affect the alleged eclecticism of elite taste. To the extent that a large amount of mass-produced and mass-consumed items are not clearly connected to the class divisions that they precisely contribute to hiding (Gartman 1991), the taste for mass culture displayed among the upper class does not substantially weaken these class divisions. In another words, the fact that the culturally well-to-do also increasingly consume the most common and widely advertised mass-produced cultural items might be rather trivial. Wine connoisseurs also drink tap water.

We can therefore see that despite the particular controversies Bourdieu has left behind him, his approach continues to have power, even in very different conditions, but that we need to be attentive to new perspectives. Whereas taste eclecticism of the elite does not abolish cultural domination, cultural domination is certainly more difficult to exert in a media-saturated environment where the dominant must constantly reassert their domination against the onslaught of a growing diversity of cultural prescribers.

References

Ahearne, J. (2006) 'Public intellectuals and cultural policy in France', *International Journal of Cultural Policy*, 12(3): 323–339.

Bennett, T. (2007) 'Habitus clivé: aesthetics and politics in the work of Pierre Bourdieu', *New Literary History*, 38(1): 201–228.

Bjørnsen, E. (2012) 'Norwegian cultural policy—A civilising mission? The Cultural Rucksack and abstract faith in the transforming powers of the arts', *Poetics*, 40(4): 382–404.
Boltanski, L. and L. Thévenot (2006) *On justification: economies of worth*, Princeton, NJ: Princeton University Press.
Boullier, D. (1988) 'Les styles de relation à la télévision', *Réseaux*, 6(32): 7–44.
Bourdieu, P. (1975) 'La lecture de Marx. Ou quelques remarques critiques à propos de "Quelques critiques à propos de 'Lire le capital'", *Actes de la recherche en sciences sociales*, 5(6): 65–79. [*Marx reading. 'Some critical remarks on "Reading the Capital"'*]
—— (1983) 'The field of cultural production, or: the economic world reversed', *Poetics*, 12(4-5): 311–356.
—— (1996) *The rules of art: genesis and structure of the literary field*, Stanford, CA: Stanford University Press.
—— (2000) *Pascalian meditations*, Stanford, CA: Stanford University Press.
—— (2004) *Esquisse pour une auto-analyse*, Paris: Editions Raisons d'agir.
—— (2013) *Manet, Une révolution symbolique: Cours au collège de France (1998-2000)*, Paris: Le Seuil.
Bourdieu, P., A. Darbel and D. Schnapper (1990) *The love of art: European art museums and their public*, Stanford, CA: Stanford University Press.
Bourdieu, P. and J.C. Passeron (1977) *Reproduction in education, culture and society*, London: Sage.
—— (1979) *The inheritors: French students and their relation to culture*, Chicago: University of Chicago Press.
Calhoun, C. (2002) 'The class consciousness of frequent travellers: toward a critique of actually existing cosmopolitanism', *The South Atlantic Quarterly*, 101(4): 869–897.
—— (2007) *Nations matter: culture, history and the cosmopolitan dream*, London: Routledge.
Coulangeon, P. (2004) 'Classes sociales, pratiques culturelles et styles de vie: Le modèle de la distinction est-il (vraiment) obsolète?', *Sociologie et sociétés*, 36(1): 59–85.
—— (2013) 'Changing policies, challenging theories and persisting inequalities: social disparities in cultural participation in France from 1981 to 2008', *Poetics*, 41(2): 177–209.
Coulangeon, P. and J. Duval (2014) 'Introduction', *The Routledge companion to Bourdieu's Distinction*, Oxford: Routledge, Taylor & Francis Group Ltd.
Coulangeon, P. and Y. Lemel (2007) 'Is 'Distinction' really outdated? Questioning the meaning of the omnivorization of musical taste in contemporary France', *Poetics*, 35(2): 93–111.
—— (2009) 'Les pratiques culturelles et sportives des Français: arbitrage, diversité et cumul', *Économie et statistique*, 423(1): 3–30.
De Saint-Martin, M. (2014) 'From 'Anatomie du goût' to La Distinction: attempting to construct the social space. Some markers for the history of the research', in P. Coulangeon and J. Duval (eds.), *The Routledge companion to Bourdieu's Distinction*, Oxford: Routledge, Taylor & Francis Group Ltd.
Donnat, O. (1994) *Les français face à la Culture: de l'exclusion à l'éclecticisme*, Paris: La Découverte.
—— (2003) 'La question de la démocratisation dans la politique culturelle française', *Modern & Contemporary France*, 11(1): 9–20.
—— (2011) 'Pratiques culturelles, 1973–2008. Dynamiques générationnelles et pesanteurs sociales', *Culture études*, (7): 1–36.
Dubois, V. (1999) *La politique culturelle: genèse d'une catégorie d'intervention publique*, Paris: Editions Belin.
—— (2011) 'Cultural capital theory vs. cultural policy beliefs: how Pierre Bourdieu could have become a cultural policy advisor and why he did not', *Poetics*, 39(6): 491–506.
Dubois, V. and D. Georgakakis (1993) 'Sciences sociales et action culturelle', *Politix* (24): 57–77.
Dubois, V. and P. Laborier (2003) 'The 'social' in the institutionalisation of local cultural policies in France and Germany', *International Journal of Cultural Policy*, 9(2): 195–206.
Duval, J. (2006) 'L'Art du réalisme. Le champ du cinéma français au début des années 2000', *Actes de la Recherche en Sciences Sociales*, 1–2 (161–162): 96–115.
—— (2011) 'L'offre et les goûts cinématographiques en France', *Sociologie*, 2(1): 1–18.
Ferry, L. and A. Renaut (1985) *La pensée 68*, Paris: Gallimard.
Finkielkraut, A. (1987) *La défaite de la pensée*, Paris: Gallimard.
Gans, H.J. (1999) *Popular culture and high culture: an analysis and evaluation of taste*, New York: Basic Books.
Gartman, D. (1991) 'Culture as class symbolization or mass reification? A critique of Bourdieu's *Distinction*', *American Journal of Sociology*, 97(2):421–447.
Girard, A. and G. Gentil (1983) *Cultural development: experiences and policies*, Paris: Unesco Publication.
Glévarec, H. (2010) *La Culture de la chambre: Préadolescence et Culture contemporaine dans l'espace familial*, Paris: La Documentation Française, Ministère de la Culture et de la communication, Département des études, de la prospective et des statistiques, Collection questions de Culture.

Glévarec, H. (2013) *La Culture à l'ère de la diversité. Essai critique trente ans après La Distinction*, Paris: Éditions de l'Aube.
Glévarec, H. and M. Pinet (2012) 'Tablatures of musical tastes in contemporary France: distinction without intolerance', *Cultural Trends*, 21(1): 67–88.
Glévarec, H. and M. Pinet (2013) 'De la distinction à la diversité culturelle. Eclectismes qualitatifs, reconnaissance culturelle et jugement d'amateur', *L'Année sociologique*, 63(2): 471–508.
Grignon, C. and J.-C. Passeron (1989) *Le savant et le populaire. Misérabilisme et populisme en sociologie et en literature*, Paris: Gallimard/Seuil, collection Hautes Etudes.
Heinich, N. (1998) *L'Art contemporain exposé aux rejets: études de cas*, Paris: Jacqueline Chambon.
Hennion, A. and J.-M. Fauquet (2001) 'Authority as performance: the love of Bach in nineteenth-century France', *Poetics*, 29(2): 75–88.
Hennion, A., S. Maisonneuve and E. Gomart (2000) *Figures de l'amateur: formes, objets, pratiques de l'amour de la musique aujourd'hui*, Paris: La Documentation française.
Herpin, N. (1980) 'Bourdieu Pierre, La distinction, critique sociale du jugement', *Revue française de sociologie*, 21(3): 444–48.
Horkheimer, M. and T.W. Adorno (2002) 'The culture industry: enlightenment as mass deception', in G.S. Noerr (ed.), *Dialectic of enlightenment: philosophical fragments*, Stanford, CA : Stanford University Press.
INSEE (2011) *Tableaux de l'économie française*, Paris: Institut national de la statistique et des études économiques.
Lahire, B. (2003) 'From the habitus to an individual heritage of dispositions: towards a sociology at the level of the individual', *Poetics*, 31(5): 329–355.
—— (2004) *La Culture des individus: dissonances culturelles et distinction de soi*, Paris: Editions La Découverte.
—— (2008) 'The individual and the mixing of genres: cultural dissonance and self-distinction', *Poetics*, 36(2): 166–188.
—— (2011) *The plural actor*, Cambridge: Polity.
—— (2014) 'Culture at the level of the individual: challenging transferability', in P. Coulangeon and J. Duval (eds.), *The Routledge companion to Bourdieu's Distinction*, Oxford: Routledge, Taylor & Francis Group Ltd.
Lebaron, F. and B. Le Roux (eds) (2014) *Pratiques culturelles et espace social. La méthodologie de Pierre Bourdieu en action*, Paris: Dunod.
Le Roux, B., H. Rouanet, M. Savage and A. Warde (2008) 'Class and cultural division in the UK', *Sociology*, 42(6): 1049–1071.
Levine, L.W. (1988) *Highbrow/lowbrow: the emergence of cultural hierarchy in America*, Cambridge, MA: Harvard University Press.
Lizardo, O. and S. Skiles (2012) 'Reconceptualizing and theorizing "omnivorousness" genetic and relational mechanisms', *Sociological Theory*, 30(4): 263–282.
Macé, E. and E. Maigret (2005) *Penser les médiacultures*, Paris: Armand Colin/INA.
Marcuse, H. (1964) *One-dimensional man: studies in the ideology of advanced industrial society*, Boston: Beacon Press.
Mauger, G., C. Fossé-Poliak and B. Pudal (1999) *Histoires de lecteurs*, Paris: Nathan.
Mauger, G. and C. Fossé-Poliak (1998) 'Les usages sociaux de la lecture', *Actes de la recherche en sciences sociales*, 123(1): 3–24.
Morley, D. (1992) *Television, audiences, and cultural studies*, London and New York: Routledge.
Octobre, S. (2011) 'Du féminin et du masculin: genre et trajectoires culturelles', *Réseaux* 168–169 (4–5): 23–57.
Pasquier, D. (2005) *Cultures lycéennes: la tyrannie de la majorité*, Paris: Autrement.
Peterson, R.A. (1992) 'Understanding audience segmentation: from elite and mass to omnivore and univore', *Poetics*, 21(4): 243–258.
Peterson, R.A. and A. Simkus (1992) 'How musical tastes mark occupational status groups', in M. Lamont and M. Fournier (eds.) *Cultivating differences. Symbolic boundaries and the making of inequality*, Chicago: University of Chicago Press: 152–186.
Prieur, A. and M. Savage (2013) 'Emerging forms of cultural capital', *European Societies*, 15(2): 246–267.
Rancière, J. (1991) *The ignorant schoolmaster: five lessons in intellectual emancipation*, Stanford, CA: Stanford University Press.
—— (2012) *Proletarian nights: the workers dream in nineteenth century*, London: Verso.
Rouanet, H., W. Ackermann and B. Le Roux (2000) 'The geometric analysis of questionnaires: the lesson of Bourdieu's La Distinction', *Bulletin de méthodologie sociologique*, 65(1): 5–18.

Santerre, L. (2000) 'De la démocratisation de la Culture à la démocratie culturelle', in G. Bellavance (ed.), *Démocratisation de la Culture ou démocratie culturelle? Deux logiques d'action publique*, Sainte-Foy: Presses de l'Université de Laval.

Sapiro, G. (2002) 'The structure of the French literary field during the German occupation (1940–1944): a multiple correspondence analysis', *Poetics*, 30(5): 387–402.

—— (2003) 'The literary field between the state and the market', *Poetics*, 31(5): 441–464.

Schwartz, O. (1990) *Le monde privé des ouvriers. Hommes et femmes du Nord*, Paris: Presses universitaires de France.

Voisin, A. (2013) 'Des jeunes "univores"? Musique, ethnicité et (il)légitimité culturelle dans l'East-End londonien et en Seine-Saint-Denis', in P. Coulangeon and J. Duval (eds.), *Trente ans après La Distinction de Pierre Bourdieu*, Paris: La Découverte.

Wagner, A.-C. (1998) *Les nouvelles élites de la mondialisation: une immigration dorée en France*, Paris: Presses universitaires de France.

—— (2007) 'La place du voyage dans la formation des élites', *Actes de la recherche en sciences sociales*, (5): 58–65.

—— (2010) 'Le jeu de la mobilité et de l'autochtonie au sein des classes supérieures', *Regards Sociologiques*, (40): 89–98.

Weenink, D. (2008) 'Cosmopolitanism as a form of capital', *Sociology*, 42(6): 1089–1106.

Wilensky, H.L. (1964) 'Mass society and mass culture: interdependence or independence?', *American Sociological Review*, 29(2): 173–197.

2
A post-Bourdieusian sociology of valuation and evaluation for the field of cultural production[1]

Stefan Beljean, Phillipa Chong and Michèle Lamont[2]

Introduction

In recent years, social scientists have seen an upsurge of interest in the sociology of valuation and evaluation (SVE). In Europe, leading sociologists have increasingly focused their attention on the topic. For instance, shortly after having been elected at the Collège de France in 2013, the sociologist Pierre-Michel Menger gave his first year of seminars on 'Evaluation in the sciences, the arts and organizations', while a very different type of sociologist, Luc Boltanski, has turned his attention to organizational forms used to present and classify cultural objects.[3] At the same time, American sociologists focus on the study of central cultural processes tied up in evaluation such as quantification (Espeland and Stevens 2008), commensuration (Espeland and Stevens 1998), standardization (Epstein 2007; Timmermans and Epstein 2010), or classification (Fourcade and Healy 2013). Sociological subfields such as cultural sociology and economic sociology, where evaluation figures prominently, are bustling with activity and energy and have experienced considerable growth over the past decades. Collective volumes on evaluation are multiplying (e.g. Beckert and Musselin 2013; Berthoin Antal, Hutter and Stark 2015) while sessions on the sociology of evaluation attract large and enthusiastic crowds at European and American professional sociological meetings alike.[4] And a newly launched international journal concerned with (e)valuation, *Valuation Studies* (http://valuationstudies.liu.se), has generated considerable interest across research communities. Such synchronized movements suggest that clearly, something is in the air.

These various developments are in part linked to a number of empirical macro-social changes concerning the ways in which values are defined and assessed in contemporary society (see e.g. Kjellberg and Mallard 2013).[5] Intellectually, they owe much to Bourdieu and the profound influence he has had on sociology through his inquiries into cultural production and consumption in symbolic and cultural fields (art, science, culture, knowledge, fashion and more; see e.g. Bourdieu 1993). Bourdieu's work has put questions of evaluation and valuation at the centre of sociologists' attention and introduced an analytical framework for studying markets for symbolic goods from which many scholars have taken inspiration. Thus, in the last twenty years, we have seen a proliferation of Bourdieu-inspired research on (e)valuation and fields of cultural production (Lamont 2012a; Coulangeon 2016).

But while many scholars have embraced Bourdieu's approach to (e)valuation, others have positioned themselves more critically toward his work. Instead of seeing in Bourdieu's writing a comprehensive and definitive analytical framework, these scholars have been working on the blind spots of his contribution, digging in new directions that became salient because of the distinctive angles that Bourdieu adopted to approach evaluation (see e.g. Hennion 2001; Hesmondhalgh 2006; Lamont 2009; Born 2010; Prior 2011; Silva and Warde 2010). The work of these scholars – as well as the various new developments cited above – indicate that we are already well on our way in developing a 'post-Bourdieusian' sociology of valuation and evaluation.

Up until recently, however, this post-Bourdieusian sociology of valuation and evaluation has developed without much theoretical integration. Scholars have worked on different aspects and sub-processes involved in (e)valuation, but only little effort has been made to bring different lines of work in dialogue with each other. As a result, much of this new line of research has remained confined to a succession of case studies, in which the added value from one project to the next was either unclear or not made explicit.

To remedy this situation, Lamont (2012a) recently made a call for more *comparative* research of valuation and evaluation with the goal of moving the field toward more cumulative theory building. Building on Karin Knorr-Cetina's (1999) notion of machinery of knowledge and on her collaborative work with sociologists of knowledge Charles Camic and Neil Gross (2011), Lamont outlined an agenda for such a research program that centres around the study of various types of *constraints* that shape the form and outcome of (e)valuation processes. The idea is to use the analytical focus on these constraints to compare evaluation processes in various types of contexts and evaluations of different types of cultural objects.

In this short essay, we build on this idea. We do so by focusing on three *constraints* that have tended to receive little attention in the work of Bourdieu and followers, but which we regard to be particularly important analytical dimensions for a comparative sociology of evaluation and valuation. These dimensions are: 1) the standards of evaluation in fields of cultural production; 2) the self-concepts of evaluators; as well as 3) the agency of objects in evaluation.

The body of this paper discusses recent empirical work on each of these three constraints and offers directions for future scholarship. We centre our attention on recent developments in the sociology of *cultural production*, as other chapters in this volume deal with cultural consumption.[6] In addition, we also offer a discussion of research at the intersection of economic sociology and organizational research that has made important contributions to the sociology of valuation and evaluation, but which has developed largely independently from the influence from Bourdieu. We argue that establishing more bridges between this literature and the sociology of art and culture is a necessary precondition for the development of a more integrated research agenda for the sociology of valuation and evaluation. Before we delve into our analysis, however, we start with a short discussion of Bourdieu's legacy to the sociology of arts and culture.

The 'classical' model

One of Bourdieu's major contributions to the sociology of art and culture was what we dub his "classical model" of the field of cultural production (Bourdieu 1993, 1996). According to this model, the field of cultural production is divided into opposite poles which are each governed by two distinct sets of standards of evaluation: On the one hand, there is the (sub-)field of large-scale production which revolves around economic standards of evaluation, while on the other hand, there is the (sub-)field of restricted production which is oriented toward aesthetic standards of evaluation.

A key goal that Bourdieu pursued in his work on the field of art in France was to convey the historical contingency of this particular structuration of the field of cultural production. More specifically, he aimed to show how the idea of artistic autonomy – which lies at the fundament of the sub-field of restricted production – is far from transcendent and universal, but only emerged at a particular point in time and under particular historical circumstances.

However, this important point has largely been overlooked in survey-based Bourdieu-inspired research on cultural production. Indeed, as scholars applied his framework to various national cases, the historical character of his argument often got lost. Instead, many approached Bourdieu's model as a ready-made theoretical framework to be transposed to an ever-larger set of empirical settings. This has led to a gradual reification of Bourdieu's classical two-pole model of the structure of symbolic and cultural fields (but note the proliferation of excellent Bourdieu-inspired French historical studies of cultural fields: e.g. Sapiro 2003; 2010 in particular). Further, such highly standardized and predictable applications have focused scholarly attention away from a number of important dimensions of evaluation processes, such as the role of self-concepts of evaluators or the substantive content of criteria of evaluation. In the following section, we point to three new lines of work by a new generation of scholars who have started to bring these dimensions of evaluation back into focus.

Recent criticisms and revisions

New research on standards of evaluation in fields of cultural production

First, new work in cultural sociology is focusing attention on standards of evaluation in fields of cultural production, a topic that Bourdieu approached through a simple model: He posited a clear opposition between economic and aesthetic criteria of evaluation which for him were the product of the dualistic structure of the field of cultural production, that is, the fundamental opposition between pure art and commercial mass production. Again, this view has become part and parcel of much empirical research in the sociology of art and culture.

New work, however, is challenging this classical view of the relation between criteria of evaluation and the structure of fields of cultural production. Evidence from recent case studies indicates that even genres that are clearly geared toward either mass-production (such as stand-up comedy) or restricted production for peers or experts (such as poetry) exhibit a great deal of internal diversity, such that they encompass a broad range of possible positions that are *more* or *less* market (or art) oriented – with the result that cultural products are often evaluated against economic and aesthetic criteria of evaluation at the same time (see e.g. Craig and Dubois 2010; Kersten and Verboord 2013; Beljean 2014). These findings suggest that Bourdieu's model may have overstated the contrast between restricted production and large-scale cultural production, and that there is a need for a more refined understanding of these two modes of cultural production.

Further, empirical findings suggest that there is no fundamental opposition between the logic of 'art for money' and the logic of 'l'art pour l'art', and that these two logics are often intertwined. Michael Hutter (2013), for example, considers how the meeting of artistic and commercial logics can be productive and a source of innovation. An exemplar of this generative potential is the translation of Japanese artist Takashi Murakami's graphic otaku motif onto Louis Vuitton luxury-brand handbags.

A second literature invites us to go beyond Bourdieu's classical model, and its emphasis on the opposition between profit-orientation and autonomy, and to consider other structuring principles that shape how cultural products are evaluated. One example comes from research on evaluation processes in a cultural industry. In a study of intermediaries in the industry for stand-up comedy in the United States, Beljean (2014) finds that there are systematic differences in how market intermediaries evaluate comedians across different vertically stratified tiers of the comedy industry. For example, intermediaries who cater to the top tier of the industry tend to be primarily concerned with the renown of comedians and their ability to sell tickets, while intermediaries in the mid-tier of the market are more concerned about comedians' ability to adapt their material to different types of crowds.[7] However, these differences cannot be simply explained by the degree of autonomy of different market tiers, as a standard Bourdieusian account would have it. Rather, these differences need to be understood in the light of the 'superstar' structure (Rosen 1981) of the comedy industry, which creates different dynamics of supply and demand across different market tiers.

These new lines of work point to promising directions for future research such as the value of studying standards of evaluation in fields of cultural production *inductively*, rather than through the preconceived lens of field analysis or another theoretical framework. Such an approach can help us to identify unanticipated empirical patterns and to eschew reifying theoretical assumptions such as Bourdieu's distinction between economic and aesthetic criteria of evaluation. It can also shed light on how various criteria of evaluation are intertwined, thus generating a more accurate and comprehensive understanding of how cultural products are evaluated. Another promising topic is considering the relation between evaluation and the structure of cultural fields beyond the opposition between profit-orientation and autonomy, so as to identify other principles of structuration that shape the criteria of evaluation against which cultural products are evaluated, such as disciplinary boundaries (Guetzkow, Lamont and Mallard 2004; Mallard, Lamont and Guetzkow 2009) or market forces (Beljean 2014).

Neo-phenomenological studies of valuation and tasting practices

Second, in response to criticisms of Bourdieu's work for his lack of attention to actual evaluative practices and deliberations 'on the ground', new studies of evaluation engage in close-up empirical (ethnographic and interview-based) analysis of evaluative practices and judgment.[8] This interactional focus has manifested itself in studies that emphasize (i) how self-concepts shape evaluative practice and (ii) the agency of objects in evaluation (i.e. the role of non-human supports).

Self-concepts in evaluation

Work on self-concepts considers both the formation of the evaluator's subjectivity and how individuals' self-understandings shape their evaluative behaviour. Self-concepts refer to the narratives that individuals tell to themselves and the world about the types of people they are (Epstein 1973; Leschziner 2015). Research shows that people not only construct and 'tell' these narratives, but also that these self-understandings can shape action to the extent that people may be drawn to activities that resonate with their self-concepts (Gross 2002), and the content of self-concepts reflect constraints people face (Leschziner 2015). People's narratives, thus, matter insofar as they contribute to actors' intersubjective construction of reality and shape their evaluative practices. This literature also considers the intellectual and organizational conditions that make specific types of evaluative selves possible (e.g. Lamont 2009 on peer review in the US).

In his theory of symbolic fields, Bourdieu (1993; 1996) focuses on how people behave in ways to maximize their strategic self-interests based on their field position. But new work on evaluation suggests that self-interest is not all that matters. Lamont (2009) argues that we need to move beyond considerations of self-interest to examine neglected aspects of evaluation, including how evaluators understand their role and the emotional consequences of their work. Using the world of scientific peer review as her case study, she finds that peer review represents more than just an opportunity for panellists to advance their research agendas or reproduce their positions in the academic field. Panellists are driven by the desire to contribute to collective problem solving, and they derive feelings of pleasure and validation from the process of serving as experts whose opinions matter.

Chong (2013) offers a phenomenology of fiction reviewing as a study of evaluative identity and practice. She traces the concrete steps that reviewers take to guarantee the legitimacy of their professional evaluations by moving beyond their idiosyncrasies as readers to offer a general assessment, which both enables and sustains reviewers' self-concept as fair judges. In a related study, Chong (2015) studies the various factors critics weigh when considering whether or not to write a negative review. Her interviews with critics reveal how a complex mix of pleasure and anxiety, competition and stewardship, empathy and self-preservation all come to bear on critics' evaluative practices.

Empirical analyses in this vein demonstrate the value of considering actors' subjective experiences for a fuller portrait of evaluative practice (also Gross 2008; Heinich 2005). This line of work emphasizes the value of empirical studies of evaluation as an identity and practice, one that reveals multidimensionality and variability in the orientation of evaluators. This strongly contrasts with the Bourdieusian approach to identity which has remained largely underdeveloped (Alexander 1995).[9]

The place of subjectivity in evaluation has been understudied because of its historical understanding as a foil obscuring 'objective' ways of knowing. This has resulted in what Shapin (2012) calls a 'dustbin' conception of subjectivity as a heterogeneous bucket of meaning about which nothing coherent can be said.[10] But by taking evaluators' experience of evaluation and their self-concepts as analytical points of departure, work considering the phenomenology of tasting and evaluation can shed new light on the practical, cultural and emotional dimensions of evaluation – dimensions too often obscured within the final judgments themselves.

Bringing objects back in

Rich ethnographic and phenomenological studies have produced insights on the subject-object relation: that is, how subjects learn to appreciate and evaluate cultural objects and how cultural objects exert influence on evaluating subjects. This approach is in keeping with the new sociology of art (cf. Becker *et al.* 2006), which grapples with how to meaningfully incorporate art objects into social analysis rather than just reducing them to mere proxies for other 'social variables.' The goal is to recognize not only how art objects are shaped by society, but also what forms of agentic power and distinctive properties they wield (while still eschewing 'charismatic' ideologies about art or artists). This work also aligns with an actor-network-theory inspired view of evaluation as a socio-material process wherein the properties of the object being evaluated and the evaluating agent are coproduced (also see Boltanski and Esquerre 2014).

Hennion's (2004) theory of attachment, developed based on his empirical work on amateurs, is exemplary here. He rejects the idea that taste and judgment simply reflect other social factors. Rather than emphasize that taste is a product of broader societal classification systems, Hennion argues for a performative approach to taste that considers how people, their bodies and the objects they evaluate coproduce one another. Much in line with French contemporary pragmatist thinking (Barthe *et al.* 2013), he takes taste and judgment seriously as techniques that people learn, and with which they actively engage. In his study of amateur wine-tastings, for example, he emphasizes how people in such group settings physically and socially coproduce the objects they are tasting: the physic-chemical properties of a wine act on the taster and the taster's status is defined by the way she attends to the act of drinking the wine (i.e. taking a moment to sniff and pucker while sipping).

Similarly, in the United States, Benzecry (2011) looks at how individuals fashion themselves into members of a community of cultural appreciators. Specifically, he studies opera fans and examines how they learn, in quite practical ways, to deepen their passion for and attachment to opera. This includes learning the acceptable practices for appreciating and valuing opera through informal talk, attending conferences and experiencing opera house performances. Benzecry traces how opera fans move from their initial, visceral reactions to opera to consciously learning how to deepen their engagement with the art form. This contrasts with Bourdieu's approach in that it foregrounds the beguiling properties of opera itself as a cultural object and how it attracts people to learn more about it, rather than suggesting that people are only attracted to opera as part of the corpus of 'legitimate' culture. Furthermore, this approach allows Benzecry to acknowledge opera fans' experience at times of being stigmatized for enjoying this particular form of cultural participation – something that is hard to reconcile with a straightforward cultural capital argument.

In summary, then, recent research demonstrates the value of looking at taste and cultural discernment not only as mechanisms for reproducing inequality, but also as nuanced interactional processes. Specifically, new work seeks to balance Bourdieu's insights by bringing cultural objects themselves and their evaluators 'back in,' so to speak. The point is not to return to a view of art as having inherent or charismatic value, but to relocate within the frame of analysis the agency, identity and emotions of evaluative actors and their practices. Such research also promises to be relevant for other fields where professional evaluations routinely carry influence.

New perspectives from organizational research and economic sociology

In this last section of our paper, we broaden our focus and examine developments beyond the sociology of art and culture. This is essential because the study of (e)valuation processes in cultural domains is no longer the sole purview of sociologists of art and culture. Rather, over the last ten to twenty years, we have seen a growing body of literature on cultural production and (e)valuation emerging in economic and organizational sociology.

This literature has developed largely independently from the influence of Bourdieu's work. Rather than building on Bourdieu's theory of the field of cultural production, economic sociologists and organizational scholars have turned to the study of cultural markets primarily to answer theoretical questions germane to their own subfields.

Economic sociologists have aimed to identify mechanisms through which value is 'socially constructed' and to challenge standard theories of valuation in economics (see e.g. Velthuis 2005; Karpik 2010; Beckert and Aspers 2011). Organizational scholars, in turn, have developed an interest in cultural markets to better understand processes and dynamics that are central to organizational theories of legitimacy, diffusion and reputation (see e.g. Bielby and Bielby 1994; Zuckerman et al. 2003; Rao et al. 2005; Phillips 2013).

The result is a number of significant contributions to the development of a post-Bourdieusian sociology of evaluation and valuation. Most importantly, these scholars have introduced new theoretical and analytical perspectives to the study of fields of cultural production – perspectives that have their origin outside the sociology of art and cultural production. For instance, one strand of work in organizational research is drawing from general theories of categorization and identity (see Negro et al. 2010 or Vergne and Wry 2014, for a review of this research paradigm). Scholars have built on these theories to examine how membership in certain cultural categories (such a genres), as well as their clarity or ambiguity, affects the evaluation of cultural products (see e.g. Zuckerman et al. 2003; Hsu 2006). In doing so, these scholars have moved away from an orthodox Bourdieusian interpretation of categories in markets for symbolic goods as 'weapons' in positional struggles for power to an understanding of categories as 'coordination devices' between market participants.[11]

Another line of research at the intersection of economic sociology and organizational research has borrowed from sociological theories of status to explain differences in how cultural products are evaluated in markets for symbolic goods (e.g. Benjamin and Podolny 1999; Yogev 2010), while still other scholars have built on sociological theories of social influence to develop a better understanding of how consumers and intermediaries in cultural markets manage to reach agreement in their evaluations despite an absence of reliable markers of quality (see e.g. Mark 2003; Salganik et al. 2006; Godart and Mears 2009).

Last, but not least, organizational scholars and economic sociologists also need to be credited for correcting a bias in favour of high culture that critics have identified in Bourdieu's work: While Bourdieu – as well as his followers – have paid only little attention to the subfield of large-scale cultural production (see e.g. Hesmondhalgh 2006), these social scientists have extended empirical sociological research on valuation processes to a broad range of *cultural industries*.

We draw attention to these developments here because we believe that the work by economic sociologists and organizational researchers can guide and enrich future research on (e)valuation processes in cultural fields in at least two important ways. First, the work of these scholars provides a model for how to theorize processes of valuation and evaluation in cultural fields most productively. Bourdieu famously conceptualized the field of cultural production as 'the economic world reversed' – in which disinterestedness is valued over the pursuit of short-term material gains (Bourdieu 1983). But by doing so, he may have put more emphasis on the particularities of cultural fields than needed. For there is no reason to assume that valuation processes in fields of cultural production are a priori distinct from valuation processes in any other domains of society. In contrast to Bourdieu, newer work emerging from these fields does not treat fields of cultural production as fundamentally distinct from other domains of research. Rather, it draws on theoretical tools and frameworks derived from general sociological theories such as organizational theory, labour market theory or status theory to consider valuation processes in cultural fields together with valuation processes in other domains of society, such as education, business or politics. Thus, it opens up the possibility for general theory-building across substantive areas of research as a complement to domain-specific theories of valuation in fields of cultural production.[12]

Second, the work of economic sociologists and organizational scholars also underscores the importance of acknowledging and theorizing the role of *formal organizations* in cultural markets. This is important because in many cultural markets, it is *members of formal organizations* who produce, classify and evaluate cultural products, not atomized individual producers or critics. This matters because the status of formal organizations, their relation to other organizations, as well as their internal politics and practices are all likely to affect how cultural products are evaluated. Hence, the adoption of organizational perspectives is absolutely essential for developing a proper understanding of (e)valuation processes in cultural markets. Many of the empirical studies cited above provide excellent illustrations for this (see e.g. Zuckerman *et al.* 2003). Yet, to date, such organizational perspectives have been primarily deployed in research on *cultural industries*. A key task for future research therefore will be to adopt similar perspectives for the study of cultural fields that fall on the opposite pole of the field of cultural production: high culture art fields and fields of restricted production.

Such a focus is particularly timely given important structural changes in the organization of many art worlds. In the last decade, we witnessed a growth of professional and organizational structures in countless cultural fields, with the result that more and more fields that used to be structured by an ideology of disinterestedness now look increasingly like market-oriented cultural industries (e.g. for the case of the literary field, see Thompson 2010; Verboord 2011). Common markers of this transformation are the emergence of third-party market mediators such as agents or managers, a growing involvement of large media corporations or the widespread use of marketing practices. In the light of these developments, we consider it highly important that scholars build more bridges between traditional Bourdieu-inspired research on cultural production and research in economic sociology and organizational research.

Conclusion

With the brief 'tour d'horizon' offered in this paper, we aim to generate enthusiasm and further discussion around a future agenda for the sociology of valuation and evaluation. Building on Lamont's recent call for a comparative sociology of valuation and evaluation (2012b), we have highlighted three important types of *constraints* that are exercised on (e)valuation – 1) *the criteria of evaluation*; 2) *the self-concepts of evaluators*; and 3) the *roles of object and non-human supports* – and discussed how these three constraints could serve as points of comparison for future scholarship. These analytical levels are among the most important to consider across different contexts and different types of cultural objects. Thus, we urge our colleagues to work toward theory building while focusing on these promising topics.

But even though we share a firm conviction in the value of comparative lenses for gaining new theoretical insights in the study of cultural processes (Lamont *et al.* 2014), the multifarious development of the field is likely to follow its own logic. Hence, we want to encourage scholars to think about the blind-spots of, not only the Bourdieusian theoretical framework, but also of the lenses currently used in sociological research on evaluation and valuation. For path dependency is not easily avoided when it comes to the formulation of theoretical problems, as Thomas Kuhn (1970) powerfully argued almost fifty years ago.

Notes

1 We gratefully acknowledge Heather Haveman and Mike Savage for providing comments on this paper.
2 Harvard University.
3 www.college-de-france.fr/site/pierre-michel-menger/#seminar; Luc Boltanski et Arnaud Esquerre. "La "Collection", une forme neuve du caplitalisme. La mise en valeur economique du passé et ses effets." *Les Temps Modernes*, 679(3), p. 5.

4 Most recently, the sessions organized by the Science, Knowledge and Technology section at the meetings of the American Sociological Association in San Francisco in August 2014 and the meetings of the German Sociological Association held in Trier in October 2014.
5 These macro-social changes include, among other things, the rise of new public management, the impact of neoliberalism or new developments in information technology (Kjellberg and Mallard 2013).
6 Note, however, that much of our argument also applies to cultural consumption, as there is a "homology" between Bourdieu's sociology of cultural production and his sociology of cultural consumption (Hesmondhalgh 2006: 216)
7 Note, however, that this strong focus on "economic" criteria of evaluation in the professional evaluations of market intermediaries stands in contrast to consumers' evaluation of comedy. Existing research on comedy consumers in the UK suggests that taste-based "symbolic boundaries" are particularly strong among consumers of comedy because of the personal and subjective nature of humor (Friedman 2014).
8 Interestingly, this shift toward more inductive and close-up empirical analysis can also be observed in the work of scholars who continue to study (e)valuation processes in fields of cultural production through the lens of an orthodox Bourdieusian framework of analysis, see e.g. Nylander (2013) or Friedman (2014).
9 But see Steinmetz's (2006) argument of a more Freudian take on Bourdieu's concept of *libido sciendi*.
10 Shapin (2012) argues for a phenomenology of taste, but he is more interested in the inter-subjectivity of taste in terms of classification systems and chemical properties of food: that taste has both a cultural and a natural basis.
11 This difference points to an important underlying difference in the treatment of question of power and domination in the work of Bourdieu and organizational scholars. While Bourdieu has been criticized for putting *too much* emphasis on antagonistic dynamics in cultural fields, organizational scholars might be criticized for paying *too little* attention to the question of power and domination.
12 For an example of such a domain-crossing approach to theory-building, see Lamont, Chong and Bourgoin (2014) who compare customary rules of evaluation across three settings: fiction reviews, peer review and management consulting. Lamont, Chong and Bourgoin argue that what is understood to be a legitimate evaluation in these three settings is shaped by three main factors: 1) the agent conducting the evaluation (who can do it, how are they certified, how to do gain their competence? etc.); 2) the object being evaluated (how clearly bounded is it, how are the comparans defined? etc.); and 3) the audiences (is it single or plural? a client or a peer? etc.).

References

Alexander, J. (1995) *Fin de Siècle Social Theory: Relativism, Reduction, and the Problem of Reason*, London: Verso.
Barthe, Y., D. de Blic, J. Heurtin, É. Lagneau, C. Lemieux, D. Linhardt, C. Moreau de Bellaing, C. Rémy and D. Trom (2013) 'Sociologie Pragmatique : Mode d'Emploi', *Politix*, 103(3): 175.
Becker, H. (1982) *Art Worlds*, Berkeley, CA: University of California Press.
Becker, H., R. Faulkner and B. Kirshenblatt-Gimblett (2006) *Art from Start to Finish*, Chicago: University of Chicago Press.
Beckert, J. and P. Aspers (2011) *The Worth of Goods*, New York: Oxford University Press.
Beckert, J. and C. Musselin (2013) *Constructing Quality*, Oxford: Oxford University Press.
Beljean, S. (2014) 'You Gotta Make People Laugh. Stratification and Standards of Evaluation in the Stand-up Comedy Industry', paper presented at Conference of Eastern Sociological Association, February, Baltimore, USA.
Benjamin, B. and J. Podolny (1999) 'Status, Quality, and Social Order in the California Wine Industry', *Administrative Science Quarterly*, 44(3): 563.
Benzecry, C. (2011) *The Opera Fanatic*, Chicago: University of Chicago Press.
Berthoin Antal, A., Hutter, M. and D. Stark (2015) *Moments of Evaluation*, New York: Oxford.
Bielby, W. and D. Bielby (1994) "'All Hits Are Flukes': Institutionalized Decision Making and the Rhetoric of Network Prime-Time Program Development', *American Journal of Sociology*, 99(5): 1287–1313.
Boltanski, L. and A. Esquerre (2014) 'La "Collection", Une Forme Neuve du Capitalisme. La Mise en Valeur Économique du Passé et Ses Effets', *Les Temps Modernes*, 3(679): 5–72.
Born, G. (2010) 'The Social and the Aesthetic: For a Post-Bourdieuian Theory of Cultural Production', *Cultural Sociology*, 4(2): 171–208.

Bourdieu, P. (1983) 'The Field of Cultural Production, or: The Economic World Reversed', *Poetics*, 12(4): 311–356.
—— (1993) *The Field of Cultural Production*, New York: Columbia University Press.
—— (1996) *The Rules of Art*, Stanford, CA: Stanford University Press.
Camic, C., N. Gross and M. Lamont (2011) *Social Knowledge in the Making*, Chicago: University of Chicago Press.
Chong, P. (2013) 'Legitimate Judgment in Art, the Scientific World Reversed?: Critical Distance in Evaluation', *Social Studies of Science*, 43(2): 265–281.
—— (2015) 'Playing Nice, Being Mean, and the Space in Between: Book Critics and the Difficulties of Writing Bad Reviews', in B. Antal, M. Hutter and D. Stark (eds.) *Moments of Valuation: Exploring Sites of Dissonance*, New York: Oxford University Press.
Coulangeon, P. (2016) 'The Sociology of Cultural Participation in France Thirty Years after Distinction', in L. Hanquinet and M. Savage (eds.) *Routledge International Handbook of the Sociology of Art and Culture*, London: Routledge.
Coulangeon, P. and J. Duval (2013) *Trente ans Après La Distinction de Pierre Bourdieu*, Paris: Editions la Découverte.
Craig, A. and S. Dubois (2010) 'Between Art and Money: The Social Space of Public Readings in Contemporary Poetry Economies and Careers', *Poetics*, 38(5):441–460.
Epstein, S. (1973) 'The Self-Concept Revisited: Or a Theory of a Theory', *American Psychologist*, 28(5): 404–416.
—— (2007) *Inclusion*, Chicago: University of Chicago Press.
Espeland, W. and M. Stevens (1998) 'Commensuration as a Social Process', *Annual Review of Sociology*, 24(1):313–343.
—— (2008) 'A Sociology of Quantification', *European Journal of Sociology*, 49(03): 401–436.
Fourcade, M. and K. Healy (2013) 'Classification Situations: Life Chances in the Neo-Liberal Era', *Accounting, Organizations and Society*, 38: 559–572.
Friedman, S. (2014) *Comedy and Distinction*, New York: Routledge.
—— (2014) 'The Hidden Tastemakers: Comedy Scouts as Cultural Brokers at the Edinburgh Festival Fringe', *Poetics*, 44(3): 22–41.
Godart, F. and A. Mears (2009) 'How Do Cultural Producers Make Creative Decisions? Lessons from the Catwalk', *Social Forces*, 88(2): 671–692.
Gross, N. (2002) 'Becoming a Pragmatist Philosopher: Status, Self-Concept, and Intellectual Choice', *American Sociological Review*, 67(1):52–76.
—— (2008) *Richard Rorty: The Making of an American Philosopher*, Chicago: University of Chicago Press.
Guetzkow, J., M. Lamont and G. Mallard (2004) 'What Is Originality in the Humanities and the Social Sciences?', *American Sociological Review*, 69(2): 190–212.
Heinich, N. (2005) *L'élite artiste: Excellence et singularité en régime démocratique*, Paris: Gallimard.
Hennion, A. (2001) 'Music Lovers: Taste as Performance', *Theory, Culture and Society*, 18(5):1–22.
—— (2004) 'Une Sociologie Des Attachements', *Sociétés*, 85(3):9–24.
Hesmondhalgh, D. (2006) 'Bourdieu, the Media and Cultural Production', *Media, Culture and Society*, 28(2): 211–231.
Hsu, G. (2006) 'Jacks of All Trades and Masters of None: Audiences' Reactions to Spanning Genres in Feature Film Production', *Administrative Science Quarterly*, 51(3): 420–450.
Hutter, M. (2013) 'Translation and Dissonance. Complementary Modes of Innovation in the Creative Economy', paper presented at conference for *Valorizing Dissonance: Cultural Perspectives on Newness*, Social Science Research Center Berlin (WZB) June, Berlin, Germany.
Karpik, L. (2010) *Valuing the Unique*, Princeton, NJ: Princeton University Press.
Kersten, A. and M. Verboord (2013) 'Dimensions of Conventionality and Innovation in Film: The Cultural Classification of Blockbusters, Award Winners, and Critics' Favourites', *Cultural Sociology*, 8(1):3–24.
Kjellberg, H. and A. Mallard (2013) 'Valuation Studies? Our Collective Two Cents', *Valuation Studies*, 1:11–30.
Knorr-Cetina, K. (1999) *Epistemic Cultures*, Cambridge, MA: Harvard University Press.
Kuhn, T. (1970) *The Structure of Scientific Revolutions*, Chicago: University of Chicago Press.
Lamont, M. (2009) *How Professors Think*, Cambridge, MA: Harvard University Press.
—— (2012a) 'How Has Bourdieu Been Good to Think With? The Case of the United States', *Sociological Forum*, 27(1):228–237.

—— (2012b) 'Toward a Comparative Sociology of Valuation and Evaluation', *Annual Review of Sociology*, 38(1):201–221.
Lamont, M., S. Beljean and M. Clair (2014) 'What Is Missing? Cultural Processes and Causal Pathways to Inequality', *Socio-Economic Review*, 12(3): 573–608.
Lamont, M., P. Chong and A. Bourgoin (2014) 'Capturing Worlds of Worth: Fiction Reviewing, Management Consulting and Scholarly Evaluation Compared', paper presented at the Annual Meetings of the American Sociological Association, August, San Francisco, CA.
Leschziner, V. (2015) *At the Chef's Table: Culinary Creativity in Elite Restaurants*, Palo Alto, CA: Stanford University Press.
Mallard, G., M. Lamont and J. Guetzkow (2009) 'Fairness as Appropriateness', *Science, Technology and Human Values*, 34(5): 573–606.
Mark, N. (2003) 'Culture and Competition: Homophily and Distancing Explanations for Cultural Niches', *American Sociological Review*, 68: 319–345.
Negro, G., Ö. Koçak and G. Hsu (2010) 'Research on Categories in the Sociology of Organizations', *Research in the Sociology of Organizations*, 31: 3–35.
Nylander, E. (2013) 'Mastering the Jazz Standard: Sayings and Doings of Artistic Valuation', *American Journal of Cultural Sociology*, 2(1): 66–96.
Phillips, D.J. (2013) *Shaping Jazz: Cities, Labels, and the Global Emergence of an Art Form*, Princeton, NJ: Princeton University Press.
Prior, N. (2011) 'Critique and Renewal in the Sociology of Music: Bourdieu and Beyond', *Cultural Sociology*, 5(1): 121–138.
Rao, H., P. Monin and R. Durand (2005) 'Border Crossing: Bricolage and the Erosion of Categorical Boundaries in French Gastronomy', *American Sociological Review*, 70(6): 968–991.
Rosen, S. (1981) 'The Economics of Superstars', *The American Economic Review*, 71(5): 845–858.
Salganik, M., P. Sheridan Dodds and D.J. Watts (2006) 'Experimental Study of Inequality and Unpredictability in an Artificial Cultural Market', *Science*, 311(5762):854–56.
Sapiro, G. (2003) 'The Literary Field Between the State and the Market', *Poetics*, 31(5): 441–464.
—— (2010) 'Globalization and Cultural Diversity in the Book Market: The Case of Literary Translations in the US and in France', *Poetics*, 38(4): 419–439.
Shapin, S. (2012) 'The Sciences of Subjectivity', *Social Studies of Science*, 42(2): 170–184.
Silva, E. and A. Warde (eds.) (2010) *Cultural Analysis and Bourdieu's Legacy*, London: Routledge.
Steinmetz, G. (2006) 'Bourdieu's Disavowal of Lacan: Psychoanalytic Theory and the Concepts of "Habitus" and "Symbolic Capital"', *Constellations*, 13(4): 445–464.
Thompson, J. (2010) *Merchants of Culture*, Cambridge, UK: Polity.
Timmermans, S. and S. Epstein (2010) 'A World of Standards but Not a Standard World: Toward a Sociology of Standards and Standardization', *Annual Review of Sociology*, 36(1): 69–89.
Velthuis, O. (2005) *Talking Prices*, Princeton, NJ: Princeton University Press.
Verboord, M. (2011) 'Market Logic and Cultural Consecration in French, German and American Bestseller Lists, 1970-2007', *Poetics*, 39(4): 290–315.
Vergne, J.-P. and T. Wry (2014) 'Categorizing Categorization Research: Review, Integration, and Future Directions', *Journal of Management Studies*, 51(1): 56–94.
Yogev, T. (2010) 'The Social Construction of Quality: Status Dynamics in the Market for Contemporary Art', *Socio-Economic Review*, 8(3): 511–536.
Zuckerman, E.W., T.-Y. Kim, K. Ukanwa and J. von Rittmann (2003) 'Robust Identities or Nonentities? Typecasting in the Feature-Film Labor Market', *American Journal of Sociology*, 108(5): 1018–1074.

3
Contesting culture
Bourdieu and the strong program in cultural sociology

Marco Santoro and Marco Solaroli[1]

Introduction

Notwithstanding Pierre Bourdieu's profoundly influential oeuvre and globally recognized dominant status in the social sciences, the humanities and cultural studies (Santoro 2008a; 2011; Silva and Warde 2010), there can be no doubt whatsoever that the Bourdieusian theory has almost no currency in the 'strong program' (henceforth SP) in cultural sociology aggressively advanced by Jeffrey Alexander and his 'school' since the late nineties (see Alexander and Smith 1998, 2002, 2010; Alexander 2003; Alexander, Jacobs and Smith 2011a; Rodrigo, Carballo and Ossandón 2008). From an SP perspective, what previous programs (including Bourdieu's) are lacking is a sense of culture as the deepest structure of social life, the inner engine of social action, and the constitutively meaningful dimension of society. Indeed, the claim of a strategic positioning of culture at the centre of the sociological enterprise of understanding human conduct and life lies at the core of the so-called 'strong program'.

Given his centrality in the field since at least the end of the eighties, when something like a 'cultural turn' in sociology started (e.g. Chaney 1994; DiMaggio 2000; Friedland and Mohr 2004; Santoro 2008b), it is unsurprising that Bourdieu's 'failed theoretical synthesis' was the target of Alexander's (1995) direct, highly critical intervention. Interestingly, this criticism followed a previously positive reading of Bourdieu's work as one of the most important contributions towards the renewal of the sociological analysis of culture after Parsons (Alexander 1990). The reasons for such a change in attitude are many – from supposed personal resentment (Wacquant 2001), to theoretical refinement and strategic repositioning in scholarly fields – but the final result is clear: Bourdieu's theory would be the vector of a 'weak' and even contradictory understanding of culture, and too 'flawed' to serve as a profitable guideline for doing cultural analysis.

However, even if Bourdieu has been one of the main targets of Alexander's criticism, one could seriously doubt Bourdieu has nothing serious to offer to a research program aimed at refocusing sociology around the foundational category of culture (including symbols and meanings) – what Alexander and colleagues have called 'cultural sociology' as different from a 'sociology *of* culture', i.e. a sociology in which culture is just one among many variables, and an analytically dependent one. One could ask, for example, if it is true that the culture concept's status in Bourdieu is that of a dependent variable – considering also that Bourdieu has since the sixties criticized the language of variables. One could also wonder if what the 'strong program' aims to offer to sociology and cultural theory could not be accommodated into more established lines of thought and research – in other words, if the 'strong program' and 'cultural sociology' as its sociological expression could be more labels in the academic market of ideas (or better in the intellectual game of position-taking and winning) (see Patterson 2014). Clearly, this is not equivalent to arguing that the 'strong program' has nothing to offer to sociologists of culture. In fact, on the one hand, a fair and serious account could not fail to appreciate how this research program has so far contributed fertile theoretical ideas, empirical analyses and epistemological debates. However, on the other hand, it equally could not push forward to claim that it has produced a 'symbolic revolution' in sociology.

Our chapter argues that the field of cultural sociology/sociology of culture (let us use the two formulas together for now) is much more integrated and dialogical than many of its practitioners like to claim, and that there is still large room for confrontation and even accommodation among supposedly opposed perspectives and even 'schools'. Moving from a brief reconstruction of the genesis and development of the 'strong program' in the field of contemporary sociology *vis-à-vis* Bourdieu's increasing global influence, but also from a recognition that intellectual life has a fractal nature in which the same distinctions reproduce themselves in cyclical ways at different levels (see Abbott 2001), this chapter aims to uncover the points of departure and distinction but also the spaces of potential convergence and mutual strengthening between Bourdieu's social theory of culture and Alexander's self-claimed 'strong program' in cultural sociology.

Section two presents the way in which the 'strong' program in cultural sociology theoretically positions itself *vis-à-vis* so-called 'weak' programs in sociology of culture. Section three critically reconstructs the historical development of the strong program's theoretical toolbox, focusing in particular on its major concepts – such as relative autonomy of culture, culture structure, codes, narratives, performance and iconicity – and reading them through a comparatively Bourdieusian lens. Section four offers a critically constructive assessment of the strong program *vis-à-vis* Bourdieu, offering an interpretation of their analogies and differences based on the notion of 'fractalization' of cultural theory. Section five suggests potential bridge-building approaches, by presenting recent empirical integrations between Bourdieu's field-theory and the SP's conceptual toolkits, aimed at overcoming the flaws of each position with the strengths of the other. Finally, the conclusions insist on three major points of critical confrontation, suggesting the need of future efforts aimed at 'stronger' theory building.

What's in a name: ('Strong') cultural sociology vs. ('weak') sociology of culture

The 'strong program' in cultural theory owes its name to the challenge developed by British sociologists David Bloor and Barry Barnes in the sociology of knowledge. As it is well known, this 'strong program' was framed directly in opposition to a supposedly 'weak' Mertonian sociology of science. This strong program refused to treat 'good science' by one standard (immune to sociological intervention) and bad science by another. Instead of a rational reconstruction in Popperian or Lakatosian style, it aimed at studying science as a 'social construction', exactly like any other type of knowledge i.e. belief (Barnes, Bloor and Henry 1996).

Explicitly referring to this previous move, Alexander and Smith (1998; 2002) argued for a fuller inclusion of culture as the realm of meanings into the sociological project (Alexander and Smith 1993; Alexander 1996; Smith 1998)[2] as part of a self-claimed strong program.

This implied that some other program can be called 'weak'. As we have seen, in science studies Mertonian sociology of science was the weak program against which Bloor advanced his 'strong program'. Indeed, there are actually four big (supposedly) 'weak programs' against which Alexander and Smith originally contrasted their proposal. They are Foucaultian social theory, British Cultural Studies (BCS), an eclectic (and mostly American) 'production and reception of culture' research stream and, last but not least, Bourdieu's work. Not really a minor pantheon indeed: suffice it to recall that Foucault is probably the most quoted social thinker of the last thirty years, the British Cultural Studies are commonly (and worldwide) recognized as one of the most influential enterprises in the social and human sciences of the second half of the twentieth century and Bourdieu has been the most cited sociologist in the world since the 1990s, at least in the English speaking world (Santoro 2008a; Gorski 2013a). In Bourdieusian terms, we could say these were the dominant programs in the burgeoning field of cultural sociology (or sociology of culture, as the two expressions were at the time interchangeable), where however also other more focused (and less theoretically ambitious) intellectual projects centred on meaning-making were taking shape within American Sociology (e.g. Peterson's 'production of culture' perspective and Becker's 'art world' approach, the latter surprisingly absent in the original manifesto)[3]. Claiming a superior status for a program yet to be born was at minimum risky, if not bold. However, one could at least try to assess (i) if their claim to superiority relies upon a promising new toolkit, and (ii) if their criticism against existing models, methods and concepts is sufficiently grounded in a balanced assessment of their values/merits as well as of their limits. This section will discuss the latter point, leaving the former to the next one.

While recognizing the writings of Foucault, BCS and Bourdieu as useful, even crucial contributions to the production of a cultural turn in sociology, i.e. to the acknowledgment that 'meanings count', and that social life cannot be reduced only to such materialist elements as power, interest and class[4], Alexander and Smith also claimed that none of them takes meanings seriously enough to admit the power of culture to shape social life, including politics and the economy. To be sure, Alexander and Smith (2010: 14) recognized their role in developing 'theoretically informed, non-empiricist explanations where concepts could play a stronger role than variables', but none of them is deemed courageous enough to claim *the autonomy of culture* a priori. For Alexander and Smith, this claim is indeed the pivotal criterion for deciding the strength (and symmetrically the weakness) of research programs, and indeed it is exactly around this point that a cleavage between programs can be noticed. What arguably makes the 'strong program' stronger is exactly the notion that, analytically, culture (i.e. the cultural dimension of social life) is potentially autonomous from social forces and social structures, and exists beyond, beside and behind them – therefore asking for an autonomous investigation, independently from other dimensions/spheres.

Moreover, there are two further features identifying a SP, two 'methodological characteristics' (see Table 3.1). The first is a 'commitment to hermeneutically reconstructing social texts in a rich and persuasive way'; this is the commitment to what the authors conceive as a 'Geertzian thick description'. The second is a commitment 'to anchor causality in proximate actors and agencies, specifying in detail just how culture interferes with and directs what really happens' – in their words: 'We would argue that it is only by resolving issues of detail – who says what, why, and to what effect – that cultural analysis can become plausible *according to the criteria of a social science*' (Alexander and Smith 2002: 138; emphasis added). Let us discuss both.

Thick descriptions oppose to thin ones, of course. The implicit statement is therefore that scholars in supposedly 'weak' programs limit themselves by stopping 'too early' in

Marco Santoro and Marco Solaroli

Table 3.1 The 'deep antinomies' in cultural theory according to Alexander and Smith

	Weak	Strong
Epistemology	Culture as superstructure (culture as 'soft' variable)	Autonomy of culture (culture as 'hard' variable)
Method/1	Thin description [?]	Thick description
Method/2	[?]	Specified causal mechanisms anchored in proximate actors/agencies

their analytical accounts, and please themselves with superficial, i.e. not enough deep, reconstruction of fragments of social life. Moreover, they miss the opportunity to reconstruct the stratification of meanings, and the interplay among meanings, which makes any social occurrence what it is. Is this true for Bourdieu? His distance from Geertzian thick description is well known. Textualization is not a strategy Bourdieu would recommend (e.g. Bourdieu 2000a), for the very simple reason that people in real life don't textualize: it is an instantiation of 'scholastic fallacy' – to quote Bourdieu (1998a) – which would introduce in social life an attitude, a disposition that only masters of cultural analysis may have. But real agents aren't or rather cannot be masters of cultural analysis of texts exactly *qua* agents – neither are scholars such as Geertz masters of texts when acting as social agents engaged in practical agency. People never relate to social codes as if they were texts, and scholars using the metaphor of text are at risk of confusing the intellectual (scholastic) relation to world with the practical one. Thus, on the one hand, the commitment to 'Geertzian thick description' risks implying a kind of sociological analysis that goes systematically too far from what social agents may ever do in their competent cultural practices. On the other hand, rejecting this approach – as Bourdieu does – doesn't necessarily entail 'thin' description. In fact, in contrast to thick description *à la Geertz* (and *a fortiori* more traditional ethnography carried out through participant observation), Bourdieu has proposed what he named 'participant objectivation', as the objectivation of the subject, the operations of objectivation and the latter's conditions of possibility (Bourdieu 2003) – thus as a viable method for capturing meaning structures without losing reflexivity. At the same time, Bourdieu himself practiced what could be called a dense, even thick description, in the sense of deep, stratified interpretation, early in his trajectory, in his fieldwork in Algeria and in his native Béarn, but also later, in sociological pieces of work including sections of *Distinction* (Bourdieu 1984) and *Homo Academicus* (Bourdieu 1988). Indeed, the presence and relevance of a Bourdieusian strand of ethnographic research (e.g. Wacquant, Bourgeois, etc.) bears witness to the compatibility of Bourdieu's tools with deep-lived research experiences. In sum, the problem is not 'thickness', but textualization as an unreflexive method.

With respect to the third methodological point, it is worth noting that, in the SP's 'manifesto', Alexander and Smith pay homage to what is clearly a legacy of the Lazarsfeldian language of variable – a pillar of US mainstream sociology at least since the fifties. Interestingly, they do this not while doing sociological analysis but as a rhetorical move:

> To speak of the sociology of culture is to suggest that culture is something to be explained, by something else entirely separated from the domain of meaning itself. To speak of the sociology of culture is to suggest that explanatory power lies in the study of the 'hard' variables of social structure, such that structured sets of meanings become superstructures

and ideologies driven by the more 'real' and tangible social forces. In this approach, culture becomes defined as a 'soft' not really independent variable.

(2002: 136)

Paradoxically, the 'language of variable' is exactly what (the *French* scholar) Bourdieu has distanced himself for almost all his career[5] looking for strategies of analysis that could recognize and capture the intrinsically *relational* nature of social life. Field analysis, with MCA (multiple correspondence analysis) as its methodological complement, is Bourdieu's response to American variable analysis: rather than seeking to explain supposedly 'dependent' variables through the causal force of some 'independent' variable, field analysis tries to discover the complex web of relations among different entities (Bourdieu 1993; 1996a; Savage and Silva 2013: 114; Lebaron 2009). Bourdieu couldn't approve the previous description of the sociology of culture simply because he wouldn't ever make use of the 'language of variables' and the social ontology that language presumes – what Andrew Abbott once famously described as the 'general linear reality' (2001).

This doesn't mean that Bourdieu escapes the search for mechanisms, for 'proximate causes specifying in detail just how culture interferes with and directs what really happens'; indeed, we could say that as a realist theorist (Potter 2000; Gorski 2013b), Bourdieu has always looked for those social mechanisms capable of accounting for the emergence of a certain pattern or situation. Still, it would be impossible to understate the place Bourdieu's sociological work recognizes and concedes to individuals, be they well-known historical actors (Flaubert, Manet, etc.) or more ordinary people, variously located in the social space.

Almost a decade after their first 'manifesto' of the strong program (2002), Alexander and Smith (2010) were able to assess and discuss achievements in the field around what has become an established albeit not dominant research program, or – as they say – paradigm. In their words:

> The Strong Program has created new tools that allow generalization or create transmissible theory…. In line with the Kuhnian model of the paradigm as an exemplar or concrete research strategy, the Strong Program has developed a range of middle-range theoretical concepts and models. These can be taken up and used by scholars in various local and topical settings. Modified and elaborated, new middle-range theorizing will be generated in turn.
>
> *(2010: 16)*

It is worthwhile noting that Mertonian 'middle-range theorizing' figures prominently in this recent self-description of the SP. (From this point of view, the SP in cultural theory seems reluctant to move too far away from a pillar of the weak programs in both science and cultural studies). Moreover – a second and more crucial difference between the SP in cultural theory and the SP in science studies – whereas Bloor asked for the submission of scientific knowledge to the same set of principles used to explain false knowledge in the assumption that knowledge is always and necessarily social, Alexander and Smith asked for the positioning of culture at the heart of the sociological enterprise as both a truly sociological object to be analyzed in its inner constitution and as a force in itself, capable of producing effects on its own. Their proposal was thus twofold: 1) previous sociological approaches to cultural studies – including the most influential ones – were unable or unwilling to really enter the cultural realm, leaving it to humanities, as Merton's sociology of science was unable/unwilling to consider science itself as a sociological object, reducing itself to a science of the social conditions of science production and leaving the mission of explaining the content of (true) science to the philosophers of science, i.e. epistemology; 2) culture was not an object like others, but a sort of meta-object, i.e. what societies (as social structures) are really made of. The SP in cultural theory asked sociologists to 'go into' culture as the deepest structure of social life.

We see some tension between these two injunctions. According to the first, in order to enter the cultural constitution of society, sociologists should give culture (i.e. meaning systems) analytical autonomy. According to the second, however, it would be impossible to sharply distinguish between culture and social life as the former lies at the basis of the latter, making it possible to exist as such. As McLennan (2004) already recognized, the strong program's ambition to offer a thick description of culture structures, codes and narratives can be possible only by accepting that they possess – in Alexander's terms – a 'musicality' and drive of their own, an analytical 'autonomy'. However,

> the significance of such structures and the intensity of the tunes cannot be properly gauged without putting them in the context of the entire social life of the groups under examination, in other words in relation to those very factors that Alexander, unaccountably, seems bent on relegating in importance: 'group processes', 'self-interested ideologies', 'networks', and, yes, the 'reproduction of social relations' in a given type of societal formation. These things, granted, are by no means 'outside' the realm of meanings, but neither can they be posed as congeries of meanings *rather than* practices, behaviours, structures, or relations.
>
> *(McLennan 2004: 82; see also Lizardo 2010b; Gans 2012)*

As we will show, this tension opens the door to strategies of integration between the (supposedly) strong and the (supposedly) weak programs that sponsors of the former typically (and strongly, even aggressively) refuse. We will now discuss this tension in greater detail, suggesting how it could be epistemologically accommodated and empirically managed.

The strong program: A critical reconstruction

In the previous section, we have suggested that the criticism of SP against existing models, methods and concepts doesn't seem sufficiently grounded on a balanced assessment of their values/merits as well as of their limits – at least with respect to Bourdieu (but the same could be argued for Peterson: see Santoro 2008b). This comes as no surprise. After all, this is what intellectual manifestos typically do, that is, carving out a position for themselves *vis-à-vis* other already existing stances, framing the latter in terms that sound 'negatively' consistent with the proposed agenda[6]. In this section we will present the pillars of the strong program as they have been developed since the early 1990s, and increasingly in the 2000s, also through a number of 'turns'.

The relative autonomy of culture

The central tenet of the SP is the claim to the *analytical autonomization* of culture as a necessary condition for understanding it and assessing its power. The relevant distinction is here between 'concrete' and 'analytical' autonomy – an old heritage from Parsons brought back to life for other purposes (Kane 1991). Whereas concrete autonomy refers to empirically observable instances of cultural primacy (in the sense of symbols' and ideas' independent influence upon social life), analytical autonomy refers to a much deeper epistemological commitment to cultural processes and objects as dominant forces in society.

This clearly contrasts with Bourdieu's program, where such concepts as habitus, field and cultural capital have been typically developed in order to grasp both the socio-structural *and* the cultural, taken as irremediably intertwined and co-constitutive dimensions of social life. Consider the following example. The Mafia is said to be a (social, economic, political, criminal) presence in such places as Italy, Russia, Japan, China and the United States. But what is Mafia? Is it a complex of symbols, values and norms, or is it a system of social relations? Is it a way of thinking manhood and moral conduct, or a social organization specialized in crime? According to a Bourdieusian approach, we should investigate Mafias as systems of *both* social and symbolic relations, because it is only in the matching of a certain structure of (historically constructed) social relationships with a certain structure of (historically formed) symbols and values that we can discover or identify 'Mafias' as an (emergent) social phenomenon. Now, according to SP we should analytically identify and insulate its symbolic elements from others (e.g. economic or political ones) and reading them as a self-contained structure in order to grasp the Mafia in its deepest and most consequential aspect as a social phenomenon. For Alexander and the SP followers, the insulation of the cultural dimension is a *sine qua non* condition for understanding what a social reality is, how it works and how it could circulate and penetrate social life. The problem with the SP stance is that in order to reach culture at its deepest, its followers have to *analytically but also arbitrarily* separate some elements from others, treating them as 'cultural' (i.e. meaningful and meaning-producing), whereas it may be the case that only in their completeness and totality they could become socially meaningful. To continue with the Mafia example, what about honour as a symbolic principle when not embedded in (concrete) systems of social relations that make honorific behaviour and a 'code of honour' meaningful to at least some social agents?

This is what 'constitutivism' (Olick 2011) as an intellectual stance would oppose to the argument that we have to analytically insulate culture in order to understand it at its deepest. According to constitutivists, social reality is constituted of both social and symbolic relations, and we couldn't separate them without missing both their reciprocal, mutual making and re-making, i.e. ontological interdependence. Bourdieu is not alone in invoking the idea of the mutual constitution of social and cultural reality. His position is shared with social theorists such as Norbert Elias and Anthony Giddens, neo-institutionalists such as Paul DiMaggio, former structural sociologists such as Harrison White (2008) and Richard Peterson (DiMaggio 2000; Santoro 2008b). According to Alexander and Smith, all these scholars belong to the club of 'weak program' followers. However, it could be argued that what the 'strong' program labels as 'weak' programs may be elaborated and long-thought assertions of different solutions to the same concerns: they are not failing programs for cultural research in social life, but differently committed programs of social analysis of cultural life.

For all his commitment to a constitutive solution, however, we should concede that Bourdieu was aware that you cannot assert mutual constitutiveness of A and B without having at least some ideas of what A and B are. Indeed, in Bourdieu we can find various instances of analytical autonomy pragmatically granted to culture – for example the unmasking of economic interests behind and beneath gratuitous or ideal ones. His whole research on cultural fields is driven by the intellectual interest in revealing the practical logic governing the production as well as consumption of cultural, i.e. symbolic goods in spite of the rhetoric of the gift, of the genius and the sacredness, which have been historically dominating in these fields at least since the Renaissance (in Europe and the Western world, to be sure) (Bourdieu 1993; 1996a). In order to highlight the practical dimension of cultural production, or the status dimension of cultural consumption, or even the symbolic dimension of power, Bourdieu has to analytically identify the economic or better the material as different from the cultural side of human agency. And in a parallel way, when dissecting the economic field (e.g. Bourdieu 2005a), Bourdieu highlights such cultural aspects as symbolic values, practices and tastes usually neglected by economists and even economic sociologists – an approach arguably not so foundationally different from recent work done by Alexander (2011b) on the market.

However, it is possible to interpret such an approach as a matter of intellectual strategy, or heuristic move (Abbott 2004), rather than philosophical commitment. Admittedly, Bourdieu sometimes did not maintain what he promised to do – i.e. to fully commit himself to the (constitutive) stance of mutual constitution of social structure and culture – ending up supporting a sort of primacy of the material over the symbolic, or of the economic over the cultural. But even if Bourdieu sometimes fails in remaining totally faithful to his commitments to a (sort of Weberian) multidimensional approach in his own research, this doesn't necessarily imply that also the assumptions or commitments undergirding his research and above all his general theoretical stance were flawed. What Bourdieu at his best says is that materiality and symbolism, as well as body and mind, and social structure and meaning structures, are deeply intertwined, and that only in their mutual relation do they constitute themselves, and exist even as an analytically manageable object of knowledge.

Instead of positing in advance, as a theoretical pre-condition and a methodological super-rule, the notion of the analytical autonomy of culture, Bourdieu analytically considered the issue of the *autonomy of the (cultural) field*. It is of course a concrete type of autonomy what Bourdieu had in mind in his field analyses, but it is from an analytical point of view that he moved to its description and theorizing. Autonomy – *relative* autonomy to be sure – is a possible feature of the field as an analytically constructed space, or better a state of those fields which have gained enough structuration and institutionalization to impose their principles of vision and division upon other fields, or at least to encapsulate their own principles of working from the influence of other fields. As a field property, relative autonomy is always embedded in social relations, even when the field is a cultural one (e.g. the music field). Moreover, as a field property, we could say relative autonomy is always embedded in cultural codes, as it pertains to systems of vision and division, e.g. to sets of principles of perception and classification (Bourdieu 1993; 1996a). What Bourdieu rejected, at least since the mid-sixties, is a purely structural analysis of cultural codes, as French structuralism promoted.

Culture structures: codes and narratives

As we have seen, the strong program is interested in the structure, dynamics and power of what could be called the 'cultural order', as analytically opposed to the more sociologically traditional 'social order'. From this perspective, any cultural-sociological attempt of articulating a 'thick description' requires the identification and mapping out of the 'culture structures' that shape social life through an initial 'analytical bracketing' of non-symbolic social relations. As the first explicit manifesto of the strong program explained:

> This bracketing out, analogous to Husserl's phenomenological reduction, allows the reconstruction of the *pure cultural text*, the theoretical and philosophical rationale for which Ricoeur … supplied in his important argument for the necessary linkage between hermeneutics and semiotics … It is the notion of the culture structure as a social text that

allows the well-developed conceptual resources of literary studies — from Aristotle to such contemporary figures as Frye ... and Brooks ... — to be brought into social science.
(Alexander and Smith 2002: 137–138; emphasis added)

What exactly is the 'pure cultural text' – and whether it can be reconstructed – is far from clear. In fact, we can see here at work exactly the kind of intellectual strategies Bourdieu has for long studied where he shows that 'purity' is a label through which scholars try to control a certain research field while excluding others, supposedly working on 'polluted' aspects of the same object, e.g. 'pure economics', the 'pure theory of law', the 'pure aesthetic gaze' and so on.[7] Let us leave this on one side, however, and see how Alexander and followers pursue their program.

Drawing on hermeneutics, post-structuralism and semiotic theory, and its applications particularly in literary studies and symbolic anthropology – from Ricoeur to Lévi-Strauss, Barthes and Sahlins – the strong program aims at overcoming the traditional divide between hermeneutics and structuralism (see the 2002 manifesto, which was explicitly entitled 'Elements of a Structural Hermeneutics') in order to understand the cultural processes and meanings that precede, surround, inform, shape and arguably 'co-cause' social actions. Such causal forces are described in terms of 'binary codes' and 'cultural narratives' – the foundational components of the culture structure that must be identified and re-constructed in order to investigate its 'internal design' and its patterns of meanings. Thanks to this theoretically integrative move, meanings can be conceived as arising from symbolic systems that are internally structured through patterns of binary oppositions, and socially circulating via their own meaning-bearers, the cultural narratives. On the one hand, in fact, 'binary codes are responsible for classifying the world and so doing according to moral criteria, detailing the qualities and attributes of the sacred and the profane, polluted and pure'; on the other hand, 'narrative structures place actors and events into plots, allocate moral responsibility, causality, and agency, shape outcome expectations and in some cases provide exemplary models for action' – as a consequence, 'binary codes provide building blocks, but narratives add subtlety to our understandings of the world and convert situations into scenarios' (Smith 2005: 14). Culture structures thus come to be analytically conceivable as an interplay of codes and narratives.

As such, binary codes (e.g. 'friend/enemy', 'good/evil', 'rational/irrational', etc.) and cultural narratives constitute the powerful foundations of the cultural structure through which what Durkheim called the 'collective conscience' emerges and influences the more concrete realms of social life: 'narratives, just like binary codes, circulate and are contested in the collective conscience/public sphere, and in this process can shape history' (Alexander and Smith 2010: 17). From a SP perspective, studying public culture thus implies deciphering the narratives' power to capture the meaningful symbolic texture of collective consciousness – the power to 'narrate the social' (Sherwood 1994). Even if it was not yet labelled as 'strong', this cultural-sociological tool-kit was implicitly sketched out in the late 1980s by Alexander with his neo-Durkheimian interpretative analysis of the Watergate (Alexander 1988), but it took a more explicit and analytically refined form in the early 1990s, when a deep commitment to a cultural approach to civil society, which included an interest for the (coded) narratives of the public sphere, emerged (Alexander and Smith 1993; Alexander 1992; see Alexander 2006).[8] Over the years, this theoretical framework has been applied to a variety of empirical contexts in more systematic ways (e.g. Ku 1999; Jacobs 2000), as well as on related topics such as war and conflict (see Smith 1991; 2005; Alexander 2004b; 2007). More recent and influential work has focused on the concept of 'cultural trauma', including Alexander's own study of the Holocaust (Alexander 2002; 2003; Alexander *et al.* 2004; Eyerman 2001).

Through such codes and narratives, social groups come to make sense of their world, understand their past and envision their future. But how does meaning-making *really* take place? If meaning-making systematically builds on pre-existing and deeply rooted culture structures, then how should we seriously account for those contingent meanings generated by situated social interactions, or interaction rituals, thus emerging (mainly, or at least also) from personal influence or collective dynamics? And how should we account for change? The SP advocates have repeatedly claimed that they consider the relation between culture structures and social interactions as a dialogical one. However, effectively linking large-scale cultural issues such as those of civil discourse or cultural trauma to a variety of local and different institutional and interactional contexts (that is, to smaller-level social interactions, political struggles, or even subcultural dynamics) would require finely grained and deeply articulated analytical models, that only further empirical research might help to develop, in order to overcome what Emirbayer (2004: 10) sees as a potential limit of the strong program, i.e. 'a static quality to Alexander's cultural sociology and a lack of attention to how cultural formations themselves emerge in dynamic relation with other such configurations' – that is, a potential inability to account for dynamics of change in cultural structures and narratives due to the SP's reliance on Saussurean structuralism's binary categories.

As noticed by supporters of the SP, the focus on narrative resonates with a much wider intellectual movement started in the eighties and established in the nineties, when a handful of sociologists and social historians began to talk and write about the possibilities and the promises of a *narrative* mode of historical sociology, able to merge the claims to generalization and theory-building typical of comparative historical sociology with the sensitivity for temporality, events and contingencies (Barbera and Santoro 2007). Scholars like Abbott, Somers, Sewell and even a former champion of structural sociology like H.C. White, among others, have insisted on the constitutive role of narratives as well as storylines and plots in social life. Drawing (similarly to the SP) on Sahlins' pioneering work in historical anthropology, as well as on classics of structuralism (e.g. Lévi-Strauss and Barthes) and of narratology (e.g. Propp, Greimas and Ricoeur), in the last twenty years these scholars have generated a deep rethinking of the relationship between time, temporality and social structure. Interestingly, many of them have moved from a refinement and adjustment of Bourdieu's practice theory – of his 'genetic structuralism' – seen as a crucial tool for advancing sociological thinking along the temporal dimension.

After all, Bourdieu has blamed structuralist theory exactly for its insensitivity to temporality and historicity as well as for its faith in the causal power of theoretically discovered and totally abstract 'rules' supposedly existing and exerting their effects inside the mind of social agents. Indeed, in his intellectual trajectory, Bourdieu has dismissed structuralism and its search for binary oppositions (although it was a strong reference in his early anthropological work, e.g. the analysis of the Kabyle house), and moved on to a pragmatist approach whose perceptual lens are set arguably more on 'continua and transformations rather than on binary oppositions' (Wagner-Pacifici 2000: 224; see Heilbron 2011).[9] However, it is also obviously true that people in their practical life often think through binary oppositions, and locate themselves according to them. The concept of field is pivotal as a conceptual and methodological means to come to terms with this double bind: the necessity to analytically move beyond the doxa – where binary oppositions abound – and the need to recognize what the doxa is mainly made of. This allows us to move on to the next step.

Performance

In the early 2000s Alexander developed what is arguably his most advanced theoretical synthesis in terms of a model of 'cultural pragmatics', that is, a macro-sociological model of social action as cultural performance 'between ritual and strategy' (Alexander 2004a; Alexander, Giesen and Mast 2006). Over the years, such a model has been empirically applied and analytically refined on a variety of case studies, from the terroristic attacks of September 11 (Alexander 2004b) to Obama's election (Alexander 2010) and the so-called Arab Spring (Alexander 2011a). Explicitly aiming to transcend the historical division in the sociology of culture between 'structuralist theories that treat meaning as a text and investigate the patterning that provides relative autonomy and pragmatist theories that treat meaning as emerging from the contingencies of individual and collective action', Alexander argues that 'the materiality of *practices* should be replaced by the more multidimensional concept of *performances*' (Alexander 2004a: 527; see also Alexander 1995).[10] Moving from a creative re-reading of well-known insights from Turner and Goffman among others, Alexander's model of cultural pragmatics focuses on the different ways in which social actions performatively put texts (scripts) into practice. Analysing social performances as theatrical ones, Alexander roots the performances on a system of collective representation that backgrounds every performative act – a system composed by deep (and maybe, at least relatively, unconscious?) background symbols, as well as foreground scripts, which are the immediate referential text for action. Of course, such a cultural background is structured by binary codes and more or less widespread (dominant) narratives.

Whereas performance theory is set forth as a 'stronger' alternative to practice theory, we would suggest that (Alexander's) performances emerge from scripts (which are in turn shaped by background representations) as much as (Bourdieu's) practices emanates from habitus (and cultural capital). As well known, the concept of 'practice' was gradually and consistently articulated by Bourdieu in the 1970s (see Bourdieu 1977; 1990a). In fact, however, notwithstanding the crucial role played by the concept of practice in Bourdieu's theoretical tool-kit, finding an explicit definition of 'practice' within Bourdieu's oeuvre is not an easy task. If, on the one hand, habitus can be defined as a (more or less consciously) practice-generating set of socially and culturally acquired dispositions (a definition still looking 'vague and incomplete' to some (e.g. Mukerji 2014: 349), on the other hand, the concept of 'practice' is used sometimes interchangeably with slightly different accepted meanings including 'practical sense' ('structured practices') and 'performance' ('performed practices').

Echoing equally sharp but more constructive critical readings (e.g. Sewell 1992; Calhoun 1995; Warde 2004), Alexander's 'cultural pragmatics' suggests how Bourdieu's concepts of habitus and practice might turn out to be too analytically poor when empirically applied to case studies within increasingly complex, differentiated, late-modern societies[11]. At the same time, when compared with the structuring power of habitus and cultural capital, such a concept as 'script' could – quite paradoxically, given Alexander's original theoretical ambitions – turn out to be conceivable only in quite strictly static terms, as the socially orienting surface element of a deeper cultural world which pre-exists social actions, practices and performances, almost independently, apparently without any necessarily direct social anchorage.

On this basis, Alexander's model of cultural pragmatics reveals at least three grey areas, which might be enlightened by a closer confrontation and potential integration with Bourdieu's concepts of field and habitus. Firstly, Alexander's model includes 'social powers' shaping both the narrative scripts and the performance's efficacy: 'The distribution of power in society – the nature of its political, economic and status hierarchies, and the relations among its elites – profoundly affects the performance process' (Alexander 2004a: 532). However, Alexander reduces these 'social powers' to three categories: productive, distributional and hermeneutic powers, without offering a tool-kit for systematically 'entering' these powers. At the same time, Alexander explicitly draws on Bourdieu's early theoretical insights on the social construction of the judgment of aesthetic taste (Bourdieu 1990d), by noting how 'the connoisseur's poised display of aesthetic judgment might be thought of as a successful performance' since "the virtuosi of the judgment of taste", [as] Bourdieu wrote, 'present their knowledge of art casually, as if it were natural' (Alexander 2004a: 549). Following these traces, Alexander notes how performative efficacy – in the sense of what could be called 'performative naturalness' – must be subsequently and accordingly interpreted, evaluated, and consecrated as such:

> Each of the de-fused elements of performance eventually becomes subject to institutions of independent criticism, which judge it in relation to criteria that establish not only aesthetic form but also the legitimacy of the exercise of this particular kind of performative power. Such judgments issue from 'critics,' whether they are specialized journalists employed by the media of popular or high culture or intellectuals who work in academic milieu.
>
> *(Alexander 2004a: 558; see Alexander 2012)*

Interestingly, such a conceptual framework strongly and quite paradoxically recalls Bourdieu's own work on the fields of cultural production, on cultural intermediaries and especially on symbolic power (Bourdieu 1993; 1996a; 1991). But at the same time, at this analytical level, it only evokes the interplay of different social powers. Bourdieu's model of the cultural field could arguably help to better situate, further differentiate and relate among themselves the actors, their strategies of construction of 'authenticity' and the process of consecration (or denigration) within a given field and in the relationships among different fields – e.g. the 'media' field, the 'popular or high culture' field or the 'intellectual' and 'academic' fields.

Moreover, according to the model of cultural pragmatics, scripts play a crucial role, as the performative process aims at 'fusing the script in two directions with background culture on the one side and with audience on the other. If the script creates such fusion, it seems truthful to background representations and real' (Alexander 2004a: 551) – and thus the performance will be successful. However, in terms of production, a number of questions about the socio-historical genesis of these scripts and background representations remain unanswered, and a number of features under-investigated: where do these scripts come from? What are the most diffused and influential scripts? Why are they so? Who has 'written' them? Who is the contemporary master, the Aristotle of script-writing, in a given performance genre? And most importantly, how do the actors embody and enact them? Scripts – the SP claims – can also be unwritten, even hidden. In both cases, however, Alexander's model of performance arguably 'omits crucial features, namely embodiment, creativity and imagination' (Snow 2010: 78). In this context, and particularly in terms of embodiment, the concept of habitus could help to reconstruct and better describe what Bourdieu (1982) – in a famously meta-reflexive academic *performance* – described as the 'embodied history' of social actors, and thus to even account for the dynamics of change of codes, scripts and performances themselves over time.[12]

Finally, beyond theoretical divergences as well as potentially integrative analytical refinements, it is possible to point out an apparently shared lacuna in both Bourdieu's and Alexander's cultural models, that is their relative lack of attention for audiences and publics, evoked more as phantasmal presences than empirical, historical entities endowed with agency. From this point of view, both models could paradoxically be strengthened – and both programs be made even 'stronger' – by looking at (and going back to) the audience studies tradition inaugurated by the (supposedly 'weak') Birmingham school.

Iconicity

Over the last few years, an 'iconic turn' has been announced within the SP (Alexander 2008a; 2008b; Alexander, Bartmanski and Giesen 2012; Bartmanski 2015). Drawing on Durkheim's classic insights on totemism, according to which 'collective feelings become fully conscious of themselves only by settling upon external tangible objects' (Durkheim 1995 [1912]: 421), the iconic turn sets out to develop a cultural-sociological approach to visual-material culture, treating icons as 'agentic, relatively autonomous performers' (Bartmanski and Alexander 2012: 6). Analytically, the iconic turn is mainly characterized by what Alexander defines as a potentially powerful interaction between aesthetic *surface* and discursive-moral *depth*. From this perspective, icons can be defined as 'symbolic condensations that root social meanings in material form, allowing the abstractions of cognition and morality to be subsumed, to be made invisible [*sic*], by aesthetic shape. Meaning is made iconically visible, in other words, by the beautiful, sublime, ugly, or simply by the mundane materiality of everyday life' (Alexander 2008a: 782). Iconicity thus deals with 'experiencing material objects, not only understanding them cognitively or evaluating them morally but also feeling their sensual, aesthetic force' (Bartmanski and Alexander 2012: 1), whereas a cultural sociology of iconicity should aim at 'broadening sociological epistemology in an aesthetic way' (Bartmanski and Alexander 2012: 5).

Through a variety of case studies – including iconic photographs, intellectuals, festivals and wines (see Alexander, Bartmanski and Giesen 2012; Bartmanski 2015) – the iconic turn has aimed at deconstructing the power of specific visual-cultural objects to symbolically condense deep meanings in a peculiar material form. In so doing, the 'iconic turn' arguably represents also the strategic attempt of taking a distinctive position *vis-à-vis* a bulk of research increasingly carried out in the social sciences and the humanities, especially in the rapidly expanding interdisciplinary field of visual culture and material culture studies (Solaroli 2015).

However, in this intellectual turn, the SP has either ignored or only reluctantly addressed some already existing work in the social sciences that paid attention not only to social practices of production and consumption but also to material-cultural objects as both signified and signifiers, with their own objectifying power. This is the kind of work done in part also by Bourdieu, both in the 1960s and 1970s and in his later sociological investigations on art and culture. For example, in his book on photography (Bourdieu 1990c), Bourdieu focused not only on photographic practice and its wider position within the hierarchy of cultural legitimacy, but also on the different aesthetic styles emerging within different spheres of action, e.g. family photography. Interestingly, Alexander (2008b) has proposed to develop also a cultural-sociological investigation on the iconic relevance of family photography, where a more direct confrontation with Bourdieu's early, often unnoticed but fertile insights would prove enriching. A second example is offered by Bourdieu's own translation of – and postface to – art historian Erwin Panofsky's *Architecture Gothique et Pensée Scolastique* (Bourdieu 2005b), a book that unveiled the homologies between, on the one hand, the architectural-cultural production of the symbolic-material forms of Gothic cathedrals and, on the other hand, scholastic philosophy, showing how the former was deeply shaped by the latter (and, as such, it was crucial in the development of Bourdieu's influential notion of habitus; see Lizardo 2010a). However, even though Panofsky is largely considered a founder of modern iconology (thus underpinning the iconic turn), Bourdieu's interpretative insights are neglected in the SP's reframing. Similarly, it is worth noting that a seemingly profound – yet almost unacknowledged – influence on Alexander's own theorizing of iconicity as surface/depth was the aesthetic theory of surface/depth developed by Shusterman (2002), following a constructive engagement with Bourdieu's theories (Shusterman 1999) (see Solaroli 2015).

The fault lines and the false line, or, the fractalization of cultural studies

Let's go back to Table 3.1. We are now in a better position to comment on it considering the case of Bourdieu. Indeed, Bourdieu has never made a case for culture as a superstructure or a soft variable, nor has he committed himself to something that he could have labelled as 'thin description'. He would not accept the charge he has 'hedge[d] and stutter[ed]' on the issue of 'specifying in detail just how culture interferes with and directs what really happens' (Alexander and Smith 2002: 138). Possibly, the more explicit misunderstanding of Bourdieu is apparent in the following statement that concludes Alexander and Smith's discussion of the French scholar's work:

> In the final analysis what we have here is a Veblenesque vision in which culture provides a strategic resource for actors, an external environment of action, rather than a text that shapes the world in an immanent fashion. People use culture, but they do not seem to really care about it.
>
> *(Alexander and Smith 2002: 141)*

Indeed, this is exactly what, as Bourdieu continuously alerted, would be a misreading of his work, i.e. a 'Veblenesque' reading, especially of his research on class and status (and distinction, to be sure) (Bourdieu 1984).[13] To discuss this, let us look at the 'weak vs. strong' dilemma as something worthy of attention in itself and read it as one of a series of distinctions and contrasts that commonly proliferate in intellectual life.

Structural hermeneutics (the first label attached to the strong program) looks indeed as a partial mirror of what Bourdieu has called constructivist structuralism, a label he reserved for his own research program (Bourdieu 1990b). Indeed, what is for Bourdieu a dialectical overcoming of subjectivism (i.e. phenomenology, hermeneutics) and objectivism (i.e. structuralism) as a third mode of knowledge (Bourdieu 1977) is in the SP a re-composition and combination of structuralist methods with hermeneutical insights. Whereas in its synthetic project, Bourdieu moves from what he conceives as objective (and objectified) structures (that is, first mode of knowledge in order to break with the doxa), the SP emphasizes and gives priority to hermeneutics and phenomenology (which in Bourdieu's theory of sociological knowledge figures as just a second step toward praxeology, another label he used to identify his program). However, in the years following the first SP manifesto, Alexander too has moved toward a second step, making a performative turn from which a new theoretical model was born: cultural pragmatics (see *supra*).

With this second move, Alexander locates himself in a sort of circuit or spiral – and a recursive one – where Bourdieu is also easily locatable. In a word, both intellectual stances are locatable in what mathematicians name a *fractal structure*, i.e. a never-ending pattern. Fractals are infinitely complex patterns that are self-similar across different scales and are created by repeating a simple process over and over in an ongoing feedback loop. As Andrew Abbott has shown, intellectual debates have a fractal form that cannot be overcome and is responsible for

Contesting culture

their never-ending deployment (Abbott 2001; 2004). In other words, and with respect to our case study, there is *always* someone who may be *more* structuralist, or more hermeneutical, or more pragmatist, than you. Far from being a crude opposition between opposite stances (weak vs. strong), the tension is a cyclical and recursive one, as Figure 3.1 shows.

If our reading holds true, then the whole play of strong and weak programs could be interpreted more as an instance of genuine intellectual positioning than as the expression of deep antagonism in theoretical presuppositions, as a fault line in paradigmatic assumptions.[14] Indeed, structural hermeneutics shares with genetic i.e. constructivist structuralism a wide array of presuppositions which should be, we contend, more appreciated especially by researchers and practitioners of sociology:

- they are both post-positivistic;
- they are anti-empiricist;
- they are multidimensional;
- they are synthesizing programs (against traditional 'twos' – subject vs. object, action vs. structure, ideal vs. material, and so on);
- they insist on their scientific status (and remain faithful to the modernist notion of science as a special kind of knowledge able to identify some truth).

Although Bourdieu could be blamed for too often leaving aside the cultural object itself, he clearly was not insensitive to issues of cultural content, as it is shown by his many works on Kabyle culture (e.g. his analysis of the Kabyle house, of the Kabyle calendar or of the Kabyle cultural system of honour) and his (internal) analysis of Flaubert's *Sentimental Education*, including its plot and system of characters. That said, it is arguable that Bourdieu is often more interested in the structure and form of culture than in its historical contents, considering structure and form what sociology – as *science* i.e. generalized and generalizable, if not universal, knowledge – should privilege. But one thing is what an author has done in his own research trajectory, another is what a research program permits one to do – and Bourdieu's

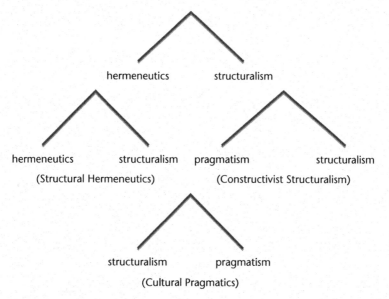

Figure 3.1 The fractalization of cultural theory

research program doesn't prevent its followers/users from engaging in cultural content/code analysis, maybe with the help of other tools compatible with Bourdieu's. In the field of literary criticism – e.g. Boschetti's (2001) study of Apollinaire's poetry – many studies have been undertaken using Bourdieu's toolbox, and literary criticism could hardly be blamed for not taking cultural content seriously.

Moreover, what the SP names 'culture structures' could be found in Bourdieu's lexicon under the label of 'mental structures', that is taxonomies and forms of classification, as in his sociological analysis of academic judgment and of the French 'dominant ideology' (Bourdieu 1996b; Bourdieu and Boltanski 1976). However, most importantly, Bourdieu doesn't assert the need of a radical decoupling of culture from social structure. The social-structural is so deeply enmeshed in the symbolic that separating them even at the analytical level – as far as it is possible – would not turn out to be very fertile. At the same time, in his empirical research Bourdieu has sometimes distinguished the two planes – as in *Distinction* where he makes two separate analysis, one for the social structure (i.e. the social space where classes, class fractions and professional categories exist) and the other for the cultural system (e.g. the reference objects of taste, or the space of lifestyles) (Bourdieu 1984). This is indeed possibly a source of weakness in *Distinction*, partially contrasted and reduced by the writing strategies Bourdieu employs and the theoretical work he accomplishes in order to make sense of his empirical data.[15]

Building bridges

After critically reviewing the main tenets of the SP, and having suggested how the SP could be read as a (still evolving) subfield, in this section we illustrate a few instances of recent empirical attempts to creatively work with both Bourdieu's and the SP's conceptual toolkits. Resonating with the suggestion that they could benefit from 'each other in ways that have yet to be recognized, for their standpoints on culture can be viewed as complementary rather than fundamentally incommensurable' (Kurasawa 2004: 60), such a stream of research concretely shows how their seemingly opposite theoretical positions may be consistently used in the practice of social research to get better and richer understandings of socio-cultural processes.

Cultural field and civil sphere

Both Bourdieu and Alexander move from classic differentiation theory and understand (modern) societies as differentiated social spaces, for instance through Bourdieu's theory of the fields (e.g. Bourdieu 1993; 1996a).

According to Alexander, however, Bourdieu's field theory 'failed to appreciate the importance of the difference between an analytical construction that involves real, if relative, autonomy for elements in various institutional *fields* and one that rests upon the notion of homology, which denies it'; therefore, on this basis, Alexander would call for an alternative, 'which recognizes the disjunctive tensions yet simultaneous interdependencies between levels of organization and subsystems in societies that are differentiated to some degree' (Alexander 1995: 163).

However, within the SP, Alexander has mainly focused on one historical instance of this differentiation process: the 'civil sphere' (Alexander 2006). But what is a *sphere*? Are there general principles of 'spheres'? In other words, is 'sphere' an analytical concept or an historical one? For example, it could be argued that the coded narratives shaping the discourse of the civil society can be effective for constructing solidarity, but their performative success depends on a mixture of cultural-institutional factors – or, more precisely, institutional field dynamics and effects (see Pérez-Diaz 2014). Such dynamics are significantly played out in and by the field of media, which act as a sort of constitutive engine for narratives, making possible the public circulation of information, symbols and collective representations, thus contributing to ongoing social efforts of weaving the (Geertzian) 'webs of meaning'.

Both Alexander (1981; Alexander and Jacobs 1998) and Bourdieu (1994; 1996; 2000b) have done influential research on the social and cultural role of news media, in relation to other realms such as economy, politics and the academia. According to both Bourdieu and Alexander, in fact, the relevance of the mass media has historically increased in society, but for Bourdieu, other cultural fields have consequently lost their autonomy, since they are increasingly influenced by the media. However, even if Bourdieu 'shares with Parsonian systems theory the crucial elements of the problematic of differentiation theory, derived from Weber and Durkheim', and thus he 'expresses a normative preference for the autonomy of fields', contrary to Alexander (1981) he does not assume 'an evolutionary process of development toward greater differentiation: fields change through a process of struggle among the agents working within them, and the direction of change is not predetermined' (Hallin and Mancini 2004: 81). In a few words, whereas Alexander posits increasing differentiation, Bourdieu sees increasing de-differentiation of the news media *vis-à-vis* other fields, e.g., in particular, the economic one.[16] On this basis, even if, drawing on differentiation theory, Alexander 'has advanced what is probably the most developed contemporary application of this perspective to media studies' (Hallin 2005: 224), which is nonetheless 'largely silent about markets' (Hallin 2005: 232), Bourdieu's field theory 'captures a key ambiguity and ultimately a key failing of differentiation theory as articulated by Alexander', and thus it represents 'a potentially more open framework for understanding change in the relations of media to other social structures' (Hallin 2005: 230–231).

Quite interestingly, the most influential (yet, as we have just seen, easily criticizable) work on news media realized by Alexander (1981) belongs to his post-functionalist, pre-SP phase. In fact, within the strong program, and particularly within its research on the civil sphere, even if media are usually considered to play a crucial social role that might be revealing in (SP-)theoretical terms, as 'in the media, we find not only factual information about public actors and their speech but also cultural structures – public meanings themselves' (Alexander 2010: 292) – analytically they seem to occupy a secondary and empirically understated position. On the one hand, as it comes out, a considerable amount of SP research is based on news media reports, which 'provide information … by telling stories, stringing independent observations into broader binary codes and narrative configurations … they are culturally constructed symbolic representations' (Alexander 2010: 289). On the other hand, however, notwithstanding its potential utility in specific empirical contexts, such an approach lacks a more deeply organic analytical framework which could help to interpret those 'stories' and 'narrative configurations' by tracing those news reports back to the structure and internal workings of the media as organizations and institutions (e.g. Alexander 2010; 2011a; Smith 2005).

On this basis, as media research clearly suggests, it could be argued that one of the less developed parts of the strong program is precisely a meso-level theory of social organization and of social positioning – exactly what field theory can offer. In fact, since the second half of the 1990s, while Alexander and colleagues were gradually advancing the proposal for a 'strong' research program in cultural sociology, Bourdieu's field-theory has been increasingly applied, refined and diffused within the sociology of media and political communication, convincingly entering the research on news production, where it has been articulated through the concept of the 'journalistic field' (Bourdieu 2000b; Benson 1999; Benson and Neveu 2005). So far, theoretically, this bulk of research has suggested also potentially fertile integration between supposedly 'not-strong' programs such as Bourdieu's field theory and neo-institutionalism (Benson 2006), while, empirically, it has dealt with crucial contemporary issues such as the configuration between news media, immigration and the civil society (or civic field) (Benson 2013).

Over the last decade, this work has offered very rich explanations of the media field's internal workings as well as of the interrelations between the media and other fields. However, as Couldry (2003) suggested, there has been less effort in reconciling this work's and other research on the 'symbolic power' of media in a broader sense, that is, on their role as vectors of wider and deeper symbolic meaning and interpretive force. More recently, however, new studies emerged, which turn out to be particularly precious in this context, as they tried to strengthen the strong program looking for aid in the Bourdieusian theory of social fields. This is the case of the work on media, culture and the public sphere – particularly on media intellectuals and the so-called 'space of opinion' – developed by Jacobs and Townsley (2011), which draws on both Alexander and Bourdieu. As Townsley (2011: 296) clarified, 'thinking about the internal structure of the public sphere in terms of cultural fields ... is productive in several ways':

> if we step back from Alexander's vitriolic critique of Bourdieu and consider what the tradition of field analysis might tell us about solidarity, one useful idea is that groups must be imagined and represented through processes of social communication in the public sphere before they can become conscious of themselves as groups. Thus, individuals engage in 'group-making practices' to persuade others to view themselves as group members and to act accordingly (Bourdieu 1985). This is a useful insight because it underlines the fact that many of the practices that produce solidarity are intellectualizing practices; that is, those who engage in group-making practices are typically intellectuals of some kind since these are agents who specialize in those practices of representation that divide group members from nonmembers.
>
> *(Townsley 2011: 299)*

Field-theory could thus offer the SP a crucial meso-level integrative analytical and conceptual framework. As Alexander, Jacobs and Smith (2011b: 16) concede, while describing Jacobs and Townsley's work, 'a successful or "fused" performance requires more than the skilled alignment of background representations, foregrounded scripts, actor, role, and scene. For real transformation to occur, audiences in different cultural fields must come to believe not only that a performer is authentic, but also that his or her presence holds out the promise that their particular cultural field can increase its autonomy and its influence.'

Cultural field and cultural trauma

Our second example of how 'strong' and 'weak' programs complement each other and could be put in fruitful dialogue comes from a study on Italian popular music (Santoro 2006; 2010). The study moves from a tragic event – the suicide of a well reputed and innovative singer-songwriter in 1967 – to explain the rise in status of song as a cultural genre, apparent in the Italian culture since the eighties, as well as the invention and institutionalization of a new, original cultural category, i.e. *canzone d'autore* ('author's song'), as a means of classification, evaluation and appreciation in the field of popular music production in Italy.

Of course, suicide is not an exceptional cause of death in the art world. What makes the suicide of the singer-songwriter Luigi Tenco exceptional is that it occurred in the course of a music festival, indeed the most important music festival in Italy (the Festival of Sanremo, broadcast from both radio and television) and that his official motivation was not personal troubles but a protest against that Festival and the world it represents, i.e. the world of song or 'light music' (*musica leggera*) as irremediably embedded in market and industrial logics.[17] In our reading, what makes Tenco's suicide a really, even 'strongly' meaningful event is that it occurred inside a world and against a world supposedly 'light', 'entertaining' and 'escapist.' The issue was not simply why Tenco committed suicide, but what that seemingly meaningless, 'crazy' suicide had to mean for all his fans, other musicians and more in general the festival's audience and Italian people. How can a deep and tragic event as a suicide find its place in what should be the epitome of joy and lightness, i.e. a festival of popular music? Indeed, just after the suicide, a long-lasting process of interpretation and decoding/encoding – we may say a 'spiral of signification' – started and rapidly translated that exceptional and apparently idiosyncratic event into a collective *cultural trauma*, a crisis in the common cultural understanding of what songs are and what is at stake even in a song festival. The crisis asked for a new interpretation, a new understanding of songs and of cultural life more generally. In the process of meaning-making started by the suicide, a series of other meanings – organized meanings, that is codes and culture structures – were mobilized: the Catholic conception of pity but also of guilt, the (Marxist, or better Frankfurt) notion of capitalist exploitation of cultural life, conservative (even post-fascist) ideas about the degeneration of youth and their loss of true values and so on.

In this play of cultural codes, however, only a few survived to have an impact on the story. The huge debate following Tenco's death has made visible an emerging culture structure which meshed together religious meanings (death as something imbued with deep values but also suicide as sinful and in need of expiation and repair) with socio-critical motives (culture industry as a profit-making machine insensitive to artistic merits and quality). This culture structure found a strategic 'carrier group' in a handful of people – including fans, other singer-songwriters and music journalists[18] – who in 1972 organized themselves in the same town of Sanremo as 'Club Tenco' and started in 1974 a new festival, the 'Rassegna della canzone d'autore' as a radical alternative (also in the name: not indeed a 'feast' but an 'exhibition', a 'show') to the Sanremo song festival: no links with the big music industry, no competition among musicians (but a strong commitment to solidarity and mutual collaboration), no professional or bureaucratic organization. The Club Tenco was (and still is) a non-profit organization founded and for many years financially supported by a man already in his fifties, Amilcare Rambaldi, a flower merchant who happened to be the same person who, as a socialist local representative in the years after the war, had proposed the creation of a festival of popular music to the city council of Sanremo. This suggestion led to the emergence of the Festival of Sanremo in 1951 under the aegis of other people. It was a feeling of guilty, Rambaldi himself revealed, that incited him to act again in this field after twenty years but this time 'in the name of Tenco' to make his reputation and his message survive after him. This feeling can be seen as firmly embedded in the Christian conception of human life deeply rooted in the Italian culture that could also resonate with the humanistic socialism Rambaldi embraced as a young man fighting against fascism (and antifascism still works as an ideological reference for Club Tenco).

The case study illustrates a general theoretical point about social and cultural structures: fields and institutions can be born from cultural traumas, but structures (institutions, organizations, role systems, social networks etc.) are needed for an even strongly meaningful event to have lasting impacts. From a 'strong program' perspective, the key aspect of this case study is that field and institutions emerge out of (in this case, suicide) trauma narration and deeply rooted systems of meaning. Also, they survive as loci of deeply felt ties of solidarity. The story could be seen as a demonstration that the 'strong' (i.e. deep meanings, inner feelings, emotions, drama) drives the 'weak' (institution building, social networks, role systems, capitals, etc.). However, the story can also be read from a 'weak' perspective as a demonstration of the mutually constitutive role of culture and social structure: what would deep meanings be without social organization, institution building and capitals? Could ideas about authenticity and quality in popular music develop and have an impact unless well located agents endowed with the 'right' resources (capitals) act in their name and use them as symbolic tokens in their struggle for classification and hegemony in a field? Would there be 'canzone d'autore' if Tenco's death had only triggered a mobilization of young fans (as it occurred in the first months after the suicide) and not also a mobilization of a large number of people endowed with enough economic and symbolic capital to have an impact in the music field? We can also see from comparative cases that without the 'weak' components of organization and institution, suicides have no lasting impact: a case in point is the rock star Kurt Cobain who in the early nineties committed a suicide able to produce something like a cultural trauma among youth all over the world, but never generated – also because of his wife and rock singer Courtney Love's reluctance to invest in his memory – a new institutional system, missing probably the opportunity to become a turning point in the history of popular music.

What this case study shows is the necessity to address social things with a strong sensitivity to both meaning systems (with all their complexities and idiosyncrasies) and institution building, to both cultural codes and cultural fields, i.e. social space. Meanings may be strongly organized in codes and deeply lived feelings, but it is hard for them to survive and have a deep and durable impact if they are not encoded and embedded in social organizations – which is exactly what such concepts as fields, capital and more in general social structure can capture.

Cultural field and iconic power

As we have seen, the SP theory of 'iconic consciousness' and 'iconic power' has proposed a cultural-sociological approach to the processes and objects of visual-material culture, arguably aiming at relatively renewing the existing conceptual tool-kits available in both visual and material culture studies. The approach at the basis of the iconic turn is represented by the synthetic formula of the interplay between 'aesthetic-material surface' and 'moral-discursive depth'. But how is 'iconic power' constructed? Analytically, the SP 'iconic turn' reconstructs the performative symbolic associations between (potential) icons and wider (and deeply coded) cultural narratives, often empirically drawing on their dynamics of circulation in the public culture and integrating the analysis with a focus on the sensorial affordances of the icons' material surfaces. From this perspective – tracing the performative success (or failure) of an icon directly back to its aesthetic qualities and other wider cultural factors – the role of micro- and meso-level social production (instead of macro-level cultural construction) of the cultural icons seems to be scarcely relevant and comes to be downplayed. Actually, however, such a process could have a crucial role in shaping a given cultural object, its forms, its meanings and its iconic potential – and thus its wide social circulation and public relevance.

For example: What about the photographer who shot an 'iconic' photograph and the practices of selection, framing and presentation on the press? What about the artistic director and the institutional ecology of an 'iconic' festival? Any analytical attempt to explicate the iconic status and the cultural power acquired by specific objects and events should not escape from investigating in detail how those objects and events themselves were previously socially produced and organized, and how such a process of production played an arguably crucial role in the relationship between the specific aesthetic form of a given cultural object, its wide circulation and public relevance and the following construction and crystallization of its iconic power.

On this basis, suggesting that the construction of iconic power depends on a complex array of both social and symbolic processes, a few empirical studies have recently aimed at offering a more analytically refined and systematic scenario (see Solaroli 2015 for a review). For example, focusing on humanitarian visuality – that is, images of suffering persons and groups during humanitarian crises – Kurasawa (2015) developed the conceptual framework of the 'iconological field', defined as 'a socio-political and aesthetic space of humanitarian visuality' in which 'institutional actors involved in the circulatory networks of visual representation of large-scale crises and emergencies – namely, news media and humanitarian aid organizations – are hierarchically located in relation to each other according to the kind of aesthetic style that they favour in their portrayals of such crises and emergencies ... and to the ideological coding and meanings that that they inscribe onto these images'. Such a conceptual framework suggests that instead of dismissing theoretical paradigms that give rise to analytical internalism or externalism, it would be more theoretically fertile 'to extract some of their most fruitful insights and assemble them in a hybrid manner that addresses the flaws of one paradigm by correcting it via the use of the strengths of another'. Therefore, a more organic cultural-sociological approach to icons should be developed 'by binding endogenous and exogenous aspects of the image's signifying processes together, in order to eschew the visual self-referentiality of internalist tendencies and the socio-political structural determinism of their externalist counterparts'. From this perspective, which explicitly aims at critically integrating Bourdieu's concept of the cultural field with Alexander's concept of iconicity, the question of an image's or an object's iconic power must be traced back to its symbolic structure and its visual convention within a pre-existent cultural iconographic background, as well as – just crucially – to the cultural processes, institutions and networks of social actors who conflictually frame its meaning(s) within and through multiple cultural (sub)fields. As these few empirical insights suggest, the strong program's cultural-sociological approach to iconic power could become more analytically systematic and conceptually refined by fertilely integrating its innovative insights with field theory-oriented research outputs, in a strategic and 'stronger' approach aimed at overcoming the flaws on one position with the strengths of the other.

Conclusions

In this chapter, we have outlined the main points of divergence between Bourdieu's cultural theory and the so-called strong program in cultural theory set forth by Jeffrey Alexander and his students in the nineties, which became an established albeit not dominant subfield in the cultural-sociological field in the following fifteen years, with an academic basis (Yale Center for Cultural Sociology), a book series (for Palgrave), a handbook (*Oxford Handbook of Cultural Sociology*), and since 2013 also a journal (*American Journal of Cultural Sociology*). After reviewing the main pillars of the SP using Bourdieu's sociological toolbox as a foil, we have suggested interpreting the antagonism between strong and (supposedly) weak programs, especially Bourdieu's, as an instantiation of a much wider mechanism widespread in intellectual life, that is, the proliferation of fractal distinctions, therefore bifurcations, among positions continuously reproducing themselves at different scales. In this final section we would like to insist upon just three points:

1) The strong program in cultural sociology inevitably builds on the shoulders of Bourdieu, for merely temporal reasons: when Bourdieu's first cultural theoretical elements were sketched out, (post-)structuralism was quite relevant, especially in France; when the SP has been launched, Bourdieusian cultural theory was already well established. This means that the relationship between Bourdieu and SP should not be read without historicizing it, trying to distinguish between genuine theoretical difference and mere temporal distance, and to acknowledge the different temporalities through which the two intellectual projects developed also in relation with different states of the fields of the social science and of the humanities.

2) The SP has unquestionably offered new tools and it has contributed to foster debate and research in sociology about culture and meaning introducing new issues and themes, and this is something we should be grateful to Alexander and his associates. Along with these merits, we should also recognize weaknesses. SP has an analytically underdeveloped meso-level dimension of social structure (e.g. institutions, organizations, etc.), it lacks an adequate set of concepts and tools to describe and analyze it (e.g. field), and thus it has troubles in grasping the relatively durable structuring of social relations. Concepts like 'field' and 'network of social relation' have no corresponding terms in the SP, whose followers seem arguably more interested in developing tools for doing analysis of cultural codes, narratives and structures, rather than in offering viable alternatives to Bourdieu's sociocultural analysis.

3) Indeed, in its confrontation with Bourdieu, the strong program has long aggressively castigated a caricatured 'straw-person' instead of engaging in fair confrontation with a complex, multifaceted and rich thinker. In sociological (Bourdieusian) terms, this strategy could work at the beginning of the story, when a position in the field of cultural sociology was still to be carved out, but it cannot work always without turning out to be intellectually limiting. We would like to recall here these words by a prominent American sociologist *of* culture (but maybe a cultural sociologist?) who happened to come from the same intellectual milieu of Alexander:

> One lesson for all of us is to stop building our own lines of theorizing by assailing external enemies, and instead to start grappling with the difficult questions that come out of our own conceptions of culture. If we stop exaggerating our theoretical differences for rhetorical advantage, we find that the theoretical difficulties we face have some common elements, even when theorists begin from very different starting points.
> *(Swidler 1996: 9)*

We do not contend that Bourdieu's social theory is without problems. The SP has pointed to a few of them – especially when noting that, notwithstanding his claims to the contrary and his efforts in (re)introducing the symbolic in social theory, Bourdieu seemed to have a marked tendency to give primacy to materially conceived social conditions considered as a kind of a priori of social life. However, as Gorski (2013b: 358–359) recently noted, 'a superficial and decontextualized reading of his work might suggest he is firmly aligned with ... the materialists against the culturalists. But this is a polemical and political stance rather than an epistemological and ontological one'.

In fact, with all its (much debated) weaknesses, there can be no doubts whatsoever that Bourdieu's conceptual framework is still very well worth preserving. The SP tends to treat

Bourdieu as an instance of a degenerative research program in Lakatos' sense, when it is clear that even if flawed in some points (and therefore in need of revision and refinement), Bourdieu's social theory still works well as a progressive research program, that is as a program able to foster our knowledge of social life and its working – at least while we are waiting for a more consistent and powerful theoretical system (or toolbox) to be developed in the future within the social sciences.

Notes

1 This article was written as a result of an intellectual exchange in which both authors were equally involved. However, for bureaucratic reasons, we declare that Marco Santoro wrote sections: 'What's in a name: ('strong') cultural sociology vs. ('weak') sociology of culture', 'The relative autonomy of culture', 'The fault lines and the false line, or, the fractalization of cultural studies', 'Cultural field and cultural trauma'; Marco Solaroli wrote sections: 'Culture structures: codes and narratives', 'Performance', 'Iconicity', 'Cultural field and civil sphere', 'Cultural field and iconic power'; the 'Introduction' and 'Conclusions' were written together.
2 The unofficial beginnings of the SP could be dated back to the mid-eighties, when at UCLA Alexander started a series of seminars and meeting with a few PhD students, focusing on the analysis of culture in the social sciences. For early products of this initial endeavour, see for example Alexander (1990), Rambo and Chan (1990), Smith (1991) and Kane (1991).
3 The phrase 'strong program' worked clearly as a label for discrediting what automatically would become 'weak programs,' where the latter typically albeit not exclusively referred to European (or Europe-based) intellectual movements.
4 Indeed, we should say that it is not power, interest and class as such to be materialist elements, but the way in which they have for long been conceived in the social science, at least in sociology, especially after the demise of functionalism in the sixties. The cultural turn (in history earlier than in sociology) has underlined the cultural (especially linguistic) embeddedness of all of them, including class (see Stedman Jones 1983; Sewell 1980).
5 We should recall that in *The Love of Art*, originally published in French in 1966, Bourdieu (1997) employs the language of variables to make sense of his survey data – so much that, it seems, he gained the approval of Lazarsfeld himself (whose seminars at the Sorbonne, however, Bourdieu intentionally never attended).
6 A sociological analysis of intellectual manifestos as cultural objects would be of help here: this is something the new sociology of ideas should pursue along with other topics, e.g. conferences (see Gross and Fleming 2011).
7 On Bourdieu as a theorist of purity and impurity, see Duschinsky and Lampitt (2012).
8 In retrospect the 'discourse of the civil society' (Alexander and Smith 1992) clearly represented one of the very first test-bed of the theoretical vision, the analytical approach, and the conceptual vocabulary of the SP, where to empirically observe the collective conscience at work, and therefore where to theoretically develop new metaphors and better conceptualize the foundational elements and analytical tools.
9 In this context, it is interesting to note that a few years before Alexander's conceptualization of the 'cultural pragmatics' model (see *infra*), Wagner-Pacifici (2000) had already explicitly advanced the suggestion to develop a 'combined project' requiring 'both the insights and tools of a general Structuralist approach and the insights and tools of Pragmatism' (Wagner-Pacifici 2000: 9), articulating a processual analysis of coded narratives as the connecting 'bridges of meaning' between the two.
10 As Eyerman (2004: 29-20) claimed: 'Human action is cultural praxis, scripted yet potentially transformative, rule-governed yet also rule-making, practical yet also creative. The task of cultural sociology is to grasp all these dimensions.' The task is thus to infuse social actions with 'culture', by unveiling the ways in which background cultural representations, narratives and structures inform, regulate and eventually shape social actions.
11 Interestingly, Alexander's criticism of Bourdieu's practice theory is close to Hedstrom's (2005), one of the strongest advocates of the so-called analytical sociology – a research program that would arguably posit itself very far away from the SP.
12 For a critical comparison of the concepts of code and habitus, see Harker and May (1993).

13 Alexander's confrontation with Bourdieu, dating back to 1995 (Alexander 1995), precedes indeed the proposal of a 'strong program' in cultural studies and in some way contributed to direct it. The long essay (published as a book chapter in English and as an autonomous booklet in French) Alexander wrote for denouncing the *failure* of Bourdieu's in synthetizing previous intellectual traditions (a text that has all the features to be read as an essay *against* Bourdieu) has been the object of sustained criticism itself, because of its apparent biases and a certain misinformation. Wacquant (2001) is just the most provocative and radical of its commentators, but others could be listed along (e.g. Potter 2000; Gartman 2007; Santoro 2011).

14 To be sure, this is also something Bourdieu indulged in his intellectual positioning, for example with respect to symbolic interactionism and specifically Becker's sociology of the arts, charged of being not sufficiently detached from surface details and common sense: we could say in sum that, for Bourdieu, Becker was 'too weak'.

15 A seemingly major source of distance between Bourdieu and Alexander is their different commitment to politics or better to a theoretically oriented vision of political life: whereas Bourdieu sees politics in realist ways as an arena, a sphere of interest and struggle, Alexander has a more positive vision focused on solidarities and dialogue in public spheres. Actually, it could be argued that behind their different theories and visions there exists one important, and deeper, theoretical stance: civic republican theory. Indeed, as Goldberg (2013) has shown, Bourdieu developed a theory of democratic politics that is at least as indebted to civic republicanism as to Marxism (see also Wacquant 2005). As Goldberg demonstrates, Bourdieu was familiar with the civic republican tradition *via* both Machiavelli's version of republicanism and Durkheimian social theory – embedded as it was in French republican tradition. Not only such a pivotal concept as field autonomy, but also Bourdieu's view of universalism, and his understanding of how solidarity is generated and preserved, are readable as sociological reformulations of originally republican ideas. Interestingly, this interpretation of Bourdieu's political sociology disavows Alexander's claim that Bourdieu's work lacked the three indispensable elements for a theory of democratic politics, i.e. a conception of civil society, moral universalism and solidarity. Therefore, from this perspective, Bourdieu and Alexander do not look as much opposed in their thinking as the latter has been strenuously claiming over the last twenty years.

16 Striking a balance between the two positions, on the basis of a comparative research in Western countries, Hallin and Mancini (2004) have highlighted how the news media are becoming less differentiated *vis-a-vis* the economic field, even as they are becoming more differentiated *vis-a-vis* the political field.

17 Tenco's song had been rejected by the popular jury in the first evening of the three-day long festival, and even the committee of quality which was supposed to save the best of the discarded songs didn't select it.

18 Among earlier supporters of this interpretation to be counted is also the Nobel prize and poet Salvatore Quasimodo, a symptom of how the tragic death puzzled and asked for interpretation in fields other than music.

References

Abbott, A. (2001) *Chaos of Disciplines*, Chicago: University of Chicago Press.
—— (2004) *Methods of Discovery*, New York: Norton.
Alexander, J.C. (1981) 'The mass news media in systemic, historical and comparative perspective', in E. Katz and T. Szecskö (eds.), *Mass Media and Social Change*, Beverly Hills, CA: Sage.
—— (1988) 'Culture and political crisis: "Watergate" and Durkheimian sociology', in J. Alexander (ed.), *Durkheimian Sociology: Cultural Studies*, Cambridge: Cambridge University Press.
—— (1990) 'Introduction: understanding the "relative autonomy"' of culture', in J.C. Alexander and S. Seidman (eds.), *Culture and Society: Contemporary Debates*, Cambridge: Cambridge University Press.
—— (1992) 'The promises of a cultural sociology: technological discourse and the sacred and profane information machine', in R. Münch and N.J. Smelser (eds.), *Theory of Culture*, Berkeley, CA: University of California Press.
—— (1995) 'The reality of reduction: the failed synthesis of Pierre Bourdieu', in *Fin de Siècle Social Theory: Relativism, Reduction, and the Problem of Reason*, London and New York: Verso.
—— (1996) 'Cultural sociology or sociology of culture? Towards a Strong Program', in ASA *Culture* newsletter, 10.

—— (2002) 'On the social construction of moral universals', *European Journal of Social Theory*, 5(1): 5–85.
—— (2003) *The Meanings of Social Life: A Cultural Sociology*, Oxford: Oxford University Press.
—— (2004a) 'Cultural pragmatics: social performance between ritual and strategy', *Sociological Theory*, 22(4): 527–573.
—— (2004b) 'From the depths of despair: performance, counterperformance, and "September 11"', *Sociological Theory*, 22(1): 88–105.
—— (2006) *The Civil Sphere*, Oxford: Oxford University Press.
—— (2007) 'Power and performance: the war on terror between the sacred and the profane', EUI Robert Schuman Centre for Advanced Studies Distinguished Lecture: www.eui.eu/RSCAS/WP-Texts/200711-DL_Alexander.pdf.
—— (2008a) 'Iconic consciousness: the material feeling of meaning', *Environment and Planning D: Society and Space*, 26(5): 782–794.
—— (2008b) 'Iconic experience in art and life. Surface/depth beginning with Giacometti's *Standing Woman*', *Theory, Culture and Society*, 25(5): 1–19.
—— (2010) *The Performance of Politics: Obama's Victory and the Democratic Struggle for Power*, Oxford: Oxford University Press.
—— (2011a) *Performative Revolution in Egypt*, New York: Bloomsbury.
—— (2011b) 'Market as narrative and character: For a cultural sociology of economic life', *Journal of Cultural Economy*, 4(4): 477–488.
—— (2012) 'Iconic power and performance: the role of the critic', in J.C. Alexander, D. Bartmanski and B. Giesen (eds.), *Iconic Power. Materiality and Meaning in Social Life*, New York: Palgrave.
Alexander, J.C. and R. Jacobs (1998) 'Mass communication, ritual and civil society', in T. Liebes and J. Curran (eds.), *Media, Ritual and Identity*, London: Routledge.
Alexander, J.C. and P. Smith (1993) 'The discourse of American civil society: a new proposal for cultural studies', *Theory and Society*, 2(2): 151–207.
—— (1998) 'Sociologie culturelle ou sociologie de la culture? Un programme fort pour donne au sociologie son second souffle', *Sociologie et Sociétés*, 30(1): 107–116.
—— (2002) 'The Strong Program in cultural theory. Elements of a structural hermeneutics', in J.H. Turner (ed.), *Handbook of Sociological Theory*, New York: Springer.
—— (2010) 'The Strong Program: origins, achievements, and prospects', in J.R. Hall, L. Grindstaff, M.-C. Lo (eds.), *Handbook of Cultural Sociology*, New York: Routledge.
Alexander, J.C., R. Eyerman, B. Giesen, N. Smelser and P. Sztompka (eds.) (2004) *Cultural Trauma and Collective Identity*, Berkeley, CA: University of California Press.
Alexander, J.C., B. Giesen and J. Mast (eds.) (2006) *Social Performance. Symbolic Action, Cultural Pragmatics, and Ritual*, Cambridge: Cambridge University Press.
Alexander, J.C., R. Jacobs and P. Smith (eds.) (2011a) *The Oxford Handbook of Cultural Sociology*, Oxford: Oxford University Press.
—— (2011b) 'Introduction: cultural sociology today', in J.C. Alexander, R. Jacobs and P. Smith (eds.)
Alexander, J.C., D. Bartmanski and B. Giesen (eds.) (2012) *Iconic Power. Materiality and Meaning in Social Life*, New York: Palgrave.
Barbera, F. and M. Santoro (2007) 'Introduction to the symposium: narratives, temporality, and sociology', *Sociologica*, 2.
Barnes, B., D. Bloor and J. Henry (1996) *Scientific Knowledge: A Sociological Analysis*, Chicago: University of Chicago Press.
Bartmanski, D. (2015) 'Modes of seeing, or, iconicity as explanatory notion. Cultural research and criticism after the iconic turn in social sciences', *Sociologica*, 9(1).
Bartmanski, D. and J.C. Alexander (2012) 'Introduction. Materiality and meaning in social life: toward an iconic turn in Cultural Sociology', in J.C. Alexander, D. Bartmanski and B. Giesen (eds.), *Iconic Power. Materiality and Meaning in Social Life*, New York: Palgrave.
Benson, R. (1999) 'Field theory in comparative context: a new paradigm for media studies', *Theory and Society*, 28(3): 463–498.
—— (2006) 'News media as a "journalistic field": what Bourdieu adds to new institutionalism, and vice versa', *Political Communication*, 23(2): 187–202.
—— (2013) *Shaping Immigration News: A French-American Comparison*, Cambridge: Cambridge University Press.
Benson, R. and E. Neveu (eds.) (2005) *Bourdieu and the Journalistic Field*, Cambridge: Polity.
Boschetti, A. (2001) *La poésie partout. Apollinaire, homme-époque (1898-1918)*, Paris: Seuil.

Bourdieu, P. (1977) *Outline of a Theory of Practice*, Cambridge: Cambridge University Press.
—— (1984) *Distinction. A Social Critique of the Judgement of Taste*, Cambridge: Harvard University Press.
—— (1982) *Leçon sur la Leçon*, Paris: Editions de Minuit.
—— (1985) 'The social space and the genesis of groups', *Theory and Society*, 14(6): 723–744.
—— (1988) *Homo Academicus*, Stanford, CA: Stanford University Press.
—— (1990a) *Logic of Practice*, Stanford, CA: Stanford University Press.
—— (1990b) *In Other Words. Essays Towards a Reflexive Sociology*, Stanford, CA: Stanford University Press.
—— (ed.) (1990c) *Photography: A Middle-Brow Art*, Cambridge: Polity.
—— (1990d) 'Artistic taste and cultural capital', in J.C. Alexander and S. Seidman (eds.), *Culture and Society: Contemporary Debates*, Cambridge: Cambridge University Press.
—— (1991) *Language and Symbolic Power*, Cambridge: Polity.
—— (1993) *The Field of Cultural Production*, New York: Columbia University Press.
—— (ed.) (1994) 'L'emprise du journalisme', special issue, *Actes de la recherche en sciences sociales*, 101–102.
—— (1996a) *The Rules of Art. Genesis and Structure of the Literary Field*, Stanford, CA: Stanford University Press.
—— (1996b) *The State Nobility*, Cambridge: Polity.
—— (1997) *The Love of Art*, Cambridge: Polity.
—— (1998a) *Practical Reason*, Stanford, CA: Stanford University Press.
—— (1998b) *On Television*, New York: New Press.
—— (2000a) *Pascalian Meditations*, Cambridge: Polity.
—— (2000b) 'The political field, the social science field, and the journalistic field', in R. Benson and E. Neveu (eds.) *Bourdieu and the Journalistic Field*, Cambridge: Polity.
—— (2003) 'Participant objectivation', *The Journal of the Royal Anthropological Institute*, 9: 281–294.
—— (2005a) *The Social Structures of the Economy*, Cambridge: Polity.
—— (2005b) 'Postface to Erwin Panofsky, *Gothic Architecture and Scholasticism*.' in B.W. Holsinger (ed.), *The Premodern Condition: Medievalism and the Making of Theory* (pp. 221–242), Chicago: University of Chicago Press.
Bourdieu, P. and L. Boltanski (1976) 'La production de l'idéologie dominante', *Actes de la recherche en sciences sociales*, 2(2–3): 3–73.
Bourdieu, P. and L. Wacquant (1992) *An Invitation to Reflexive Sociology*, Chicago: University of Chicago Press.
Calhoun, C. (1995) *Critical Social Theory*, New York: Wiley.
Chaney, D. (1994) *The Cultural Turn: Scene Setting Essays on Contemporary Cultural History*, London: Routledge.
Couldry, N. (2003) 'Media meta-capital: extending the range of Bourdieu's field theory', *Theory and Society*, 32(5–6): 653–677.
DiMaggio, P. (2000) 'The Production of scientific change: Richard Peterson and the institutional turn in cultural sociology', *Poetics*, 28(2–3): 107–136.
Durkheim, E. (1995) *The Elementary Forms of Religious Life*, New York: Free Press.
Duschinsky, R. and S. Lampitt (2012) 'Managing the tensions of essentialism: purity and impurity', *Sociology*, 46(6): 1194–1207.
Emirbayer, M. (2004) 'The Alexander School of Cultural Sociology', *Thesis Eleven*, 79(1): 5–15.
Eyerman, R. (2001) *Cultural Trauma: Slavery and the Formation of African-American Identity*, Cambridge: Cambridge University Press.
—— (2004) 'Jeffrey Alexander and the cultural turn in social theory', *Thesis Eleven*, 79: 25–30
Friedland, R. and J. Mohr (eds.) (2004) *Matters of Culture*, New York: Cambridge University Press.
Gans, H. (2012) 'Against culture versus structure', *Identities: Global Studies in Culture and Power*, 19(2): 125–134.
Gartman, D. (2007) 'The strength of weak programs in cultural sociology: a critique of Alexander's critique of Bourdieu', *Theory and Society*, 36: 381–413.
Goldberg, C.A. (2013) 'Struggle and solidarity: civic republican elements in Pierre Bourdieu's political sociology' *Theory and Society*, 42(4): 369–394.
Gorski, P. (2013a) 'Bourdieu as a theorist of change', in P. Gorski (ed.), *Bourdieu and Historical Analysis*, Durham, NC: Duke University Press.
—— (2013b) 'Bourdieusian theory and historical analysis: maps, mechanisms, and methods', in P. Gorski (ed.), *Bourdieu and Historical Analysis*, Durham, NC: Duke University Press.
Gross, N. and C. Fleming (2011) 'Academic conferences and the making of philosophical knowledge', in C. Camic, N. Gross and M. Lamont (eds.), *Social Knowledge in the Making*, Chicago: Chicago University Press.

Hallin, D. (2005) 'Two approaches to comparative media research: field theory and differentiation theory', in R. Benson and E. Neveu (eds.), *Bourdieu and the Journalistic Field*, Cambridge: Polity.
Hallin, D. and P. Mancini (2004) *Comparing Media Systems. Three Models of Media and Politics*, Cambridge: Cambridge University Press.
Harker, R. and S.A. May (1993) 'Code and habitus: comparing the accounts of Bernstein and Bourdieu', *British Journal of Sociology of Education*, 14(2): 169–178.
Hedstrom, P. (2005) *Dissecting the Social: On the Principles of Analytical Sociology*, Cambridge: Cambridge University Press.
Heilbron, J. (2011) 'Practical foundations of theorizing in sociology: the case of Pierre Bourdieu', in C. Camic, N. Gross and M. Lamont (eds.), *Social Knowledge in the Making*, Chicago: Chicago University Press.
Jacobs, J. (2000) *Race, Media, and the Crisis of Civil Society*, Cambridge: Cambridge University Press.
Jacobs, R. and E. Townsley (2011) *The Space of Opinion. Media Intellectuals and the Public Sphere*, Oxford: Oxford University Press.
Kane, A. (1991) 'Cultural analysis in historical sociology: the analytical and concrete forms of the autonomy of culture', *Sociological Theory*, 9(1): 53–69.
Ku, A. (1999) *Narrative, Politics, and the Public Sphere*, Aldershot: Ashgate.
Kurasawa, F. (2004) 'Alexander and the cultural refounding of American sociology', *Thesis Eleven*, 79(1): 53–64.
—— (2015) 'How does humanitarian visuality work? A conceptual toolkit for a sociology of iconic suffering', *Sociologica*, 9(1).
Lebaron, F. (2009) 'How Bourdieu "quantified" Bourdieu: the geometric modelling of data', in K. Robson and C. Sanders (eds.), *Quantifying Theory: Pierre Bourdieu*, New York: Springer.
Lizardo, O. (2010a) 'Pierre Bourdieu as a post-cultural theorist', *Cultural Sociology*, 5(1): 1–22.
—— (2010b) 'Beyond the antinomies of structure: Levi-Strauss, Giddens, Bourdieu, and Sewell', *Theory and Society*, 39(6): 651–688.
McLennan, G. (2004) 'Rationalizing musicality: a critique of Alexander's "Strong Program" in Cultural Sociology', *Thesis Eleven*, 79(1): 75–86.
Miller, D. (2005) 'Materiality: an introduction', in Id. (ed.), *Materiality*, Durham, NC: Duke University Press.
Mukerji, C. (2014) 'The cultural power of tacit knowledge: inarticulacy and Bourdieu's habitus', *American Journal of Cultural Sociology*, 2(3): 348–375.
Olick, J. (2011) 'What is "the relative autonomy of culture?"', in J.R. Hall, L. Grindstaff and M.-C. Lo (eds.), *Handbook of Cultural Sociology*, New York: Routledge.
Patterson, O. (2014) 'Making sense of culture', *Annual Review of Sociology*, 40: 1–30.
Pérez-Diaz, V. (2014) 'Civil society: a multi-layered concept', *Current Sociology*, 62: 812–830.
Potter, G. (2000) 'For Bourdieu, against Alexander: the reality of reduction', *Journal for the Theory of Social Behaviour*, 30(2): 229–246.
Rambo, E. and E. Chan (1990) 'Text, structure and action in cultural sociology', *Theory and Society*, 19(5): 635–648.
Rodrigo, C., F. Carballo and J. Ossandón (2008) 'Performing cultural sociology: a conversation with Jeffrey Alexander', *European Journal of Social Theory*, 11: 523–542.
Santoro, M. (2006) 'The Tenco Effect. Suicide, Sanremo and the rise of the canzone d'autore', *Journal of Modern Italian Studies*, 3: 342–65.
—— (2008a) 'Putting Bourdieu in the global field' *Sociologica*, 2(2).
—— (2008b) 'Culture as (and after) production', *Cultural Sociology*, 2(1): 7–31.
—— (2010) *Effetto Tenco. Genealogia della canzone d'autore*, Bologna: il Mulino.
—— (2011) 'From Bourdieu to cultural sociology', *Cultural Sociology*, 5(1): 3–23.
Savage, M. and E.B. Silva (2013) 'Field analysis in cultural sociology', *Cultural Sociology*, 7(2): 111–126.
Sewell, W.H. Jr. (1980) *Work and Revolution in France*, Cambridge: Cambridge University Press.
—— (1992) 'A theory of structure', *American Journal of Sociology* 98 (1): 1–29.
Sherwood, S. J. (1994) 'Narrating the social', *Journal of Narrative and Life History* 4(1–2): 69–88.
Shusterman, R. (ed.) (1999) *Bourdieu. A Critical Reader*, Oxford: Blackwell.
—— (2002) *Surface and Depth. Dialectics of Criticism and Culture*, Ithaca, NY: Cornell University Press.
Silva, E.B. and A. Warde (eds.) (2010) *Cultural Analysis and Bourdieu's Legacy: Settling Accounts and Developing Alternatives*, London: Routledge.
Smith, P. (1991) 'Codes and conflict', *Theory and Society* 20(1): 103–138.

—— (ed.) (1998) *The New American Cultural Sociology*, Cambridge: Cambridge University Press.
—— (2005) *Why War? The Cultural Logic of Iraq, the Gulf War, and Suez*, Chicago: University of Chicago Press.
Snow, P. (2010) 'Performing society', *Thesis Eleven*, 103(1): 78–87.
Solaroli, M. (2015) 'Iconicity: a category for social and cultural theory', *Sociologica*, 9(1).
Stedman Jones, G. (1983) *Languages of Class*, Cambridge: Cambridge University Press.
Swidler, A. (1996) 'Commentary', ASA *Culture* newsletter, 10(3–4): 9.
Townsley, E. (2011) 'Media, intellectuals, the public sphere, and the story of Barack Obama in 2008', in J. Alexander, P. Smith and R. Jacobs (eds.), *The Oxford Handbook of Cultural Sociology*, Oxford: Oxford University Press.
Wacquant, L. (2001) 'Further notes on Bourdieu's "Marxism"', *International Journal of Contemporary Sociology*, 38: 103–109.
Wacquant, L. (ed.) (2005) *Pierre Bourdieu and Democratic Politics: The Mystery of Ministry*, Cambridge: Polity.
Wagner-Pacifici, R. (2000) *Theorizing the Standoff*, Cambridge: Cambridge University Press.
Warde, A. (2004) 'Practice and field: Revising Bourdieusian concepts', CRIC discussion paper n. 65.
White, H. (2008) *Identity and Control* (second edition), Princeton, NJ: Princeton University Press.

4

The cultural omnivore thesis
Methodological aspects of the debate

Irmak Karademir Hazır and Alan Warde

Introduction

The concepts of 'the cultural omnivore' and 'cultural omnivorousness', coined by Richard Peterson in 1992, have become central to sociological controversies about cultural dynamics. The terms refer to repertoires of cultural practice, emerging in the late twentieth century, which are marked both by an increased breadth of cultural tastes and participation and by a willingness to transgress previously entrenched boundaries between hierarchically ranked cultural items or genres. 'Eclecticism' is sometimes preferred as an alternative designation.[1] As also discussed by Hanquinet and Savage in Chapter 1, this debate has become an obligatory point of passage for empirical studies in cultural sociology concerned to map taste and participation. The omnivore concept arose from a somewhat technical question of audience segmentation for the arts in the USA, but quickly became part of a wider concern about the contemporary importance of social class hierarchy, and especially the patterns of cultural consumption of the higher echelons of the middle class. The issue was whether people of high socio-economic status had distinctive cultural tastes, if so whether these were diverse or exclusive, and whether this led to a sense of social or aesthetic superiority. A contrast was implied with an ideal-typical picture of the past when the middle class espoused high culture and denigrated popular culture – for which they were sometimes deemed 'snobs' by members of other classes. These issues were explored against a background of great turbulence in the production of culture which led some, of postmodernist persuasion, to argue that cultural boundaries had dissolved (e.g. Firat and Venkatesh 1995).

The debate has proved important because it provides a focus for general controversies about contemporary social and cultural change. It challenges and refines understandings of the relationship of culture to power, consequential for debates on social stratification. At stake are sociological understandings, inter alia, of change in social hierarchy and cultural hierarchy and the relationship between these and the consequences of cultural difference, whether difference entails hierarchy, strategies for distinction and the value of cultural competence in social relations and competition. The debate revolves around a concentrated set of core issues. Replication of inquiries in different situations has delivered results which can be compared across countries, across time and across cultural fields. The consequent substantial stream of empirical research provides a significant base of evidence concerning cultural consumption which permits analysis of the relationship between people's personal and social characteristics and their taste profiles across several domains – music, reading, TV, art appreciation, film, etc. The profusion of empirical research has stimulated theoretical conjecture and dispute. It has also generated a sophisticated discussion of methodologies associated with the application of the concept. It is to the last of these that this chapter is primarily addressed.

Theoretical and historical context of debate

The concept of the cultural omnivore first saw the light of day in 1992 (Peterson 1992; Peterson and Simkus 1992). It arose from interests in audiences for culture in the USA. Debate about the quality of mass culture, which raged in the 1950s and 1960s, had continued to provide the platform for consideration of the relationship between elite culture and the commercial and popular cultural forms associated with television, film, popular music, etc. Gans (1999 [1974]) argued that a perceived hierarchy of 'taste cultures' existed in the USA which, he maintained, ran parallel to rankings of social status and prestige. American sociology knew from other sources also that people of high socio-economic status funded and fostered high culture (DiMaggio 1987). Taste and social position roughly coincided. However, Gans (1999: 143) observed, 'There seems to be less resentment about cultural inequality than about other kinds of inequality' (i.e. cultural inequalities had less resonance in the USA than did money or power).

That context explains Peterson's empirical approach. His study of musical taste with Simkus identified an unexpected trend. Those who most obviously were immersed in what Gans called the Upper or Upper-Middle taste cultures were apparently beginning to take a broader and more intense interest in less refined taste cultures. The paper by Peterson and Simkus (1992: 169) gave an initial definition of the omnivore. They identified:

> mounting evidence that high-status groups not only participate more than do others in high-status activities but also tend to participate more often in most kinds of leisure activities. In effect, elite taste is no longer defined as an expressed appreciation of the high art forms (and a moral disdain or bemused tolerance for all other aesthetic expressions). Now it is being redefined as an appreciation of the aesthetics of every distinctive form along with an appreciation of the high arts. Because status is gained from knowing about and participating in (that is to say, by consuming) all forms, the term omnivore seems appropriate.

Subsequent definitions were various, but note that the terms used include 'elite', marking the origin of the position in the debate about mass culture, and the 'high-status groups' who appreciate the high arts and the 'aesthetics of every distinct form'.

This formulation explains the method employed to operationalize the concept in a particularly clear and much cited article. Peterson and Kern (1996), using two surveys conducted in 1983 and 1992 in the USA, detected a trend for persons with highbrow cultural tastes in music (measured as having professed to like both opera and classical music and to like one of these genres best of all types of music) to also claim to like an increasing number of middle- and lowbrow genres. (American sociology had earlier adopted the terms highbrow, middlebrow and lowbrow to characterize hierarchically ranked blocks of taste and participation.) They noted that while people with low- and middlebrow tastes also claimed to like more genres in 1992 than in 1983, the rate of increase was fastest among those holding highbrow tastes. The article demonstrated that this emerging omnivore pattern was most prevalent among people of high socio-economic status. They made a number of remarks in specification of the content of omnivorous tastes, which in light of subsequent debate proved neither sufficiently precise nor necessarily consistent: 'it is antithetical to snobbishness, which is based fundamentally on rigid rules of exclusion' (1996: 904); it is not 'liking everything indiscriminately', but 'an openness to appreciating everything'; and it 'does not imply an indifference to distinctions', for the highbrow does not necessarily fully embrace the lowbrow forms, but merely seeks to 'appreciate and critique in the light of some knowledge of the genre'. These comments left open many questions about the forms and extent of discriminating tastes, of openness and of markers of distinction, and a legacy of problems about how to measure the extent and dispersion of omnivorousness. For this was a pioneering and preliminary study which used a part of a data set, designed for other purposes, which referred solely to eighteen genres of music over a nine-year period in the USA. The findings were, however, sufficiently intriguing to spark both re-studies about class and taste, and extrapolation to other areas where middle-class behaviour might be changing. Among these putative changes were less denigration of popular culture, fewer dislikes among the middle class of popular items, less class consciousness, greater tolerance, etc. Peterson and Kern attributed the growth of omnivorousness to structural changes which have made different cultural forms more widely available, 'a historical trend towards greater tolerance of those holding different values' (1996: 905), the decline of a single standard in the art world, the effect of generational politics as tastes developed from the 1950s onwards and a change in the operation of status group politics.

The omnivore thesis rapidly gained traction as further investigations into contemporary cultural taste and practice identified it as a plausible description of how social position and cultural preferences had become realigned in a period of apparently rapid cultural change. Once brought into contact with European sociology, however, it became much more contentious. Peterson's early formulations painted a contrasting picture to Pierre Bourdieu's highly influential account of the relationship between socio-economic position and cultural competence. Bourdieu's (1984) account of how and why different social classes had predictably different tastes was initially not addressed directly by Peterson, because of the latter's point of departure being the relationship between elite and mass as described in mass culture theory.[2] Bourdieu's work had little currency in the USA at the time (Sallaz and Zavisca 2007). *Distinction: a social critique of the judgment of taste* (1984) was couched in different, and uncongenial, theoretical terms and had been formulated with respect to cultural practice in Europe, and specifically France. With key concepts of practice, field, habitus and types of capital, Bourdieu mapped consumption and taste onto the social distribution of economic and cultural capital. Taste was viewed as an asset in social struggles for domination, with cultural tastes symbolizing and reinforcing class divisions; dominant classes defined their own taste as good taste, thus rendering it 'legitimate' taste, and then imagined that it justified their superiority. Bourdieu asked insistent questions about the consequences of taste for social inequality and political alignments.

The incommensurable aspects of the accounts of Peterson and Bourdieu raise fundamental sociological questions which have driven research and analysis for almost two decades. With the accumulating evidence largely showing a significant but ambiguous association between cultural preferences and social position, there is much to dispute regarding its theoretical interpretation. Several major issues are at stake. One is whether a recognisable and widely shared classification of cultural forms persists. If hierarchy is waning, is this a temporary transition – which Bourdieu could understand perfectly well as a round of social struggle for the legitimization of a new type of symbolic capital – or a terminal state of permanent equivalence and pluralization of cultural forms? A second question concerns the socio-economic determination of taste. Since scarcely anyone claims that socio-economic differentiation has disappeared altogether – it is, rather, a tendency, though one which some consider irreversible – what is the strength, nature and direction of the association over time? A third question concerns institutional settings.

Omnivorousness might be specific to the cultural formation of the USA, and societies subject to Americanization, a tendency linked to the decline of snobbishness in a society where class, and its expression through culture, was always somewhat less pronounced than in most of Europe.

Addressing these matters empirically requires a complex series of connected investigations. There is not a single explanatory problem but several, and these have kept cultural sociology fruitfully occupied for a couple of decades. Many substantive and technical problems of measurement have been thrown up by attempts to evaluate the importance of omnivorousness.

They include:

- Agreeing a definition of omnivorousness is difficult. Is an omnivore best identified by the scale or exceptional volume of likes and participation? Or is the key feature the composition of their tastes: the crossing of boundaries between high culture and popular culture? And does frequency of engagement signify anything?
- Equally contentious is the subsequent operationalization of omnivorousness. Should it be measured as participation, knowledge or preferences? And in the last instance, does it refer only to likes, or are dislikes more significant?
- Given the profuseness of cultural practice, which cultural domains and items are important? Clearly there are limits to generalizations based on the study of music alone, but are all practices relevant? Is looking for the distribution of preferences for genres of cultural forms sufficient, or is it better to identify particular items or artists?
- Problems also arise over identification of social position and interpretation of any socio-demographic correlates of taste. Should sociologists be looking for measures of class, as Bourdieu might require, or of status, as Weberians would prefer, or is education an acceptable proxy, which many studies employed to approximate to socio-economic status? Perhaps other key features behind tastes – gender, ethnicity, age or generation – are obscured by the founding interest in socio-economic status.
- Even if these difficulties could be resolved, can the meaning of statistical associations indicated by survey data be divined without qualitative inquiry into experience of participation in the cultural realm?
- Finally, the thesis hangs on a diagnosis of change which calls for reliable historical or processual proof of tendencies and trends towards omnivorousness. The cultural preferences of individuals may always have been uneven and eclectic, even in contexts where there was social consensus about the superior value of high culture (Lahire 2008). Evidence of both individual and institutional change is needed to demonstrate specifically new patterns of cultural experience at the end of the twentieth century.

In the remainder of the chapter, as we were commissioned to do, we trace threads in the on-going debate regarding issues of method and measurement in an attempt to clarify sources of confusion and disagreement in one of cultural sociology's most interesting and coherent debates.

Measurement issues

The variation in the operationalization of omnivore profiles and in the methods of measurement is widely acknowledged but has yet to be systematically analysed. We decided that reviewing the articles written on this topic would be an appropriate starting point, since the debate has mainly taken place in journals. We limit our search to the journals indexed in the SSCI and AHCI databases and to the time period between 1992 and 2013. We omitted the articles in which our keyword 'omnivore' used to indicate a condition other than cultural eclecticism

Table 4.1 Articles on omnivorousness 1992–2013, by type of content

Type of article	Count	Percentage
Empirical	68	54.8
Commentary	56	45.2

(such as eating both vegetables and meat). Finally, our list included 124 articles on cultural omnivorousness which drew on different conceptualizations, operationalization and measurement techniques. Sixty-eight of these articles were empirical, that is to say, omnivorousness was measured directly using first-hand or secondary data (see Table 4.1). In the others, the discussion was either theoretical, or the issue of omnivorousness was marginal to the papers' main purposes. To explore the measurement dynamics in this debate, we categorized the articles drawing on empirical data on several dimensions. We first recorded the national contexts in which the research was conducted. Then, we identified the type of the data utilized (cross-sectional, longitudinal, etc.) to see if measuring a change in the cultural repertoires in time was a concern or not. Furthermore, we listed different types of method applied in these articles (qualitative or quantitative, mixed methods), and the way omnivorousness was operationalized (knowledge, taste, participation).

As seen in Table 4.2, half of the articles in which omnivorousness is measured take participation as a proxy for cultural appreciation. One-quarter examines taste, and only in one per cent of the empirical papers was knowledge taken as a proxy for cultural appreciation. Combining two proxies is uncommon; 10 per cent use participation and taste, 4 per cent taste and knowledge and 1.5 per cent participation and knowledge. Only in 7 per cent of the articles were participation, taste and knowledge measured concurrently to calculate the degree of omnivorousness. Practical considerations, particularly regarding availability of data, have necessarily affected the operationalization of eclectic repertoires. Especially the articles which re-use the national surveys conducted routinely for wider purposes (e.g. Public Participation in the Arts Survey in the US) have to adjust their operationalization to variables at hand.

However, variation in the proxies also stems from researchers' different views about their appropriateness. Some researchers argue that participation in cultural practices requires economic investment and is limited by the availability of events and, in line with the original studies of Peterson (Peterson and Kern 1996; Peterson and Simkus 1992), many newer investigations therefore consider self-reported tastes as the most appropriate measure of cultural appreciation (e.g. Purhonen, Gronow and Rahkonen 2010; Graham 2009). Others, for the same reasons, consider participation a better proxy of appreciation (e.g. López Sintas and García Álvarez 2002; van Rees, Vermunt and Verboord 1999); practical involvement represents investment of time and money and thus some level of commitment. Respondents' knowledge of different genres on the other hand, despite its significance in demonstrating the condition of 'openness to appreciate everything', has rarely been taken as a primary measure (a notable exception is Veenstra [2005]). It should be noted that choosing one proxy over another is likely to generate different

Table 4.2 Measurement of omnivorousness in empirical articles

	Participation	Taste	Knowledge	P+T	T+K	P+K	P+T+K
Percentage	49	26	1	10	4	1	7

correlations between the level of omnivorousness and other variables. For instance, Warde and Gayo-Cal (2009) show that socio-demographic characteristics relate differently to alternative measures; declared taste is less strongly influenced by socio-demographic features than participation and, in addition, using different operationalizations interchangeably is likely to blur findings. It is also important to think about how far the operationalization suits the explanatory hypothesis. For instance, in relation to the characteristics of eclectic repertoire owners, if significance is attributed to social networking or the self-confidence required for stepping out of one's comfort zone, this can only be explored in relation to measures of public participation rather than through taste or knowledge.

Another significant dimension of variation reflects different criteria for identifying 'openness' to diversity. A number of researchers consider the *volume* of tastes, participation or knowledge to be a sufficient marker of an omnivorous profile (Peterson 2005). This means that a respondent who likes, engages or knows more than the average number of genres or items is considered omnivorous, regardless of the positions of those genres in the hierarchy of tastes (e.g. Peterson and Kern 1996; for a comparison of volume and composition measurements see Purhonen, Gronow and Rahkonen 2010). However, omnivorousness, according to its original definition, was about crossing hierarchical boundaries and thus about the composition of tastes. Therefore, examining the contents of cultural profiles is critical for understanding the processes and consequences of cultural appreciation, notwithstanding the fact that most studies show also that high socio-economic status is directly associated with high volume. Researchers convinced that composition matters then need to determine relevant boundaries. Some draw on the accumulated knowledge of what constitutes legitimate taste (e.g. Lizardo and Skiles 2009; Ollivier, Gauthier and Truong 2009), others resort to their own data sets to extract the genres that are more liked by highly educated respondents via methods such as multiple correspondence analysis (e.g. López Sintas and Katz-Gerro 2005; Warde 2011; Savage and Gayo-Cal 2011). The latter approach is more demanding, but it is more receptive to changes in taste hierarchies as well as to differences between national cultural fields. However, measuring omnivorousness by first identifying the highbrow genres (*a priori* or inductively) and then focusing on those who show openness to lowbrow genres in addition to highbrow tastes may have shortcomings. Various studies show that different types of omnivorousness can be manifested in crossing horizontal boundaries (between, for example, the old and the new) within the realms of legitimate taste (e.g. Bellavance 2008; Bergman and van Eijck 2009). Others identify lowbrow eclecticism (e.g. Bennett *et al.* 2001). Such problems of multiple forms of boundary crossing caused Peterson (2005: 265) latterly to propose not to 'bind breadth and brow-level together by definition, but to see omnivorousness as a measure of the breadth of taste and cultural consumption, allowing its link to status to be definitionally open'.

The field of consumption chosen to measure omnivorousness deserves critical assessment. In 38 per cent of the empirical articles compiled, only music is examined (see Table 4.3). Twenty-five per cent of the papers take a single domain other than music, such as reading or visual arts, while 37 per cent of the articles investigate tastes in multiple fields. Music has thus strongly shaped the debate. It is a very special domain; almost everyone listens to music, many

Table 4.3 Distribution of the empirical articles: Field(s) of consumption chosen to measure omnivorousness

	Music	Single field other than music	Multiple fields	Total
Percentage	38	25	37	100

very enthusiastically. People express stronger likes and dislikes and are capable of distinguishing many more genres than might be expected in other domains. It is widely accessible, embedded in the institutional-school curriculums, and its ways of consumption are strongly affected by constant technological advancements. Moreover, it is more common to speak of 'brow' categories in music, and perhaps researchers' continuing enthusiasm about music partially stems from the appeal of engaging with the findings of a series of previous studies. These qualities of the music field all suggest that the extent to which we are justified in extrapolating from openness in musical taste to other cultural domains without actually examining sufficient of them closely is very questionable, as Lahire (2008) notes. In addition to this issue, it is important to recognize that the evidence collected is mostly relevant to middle-class practices, overlooking the recreational pursuits specific to other classes who consequently may be misleadingly presented as inactive.

The concept of the omnivore presumes the present to be different from the past (scarcely anyone would contend that openness was a quality of culturally cultivated elites in the mid-twentieth century which had merely lain undiscovered until 1992 – although the matter remains unproven), yet change is hard to measure satisfactorily. The debate perforce draws disproportionately on cross-sectional data. Eighty-five per cent of the papers reviewed draw on a data set referring to a single point in time. Hence, much of the empirical material cannot directly provide the ground for discussing the dynamics of change. The limited availability of time-series data mitigates against employing research designs with temporal perspectives. Thus, the exceptions (e.g. DiMaggio and Mukhtar 2004; Jaeger and Katz-Gerro 2010; Katz-Gerro and Jaeger 2013; López Sintas and Katz-Gerro 2005; Ollivier et al. 2009; van Eijck and Knulst 2005) which mobilize cross-sectional survey evidence about specific populations at several points in time are especially valuable for understanding the direction of change. For instance, López Sintas and Katz-Gerro's analysis of art participation in the USA between 1982 and 2002 identifies different types of omnivorousness, each of which has been developing unevenly in time. It is thus made apparent that change in cultural appreciation has not been a simple unilateral trend (i.e. decline of traditional highbrow participation) but that different types of cultural eclecticism with different trajectories were at play.

Another important finding of our scoping review is that the debate has not yet benefited sufficiently from cross-national comparisons. Only a few studies attempt to measure omnivorousness in more than one national context (e.g. Fishman and Lizardo 2013; Lizardo and Skiles 2009; Katz-Gerro 2002), and few discuss their findings with an eye to confounding peculiarities of national cultural profiles. As Peterson (2005) claims, comparative research faces obvious methodological difficulties, such as the wording of the research instrument or incomparable classifications (socio-economic status variables or genres) which make comparative endeavours less appealing (see Purhonen and Wright 2013). Another feature of the debate is its Eurocentrism. Only a few papers discuss non-European contexts (e.g. Brazil by Hedegard 2013; South Korea by Yoon et al. 2011; and South Africa by Snowball et al. 2010) (see Table 4.4) and see Gayo's chapter in this handbook. As in the case of unbalanced focus on certain fields and on cross-sectional data, knowing little about the change in cultural hierarchies outside of Europe and North America poses challenges to the generalizability of the main findings and to the refinement of the concept.

Eighty-three percent of the papers that we scanned draw on the quantitative analysis of surveys. Qualitative analysis is used in 10 percent of our population. Only 7 percent of them adopt a mixed-methods design, for example Zavisca (2005), Warde et al. (2007), Savage and Gayo-Cal (2011) and Friedman (2012). Yet, in these works the qualitative material unpacks significant processes in cultural appreciation, such as the role of different art forms in the

Table 4.4 Distribution of empirical articles by countries studied

First 10 Countries	Percentage
USA	37
UK	22
Netherlands	11
Canada	8
Spain	8
Australia	6
Israel	5
Belgium	4
Denmark	4
Finland	3

respondent's biography and the reasons behind respondents' particular preferences. However, even in studies drawing primarily on qualitative material, omnivorousness is usually first measured quantitatively and then the evidence from the interviews is discussed in relation to the scores that people got on the omnivorousness scales. Most of the time, the emphasis of those papers is on the meaning of the qualitative differences between quantitatively identified omnivorous profiles (e.g. Ollivier 2008; Warde *et al.* 2007). It is important to note that some critiques of the omnivore thesis reject quantitative analysis altogether (e.g. Atkinson 2011), arguing that identification of eclecticism is merely an artefact of the survey method which is shown to be mistaken by individuals' own narratives. We do not share this view, believing that quantitative studies do usefully reflect aggregate patterns, and that mixed methods studies generate complementary results, yet it is clear that qualitative studies have made significant contributions to our understanding of eclectic repertoires. For instance, Ollivier uncovered four different types of openness to diversity (humanist, practical, indifferent, populist) in each of which the meanings attached to openness were distinct. Her qualitative analysis of these repertoires challenges the association between openness and egalitarian tolerance which is frequently presumed in the debate, for she demonstrates clearly that 'openness to cultural diversity entails neither the disappearance of cultural boundaries nor the flattening of social and artistic hierarchies' (2008: 144).

A final point regarding methodological trends concerns the operationalization of openness. In most of the papers, as in Peterson's own study, integration of lowbrow genres into upper-class taste portfolios is framed as 'openness'. However, partly because of the qualities of the research instruments employed, there is limited analysis of whether or not eclecticism brings with it openness as a general social, cultural or political disposition. Despite some notable exceptions, which carefully scrutinize the relationship of tolerance and taste profiles (e.g. Bryson 1996; Roose *et al.* 2012; van Eijck and Lievens 2008; Warde 2011), correspondence between liking

Table 4.5 Methodological approaches to measuring omnivorousness in empirical articles

Technique	Percentage
Quantitative	83
Qualitative	10
Mixed methods	7

lowbrow genres and being less defamatory about the tastes or morals of other social groups is frequently presumed without pausing to measure tolerance or advance other proof.

Shifts in emphasis

There have been significant shifts in emphasis in the debate over the last two decades. Before passing into details of these changes, let us note that there is very little sign that the interest in this topic is waning. The volume of articles published has increased gradually, with an apparent peak in the year 2011. The variety of topics discussed in relation to omnivore profiles also increased dramatically in time. To grasp the dynamics of this change, we used a word cloud generator to compare the keywords in the articles published between 1992–2002 and 2002–2013. We found out that many new associated key words, such as cosmopolitanism, multiculturalism, time, discourse, mobility and field, appeared as the debate progressed. Omnivore profiles are problematized and addressed in less orthodox ways, such as in Hedegard's paper (2013), entitled 'Blackness and experience in omnivorous cultural consumption: evidence from the tourism of capoeira in Salvador, Brazil', and Allington's paper (2011), entitled 'Distinction, intentions, and the consumption of fiction: negotiating cultural legitimacy in a gay reading group'. Studies like these, likely to proliferate in the coming years, concentrate on eclectic profiles under specific conditions and make links to wider issues (e.g. cosmopolitanism, ethnicity) without much concern for precision in measurement of omnivorousness. Nevertheless, a substantial proportion of the papers core to the debate open their discussion with more or less similar theoretical remarks and then measure omnivorousness in a national setting with data about established cultural domains.

Although the debate is overwhelmingly focused on the West, the geographical frame of reference is gradually expanding. The initial studies were conducted mainly in the United States, then spreading across Europe, but recent contributions come from Latin America, South Africa and Korea. As Peterson (2005) suggested, nations beyond Europe have their own art traditions, and we need data from the Islamic world, Africa and Asia to explore the current relationship between high culture and cultural stratification in those regions. The continuing spread of the debate also led to greater diversity in the cultural fields under investigation. Music still occasions most interest, yet compared to the initial periods of the debate, more other realms are being discussed. By contrast, there seems no systematic trend to innovation in operationalization; participation, taste, knowledge, breadth, volume and composition remain the main indicators.

Measurement techniques have evolved. The early studies used very similar quantitative techniques. The original objective was to find and characterize omnivorous profiles and to determine systematic relationships within the changing tastes of people of high socio-economic status (driven by questions of class, power and privilege). Subsequently, the use of mixed methods revealed how different measurement instruments can compensate for each other's weaknesses and unpack both systematic trends and people's rationales for their cultural consumption (e.g. Bennett et al. 2009; Cveticanin 2012). The in-depth analysis of omnivorous repertoires revealed distinct forms of eclecticism which correlated differently with respondents' socio-economic characteristics, leading to greater sophistication in measurement and analysis. Interest in cross-national comparative analysis and the use of longitudinal data are both growing apace with direct consequences for the future direction of research. As Fishman and Lizardo's (2013) comparison of Spain and Portugal shows, comparative designs make us question the peculiarities of the national and institutional mechanisms influencing cultural appreciation, a feature rarely visible in cross-sectional, non-comparative designs. Last but not least, as the debate has flourished, omnivorousness has begun to be analysed in relation to multiple social divisions. Class-based hierarchy has been central, but emphasis on other divisions, such as gender and ethnicity, is growing, refining our understanding of the social processes that affect and are affected by changes in cultural practices.

Before passing to our recommendations for future research, we would like to underline a few important features of the current omnivore debate. First of all, despite increased numbers of contributions to the debate, we do not seem to be any closer to agreement on the definition or measurement of cultural omnivorousness. Such a lack hampers progress and makes much needed comparisons across nations and over time more difficult. Yet it is important to note that, however measured, and whichever statistical techniques are employed, quantitative studies persistently have tended to identify groups of omnivores in Europe and the USA who have higher socio-economic status and who are also more active in their cultural participation. Omnivores have also been found in other national contexts when quantitative measures have been applied. However, in many such studies the dependent variable often lacks subtlety and there is a tendency to over-extrapolate from constructed clusters of taste to personal dispositions. Qualitative inquiries have compensated to some degree and have usefully identified different types of omnivore. Yet, as Lizardo and Skiles (2012) argue, while studies repeatedly find data confirming the existence of clusters of tastes with omnivorous characteristics, theoretical explanation of the origins and reproduction of omnivorous orientations is rudimentary. Their proposed solution identifies some mechanisms that explain the origins and development of an omnivorous aesthetic disposition from which they are also able to account for its distribution within populations. Their argument might be further strengthened by taking into account institutional contexts and national policies using comparative and historical analysis. This, in turn, would permit better assessment of the validity of the widely presumed association of omnivores with cultural openness and univores with cultural intolerance.

Agenda

We have sought to identify measurement trends and variations in the operationalization of omnivorousness, as well as to reflect on the influences of different methodological approaches on conclusions to date. The systematic analysis of articles published between 1992 and 2013 reveals gaps in the literature and suggests lines for further research. Admittedly, our formal sample has limitations: it draws only on the journals listed in the SSCI and AHCI, which include few journals published in languages other than English, and contributions published in books have not been systematically reviewed. Nevertheless, the sample probably represents the debate satisfactorily, for it has mainly proceeded by means of journal articles published in English.

A controversy with a robust evidence base in cultural sociology might yet benefit from further investigation of the ways in which omnivorous repertoires are formed, transmitted and experienced. In terms of formation, there is a need to reflect on the conditions that foster openness and on how eclectic repertoires come to differ from each other. For instance, Friedman's (2012) paper on taste in comedy demonstrates that repertoires of middle-class respondents with lower-class backgrounds become more eclectic as they integrate highbrow tastes into their schemes of cultural appreciation (omnivorousness from below). When compared to the established upper-middle classes' openness towards lower ranks (omnivorousness from above), this type of eclectic taste in humour yields different tensions and exhibits different characteristics. More studies like Gripsrud et al.'s (2011) comparison of children's with parents' cultural tastes and Lizardo and Skiles's (2012) analysis of mechanisms generating omnivorousness would contribute to grasping fully the role of social reproduction in the changes observed in cultural appreciation.

Explanations of transmission would also be enhanced by better institutional analysis and greater attention to the cultural context of nation-states or local circumstances. We now have fair knowledge about changes in profiles, but less about the conditions fostering the trends. Lizardo and Skiles's paper (2009) comparing TV and music tastes and van Eijck and van Rees's (2010) comparison of TV viewing and reading, for example, show that cultural domains have distinctive conditions of production and consumption, influenced by specific changes in technology, cultural policies, etc. Conditions of production in specific fields of consumption certainly influence consumers' behaviour. So too do the institutional policies materialized in school curricula or state funding of culture. Unfortunately, few contributors refer in detail to these issues, tending to divorce the results of their empirical investigation from historical, contextual and institutional setting. Explication of the interrelationship between conditions of cultural production, prevalent institutionalized cultural repertoires and the tastes of individuals would allow better comprehension of the dynamics of change and the more refined understanding of the differences between national and local contexts. For instance, why is the boundary of highbrow taste located towards the bottom of the class structures in Italy and West Germany, separating the working class from other classes, as Katz-Gerro (2002) found, rather than between the salariat and the rest? Or, why is the crossing of genre boundaries common among the holders of low institutionalized cultural capital in Serbia but not in West European countries (Cveticanin 2012)?

Research might also explore further how omnivorousness is experienced and why exactly eclecticism is valued highly. Is omnivorousness a unified disposition or more a result of pluralization of experience? This might help determine the extent to which omnivorousness is a form of distinction rather than an attitude of tolerance. The Bourdieusian version of omnivorousness as mark of distinction would, for example, be strengthened if it were shown that eclectic dispositions exhibited homology across fields or that the association between the liking of popular genres was weakly associated with openness or inclusive evaluative schemes. It also remains to be shown the manner and extent to which an omnivore repertoire generates advantages in other social domains. Finally much may yet be gained from extended use of mixed method research designs, for drawing both on surveys and on individuals' own accounts helps to avoid unnecessary methodological disputes and to reconcile information about the experiences, evaluations, rationales and biographies of individuals with the aggregate patterns of taste at the level of groups and populations.

In sum, the omnivore debate has proceeded at a relatively high level of methodological sophistication when compared with other debates in the area of the sociology of art and culture. It has been refined in many respects since its initial formulation, although it remains based largely on inductive observation with no strong theoretical underpinning. Many different techniques and measures have been used, and in general evidence supports the presence of an omnivorous disposition among social groups with high socio-economic status. It seems plausible to interpret an omnivorous disposition as a prevalent form of cultural orientation among those in positions of greater privilege since the late twentieth century in Western Europe and North America. Because the existing literature is mostly based on cross-sectional investigations, there is a tendency to treat omnivorousness as the highest or last, rather than just the latest, point of cultural development. We believe that it might possibly be better conceived as a stage in the development of post-industrial capitalist societies. It seems likely that it will prove to be a temporary phenomenon, generated as a result of systematic change in education and commercial cultural production systems during a period of globalization and informatization. However, it may be some years before such a conjecture can be confirmed or rejected, for we have as yet neither the historical perspective not the relevant data to determine decisively the specificity of recent trends. Meanwhile, the prospect for a resolution to current controversies would be much enhanced if more reliable longitudinal and comparative data could be compiled and analysed.

Notes

1 However, eclecticism does not capture the importance of increased volume or intensity of cultural engagement.
2 In his 2005 overview of the debate, Peterson argues that their original 1992 study 'expected to replicate Bourdieu's earlier findings' (p. 259). Yet, in the earlier writings of Peterson, the dialogue between the omnivore thesis and Bourdieu's works are actually limited, but gradually it has intensified as many new contributors to the debate moved the emphasis away from mass culture towards culture and distinction dynamics.

References

Allington, D. (2011) 'Distinction, intentions, and the consumption of fiction: Negotiating cultural legitimacy in a gay reading group', *European Journal of Cultural Studies*, 14 (2): 129–145.
Atkinson, W. (2011) 'The context and the genesis of musical tastes: Omnivorousness debunked, Bourdieu buttressed', *Poetics*, 39: 169–186.
Bellavance, G. (2008) 'Where's high? Who's low? What's new? Classification and stratification inside cultural "Repertoires"', *Poetics*, 36: 189–216.
Bennett, T., M. Emmison and J. Frow (2001) *Accounting for Tastes: Australian Everyday Cultures*, Cambridge: Cambridge University Press.
Bennett. T., M. Savage, E. Silva, A. Warde, M. Gayo-Cal and D. Wright (2009) *Culture, Class, Distinction*, London: Routledge.
Bergman, M. and K. van Eijck (2009) 'Visual arts appreciation patterns: Crossing horizontal and vertical boundaries within the cultural hierarchy', *Poetics*, 37(4), 348–365.
Bourdieu, P. (1984) *Distinction: A Social Critique of the Judgement of Taste*, Cambridge: Harvard University Press.
Bryson, B. (1996) '"Anything but heavy metal": Symbolic exclusion and musical dislikes', *American Sociological Review*, 6: 884–899.
Cveticanin, P. (ed.) (2012) *Social and Cultural Capital in Serbia*, Sven Nis, Serbia.
DiMaggio, P. (1987) 'Classification in art', *American Sociological Review*, 52:440–455.
DiMaggio, P. and T. Mukhtar (2004) 'Arts participation as cultural capital in the United States, 1982–2002: Signs of decline?', *Poetics*, 32: 169–194.
Firat, F. and A. Venkatesh (1995) 'Liberatory postmodernism and the reenchantment of consumption', *The Journal of Consumer Research*, 22 (3): 239–267.
Fishman, R. and Lizardo O. (2013) 'How macro-historical change shapes cultural taste: Legacies of democratization in Spain and Portugal', *American Sociological Review*, 78(2): 213–239.
Friedman, S. (2012) 'Cultural omnivores or culturally homeless? Exploring the shifting cultural identities of the upwardly mobile', *Poetics*, 40(5): 467–489.
Gans, H. (1999) *Popular Culture and High Culture: An Analysis and Evaluation of Taste* (second edition), New York: Basic Books.
Graham, R. (2009) 'The function of music education in the growth of cultural openness in the USA', *Music Education Research*, 11(3): 283–302.
Gripsrud, J., F.J. Hovden and H. Moe (2011) 'Changing relations: Class, education and cultural capital', *Poetics*, 39: 507–529.
Hedegard, D. (2013) 'Blackness and experience in omnivorous cultural consumption: Evidence from the tourism of capoeira in Salvador, Brazil', *Poetics*, 41: 1–26.
Jaeger, M. and T. Katz-Gerro (2010) 'The rise of the eclectic consumer in Denmark, 1964–2004', *The Sociological Quarterly*, 51: 460–483.
Katz-Gerro, T. (2002) 'Highbrow cultural consumption and class distinction in Italy, Israel, West Germany, Sweden and the United States', *Social Forces*, 81: 207–229.

Katz-Gerro, T. and M. Jaeger (2013) 'Top of the pops, ascend of the omnivores, defeat of the couch potatoes: Cultural consumption profiles in Denmark 1975–2004', *European Sociological Review*, 29(2), 243–260.

Lahire, B. (2008) 'The individual and the mixing of genres: Cultural dissonance and self distinction', *Poetics*, 36: 166–188.

Lizardo, O. and S. Skiles (2009) 'Highbrow omnivorousness on the small screen? Cultural industry systems and patterns of cultural choice in Europe', *Poetics*, 37: 1–23.

—— (2012) 'Reconceptualizing and theorizing 'omnivorousness': Genetic and relational mechanisms', *Sociological Theory*, 30(4): 263–282.

López Sintas, J. and E. García Álvarez (2002) 'Omnivores show up again: The segmentation of cultural consumers in Spanish social space', *European Sociological Review*, 18: 353–368.

López Sintas, J. and T. Katz-Gerro (2005) 'From exclusive to inclusive elitists and further: Twenty years of omnivorousness and cultural diversity in arts participation in the USA', *Poetics*, 33: 299–319.

Ollivier, M. (2008) 'Modes of openness to cultural diversity: Humanist, populist, practical and indifferent omnivores', *Poetics*, 36(1): 127–147.

Ollivier, M., G. Gauthier and H.A. Truong (2009) 'Cultural classifications and social divisions: A symmetrical approach', *Poetics*, 37: 456–473.

Peterson, R. (1992) 'Understanding audience segmentation: From elite and mass to omnivore and univore', *Poetics*, 21: 243–258.

—— (2005) 'Problems in comparative research: The example of omnivorousness, *Poetics*, 33: 257–282.

Peterson, R. and R.M. Kern (1996) 'Changing highbrow taste: From snob to omnivore', *American Sociological Review*, 61(5), 900–907.

Peterson, R. and A. Simkus (1992) 'How musical tastes mark occupational status groups', in M. Lamont and M. Fournier (eds.), *Cultivating Differences: Symbolic Boundaries and the Making of Inequality*, Chicago and London: University of Chicago Press.

Purhonen, S. and D. Wright (2013) 'Methodological issues in national-comparative research on cultural tastes: The case of cultural capital in the UK and Finland', *Cultural Sociology*, 7(2), 257–273.

Purhonen, S., J. Gronow and K. Rahkonen (2010) 'Nordic democracy of taste? Cultural omnivorousness in musical and literary taste preferences in Finland', *Poetics*, 38(3), 266–298.

Roose, H., K. van Eijck and J. Lievens (2012) 'Culture of distinction or culture of openness?: Using a social space approach to analyse the social structuring of lifestyles', *Poetics*, 40(6), 491–513.

Sallaz, J. and J. Zavisca (2007) 'Bourdieu in American sociology, 1984–2004', *Annual Review of Sociology*, 33: 21–41.

Savage, M. and M. Gayo-Cal (2011) 'Unravelling the omnivore: A field analysis of contemporary musical taste in the United Kingdom', *Poetics*, 39: 337–357.

Snowball, J.D., M. Jamal and K.G. Willis (2010) 'Cultural consumption patterns in South Africa: An investigation of the theory of cultural omnivores', *Social Indicators Research*, 97(3): 467–483.

van Eijck, K. and W. Knulst (2005) 'No more need for snobbism: Highbrow cultural participation in a taste democracy', *European Sociological Review*, 21(5): 513–528.

van Eijck, K. and J. Lievens (2008) 'Cultural omnivorousness as a combination of highbrow, pop, and folk elements: The relation between taste patterns and attitudes concerning social integration', *Poetics*, 36(2–3), 217–242.

van Eijck, K. and K. van Rees (2010) 'Media orientation and media use: Television viewing behavior of specific reader types 1975–1998', *Communication Research*, 27: 524–616.

van Rees, K., J. Vermunt and M. Verbood (1999) 'Cultural classifications under discussion: Latent class analysis of highbrow and lowbrow reading', *Poetics*, 26: 349–365.

Veenstra, G. (2005) 'Can taste illumine class? Cultural knowledge and forms of inequality', *Canadian Journal of Sociology*, 30(3): 247–279.

Warde, A. (2011) 'Cultural hostility re-considered', *Cultural Sociology*, 5(3): 341–366.

Warde, A. and M. Gayo-Cal (2009) 'The anatomy of cultural omnivorousness: The case of the United Kingdom', *Poetics*, 37: 119–145.

Warde, A., D. Wright and M. Gayo-Cal (2007) 'Understanding cultural omnivorousness: Or, the myth of the cultural omnivore', *Cultural Sociology*, 1(2): 143–164.

Yoon, T.I., K.H. Kim and H.J. Eom (2011) 'The border-crossing of habitus: Media consumption, motives, and reading strategies among Asian immigrant women in South Korea', *Poetics*, 35(2–3): 70–98.

Zavisca, J. (2005) 'The status of cultural omnivorism: A case study of reading in Russia', *Social Forces*, 84(2): 1233–1255.

5

After omnivorousness

Is Bourdieu still relevant?

Omar Lizardo and Sara Skiles

A fundamental ambiguity runs through the theoretical foundations of the sociology of taste. Most contemporary analysts consider Pierre Bourdieu's *Distinction* as the foundational work in the field. Yet, the approach taken by empirical researchers in relation to this work ranges from outright dismissal as an outdated theoretical position to the acknowledgement of partial influence in need of being transcended. This ambiguous relationship to Bourdieu's work has become even more salient in light of the empirical discovery of patterns of omnivorousness – taste among high-status persons that cuts across the fine and popular arts divides. This is usually interpreted as posing insurmountable difficulties for Bourdieu's original account, according to which elites reject popular culture and should be expected to consume only 'high' culture. In this chapter we argue that this portrayal of Bourdieu's work is based on widespread misunderstandings regarding the conceptual foundations of his theory of taste. We show that the depiction of the expected patterns of taste of high cultural capital persons offered by Bourdieu is much more compatible with recent considerations in the sociology of taste than has been acknowledged in the literature.

Enter omnivorousness, exit Bourdieu?

Supported by ample empirical evidence, the omnivore thesis has unarguably become the dominant paradigm in the sociology of taste (Peterson 2005; Lizardo 2008; Warde *et al.* 2008). In Peterson's (1997: 87) influential formulation, being 'high status' no longer requires being 'snobbish,' but 'means having cosmopolitan "omnivorous" tastes'. In this way, 'aesthetics of elite status' have been 'redefined as the appreciation of all distinctive leisure activities … along with the appreciation of the fine arts' (1992: 252). DiMaggio and Mukhtar (2004: 171) echo this sentiment in noting that the 'new cultural capitalists are the "omnivores," men and women who are comfortable speaking about and participating in high and popular culture and everything in between … [high] status now inheres in cosmopolitanism and broadly inclusive tastes' (DiMaggio and Mukhtar 2004: 189).

The omnivore/univore thesis has in many ways displaced or become a strong competitor to Bourdieu's theory of taste as the central organizing framework for empirical work in the field. The question that emerges is: What is the relationship between the new paradigm and the previously dominant one?

Most contemporary researchers frame the omnivore thesis as a *surprising* and *unexpected* empirical pattern given the context of particular interpretations of Bourdieu's work on class and lay aesthetics, which allegedly proposes a clear-cut division between the fine arts and popular culture, and thus suggests that cultural elites would invariably reject the latter types of cultural goods (Bryson 1996; Chan and Goldthorpe 2007a, 2007b). Thus, Peterson notes in this regard that the findings associated with omnivorousness are in 'dramatic difference from the earlier findings by Pierre Bourdieu in France' (2005: 260). Vander Stichele and Laermans categorically conclude that in spite of the influence of Bourdieu's early research, 'it is questionable whether his theoretical framework still corresponds to contemporary social reality'. They reach this conclusion based on the fact that 'empirical doubts have been raised regarding Bourdieu's claim that the bourgeoisie or dominant class primarily affirms its high social status via the public and private consumption of so-called high or legitimate culture' (2006: 45–6).

Van Eijck proposes that 'Bourdieu's notion that a high status implies snobbery and, thereby, a consistent aversion to popular culture, has been inadequate for decades, at least outside France' (2001: 1164). Chan and Goldthorpe (2007a: 14) are the most forceful, concluding that

> [w]e would ally ourselves with proponents of the omnivore–univore argument who claim that, whatever validity the ideas of symbolic 'struggle' and 'violence', as advanced by Bourdieu and his followers, may have had for the earlier history of modern societies, they appear out of place the contemporary world.

This entire line of reception[1] is aptly summarized by Coulangeon and Lemel (2007:94) when they note that '[t]he increasing renown of this new theoretical construct [omnivorousness] has often been interpreted as an invalidation of Bourdieu's sociology of taste'.

In what follows, we argue that this portrayal of Bourdieu's work is based on widespread misunderstandings regarding the conceptual foundations of his theory of taste (but see Holt 1997; Warde 2005; and Atkinson 2011 for exceptions to this line of interpretation). We show that the depiction of the expected patterns of taste of high cultural capital persons offered by Bourdieu is much more compatible with recent considerations in the sociology of taste, such as the 'omnivorousness' phenomenon, than has been acknowledged in the literature.

Bourdieu's theory of taste revisited

As suggested by the passages quoted above, one of the main reasons offered to justify the diagnosis of the increasing irrelevance of Bourdieu in the wake of the discovery of 'omnivore' patterns of cultural choice involves the claim that two basic presuppositions stand at the centre of Bourdieu's theory of taste:

Proposition 1: The primary way in which 'high-status' people consume culture according to Bourdieu and the evidence that he presents can be characterized as snobbish exclusiveness: that is, 'high-status' people dislike more things than low-status people, and in particular, they dislike the popular culture that the working classes consume (Bryson 1996; Chan and Goldthorpe 2007a, 2007b; Erickson 1996).

Therefore,

Proposition 2: Distinction is primarily a book about how 'high-status' people use 'highbrow' culture to draw symbolic boundaries that separate them from 'low-status' people and their 'lowbrow' cultural taste.

In what follows we propose that, contrary to popular opinion, neither of these claims are at the centre of Bourdieu's overall argument.

Is high-status exclusiveness a key element of Bourdieu's theory of taste?

Rather than being self-evident, it is at the very least curious that the omnivore thesis is considered so at odds with Bourdieu's theory of taste as to make it completely irrelevant for the current situation. Interestingly, in their influential article, Peterson and Kern (1996: 904) never took their findings to imply a *refutation* of Bourdieu, but simply a partial *reformulation*. They were careful to note that Bourdieu's theory is perfectly consistent with a notion of 'discriminating omnivorousness,' provided that 'the ethnocentrism central to snobbish elitism is replaced by cultural relativism', Peterson and Kern (1996: 904) do seem to provide ammunition for current misinterpretations, however, when they add that when Bourdieu differentiates between working-class and 'high-status' aesthetic consumption practices, he tends to portray the latter 'in ways that most easily fit a monolithic symbolic landscape appropriate to the era of the elitist snob'. Nevertheless, we argue that Peterson and Kern's ultimate verdict as to the compatibility of their findings with Bourdieu's taste theory is ambiguous at best, a conclusion that is at odds with the 'death knell' interpretation regarding the consequences of high-status omnivorousness for Bourdieu's theory of taste.

In her equally influential article, Bryson (1996: 886) provides a clearer cut example of what has become the dominant line of interpretation of Bourdieu's argument. In developing what she refers to as the "high-status exclusiveness" hypothesis, she notes that according to Bourdieu '[t]he *crux of symbolic exclusion is dislike ... and exclusion is more important to high status individuals than to others*' (italics added).

Most subsequent evaluations have tended to focus on this aspect of Bryson's interpretation of Bourdieu, which requires the strong claim that elites express dislikes more liberally than do individuals in the dominated class. López-Sintas and Katz-Gerro (2005: 300) lay out a common interpretation of Bourdieu's discussion of highbrow taste patterns: 'Bourdieu's theory predicts a distinct and univorous consumption pattern for the upper classes, who adopt cultural tastes that are considered highbrow to establish a distinction between them and others'. Bourdieu's work in *Distinction* is used as evidence for the conclusion that high-status persons consume certain things and not others strategically, with the intent of distancing themselves from others of lower status: 'Bourdieu's emphasis on aesthetic distancing is asymmetric, focusing more on high-status people distancing themselves from low-status people than vice versa' (Mark 2003: 325). Van Eijck (2001: 1144) agrees, noting Bourdieu's finding 'that a high status implies snobbery, and, thereby, a consistent aversion to popular culture'.

Scholars routinely conclude that the omnivore phenomenon flies in the face of Bourdieu's own findings and theory: omnivorousness among high-status groups 'represents a potential repudiation of Bourdieu's framework for identifying social classes' (Veenstra 2005: 261). Omnivorous consumption 'blurs the expected relationship between social position and cultural practice on which the sociology of taste has relied from the time of Thorstein Veblen up to that of Pierre Bourdieu' (Bellavance 2008: 1–2). Research done in the wake Peterson's proposal 'has clearly demonstrated that the present socio-cultural reality indeed differs from the one depicted in *Distinction*' (Vander Stichele and Laermans 2006: 46). But is this an accurate interpretation of Bourdieu's substantive claims in *Distinction*?

The following commonly referenced passage in *Distinction* appears to be consonant with this now standard interpretation:

> Tastes (i.e. manifested preferences) are the practical affirmation of an inevitable difference. It is no accident that, when they have to be justified, they are asserted purely negatively, by

the refusal of other tastes. In matters of taste, more than anywhere else, all determination is negation; and tastes are perhaps first and foremost distastes.... The most intolerable thing for those who regard themselves as the possessors of legitimate culture is the sacrilegious reuniting of tastes which taste dictates shall be separated

(Bourdieu 1984: 56–7, quoted in Bryson 1996: 886)

This appears to confirm propositions (1) and (2) above: dominant class members express lots of distaste, and (by implication) those rejected tastes have to be those which are more likely to be expressed by individuals in the dominated class.

We suggest, however, that such a reading represents a fundamental *misreading* of the argument. First, it is not logically necessary to go from Bourdieu's conditional generalization regarding the role of the negation of other tastes as one of the primary ways that aesthetic choices are *justified* to the empirical claim that one 'class' of individuals is more likely to express dislikes than another.[2] Bourdieu is actually talking about the ways that taste operates for *all classes*, and nowhere does he say that taste justification through the negation of other tastes is going to be the exclusive (or even statistically more likely) purview of dominant classes. Instead, he posits that this cultural boundary drawing mechanism via negation of different tastes operates equally across all classes and serves to produce (and re-produce) divisions across the *entire* social field.

This interpretation is supported by the fact that Bourdieu continues the above passage by noting that: 'Aesthetic intolerance can be terribly violent. Aversion to different lifestyles is perhaps one of the strongest barriers between the classes; class endogamy is evidence of this'. Notice that Bourdieu speaks of aversion to different lifestyles as a purview of *all* classes without singling out elites, which is the reason why he uses class endogamy as an empirical index of this fact (Illouz 1998: 248). Recent research that shows that cultural dislikes are more evenly distributed across the class structure of the contemporary US than was initially surmised in Bryson's research (e.g. Tampubolon 2008: 252) are thus consistent with Bourdieu's original proposal.

The second part of the quote, however, appears to claim unequivocally that 'high-status' people are more averse to the 'sacrilegious reuniting of tastes which taste dictates shall be separated', apparently serving to categorically establish proposition (2) above. This reading, however, is incomplete at best. Most commentators and empirical researchers read Bourdieu's phrase 'possessors of legitimate culture' as denoting 'high-status' people, but this is not quite the case. Bourdieu continues: '[t]his means that the games of artists and aesthetes and their struggles for the monopoly of artistic legitimacy are less innocent than they seem.... The *artist's lifestyle* is always a challenge thrown at the *bourgeois life-style*' (Bourdieu 1984: 57, emphasis added).

In this context, it becomes clear that by 'possessors of legitimate culture' Bourdieu meant *cultural producers*, in particular the producers of the aesthetic goods valued by members of the bourgeoisie, or what Goffman (1951: 303–304) referred to as 'curator groups', not 'high-status' classes, as has been assumed in standard readings. Furthermore, the 'aversion' that this group displays to the 'mixing' of tastes *is not directed downwards to the 'lower' classes,* but instead *horizontally* toward the only fraction of the dominant class that would unambiguously deserve to be called 'high status', namely the bourgeoisie, or members of the temporally dominant professions, and owners and managerial staff of the larger industries.

For Bourdieu, cultural and symbolic producers, who display the most self-consciously *aesthetic* 'stylization of life' (in Weber's [1994:114] sense), are always on the lookout to keep their consumption practices 'pure', not from the possible influence of the 'lower' classes (who are too far away in social space and lack the requisite symbolic capital to be any real threat), but from the economically powerful or the truly dominant ('high-status') classes who are closer to them in social space and therefore represent much more of a threat. These attempts at 'distinction' on the part of the 'cultural bourgeoisie' have little to do with 'high-status snobbery', if this is defined as an austere rejection of everything but the most 'refined' pursuits. Instead, this a rejection of the impeding *commercialization* and *standardization* of initially 'alternative' lifestyle choices developed by groups of cultural producers as a self-conscious rejection of the 'instrumental rationality' of the market (Bourdieu 1983; Lamont 1992).

This largely *horizontal* boundary-drawing dynamic is incomprehensible given the mistaken understanding of *Distinction* as suggesting only a dominant/dominated class difference, which (as we elaborate below) implicitly rests on a unidimensional conception of class differentiation. This interpretation is fundamentally at odds with Bourdieu's multidimensional conception of social space. Instead, as Bourdieu unequivocally noted, '[e]xplicit aesthetic choices are in fact often constituted in *opposition* to the choices of the groups *closest* in social space, with whom the competition is most direct and most immediate' (Bourdieu 1984: 60, emphasis added).

To support the claim that *Distinction's* primary focus is on the 'cultured' classes' *rejection* of 'lower' class culture, most researchers cite the 'beautiful photographs' quasi-experimental survey, the results of which are reported in the first chapter of *Distinction* (1984: 36–7). The basic claim is that here Bourdieu attempts to provide empirical evidence that the 'cultured' classes *unconditionally* reject the tastes of the working classes, from whom they wish to 'distinguish' themselves. Because of the importance that this material has acquired in interpretations of Bourdieu's theory of taste, we turn to a consideration of it next. We show that this example has been largely misread by current commentators, and that its implications for understanding the relationship between class and lifestyle choices have therefore been largely under-exploited (but see Holt 1997; Johnston and Baumann 2007:196–200; Prieur and Savage 2013).

What makes a beautiful photograph?

The 'beautiful photographs' quasi-experimental survey[3] was designed to ascertain the extent to which the 'aesthetic disposition' (the ability to take an 'aesthetic stance' towards everyday life objects and not yet officially legitimated cultural goods; more fully defined below) was unequally distributed among the different class fractions. Bourdieu's results are usually interpreted as implying that the higher status classes 'refuse' the tastes of popular admiration, and therefore high-status (or 'cultured') individuals should be expected to be more exclusive in their tastes (Bryson 1996: 886). For instance, Bourdieu (1984: 35) himself notes that '[t]he higher the level of education, the greater is the proportion of respondents who, when asked whether a series of objects would make beautiful photographs, refuse the ordinary objects of popular admiration'. To the best of our knowledge, this is the paradigmatic example in the literature on taste and culture consumption in which the 'snob thesis' imputed to Bourdieu is supported with empirical results.

However, this is not the only possible or even most reasonable reading of the evidence that Bourdieu presents. Notice that while Bourdieu claims that high-status people *are relatively more likely* to reject the objects of working class admiration as being capable of making a beautiful photograph *in comparison to other objects*, he *does not claim* the following two things, which would be logically required for the pure 'snob thesis' to hold: (1) that high-status persons rejected *more objects as capable of being beautiful* than working-class persons did and (2) that working-class and petit bourgeois persons *did not reject* the objects chosen by high-status individuals. The first claim is necessary to support the 'highbrow snobbishness' thesis, and the second to support the 'differential highbrow exclusiveness' thesis – the claim that high-status people are more likely to express dislikes than low-status people are (Bryson 1996).[4]

However, Bourdieu did not claim (1) and (2) above because his data contradict these assertions, and he was well aware of it (Holt 1997: 100; Prieur et al. 2008: 50). First, in regards to (1) above, the results from the beautiful photographs survey show that while it is true that high-status informants were statistically more likely to reject the objects of popular admiration (a first communion, a sunset) in comparison to their endorsement of other objects, they selected *more* objects as capable of being considered beautiful than did working class respondents. In other words, high cultural capital respondents were able to make use of their greater command of the 'aesthetic disposition' to extend the adjective 'beautiful' (and thus aesthetically acceptable) to a *wider range* of objects than were working class respondents. In turn, low-status respondents showed a much more *restricted* capacity to deem unconventional objects as beautiful, thus *deeming a larger number of objects as incapable of being aestheticized* in comparison to respondents with high education backgrounds.

Second, it is clear from Bourdieu's interview data that working-class informants rejected most of the 'mundane' objects chosen by high-cultural-capital respondents as capable of making a beautiful photograph, and were fairly vocal in saying so (Bourdieu 1984: 44–7). This undermines the canonical interpretation of Bourdieu's argument: that elites are *more likely* to be exclusionary, and that this exclusion is primarily directed toward the 'bottom' of the status order. Instead, Bourdieu suggests and finds that cultural boundaries are drawn by both the upper class (*vis-à-vis* the working class *habitus*) *and* the working class (*vis-à-vis* 'Bourgeois' tastes and values). He refers to the working class contrarian stance toward aestheticized goods and performances as an '*anti*-Kantian aesthetic' (Bourdieu 1984: 41–51). This stance subordinates 'form to function' and practicality (Bourdieu 1984: 42), thus inherently conflicting with the formalist aestheticism of the cultured classes, for whom form and content are in principle separable, giving any object the potential to have the 'aura' of the work of art as long as it is (re)presented aesthetically. These latter class fractions are more likely to accept formal aesthetic experimentation on the part of artistic producers for its own sake, rather than tying it to a practical purpose and thus rejecting it as pointless.

The emergence of widespread misconceptions regarding the core argument of *Distinction* appears even more puzzling in light of the fact that the entire book is sprinkled with quantitative survey evidence that contradicts the notion that high-status classes were shown to be 'snobs', and which demonstrates that French respondents were already in the 1960s behaving as one would expect given the theoretical framework laid out by DiMaggio (1987), or the findings reported for American respondents of the same era by Wilensky (1964). That is, highly-educated respondents (especially those whose educational capital outweighed their economic capital) consumed more culture of all forms, displayed more cultural knowledge of theatre, painting and cinema, and reported engaging in more activities (highbrow and 'middlebrow') than respondents of lower educational standing. The empirical evidence that Bourdieu presents throughout the study[5] demonstrates that he did not conceive of high-status consumers as 'snobs'.

The 'beautiful photograph' data reveal an even bigger surprise for proponents of the standard portrayal of the argument laid out in *Distinction*. Bourdieu reports that there is indeed a class fraction that is 'most inclined to say that *all* the objects mentioned could make a beautiful photograph' (Bourdieu 1984: 61). We interpret this as a fairly 'open-minded' attitude toward aesthetic appreciation consistent with the 'intellectualized aestheticism' that Peterson and Kern (1996: 904) see as responsible for the rise of omnivore taste among dominant classes. This group is contrary to the standard high-status snob reading of *Distinction*, itself part of the 'high-status' class (or at least we would like to believe): *higher education teachers*. This is the group, along with '[t]he intellectuals [and the] artists, [who] seem to hesitate between systematic refusal of what can only be, at best, a middle-brow art [photography], and a *selective acceptance which manifests the universality of their culture and their aesthetic disposition*' (Bourdieu 1984: 60, emphasis added).

These high cultural capital respondents' propensity to consider a wide variety of objects as being deserving of aesthetic appreciation, as Peterson (1992) has argued and as we elaborate below, is the dispositional basis of 'cosmopolitan' omnivore taste (Holt 1997, 1998). As Bourdieu (1984: 40) notes in perfect agreement with this view, this generalized aesthetic disposition should be the primary focus of attention since 'nothing more rigorously distinguishes the different classes than the disposition objectively demanded by the legitimate consumption of legitimate works ... and the ... capacity to constitute aesthetically objects that are ordinary or even "common" or to apply the principles of a "pure" aesthetic in the most everyday choices of everyday life'. Bourdieu considered the 'tolerant' capacity to transpose the aesthetic disposition to different realms as differently distributed across class fractions, and in this respect he is in agreement with most contemporary interpretations of the omnivore taste evidence (Peterson 1992; Bryson 1996; Emmison 2003; Ollivier 2004; Warde *et al.* 2008).

Consider, for instance, the *main* (when it comes to arts participation and cultural choices) piece of empirical analysis in *Distinction,* a multiple correspondence analysis (MCA) of various measures of arts consumption and cultural competence along with a select set of socio-demographic markers (Bourdieu 1984: 260–7). Does Bourdieu find that the 'cultured' classes, the keepers of 'legitimate culture' – and the ones most likely to be attracted to 'the works demanding the "purest" aesthetic disposition' (ibid. 263) – are incorrigible snobs who summarily reject middlebrow culture? The answer is *no.* Instead he notes that these class fractions are the ones '*most capable of applying this aesthetic disposition to less consecrated areas,* such as song or cinema', (emphasis added) and are *also* 'interested in abstract painting, visit the Modern Art Museum and expect their friends to be artistic' (ibid. 263). If that does not sound like a description of the taste patterns of cosmopolitan omnivores, we are at a loss as to what would constitute it.

For Bourdieu, the 'puzzling' phenomenon that there existed certain class fractions (those endowed with the most cultural capital from the family environment) who appear to be systematically (and routinely) able to extend their aesthetic disposition *away* from 'the most legitimate areas' of cultural practice in order to consume products hailing from *less*-artistically legitimate cultural sectors, constituted one of the *two* core findings reported in *Distinction* (or one of the 'two basic facts' established by the investigation), and Bourdieu was very clear in saying so (Bourdieu 1984:13). What is surprising about this, given the contemporary opposition between Bourdieu and omnivorousness, is that the differential social distribution of this competence is precisely what is thought to be behind the empirical phenomenon of omnivorousness (Peterson and Kern 1996; Holt 1998; Ollivier 2008). Accordingly, the claim that Bourdieu's theory of taste is incapable of addressing this phenomenon loses most of its force, given the fact that the ability of the cultured classes to incorporate less legitimate cultural forms into their consumption repertoire is one of the core empirical findings that Bourdieu's theory taste is *designed* to explain (Bourdieu 1984: 63).

Is Bourdieu's 'homology' thesis compatible with omnivorousness?

The conception of a high status exclusive consumption pattern represents the first facet of the received view that has marred the understanding of *Distinction*. The second facet revolves around the stubborn but largely unsubstantiated claim that the core of the book deals with the contrast between dominant classes versus the dominated classes. This part of the standard account is particularly damaging, since it has prevented an understanding and empirical assessment of Bourdieu's *actual* class theory (as he had hoped when speculating about possible cross-national extensions of his class-theoretical framework [Bourdieu 1991a, 1991b, 1991c]). Further, it has resulted in the diffusion of a conception of Bourdieu's theory of class as primarily relying on a dichotomous (or single linear continuum) view of classes revolving around a single axis of stratification.

For instance, Chan and Goldthorpe (2007a, 2007b), using micro-level data for a representative sample of the British population, purport to test Bourdieu's 'homology' thesis, which they claim implies the existence of a single 'dominant class' that only consumes high-status culture and rejects all of the rest. Not surprisingly, their data fail to support this hypothesis, instead showing that high-status people consume both popular and traditionally high-status culture. From these results they conclude that Bourdieu's homology thesis is wrong and represents an outdated view of the relationship between social position and culture consumption in modern societies.

Chan and Goldthorpe's research is exemplary of the various fallacies and misunderstandings regarding Bourdieu's theory of taste that we have attempted to highlight in this paper. Not only do they fatally misunderstand what Bourdieu meant by 'homology', and thus interpret Bourdieu's theory in the traditional manner as implying an impregnable separation of high and popular culture, but they uncritically attribute to Bourdieu the standard dichotomous reading of the class structure of late-modern societies as consistent of a binary separating 'high status' from 'low status' classes, and which Bourdieu spent the bulk of *Distinction* trying to do away with.

As argued by some commentators (Wacquant 2005:140–6; Lizardo 2006; DiMaggio 1979:1465) and in Bourdieu's most synaptic (and didactic) attempts to present his class theory (Bourdieu 1990:122–134),[6] Bourdieu thought of the class structure of late modern societies as divided by both *horizontal* and *vertical* boundaries. While in most empirical applications Bourdieu worked (for both theoretical and methodological reasons) with a *bi-dimensional space,* he never suggested that there were *only* two dimensions to this space (in *Distinction* he speaks of a 'three-dimensional space'), only that due to historical reasons, these two dimensions had become the most important in late modern societies (Bourdieu 1996; Wacquant 2005). This is of course an empirical claim that can be put to the test. Bourdieu presents his bi-dimensional models as follows: 'agents are distributed within [multidimensional space], in the first dimension, according to the *overall* volume of capital that they possess and, in the second dimension, according to the *composition* of their capital – i.e. according to the relative weight of the different assets within their total assets' (Bourdieu 1985: 724).

Bourdieu's multidimensional account, in particular his emphasis on the 'chiastic structure' of the dominant class, separates the anti-bourgeois aestheticism of the cultural producers from the ambivalent attitude (Bourdieu 1984: 316) towards the arts and intellectual matters (removed from the profit motive) of members of the 'temporally dominant' occupations and the business-oriented classes, and both of these from the sometimes dismissive attitude toward the most ethereal artistic pursuits demonstrated by the large employers, high-skill technicians and business managers (Bourdieu 1984; Erickson 1996).

For Bourdieu, this rift between 'artists' and 'Bourgeois' (Bourdieu 1984: 176) lifestyles and consumption practices was at the core of cultural conflict and the contest for 'symbolic capital' in the larger struggle for symbolic recognition in the class field. Furthermore, Bourdieu theorizes that since in late-modern societies, cultural capital (measured in large part by educational attainment) continues to be subordinate to the market logic of profit represented by economic capital, those whose only claim to standing rests on cultural (educational) capital (the 'dominated' fraction of the dominant class) would tend to develop oppositional attitudes to the status quo and would attempt to use their facility and greater dominance of cultural and symbolic resources to mark their difference from members of the dominant class.

That is, regardless of the specific historical and institutional arrangements that serve to define certain patterns of culture consumption as high status (or in specific historical or cross-national redefinitions of the high status/low status boundary [DiMaggio 1991]), the homology thesis would predict that we should find that the position of each occupational status group on a multidimensional space composed of lifestyle practices should be largely derivable from their position in the objective hierarchy of cultural and economic resources.

As Wacquant (2000: 115) notes:

> To uncover the social logic of consumption thus requires establishing, not a *direct link between a given practice and a particular class category* (e.g. horseback riding and the gentry), but the *structural correspondences* that obtain between *two constellations of relations, the space of lifestyles and the space of social positions* occupied by the different groups (emphasis added).

Yet, most contemporary analysts have ignored this conception of what the homology thesis implies. They have thus chided Bourdieu for a 'prediction' that he in fact never made and have produced data that 'contradict' a homology thesis – high-status classes consume 'high status' cultural products – that Bourdieu in fact never stated in that naïve form. For instance, Coulangeon and Lemel (2007: 108) conclude that 'our results do not concur with the strict understanding of the homology thesis: highbrow taste in music only concerns a minority, and 'pure' highbrow music fans appear to be very rare, even in high-status groups'. Verdaasdonk claims that 'the homology thesis predicts that the higher the degree of "cultural legitimacy" of a product, the greater the chance that it will be preferred by members of the dominating class; conversely, the lower a product's "cultural legitimacy", the greater the chance that it will appeal to the tastes of members of the dominated class' (2003: 359).

These conclusions only make sense when 'homology' is interpreted in its naïve sense as implying a one-to-one correspondence between an allegedly unidimensional hierarchy of cultural goods and an equally unidimensional social hierarchy of positions. De Nooy's characterization of homology as 'the projection of one space onto another, which is deemed possible because they reflect the same basic (i.e., objective) relations, namely, the distribution of different kinds of capital or power' (2003: 313), is consistent with Bourdieu's intention. However, this more sophisticated notion of homology has played almost no role in driving current research and theory in the sociology of taste, in spite of recent recognition of the overtly 'relational' nature of Bourdieu's conceptualization and the futility of interpreting his results as implying the historical fixity in the *content* of cultural choice patterns (Prieur and Savage 2013: 249). This is in line with recent proposals that have questioned the wisdom of the persistent focus of the sociology of taste on the question of whether high-status people dislike low-status cultures, since 'one could equally ask the question whether high-status people dislike *each other's cultures*' (Tampubolon 2008: 260). For instance, Tampubolon finds a divide within the high-status class by age with regard to taste for heavy metal music, illustrating a non-homogeneous high-status audience segmentation that distinguishes certain high-status individuals from others. We argue that this last issue is precisely what was at the centre of Bourdieu's theoretical project; and this is precisely what Bourdieu finds in the main piece of empirical analysis in *Distinction* (1984: 260–7).

Note, however, that recent research has put into question whether the axis of differentiation based on the *composition* of capital is as important (e.g. second only to the axis indexed by overall volume of capital) as Bourdieu implied. For instance, Bennett *et al.* (2009), in their exemplary analysis of British data from the 'Cultural Capital and Social Exclusion' project, find that an axis analogous to Bourdieu's second axis only shows up in the fourth dimension of their Correspondence Analysis results. Hanquinet *et al.* (2014) argue that the 'modernist' boundary between art and the market (and by implication the cultural and economic capital as oppositional sources of legitimacy) have been blurred in the postmodern turn towards playful transgression and blurring of this very distinction. The implication is precisely that the members of the cultural bourgeoisie are now as embedded in the market as members of the professions and the possessors of the sorts of 'technical capital' traditionally rewarded in the market (Bourdieu 2005: 117).

Omnivorousness and the aesthetic disposition

Most analysts fail to appreciate the fact that Bourdieu's theory of taste constitutes a *cognitive sociology* of class differences in aesthetic dispositions (Lizardo and Skiles 2012). As such, the contemporary relevance of the theory cannot be fully estimated – short of devolving into pseudo-Veblenian platitudes – without noting the role that the notion of the *aesthetic disposition* plays in it. For Bourdieu, the aesthetic disposition was a *generalized* cognitive scheme (a set of habits of perception and appreciation) whose origins were class-marked (because it is mainly fostered in the domestic and scholastic environments). Habitual, long-lasting command of the aesthetic disposition provides members of culturally-privileged class fractions with the ability to *extend* and *transpose* the 'aesthetic' form of appreciation initially reserved for symbolic goods produced in the fine-arts field (artistically 'legitimate' according to Bourdieu), to *any* and *all* objects, including common – and less legitimate – ones. This is the proper theoretical interpretation of the 'beautiful photographs' data from the point of view of the practice theory. For instance, Bourdieu defines the aesthetic disposition as 'the *capacity* to consider in and for themselves, as *form* rather than *function*, not only the works designated for such apprehension, i.e. legitimate works of art, *but everything in the world, including cultural objects which are not yet consecrated*' (Bourdieu 1984: 3, emphasis added).

It is this propensity to transpose the cognitive scheme toward new objects and not the propensity to fix the scheme on its initial prototypical objects (e.g. fine art) that is the key marker of distinction according to Bourdieu. The capacity for permanent extension of the aesthetic disposition (and constant deployment toward the assimilation of new cultural objects) thus accounts for class differences in the quality and quantity of cultural choices. This also explains the phenomenon noted by Bourdieu and subsequent researchers of differences in engagement with all forms of arts among members of specific high and middle status occupations, such as primary and secondary education teachers and other cultural and symbolic producers (Bourdieu 1984; DiMaggio and Useem 1978:188).

The aesthetic disposition is primarily constituted by the ability to perceptually separate *content* (or function) from *form* during everyday aesthetic judgments. Because aesthetic judgments (and thus 'acceptance' of given aesthetic forms) are seen as driven by formal and not 'substantive' (or content-based) considerations, those who wield the aesthetic disposition are (socio)logically inclined to *consider a wider variety* of aesthetic objects, contents, and performances as capable of being 'beautiful' and thus likely to be appreciated (Holt 1998). Accordingly, one way to 'save' Bourdieu's theory from its critics has been precisely to disengage the 'content' of cultural capital from its form (Holt 1997; Bryson 1996). According to this view, while Bourdieu might have been wrong about the *content* of cultural capital (specific forms of high-status pursuits) he was right about its form (aestheticized appreciation).

While we summarily agree that aestheticized appreciation is the key to Bourdieu's notion of cultural capital, we disagree with the claim that Bourdieu was wrong as to the 'content' of cultural capital. The reason for this is that suggesting the separation of content and form is a way to 'save' the theory belies a key misunderstanding. It is precisely the *ability* and *competence* required to separate content from form that is at the basis of the set of class-distributed cognitive schemes that have become valuable for providing 'multicultural capital' (Bryson 1996; DiMaggio and Mukhtar 2004; Emmison 2003). Bourdieu's theory of taste was 'formal' since its original formulation, and thus hardly requires this particular reinterpretation to be saved.

This separation of aesthetic form from content, rather than being required as an analytical move on the part of the theorist to fix the (presumably broken) theory, is precisely what needs to be explained by any sociological theory of cultural appreciation, since – as Bourdieu notes – it is what lay actors who belong to class factions rich in cultural capital routinely do as a matter of course (Illouz 1998; Holt 1997). This is consistent with DiMaggio's (1991: 144) observation that 'the role of formal education in ... [the contemporary] social structure is, as Bourdieu has argued, to inculcate *not tastes per se* but a capacity for aesthetic adaptation' (emphasis added), a capacity that has become even more crucial for the culturally privileged in the context of increasing geographic mobility (Griswold and Wright 2004; van Eijck 2000).

As we have argued, Bourdieu demonstrates in *Distinction* that increasing ability to separate content from form most clearly evinced by members of cultural-capital rich occupational groups (socio)*logically implies the generalization of aesthetic appreciation to a wide variety of possible contents.* This 'aesthetic disposition' can then be thought of as a 'transposable scheme' (Bourdieu 1984: 28), analytically distinguishable from whatever content this disposition was applied to. It is the constant deployment of this scheme by the 'cultured' class fractions which takes aesthetic acceptability away from a consideration of *what* is presented and toward how *any* content could in principle be (re)presented (Bourdieu 1984).

Because the 'cultured' class fractions are also the ones most likely to transpose this scheme to multiple contents, exposure to the material conditions that facilitate its early acquisition both in the household and in the formal educational system is bound to produce a more 'liberal' aptitude to extend the blanket of potential aesthetic value to *a wider variety* of objects and cultural products (as shown by the beautiful photographs data). This is in contrast to the *anti-Kantian* working class aesthetic that reduces form to functionality, does not separate the object represented from the manner in which it is presented, and which thus rejects most attempts at formal experimentation (Bourdieu 1984: 32–4).

This account explains the social rarity (Peterson and Rossman 2008; Ollivier 2008) of *restricting* the aesthetic disposition *only* to the domain of institutionally-prescribed aesthetic goods (what Peterson has referred to as the 'snob' ideal type). In Bourdieu's account, the more self-assured a person is in his or her command of the aesthetic disposition, *the more likely* it is that he or she will attempt to extend it to non-traditional objects (Bourdieu 1984: 63). Thus, in Bourdieu's scheme, 'snobbery,' as traditionally defined in the sociology of taste – liking only institutionally-prescribed cultural goods or what Ollivier (2008: 124) refers to as 'exclusive highbrows' – rather than being a marker of the highest form of aesthetic appreciation, is in fact a clear signal of the *late acquisition* of the aesthetic disposition. Sole consumption of the fine arts to the exclusion of less legitimate forms is thus characteristic of the 'safe' investments made by those who enter the rank of the cultured classes from less-privileged backgrounds, and whose primary source of exposure to the aesthetic disposition happens through formal schooling (Bourdieu 1984: 65).

Finally, since the essence of the 'popular aesthetic' consists in precisely *the negation* that content can be separated from form (Bourdieu 1984: 32–4), 'univore' consumption (Bryson 1997) also follows as a (socio)logical implication, since it is unlikely that the same content (stylistic, aural, linguistic, etc.) will be found in different artistic genres, such as rap and country music (Lizardo and Skiles 2012). This means that as we move down the educational attainment and the 'inherited cultural capital' (e.g. parental education) ladder, and as the chances of deploying the aesthetic disposition concomitantly decrease, we should find that the 'openness' of the person to a wide variety of aesthetic experiences will decrease. This same pattern of 'univorous' rejection of 'artistic' forms is precisely what Bourdieu found in his beautiful photograph quasi-experimental survey (Bourdieu 1984). This is also exactly what contemporary researchers find in regard to other forms of consumption of the popular and fine arts among culturally disadvantaged groups (Blasius and Friedrichs 2008; Trondman 1990; Bryson 1997).

Conclusion

In contrast to the received picture of *Distinction* as an outmoded and irrelevant work, we have shown that *both* the theoretical and empirical patterns reported in *Distinction* continue to have relevance for contemporary theory and research in the sociology of taste, and in many ways represent a largely under-exploited resource. In particular, we argue that Bourdieu's account may help us shed further light on the phenomenon of high-status omnivorousness (Peterson 1992; Peterson and Kern 1996). As such, our aim has been neither to create artificial divisions between theoretical schools nor to attempt to 'reduce' all subsequent work to a Bourdieuian 'master scheme', but to show how Bourdieu's original findings and more recent theoretical proposals and empirical discoveries (Peterson 1992; Lamont 1992; Holt 1998) are *complementary* and capable of being integrated, once we get past the original misunderstandings that block appreciation of the relevance of Bourdieu's work for the contemporary situation.

Notes

1 Also see Bellavance (2008:2), López-Sintas and Katz-Gerro (2005: 300) and Veenstra (2005: 261) for other examples of this interpretation of the inadequacy of Bourdieu's theory of taste to account for omnivorous taste patterns.
2 That would imply that one class is chronically obliged to justify their tastes more often, and according to Bourdieu, high-status classes would be less likely to be required to justify their tastes, since these are taken to be naturally better and therefore require little justification.
3 In a preliminary survey, subjects were shown actual photographs before being asked: 'Given the following subjects, is a photographer more likely to produce a beautiful, interesting, meaningless or ugly photo: a landscape, a car crash, [pebbles, a pregnant woman] etc.?' In the large-scale survey, the interviewers simply named the objects.
4 We have seen in this last regard that Bourdieu thought of the expression of dislikes as common to all classes in their attempts to draw symbolic boundaries, or 'fences' (Douglas and Isherwood 1996) between themselves and other classes.
5 For example, Bourdieu reports that 'cinema-going', a putatively 'popular', or in Bourdieu's terms 'less consecrated', activity, is directly related to education, urban-residence, income and youth (1984: 26). These are the same correlations that scores of subsequent studies have found in more recent data in relation to popular consumption activities akin to going to the movies. Thus there is nothing 'unusual' (or particularly 'French') about Bourdieu's 1960s sample of respondents.

References

Atkinson, W. (2011) 'The context and genesis of musical tastes: Omnivorousness debunked, Bourdieu buttressed', *Poetics*, 39: 169–186.
Bellavance, G. (2008) 'Where's high? Who's low? What's new? Classification and stratification inside cultural "repertoires"', *Poetics*, 36: 189–216.

Bennett, T., M. Savage, E. Silva, A. Warde, M. Gayo-Cal and D. Wright (2009) *Culture, Class, Distinction*, London: Routledge.

Blasius, J. and J. Friedrichs (2008) 'Lifestyles in distressed neighborhoods: A test of Bourdieu's "taste of necessity" hypothesis', *Poetics*, 36: 24–44.

Bourdieu, P. (1983) 'The field of cultural production, or: The economic world reversed', *Poetics*, 12: 311–356.

—— (1984) *Distinction: a Social Critique of the Judgment of Taste*, Cambridge, MA: Harvard University Press.

—— (1985) 'The social space and the genesis of groups', *Theory and Society*, 14: 723–744.

—— (1990) *The Logic of Practice*, Cambridge: Polity Press.

—— (1991a) 'First lecture. Social space and symbolic space: introduction to a Japanese reading of Distinction', *Poetics Today*, 12: 627–638.

—— (1991b) 'Fourth lecture. Universal corporatism: the role of intellectuals in the modern world', *Poetics Today*, 12: 655–669.

—— (1991c) 'Second lecture. The new capital: introduction to a Japanese reading of state nobility', *Poetics Today*, 12: 643–653.

—— (1996) *The State Nobility: Elite Schools in the Field of Power*, Cambridge: Polity Press.

—— (2005) *The Social Structures of the Economy*, Cambridge: Polity Press.

Bryson, B. (1996) 'Anything but heavy metal': symbolic exclusion and musical dislikes', *American Sociological Review*, 61: 884–900.

—— (1997) 'What about the univores? Musical dislikes and group-based identity construction among Americans with low levels of education', *Poetics*, 25: 141–156.

Chan, T.W. and J.H. Goldthorpe (2007a) 'Social stratification and cultural consumption: Music in England', *European Sociological Review*, 23: 1–19.

—— (2007b) 'Social stratification and cultural consumption: The visual arts in England', *Poetics*, 35: 168–190.

Coulangeon, P. and Y. Lemel (2007) 'Is 'Distinction' really outdated? Questioning the meaning of the omnivorization of musical taste in contemporary France', *Poetics*, 35: 93–111.

De Nooy, W. (2003) 'Fields and networks: Correspondence analysis and social network analysis in the framework of field theory', *Poetics*, 31: 305–327.

DiMaggio, P. (1979) 'Review essay: On Pierre Bourdieu', *American Journal of Sociology*, 84: 1460–1474.

—— (1987) 'Classification in art', *American Sociological Review*, 52: 440–455.

—— (1991) 'Social structure institutions and cultural goods: The case of the United States', in P. Bourdieu and J. Coleman, *Social Theory for a Changing Society*, Boulder, CO: Westview Press.

DiMaggio, P. and T. Mukhtar (2004) 'Arts participation as cultural capital in the United States, 1982–2002: Signs of decline?', *Poetics*, 32: 169–194.

DiMaggio, P. and M. Useem (1978) 'Cultural democracy in a period of cultural expansion: The social composition of arts audiences in the United States', *Social Problems*, 26: 179–197.

Douglas, M. and B. Isherwood (1996) *The World of Goods: Towards an Anthropology of Consumption*, New York: Routledge.

Emmison, M. (2003) 'Social class and cultural mobility: Reconfiguring the cultural omnivore thesis', *Journal of Sociology*, 39: 211–230.

Erickson, B.H. (1996) 'Culture, class, and connections', *American Journal of Sociology*, 102: 217–252.

Goffman, E. (1951) 'Symbols of class status', *British Journal of Sociology*, 2: 294–304.

Griswold, W. and N. Wright (2004) 'Cowbirds, locals, and the dynamic endurance of regionalism', *American Journal of Sociology*, 109: 1411–1451.

Hanquinet, L., H. Roose and M. Savage (2014) 'The eyes of the beholder: Aesthetic preferences and the remaking of cultural capital', *Sociology*, 48: 111–132.

Holt, D.B. (1997) 'Distinction in America? Recovering Bourdieu's theory of tastes from its critics', *Poetics*, 25: 93–120.

—— (1998) 'Does cultural capital structure American consumption?', *Journal of Consumer Research*, 25: 1–25.

Illouz, E. (1998) *Consuming the Romantic Utopia: Love and the Cultural Contradictions of Capitalism*, Berkeley, CA: University of California Press.

Johnston, J. and S. Baumann, S. (2007) 'Democracy versus Distinction: A study of omnivorousness in gourmet food writing', *American Journal of Sociology*, 113: 165–204.

Lamont, M. (1992) *Money, Morals, and Manners*, Chicago: University of Chicago Press.

Lizardo, O. (2006) 'The puzzle of women's 'highbrow' culture consumption: Integrating gender and work into Bourdieu's class theory of taste', *Poetics*, 34:1–23.

—— (2008) The question of culture consumption and stratification revisited', *Sociologica: Italian Online Sociological Review*, doi 10.2383/27709.
Lizardo, O. and S. Skiles (2012) 'Reconceptualizing and theorizing "omnivorousness": Genetic and relational mechanisms', *Sociological Theory*, 3: 261–280.
López-Sintas, J. and T. Katz-Gerro (2005) 'From exclusive to inclusive elitists and further: Twenty years of omnivorousness and cultural diversity in arts participation in USA', *Poetics*, 33: 299–319.
Mark, N.P. (2003) 'Culture and competition: Homophily and distancing explanations for cultural niches', *American Sociological Review*, 68: 319–45.
Ollivier, M. (2004) 'Towards a structural theory of status inequality: Structures and rents in popular music and tastes', *Research in Social Stratification and Mobility*, 21: 187–213.
—— (2008) 'Modes of openness to cultural diversity: Humanist, populist, practical, and indifferent', *Poetics*, 36: 120–147.
Peterson, R.A. (1992) 'Understanding audience segmentation: From elite and popular to omnivore and univore', *Poetics*, 21: 243–258.
—— (1997) 'The rise and fall of highbrow snobbery as a status marker', *Poetics*, 25: 75–92.
—— (2005) 'Problems in comparative research: The example of omnivorousness', *Poetics*, 33: 257–282.
Peterson, R.A. and R.M. Kern (1996) 'Changing highbrow taste: From snob to omnivore', *American Sociological Review*, 61: 900–907.
Peterson, R.A. and G. Rossman (2008) 'Changing arts audiences: Capitalizing on omnivorousness', in *Engaging Art: The Next Great Transformation of America's Cultural Life*, New York: Routledge.
Prieur, A., L. Rosenlund and J. Skjott-Larsen (2008) 'Cultural capital today: A case study from Denmark', *Poetics*, 36:45–71.
Prieur, A. and M. Savage (2013) 'Emerging forms of cultural capital', *European Societies*, 15: 246–267.
Tampubolon, G. (2008) 'Revisiting omnivores in America circa 1990s: The exclusiveness of omnivores?', *Poetics*, 36: 243–264.
Trondman, M. (1990) 'Rock taste – on rock as symbolic capital …', in U. Carlsson and K. Roe, *Popular Music Research*, Gothenburg: NORDICOM.
Vander Stichele, A. and R. Laermans (2006) 'Cultural participation in Flanders: Testing the cultural omnivore thesis with population data', *Poetics*, 34:45–64.
van Eijck, K. (2000) 'Richard A. Peterson and the culture of consumption', *Poetics*, 28: 207–224.
—— (2001) 'Social differentiation in musical taste patterns', *Social Forces*, 79: 1163–1185.
Veenstra, G. (2005) 'Can taste illumine class? Cultural knowledge and forms of inequality', *Canadian Journal of Sociology*, 30: 247–279.
Verdaasdonk, H. (2003) 'Valuation as rational decision-making: A critique of Bourdieu's analysis of cultural value', *Poetics*, 31: 357–374.
Wacquant, L.J.D. (2005) 'Symbolic power in the rule of the "state nobility"' in L.J.D Wacquant, *Pierre Bourdieu and Democratic Politics: The Mystery of Ministry*, Malden: Polity Press.
Warde, A. (2005) 'Consumption and theories of practice', *Journal of Consumer Culture* 5: 131–153.
Warde, A., D. Wright and M. Gayo-Cal (2008) 'The omnivorous orientation in the UK', *Poetics* 36: 148–165.
Weber, M. (1994) *Sociological Writings*, New York: Continuum.
Weininger, E.B. (2005) 'Foundations of Pierre Bourdieu's class analysis', in Erik Olin Wright (ed.), *Approaches to Class Analysis*, Cambridge: Cambridge University Press.
Wilensky, H.L. (1964) 'Mass society and mass-culture: Interdependence or independence?', *American Sociological Review*, 29:173–197.

6

A critique of the omnivore

From the origin of the idea of omnivorousness to the Latin American experience

Modesto Gayo

Towards an understanding of the omnivore: Origin, context and definition

In the early 1990s, when the influence of Bourdieusian sociology was spreading worldwide in the sociology of culture, and in the social sciences more generally, an idea emerged that over the years would come to be understood as a fundamental critique of Bourdieu's contribution. This was the idea of the 'omnivore', coined as a provisional term for a social pattern that was interpreted as a new departure or, at the very least, as a significant expression of deep and long-lasting social change. US scholar Richard Peterson is the accepted creator of the notion of the omnivore (Peterson 1992, 1997), an idea that he developed initially with two colleagues, Simkus (Peterson and Simkus 1992) and Kern (Peterson and Kern 1996), in two different studies. In those contributions, the idea of the omnivore was spelt out quite clearly, even though many of the conceptual, explanatory and methodological issues were underdeveloped.

It is crucial to understand that the idea of the omnivore was developed from a position of high status and strong legitimacy in North American sociology. By the early 1990s, Peterson was already a leading figure in US academic circles, specifically in the sociology of culture. His work on cultural industries and cultural production was widely known and recognized by his peers (Battani and Hall 2000; Hirsch and Fiss 2000; Zolberg 2000), and had been published in significant collections or prestigious journals such as *American Sociological Review* and *Poetics*. This legitimacy of origin provided a privileged platform for dissemination of the notion of the omnivore.

Two additional contextual factors shaped the evolution of the concept of the omnivore. The first was its appearance at a time of crisis in critical sociology, faced as it was with the apparent rise of a new world order in which class conflict had diminished (Pakulski and Waters 1996). The new politics of the 1970s and 1980s were supposed to have superseded industrial social class struggles, a view that sociological thinking came belatedly to reflect. Second, the omnivore idea can also be seen as a manifestation of the uneasy relationship of the United States and its population to the very idea of class; and a related unwillingness on the part of North American scholars to accept the validity of Bourdieu's homology thesis (Lamont 1992).

Conceptually speaking, the idea of omnivorousness is quite simple, although later scholarly interpretations of it have varied. The original idea can be usefully summed up by the notion of omnivores as highbrows who also consume mass or popular culture. While this is the most common interpretation of the omnivore, other derivations include definitions of omnivores as:

- First, persons of high status who do not participate in elite expressions of art (Peterson and Simkus 1992). Here, engagement in highbrow or elite art activities in higher status groups is limited to a minority of the group's members, i.e. most of those people do not show culturally elitist behaviour.
- Second, upper-middle-class individuals who consume more popular culture than do working-class people (Peterson and Simkus 1992; Warde *et al.* 2008; Warde and Gayo 2009; Katz-Gerro and Jaeger 2013). This notion emphasizes the high level of across-the-board cultural engagement shown by higher status groups, spanning consumption of both elite and mass cultural forms. Being a fully fledged omnivore is not only about crossing frontiers of class and taste: it also has to do with a good knowledge of more popular cultural expressions and a real participatory engagement with them.
- Third, upper-middle-class individuals consuming more mass culture than before (Peterson and Kern 1996; Peterson 2002). In this understanding, the omnivore is seen as the product of a historical trend linked to the growing prominence of popular culture, having as much to do with change over time as with status and social rank. From this perspective, omnivorousness is symptomatic of a deep social change held to be taking place in the second part of the twentieth century in the United States, and more widely within advanced post-industrial societies (Peterson and Simkus 1992). That change leads to a decline in the absolute numbers of exclusively snobbish or highbrow cultural consumers, with snobs therefore becoming a minority within the already relatively small high-status groups.
- Fourth, although there is resistance to recognizing that the omnivore is not confined to the educated upper middle class, it is sometimes acknowledged that lower social classes or working-class people are increasingly involved in cultural activities. Peterson and Kern (1996) showed that within this trend people in general – including individuals of lower status – were more open than before to appreciation of more, and more varied, styles. Omnivorousness would in this case be part of a general trend in society, affecting all social groups (Peterson 2005). However this conception has not been developed extensively: the working classes were mostly condemned to being univores, while the theoretical debates remained almost blind to their historical transformation.

This plurality of meanings ascribed to the concept of the omnivore has to be foregrounded because from the very start the idea of the omnivore was employed to argue against Bourdieu. Indeed, the idea of a fundamental antagonism remains widespread among scholars. However, this need not be so. When 'omnivorousness' is used simply as a device to explore how engaged middle-class people are with popular culture (Warde and Gayo 2009), it ceases to be necessarily an anti-Bourdieusian resource. It might instead become a way to describe and demonstrate how culturally powerful middle-class individuals are, allowing us to reaffirm the importance of cultural capital.

The theory of omnivorousness?

The omnivore is not, in and of itself, a theory, nor even a hypothesis. At best, it was the name given to an empirical finding. At worst, it became a construct or projection by a certain kind of anti-Bourdieusian scholar. Whatever the case, it became a very common term in works of US and European origin in the field of the sociology of practices and tastes. This helped to turn the omnivore into the lens through which it was understood that social differences became more blurred, with previously class-stratified societies giving way to new lifestyles. In this sense, omnivorousness posited as a pattern of taste plays a similar role to the idea of homology in Bourdieusian thinking. Both are explained by, rather than explanatory of, the social processes or histories in which they are embedded. Each functions as a sociological account of key advanced Western societies such as France and the United States.

The cultural omnivore was a further reiteration of the familiar motif within US sociology which proclaimed that the generation born after the Second World War was more prosperous, educated, open and tolerant than previous generations of North Americans (Brint 1984,1985; Inglehart and Rabier 1986; Inglehart 1991). In fact, writing about the omnivore makes explicit conceptual and explanatory connections between omnivorousness and concepts like cultural openness and, above all, tolerance. Thus, the omnivore is generally seen to be a tolerant highbrow individual. This association with tolerance doubtless heightens the attractiveness of the idea of omnivorousness, allowing it to be viewed as a celebrated liberal value of our days.

Very surprisingly, the idea of tolerance is not critically appraised in most of the literature on the omnivore. So the main problem here goes beyond the fact that the concept of the omnivore is not only used, but assumed as true, with examples eagerly sought and greeted with both relief and acclaim when found (Chan and Goldthorpe 2007a, 2007b; Katz-Gerro and Jaeger 2013). Equally as significant a problem is that the explanatory basis for the notion of the omnivore is rarely even articulated, much less conceptually elaborated and criticized (van Eijck 2000; Warde *et al.* 2007). In other words, tolerance is accepted instinctively as a celebration of a very modern, highly praiseworthy type of individual. From that perspective, the notion of tolerance probably serves the purpose of freeing people from the rules of history or the chains of society. Individuals are freed to make their own choices according to authentic preferences, leaving behind the weight of Bourdieusian homology, that is, the connection between cultural practices and the accumulation of capital. The difficulty with this is that most of this rationale is extremely speculative, as it has never been conclusively demonstrated that the omnivore is in fact an exemplary model of tolerance.

Moreover, even though the omnivore is presented in society as contradicting Bourdieu's analysis about the relation between class and culture, omnivorousness took for granted the Bourdieusian understanding of what highbrow culture is. Peterson and Kern's contribution (1996) is a case in point. The authors proposed that high culture could be understood and measured as a liking for classical music or opera, signing off on a rather limited definition of refinement or assignation of value to particular cultural expressions. This has been a common way of proceeding, and its implications have included a lack of consideration, in much research about cultural practice and social class drawing on the notion of the omnivore, of the idea of distinction. In other words, issues of legitimacy, recognition or the status of cultural practices were neglected. By implication, Bourdieu was partially right in his thinking, at least with respect to the unequal social value of specific cultural practices. Those assumptions could have become problematic, but did not. As a result, the idea of the omnivore contributed to a reduction of the debate about the relation between cultural engagement and social class to a narrower, one-dimensional, discussion about the homology thesis. In the course of this discussion, it was common for scholars to provide evidence showing the democratic nature of the cultural consumption or practices of the educated middle class. In this respect, scholars who favour the notion of omnivorousness have tended to echo Bourdieu in taking it for granted that highly regarded and recognized cultural practices were a matter of interest for the middle classes. In fact, the central point has been considering the expansion of the content of such practices through the incorporation into everyday middle-class life of more popular or mass cultural activities.

Empirical tools and methodological issues

One particularly indicative illustration of the ideologically charged nature of the debate about the omnivore comes from reflecting on the methodologies used by most of those who have given support to the idea. The vast majority have been reluctant to use those statistical techniques commonly associated with Bourdieu, in particular, multiple correspondence analysis (MCA). Put succinctly, the empirical history of the idea of the omnivore started with a regression model (Peterson and Kern 1996) and ended up being tested and supported by latent class analysis (LCA) (López-Sintas and Katz-Gerro 2005; Vander Stichele and Laermans 2006; Chan and Goldthorpe 2007a, 2007b). Anti-Bourdieusians never wanted to be trapped in Bourdieu's perspective, and using other statistical techniques was seen as a way to identify empirical flaws in his thinking. However, from the very beginning, the idea of the omnivore was based on a rudimentary pattern with very thin evidence base.

As mentioned above, the idea of the omnivore takes the distinction between high and low cultures for granted. Within this line of research, that differentiation was never developed as an important object of study in its own right. In fact, a very Bourdieusian status hierarchy of cultural practices was assumed. Therefore, from the very beginning the debate was about the crossing of cultural boundaries of taste, rather than about the frontiers of taste themselves. As such, those 'sacred' limits seemed to endure endlessly through time and space, something which constitutes a largely unchallenged element of the whole debate about class and culture.

It is important to recognize the scarcity of empirical work or data in the realm of cultural practices, mainly collected through national or local surveys. Only very recently have national surveys been conducted in many Western countries, such that at least some country-level data now exists for all Europe, Latin America, Australia and the United States. However, in most cases there have been few iterations of each national study. Data rich settings such as France have been more the exception than the rule. This empirical limitation sets the parameters of the debate, meaning that some of the claims of those scholars who have promoted the idea of the omnivore remain weak or insufficiently grounded.

One of their crucial claims is that cultural omnivorousness as a historical trend has been growing over the past few decades, at least between the 1960s and 1990s. This claim was originally based solely on a very thin comparison between two national surveys, each conducted only in the US, at the start of the 1980s and 1990s, respectively (Peterson and Kern 1996). These authors found that those people who liked classical music had shown a tendency to open their tastes in favour of more popular musical expressions. That was consistent with the idea of the development of a more open and tolerant society, and it is probably that consistency which contributed to making the claim seem plausible. However, it is undeniable that the evidence was still quite weak at this point in time. Not a single attempt was made to measure change within the ten-year time period between the two surveys, nor was there any reference made to data from before the decade in question. Moreover, when, Peterson and Rossman attempted ten years later, in 2002, to test whether that trend towards openness was still in place, they found that the tendency was in fact at that moment in decline (Rossman and Peterson 2005). Instead of concluding that there might therefore be some doubt about the previous findings, comparing 1982 and 1992, Peterson and his colleague chose to claim that over the later period, 1992 to 2002, omnivorousness simply underwent a change in direction, now on the wane. From this perspective, the era of tolerance simply appeared to be coming to an end.

It is striking that an idea that started with a very strong focus on change, using methodologies that tried to address this dimension, ended up being worked in a way that was very much disconnected from any longitudinal analysis. Other than in a very small number of works, the omnivore was measured as a pattern existing at a particular moment in time. Its interpretation was very much oriented against Bourdieu and his followers, and as regards its empirical basis, it was conveniently forgotten that the term omnivorousness had been coined to depict a putative historical trend of change.

Critiques of omnivorousness

Even though the idea of the omnivore has been widely accepted by both anti-Bourdieusians and, sometimes, by Bourdieu's own followers (Warde *et al.* 2007; Bennett *et al.* 2009; Savage and Gayo 2011), it has not been untouched by critiques. These critical comments are varied in both origin and intentions, as will be seen below. In general, they never put into question the importance of omnivorousness; instead they pursue lines of enquiry that will make the attractiveness or desirability of the notion for cultural scholars clear. In other words, most of the critiques are about shedding light on the limited reach of omnivorousness in actual behaviours. To that end, it has been taken for granted that not the snob but the more modern and tolerant high cultural omnivore is a normative, and generally accepted or expected, model of cultural behaviour in a culturally renewed and more open society.

A first important critique of the omnivore came very unexpectedly from its creator, Richard Peterson. As we have seen above, their follow-up study (Rossman and Peterson 2005) attempted to test the continued validity of the pattern of increasing omnivorousness previously discovered by Peterson and Kern (1996). Their finding of decreasing cultural omnivorousness for the US in 2002 when compared to 1992 led them to conclude that the omnivore was a pattern characteristic of a particular period – the last decades of the twentieth century – and subsequently in decline. While their piece has elements of a farewell to omnivorousness, it was unclear whether they thought that this change reinstated Bourdieu's more traditional 'homology thesis'.

A second critique has to do with the actual patterns of cultural participation and taste exhibited by real omnivores. Identified through the use of national surveys of culture, in cases including Great Britain, England and Quebec, these patterns were shown to be extremely heterogeneous (Warde *et al.* 2007; Ollivier 2008; Tampubolon 2010). The conclusion drawn was that there are different types of omnivore. The significance of this is not the plurality itself, but the difficulty associated with the fact that only some of those who show an omnivorous cultural practice are 'real' Petersonian omnivores, that is, snobs who also incorporate mass or more popular cultural expressions in their tastes and activities. It therefore became evident that omnivorousness is not necessarily a measure or a guarantee of a highly educated, modern and tolerant cultural engagement.

A third critical comment was oriented towards broadening the notion of the omnivore, to reduce its association with upper-middle-class practices. Thus it was argued that working class cultural patterns had undergone very important changes over the last decades, also in the direction of making 'workers' more omnivorous than they had been in the first part of the twentieth century (Peterson 2005).

A fourth line of critique concerns Peterson's interpretation of Bourdieu's ideas. Specifically, it calls into question whether Bourdieu really ever ruled out the possibility of people from high-status groups enjoying popular expressions of culture in their everyday lives (Bryson 1996; see Lizardo in this volume). Bryson also argued that the tastes displayed by well-off and highly educated people are actually less exclusive than those of lower-status individuals. Such a finding would transform the trend described by the idea of the omnivore into something to be demonstrated instead of an assumed or given point of departure. In other words, omnivorousness would become a discussion about a possible historical trend, opening the possibility that Bourdieu was misinterpreted.

The Latin American experience and the historical embeddedness of the idea of the omnivore

The Latin American reception of the idea of the omnivore demonstrates how embedded the notion was in a particular intellectual context in which it played a very specific role. As we have seen above, North American academia viewed the omnivore from the beginning as an expression of liberal beliefs. It was accordingly deployed as a weapon or argument against those scholars who resisted changing their view of social class as key for understanding how Western societies work. Sociology as a discipline, and sociologists or scholars working in this area, have been heavily influenced by discourses of social change, historically rooted in social class struggles and their institutionalization in political parties, trade unions and social movements (Burawoy 2005). So deeply implanted is this idea that it very likely constitutes common sense for many sociologists in Europe and the United States. However, it is essential to understand that in Latin America, the type of critical analysis and research that European and North American scholars usually associate with the sociology of culture was mostly led by anthropologists. This does not mean that sociologists have not been significantly involved in research and debate on culture across Central and South America (see for example Brunner et al. 1989; Catalán and Torche 2005; Gayo et al. 2009; Gayo 2013). The point is rather that most of the leading ideas within the revival of social scientific study of culture since the 1980s and 1990s, in Latin America, have been produced and promoted by scholars identified with, and working within, the discipline of anthropology. This dominance of the anthropological view is intimately connected with other reasons why importation of the idea of the omnivore into Latin America academia has confronted many difficulties.

One of these difficulties has been the successful installation of the idea of 'hybridity', elaborated and defended by renowned Latin American scholar García Canclini (Nivón, 2012). This concept has become a key term in the Latin American academic and political lexicon relating to culture. It fits very well with a tradition of studies that recognizes the extremely long-lasting and significant influence of the region's history of colonization. In more recent times, hybridity has also been useful for conceptualizing migratory processes, not least those occurring within Latin America. This fact goes hand in hand with a strong analytical and interpretive focus on national cultures and the influence of globalization (García Canclini 2004).

The Mexican experience in this regard has become very significant, at a time when thinking about the historical constitution of Latin American societies has become important (Mejía Arango 2009).

Furthermore, an approach informed by a tradition of cultural studies very much linked to the anthropological view has featured very centrally in research on culture in Latin America. This has proved an additional obstacle to wide engagement with debates about the omnivore, for reasons that may become clearer if we understand that Latin American experts on culture, even sociologists, were usually trained in a tradition very much influenced by French critical social science thinking and the centrality of the essay or a sort of humanistic reflection, instead of using empirical methods. Additionally, even where more 'hard-science' approaches were taken, qualitative anthropological methodologies predominated (Sunkel 2006). Scholarly construction of the idea of the omnivore, by contrast, has been largely led by statistical procedures, with little consideration or adoption of ethnographic approaches as a methodological alternative.

Regarding the methodological point, Latin America has also suffered until very recently from a dearth of statistics. This absence has made it very difficult to engage with debates in which numbers have been at the very core of the discussion, as has been the case with much research on omnivorousness. Today, we can perhaps see the beginnings of a possible change, as national surveys on culture have now been conducted in countries including México, Chile, Uruguay, Colombia and Argentina. Unfortunately, dataset access is very often restricted and/or available only on a paid-for basis.

The idea of the omnivore therefore had to compete, on arrival, with anthropological hegemony in Latin American social scientific study of culture and also with the type of theoretical currents and thematic foci in vogue at the time in the region. Chile offers one useful example, as a country in which, in the 1990s, social change was largely being understood through variants of the theory of individualization (PNUD 2002). Since individualization had, as a theory, staunchly rejected any emphasis on social classes from the moment of its inception (Beck and Beck-Gernsheim 2002), it was not particularly receptive to an agenda focused on the relationship between class and culture.

Another reason for the relative lack of acceptance of the idea of the omnivore may be the persistence of evident social inequalities in Latin America that are moreover mainly economic rather than cultural (Corporación Latinobarómetro 2013). Latin American societies are totally informed by class. While it is true that there have been historical processes of construction of a sort of egalitarianism around the idea of a middle class, these have been only partially successful (Franco *et al.* 2010). Class inequality has certainly been taken into account by Latin American experts on culture. It has not, however, been afforded in-depth or systematic treatment, often constituting a secondary topic of analysis and/or being treated as one variable among others such as gender, race or education (Sunkel 2006).

The idea of the omnivore hinges on the European confrontation between middle-class and working-class cultures, in which the former is seen as superior or more legitimate in a Weberian sense, whereby middle-class culture is highly valued or recognized by working class people. Latin America however combines a more diffuse notion of the nature of the working class, and a less sharp self-consciousness of membership in it, with high levels of attention and value placed on popular culture by cultural scholars (Facuse 2011; Sunkel 2006). Popular culture is often seen as an expression of resistance to the imposition or inculcation of a hegemonic culture that only benefits an alien and/or privileged elite minority. Scholarly discourse about democratizing social change has therefore been conducted not through reworking the link between middle class and mass culture, as with the omnivore, but rather through a valorization of the performers and representatives of expressions of popular culture (Facuse 2011; Tijoux *et al.* 2012).

An additional difficulty has to do with the way Bourdieu's contribution has been translated into actual social thinking about culture in Latin America. While Bourdieu has certainly been read, interpreted and used by researchers working in this region, the incorporation of his ideas has been restricted or partial. While examples do exist of studies of cultural practice that show a genuine interest in the influence of economic and cultural capital, most pay attention only to the homology thesis (Gayo *et al.* 2009). This line of research has been mostly led by anthropologists, and only in the past decade have new ways of looking at cultural practices been explored. This has mainly been as a result of the advent of scholars with expertise in the sociology of culture, some trained in the United Kingdom, France, or, to a lesser extent, the US. These researchers are more familiar with the idea of the omnivore, and their contributions have been crucial in introducing or bringing the notion to Latin American sociological debates on culture (Gayo *et al.* 2009; Torche 2010). However, since these scholars are relatively new, the impact of their contributions has not yet been fully felt in the field of the sociology of culture in Central and South America. On the other hand, Bourdieu has been very influential in the sociology of education, helping to introduce topics such as the relationship between parental capital and children's school success. Bourdieu's main Latin American following has in other words been more focused on education than on questions of cultural activism and taste.

The recent nature of the incorporation of 'new' debates such as that of the omnivore to Latin America also, by definition, means that these have not reached the point of intellectual maturity that they currently enjoy in Europe and the United States. The development of a critical mass of knowledge and ideas about Bourdieu's contribution, a prerequisite for reaching such a point, is still incipient, particularly in the sociology of culture, where this area of research has not moreover been a priority. Other topics, such as education and work, have been seen as more fundamental for understanding Latin American societies.

If the idea of the omnivore was rooted, as we have seen, in the uneasiness of North Americans with the French homology thesis, Latin America displays no similar feeling or spirit of rivalry with France. Nor is France necessarily viewed primarily as a society riven with social inequalities and class culture. On the contrary, France is often admired within Latin America as a place of high culture, economic development and modernity. North American sociology has moreover had a very limited influence on Latin American critical sociology, which has mostly been shaped by European thinking, in which the omnivore does not feature.

The Latin American social sciences have of course been very much affected by the region's political history. In particular, the history of authoritarianism and dictatorships has limited the development of sociology, and of critical thinking in general. Recent authoritarian regimes opposed a wide and open institutionalization of the social sciences. However Mexico, Argentina, Brazil and to a lesser extent cases like Chile have seen a blossoming of the disciplines of sociology and anthropology as democracy has become the rule over the past three decades, although neoliberal ideas have not promoted powerful critical agendas.

Notwithstanding all of these conditioning factors, we do find examples in the region of using the idea of the omnivore, mostly by sociologists trained in US or European universities. A handful of scholars working on culture and researching Latin American countries introduced the idea of the omnivore in contexts where that notion was very alien to the way the academic field of the study of culture had developed over the preceding thirty years. The very limited use of the omnivore idea accordingly mirrors the trajectory of those researchers, who have developed a very restricted version of omnivorousness, something which can be explained by their participation in particular international academic networks and agendas (Torche 2010). In its current state, the Latin American omnivore is more an imitation than a proper 'aboriginal' type of cultural consumer or practitioner.

Evaluating research outcomes: Omnivorousness as a dead end

The idea of the omnivore has reached a point of stasis, which can be understood as a *'cul de sac'* signalling the end of the road for a line of research quite homogeneous and densely populated. The scarcity of new ideas points not only to a lack of sociological imagination, but also, more importantly, to the theoretically limited nature of a concept around which few ideas have blossomed.

The omnivore began as a description of a pattern of taste and cultural practice that could genuinely help to shed light on issues probably undervalued by Bourdieu's work. To that extent, it was successful in bringing to the fore less snobbish ways of looking at culture from the vantage point of the privileged upper middle class. Although the history of the relationship between class and culture has not been researched extensively enough to allow the drawing of definitive general conclusions, there was sound enough evidence for omnivorousness to demonstrate a reasonably peaceful cohabitation of highbrow and mass or popular culture. The slew of subsequent scholarly contributions in favour of the same idea is however difficult to justify from the intrinsic academic value of the evidence provided and reasoning applied, for several reasons.

Firstly, the argument was presented as a reaction against Bourdieu. It is however unconvincing to contend that the mere existence of the omnivore necessarily calls the idea of homology into question. In other words, the value assigned to the idea of the omnivore is based upon a particular interpretation of the homology thesis, or the Bourdieusian understanding of the relation between class and culture. From the standpoint of those who advocate the thesis of the omnivore, Bourdieu's work holds that social classes would have exclusive and incompatible cultural practices. However, this is a very restricted understanding of Bourdieu's work (Bryson 1996).

Secondly, in many works favouring the idea of the omnivore, the data analysed was very poor. In this respect, it has been common to base claims about the omnivore pattern on the use of only a very few variables (Chan and Goldthorpe 2007a, 2007b). The results of this type of analysis doubtless produced evidence of a mixing of tastes, but at the same time betrayed a lack of interest in the process of distinction, that is, in social field analysis, and in class analysis more generally. The role of social classes in accounting for people's cultural practices was downplayed. Bourdieu's thinking is more about this 'classist' way of looking at cultural patterns, and the question of whether his theoretical approach, based on capital, is in fact incompatible with a *de facto* mixing of cultural practices is, at least, uncertain or open.

Thirdly, in terms of the productivity and originality of articles and contributions arguing in favour of the omnivore, we have seen very repetitive findings whose potential contribution to the evolution of theory remains unclear. If it is simply the case that all or most cultural expressions are now accessible and popular, it might be concluded that culture has ceased to play a relevant role in the construction of, and interplay between, social classes. This would render culture a less attractive topic for sociologists whose views are shaped by traditions such as the Bourdieusian school, very much concerned as it is with inequalities, stratification and social classes. In other words, the omnivore might have contributed to a trend towards closing down lines of research linked with critical sociological thinking.

Fourthly, one of the main hindrances for theoretical work based on the omnivore is that the concept lacks a proper explanatory level. We can play with very simple, or more complex, notions of omnivorousness, but we do not know much about its connections with other social variables. There is quite a lot of speculation about the social characteristics and changes which have supposedly fed the emergence of the omnivore (Peterson and Kern 1996), but there is little actual analysis of its history, such as could open up other important lines of research, including potential lines of critique.

Taken together, these objections suggest that omnivorousness was less about a social relation than about something occurring at the level of the individual. Even if there was evidence of an increasingly tolerant standpoint at this level, further work on the notion neglected to call into question the actual significance of cultural practices in the formation of social hierarchies. This omission was supposedly rectified by demonstrating over and over how common it is in modern societies for people to combine tastes that were considered incompatible just a few decades earlier. However, the discovery or portrayal of those 'successful' and 'welcome' combinations of tastes have not per se resolved the question of whether or not the formation and reproduction of social hierarchies is still connected with disputes over cultural capital.

Concluding remarks

The notion of the omnivore was coined in a pragmatic manner to demonstrate that US society was increasingly open or tolerant from a cultural perspective. From the 1950s and 1960s onwards, a new generation of young people showed that very diverse tastes could coexist not only in the same society, but moreover within the cultural practices of many individuals. Well educated young people, particularly, combined highbrow practices with others considered more massive and popular. These people became the quintessential omnivores. The idea was rapidly successful, not least because it came from a legitimated position in the academic field, and it became particularly popular amongst anti-Bourdieu scholars.

However, the idea of the omnivore presented serious difficulties. On the one hand, it has neither developed nor contributed to the development of a realistic theoretical alternative to Bourdieu's work. The concept has been clearly under-theorized, probably because it was taken at face value as a self-evident, empirical pattern that challenged the ideas about the relationship between class and culture promoted by the Bourdieusian school. In point of fact, the underlying evidence for the notion was thin or unclear from the very beginning. The longitudinal aspect of omnivorousness was never researched or well developed, while the variables used for its analysis were usually scarce and not very well justified. Such analyses moreover took for granted an old distinction between high and low culture, leading to 'very evident' conclusions that have been widely accepted even though more work clearly needs to be done about the social status and recognition of cultural practices.

It is important to acknowledge that the interest in the idea of omnivorousness is rooted in a particular academic field and scholarly culture, within which what it is at stake is the value of particular sociological stances. The current moment is one in which the relevance of social class analysis is in dispute, with the Bourdieusian approach as only one example. One way to understand the radical significance of this particular intellectual context is to look to scholarship in and from areas of the world which have had a weak connection with the omnivore debate. The Latin American experience can be instructive in this regard. If the idea of the omnivore evolved fundamentally from the 1990s onwards, leading scholars of culture in Latin America did not engage much with this notion. From the 1980s onward, they were instead working within a political and intellectual paradigm in which the concept of 'hybridity' played a central role. This concept was not particularly rooted in class, emphasizing rather the ways in which national cultures had been constituted through constant information flows and encounters between populations with different origins. Phenomena such as migration and globalization were key elements in this whole rationale. These studies were mainly led by anthropologists, to whom the idea of the omnivore has been quite alien.

Finally, the idea of the omnivore came about in a very pragmatic way, based upon thin evidence and some intuition and speculation. It was nonetheless surprisingly successful, and became very widely used. While it may have started out as little more than a pattern, for many scholars it acquired the status of a paradigm, seen as a synthesis of a tolerant and culturally democratic historical moment, the 'age of the omnivore'. That success was frequently interpreted as a clear symptom of the end of the reign of Bourdieu. However, the shaping of the idea of the omnivore was very Bourdieusian, while never developing a deep theoretical basis in its own right. In the end, and quite paradoxically, by not being able to gain the status of a theory, the omnivore may have helped to keep Bourdieu's contribution to sociological thinking alive.

Acknowledgements

This chapter was written with the support of the Chilean government, via FONDECYT project no. 1130098, entitled 'Capital cultural y territorio en Chile. La estructuración territorial del espacio social más allá de los capitales'.

References

Battani, M. and J. Hall (2000) 'Richard Peterson and cultural theory: From genetic to integrated and synthetic approaches', *Poetics*, 28: 137–156.
Beck, U. and E. Beck-Gernsheim (2002) *Individualization*, London: Sage.
Bennett, T., M. Savage, E. Silva, A. Warde, M. Gayo-Cal and D. Wright (2009) *Culture, Class, Distinction*, London: Routledge.
Brint, S. (1984) '"New-class" and cumulative trend explanation of the liberal political attitudes of professionals', *American Journal of Sociology*, 90(1): 30–69.
—— (1985) 'The political attitudes of professionals', *Annual Review of Sociology*, 11: 389–414.
Brunner, J.J., A. Barrios and C. Catalán (1989) *Chile: transformaciones culturales y modernidad*, Santiago de Chile: Facultad Latinoamericana de Ciencias Sociales (FLACSO).
Bryson, B. (1996) '"Anything but heavy metal": Symbolic exclusion and musical dislikes', *American Sociological Review*, 61(5): 884–899.
Burawoy, M. (2005) '2005 ASA presidential address: For public sociology', *American Sociological Review*, 70(1): 4–28.
Catalán, C. and P. Torche (eds.) (2005) *Miradas y perspectivas. Consumo cultural en Chile*, Santiago de Chile: Publicaciones INE, Consejo Nacional de la Cultura y las Artes.
Chan, T.W. and J.H. Goldthorpe (2007a) 'Social stratification and cultural consumption: The visual arts in England', *Poetics*, 35: 168–190.
—— (2007b) 'Social stratification and cultural consumption: Music in England', *European Sociological Review*, 23(1): 1–19.
Corporación Latinobarómetro (2013) *Informe 2013*, Santiago, Chile. Available online at www.latinobarometro.org/documentos/LATBD_INFORME_LB_2013.pdf (accessed 26 March 2014).
Facuse, M. (2011) 'Poesía popular chilena: Imaginarios y mestizajes culturales', *Atenea*, 504, II semestre: 41–53.
Franco, R., M. Hopenhayn and A. León (eds.) (2010) *Las clases medias en América Latina*, México DF: Siglo XXI, CEPAL.
García Canclini, N. (2004) *Diferentes, desiguales y desconectados: Mapas de la interculturalidad*, Barcelona: ed. Gedisa.

Gayo, M. (2013) 'La teoría del capital cultural y la participación de los jóvenes: El caso chileno como ejemplo', *Última Década*, CIDPA Valparaíso, 38, July: 141–171.

Gayo, M., B. Teitelboim and M.L. Méndez (2009) 'Patrones culturales de uso del tiempo libre en Chile. Una aproximación desde la teoría bourdieuana', *Revista Universum* 24(2): 42–72.

Hirsch, P.M. and P.C. Fiss (2000) 'Doing sociology and culture: Richard Peterson's quest and contribution', *Poetics*, 28: 97–105.

Inglehart, R. (1991) *El cambio cultural en las sociedades industriales avanzadas*, Madrid: Siglo XXI, CIS.

Inglehart, R. and J.-R. Rabier (1986) 'Political realignment in advanced industrial societies: From class-based politics to quality-of-life politics', *Government and Opposition*, 21(4): 456–479.

Katz-Gerro, T. and M.M. Jaeger (2013) 'Top of the pops, ascent of the omnivores, defeat of the couch potatoes: Cultural consumption profiles in Denmark 1975–2004', *European Sociological Review*, 29(2): 243–260.

Lamont, M. (1992) *Money, Morals and Manners: The Culture of the French and American Upper-Middle Class*, Chicago: The University of Chicago Press.

López-Sintas, J. and T. Katz-Gerro (2005) 'From exclusive to inclusive elitists and further: Twenty years of omnivorousness and cultural diversity in arts participation in the USA', *Poetics*, 33: 299–319.

Mejía Arango, J.L. (2009): 'Apuntes sobre las políticas culturales en América Latina, 1987–2009', *Pensamiento Iberoamericano*, 4: 105–129.

Nivón, E. (ed.) (2012) *Voces híbridas. Reflexiones en torno a la obra de García Canclini*, México DF: Siglo XXI Editores, Universidad Autónoma Metropolitana.

Ollivier, M. (2008) 'Modes of openness to cultural diversity: Humanist, populist, practical, and indifferent', *Poetics*, 36: 120–147.

Pakulski, J. and M. Waters (1996) *The Death of Class*, Thousand Oaks, CA: Sage.

Peterson, R. (1992) 'Understanding audience segmentation: From elite and mass to omnivore and univore', *Poetics*, 21: 243–258.

—— (1997) 'The rise and fall of highbrow snobbery as a status marker', *Poetics*, 25: 75–92.

—— (2002) 'Roll over Beethoven, there's a new way to be cool', *Contexts*, 1: 34–9.

—— (2005) 'Problems in comparative research: The example of omnivorousness', *Poetics*, 33: 257–282.

Peterson, R.A. and R.M. Kern (1996) 'Changing highbrow taste: From snob to omnivore', *American Sociological Review*, 61(5): 900–907.

Peterson, R.A. and A. Simkus (1992) 'How musical tastes mark occupational status groups', in M. Lamont and M. Fournier (eds.), *Cultivating Differences*, Chicago: The University of Chicago Press, pp. 152–187.

PNUD (2002) *Informe sobre Desarrollo Humano en Chile. Nosotros los chilenos: un desafío cultural*, Santiago de Chile.

Rossman, G. and R. Peterson (2005) 'The instability of omnivorous cultural taste over time', paper presented at the annual meeting of the American Sociological Association, Philadelphia, 12 August.

Savage, M. and M. Gayo (2011) 'Unravelling the omnivore: A field analysis of contemporary musical taste in the United Kingdom', *Poetics*, 39: 337–357.

Sunkel, G. (2006) *El consumo cultural en América Latina*, Bogotá: Convenio Andrés Bello.

Tampubolon, G. (2010) 'Social stratification and cultures hierarchy among the omnivores: Evidence from the Arts Council England surveys', *The Sociological Review*, 58(1): 1–25.

Tijoux, M.E., M. Facuse and M. Urrutia (2012) 'El Hip Hop: ¿Arte popular de lo cotidiano o resistencia táctica a la marginación?', *Polis*, 33: 429–449.

Torche, F. (2010) 'Social status and public cultural consumption: Chile in comparative perspective', in T.W. Chan (ed.), *Social Status and Cultural Consumption*, Cambridge (UK) and New York: Cambridge University Press, pp. 109–136.

Vander Stichele, A. and R. Laermans (2006) 'Cultural participation in Flanders: Testing the cultural omnivore thesis with population data', *Poetics*, 34: 45–64.

van Eijck, K. (2000) 'Richard A. Peterson and the culture of consumption', *Poetics*, 28: 207–224.

Warde, A. and M. Gayo (2009) 'The anatomy of cultural omnivorousness: The case of the United Kingdom', *Poetics*, 37: 119–145.

Warde, A., D. Wright and M. Gayo (2007) 'Understanding cultural omnivorousness, or the myth of the cultural omnivore', *Cultural Sociology*, 1(2): 143–164.

—— (2008) 'The omnivorous orientation in the UK', *Poetics*, 36(2): 148–165.

Zolberg, V.L. (2000) 'Richard Peterson and the sociology of art and literature', *Poetics*, 28: 157–171.

7
Age-period-cohort and cultural engagement

Aaron Reeves

Introduction

A crucial question for cultural sociologists is how patterns of taste and cultural practice vary across time (Reeves 2014; Jaeger and Katz-Gerro 2010). Does cultural engagement increase with age (Scherger 2009)? Have there been historical shifts in the nature of cultural capital? Has snobbery declined since the 1980s? Despite this interest, the relationship between time and taste remains under-examined. Understanding this association requires that researchers attend to three distinct dimensions of time: age (how old people are when data collection occurs), period (when data collection occurs), and cohort (the year or period in which people were born) (Yang et al. 2008). Differences between age-period-cohort (APC) effects are described in this fictional dialogue, adapted from Suzuki (2012: 452):

> A: I don't enjoy the cinema anymore. Guess I'm just getting old. [Age effect]
> B: Do you think it's just what has been available? The films have been pretty poor this year. [Period effect]
> A: Maybe. What about you?
> B: Actually, I have been dissatisfied too! I haven't seen anything I really enjoyed either.
> A: You're kidding. Almost all the new releases seemed aimed at your age group. I would have loved those films when I was your age.
> B: Oh, really?
> A: Yeah, young people these days are never satisfied. We were not like that. [Cohort effect].

Cultural sociology has examined extensively the association between taste and a range of social and political dimensions, including class, status, gender, religion and political ideology (Bourdieu 1984; Chan 2010; Bennett et al. 2009), and yet, despite this broad and growing literature, much less attention has been directed toward temporality more broadly.

There are three primary reasons for this neglect: first, inadequate data. Until recently there have been very few repeated cross-sectional surveys of cultural practice conducted with sufficient regularity. Individual-level longitudinal data sets which follow particular respondents over time while measuring taste are even rarer. Second, traditional linear regression models are unable to resolve the identification problem in estimating age-period-cohort effects. The identification problem is, in short, the logical impossibility of including measures of age, period and cohort in the same mathematical model. Thus, identifying the effect of age on omnivorousness – the extent to which people's taste ranges across different genres – is impossible in that framework. Third, not only is there a methodological problem in estimating age-period-cohort effects, there are also theoretical challenges in how sociologists conceptualize the relationship between these three variables (Lizardo and Skiles 2012). Cultural sociologists in particular should be concerned with these issues because of the potential cohort effects on taste.

Three recent developments make this an excellent time to reconsider age-period-cohort effects in relation to cultural sociology. The availability of good data – which captures individuals over time and which measures cultural preferences and practice at regular (e.g. annual) intervals – is increasing. In tandem, over the last decade there have been a number of important contributions to the methodological literature on age-period-cohort effects which alter the kinds of questions that can now be asked (Luo 2013a, 2013b). Finally, insights from cognitive sociology, particularly as applied to Bourdieu's sociological apparatus, have provided new ways of thinking about how cultural preferences are generated and maintained while situating such discussions in broader debates about social change (Vaisey 2009).

In this chapter, I bring together some of these developments by discussing the age-period-cohort identification problem in light of the specific theoretical concerns of cultural sociology. This chapter will firstly outline some of the challenges age-period-cohort analysis poses for Bourdieu's work while situating these debates in the context of the omnivore thesis (see also, the papers by Karademir Hazır and Warde and by Gayo in this volume). Secondly, I will outline the identification problem associated with estimating age-period-cohort effects while summarizing some of the recent methodological innovations attempting to solve it. Thirdly, I will discuss the implications of these methodological and theoretical issues for conceptualizing age-period-cohort effects in the context of Bourdieu's work. Fourth, I will explore the implications of these theories for how researchers think about age-period-cohort effects in relation to the omnivore thesis.

Bourdieu, time and omnivores

Bourdieu was concerned with the composition of social practices in the context of processes of socio-cultural change. His interest in cultural engagement is centred around a set of questions pertaining to how and why certain cultural dispositions are associated with specific social groups (Bourdieu 1984; Bourdieu and Passeron 1979). For example, his concept of the habitus captures both how and why highbrow cultural practices are more common among elite groups but not others. Bourdieu (1984) defines habitus as 'a structuring structure', in that it organizes the social world and classifies it, and as 'a structured structure', in that this classificatory system is itself the product of 'internalization of the division into social classes'. Cultural practices differ across social classes because the classificatory systems that determine which practices are highly valued (or not) are grounded in social position.

Bourdieu's theory of social change is far less concerned with how such change might occur; instead he wants to understand why socio-cultural norms and structures are reproduced. This leads Bourdieu to theorize, again using the habitus, the conditions that facilitate or inhibit such change in general. The habitus has a critical role in perpetuating and reproducing the socio-cultural norms and social structures that link social position and patterns of cultural practice. In this sense, the habitus is a stable way of relating to the world that develops during the early years and which adapts to commonly changing circumstances, such as age.

Much of the secondary literature utilising Bourdieu's work has been principally concerned with the association between social position and the composition of social and cultural practices. Due to this emphasis on stratification, the implications of his work for examining how age, period and cohort effects have not been fully developed. Part of the reason for this neglect is that Bourdieu himself does not directly address these debates, and his account of the influence of age is under-developed. For example, Bourdieu's focus on the 'objective gap between the slope of [the] actual trajectory' of an individual through the social space and 'the modal trajectory of their group of origin' (1996: 185) suggests that he would anticipate a primarily smooth age trajectory. That is, he would anticipate the individual to follow the trajectory of the group of origin with relatively little deviation over time. Although Bourdieu acknowledged that changes to the cultural field could occur, with implications for the relationships between habitus and cultural practice (i.e. what is considered to be culturally valuable), he believes such changes are uncommon and represents them as a form of 'crisis'. While this may be accurate, as Bottero (2009) observes, this notion of 'crisis' (or period effect) is not explored in detail and so stability rather than change is emphasized. In addition, Bourdieu's vision of the habitus does not fully account for change across cohorts. To extend the crisis example, how will changes to the cultural field influence the habitus of those socialized under new cultural regimes?

This gap in Bourdieu's account is particularly evident in connection with the omnivore thesis; the most prominent example of the post-Bourdieusian research stream (Peterson and Kern 1996; Peterson and Simkus 1992). The omnivore thesis has an important place in this age-period-cohort debate because it is at the centre of the critique of Bourdieu-inspired cultural sociology and because it makes specific and testable claims.

Central to the omnivore thesis is the contention that educated and professional individuals are more likely to express preferences for cultural items and activities that cut across traditional status boundaries between, for example, music genres (Peterson and Kern 1996; Peterson and Simkus 1992). This new type of cultural consumer was the hypothesized consequence of profound socio-cultural changes during or just prior to the 1980s which altered status-group dynamics and cultural norms (Peterson and Kern 1996). Omnivores were products of something other than age effects because people had previously aged without becoming omnivorous. They therefore emerged from a mixture of period and cohort effects. Despite these claims, very little work has examined whether any of these factors did, in fact, contribute to the rise of the omnivore and there remains a great deal of conceptual ambiguity around what precisely defines this type of cultural consumer (van Rees et al. 1999).

In contrast to Peterson, the implications of Bourdieu's thinking are to suggest that omnivorousness is not a new phenomenon. As far back as *The Inheritors* (published in 1964 in France) Bourdieu and Passeron (1979) were drawing attention to groups of students who were blending high- and lowbrow cultural goods. Bourdieu's concept of habitus, with its emphasis on the development of cognitive structures during the formative years of a child's life, suggests that period effects occurring in mid-life should not radically alter the stable dispositions that influence patterns of cultural practice. Period effects will only influence patterns of cultural engagement to the degree to which they reconfigure the structure of the cultural field, i.e. instigate a 'crisis'. Hence, cohort effects and, to a lesser extent age effects, are more important for Bourdieu than period effects: suggesting that the rise of the omnivore will likely be overemphasized in the work of Peterson (Jaeger and Katz-Gerro 2010).

In summary, Bourdieu's account of socio-cultural change does not clearly articulate how age-period-cohort effects may interact with the habitus in shaping cultural practice over time. Of course, this neglect is understandable. Bourdieu did not have longitudinal data, and there are longstanding theoretical and methodological challenges associated with estimating APC effects. However, key questions in the omnivore debate can only be resolved through examining age-period-cohort effects, and so addressing these methodological and theoretical questions becomes particularly important.

Interpretation of the habitus: Insights from the APC

Age-period-cohort analysis and the identification problem

Variation in omnivorousness or cultural participation over time can be explained in terms of age, period and cohort (APC) effects (Yang 2007). These apparently simple concepts need to be explained in more detail. Change associated with reaching a particular age (e.g. turning 40), regardless of the year of birth, is an age effect. Age effects are regular changes which are observed across time and place. Although changes in health are not strictly age effects, they are frequently associated with it (Yang 2007: 20). Age is a crucial dimension in social science research, associated with a wide range of sociological outcomes (Voas and Crockett 2005). Period effects are the consequence of changes in a society at a particular point in time that affect all age groups simultaneously (e.g. WWII). These social and historical changes can affect an individual's political views, vocabulary and health (Wilson and Gove 1999). Cohort effects are changes which occur across groups of individuals who experience a similar event (such as birth in the same year). Birth cohort 'membership may be thought to index the unique historical period in which a group's common experiences are embedded' (Alwin 2012: 23). Cohorts reflect the formative effects of exposure to social events in one's early childhood that persist over time (Ryder 1965).

Estimating distinct APC effects is far from simple because the original APC accounting model suffers from an identification problem. Imagine a 50-year-old woman named Sheila who participates in a survey in 2010. Based on these two facts, she must have been born in 1960. Cohort is completely determined by age and period:

Eq. 1   Cohort = period − age.

This rather obvious equation gestures toward a larger problem. Because age is a perfect function of the other two time dimensions it is not separable from the others in relation to an outcome of interest. If a researcher has individual-level, cross-sectional data collected in 2005 they may decide to estimate a multivariate statistical model to predict cultural participation. Such models may (and very often will) include a measure of age. The researcher may even conclude that as age increases by one year the likelihood of omnivorousness also increases by a specified amount (e.g. β coefficient) and yet the researcher cannot know from this data alone whether this is an age effect or whether this is a cohort effect. In other words, because age = period − cohort and cohort = period − age, there is no certainty that the causal effect of age on cultural participation has been identified; it can reflect something more than the ageing process. Traditional multivariate regression models cannot solve this problem because there is more than one solution to the equation. Although such a model will, under some conditions, produce estimates of these APC parameters, a researcher cannot be certain they approximate the true value.

Consequently, it is impossible to uniquely 'identify' the causal effect of APC on, for example, omnivorousness using this approach.

The APC identification problem has spawned a large literature proposing technical solutions to this estimation problem (Glenn 2005). In response there are those who repeatedly affirm the futility of this quest for a technical solution to this logical and conceptual problem (Luo 2013a; Bell and Jones 2014). A few dimensions of this ongoing and, at times, heated debate offer key insights into how researchers might examine the APC effects associated with the omnivore thesis.

Early attempts to overcome this identification problem used a statistical constraint of some kind (Yang et al. 2008). These constraints may fix the value of one of the three variables in a multivariate model or constrain one of the parameters in the model in order to make the coefficients estimable. Examples of this technique include constrained generalized linear models (Mason et al. 1973) or the intrinsic estimator (Yang et al. 2008). While the details of these methods are not of primary importance, the problem with these approaches is that the choice of the constraint must be based on theory or information external to the available data and the model (Glenn 2005; Luo 2013b). However, such theoretical information is almost never available (Bell and Jones 2014), and so these methods require strong theoretical assumptions in order to be able to identify APC effects, assumptions that are rarely justified or even verifiable.

Those who have remained sceptical to these technical solutions to the APC identification problem have advocated the use of graphical approaches (Voas and Crockett 2005; Reeves 2014) using data visualization and pre-existing theory to test key assumptions (Figure 7.1). For example, if we were to plot the levels of omnivorousness over time in a line graph (with time on the x-axis and the proportion of omnivores in the population on the y-axis), then there are a number of potentially observable patterns. If different cohorts consistently increase in omnivorousness with age then this would be an age effect (Figure 7.1). If each cohort's likelihood of being omnivores did not change as they aged, but all cohorts were different from each other, then this would likely be a cohort effect (Figure 7.1). Finally, a period effect could be a break in the trend observed across all cohorts (Figure 7.1). Other combinations are also possible (Voas and Crockett 2005). These methods are therefore useful because researchers are rarely completely ignorant of the plausible APC-related mechanisms that may be shaping cultural engagement and can bring theoretical insight to bear on interpreting these visualisations of APC effects.

In sum, technical solutions to the APC identification problem are not generally applicable but only work under certain theoretically justified conditions. In examining the rise of the

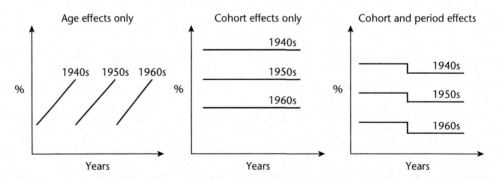

Figure 7.1 Hypothetical examples of age, period, and cohort effects by decade of birth

Notes: Decades represent birth cohorts.

omnivore it is inadequate to simply estimate APC effects using, for example, the intrinsic estimator without carefully considering whether such an approach is identifiable given the assumptions necessary to use this procedure.

Theorizing age-period-cohort effects

In all of these approaches to the APC identification problem theory therefore needs to play a central role. It justifies assumptions in the constraints approach, it explains the choice of methods (e.g. when using the intrinsic estimator and hierarchical APC models), and it helps researchers interpret the patterns observed using the graphical approach. These theoretical issues not only apply to estimating the causes of APC effects but also to the categories themselves. Criticism of these technical solutions has not only been statistical but it has also raised questions about how these effects are conceptualized, prompting reflection on the sociological theories of social change, e.g. Bourdieu's habitus and the omnivore thesis.

Conceptualizing age effects

Early APC research argued that understanding social change (such as the rise of the omnivores or changes in the pattern of cultural practice) required only that analysts consider age and period: changes between age groups over time (Ryder 1965). One of the challenges with thinking through the implications of age for cultural practice is that the distinction between age effects and the association between age and certain life periods or particular social events is not always clear (Yang 2007). According to one perspective, age effects should be consistent across countries and for different cohorts within that country: suggesting that age effects are likely to be biological and unlikely to be altered by social and cultural factors. Observing this type of age effect in the context of cultural engagement is, however, unlikely because cultural practice is inevitably connected with a variety of other social and institutional processes that are intertwined with the biological process of ageing. Consequently, sociological examination of age effects requires careful examination of the social roles, the institutional structures and biological changes associated with aging across societies. As such, ageing is an embodied process enforcing constraints on activity through the onset of poor health, but these constraints are also shaped by institutions and social roles that may facilitate or restrict cultural activity (Evans 2003).

Consider the following illustration of age effects using repeated cross-sectional surveys from the UK. Here I create a crude measure of arts omnivorousness from the UK's Taking-Part survey. This is a frequency or volume measure of arts participation within the last 12 months capturing whether respondents self-report having participated in any of the 22 activities listed (range 0–20; no respondents participated in all 22 activities). The measure assumes that participating in a greater number of arts activities is a form of omnivorousness. This, of course, ignores the composition of the arts activities (i.e. are they highbrow activities or not) but these types of volume measures are frequently used in the empirical literature (Warde et al. 2007). The data suggest that the number of arts activities remain fairly stable (around 2.5 activities) until age 60, at which point it declines rapidly (Figure 7.2). This decline is observed in all three periods and could be evidence of an age effect.

Period or cohort effects?

While period effects also influence temporal variation in cultural practice, there is some debate regarding what constitutes a period effect. Alwin and McCammon (2003) observe

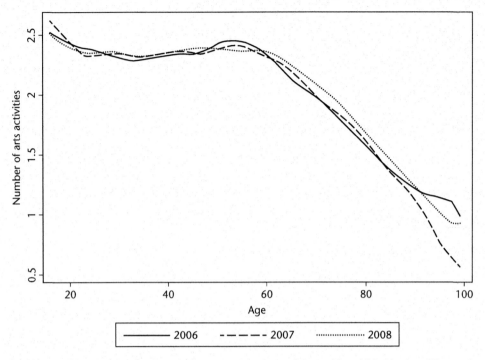

Figure 7.2 The number of arts activities respondents participated in within the last 12 months in the UK, 2006–2008

Note: Years represent time when data was collected.

that period effects can influence a specific age cohort or collection of age cohorts uniformly at the same time. In contrast, Luo (2013a) argues that period effects must influence all age groups at the same time, otherwise they are cohort effects. For example, the rise of digital technology may constitute a period effect. It is a form of cultural engagement that was not available to some generations and then, relatively quickly, became (potentially) available to the vast majority of people. Some period effects might be short-lived, and others may persist. Those who have documented the rise of the omnivore have usually examined the proportion of omnivorousness within a population over time. For example, Peterson and Kern document a rise in the proportion of people who blend high- and lowbrow musical preferences in 1982 and 1992. At first blush, these results might indicate a period effect, but drawing such a conclusion would ignore potential differences in omnivorousness across cohorts.

Taking this approach – that is, ignoring cohorts – may be justified under some circumstances but it makes some important assumptions about how cultural preferences change within individuals over time. For example, assuming that the rise in omnivorousness is occurring across all cohorts makes assumptions about the genetic (early socialization which cultivates dispositions) and relational (conditions in later life that activate cultural dispositions) mechanisms that shape cultural practices across the life course (Lizardo and Skiles 2012). For example, such an approach would ignore the possibility that this growth in omnivorousness is driven by cohort replacement rather than a general rise across all cohorts. In short, making the claim that there has been a period effect which has influenced all groups to the same extent is a strong conclusion because it would need to show that a range of other factors are not the explanation, such as the influence of technological change on both socialization and the context of adult cultural practice (Tepper and Ivey 2008). Further, this claim would suggest that the rise of higher education has not played a role (Fishman and Lizardo 2013) or that changing gender roles have not shaped socialization and the norms surrounding adult cultural engagement (Lizardo 2006b). Finally, making the claim of a period effect would suggest that changes in economic resources and parenting styles have also had no influence on omnivorousness (Lareau 2003). Of course, Peterson and Kern do not make this claim, but what this example illustrates is the importance of considering both the genetic and relational mechanisms the shape cultural practice.

This complexity is evident in a recent study of cultural engagement over time in the UK where Figure 7.3 in Reeves (2014) shows that the rise in omnivorousness is predominantly observed in the youngest three cohorts (born in 1960–1969, 1970–1979 and 1980–1995). In particular, the rise occurs first in the 1960s cohort and is then followed by these subsequent cohorts. These patterns suggest that while there have been period effects, the impact of these societal wide changes have influenced some cohorts more than others. Consequently, there are good reasons to assume that cohorts are very likely quite different from each other and that such differences will change the response of particular groups to these period effects.

Conceptualizing cohort effects and the possibility of interactions

If cultural sociology needs to think carefully about cohorts, how then should cohorts be conceptualized? Birth cohort effects are frequently assumed to be distinct from, or net of, age. In this view, cohorts are shaped by the 'conditions, barriers, and resources' into which they are born and under which they mature (Keyes *et al.* 2010: 1100). This idea stresses the

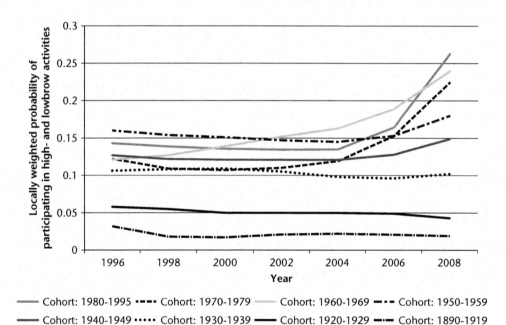

Figure 7.3 The likelihood of consuming a broad range of cultural activities in the UK across cohorts, 1996–2008

Source: British Household Panel Survey. See Reeves 2014 for details.

importance of development during childhood and adolescence, but it is an empirical and theoretical question which ages during those early years are most important.

The APC accounting model, which takes the form described earlier (age = period - cohort), assumes that cohort effects are established at some point during those early years. As Ryder observed, 'each new cohort makes fresh contact with the contemporary social heritage and carries the impress of the encounter through life' (Ryder 1965: 844). Ryder (1965) is often read as arguing that cohort effects are constant across the life course and as a consequence cohort effects have often been conceptualized as 1) independent of age and period and 2) a stable factor influencing individuals from birth to death. However, Ryder also wrote, 'transformations of the social world modify people of different ages in different ways; the effects of these transformations are persistent. Through this process a cohort meaning is implanted in the age-time specification' (Ryder 1965: 861). In this view, cohort effects may not be constant throughout the life course, but there may be some trajectory that is cohort dependent and with which age and period interact (Luo 2013b). That is, the democratization of highbrow culture (a period effect) may have increased omnivorousness but only among specific cohorts (Scherger 2009; Hanquinet et al. 2014). Some may have become more egalitarian, while others may have become even more likely to reject lowbrow culture. Thus, social change is not merely a matter of cohort replacement but also a dynamic interaction between cohort, age and the contemporary social and historical context (period).

While recognizing the theoretical importance of cohorts, Luo (2013b) has sought to move away from conceptualizing cohorts as constant and independent of period and age. For example, the effect of being a young adult when the civil rights movement was sweeping through America may matter for cultural preferences, but it is not necessary to assume that those effects persist unchanged into later life for that birth cohort. Instead, Luo argues that cohorts can be conceptualized as an 'age-by-period interaction' (Luo 2013b: 1987). Any historical change, such as the democratization of culture, that influences all people uniformly is not a cohort effect – instead it is pure period effect. Historical (or social) changes that only influence a small number of people, perhaps young children – and, by implication, those that are born after them – will create differences between generations; and these are cohort effects. According to Luo, this approach allows social scientists the flexibility to consider cohort effects as the product of both age effects and period effects.

Yet if cohort effects are the product of both age effects and period effects, how can cohort and, for example, period effects be distinguished? Returning to the example of the democratization of culture, there are two possible processes through which such changes can influence social groups. New cultural practices can be taken up by younger generations first and then spread to older generations through cohort replacement or through the social networks across various groups over time (Lizardo 2006a). If the spread of omnivorousness is through cohort replacement, then it is not a period effect because it never reached some cohorts. In contrast, if omnivorousness spread through all cohorts within a relatively short period of time then this would likely be a period effect.

Habitus as class-based cohort effect

These methodological and theoretical debates have important implications for Bourdieu's conception of the habitus, which is the context in which the dynamic interaction between contemporaneous social change (i.e. period effect) and the persistent influence of socialization (i.e. cohort effect) plays out.

Bourdieu's habitus draws on Piaget's notion of genetic structures that are relatively stable but which are not fixed (Lizardo 2004). The habitus is a set of socially produced cognitive structures, commonly called dispositions, used to explain how social structures shape the logic of our judgments and also the logic of everyday practice. These cognitive structures are constituted via the experience of objective probabilities, and so only those who inhabit similar positions in the social space will emerge with similar habitus. The habitus emerges from and reproduces the differential association of people (Bourdieu 1984), and so those habitus which are most different from each other are also, of necessity, those positions in the social space which are most distant. Accidental interaction between these dissimilar groups is possible but these individuals 'will not get on together, will not really understand each other, will not appeal to one another' (Bourdieu 1998: 11). Differential association creates separate paths through life, and therefore unique patterns of cultural practice. Hence the habitus is a set of cognitive structures that are the product of a particular social location. These cognitive dispositions are structured (because they are the product of social structures and reflect those structures) and they are structuring (because they reproduce those structures through action).

To the extent that the objective probabilities change over time, then we would expect to see cohort effects. The environmental and material conditions in which the habitus is developed consist of economic, educational and social opportunities that make the acquisition of certain dispositions toward culture more or less likely (Lizardo and Skiles 2012). For example, the rapid expansion of both economic wealth and the accessibility of higher education could have profound cohort effects in relation to omnivorousness.

Yet, Bourdieu's more important point is that these cognitive structures are group specific as well as cohort specific. Changes to environment and material conditions that shape objective probabilities will differ depending on the individual's position within society. For example, the expansion of higher education benefited young men first and then young women. Some groups continue to have lower admission rates to university. Similarly, while standards of living have risen in the UK since WWII, the degree to which economic growth has benefitted those in deprived social circumstances has varied over time. This, of course, is not to suggest that such structures are unchangeable but rather that these early years form an important set of initial conditions through which all other subsequent adaptions to the habitus are made. This interaction between cohort specific changes and the extent to which certain classes experienced those cohort effects suggests that the habitus can be interpreted through the lens of APC as a class-based cohort effect.

This has a number of implications for how researchers think about documenting cohort effects associated with omnivorousness. First, the habitus is a product of the era in which a child matured (parenting styles that were in vogue, educational and cultural opportunities and tastes, access to resources, etc.). Second, the habitus is also responsive to changes associated with age. Social ageing 'leads agents to adjust their aspirations ... become what they are and make do with what they have' (Bourdieu 1984: 110). Third, contemporary changes in the structure of society require adaptation within the habitus, suggesting that current dispositions are the product of the period during which an individual grew up, their current age and the changes in the contemporary period (Lizardo and Skiles 2012). Similar to Luo, one could argue that the habitus (omnivore disposition) should be considered as an interaction between cohort and period.

Age-period-cohort modelling: Implications for the omnivore debate

In previous sections, I have argued that the APC problem is a theoretical problem as much as it is a methodological problem, and that the rise of the omnivores provides one useful test case of these issues. In this section, I want to explore this connection in more detail. Because omnivores (the cultural egalitarians who mingle high- and lowbrow forms of culture, although in a quite discriminant way) are operationalized in terms of the composition of their cultural practices they have frequently been defined in terms of 'openness' (Ollivier 2008). But where does this openness come from, and is it due to APC effects?

Peterson and Kern's (1996) aforementioned hypothesis posits that age is unlikely to be the primary explanation of why omnivores emerge during the 1980s. Instead they argue that changes in the politics of exclusion, social values, the art world, generational politics and status-group politics have all led to the emergence of this group. The politics of cultural exclusion has changed over the last 50 years with greater access to higher education and increased economic prosperity which, in turn, has increased access to highbrow culture. Concurrently the mass media have mixed aesthetic tastes and popularized certain forms of folk or lowbrow culture. Societal values have also shifted away from exclusionism toward greater tolerance. The rise of modernism and then post-modernism in the art world also expanded the scope of what could be considered aesthetically praiseworthy despite attempts to stabilize the artistic canon. Youth movements in the 1950s and 1960s shifted the cultural trajectories of maturing adults. Instead of transitioning toward elite arts from popular styles, they became less likely than previous cohorts to make that shift. Peterson and Kern (1996) also argue that dominant status groups stopped defining popular culture as crass and instead begun to gentrify certain aspects of it, a trend documented in more recent work (Skeggs 2005).

This set of factors suggests a number of empirically verifiable claims – assuming data were available. The rise of higher education should increase the proportion of highbrow consumers, which, in the US at least, appears not to have occurred (Peterson 2005). Upward social mobility should increase omnivorousness by encouraging individuals to blend the cultural practices of their position of origin with the cultural practices of their position of destination (Daenekindt and Roose 2014). The rise of omnivorousness should be correlated, but presumably with a time lag, with changes in the art world, such as the rise of post-modernism. However, the final two factors regarding youth movements in the 60s and the rise of cultural gentrification are difficult to identify because they are also the products of other socio-cultural changes which may have also prompted increased omnivorousness.

What remains unclear from these speculations is the mechanisms that link these changes with particular groups. For example, who will be influenced by changes in the art world and when? Is the impact of social mobility due to changes in occupational status or the rise of higher education? What changed in the 50s and 60s that prompted younger members of the middle classes to reject elite highbrow culture as they matured? Further, even if such associations could be documented they fail to articulate how such changes would impact behaviour and, more specifically, which groups would experience these shifts. In short, while these speculations provide a useful set of possible explanatory factors, they fail to develop a theory of change in cultural practice.

Because these changes are likely to have influenced some social classes more than others (i.e. class-based cohort effects), Bourdieu may be particularly helpful here. Below I summarize some of the empirical evidence around temporal variation in omnivorousness while considering how this Bourdieusian approach to APC effects may help interpret the existing literature.

Age and omnivores

As I have argued, in both Bourdieu's work and Peterson's work, age is an underdeveloped factor shaping cultural practice and, potentially, omnivorousness. Cultural sociologists are concerned with age effects associated with how certain life periods bring with them an increased likelihood of having children, going to university or retiring, events which also impact leisure time and cultural engagement (Reeves 2014). Evidence associating age with cultural practice appears to vary somewhat depending on the type of activity (Scherger 2009). Music omnivores in the UK and the US were older than those with narrower music tastes (Chan and Goldthorpe 2007; Alderson et al. 2007), while in France middlebrow omnivores were more common among younger cohorts (Coulangeon and Lemel 2010). Younger cohorts are less likely to participate in traditional forms of cultural practice, such as classical music (Bennett et al. 2009) or other highbrow genres (Goldberg 2011). Warde observes that younger respondents 'eat-out' at a wider range of restaurants and more often (Warde et al. 1999). There is no clear association between age and consuming theatre, dance and/or cinema (Chan and Goldthorpe 2005). Finally, some forms of omnivorousness are more common among younger people (Peterson and Kern 1996; Jaeger and Katz-Gerro 2010).

What explains these patterns? Those who are under the age of 30, or even 25, are likely to have more disposable time because they do not have extensive family commitments. They are more likely to be in education (particular university education) which is correlated with broader cultural practice. Yet, there are mixed results concerning the impact of time constraints and cultural practice. Qualitative data indicate that limited time is one of the primary reasons individuals give for not participating more in leisure activities (Charlton et al. 2010) while quantitative evidence using time-use diaries indicates that time constraints do not impinge on cultural practice (Sullivan and Katz-Gerro 2007).

Disentangling these age effects requires further analysis around three issues. First, cross-national comparisons: Some of the results already discussed indicate that patterns of music and omnivorous consumption vary across national contexts and explain these different patterns. Second, examining age effects for specific activities: Chan and Goldthorpe's observation that age has no association with attending the theatre, dance productions or going to the cinema may reflect differences between these activities rather than the lack of an association when they are measured jointly (Chan and Goldthorpe 2005; Bennett et al. 2009). Third, as noted earlier, previous studies have not carefully considered whether age effects are actually period or cohort effects. For example, most of these studies have used multivariate regression analysis with cross-sectional data and so are unable to identify age effects. Although those who are younger are more likely to participate in a wide variety of cultural activities, it is unclear how this young-adult disposition translates across the life course when children and employment arrive (Sullivan and Katz-Gerro 2007).

In fact, this has been a challenge in the majority of those studies exploring this thesis (Chan 2010; Lizardo 2006a). Viewing omnivorousness longitudinally suggests the need to examine both coherence and persistence in longitudinal patterns of cultural practice while making space for variation in response to changing family and economic circumstances (Lahire 2010). For Bourdieu, the habitus would encourage responses to these common changes associated with age in ways that are consistent with the class of origin. Hence, although the degree of omnivorousness may not be constant during such transitions, alterations in the degree of omnivorousness due to age effects would be largely consistent with those who possess a similar habitus.

Period and omnivores

With respect to omnivorousness, two distinct period effects need to be disentangled: material access and socio-cultural change (Scherger 2009).

Material access to cultural practices, such as changes in geographical access, could influence cultural practice. The UK Film Council's statistical report for 2010 demonstrates that there is a close, positive correlation between screen density per person and the number of cinema admissions (Perkins *et al.* 2011). Additionally, financial access may also play a role. Between 1978 and 1984, during the recession of the early 80s, cinema admissions dropped from 130 million to 54 million, a decline that was unrelated to screen density.

Both of these may explain the rise of the omnivore. The expanding availability of highbrow culture coupled with the pervasiveness of lowbrow culture in the mass media may then have facilitated blending both forms of practice. Over the last 60 years, there has been massive economic growth in most western societies coupled with, in many countries, the expansion of welfare states which redistribute wealth through taxation. If economic wealth allows participation in forms of culture that might require greater financial outlays, such as visiting the opera, then economic growth may also increase omnivorousness. Interestingly, these economic factors do not appear to have had a substantial influence. For example, between 1964 and 2004 Denmark experienced economic growth and the expansion of redistributive policies, improving living standards (Jaeger and Katz-Gerro 2010). However, the number of 'eclectic' or omnivorous consumers has only slightly increased and there has not been a reduction in the social gradient in omnivorousness. In short, while changes in material access might have a minor influence on cultural engagement, there is no good evidence that such period effects radically alter the trajectories of cultural consumption over a short period of time.

For Bourdieu, this is unsurprising. Greater economic capital does not necessarily lead to a change in the dispositions that constitute the habitus. Greater financial resources may intensify the omnivorousness of those predisposed to be omnivores – increasing the voraciousness – but it may not increase the likelihood of omnivorousness among those who do not value this pattern of cultural practice.

The second type of period effect is socio-cultural change. Peterson and Kern argue that changes in status politics may explain the rise of the omnivore. If, as discussed previously, diffusion of these new cultural values occurs through cohort replacement, then they are best categorized as cohort effects, whereas if they diffused within a short period across all cohorts then they could plausibly be described as period effects. Because of the nature of cultural values and attitudes, it is most likely that socio-cultural change will actually be diffused via cohort replacement and therefore is a cohort effect, to be discussed in more detail in the cohort section below. More research is needed to understand the impact of accessibility through the media but broadly speaking, changes in cultural engagement do not appear to be driven by period effects, as Peterson and Kern suggested.

Cohort and omnivores

Examination of cohort effects that may be linked with changing socio-cultural norms has not yet been widely taken up in the empirical literature, with two important exceptions. The first is Jaeger and Katz-Gerro's (2010) paper on the rise of eclectic consumer in Denmark and the second is Fishman and Lizardo's (2013) work examining Spain and Portugal. Jaeger and Katz-Gerro observe that in Denmark between 1964 and 2004 there was a small rise in the number of eclectic (omnivore) consumers but which has remained around 10 per cent of the population since the 1970s (Jaeger and Katz-Gerro 2010). This small cohort effect indicates that while the proportion of omnivores has increased, this rise has not occurred across all social groups, a finding consistent with Bourdieu's vision of class-based cohort effects (ibid.). Whilst acknowledging that the rise in omnivorousness is largely unrelated to economic growth or the expansion of the welfare state, Jaeger and Katz-Gerro do not offer a clear explanation for this cohort effect.

Fishman and Lizardo (2013) are also sceptical that economic growth or financial barriers are the major drivers of increasing omnivorousness. Instead they argue that omnivorous consumption is a product of institutional and ideological variation between countries that become embodied within education systems. Comparing the different democratic transitions in both Spain and Portugal, Fishman and Lizardo observe that omnivorousness becomes more common among Portuguese people than Spanish individuals but only among those born after the divergent trajectories to democracy in these two countries. They trace the institutional implications of these democratic trajectories and demonstrate that the egalitarianism of the Portuguese democratic transition shapes secondary educational systems, creating cultural norms that are distinct from their previously similar neighbours. In short, these education systems mediated the association between political and ideological changes and individual dispositions. Changes in pedagogy and curriculum influence the omnivorous disposition but only among those who were still in secondary education (and, of course, subsequent cohorts).

Fishman and Lizardo's paper offers a provocative hypothesis regarding the implications of education institutions for cohort effects, but more work is needed to understand the influence of family background on these class-based cohort effects that are central to Bourdieu's work. Further, there are substantial gaps in our understanding of how different cohorts will then respond to contemporary socio-cultural change later in life. These are themes that need to be addressed in future work.

Conclusion

This discussion has important implications for future research. First, by bringing together methodological debates around APC with empirical and theoretical work in cultural sociology, it raises some of the methodological challenges with estimating age-period-cohort effects. These challenges require careful consideration in future research that is trying to unpack the rise of the omnivore – and similar empirical problems – but these concerns also pertain to more traditional approaches to analysing APC effects using multivariate regression. Second, these methodological debates also have theoretical implications for how APC effects are conceptualized. I have argued that Bourdieu's account of the habitus suggests that the habitus can be usefully framed as a class-based cohort effect that is responsive to age effects and period effects. Third, these debates should also shape future research into the rise of the omnivore. Peterson and Kern have offered a number of plausible hypotheses explaining the emergence of this group, and yet these remain largely unexamined nearly 20 years later. APC effects remains an understudied area in cultural sociology, but the current context provides a germane moment in which to re-think how these important conversations may help cultural sociologists answer questions central to the field.

References

Alderson, A.S., A. Junisbai and I. Heacock (2007) 'Social status and cultural consumption in the United States', *Poetics*, 35: 191–212.

Alwin, D.F. (2012) 'Integrating varieties of life course concepts', *Journals of Gerontology Series B-Psychological Sciences and Social Sciences*, 67: 206–220.

Alwin, D.F. and R.J. McCammon (2003) 'Generations, cohorts, and social change', in J.T. Mortimerand M.J. Shanahan (eds.), *Handbook of the life course*, New York: Kluwer.

Bell, A. and K. Jones (2014) 'Another 'futile quest'? A simulation study of Yang and Land's hierarchical age-period-cohort model', *Demographic Research*, 30: 333–360.
Bennett, T., M. Savage, E. Silva, A. Warde, M. Gayo-Cal and D. Wright (2009) *Culture, class, distinction*, London: Routledge.
Bottero, W. (2009) 'Relationality and social interaction', *British Journal of Sociology*, 60: 399–420.
Bourdieu, P. (1984) *Distinction: a social critique of the judgement of taste*, London: Routledge and Kegan Paul.
—— (1996) *The state nobility: Elite schools in the field of power*, Oxford: Polity.
—— (1998) *Practical reason: On the theory of action*, Cambridge: Polity Press.
Bourdieu, P. and J.-C. Passeron (1979) *The inheritors: French students and their relation to culture*, Chicago and London: University of Chicago Press.
Chan, T.W. (2010) *Social status and cultural consumption*, Cambridge: Cambridge University Press.
Chan, T.W. and J.H. Goldthorpe (2005) 'The social stratification of theatre, dance and cinema attendance', *Cultural Trends*, 14: 193–212.
—— (2007) 'Social stratification and cultural consumption: Music in England', *European Sociological Review*, 23: 1–19.
Charlton, A., M. Potter, S. Mcginigal, E. Romanou, Z. Slade and B. Hewitson (2010) 'Barriers to participation: Analysis to inform the development of the 2010/11 Taking Part Survey', in Department for Culture, M., and Sport (ed.), London: DCMS.
Coulangeon, P. and Y. Lemel (eds.) (2010) *Bourdieu's legacy and the class-status debate on cultural consumption: Musical consumption in contemporary France*, Cambridge: Cambridge University Press.
Daenekindt, S. and H. Roose (2014) 'Social mobility mobility and cultural dissonance', *Poetics*, 42: 82–97.
Evans, J.G. (2003) 'Age discrimination: Implications of the ageing process', in S. Fredman and S. Spencer (eds.), *Age as an equality issue*, Oxford: Hart.
Fishman, R.M. and O. Lizardo (2013) 'How macro-historical change shapes cultural taste: Legacies of democratization in Spain and Portugal', *American Sociological Review*, 78: 213–239.
Glenn, N.D. (2005) *Cohort analysis*, Thousand Oaks, CA and London: Sage.
Goldberg, A. (2011) 'Mapping shared understandings using relational class analysis: The case of the cultural omnivore reexamined', *American Journal of Sociology*, 116: 1397–1436.
Hanquinet, L., H. Roose and M. Savage (2014) 'The eyes of the beholder: Aesthetic preferences and the remaking of cultural capital', *Sociology – the Journal of the British Sociological Association*, 48: 111–132.
Hobcraft, J.N., J.W. Mcdonaldand S.O. Rutstein (1984) 'Socio-economic factors in infant and child mortality: A cross-national comparison', *Population Studies: A Journal of Demography*, 38: 193–223.
Jaeger, M.M. and T. Katz-Gerro (2010) 'The rise of the eclectic cultural consumer in Denmark, 1964–2004', *Sociological Quarterly*, 51: 460–483.
Keyes, K.M., R.L. Utz, W. Robinson and G.H. Li (2010) 'What is a cohort effect? Comparison of three statistical methods for modeling cohort effects in obesity prevalence in the United States, 1971–2006', *Social science and medicine*, 70: 1100–1108.
Lahire, B. (2010) *The plural actor*, Cambridge: Polity.
Lareau, A. (2003) *Unequal childhoods: Class, race, and family life*, Berkeley, CA: University of California Press.
Lizardo, O. (2004) 'The cognitive origins of Bourdieu's habitus', *Journal for the Theory of Social Behaviour*, 34: 375–401.
—— (2006a) 'How cultural tastes shape personal networks', *American Sociological Review*, 71: 778–807.
—— (2006b) 'The puzzle of women's "highbrow" culture consumption: Integrating gender and work into Bourdieu's class theory of taste', *Poetics*, 34: 1–23.
Lizardo, O. and S. Skiles (2012) 'Reconceptualizing and theorizing 'omnivorousness': Genetic and relational mechanisms', *Sociological Theory*, 30: 263–282.
Luo, L.Y. (2013a) 'Assessing validity and application scope of the intrinsic estimator approach to the age-period-cohort problem', *Demography*, 50: 1945–1967.
—— (2013b) 'Paradigm shift in age-period-cohort analysis: A response to Yang and Land, O'Brien, Held and Riebler, and Fienberg', *Demography*, 50: 1985–8.
Mason, K.O., W.M. Mason, H.H. Winsborough and K. Poole (1973) 'Some methodological issues in cohort analysis of archival data', *American Sociological Review*, 38: 242–258.
Ollivier, M. (2008) 'Modes of openness to cultural diversity: Humanist, populist, practical, and indifferent', *Poetics*, 36: 120–147.
Perkins, S., N. Maine and S. Little (2011) BFI Statistical Yearbook 2011, *British Film Institute* (ed.), London: BFI.

Peterson, R.A. (2005) 'Problems in comparative research: The example of omnivorousness', *Poetics*, 33: 257–282.
Peterson, R.A. and R.M. Kern (1996) 'Changing highbrow taste: From snob to omnivore', *American Sociological Review*, 61: 900–907.
Peterson, R.A. and A. Simkus (1992) 'How musical tastes mark occupational status groups', in M. Lamont and M. Fournier (eds.), *Cultivating differences: Symbolic boundaries and the making of inequality*, Chicago: University of Chicago Press.
Reeves, A. (2014) 'Cultural engagement across the life-course: Examining age-period-cohort effects', *Cultural Trends*, 23: 273–289.
Ryder, N.B. (1965) 'The cohort as a concept in the study of social-change', *American Sociological Review*, 30: 843–861.
Scherger, S. (2009) 'Cultural practices, age and life-course', *Cultural Trends*, 18: 23–45.
Skeggs, B. (2005) 'The re-branding of class: Propertising culture', in F. Devine, J. Scott, M. Savage and R. Crompton (eds.), *Rethinking class: Culture, identities and lifestyles*, Basingstoke: Palgrave Macmillan.
Sullivan, O. and T. Katz-Gerro (2007) 'The omnivore thesis revisited: Voracious cultural consumers', *European Sociological Review*, 23: 123–137.
Suzuki, E. (2012) 'Time changes, so do people', *Social science and medicine*, 75: 452–6; discussion 457–8.
Tepper, S.J. and W. Ivey (2008) *Engaging art: The next great transformation of America's cultural life*, New York: Routledge.
Vaisey, S. (2009) 'Motivation and justification: A dual-process model of culture in action', *American Journal of Sociology*, 114: 1675–1715.
van Rees, K., J. Vermunt and M. Verboord (1999) 'Cultural classifications under discussion – Latent class analysis of highbrow and lowbrow reading', *Poetics*, 26: 349–365.
Voas, D. and A. Crockett (2005) 'Religion in Britain: Neither believing nor belonging', *Sociology – the Journal of the British Sociological Association*, 39: 11–28.
Warde, A., L. Martens and W. Olsen (1999) 'Consumption and the problem of variety: Cultural omnivorousness, social distinction and dining out', *Sociology*, 33: 105–127.
Warde, A., D. Wright and M. Gayo-Cal (2007) 'Understanding cultural omnivorousness: Or, the myth of the cultural omnivore', *Cultural Sociology*, 1: 143–164.
Wilson, J.A. and W.R. Gove (1999) 'The intercohort decline in verbal ability: Does it exist?', *American Sociological Review*, 64: 253–266.
Yang, Y. (2007) 'Age/Period/Cohort distinctions', in K.S. Markides (ed.), *Encyclopedia of Health and Aging*, Los Angeles: Sage.
Yang, Y., S. Schulhofer-Wohl, W.J.J. Fu and K.C. Land (2008) 'The intrinsic estimator for age-period-cohort analysis: What it is and how to use it', *American Journal of Sociology*, 113: 1697–1736.

8
A social aesthetics as a general cultural sociology?

John Levi Martin and Ben Merriman

Introduction

A new cultural sociology?

Cultural sociology has often been considered a coherent approach that assumes the central role of culture in a large number of spheres of social life (see especially Alexander 2003). This is in contrast to a more narrowly defined sociology of Culture, which more often focuses on, for instance, the production, distribution, consumption and reception of what are consensually taken to be Cultural products and services, such as paintings, country music performances or haute cuisine. (We use small-c to indicate the broader, anthropological use of the word and big-C to indicate the narrower one.) The dominant understanding of cultural sociology has been one that emphasizes the importance of shared cognitions, most generally 'schema' of different sorts, up to and including shared understandings of the most transcendent values.

From such a perspective, the approach to the sociology of Culture associated with Pierre Bourdieu (especially 1984) has been seen as threatening a materialism and reductionism that would destroy any appreciation of culture as autonomous (hence Alexander's [1995] fierce critique). There is a way in which this interpretation is quite correct: as we shall see, Bourdieu's aesthetic theory mounted a sustained attack on the idea of purity, which he viewed as the greatest impurity of all, and to the extent that the plank of the autonomy of culture is used as a stand-in for such purity, there is indeed an unyielding opposition between the two perspectives.

Yet a coherent elaboration of the field theoretic perspective that Bourdieu put forward, rather than being the negation of cultural sociology, is itself a cultural sociology, a systematic account of the role of culture in a wide variety of social domains. Further, we argue that this general cultural sociology is by its nature an aesthetics – an examination of how actors respond to the qualitative properties of experience. Thus we shall argue that aesthetics, rather than being an approach suitable only to specific areas of high cultural production and consumption, is the most reasonable model for a rigorous science of what we shall call action.[1] This expansive role for aesthetics was a central tenet of the first generation of field theorists, though they influenced Bourdieu only indirectly, and is compatible with the more coherent aspects of Bourdieu's theorizing. Below, we present a brief overview of a field approach to aesthetics and then offer a rereading of Bourdieu that suggests that his work may provide the basis for an aesthetic approach to social explanation. We then argue that by focusing (as did Bourdieu in *Distinction*) on 'second-order' judgements – judgements of judgements – we may be able to demonstrate the most fundamental ways in which this social aesthetics can point towards a rigorous cultural sociology of action.

Bourdieu and Kant

We assume general familiarity with the approach of Pierre Bourdieu; here we focus on his work *Distinction*, for reasons that we make clear below. *Distinction* was, as Bourdieu sub-titled it, a social critique of the judgement of taste, especially 'pure' taste. It is tempting to view Bourdieu's critique of Kantian purity as essentially agonistic rather than theoretically constructive. But Bourdieu's critique was not merely a war of words; his barbed presentation was necessary for us to understand the role of a certain type of judgement in social action. It is not that Bourdieu was attempting to show the 'functions' of pure taste, but rather, to allow us to understand what purity of taste *is*. Just as the sacred is not made without reference to the profane, but rather is a separation from the profane, so pure taste – and the cultivation of pure taste – is a taste for purity. The pure taste is not a taste that ignores the materiality of the common, but one that flees the common, though it may also involve embracing the common ... when this is an uncommon choice (among a specific group of comparables). In sum, purity is not escape from the world – it is a (dominant) position within the world. For this reason, it can be an avenue to understanding the nature of the world.

Further, taste, whatever its degree of purity, is a disposition to make certain types of judgements regarding certain types of objects *that are already there*. We cannot understand the logic of the taste without understanding the logic that explains the dispersion and organization of the objects it encounters. To take a familiar case as analogy, we all now understand that 'race blind' policies *mean* and therefore *are* one thing in a world in which there is existing racial inequality and another in a world in which there is not. The organization of tastes, and hence of positions taken, could not be independent of the configuration of positions that we call social structure if it wanted to – that is, if the organized tastes wanted to, which means that the tasters wanted to – and they don't. People do not want their tastes to be independent of the rest of social life because those who make judgements make them about that 'rest of.' As we shall see, this is the key to making sense of *Distinction* as a general framework for cultural sociology.

A Bourdieuian cultural sociology of action?

Restricted application

It is not immediately clear that Bourdieu's work really does provide anything like a general theory of action, despite the fact that many adherents have been emboldened to treat it as such. For one thing, the specific set of social processes that interested Bourdieu are a subset of all social processes; further, to the extent that we focus on Bourdieu's theory of fields, it is, as Bourdieu himself would have no trouble acknowledging, necessarily of restricted application because not all action takes place in fields.

Given that there have been critiques of Bourdieu's theory that are based merely on this selective interest (as if focusing on objectively strategic action were to make the strong claim that *all* human action is objectively strategic), one might seek to avoid further confusion by emphasizing in what ways Bourdieu's theory is not a general theory of action. Following this tactic, one would emphasize that this approach is at its best when confronted with specific, reasonably well defined, social fields. However, there are paths towards generalization beyond such delimited fields. We want to discuss two here.

The field of power

The first is the path that Bourdieu himself took. We must understand that Bourdieu's empirical work very often analyzed the behavior of actors in well-defined fields of activities, often with clear organizational bases – for example, universities (Bourdieu 1988), art galleries (Bourdieu 1996a) and theaters (Bourdieu 1993). Such organizationally delimited or anchored fields (note that this is not the same thing as an 'organizational field') have two characteristics. First, one's 'position' may have a very clear relation to consensually understood organizational attributes: an appointment in some academic department, a partnership in some firm, a column in some media outlet.[2] People occupying positions in these fields can know in a very definite sense where they are and where they are with respect to others in the field.

Second, this analytic simplicity can lead us to propose the existence of different kinds of field-specific capital. Such capital is, in essence, a reification of position (which is just what it should be, if we follow Marx – it is a social relation made into a thing subject to appropriation by an individual); an actor, rather than being seen as occupying a particular place in a world endowed with various qualities, can be said to 'possess' a certain quantity of social substance. This simplification is often imposed by social investigators, or may reflect the way that people in a field produce their own theories about its structure. In either case, the notion of multiple specific capitals also suggests the existence of a mechanism for conversion by which, say, economic capital is exchanged for cultural capital.

And this was how Bourdieu moved to take a theory that might seem only applicable to specific fields and give it a greater span. That is, he relied on fixity of positions and identifiability of capital to attempt to situate the fields in an overall organizational topography, constructing what he called the 'field of power' (for a previous use of power as such a generalized intermediary between sectors, see Gerth and Mills 1954: 328).

The perhaps mis-named field of power is less a field and more like, on the one hand, a central train station that allows one to move from one line to another and, on the other hand, a total free-for-all: a field without the rules. Here is Bourdieu (1996b: 264f):

> The field of power is a field of forces structurally determined by the state of the relations of power among forms of power, or different forms of capital. It is also, and inseparably, a field of power struggles among the holders of different forms of power, a gaming space in which those agents and institutions possessing enough specific capital (economic or cultural capital in particular) to be able to occupy the dominant positions within their respective fields confront each other using strategies aimed at preserving or transforming these relations of power.

That is, it is like a second round in which the winners of various fields, elites associated with different sectors, strive to determine the exchange rate between their capitals, to determine what is the dominant principle of domination. In the crudest terms, for Bourdieu it tends to come down to the eternal struggle between the eggheads and the meatheads – those with cultural capital versus those with economic capital (or, most simply, us versus them, our rivals for power ... at least in France, where the eggheads have a fighting chance).

We believe that this formulation was a fundamentally flawed one. First, it took the homologies that might indeed be rather strong in France as if they were inherent to social judgement; second, it ideologically inflated the professoriate's obsession with their being sidelined by economic elites as if it was a major structuring issue of modern societies; third, it somewhat fancifully imagined that through struggle of some sort elites could affect the exchange rates of their capitals (when, as any American sociologist can tell you, the exchange rate of economic for cultural capital remains stable at precisely $0 per bushel). Fourth, and most important, Bourdieu's conception makes the most sense in a highly structured, indeed, corporatist polity, in which there actually are relatively small and well-defined sets of different elites who interact with one another (hence Bourdieu's 'state nobility'), but it is implausible to use this to account for more fundamental homologies across fields. This is readily apparent when comparing France to polities such as the US (see, for instance, Lamont 1992).

That is, Bourdieu did indeed find many fields to have homologies in which there seemed to be a differentiation between those whose capital was mainly economic and those whose capital was mainly cultural. But does this have anything to do with the struggles among the winners of each field? For although Bourdieu increasingly emphasized the field of power account as crucial for accounting for homologies, there was a simpler, more plausible, and more parsimonious account ... in his own earlier work.

And this is simply that fields are embedded in a social space, and all are in the same social space. Although some fields may recruit disproportionately from some areas of social space, and this *does* lead to interesting possibilities of complexity in terms of the formation of homologies, we can as a first approximation imagine that there will be some tendency to the overall organization of the relation of fields to one another coming from the fact of their non-independent fundaments. Here we wish to return to Bourdieu's key work on such social space (*Distinction*) and suggest that he has here in fact theorized a wide-ranging field of judgement. That is, instead of going 'up' as did Bourdieu to the 'field of power' – to see how the victors in each field divide up the spoils – we go 'down' to see the common substratum in the self-organized relations of all social actors.

Field theory and a theory of fields

First, it may help to make what may initially seem a paradoxical distinction, namely between a 'field theory' and a 'theory of fields'. Field theory is a formal approach to thinking, first developed in physics, and then applied to social psychology by scions of the Gestalt/phenomenological schools in the mid-twentieth century and resuscitated by Bourdieu in the late twentieth century. A theory of fields is a particular approach to the exploration of the substantive phenomenon of fields; it may or may not have the formal characteristics of a field theory. In fact, the most important such theory currently, that of Fligstein and McAdam (2012), does not rely on field theoretic principles, but rather focuses on common internal structural properties of fields, the relation between fields, the sorts of action that allow actors to successfully navigate or transform fields, and the relations of fields to wider political-economic structures and changes. Such a theory of fields is clearly applicable to the more institutionally defined, 'objectified' fields such as the discrete realms of production that Bourdieu often studied.

But in the field theoretic perspective, a field is a global organization of vectors (pushes and/or pulls in a certain direction) that arises from the local mutual interactions of elements.

Further, we expect such pushes and pulls to be regular aspects of human experience, as the objects that we encounter have valences (good/bad, useful/useless and so on) that we read in with their other perceivable aspects. Thus we can approach a field theoretic understanding by beginning with the nature of aesthetic perception; we here review the conclusions of the Gestalt theorists who made this connection so as to assemble key aspects of the vocabulary we will need.

Field theory and aesthetics

Objects and fields

We will argue that the field theoretic approach of Bourdieu implies a path of generalization that can only be called a social aesthetics. Interestingly, this conclusion was reached by the first generation of social field theorists, who came from the German Gestalt school, all of whom were interested in aesthetics as a way of approaching action. Aesthetics were even more central to second generation theorists such as Metzger (e.g. 1986a; 1986b). There were also Gestalt-/field-theory inspired works of art criticism, most notably Meyer (1956), but also Berleant (1970) and Arnheim (1971). Bourdieu himself was only indirectly influenced by the Gestaltists; though he had some familiarity with the work of Kurt Lewin, it was mainly through Merleau-Ponty, and to a lesser extent Sartre, that these ideas came to Bourdieu (Martin and Gregg, 2015). Rather than deriving it from a close engagement with the Gestalt theorists, Bourdieu developed an emphasis on aesthetic judgement for the same reason that the Gestalt theorists did – it is strongly implied by a field theoretic account.

Aesthetics refers here to the family of theories and vocabularies that help us account for the varied qualitative experience that persons have of objects and experiences, especially those experiences connected with pleasure and displeasure. Thus they are not theories of the sensory receptivity of persons, but about a type of duality, the relationship between the characteristics of objects and the characteristics of experience. Although the term 'aesthetics' comes from the word for *sensation*, aesthetics has always been understood to imply not mere sensation, but *judgement*, and the puzzle of aesthetics is in some ways to account for our capacity to create judgements not through, say, syllogistic reasoning, but rather our reflection upon our own experience (for example, as pleasurable as opposed to displeasurable).

Further, aesthetics rises to the challenge of accounting for experiences that are complex and rich (as opposed to simple and atomic) yet unitary, which requires some way of grasping how complexities may be intuited as unities. Two questions are always asked and must be answered together: What is it about X that makes us feel Y? And what about those tasteless jerks who *don't* feel Y in the presence of X? That is, the intersubjective validity of aesthetic perception allows us to explain our reactions by recourse to the properties of objects even as we recognize, and must account for, the fact that this intersubjective concordance stops far short of unanimity. Indeed, if unanimity did obtain, taste could not provide us with a way of navigating social life.

The Gestalt/field approach holds that, first, whatever it is about X that pleases us (say) isn't just *about* X, but is *in* it, or is it. The qualities of objects – those aspects of them that have the potential to evoke a certain sort of response upon contact with a certain form of sentient being – are as objective as anything else about them. The fact that this vinyl disk recording of Mahler's *Kindertotenlieder* will make grown men burst into tears is no different from the fact that the disk will fly 20 yards if you throw it like a Frisbee. But just like the disk will only fly if it is thrown in the proper atmosphere, so too its lachrymogenic quality is only realized when it is brought into contact with the person of a certain disposition.

What prevents this from being a tautology (this will make you cry, except if it doesn't) is that the sets of dispositions to objects are non-randomly distributed across persons, and associated with social position. Hence any aesthetics is, for a sociologist, only stabilized by becoming a sociological aesthetics (this is similar to the 'institutional' aesthetics of art theory, as implicitly adopted by Becker 1982: 145). A social aesthetics, then, does not refer to those occasions when we choose our analytical tools on the basis of their aesthetic qualities, nor when we make inquiries about experiences that would widely be understood as involving high culture (asking, say, whether the way in which men hear the Mahler songs is similar to how women hear them); instead, it refers to our use of these analytic tools outside of the straitened realm of high culture to see how our grown man reads *USA Today*, thinks about the Methodist Episcopal Church, talks about Harvard University or answers a feeling-thermometer question on 'how close do you feel to immigrants'. It is not that specifically 'aesthetic' qualities are invoked (thus not that he thinks the stained glass windows are pretty, or that immigrants are somewhat too stubby compared to classic Greek statuary). Rather, it is that we as analysts must be oriented to the same problem in everyday social life that aestheticians grapple with when attempting to account for the experience of artworks: how to study the processes whereby persons, presumably simultaneously, (1) create single virtual unities out of complex tangles that our intellect would classify as abstractions and (2) retrieve information about the qualities of these unities, information that has a veridical nature in that it allows actors to successfully orient themselves to action in concordance, complementarity or contradiction with others.

The stuff of culture

We pursue such an aesthetics by following the lines laid out by the Gestalt theorists. For them, obviously aesthetic experience was only the tip of the iceberg of our capacity for the veridical perception of the qualities of objects. The aspects of objects that were of greatest interest to the Gestalt theorists, and to a theory of action, are their 'affordances' – what we can do with them. For the Gestalt theorists, we can directly perceive that a hammer is something you grab with your hand and smack things with; that a fruit should be eaten; that a rock can be thrown. What is key is that, argued Gibson (1986), information about what objects 'afford' us is present in the 'ambient optic array' – all the reflected, organized, light flying about us. That's why we have eyes.

As a result, the first-approximation account that they derived was one in which persons are fundamentally reactive, a view which may cut against the presumptions of most sociologists. Yet it is, for that, correct – as a first approximation. Objects *do* call out for us to do things with them. The cup says 'pick me up by the handle' and 'drink me'. The problem is that someone who always obeys when a cup says 'drink me' is likely to spend a lot of time very drunk. We generally have the capacity to suppress motor responses to objects with affordances, although when distracted, our suppression may weaken (thus we may find ourselves picking up potato chips that positively scream out 'eat me' when we are talking, completely unaware that we are obeying the chip). Further, certain neurological disorders seem to weaken our central control over, say, our hands, which then respond to the affordances directly (McBride *et al.* 2013; also see Lhermitte 1986), while in other cases, distracted attention may render us insensible to otherwise obvious stimuli (Mack and Rock 1998).

Further, we recognize that there is not only individual variation in what the affordances of objects mean (to one, a photograph is charming, and to another, maudlin), but variation in the degree to which people are responsive to objects. If this latter degree varies according to socially recognizable predictors, this suggests a further role for a sociological analysis, but we lay that to the side for now. Instead, we focus on what is perhaps the simplest issue, namely the nature of the aesthetic response. We can dispense with definitions and typologies because, according to consistent field theoretic principles, as analysts, we do not need to determine the order or arrangement of objects, in the way that a typologizer decides to order unruly particulars. Instead, objects come to us already arranged. That is, consider physical objects. They are, each and every one, in one place at one time, though some (such as train cars) move around a bit. If they radiate information about their affordances, we do not need to begin by *theorizing* where they are, but merely *noting* where they are.

When it comes to social objects, the same should also be true: as the social world has its own principles of organization, we may dispense with typologizing and classifying and proceed to mapping social objects. We may not know precisely where they are, but assuming that they are *somewhere* means that we can use their interactions with persons to tell us where they are. If Arizonans can see Humphrey's Peak, the mountain is probably in Arizona. If public school teachers like mountain climbing (as they do, or at least did, in 1970s France [Bourdieu 1984: 219]), 'mountain climbing' is probably near them, whatever that may mean. Hence the duality-based technique of correspondence analysis that became the workhorse for Bourdieu's numerical explorations (Breiger 2000).

But this has a strong implication. If we are materialists, as most of us claim to be (not in the Marxist sense but simply that we think that anything that exists is either matter or energy), then anything that we study is somewhere in the world as organized stuff. The problem for us is not locating the stuff, but understanding its principles of organization. The implication is that actors are our co-researchers. If we have spilled sugar and are not sure where it is, a fine solution would be to release a number of ants. The ants will quickly trace out the constellation of the sugar distribution.[3]

Similarly, people are continually telling us about social structure, if we would only listen. They tell us how classes are organized by whom they visit (Bian et al. 2005) and most importantly, by whom they marry. We, however, tend to refuse to allow them to explain the class structure to us, and instead keep our preconceptions and find an 'imperfect association,' say, of marriage patterns – given the assumed perfection of our lousy measures. In other words, it is not that culture is an 'also' to 'structure,' nor that culture 'is often important' in 'causing' or 'reproducing' structure. It is that our best tools for the investigation of social structure involve understanding those sorts of trans-individual regularities in the distribution of subjective states that we consider culture.

In sum, our capacity for non-arbitrary intuition of the qualities of complex social objects gives us, as actors, a head start in interpreting the world, and, as analysts, a head start in interpreting action, which itself is a function of compiled interpretations of a world full of stuff. Because social objects which make up one portion of this stuff, are not always visible to analysts as unities the way they are to actors, we are unlikely to be able to understand action without piggybacking on the capacity of actors to have insight – a capacity to use superficial aspects of the world to orient oneself to things one cannot technically perceive. Thus a field theoretic account joins those who would call for a vigorous cultural sociology. The great difference, however, is that the organization is believed to be in the arrangement of the stuff of the world, the pattern of social relations, and not a shared set of complex cognitive templates.

But how do we move from such a general picture to a clearer understanding of the role of such cultural components in *action*? This returns us to the issue of judgement in *Distinction*.

The field of judgements

Judgement and social space

Distinction stands out from Bourdieu's other works in two notable ways. First, it is regularly understood to be about cultural consumption, while his other books are generally oriented toward social production and reproduction. More important for our purposes, *Distinction* makes routine use of the language of fields for specific realms of endeavour or classes of products among which choices can be made (1984: 224, 226), but organizes these using the idea of a 'space' of various lifestyle choices. The term 'space' suggests a 'neutral,' or uncharged, substrate in which various sorts of fields may be positioned, in the same way that Cartesian space could be used to identify a metric field (e.g. a magnetic one) but would not itself have any field-like properties. Bourdieu tended to rely on space metaphors when he was speaking more generally, descriptively and regarding shared fundaments for multiple fields. This would suggest a strict division, in which only the intersubjectively recognized arenas of organized striving are amenable to field analysis, which may map these positions onto locations in space.

And that is how most Bourdieuians have treated his approach. Yet at the same time as he uses space for such more general principles of structuration, Bourdieu also (1984: 230) speaks of a 'field' of social classes in which tastes can be produced in strict analogy to the production of things-for-which-we-have tastes, which suggests that the social space of lifestyle choices is itself this field – even though this clearly is not one of the 'objectified' fields that we saw being treatable by a 'theory of fields'. For this reason, we would be unlikely to propose a 'theory of fields' for something like the set of judgements that are key for *Distinction*. Indeed, the Fligstein and McAdam (2012: 3, 9) approach defines the fields in question as 'mesolevel' orders 'in which actors … interact with one another on the basis of shared … understandings about the purposes of the field'. Most would, however, deny that there are *any* such purposes in the sorts of consumptive practices that seem to be the focus of *Distinction*, and certainly not claim that there is *agreement* about them.

But it is not the consumption itself that is of interest to Bourdieu; this is in many ways a by-product of the more fundamental *judgements* involved. It was, we recall, Kant's *Critique of Judgement* that inspired Bourdieu's theoretical investigations, and he pursued the dynamics involved doggedly: subjects are invited by researchers to judge various objects; the quantitative analyses here (and in many works inspired by *Distinction*) turn on large-scale observed correlations that lump together similar persons and things. Bourdieu links these judgements – and the general principles underlying them – to position in social space (most famously, linking binary oppositions like 'sweet/dry' to class oppositions like 'working class/middle class').

Given that these judgements are of all sorts of things – foods, sports, music and so on – it would seem quite clear that we cannot propose that there is some single 'field' in which they all sit, because they are judging a completely heterogeneous set of objects. But that may be incorrect: the subjects spend a great deal of time judging the judgement of others, regularly characterizing their sense of their own position by reference to the positions occupied by others (for examples: Bourdieu 1984: 185, 258, 275, 294, 298–300, 323, 324, 326, 335, 349, 355).

This pervasive judging of other judgements leads to a kind of comparability across domains and suggests that it might not be at all implausible to gather and analyze these judgements together.

Second order judgements

There are two notable characteristics of this sort of field which we think make it of key analytic importance for a general cultural sociology. As we noted above, it is clear that here, unlike the fields of production that Bourdieu analyzes, there are no 'stakes' to wager, no 'capital' to increase. Of course, there may well be *some* people who pursue distinction as if there were an apex that could be reached (our post-post-post-post-post-modern types, say), but we know from *Distinction* that this is not true of all. Many play this game 'as losers', attempting to distinguish themselves from others by knowing their place and loving their fate.[4] And yet, we find that field theoretic principles seem completely applicable.

The second characteristic is that while the objects of first order judgements are various and quite possibly often incomparable, second order judgements (judgements of judgements) are more homogeneous. Further, we believe that the potential for recursion in such judgements is greatly limited. That is, logical considerations alone might lead us to think that we would need to distinguish

1. Objects (say, a garden gnome);
2. Judgements of objects (garden gnomes are tacky);
3. Judgements of judgements of objects (those who think 'garden gnomes are tacky' are intolerant);
4. Judgements of judgements of judgements of objects (those who think 'those who think "garden gnomes are tacky" are intolerant' are simply uncultured);
5. Judgements of judgements of judgements of judgements of objects (those who think 'those who think "those who think 'garden gnomes are tacky' are intolerant" are simply uncultured' are full of themselves).

And so on, *ad astra*. Yet we believe that this is not the case. It may well be that there can be some separation to different levels of judgement: indeed, there is some evidence for this in *Distinction* (1984: 300), precisely where one middle-class person seems to judge that gnomes are tacky but that those who judge others harshly for accepting low culture are doing something wrong (that is, he is aware of the 'racism' of such judgements, though he himself makes them). But it would seem to be limited to only a few levels and a few situations. Certainly, the hypothetical attempt to provide an example above in which these levels could be separated led not merely to alternation of valence (+, −, +, −, ...), but to altercation − otherwise unlimited recursion seems to require either multiple personality disorder or a cognitive capacity that dwarfs anything plausibly attributed to persons.[5] Indeed, we might say that without altercation, it might be impossible to separate many levels, because *approving* judgements of judgement are 'transparent' (in the way that, contra Hume, we do not need to judge that our own judgements are true). Thus we expect judgements of judgements of judgements to regularly collapse back to judgements of judgements, and so we will be able to speak simply of 'first-order' judgements (judgements of objects) and 'second-order' judgements (judgements of judgements).

Finally, we should note that judging judgements is clearly a perfect case of that sort of valenced perception that can lead to vectoral experience (as each positive judgement is a 'towards' and each negative an 'away' from the target). Thus there is a way in which the very existence of second-order judgements suggests the possibility of a general field approach to at least one aspect of culture.

How can judgements form a field?

It is for this reason, we believe, that in *Distinction* Bourdieu moves effortlessly from the discussion of this social space to the theoretical principles that require the identification of a field (e.g. 110). Field theoretic analyses are applicable for the set of second-order judgements, not only because these are vectorial, but because they have a non-random organization that is accessible to actors' experience.

It is, we recall, the suggestion of Gestalt and field theories that objects in the world afford us certain felt imperatives about their use. The organization of these objects is social in two ways: first, in any literal sense, the ways in which objects are spatio-temporally distributed, and in which access to them is distributed across persons, is the result of at least partially non-random social processes. Whether it is the placement of a Monet next to a Renoir in a room in a museum or the very placement of the museum, its distance to forms of transport, its hours and admissions policies, we are seeing the results of some of the myriad social processes structuring the organization of things in the world. Second, if Bourdieu was in the slightest bit correct about anything, the *responses* that people have to such objects are differential in a way that is, as a first approximation, a function of position in social space.

At this point, we must introduce what we think is an underappreciated aspect of Bourdieu's analysis of social space. Let us call the 'lemma of the environmental validity of social space' the assumption that the principles used to organize individuals by the analyst are shared by the analyzed. They may not be the only, or even the most important, such principles, but they are recognized by actors, and hence, to an empirically assessable degree, structure patterns of interaction.

The logic above suggests that the task for a cultural sociology is to provide a framework that allows us to understand how human interactions produce affordances that enable actors to orient themselves toward one another in much the same way they orient themselves to other things in the world. It is not logically necessary, but clearly convenient and plausible, that we can use social space as an analogue for geographical space when we attempt to examine how actors respond to the affordances in their environment.

It might seem difficult to go from the analyses of *Distinction* showing class preferences for certain cultural products to more important actions, paradigmatically, to the analysis of class formation itself. But to the extent that people present themselves to one another as bundles of judgements, actors can perceive the affordances of one to another. That is, the transition from first-order to second-order judgements may be what transforms a sociology of Culture into a cultural sociology.

Perception, judgement and action

A sociology of perception

What is somewhat unusual about the field theoretic approach is the direct mapping of the qualities of objects to the actions of those who confront them. Conditional on the actor's own structure (habitus), the object tells the actor what to do with it. Just as potato chips say 'eat me', so a garden gnome says to some, 'buy me' and to others, 'mock me'. This means that the field theoretic approach unites its theory of action with a particular (and we think particularly defensible) sociology of perception.

And here we believe a cultural sociology based on these aesthetic principles makes a contribution to recent efforts at reformulating a sociology of perception (Friedman 2011) and/or copresence (Campos-Castillo and Hitlin 2013). Most sociologies of perception assume that the bulk of the organization of experience comes 'post-retina', as we pass neutral sensations (one can hardly call them perceptions) through what we may call a 'Mary-Douglas-Filter' of culturally prescribed samenesses and differences. Despite this position's compatibility with core ways of thinking in sociology (see Martin 2011), this seems to require implausibly demanding processing on the part of the individual mind, in contrast to theories – like that of Bourdieu – that argue that our chunking of experience comes not via the imposition of culturally arbitrary templates but because we learn to *recognize* (and *misrecognize*) the sorts of things that are out there.[6]

What might seem at best overscrupulous concern and at worst, irrelevant navel-gazing, may be crucial for our understanding of *social* perception – how we perceive others perceiving us. The puzzle is, as Campos-Castillo and Hitlin (2013: 169) have emphasized, that we find situations in which actors experience a kind of immediacy and an illusion of co-presence even though they are actually communicating via very restricted channels (such as email), with impoverished interactants like animals (Jerolmack 2009), with non-living actants (for example, a simple program like ELIZA or with a doll [also see Cerulo 2009]), or even with entities believed by many sociologists to be wholly imaginary (Sharp 2010).

In no way should we ignore such strong results about the *imputation processes* that are involved in actors' reflections on their relations with others, which indeed may also affect their actions.[7] Further, we must understand that, as Goffman (1967: 135) put it, the 'illusion of reality' – that firm belief that we are all living in the same world – owes its existence to processes that are fragile, though susceptible to quick repair. But we do not need to choose between (on the one hand) theories that flatten all forms of orientation to the world into a single voluntaristic attribution ('if you want to think people are giraffes, well then, I guess they're giraffes to you') and theories that require that no one ever make a mistake ('we see things as they are, all the time'). Ecological psychologists like Gibson (1986) instead begin from the premise that *when* we perceive, we perceive the qualities of things (which is to say, their potentials for our experience and our action), and when we misperceive, it is such qualities that we misperceive.

So, too, we propose that a theory of social perception must start with situations of perceivability. By focusing on *attributions* of co-presence, and attempting to experimentally manipulate these, we often miss what is essential about true social co-presence, which is mutual exposedness. The person – or javascript program – on the other end of a chat line not only has a very narrow channel of communication (a single stream of ASCII characters, say), but is almost completely cloaked, with indefinite amounts of time before any information (save that a move has not yet been made) is given off.

It is for this reason, we suspect, that research along these lines has produced contradictory findings: some arguing that reduced co-presence leads to *exaggerated* social judgements (in part because of the lack of mediating non-verbal signals [Menchik and Tian 2008]), while in other cases it seems that it is high co-presence ('vividness') that produces exaggerated judgement (see Campos-Castillo and Hitlin [2013: 185] who endorse this position). But seeing co-presence as a 'treatment' that can be applied in various 'doses' (which can have 'effects') may be the wrong way of beginning; rather, we should think about *environments* that make certain forms of exposure and concealment possible.

Perception out and about

And it is this that returns us to the idea of a field. A field (the French *champ* comes from the Latin *campus*) is, at heart, an open space facilitating certain types of human actions, most importantly, cultivation and conflict.[8] And field theory is a theory that best works for situations in which people are in 'cleared land' – exposed to mutual observation, and hence primed for mutual orientation. It is not impossible that results from laboratory experiments using close-up, heavily constrained vision will tell us *something* about social perception in a field, but it is unlikely that the results can be mechanically applied, without adaptation, to action outside. As an analogy, we are able to track a limited number of distinct moving objects in our visual field at any time, but the way that we perceive the texture of a grassy plain, say, is not a compounding of such individual objects. First, it seems that (despite our attribution of distinctness to 'parts') we do not actually see the detail for any part of the grass except the most central elements (which reach the fovea), and instead 'fill in' the texture for other areas. But most important, as Gibson emphasized, we use the *vector field* that is created by movement across a texture to tell us where we are, which way we are headed and what we are likely to hit. The organization of the texture, the preservation of the principles of organization in the optic array, and the development of our sensory-motor system in a world with such principles of organization allow us to make extremely efficient inferences that we could not do deliberately.

The upshot of this side-trip into analogy is the following conclusion: we may need to begin a social theory of perception with a field perspective not because we happen to like field theory, but because the 'openness' of fields leads them to elicit broadly consensual views of reality for the actors within them. We can thereby dispense with overly scrupulous attention to attribution, and, without denying that there are always errors, determine why social judgement works for action as well as it does.

There is a second implication. Given the 'lemma of the environmental validity of social space' above – one which we believe no sociologist would deny – we can trust that we can 'hang' judgements on social space, but *not* simply for our analytic purposes, the way we might regress counts of hen pecks on certain aspects of their social situation. Rather, we are making the claim that *actors* make a similar 'hanging' which means that they *experience the judgements of others as socially organized*. Given that we have already concluded that judgements of judgements are, substantially, judgements, we understand that, first, they are immediate responses to the qualities of that which is judged (though we recognize that these qualities, being relations between perceiver and perceived, vary predictably across social space), which allows us to focus on what actors *do* – how they respond to objects and judgements – and not how they may be forced to defend these to interlocutors, whether hostile or friendly, lay or professional.[9]

Advantages of a focus on judgements

In addition to the contributions made to a sociology of perception, we believe that such a general cultural sociology founded on the field of judgements has two other advantages. For one, somewhat counterintuitively, we may find that a more emically adequate approach to cognition, one that begins with first person, qualitative experience, allows us to dispense with the individual as unit of analysis. This in turn might allow us to produce strong theoretical statements about social perception and its relation to action *without* handling the complex, and potentially intractable, problems of a complete sociology of perception. We may get analytic clarity whenever we reduce the number of elements, but especially so when our subjects and direct objects in a theory of action are properly consubstantial – that is, they are the same sort of thing. Philosophers always had a hard time explaining how mind could know matter, but a very easy one explaining how mind could know mind (as long as the relation was unmediated by matter). Somewhat similarly, if we accept Bourdieu's argument that we judge objects through embodied dispositional principles, then to the extent that sexual fields are bodies judging bodies, they may have this analytic flatness that allows for the development of a parsimonious theoretical vocabulary (Martin 2013; also see Green 2011).

James Coleman (1990: 8) famously argued that every 'macroscopic' social relationship (say, between two variables in a social configuration, M1 and M2) was only a rough proxy that needed to be re-cast as three relations: first, one from the seeming macroproperty to the actual microcomponents of individual characteristics and actions (M1→m1; imagine a 'down arrow'); second, a rigorous and plausible connection from these microelements to others (m1→m2, 'across'); and third, an understanding of how these resultant microelements aggregate to the observed macrocomponent (m2→M2; 'up'). Thus the relation between Protestantism (M1) and capitalism (M2) discussed by Weber must be expanded to include the m1 of individual values and the m2 of individual economic behaviors. Analogously, many accounts of social action that accept the importance of subjective phenomenology seem to be drawn to a similar 'down-over-up' path (_/) in which we must go into the subjectivity of the actor, disassemble it into recognizable components (such as 'schemata,' 'values,' 'heuristics' or 'tools'), link these in some way (often undertheorized), and then return up to the level of the actor. To the extent that we focus on second-order judgements, we may be able to take a 'high road' in which we directly link judgement to judgement, avoiding the necessity of opening up heads.

Second, focusing on second-order judgements can help correct possibly misleading conclusions that sociologists have derived from sociological studies of judgement. If only for reasons of tractability, studies have tended to focus on *asymmetric* processes: some are judges, rankers or evaluators, and others are the judged, the ranked and the evaluated. But as Lamont (2012) in particular has argued, one of the most important forms of evaluative practice is peer-evaluation, in which all judges may be judged.

The sociology of judgements (quite understandably and correctly) tends to attempt to re-politicize decisions that are effectively de-politicized. To make an algorithm that automatically ranks colleges (Espeland and Sauder 2007) is to seemingly de-politicize a choice in which power will be used to authoritatively determine allocations (on this dynamic see also Porter 1996). Sociologists (e.g. Boltanski 2011 [2009]) often attempt not only to unveil the precise mechanisms and machinations behind the stabilization of any particular set of criteria but (perhaps especially after their institutions go down a notch in the US News!) also to return these decisions to rough-and-tumble world of politics, where the rated can fight back.

We may perhaps be seeing more of this sort of rough and tumble, given that formal means for evaluating the evaluations of others are increasingly common. At Amazon, rankers are ranked, and even more, in many venues, we find that we are allowed to choose our rankers (people who liked the things you liked like this ...). Such dynamics may be required for the emergence of an orderliness that is clearly distinguishable from patterns of judgement that may be fundamentally arbitrary, or at least may be effectively *made to be* arbitrary by a sociological critique.[10]

Our argument is not that this sort of 'judgement 2.0' is now more widespread than '1.0', which would probably be impossible to determine and theoretically irrelevant anyway.

It is that such settings provide a better case for getting at the fundamental dynamics of judgement than one in which the judgement is channeled by, or attached to, exogenously defined structures that define asymmetry. That is, the characteristics of emergent order shed the most light on the nature of the elements involved when these elements swim freely in an otherwise unstructured soup. Moreover, as a descriptive matter, many evaluative practices that have been treated as asymmetric are, to a large extent, the products of group evaluative efforts in which judges devote a great deal of attention to their fellow judges and orient their actions accordingly. Thus Lamont (2009) and Huutoniemi (2012) describe the production of academic consensus by the orientation of evaluators to the judgements of *other* evaluators, rather than toward the object being judged.[11]

Finally, we note that focusing on *judgements* as opposed to either *actors* or *objects* can lead to greater clarity. Taking the former, it may well be that there are classes of judgements that share formal similarities – for example, 'sour grapes' type judgements (where the inaccessible is judged to be of low quality), or 'dismissive' type judgements, in which something unknown is assumed to be unworthy of being known. We will – solely for purposes of explication and contrary to a great deal of good data – assume a simple world of completely hierarchically ranked positions, here only three: A > B > C. These positions can 'contain' both objects and persons, which we denote O_A, O_B, O_C, and P_A, P_B, P_C, respectively; we will use >, < and = to denote relations between objects and persons; thus $P_A > O_B$, $P_C < O_A$, $P_b = O_B$. We will assume that any P_i makes a "sour grapes" judgement of O_j ($J_i(O_j) = S$) if $P_i < O_j$; makes a "dismissive" judgement of O_j ($J_i(O_j) = D$) if $P_i > O_j$; and makes an "approving" judgement of O_j ($J_i(O_j) = A$) if $P_i = O_j$. We might find regularities in judgements of judgements such that (to take i's judgement of j's approval) $J_i(A_j) = A$ if $P_i = P_j$; $= C$ if $P_i < P_j$ (C being a cynical skepticism); and $= Pt$ if $P_i > P_j$ (Pt being a supercilious patronizing acceptance). And similarly for other combinations (for example, P_B may judge P_A's dismissal of O_B as "snobbery," while joining in P_A's dismissal of O_C). If now we generalize to multiple 'worlds' of objects, in which the ordering of our persons is permuted (one may be an expert on wines but all thumbs when it comes to the viola), we may find the regularities to be preserved at the level of second order judgements and not judgements of persons.

Further, we may find that to the extent that persons do judge one another, they may be more moved by others' *style* of judgement than the content of the judgements themselves (certainly a point made by Bourdieu regarding the aesthetic abstraction and formalism of pure taste). In particular, middle-class persons may approve of judgements of objects that involve prolixity and reference, even if they do not approve of the particular references made. Conversely, the nearly instinctive dismissal response that characterizes the contrarian distinction strategy overflows into dismissals of dismissals (even if these are of objects that are mutually dismissed). And judging the form of judgements allows persons to move into mutual orientation when they do not actually have joint familiarity with enough concrete objects.[12]

We wish to take care not to assert that this approach is simply or directly suitable to all problems. Field theory cannot explain social phenomena that are not organized by a field. Fields that are generally organized by routine behavior may nonetheless still produce phenomena that require deliberate, conscious thought (Leschziner and Green 2013). And as Fligstein and McAdam (2012) would say, we must expect a form of 'rolling turbulence' to scatter our nicely arranged vectors time and time again. Nor does social action oriented toward the perceived judgements of others necessarily mean that actors fully understand one another. Error and misunderstanding are common and sociologically interesting aspects of interaction (see e.g. Gibson 2012). In addition, certain fields may be based entirely on systematic misapprehension (Bourdieu *et al.* 1994). Our sense of the judgements of others is necessarily incomplete and yet it may amount to much of what we have to go on.

Conclusion

Cultural sociology has concerned itself with the role of culture, broadly defined, in many domains of social life. This perspective has been resistant to Bourdieu's critique of the presumptions underlying taste, and the general view of the sociology of Culture has been that this critique is properly confined to cases of the production and evaluation of a relatively small class of goods. However, the extension of this Bourdieuian sociology of Culture approach to second-order judgements may provide the basis for a cultural sociology in the broader sense. The aesthetic view is ultimately an account of socially conditioned perception. Such distinguishing, judging perceptions may play a significant role not only in the evaluation of a few high status objects, but also in providing a basis for social action with respect to other judging, perceiving actors. The range of phenomena over which this perspective may be especially helpful is still being defined. However, it is immediately useful in lending greater theoretical coherence to our notions of culture. One thing that it seems almost all of us now accept is that there is no express train from social structure to social action that does not pass through perception. But the reasoning outlined here suggests that there are routes that do not pass through quasi-propositional or schematic aspects of cognition. Action informed by perception, rather than complex scripts and schemes, enables us to understand culture as made of the things of the world, rather than a world crammed inside our heads.

Notes

1. We understand the reasons why some have abandoned the term in favour of 'practice', but we think we lose more than we gain in throwing out this somewhat turbid bathwater.
2. These positions, at least in the case of France, also have clear locations in geographic space: Paris or the provinces, the Left Bank or the Right.
3. The only problem is, now we've got ants.
4. A great deal of work following Peterson (1992) and Bryson (1996) has treated this reference to other positions as a symbolic tactic of identity construction (or autoproduction). Whether or not such an approach incorrectly reduces low-status consumers to a passive null category (see Bennett 2011) seems an empirical question that requires greater precision in our investigations (along the lines of Lizardo and Skiles 2012).
5. Although speakers can easily have two levels of recursion, linguists (e.g. Johansson 2005: 238) suggest that our maximum is three or four, and this is with the substantial scaffolding of a linear grammar (which gives us a single dimension to spread out structure on, in contrast to the '0-dimensional' point of unspoken consciousness).
6. We must bear in mind, however, that not all such 'things' – social objects, that is, or nexi of relations – that are 'out there' are things we all want to defend as real. Thus entire classes of things, or so Bourdieu claimed, are only recognized because they are misrecognized (for example, the shiftiness of gypsies), hence our temptation to put them consistently in 'scare quotes'.
7. We do note that it is not obviously the case that such attributions track behaviour. We may believe that we are 'copresent' and 'fully interacting' with some X (who, say, is actually not present) when our behaviour is actually measurably different than it is with an 'actually copresent' alter. Thomas's rule – that 'if men define situations as real, they are real in their consequence' – is an important place to start, but it is not always correct, and becomes less and less correct as we get to finer grained analyses of behavior.
8. Interestingly, it may well be that the root of the Latin *campus* is an Indo-European term meaning *corner* or *bend*, as the first fields were surrounded by non-cleared land; the English and Germanic terms more obviously derive from a root meaning 'flat' or 'spread out.'

9 Much has been made about the difference between the kinds of behavior and explanation elicited by observation and interviewing (Vaisey 2009; Pugh 2013; Khan and Jerolmack 2013); while this remains an open question, it may well be that such techniques will be important for bringing to the fore gaps or contradictions in actors' self-understandings, as well as possible paths of resolution they might pursue in certain circumstances.
10 Thus for example, Rivera (2010; also see 2012) describes the gatekeeping practices at an elite club, noting that the gatekeepers make their decisions about admittance not so much by calculation as a felt sense of the appropriateness of a potential patron. They might have completely indefensible criteria, but until there is pushback, this is not known. It is precisely for this reason that there is such a temptation for asymmetric rankers to cover up the details of their procedures.
11 Clayman and Reisner (1998) characterize a similar process in evaluations of newsworthiness and Radway (1997) in evaluations of books.
12 At the same time, we note that there is reason to think that if our goal is to group persons, we may do better when we *ignore* judgements entirely and simply focus on behavior. The Netflix recommendation algorithm was improved when it was reformulated to take into account not only how viewers had *rated* movies, but the mere fact that they had viewed them at *all*. Thus focusing on the objects tells us what *worlds* people are in, in the sense of forming subgroups of persons who *can* be mutually oriented to one another, and thus induce field effects.

References

Alexander, J.C. (1995) *Fin-de-Siècle Social Theory: Relativism, Reduction and the Problem of Reason*, London: Verso.
—— (2003) *The Meanings of Social Life: A Cultural Sociology*, New York: Oxford University Press.
Arnheim, R. (1971) *Entropy and Art*, Berkeley, CA: University of California Press.
Becker, H.S. (1982) *Art Worlds*, Berkeley, CA: University of California Press.
Bennett, T. (2011) 'Culture, Choice, Necessity: A Political Critique of Bourdieu's Aesthetic', *Poetics*, 39: 530–546.
Berleant, A. (1970) *The Aesthetic Field: A Phenomenology of Aesthetic Experience*, Springfield, IL: Charles C. Thomas.
Bian, Y., R. Breiger, D. Davis and J. Galaskiewicz (2005) 'Occupation, Class, and Social Networks in Urban China', *Social Forces*, 83: 1443–1468.
Boltanski, L. (2011 [2009]) *On Critique*, translated by Gregory Elliot, Cambridge: Polity.
Bourdieu, P. (1984 [1979]) *Distinction: A Social Critique of the Judgement of Taste*, translated by Richard Nice, Cambridge, MA: Harvard University Press.
—— (1988) *Homo Academicus*, Palo Alto, CA: Stanford University Press.
—— (1993) *The Field of Cultural Production*, New York: Columbia University Press.
—— (1996a) *The Rules of Art: Structure and Genesis of the Literary Field*, Palo Alto, CA: Stanford University Press.
—— (1996b) *The State Nobility: Elite Schools in the Field of Power*, Palo Alto, CA: Stanford University Press.
Bourdieu, P., J.-C. Passeron and M. de Saint Martin (1994) *Academic Discourse: Linguistic Misunderstanding and Professional Power*, Cambridge: Polity.
Breiger, R.L. (2000) 'A Tool Kit for Practice Theory', *Poetics* 27: 91–115.
Bryson, B. (1996) '"Anything but Heavy Metal": Symbolic Exclusion and Musical Dislikes,' *American Sociological Review*, 61(5): 884–899.
Campos-Castillo, C. and S. Hitlin (2013) 'Copresence: Revisiting a Building Block for Social Interaction Theories,' *Sociological Theory*, 31(2): 168–192.
Cerulo, K.A. (2009) 'Non-Humans in Social Interaction,' *Annual Review of Sociology*, 35: 531–552.
Clayman, S.E. and A. Reisner (1998) 'Gatekeeping in Action: Editorial Conferences and Assessments of Newsworthiness', *American Sociological Review*, 63: 178–199.
Coleman, J.M. (1990) *Foundations of Social Theory*, Cambridge: Belknap Press.
Espeland, W.N. and M. Sauder (2007) 'Rankings and Reactivity: How Public Measures Recreate Social Worlds', *American Journal of Sociology*, 113(1): 1–40.
Fligstein, N. and McAdam, D. (2012) *A Theory of Fields*, New York: Oxford University Press.
Friedman, A. (2011) 'Toward a Sociology of Perception: Sight, Sex, and Gender', *Cultural Sociology*, 5(2): 187–206.
Gerth, H. and C.W. Mills (1954) *Character and Social Structure*, London: Routledge and Kegan Paul.

Gibson, D.R. (2012) *Talk at the Brink: Deliberation and Decision during the Cuban Missile Crisis*, Princeton, NJ: Princeton University Press.
Gibson, J.J. (1986 [1979]) *The Ecological Approach to Visual Perception*, Hillsdale, NJ: Lawrence Erlbaum.
Goffman, E. (1967) *Interaction Ritual. Essays in Face-to-Face Interaction*, Chicago: Aldine.
Green, A.I. (2011) 'Playing the (Sexual) Field: The Interactional Basis of Systems of Sexual Stratification', *Social Psychology Quarterly*, 74(3): 244–266.
Huutoniemi, K. (2012) 'Communicating and Compromising on Disciplinary Expertise in the Peer Review of Research Proposals', *Social Studies of Science*, 42(6), 897–921.
Jerolmack, C. (2009) 'Humans, Animals, and Play: Theorizing Interaction When Intersubjectivity Is Problematic', *Sociological Theory*, 27: 371–389.
Johansson, S. (2005) *Origins of Language: Constraints on Hypotheses*, Amsterdam: John Benjamins Publishing Company.
Khan, S. and C. Jerolmack (2013) 'Saying Meritocracy and Doing Privilege', *The Sociological Quarterly*, 54(1): 9–19.
Lamont, M. (1992) *Money, Morals, and Manners: The Culture of the French and the American Upper-Middle Class*, Chicago: University of Chicago Press.
—— (2009) *How Professors Think: Inside the Curious World of Academic Judgement*, Cambridge: Harvard University Press.
—— (2012) 'Toward a Comparative Sociology of Valuation and Evaluation', *Annual Review of Sociology*, 38: 201–221.
Leschziner, V. and A.I. Green (2013) 'Thinking about Food and Sex: Deliberate Cognition in the Routine Practices of a Field', *Sociological Theory*, 31(2): 116–144.
Lhermitte, F. (1986) 'Human Autonomy and the Frontal Lobes. Part II: Patient Behavior in Complex and Social Situations: The "Environmental Dependence Syndrome."' *Annals of Neurology*, 19: 335–343.
Lizardo, O. and S. Skiles (2012) 'Reconceptualizing and Theorizing "Omnivorousness": Genetic and Relational Mechanisms', *Sociological Theory*, 30(4): 263–282.
Mack, A. and I. Rock (1998) *Inattentional Blindness*, Cambridge: MIT Press.
Martin, J.L. (2011) *The Explanation of Social Action*, New York: Oxford University Press.
—— (2013) 'The Crucial Place of Sexual Judgement for Field Theoretic Inquiries', in A.I. Green (ed.), *Sexual Fields: Toward a Sociology of Collective Sexual Life*, Chicago: University of Chicago Press.
Martin, J.L. and F. Gregg (2015) 'Was Bourdieu a Field Theorist?', in M. Hilgers and E. Mangez (eds.), *Bourdieu's Theory of Social Fields*, London: Routledge.
McBride, J., P. Sumner, S.R. Jackson, N. Bajaj and M. Husain (2013) 'Exaggerated Object Affordance and Absent Automatic Inhibition in Alien Hand Syndrome', *Cortex*: 49(8): 2040–2054.
Menchik, D.A. and X. Tian (2008) 'Putting Social Context into Text: The Semiotics of E-mail Interaction', *American Journal of Sociology*, 114: 332–370.
Metzger, W. (1986a) 'Der Geltungsbereich gestalttheoretischer Ansätze', in M. Stadler and H. Crabus (eds.), *Gestalt Psychologie*, Frankfurt am Main: Verlag Waldermar Kramer.
—— (1986b) 'Die Entdeckung der Prägnanztendenz', in M. Stadler and H. Crabus (eds.) *Gestalt Psychologie*, Frankfurt am Main: Verlag Waldermar Kramer.
Meyer, L.B. (1956) *Emotion and Meaning in Music*, Chicago: University of Chicago Press.
Peterson, R.A. (1992) 'Understanding Audience Segmentation: From Elite and Mass to Omnivore and Univore', *Poetics*, 21(4): 243–258.
Porter, T.M. (1996) *Trust in Numbers: The Pursuit of Objectivity in Scientific and Public Life*, Princeton, NJ: Princeton University Press.
Pugh, A.J. (2013) 'What Good Are Interviews for Thinking About Culture? Demystifying Interpretive Analysis', *American Journal of Cultural Sociology*, 1: 42–68.
Radway, J.A. (1997) *A Feeling for Books: The Book-of-the-Month Club, Literary Taste, and Middle-Class Desire*, Chapel Hill, NC: University of North Carolina Press.
Rivera, L. (2010) 'Status Distinctions in Interaction: Social Selection and Exclusion at an Elite Nightclub', *Qualitative Sociology*, 33: 229–255.
—— (2012) 'Hiring as Cultural Matching: The Case of Elite Professional Service Firms', *American Sociological Review*, 77(6): 999–1022.
Sharp, S. (2010) 'How Does Prayer Help Manage Emotions?', *Social Psychology Quarterly*, 73: 417–437.
Vaisey, S. (2009) 'Motivation and Justification: A Dual-Process Model of Culture in Action', *American Journal of Sociology*, 114: 1675–1715.

9

Genre

Relational approaches to the sociology of music[1]

Jennifer C. Lena

A core objective for sociologists of culture has been to understand classification and categorization processes. Categorizing the observed world into groups of things with some perceived similarities is fundamental to human cultures and provides sociologists with insights into how particular social groups define difference and similarity, value and significance. Categorization reflects social structures, as generations of cultural anthropologists and sociologists have demonstrated.

The study of *sociocultural* classification has a long history in sociology, perhaps because category distinctions are often the nucleus for identities, hierarchies, and conflict. Sociologists have examined classification systems in diverse contexts, including organizational forms and religious communities and exploring distinctions between people based on gender, sexuality, race, and cultural tastes, among others. The transmutation of relational qualities, like poverty (which is a social relationship and not a quantity of money), into attributional qualities is a core concern of sociologists working in many areas of the discipline, but the study of how categories '"totalize" identities that are in fact often multidimensional and contradictory' (Emirbayer 1997: 308–9) is work that often falls to cultural sociologists.

In this chapter, I turn my attention to the classification of musical works into genres, illuminating some problems that result from the use of musicological categories in sociological research. I propose that we substitute a sociological specification of genre built from the careful study of how relations within music communities constitute categories of consumption. I discuss the consequences of sociological genres for two bodies of research on taste: that of the heritability of preferences and of the theorized 'omnivorousness' of elites. In tracing the roots and uses of a relational approach both in and outside of cultural sociology, I hope to illustrate both a method and a theory of use in the field.

Genre

No ordering principle is as fundamental to culture as genre. Genres are generally treated as natural objects; contested, yes, but based on the sorting of 'intrinsic' or 'objective' attributes like beats-per-minute, or narrative tropes, that link individual works. Our peers in the humanities often employ the idea of genre to focus attention to the text abstracted from the social environment of its production or consumption (*inter alia* Frow 2006). Such musicological genres include rock, pop, and jazz.

Cultural sociologists, and the sociologists of music who are my focus here, often treat genres as natural objects for the sake of expediency and to favor the emic experience of fans, artists, and other 'insiders' in music communities. Stories about socio-musical identities are usually premised on the assumption that patronage of a musicological genre makes one's experiences and opinions coherent. Musical texts reinforce the notion that musicological genres have natural boundaries by presenting linear trajectories of musical, economic, or social development in timelines, the chronological organization of chapters, and status and role designations for participants that resemble ancestry charts (e.g. 'grandfather' and 'queen'). These features do the canon-formation work for genres and, to the extent that they include discussions of boundary controversies, guide readers away from questioning the existence of a coherent whole. Treating genres and the boundaries around them as natural and inevitable effaces their core sociological attributes by portraying something constituted through dynamic relations as something objective and extra-social.

But such 'natural' philosophies of genres don't hold up under scrutiny; they 'collapse a complex, shifting social world full of debate and disagreement into an inevitable chain of events leading to the present, during which necessary transformations take place' (Lena 2012: 146). Claims for inalienable boundaries between styles cannot be sustained in the face of substantial evidence that stylistic boundaries are social constructions accomplished when people and organizations collaborate in order to re-/produce genres. Sociological genres are 'systems of orientations, expectations, and conventions that bind together industry, performers, critics, and fans in making what they identify as a distinctive sort of music' (Lena 2012: 6). Sociological genres are community structures characterized by shared musical activity, not musical performances that share musicological characteristics. That said, the music enjoyed by a particular genre community has particular (but not particularistic) musical or aesthetic traits. However, a shared appreciation of particular aesthetic characteristics is only one of the dozen traits that characterize a given sociological genre.

The dynamic, social character of boundary-making is reflected in the very arguments we have about what kinds of people and works should be included within a genre category, and patterned kinds of claims-making that are used to exert power over these inclusions. We err if we ignore the obvious fact that music history is not characterized by widespread consensus over the allocation of songs or performers to musicological genres. Instead, musical history is better characterized as punctuated by periodic arguments over the sorting of songs and groups among contiguous styles. Genre disputes illustrate how power is exerted to support 'invidious categorical distinctions which compel our obedience' (Emirbayer 1997).

After all, 'genres do not work by simply reproducing the same patterns over and over; such repetitive logic would likely have little appeal to popular music audiences' (Wakesman 2009: 8). Consider, for example, the merging of popular musical styles, the 'pop-rockization', that Regev details in his book as a form of 'expressive isomorphism' (2013:12). He observes the 'tendency within pop-rock music to merge and fuse pop-rock with other styles and genres, and the tendency of musicians and producers working in various genres of popular music to adopt and implement at least some creative practices associated with pop-rock, most notably the adoption of electric instrumentation, have contributed to a process whereby the pop-rock aesthetic became the dominant force in world popular music' (Regev 2013: 22). This fluidity of instrumentation and other creative practices across musicological genre boundaries is *characteristic* of creative fields, not exceptional.

What's at stake in getting genre right?

The consequences of relying on these musicological genres in sociological research are quite grave, which I can illustrate in reference to a recent study of intergenerational musical influence, and in the scores of articles charting the rise of 'omnivorous' tastes. In both cases, the reliance on musicological genres leads authors to mistaken conclusions.

Ter Bogt et al. (2011) study an interesting and underexplored facet of taste: how parents' listening habits in their teen years impact the preferences of their offspring. To determine if there is a correlation of musical preferences between generations of a family, the authors asked a sample of Utrechtian parents and their children to tick off their musical preferences from a list that included soul, rock, punk, hip-hop, and jazz.[2] The authors found that parents who enjoyed pop had children who preferred pop and dance; parents who preferred rock had daughters (but not sons) who enjoy rock. They concluded that 'preferences for cultural artifacts such as (popular) music show continuity from generation to generation' (2011: 297).

But is the pop music of the early 1970s the same as the pop music of the oughts? If we compare the weekly Album Top 100 charts (a conventional measure of 'pop' music) when parents were the same ages of their teens, we see some stark (musicological) differences.[3] According to dutchcharts.nl, the top performers in 1971 (for fathers) included The Rolling Stones, Paul and Linda McCartney, and Emerson, Lake, and Palmer. In July 1974, mothers enjoyed the soundtrack to Andrew Lloyd Weber's *Jesus Christ Superstar*, a compilation album of the 'RCA Nashville Sound' and Chris Hinze featuring Louis van Dyke and Jan Goudswaard playing *Sketches on Bach*. The July 2005 Top Album charts included The Black Eyed Peas, System of a Down, and Guus Meeuwis.

On first glance, both the older and more recent pop charts feature a number of rock acts (from The Rolling Stones to hard rockers System of a Down), which begs the question of whether the authors should have treated 'pop' and 'rock' as distinct genres in the survey.[4] Indeed, in their preliminary analysis, the authors found some cross loading of factors for the pop music items for parents (2011: 305). Next, the comparison reveals that music that might also be labeled as folk revival, Broadway, classical, and country appears on the pop charts in the 1970s and is replaced by rap and hard rock on the 2005 charts. The aesthetic content of this genre doesn't appear to be stable enough to use as an index of the intergenerational transmission of music tastes. I would add that the weakness of these genres as descriptors of musical content isn't an artifact of some feature of pop or rock (noting Regev's [2013] argument to the contrary). The authors excluded a number of genres (disco, soul) from the youth survey and added others (hip-hop, electronic music) to reflect the waning and waxing salience of the category titles.

We might measure taste using these categories because we think they are emic representations of taste – that they best reflect how respondents do the work of categorizing their musical preferences. But do sociologists have evidence this is the case? In a very provocative study of musical taste among students in Mississippi, John Sonnett (2013) finds that musical boundaries cohere not around musicological genres, but around processes of inclusion, exclusion, and ambivalence. Based on respondents' own ranking of artist preferences, Sonnett finds 'the primary opposition in the field of musical taste is between those who make distinctions within genres (i.e., Ambivalent) versus those who make distinctions between genres (i.e., Divider)' (25). While Sonnett's research is too preliminary in scope to offer a generalizable model of taste, it is worth noting that his results suggest that fixed-choice questions about genres are both failing to reflect the emic experience of taste for many respondents, and that obvious alternative specifications exist for how to measure cultural tastes.[5]

Musicological genre distinctions are also used in the many studies of musical omnivorousness, and here too we see scholars drawing conclusions about taste that rest on shaky foundations. In a landmark study, Peterson and Kern (1996) used data from the Survey of Public Participation in the Arts (SPPA) to demonstrate that wealthy and well-educated Americans were supplementing their traditional fondness for consecrated musical genres (opera and classical music) with a small set of popular styles. They discovered that 'highbrow snobbery' was being replaced by 'highbrow omnivorousness', particularly within younger cohorts of elites (Peterson and Kern 1996). Many studies have replicated this result in multiple countries, and across a range of cultural pursuits, including reading, art, and most recently, food and television (see Peterson 2005 for a review).

To measure musical taste, the SPPA asks respondents to tick off all the styles (e.g. classical, rock, classic rock) they enjoy from a list provided to them. The reason sociologists argue that elites are increasingly omnivorous is because younger elites in recent surveys tick off more styles, on average, than elites who completed earlier waves of the survey, or who are older. Many interpret this to mean that elite tastes have experienced fragmentation, such that older elites maintain exclusionary tastes, while younger elites adopt an ideology of equality. The later discovery of omnivorousness among non-elites (Peterson 2005; Peterson and Rossman 2008) was interpreted as an indication that the old homology between class or social position and taste was breaking down.

The more stirring alternative is that the increase in reported genre preferences is a means respondents use to indicate increased selectivity within genres, which would likely be true if taste identities cohere around inter-genre selectivity. In fact, there is a large and growing body of research that suggests that boundary work operates (for at least some of us) within and across genres. I have already noted Sonnett's (2013) excellent study of how combinations of inclusion, exclusion, and ambivalence around specific artists typify Mississippi college students' tastes, which usefully builds upon Goldberg's (2011) earlier research. Johnston and Baumann's (2007) research on foodies (omnivorous eaters) demonstrates that their preferences are not driven by cuisine, or the status of any eaterie, nor do they fail to discriminate among foods; they eat at the same places and the same foods as other eaters, but they set themselves apart with the discourse they use to describe the experience: the food they like is 'authentic', less 'processed', or 'industrial'. The time has come for more concerted attention to the categories that consumers produce through their consumption behaviour; such research may reveal the need to jettison (musicological) genre as a valid (or even reliable) variable in many studies of cultural taste.

How relational methods produce sociological categories

So, what alternatives to musicological genre categories exist? How can we construct more valid and reliable measures of taste for use by sociologists? How can we incorporate into such measures our understanding that boundaries are socially constructed, contested, manifestations of power?

Understanding the relationship between taste and aesthetic categories profitably begins with the observation of how people participate in music communities, since group membership predicts how aesthetic boundaries are drawn. That is, the study of taste relies first on the study of taste groups and how they categorize since 'processes by which genre distinctions are created, ritualized, and eroded, and processes by which tastes are produced [are] part of the sense-making and boundary-defining activities of social groups' (DiMaggio 1987: 441). An inductive approach is suited to measuring these kinds of cultural questions because we seek to understand how people order the world to produce the categories that they then treat as fixed or natural. If we examine social exchanges we begin to see the social relationships that produce, and are produced by, categorization processes.

A set of classic anthropological studies by Ward Goodenough, Thomas Schweitzer, and James Davis may offer inspiration for this relational, inductive approach to taste. In 1963, Ward Goodenough published a study of the neighborhood of Manuhoe in Papeete, the capital of the country then called French Polynesia. His study was designed as a test of theories of economic rationality, to see if cost and 'objective' utility would explain the acquisition of consumer goods within the village; he asked: would wealthier families own more expensive goods? Goodenough gathered data on 40 of the 41 households in Manuhoe and seven kinds of consumer goods they might own, including bicycles, cars, radios, stoves, and refrigerators. In contrast to what we might find if economic resources were perfectly correlated with taste, each household did not simply buy what it could afford, acquiring objects in order of expense, nor was it the case that households treated the same object as possessing the same amount of utility. Instead, social ties and cultural attitudes better explained the observed variation. Household 33 included only a widower whose food was provided by his children; although he could afford it, he had no need for a stove and so did not have one.

The method that Goodenough used to analyze these data is the same one that Thomas Schweizer used in his study of the Congo-region Mbuti people. The process, known as Guttman scaling, 'identifies the maximally transitive and consistent representation of the rows and columns of the matrix' (Schweizer 1993a: 471) into which the analyst has entered data on things like 'who owns which consumer goods'. What the scaling process yields is classes of data points where members are maximally similar to one another and maximally dissimilar to members of other groups. In such a model, we must rely purely on observation to identify groups, rather than imposing some set of expectations on what kind of households, goods, or people should end up belonging to the same group.

This approach may appear to be a kind of primitivist sociology: one assumes no characteristics of the exchanges within a population before initiating observation. The first act isn't to identify gender, race, age, or wealth, or even to trust reports of who or what belongs to the group. Rather, we start by documenting transfers of resources, goods, positions, ideas, people, and organizations through social ties. This approach has been referred to as 'relational sociology' (Emirbayer 1997) although it is worth noting that roots lie in core sociological texts by authors we now treat as progenitors of distinct theoretical traditions (itself an interesting case of classification), including Marx, Weber, Durkheim, and Simmel. Thorough and recent reviews of the application of this approach to culture (Mohr and White 2008; Goldberg 2011) emphasize the complexity of these relations and the resulting multiplicity of shared understandings (Breiger 2009; Mohr and White 2008; Mohr 2013; Mische 2011), and largely abjure the hard behaviourism of earlier network models.

One of the notable strengths of this approach is its ability to assist the researcher in identifying relationships that might be ignored or denied by interview subjects or if more assumptions were made about category salience. Speaking of his study of status relationships, Schweizer (1993a: 478) wrote: 'As participant observers we had difficulty breaking down this structure…. The frequencies and the prices of consumer items provided clues to their economic and cultural values, but the whole pattern was rather diffuse'. Using a simple observation and indexing process, we can identify patterned disparities in both access to resources and control of them, and observing the sorting behaviour that leads to categories can help us to generate a robust understanding of how some things are left out of such categories.

Consider the difficulty of measuring status without some method that allows you to identify forms of esteem or deference that are embarrassing to relate, that are based on automatic cognition (Vaisey 2009: 1688), or that would result in lower self-esteem if they were related faithfully. Studies of status rely on measures of financial success like sales (Dowd 2004) and on indexes of productivity or publication (Anheier *et al.* 1995; Craig and Dubois 2010), critical success (Allen and Lincoln 2004), and awards (Allen and Lincoln 2004; Craig and Dubois 2010). Scholars have also used name recognition (Anheier *et al.* 1995) and surveys (Craig and DuBois 2010) to evaluate peer esteem. While sales and critical acclaim reliably measure certain status dimensions, they do a poor job capturing others. Indeed, a recent study of rap artists reveals that three distinct status orders exist: one based on sales success, one based on peer esteem, and one based on aesthetic innovation and imitation (Lena and Pachucki 2013). While sales and peer esteem are relatively visible to actors in the field and made objective in charts, award shows, invitations to collaborate, interviews, and 'listicles', the aesthetic status order is more complex and less visible, yet it reflects an important dimension of the art world's social structure.

This relational approach attempts to 'take seriously what Durkheim saw but most of his followers did not: that the organic solidarity of a social system rests not on the cognition of men, but rather on the interlock and interaction of objectively definable social relationships' (Boorman and White 1976: 1442) That is, social structure is 'regularities in the patterns of relations among concrete entities; it is *not* a harmony among abstract norms and values or a classification of concrete entities by their attributes' (White *et al.* 1976: 733–4, emphasis in original). The analysis of patterns of values and attributes tells us a great deal about social life, but there are some aspects of culture they are not suited to reveal. A relational approach can help us to identify 'hidden relations' and 'the constraining and enabling dimensions of patterned relationships among social actors within a system' (Emirbayer and Goodwin 1994: 1418). As Bearman (1993: 9–10) wrote, 'Categorical models alone rarely partition people in a way that confirms with observed action, because individual activity in the world is organized through and motivated not by categorical affiliations but by the structure of tangible social relations in which persons are embedded'. While most sociologists are 'beholden to the idea that it is entities that come first and relations among them only subsequently' emerge in the analysis, we can instead 'reverse these basic assumptions and depict social reality instead in dynamic, continuous, and processual terms' (Emirbayer 1997: 281).

How relational methods produce sociological genres

Turning back to music, the process of identifying musical communities should be relatively straightforward. We can begin by identifying a data source that might document transfers of resources among music community members. Lena (2012) and Lena and Peterson (2008) treated the voluminous corpus of primary and secondary documentation of the lives of musicians, fans, administrators, organizations, and styles that exist as containing information on exchanges.

Through an iterative coding process, patterns in community structure, use of media, and discourses used by group members emerged from these histories. The organizational form (a circle or scene), scale, and locus (homes, firms, or festivals) of activity captured differences in groups' social structures. To describe differences in how groups employed material culture, the authors identified the sources of income for participants, the degree to which technology was standardized, and the use of fashion and drugs as identity markers in order to distinguish groups. Finally, several important facets of discourse were coded including the way group members articulated their 'genre ideal' or goals, the content of disputes or complaints about other musical artists, the degree of consensus in the use of argot or lingo by members of the group, and the source of the name for the musical style.

Combinations of these attributes make it possible to identify resemblances between rock and gospel, south Texas polka and salsa, while clusters of quantities of these attributes revealed developmental trajectories held in common by musical communities. Taking the simplest of these: organizational structures are often informal when the group is small, and become more formal as it increases in size. The patterned clusters of attributes reveal that four stages characterize the history of 60 musical styles created in the twentieth century United States: avant-garde, scene-based, industry-based, and traditionalist.

The first stage includes a very small group of people who occasionally make music together, never develop a name for the group, and typically fail to make money or develop fans, and quickly disband. In some cases, they grow and create a scene-based community, often located within a neighborhood from which they generate income (often from non-musical employment), fans, press attention, and a collective sense of purpose or identity. Occasionally, these groups come to the attention of record label executives or national journalists, and attention from either can catapult the community into the mainstream as an industry-based genre. Finally, some last long enough for a core group to call for album re-issues and reunion concert tours, and academics and old timers support these heritage movements with their time and money; these are traditionalist genres.

The inductive categorization process used in Lena (2012) yielded a matrix of associations that best describes classes of data points where members are maximally similar to one another and maximally dissimilar to members of other groups. But we must bear in mind that the genre forms that result are ideal-typical structures. If distinctions between attributes or finer gradations within them had been made it would have been possible to identify more than twelve attributes, or more than four genre forms. For example, 'press coverage' could have been dissembled into two dimensions: one that captured the size and demographic attributes of readers and one that reflected the content or character of specific articles.[6] The four-genre type by twelve-dimension resolution was ultimately the most parsimonious.

The four-genre forms that resulted represent a way of thinking about genre that is sociological – that is based on differences in community characteristics and not musicological ones. A striking difference with musicological genres is that the sociological approach allows us to identify and understand musicians who participate in a community at one point in time but later produce what will be seen as aesthetically dissimilar music. One such example can be found among the group of singer-songwriters who lived and worked together in Los Angeles' Laurel Canyon in the late 1960s. This group included members of the Doors; the Mamas and the Papas; Crosby, Stills, Nash, and Young; Joni Mitchell; Jackson Browne; Linda Ronstadt; Leonard Cohen; and Frank Zappa. That these diverse artists constituted a musical community is undeniable (Lena 2012: 86–9). That they produced musicologically diverse pop is similarly beyond dispute: they contributed to at least six distinct traditions: singer-songwriter rock (James Taylor), contemporary folk-pop (Joni Mitchell), cosmic country (Flying Burrito Brothers), country rock (the Eagles), psychedelic pop (the Mamas and the Papas), and adult contemporary pop/country (Linda Ronstadt). The sociological definition of genre allows us to correctly identify the existence of a genre (community) at an early point and to mark its dissolution over time.

A second advantage of the sociological definition of genre is that it helps us to understand why fans of the same music have patterned, almost routine, arguments about which performers, albums, and songs represent the 'true', or 'authentic', manifestation of the style. Debates within punk music are characteristic in this regard. Older punk fans, those who have participated in the community for many years, tend to defend the value of specific songs developed in a particular time period. Younger punks, or those newer to the music, tend to defend a punk ethos that isn't particular to music created in any isolated time or space (Lena 2012: 52). The former defines authentic punk as the *music* made in a particular period, while younger fans associate authenticity with a fidelity to what they see as the *spirit* of that era. While both groups might be described in musicological terms as 'punk fans', the former are properly understood as members of a traditionalist punk movement, while the younger fans are members of a scene-based contemporary punk community. The two are linked in the sense that they describe the music they enjoy using the same word ('punk'), but they are sociologically distinct in that they transfer few resources across the groups. They don't even share space – in Andy Bennett's recent book on aging music fans, he notes that the 'codes of crowd behaviour are not necessarily understood, or appreciated, by older punks, whose appreciation of the music, sense of association with the crowd, and acquired reading of acceptable crowd conventions are often qualitatively different' from youths' (2013: 137). Bennett's careful observation reveals that two groups exist: a traditionalist genre comprised of older music fans and a scene-based genre populated by teens, both (confusingly) employing the same musical label (e.g. punk). While sociologists have become accustomed to using musicological designations, Bennett concludes, 'the fact of generation can, in itself, produce a particular perception of the meaning and significance of a specific music genre' (2013: 122).[7]

The recognition that sociological genres do a better job of capturing community membership, taste, and behaviour provides a foundation for us to integrate existing research on fans of musicological genres with research that shows some people have broad, or inter-genre, tastes. For example, Wakesman (2009) studied fans of 'underground' or 'independent' music, noting that 'indie' now refers to a set of political, moral, and ethical values, rather than to a mode of production (that is, not to music manufactured without the assistance of 'major' record labels) (2009: 215). Fans of indie music often report their sympathy extends to music categorized within multiple musicological genres. These are not fans of punk, in particular, or of punk music made in an era, but of scene-based music from a variety of popular styles. Sociological genres help us to make sense of existing evidence that fans are oriented toward genre forms, not (necessarily) musical styles.

Broader impacts of relational approaches to the study of categorization

I have focused here on the value of relational approaches and inductive methods of category construction within the study of musical genre, but I wish to point toward the value of such approaches beyond genre. Contemporary readers may be more familiar with the relational approach as it informs some social network studies, whether they are studies of individuals linked through bonds of friendship (Milgram 1967); scientists joined by the papers they co-author (Moody 2004); or songs linked by the shared use of score elements, like musical notes (Cerulo 1995). It is the emphasis on these links or flows that makes network studies compatible with relational models.

Relational approaches are valuable in the study of other forms of categorization, including the study of law school reputations (Espeland and Sauder 2007), insurance rates (Heimer 1985), and economic behaviour (Callon 1998; MacKenzie 2006). Most provocatively, relational approaches may help us to integrate new research on cognition (Lizardo and Strand 2010) and values (Vaisey 2009; on both, see Vaisey and Lizardo 2010) with socio-biological knowledge about the body as an interactional site and more traditional research on meaning. Take musical taste as an example: preferences result (in part) from listening to music. In order to listen, humans interact with a sound-making device, sound waves interact with the environment as they travel to the ear, and with the anatomy of the ear, and then a human must choose to initiate a set of mental processes (built on a web of significances that are themselves relationally generated and maintained) in order to be attentive and to generate meaning.[8] We can pretend that timbre is an attribute of the sound waves, or that arrays of meanings are attributes of people, but in fact we are transmuting relational qualities into attributes (Vannini et al. 2010).

Moreover, these relations between sounds and objects must be seen as something more than the backdrop of social interaction, but also as constitutive of some interactional forms, and less others. Music sociologists like Grazian (2003), DeNora (2000), and Lena (2012) illuminate how sounds facilitate various forms of sociality. Subjective representations of sound are constrained by a common language. Sensory experience is produced by social learning (Keane 2003: 410) and sociologists have a great deal to learn about how socialization includes objects (Knorr Cetina 1997); we may even need to revise our notion of how experience, mental storage, and reproduction operate (Vaisey and Lizardo 2010).

Concluding thoughts

It may be important in some cases to dispense with existing cultural categories and engage in inductive work to identify groups and boundaries. This is particularly so in cases where we rely on categories we have inherited (as was the case with music genres) and when the categories we use are outmoded by rapidly changing social and cultural circumstances (as is the case with omnivorousness). It is – of course – important in situations where sociologists know very little about local social structure and cultures, or in societies where few studies have been completed on any of the three facets of culture.

Instead of relying on a set of demographic attributes, or a cluster of genres assumed to have some social value, we can understand taste as an interactive process whereby people buy, sell, and talk about culture and in so doing, constitute their similarities (or differences) with other people. Studying this process may lead us to confirm the existence of working-class, white culture as a coherent sociological object (aka 'mass culture'). On the other hand, we may find new and interesting communities of consumers that change our ways of thinking about identity and culture.

I have suggested a relational model of taste in which we simultaneously model the coordination of behaviours, discourses, and objects. The limit of this model's replicability lies in the ability of successive researchers to observe and code attributes in the same way. However, it poses no additional barriers beyond what already exists for observational or archival research. It provides an ideal framework for producing inductive categories in almost any social setting. The first order benefit to researchers is the identification of inductively produced social categories. These stand a chance of representing emic and etic orders simultaneously, while allowing the two to be segregated during analysis.

Notes

1 The first draft of this argument ('Relational and multi-method approaches to category construction') was written for the Measuring Culture Conference, hosted by the University of British Columbia in 2012. For comments on that draft, I thank the participants in the conference: Amin Ghaziani, Chris Bail, Omar Lizardo, Ashley Mears, Ann Mische, Iddo Tavory, Steve Vaisey, Fred Wherry, and especially Terry McDonnell and John Mohr, both of whom provided comments on later drafts as well. A version of this paper was presented at the second Measuring Culture Conference, at the University of California,

Santa Barbara (April 2014), and at the University of Chicago Global Literary Networks Conference (May 2014).
2 Parents and teens were given a slightly different list of genres, and the authors used Principal Components Analysis to arrive at the final units of comparison.
3 The report is unclear about the date when music interviews and demographic data were gathered. The mean teen age was 14.4, and based on the mean ages of parents, the average father was 14 in 1971, and mothers in 1974. I arbitrarily chose the final year of the 5-wave study (2005) as the baseline for teen comparisons and chose the first week of July in all three years of "mean teendom": July 3, 1971; July 1, 1974; and July 4, 2005. While my selection of the July charts was arbitrary, there's little reason to think music at the mid-year mark is an unreliable indicator of yearly patterns.
4 Are these genre boundaries recognizable to respondents? The authors address this concern in their conclusion: 'today's adolescents may love hip-hop in the abstract yet argue endlessly between Snoop Doggy Dogg and Kanye West, or they may like rock, in general, yet disagree violently between Tool and Marilyn Manson. Measuring music preferences in finer detail, that is, on the level of artists, bands or composers, may have revealed deeper and more intricate links between parental and adolescent taste as well as between music preference and social differentiation' (2011: 315). Please note the authors are in effect suggesting that their measures are not valid measures of the core phenomen on of interest: musical taste.
5 Bourdieu's (1984) research on music highlighted the importance of specific musical works, rather than named genres, and some contemporary sociologists have adopted this approach (Bennett et al. 2009), highlighting stylistic variation within genre categories (Savage and Gayo 2011).
6 It is possible that readership and content do not work in concert, but in this case there is substantial evidence to suggest that these attributes are correlated.
7 Regev cites Lena (2012) and concludes that 'the analysis of genre trajectories implies that genres cannot exist concurrently in multiple incarnations – at any given moment a genre's incarnation is either avant-garde, scene-based or industry based' (2013: 128–129), but this ignores the discussion of overlapping genre forms (2012: 62–63).
8 As McDonnell (2010: 1803) explains: 'meaning happens through the emergent process of interaction between the material and symbolic qualities of an object, the interpretant, and the context of that interaction'.

References

Allen, M.P. and A.E. Lincoln (2004) 'Critical discourse and the cultural consecration of American films', *Social Forces*, 82(3): 871–893.
Anheier, H.K., J., Gerhards and F.P. Romo (1995) 'Forms of capital and social structure in cultural fields: Examining Bourdieu's social topography', *American Journal of Sociology*, 100: 859–903.
Bearman, P.S. (1993) *Relations into Rhetorics: Local Elite Social Structure in Norfolk, England, 1540–1640*, ASA Rose Monograph Series: New Brunswick, NJ.
Bennett, A. (2013) *Music, Style and Aging: Growing Old Disgracefully?*, Philadelphia: Temple University Press.
Bennett, T., M. Savage, E. Silva, A. Warde, M. Gayo-Cal, and D. Wright (2009) *Culture, Class, Distinction*, New York: Routledge.
Boorman, S.A. and H.C. White (1976) 'Social-structure from multiple networks. 2. Role structures', *American Journal of Sociology*, 81: 1384–1446.
Bourdieu, P. (1984) *Distinction*, Cambridge, MA: Harvard University Press.
Breiger, R. (2009) 'On the duality of cases and variables: Correspondence analysis (CA) and qualitative comparative analysis (QCA)', in D. Byrne and C.C. Ragin (eds.), *The SAGE Handbook of Case-Based Methods*, Los Angeles: Sage Publications, pp. 243–259.
Burt, R.S. (2009) *Structural Holes: The Social Structure of Competition*, Boston: Harvard University Press.
Callon, M. (ed.) (1998) *The Laws of Markets*, Oxford: Blackwell.
Cerulo, K. (1995) *Identity Designs: The Sights and Sounds of a Nation*, New Brunswick, NJ: Rutgers University Press.
Cetina, K. (1997) 'Sociality with objects: Social relations in postsocial knowledge societies', *Theory, Culture and Society*, 14(4): 1–30.
Craig, A. and S. Dubois (2010) 'Between art and money: The social space of public readings in contemporary poetry economies and careers', *Poetics*, 38(5): 441–460.
DeNora, T. (2000) *Music in Everyday Life*, London: Cambridge University Press.

DiMaggio, P. (1987) 'Classification in art', *American Sociological Review*, 52(4): 440–455.
Dowd, T.J. (2004) 'Concentration and diversity revisited: Production logics and the US mainstream recording market, 1940–1990', *Social Forces*, 82(4): 1411–1455.
Emirbayer, M. (1997) 'Manifesto for a relational sociology', *American Journal of Sociology*, 103(2): 281–317.
Emirbayer, M. and J. Goodwin (1994) 'Network analysis, culture, and the problem of agency', *American Journal of Sociology*, 99(6):1154–1411.
Espeland, W., and M. Sauder (2007) 'Rankings and reactivity: How public measures recreate social worlds', *American Journal of Sociology*, 113(1): 1–40.
Frow, J. (2006) *Genre*, New York: Routledge.
Goldberg, A. (2011) 'Mapping shared understandings using relational class analysis: The case of the cultural omnivore reexamined', *American Journal of Sociology*, 116(5): 1397–1436.
Goodenough, W.H. (1963) 'Some applications of Guttmann scale analysis to ethnography and culture theory', *Southwestern Journal of Anthropology*, 19(3): 235–250.
Grazian, D. (2003) *Blue Chicago: The Search for Authenticity in Urban Blues Clubs*, Chicago: University of Chicago Press.
Heimer, C. (1985) *Reactive Risk and Rational Action: Managing Moral Hazard in Insurance Contracts*, Los Angeles: University of California Press.
Johnston, J. and S. Baumann (2007) 'Democracy versus Distinction: A study of omnivorousness in gourmet food writing', *American Journal of Sociology*, 113(1): 165–204.
Keane, W. (2003) 'Semiotics and the social analysis of material things', *Language and Communication*, 23(3–4): 409–425.
Lena, J.C. (2012) *Banding Together: How Communities Create Genres in Popular Music*, Princeton, NJ: Princeton University Press.
Lena, J.C. and M.C. Pachucki (2013) 'The sincerest form of flattery: Innovation, repetition, and status in an art movement', *Poetics*, 41(3): 236–264.
Lena, J.C. and R.A. Peterson (2008) 'Classification as culture: Types and trajectories of music genres', *American Sociological Review*, 79(1): 697–718.
Lizardo, O. (2006) 'How cultural tastes shape personal networks', *American Sociological Review*, 71(5): 778–807.
Lizardo, O. and M. Strand (2010) 'Skills, toolkits, contexts and institutions: Clarifying the relationship between different approaches to cognition in cultural sociology', *Poetics*, 38(2): 205–228.
MacKenzie, D. (2006) *An Engine, Not a Camera: How Financial Models Shape Markets*, Cambridge, MA: MIT Press.
McDonnell, T.E. (2010) 'Cultural objects as objects: Materiality, urban space and the interpretation of AIDS media in Accra, Ghana', *American Journal of Sociology*, 115(6): 1800–1852.
Milgram, S. (1967) 'The small world problem', *Psychology Today*, 2: 60–67.
Mische, A. (2011) 'Relational sociology, culture, and agency', in E.J. Scott and P. Carrington (eds.), *The Sage Handbook of Social Network Analysis*, Thousand Oaks, CA: Sage Publications.
Mische, A. and H.C. White (1998) 'Between conversation and situation: Public switching dynamics across network domains', *Social Research*, 65: 695–724.
Mohr, J.W (2013) 'Bourdieu's relational method in theory and practice: From fields and capitals to networks and institutions (and back again)', in F. Dépelteau and C. Powell (eds.), *Applying Relational Sociology*, Basingstoke: Palgrave.
Mohr, J.W. and H.C. White (2008) 'How to model an institution', *Theory and Society*, 37(5): 485–512.
Moody, J. (2004) 'The structure of a social science collaboration network: Disciplinary cohesion from 1963 to 1999', *American Sociological Review*, 69(2): 213–238.
Pachucki, M.A. and R.L. Breiger (2010) 'Cultural holes: Beyond relationality in social networks and culture,' Ms. submitted for *Annual Review of Sociology*, vol. 36., as submitted 12.2009.
Peterson, R. (2005) 'Problems in comparative research: The example of omnivorousness', *Poetics*, 33(5–6): 257–282.
Peterson, R. and R.M. Kern (1996) 'Changing highbrow taste: From snob to omnivore', *American Sociological Review*, 61: 900–907.
Peterson, R. and G. Rossman (2008) 'Changing arts audiences: Capitalizing on omnivorousness', in S. Tepper and B. Ivey (eds.), *Engaging Art: The Next Great Transformation of America's Cultural Life*, New York: Routledge.
Regev, M. (2013) *Pop-Rock Music*, Cambridge: Polity Press.
Savage, M. and M. Gayo (2011) 'Unraveling the omnivore: A field analysis of contemporary musical taste in the United Kingdom', *Poetics*, 39(5): 337–357.

Schweizer, T. (1993a) 'The dual ordering of actors and possessions', *Current Anthropology*, 34(4): 469–483.
—— (1993b) 'Actor and event orderings across time: Lattice representation and Boolean analysis of the political dispute in Chen village, China', *Social Networks*, 15(3): 247–266.
Schweizer, T., E. Klemm, and M. Schweizer (1993) 'Ritual as action in a Javanese community: A network perspective on ritual and social structure', *Social Networks*, 15(1): 19–48.
Sonnett, J. (2013) 'Indifference, ambivalence, and Distinction: A configurational analysis of musical boundaries in Mississippi', paper presented at the 2013 American Sociological Association conference, provided by the author.
Ter Bogt, T.F.M., M.J.M.H. Delsing, M. van Zalk, P.G. Christenson, and W.H.J. Meesus (2011) 'Intergenerational continuity of taste: Parental and adolescent music preferences', *Social Forces*, 90(1): 297–320.
Ter Bogt, T.F.M., Q. Raaijmakers, W. Vollebergh, F. van Wel, and P. Sikkema (2003) 'Youngers and their musical taste: Musical styles and taste groups', *Netherlands' Journal of Social Sciences*, 39(1): 35–52.
Vaisey, S. (2009) 'Motivation and justification: A dual process model of culture in action', *American Journal of Sociology*, 114(6): 1675–1715.
Vaisey, S. and O. Lizardo (2010) 'Can cultural worldviews influence network composition?', *Social Forces*, 88(4): 1595–1618.
van Eijck, K. (2001) 'Social differentiation in musical taste patterns', *Social Forces*, 79(3): 1163–1184.
Vannini, P., D. Waskul, S. Gottschalk, and C. Rambo (2010) 'Sound acts: Elocution, somatic work, and the performance of sonic alignment', *Journal of Contemporary Ethnography*, 39(3): 328–353.
Wakesman, S. (2009) *This Ain't the Summer of Love: Conflict and Crossover in Heavy Metal and Punk*, Berkeley and Los Angeles: University of California Press.
White, H.C., S.A. Boorman, and R.L. Breiger (1976) 'Social structure from multiple networks. I. Blockmodels of roles and positions', *American Journal of Sociology*, 81(4): 730–780.

10
Networks and culture

Alix Rule and Peter Bearman[1]

Introduction

Social networks invoke relations between people giving rise to social structures. Culture, broadly construed, invokes meanings. The fact that ties between people are necessarily infused with meaning and that meaning is no more than a network of people, objects, and ideas *in practice* makes the distinction between culture and networks an analytical convenience – a device for thinking about the relationships between culture and groups. In this essay we aim to show that this insight can illuminate the study of a variety of complex empirical settings, and thus provide answers to classic questions in the sociology of culture: (1) how tastes differentiate people, (2) how structures of meaning and structures of social relations co-evolve and (3) how transformations in structures of meaning articulate with and shape transformations in structures of dominance. Throughout, we use an idea from Arthur Danto that crystalizes the thought that networks and culture constitute one another.

Under the abstract definition considered here, culture is, well, pretty much everywhere. The strategy we pursue in this paper is to consider in detail a few cases – fashion, new 'economic' relations on the eve of capitalism, religious identity, the breakdown of peasant society, art, American musical tastes, and so on – that seem exemplary of the focal problems. But since culture is everywhere, the world of exemplary cases is enormous and selecting any set of individual cases from an infinite sea of possibilities will appear as arbitrary. Against this background, we simply note that we have picked cases that fall squarely into those domains we often think of when we think of culture and those domains that tend to be coded as belonging to sociological sub-disciplines that are distant from the sociology of culture, for example economic sociology. This choice is quite purposive.

In the *Journal of Philosophy*, Arthur Danto wrote: 'To see something as art requires something that the eye cannot descry ... an atmosphere of artistic theory, a knowledge of the history of art: an art world' (1964: 580). Danto, a practicing critic on the New York scene just as conceptual and pop art were first emerging, was trying to account for how an object like Andy Warhol's Brillo boxes could properly be interpreted as a work of art – and thus seeking to provide an alternative to a view of art as imitation of nature. Instead, he argued, artworks should be thought about as a special class of objects whose basic point of reference was not the world external to them, but one another. 'What in the end makes the difference between a Brillo box and a work of art consisting of a Brillo Box is a certain theory of art', Danto wrote. To apply the 'theory of art' that Danto had in mind is to see an object as joining a conversation with the art created before it.

Danto argued that '[t]he art world stands in relation to the real world in something like the relationship in which the City of God stands in relation to the earthly city. Certain objects, as well as certain individuals, enjoy a double citizenship' (1964: 582). Of course no theory of art could exist without the people who write the history books, keep the museums open, who create art objects to join the conversation, etc. They are, as Danto's allusion to Augustine suggests, a group unified by their vision. Though they see the same things visible to others – a Brillo box here, a smiley face there – what they see *in* them is different. The members of the art world are united by the way they ascribe meaning.

The idea of the art world provides a useful imagery for thinking about networks and culture – for understanding how people are related by their ascriptions of meaning, their perceptions of objects' qualities, and for understanding how objects (and ideas) are in turn related by people. Danto's art world represents, among other things, a distinctive way of defining a community.

Below we transpose Danto's art world idea to various empirical contexts, first to the (observable) worlds of art studied by sociologists, then to a more diverse collection of settings in which cultural sociologists in the largest sense have been interested. Danto's art world is an abstraction. Its value is that it helps both analysts and (we hope) readers see clearly the particular relationship between culture and groups in these more complex settings.

The art world

In closing his essay, Danto provides a formal illustration of the 'language of the art world', the atmosphere of artistic theory in which worldly objects appear as works of art. The history of art consists of a series of aesthetic possibilities that artists, or artistic movements, have worked out; imagine, Danto proposes, that we list every one of these possibilities. This list, however long, defines the universe of art-relevant qualities. Any art object, as such, either possesses or rejects each one of them (once an aesthetic quality exists, it defines a position; an artwork cannot be neutral). He proposes that we interpret a given art object, by moving down the row of qualities we have defined, and marking a '1' under every quality it possesses, and a '0' under the qualities it lacks. By running through the entire population of possible rows of 0's and 1's, we define the set of stylistic or aesthetic possibilities that exist at a given moment.

The rectangular matrix of objects × aesthetic possibilities naturally gives rise to a matrix of aesthetic possibilities and a matrix of objects through ordinary matrix multiplication, where cell entries index aesthetic possibilities that objects share, or objects that share aesthetic features[2]. It would seem that the matrix is always expanding. With each innovative new artwork, a new column is added. As art history proceeds, the art world becomes richer – and so does each individual art object, as it is endowed with qualities that it either has or lacks. For Danto, '[o]ne row of the matrix is as legitimate as another' (1964: 584). Danto is not interested in the mechanisms by which expansion occurs – how an artwork defines a new row in the art historical matrix – or how a new quality gets universally recognized by the individual citizens of the art world – or what happens to an artistic quality once no one any longer cares about it, noting that what happens in practice, is 'of almost purely sociological interest'. Right. We are precisely interested in those dynamics; especially in how rows and columns are added or deleted – or more precisely, how power shapes the art world (i.e. cultural) matrix. These are the issues we inevitably confront in the study of real social worlds and that we now consider.

Positions in the art world

Danto argues that the art world floats above the contingency of social process and that it represents the right theory of art, not the reality of it, which is irregular and messy. This representation anticipates Levi-Strauss' (1969) argument that the rules and norms of classificatory kinship – the kinship grammar – *is* the social structure and that the fact that people fail to behave in the prescribed ways, that is, to act 'ungrammatically', is unimportant. Strangely, canonical *empirical* studies of art by sociologists seem to take for granted that a Dantoesque world of art exists – a sphere somehow separate or distinctive in relation to 'the rest' of social life. (See for example: White and White 1965; Crane 1987; Alloway 1972.) The analogous notion of science as a separate and distinctive sphere of social life has been much debated (see Latour and Woolgar 1979; Merton 1973). Among this group is Pierre Bourdieu.

Take, for instance, Bourdieu's account of the field of artistic production. It is a competitive place. With the work they make, artists claim positions in this field. Making artwork *inevitably* means competing by claiming a position, much as it does when one takes a turn in chess. Unlike in chess, the actual choosing of artistic positions is motored not only by the logic of the game itself – this is Bourdieu's quarrel with Foucault – but *also* by the 'real-worldly' social significance of the positions taken. Aesthetic possibilities have social associations – some styles of art are more saleable, others more likely to be accepted into certain collections; some art is more 'pure' in that it is appreciated most by no one besides other producers and remunerated by nothing other than the rewards their recognition can construct. And so on. And yet, the social connotations of different styles are constantly shifting, as history progresses, and with the history of the field itself – that is, in response to positions previously taken. For Bourdieu, these dynamics of competition through position taking are pervasive in other spheres of social life. Each may be conceived of as distinctive inasmuch as competitors apply a unique set of qualities to the objects of their concern.

But Bourdieu insists that this is *not* a closed set: he faults social scientists for trying to define the 'contents' of art *ex ante* – for trying to draw the boundaries of the art world – arguing that struggles over *exactly* that question are what drive art making. The work that artists make comes to reflect strategic attempts to define the field, or more accurately, to define certain other types of work *out* of the field. The dynamics at play are explicitly agonistic:

> We are insisting that what can be constituted as a system for the sake of analysis is not the product of coherence-seeking intention or an objective consensus (even if it presupposes unconscious agreement on common principles) but the product and prize of permanent conflict. Or, to put it in another way, that the generative, unifying principle of this 'system' is the struggle – with all the contradictions it engenders (so that participation in the struggle which may be indicated objectively by, for example, the attacks that are suffered – can be used as the criterion establishing that a work belongs to the field of *prises de position* and its author to the field of positions.
>
> (Bourdieu 1983: 316)

In Danto's terms, this is a struggle to define the matrix of aesthetic qualities characteristic of *legitimate* artworks. If we are to transpose Bourdieu's theory into Danto's art world, the sphere of art might be seen as a competition to systematically occupy positions in the matrix of aesthetic possibility in ways that devalue the positions taken by others. Notice that for Bourdieu, the aesthetic positions occupied by artworks also attach to *individuals*, namely, the artists who make them; while social connotations tend to 'bleed' from artists onto the positions they occupy, and – conversely – from the positions onto the artworks themselves. In brief, an important conceptual elaboration on Danto's art world comes from Bourdieu's account: if the attribution of meaning may unify individuals as a community, the internal dynamics that drive meaning-making necessarily induce the differentiation of people into subgroups (Whitham 2014). Thus, whether or not one believes in a single 'language of the art world', artists both communicate with one another and distinguish themselves by the way they speak.

Similarly, at first glance, Howard Becker's 'art worlds' seem to have little to do with the transcendental matrix that Danto describes. Art worlds, for Becker, are networks of people. When we extend our gaze beyond visual art – with its hard but arbitrary line between 'the artist' and everyone else – to the production of music, dance, film, etc., it becomes especially clear that any artwork requires socially organized activity to bring it into existence as such. The existence of *conventions* is a key way that this happens. In any art world, a system of conventions gets 'embodied in equipment, materials, training, available facilities and sites, systems of notation all of which must be changed if any one component is' (Becker 1984: 36). By drawing attention to the work that goes into sustaining such systems, Becker directs us to the extensive social networks regularly activated to make aesthetic objects what they are. Latour (1988), for science, later observes the same dynamics.

Notice though that to define 'art worlds' as the networks of people required to make art, Becker also must rely on a *theory* of art, on a way of deciding what are 'legitimate' art objects. Becker thus accepts that something like Danto's matrix exists; however, he has a particular idea about the way that its contents are generated. What looks like the relevant aesthetic qualities or categories at a given moment in the history of an art world are really just the qualities that conventions around art make salient. Most often these are tacitly agreed upon, other times they need to be negotiated: 'e e cummings had trouble publishing his first book of poetry because printers were afraid to set his bizarre layouts; writers don't want a word changed' – the art that gets produced depends on how such conflicts are resolved. 'The philosophical and aesthetic problem' of knowing whose intentions should define the meaning of art is 'solved by sociological analysis', for Becker. Though 'such a solution does not, of course, solve the problem. It merely makes it the object of study' (1984: 21). In art worlds where they pontificate, aestheticians generally define ex-post what is enacted in practice (1984: 131–135).

In brief, for Becker aesthetic qualities supervene on social structures. This is not to say that those structures are easy to define precisely. It's worth considering what it means for Becker, for instance, that the audience may be part of an art world. This implies that in the appreciation of very old artworks, the relevant social structure extends across historical time, while conversely, in Becker's account, the stylistic qualities that are not actively socially recognized effectively disappear. In his later work on art worlds, Becker notes that their relevant networks are impossible to 'bound' precisely (36).

Becker inverts our perspective on Danto's art world, while preserving its basic architecture: rather than identifying the aesthetic qualities whose recognition defines a community, he urges us to see patterns of social exchange as defining a universe of aesthetically relevant qualities. Further, just as Bourdieu helps elaborate Danto's picture of the art world, by suggesting that the different sets of objects recognized as legitimate art may define sub-groups within it, Becker's work invites us to see differences in the social groupings as defining certain sets of relevant aesthetic qualities – that is, defining cannons and genres.

The conceptual elaborations of Danto's art world provided by sociologists help us appreciate the following: insofar as not all possibilities in the art world matrix are equally realized in practice, the art world has a meaningful structure. Not all aesthetically possible artworks are equally valorized, made, bought, or viewed; not all people who understand representative meaning recognize the same objects as legitimate representations. In either case, we would notice that in practice, certain cells in Danto's matrix are more active than others. Notice that the art world is easily a network: at most basic we could visualize it as either a network of objects connected by the people who constitute them as meaningful (as in Becker; also Accominotti, forthcoming), or a social network in which individuals are related by shared recognition of objects' meaningfulness (as in Bourdieu; also Giuffre 2001). We explore further analytical possibilities below.

Colloquially, people rely on 'the art world' to refer to a variety of different things: sometimes to the social context in which art is made, distributed, and sold – (often, in particular, the unseemly hierarchical elements of that context); sometimes to refer to the significant *geography* of contemporary art, its institutions etc.; sometimes, as an adjective to refer to the sensibilities of a certain people (e.g. the art world reaction to a particular film). The art world gets invoked when people want to distinguish one context from another – whether emphasis is on the cultural or the social structural element or some category of entities onto which art-relevant meanings bleed. Here, we treat the art world as a model of the relationship between meanings and the relations attached to them. As Breiger (2000) points out, by extension, these relations could be between aesthetic elements, artists and audiences (DiMaggio 1987). That is not to say that in actuality structures of meaning and relations come bundled together as pristine wholes, that they're impenetrable or immutable. Just to the contrary. Returning to our three problems posed at the start of this essay, the imagery of the art world provides, we hope, a useful vehicle for considering their various empirical relations to one another.

Taste and differentiation

How do tastes work to differentiate 'types' of people? Since even before Veblen's *Theory of the Leisure Class*, the problem has been a classic, more recently taken up by such diverse scholars as Lieberson and Bell (1992) and Katz (1988) among others. The best-known recent treatment is Bourdieu's *Distinction* (1984). Its target is the intuitive notion of *personal* taste, the idea that individual likes and dislikes are somehow ineffable, or natural. Demonstrating that patterns of preferences in cultural objects – from high culture, to sports, to 'cosmetics, clothing, home decoration' – are systematically related to, for example, people's professions, their level of education and family backgrounds, Bourdieu develops his theory of the habitus ('a virtue made of a necessity') to account for such regularity. The core argument of *Distinction* is that patterns in consumption, especially when considered across a variety of domains, communicate powerfully, compellingly and inevitably about our social location, much the way that an accent in speech communicates place of birth. This is because tastes are the result of practical dispositions shaped by early experience of one's position in the social structure.

Bourdieu's 'world' of interest is (French) late-capitalist consumer society – and its relevant objects are cultural and consumer goods quite generally. Rather than thinking of these in terms of their possible 'qualities', *Distinction* would have us think of matrix of possible 'appetites' for objects.[3] (The very cognitive informality in the way that we relate to culture is part of what makes it speak so powerfully as a social differentiator.) If we could aggregate all the appetites that a given person exhibits, as we in fact do informally, Bourdieu argues, we would be able to situate her precisely within the social structure.

Thus to properly understand the role of cultural tastes, we have to shift analytical attention away from its particular objects in themselves. Not only do we have to aggregate tastes for different things, we need to understand each one within a context of comparable choices, a 'system of differences'. What Bourdieu has in mind is explicitly similar to Danto's matrix of aesthetic qualities. 'Each of these worlds – drinks ... or automobiles, newspapers or holiday resorts – provides the small number of distinctive features which, functioning as a system of differences, differential deviations, allow the most fundamental social differences to be expressed almost as completely as through the most complex and refined expressive systems available in the legitimate arts' (Bourdieu 1984:226). The possibilities for pursuing identity through the sum total of these fields of choice – the 'space of life styles' – is 'well-nigh inexhaustible'.

Differences are legible without the subjective appreciation of the tastes of others. Insofar as we read cultural choices revealing positions of greater or lesser privilege, we can read sheer difference in taste as significant. Bourdieu urges attention to the *asymmetries* between people that increasingly refined tastes impose. Claims to increasingly specific cultural tastes (not just Dylan, but *late* Dylan; not just Châteauneuf-du-Pape, but this particular vintage) are a way of asserting increasingly fine social distinctions – since the claimant excludes other individuals who share in her appreciation of the larger category of goods. So do hierarchies in material conditions – like access to time and money – dictate the types of appetites one can devote oneself to developing, and in turn whom (socially-speaking) one can manage to exclude in such a manner. For this reason, appetites cultivated should be thought of as social investments (or alternatively, cultural capital) – since they will bear particular fruits in excluding others – while appearing to their possessors as investments in the sense of 'commitments'. If in Danto's terms, each 'field of preferences' represents a matrix of possible appetites, we could consider that the cells of that matrix are fractal in nature: each one may subdivide to yield finer systems of difference.

One could, of course, represent the same phenomenon by extending the matrix outward, including as new columns the appetites that the most discerning of connoisseurs have for the particular types of objects they enjoy. This would result in a matrix of appetites that was not uniformly filled, with some objects registering values in many columns and others only in very few. If one believed that the capacity for distinction through taste was strictly quantitative – it is not, even if some omnivores imagine otherwise – then an individual's social position would correspond to the extent of the matrix his or her tastes could occupy.

Necessarily though, the finer distinctions in taste are qualitative. For Bourdieu, struggles over taste are struggles, literally, over the *meaning* of objective, social-structural positions. This, along with the very proliferation of possibilities, can help explain why differences in taste-patterns are so legible as social distinctions, even if that is not the way that we think of them. Systems of differences offered by contemporary consumer society mean that the possibilities for distinction are so vast, that its bourgeois subjects become sensitive to the most trivial differences as differences between *individuals* – we fail to step back and see the full social picture. Conversely, when confronting so much potential difference, similarity in taste appears as a miracle – 'Taste is what brings together things and people that go together' (Bourdieu 1984: 241). What is subjectively experienced as serendipity is actually socially quite predictable. Observe that as an ethos of romantic partnership, this reproduces social structure beautifully.

Consider another treatment of the question of social differentiation through taste, this one more narrowly focused. Amir Goldberg's methodological work (2011) is oriented to helping social scientists identify communities that apply 'shared understandings'. The originality of Relational Class Analysis (RCA), the analytical method that Goldberg designs for this purpose, is that it permits detection of groups on the basis of revealed reactions to particular cultural objects, even if their evaluations of those objects are not shared. It thus allows structures of meaning to emerge as a unit of analysis. In his demonstrative case of musical taste, for example, it allows Goldberg to identify groups for whom taste in music is 'about' the same things, even when individuals' particular *tastes* differ.

Goldberg's example captures the idea that people inhabit different musical 'worlds'. Following Bourdieu, Goldberg's thought is that detecting patterns in their evaluations of objects will allow the analyst to distil the different *social* meanings that shape individuals' cultural consumption. 'In this universe of continuity', Bourdieu explains, 'the work of construction and observation is to be able to isolate (relatively) homogenous sets of individuals [...] in other words, groups organized by systems of differences' (1984: 259). Goldberg's RCA method is designed to facilitate this work of observation and construction.

RCA relies on 'scaled, attitudinal data' – for example, the Culture Module of the 1993 General Social Survey, which asked respondents to rate enjoyment of a series of 17 musical genres ('rap', 'heavy metal', 'classical', etc.) on a five-point scale. Goldberg defines his measure of covariance in strings of responses as 'relationality'. He then creates an adjacency matrix in which cell values are defined by the relationality score for every pair of individuals in his sample. We may think of this as tantamount to a social network where the strength of a tie between two individuals is based on the similarity of their respective 'theories' of music, in Danto's sense (for another approach to a similar end, see Schultz and Breiger 2010). Associations between people's preferences with respect to a certain genre, whether convergent or divergent, imply the presence of a shared criterion of evaluation.

By partitioning this social network to find the sets of individuals most interconnected with one another, Goldberg identifies three worlds of musical taste. Each is defined by variation according to a different pattern: In the group Goldberg labels 'Omni-Univore', members who like one musical genre tend also to like all the rest – while others are strictly parochial, favoring one or two genres and hating all other kinds of music. In the 'High-Low' group, 'classical' genres of music are distinguished, by those who both like and hate them, from 'popular' ones; the 'Contempo-Trad' group distinguishes musical genres with 'associations with American folklore' from more modern ones.

Goldberg looks for the meaning of musical genre in these three worlds, by relating the socio-demographic attributes of each group of GSS respondents to their evaluation of particular musical genres within each. 'The same musical genre may carry different meanings in different social contexts', Goldberg points out. 'Jazz, for example, is understood as a symbol of socioeconomic status in the High-Low group, whereas in the Contempo-Trad group it marks racial tolerance, secularism and urbanism. [Jazz's] rejection in the former group appears to be related to class identity, while in the latter to regional and racial identities' (2011: 1429–1430). In other words, by relating variation in tastes to these attributes, Goldberg imputes the categories that groups (identified through RCA) use to evaluate music.

We might debate whether these imputations are correct. It does not necessarily follow from the fact that groups share different understandings of music's meaning that the content of those meanings is given by identifiable social groups. Notice, though that if Goldberg is right, it is the salient socio-demographic groups that Americans identify differently when they report on their musical tastes. Effectively musical taste *is* American social structure.

The co-evolution of structures of meanings and relations

The way that social and institutional changes shape the recognition of aesthetic qualities is, for Danto, a matter of mere 'fashion'. The question of how changes in culture articulate with changes in social relations, however, is (or should be) of central interest to sociologists. The art world heuristic can focus our study of the processes by which structures of meaning and of social relations co-evolve.

Maybe unsurprisingly, strong examples come from the world of clothes. Take for example Kennedy Fraser's analysis of the changes in women's dress during the sixties and seventies, recorded in her compilation of fashion reporting for the *New Yorker* (1985). In Fraser's account, largely transient social upheavals spelled a permanent shift in the idiom of women's clothing: transforming a regime in which clothes were chosen for how they *looked*, into one in which they mattered for what they *meant*. In the US at mid-century, the type of clothing women wore was a signal (be it true or aspirational) of social identity – i.e. primarily age, class, and marital status. Within the bounds of social propriety, clothes communicated primarily in the idiom of form, through colours, materials, shape ('cut'), etc. During the 1960s, widespread social critique had revolutionary impact on dress: it produced new garments whose popularity cut across age and social class and led to a rare efflorescence of personal style – meaning, for Fraser, an individual sensibility which identifies its own relevant qualities.

Fraser argues that the ethos of style was too taxing for most women, and the fashion industry exerted its best marketing efforts to re-establish (profitably revisable) norms in dress – but the sixties fractured the fit between clothing and social position irreparably. So, while the freedom didn't last, the destruction of clothing's old idiom did. From the 1970s onward, norms of fashion were re-established on different terms. Fraser argues that dress became more like *costume* – once decoupled from actual social position; garments could express or allude to different identities that were in no way socially realistic for the wearer, channelling different emotional tonalities. Clothes could reference different eras and cultures, 'the movement is toward make believe, and leads us to dress up as peasants, Indians, and women of the nineteen forties' (33). 'Dislocation, mystification, revival – these were more than anything the hallmark of fashion during the 70s', Fraser remarks (241).

The process of change Fraser describes is fruitful to imagine as a shift in the social manipulation of a Dantoesque matrix of dress. Clothes, as individual garments, did not acquire new qualities in the 1970s; they had always had social significations as well as formal ones. Instead, for the average American woman, the locus of concern in choosing what to wear shifted away from the formal toward the meaningful – and consequently expanded enormously. Once women's social positions no longer constrained their clothing choices, a larger swath of the matrix of dress could and needed to be negotiated. This explains two observations that Fraser makes about fashion during the seventies: One is that the rise of meaning – and the concomitant ideological injunction to 'self-expression' in dress – only provided a shot in the arm to the fashion industry as a commercial concern: with more possibilities open to all women fashion trends could proceed more rapidly. The second is that faced with a more difficult, and less well-defined task, women actually became better dressers – at least for a period.

The sartorial assault on a social system articulated in dress that Frasers describes amounts to a random 'occupation' of positions in a matrix, where once women were constrained to certain regions of possibility. Though the assault doesn't last, the old formal idiom, which like all formal idioms depends on constraint as a frame, is destroyed – permitting a new one to emerge. The *Fashionable Mind* ends with the ironic suggestion that the 'meaningful' idiom that emerged hegemonic in 1970s fashion was itself unstable. The meanings that garments possessed, once they no longer made realistic reference to social position, vacated clothing altogether. Writing in 1980, Fraser argues that: 'By now obfuscatory style is deeply ingrained in even the most derivative and commercial dress designers ... [such that] the job of deadening visual response and baffling interpretation is virtually complete' (1985: 239).

Of course objects need not be in the world of consumption, the arts, or fashion to be culturally innovative. And co-evolution may turn out to be more than mere innovation, but truly inventive. Anticipating one of the central mechanisms – transposition across multiple networks – identified by Padgett and Powell (2012), in their penetrating analysis of the dynamics underlying the invention of new institutions, cultural objects, and meanings, Quentin Van Doosselaere (2009) describes how the invention of objects with new qualities interacts with and progressively reshapes social organization over the long *durée* – ultimately creating a new world with vastly extended boundaries. In the case that he studies, the social world is the feudal city of medieval Genoa, the cultural objects at stake are legal – equity, credit, and insurance instruments – and the waves of social reorganization built through them culminate, finally, in the rise of merchant capitalism.

The basic analytic approach is to build networks of individuals related through these respective instruments, and to measure the changes in both their social identities and the network structure over time. From archives, he collects information on the backgrounds of citizens involved together in tens of thousands of commercial agreements of different types. The commenda, for example, was an early form of equity partnership, which limited the liability of the traveling trader if he abided by the terms his partners specified. Van Doosselaere describes the network of individuals who entered into such agreements together, over the period of 1154–1315. Measurements of the network's structural evolution, and attention to the social attributes of those connected within it, reveal how the commenda was progressively embraced by different tranches of Genovese feudal society. As the use of the commenda spread through the city's increasingly stratified population, occupational homophily of those entering into such contracts developed so that, over time, as the formal economic relationships entailed by commenda agreements were recognized and leveraged by an increasingly diverse swath of citizens, they acquired additional *social* – largely feudal – meanings in Genovese society. On the other hand, with the commenda emerged another 'world' – one in which accumulation was pursued for its own sake, outside of feudal status relations. For this very reason, the commenda's use was self-limiting, thanks to 'its fixed, that is non-market driven, system of profit allocation' (210).

Though insurance was crucial to the expansion of trade in the risky Mediterranean, it was barely profitable because it did not aggregate risk widely enough. Van Doosselaere reveals that the network of insurance provision had a dense core consisting of the majority of the city's noble households. Comparing this structure to the one that would arise if ties were distributed randomly, he finds that it is in fact *less* clustered. This indicates that the provision of insurance among the nobility was not (*a fortiori*) market-driven, but instead the result of intentional spreading of ties. Van Dooselaere suggests that insurance contracts were extended on the basis of – and served to create – elite group solidarity. In short, a crucial piece of the mercantile architecture, which *later* became a commercial product, was invented by feudal elites acting in their corporate interest. The irony of course is that: 'Eventually, the expansion of trade — in a premarket society — and the cumulative nature of its profits decoupled the feudal domination from the economy, and a quantitative change became qualitative'. The merchant capitalist social organization built itself on top of the feudal social organization. 'The skillful operators were those who forged social relationships in the context of the market in order to avoid the fatal isolation inherent in capitalism' (214). Here, a new column in the matrix of objects – insurance instruments – built to solidify feudal social relations comes to create wholly new, and ultimately, with respect to the feudal system, completely destructive, social relations.

Transformations in structures of meaning and structures of domination

Earlier we mentioned that columns don't disappear in the art world, but in real life they do. In terms of Danto's matrix, domination is all about the destruction of columns.

'An attack on sacred aesthetic beliefs as embodied in particular conventions is, finally, an attack on an existing arrangement of ranked statuses, a stratification system', writes Howard Becker (1974: 174). Recall Becker's idea that the philosophical justification for meaningful aesthetic possibilities, of particular structures of meaning, is subsidiary on the role these play in coordinating particular patterns of collective action, regularizing them, and reinforcing social *structures*. For example aesthetics in painting, such an argument goes, are shaped around notions of the subjectivity of the painter, the single individual who occupies the high-status role in the production of this kind of work. This *justifies* the painter's role, as well as the 'lesser' jobs of hanging the painting, producing the paint, etc. – all also necessary for painting as an institution to survive. To the extent that we agree with Becker here, that 'sacred' aesthetics, or, in other worlds, sacred value systems, index stable forms of social organization, we should allow that they most always index power relations between individuals and groups. Given this, Becker's insight begs for attention to the way that the transformation of structures of meaning articulate with the transformation of social dominance.

One beautiful example of such attention comes from *The Bachelor's Ball,* Bourdieu's account of the collapse of peasant society in his native *département,* Bearn, through the failure of the traditional system of marriage. In his account, the process starts as the least privileged members of peasant society, women, begin refusing their subordinate role. By tradition among Bearn's peasantry, women married upward into higher status families, where they became the lowest ranking members of the society's basic economic and social unit. World War I, the devaluation of the dowry, the ability of women to find work in towns, etc. – all removed constraints upon women's exit from the peasantry. But what enabled them to appreciate alternative options was a change in their sensibilities, which let them see positive possibilities where none existed before. Living in towns, young peasant women become sensitive to the values of French consumer society. When they apply this new 'table of values' to the objects of peasant society, they find it wanting.

Young women apply their new sensibilities, most devastatingly, to other people – in particular, to prospective spouses. In an argument that Bourdieu illustrates with an ethnographic vignette of a country-dance, the denial of peasant values that begins with young women, spreads by contagion. Peasant men begin to see themselves through the eyes of women as the latter snub them and choose young men from 'the towns' for dance partners. Not able themselves to recognize the new qualities, they realize that the old matrices do not apply: none of the qualities in light of which they are attractive – the size of their farms, their dedication to work, and so on – are recognized. Domination, Bourdieu says, is the ability to reduce your subjective reality to objective truth. The peasant men who cannot dance are suddenly ineffably unattractive; moreover their own ways of seeing themselves (as good men), their roles (as the 'receivers' of wives), and their future (as the leaders of a community) are denied in the reality playing out in front of them. This hobbles their ability even to act their familiar part – it effectively erases in them the qualities that are not recognized.

Those columns are gone. Becker should be impressed with the extent to which even individuals' action is here revealed as collective. Of course, that is just because the individual is the site of incorporation for new sets of qualities, and is the target to which these new meaning structures are applied. It is also where Bourdieu's methodological focus rests. The ethnographic and interview-based approach allows the reader to experience the process as it plays out on the level of intimate personal exchanges. The scene of the dance vividly captures the collapse of the peasant social hierarchy in the transformation of a power relationship between persons. Here, the inheriting peasant son, traditionally the most powerfully positioned of individuals in Bearn's peasant society, ultimately becomes a metonym for that society as a whole. The inability of these men to marry not only represents a repudiation of the qualities the peasant world sustains, it undermines that world's material basis. When heirs cannot find spouses, the traditional family-run farm — the basic unit in the peasant economy, cannot last long. And it doesn't.

In *Relations into Rhetorics*, Bearman (1993) considers how the breakdown of kinship as a basis for social and political action among English gentry resulted in a new language for elite identity, and hence political mobilization. This new language facilitates *national* mobilization of elites for the first time, resulting in the outbreak of civil war in the 1640s — and over the longer term, in the formal transformation of power relations between England's elites and its monarch. Historical accounts linking the outbreak of the English Civil War to the interests of the nationally organized groups who acted as its protagonists have problems explaining its timing and alignments. Analytic attention in *Relations into Rhetorics* — in contrast to both the macro-lens of most historical analyses, and the ethnographic view of *The Bachelor's Ball* — focuses on the intermediary level: namely the structure of meanings that organized political identity and alliance among county elites.

Bearman argues that the breakdown of kinship as guide to political action sent local gentry looking for other means of accomplishing their goals, which included seeking patronage of elites at court. The new patterns of interaction in the elite sub-world that emerged cut across the traditional arrangements of social life represented by family, kinship, and local groups. For precisely this reason, these new relations were hospitable to an ideology of *religious* alliance — and a new structure for elite identity: that of the religiously motivated political actor. Though they emerged to give shape to local action, such religious rhetorics could for the first time channel mobilization beyond the county, something that kinship as a vocabulary of political motive could not do.

As with Padgett and Powell (2012), the argument takes shape around the analysis of two intercalated social networks. One is the network of kinship claims among the Norfolk gentry in the century preceding the outbreak of civil war. The second is the network of religious patronage in which Norfolk's elites were involved over roughly the same period. The analysis of the kinship networks reveals a crisp hierarchy during the first period of analysis (1540–1564). Such a structure is possible because kinship claims are, for one, discretionary (not all possible relations need be identified) and asymmetrical (a nephew may claim an uncle without the uncle's recognizing the nephew). In a context in which kinship relations closely indexed the structure of power and privilege, Norfolk's 'old' families, generally speaking, attempted to narrow their family trees, attributing kinship only to ancestors and descendants in the direct line. Families of lesser status attempted to broaden their trees — claiming lateral relations to more distant (and more powerful) relatives, which the latter do not typically reciprocate.

In the language developed here, kinship claims are meanings whose relevant objects are other people. By the 1600's, the structure of meaning was no longer adequate to describe the distribution of power among Norfolk's elites. In a context in which it no longer made legible an individual's social position, kinship equally became useless as what C. Wright Mills (1940) calls a 'vocabulary of motive' for political action. It no longer was useful as guide to others' interests, loyalties – in short, for predicting actions, nor could it (consequently) provided a socially coherent justification for one's own actions in the world. Emergent are profane patronage networks whose objects – clients (rectors) and positions (benefices) – happen to be 'religious'. As clients built careers moving across benefices, they linked elites into increasingly polarized patronage structures, blocks increasingly infused with religious meaning. The articulation of these new political ties as religiously motivated could make retrospective sense of activity that took place outside the vocabulary of traditional social relations – and so elites began to see themselves, and act in the world as, religiously motivated actors whose frame of reference was the nation. This, of course, eliminated all of the identity/action columns previously organized at the local level, and made a national civil war over abstract religious and ideological meanings possible.

Summary

As we noted at the start of this essay, the types of ties between people giving rise to social structures are necessarily infused with meaning. At the same moment, meaning is nothing more than a network of people, objects, and ideas *in practice*. In this regard, culture and networks are the same. The only question then is whether it is useful for a class of empirical problems centred on how groups of people and groups of meaning are tied to distinguish them analytically. Building on the imagery that Danto develops in his work on art and artistic communities, we developed a simple framework for thinking about three issues centred on the interweaving of meanings and structures that have been of interest to sociologists.

Notes

1 Support from the Interdisciplinary Center for Innovative Theory and Empirics (INCITE) at Columbia University is gratefully acknowledged. Unusually penetrating and helpful comments and suggestions from Ron Breiger greatly improved this paper, for which we are very grateful. We also thank the two editors for pushing us towards less abstraction, and hopefully more clarity. Address all correspondence to Alix Rule (alix.rule@gmail.com) or Peter Bearman (psbearman@gmail.com).
2 Ronald Breiger (2000) offers a similar formalization of the 'duality' of culture and groups, which he develops in greater mathematical depth; he demonstrates that this approach to the co-constitution of individuals and cultural elements underlies both Bourdieu's correspondence analysis and the 'mathematics of social action' of Coleman's *Foundations of Social Theory*.
3 In any case, it is impossible to know whether it is the social meaning of these appetites, rather than the qualities of the objects at which they're directed, that establish their communicative power: 'The paradox of the imposition of legitimacy is that it makes it impossible to determine whether the dominant feature appears as distinguished or noble because it is dominant, or whether what is noble or distinguished as being noble because it is dominant — because it has the privilege of defining, by its very existence, what noble or distinguished itself is, a privilege which is expressed precisely in its self-assurance — or whether it is only because it is dominant that it appears as endowed with those qualities and uniquely entitled to define them' (1984: 92).

References

Accominotti, F. (2014) 'The price of purity: Brokerage as consecration in the market for modern art', Manuscript.
Alloway, L. (1972) 'Network: The art world described as a system', *Artforum International*, 10(9).

Bearman, P.S. (1993) *Relations into rhetorics: Local elite social structure in Norfolk, England, 1540–1640*, New Brunswick, NJ: Rutgers University Press.
Becker, H.S. (1974) 'Art as collective action', *American Sociological Review*, 39(6): 767–776.
—— (1984) *Art worlds*, Berkeley, CA: University of California Press.
Bourdieu, P. (1983) 'The field of cultural production, or: The economic world reversed', *Poetics*, 12(4): 311–356.
—— (1984) *Distinction: A social critique of the judgement of taste*, Cambridge, MA: Harvard University Press.
—— (1993) *The field of cultural production: Essays on art and literature*, New York: Columbia University Press.
—— (2008) *The bachelors' ball*, Cambridge: Polity.
Breiger, R.L. (2000) 'A tool kit for practice theory', *Poetics*, 27(2), 91–115.
Crane, D. (1987) *The transformation of the avant-garde: The New York art world, 1940–1985*, Chicago: University of Chicago Press.
Danto, A. (1964) 'The artworld', *The Journal of Philosophy*, 61(19): 571–584.
DiMaggio, P. (1987) 'Classification in art', *American Sociological Review*, 52(4): 440–455.
Fraser, K. (1985) *The fashionable mind: Reflections on fashion, 1970-1982*, Boston: DR Godine.
Giuffre, K. (2001) 'Mental maps: Social networks and the language of critical reviews', *Sociological Inquiry*, 71(3): 381–393.
Goldberg, A. (2011) 'Mapping shared understandings using relational class analysis: The case of the cultural omnivore reexamined', *American Journal of Sociology*, 116(5): 1397–1436.
Katz, J. (1988) *Seductions of crime: A chilling exploration of the criminal mind–from juvenile delinquency to cold-blooded murder*, New York: Basic Books.
Latour, B. (1988) *The pasteurization of France*, Cambridge, MA: Harvard University Press.
Latour, B. and S. Woolgar (1979) *Laboratory life: The social construction of scientific facts*, Beverly Hills, CA: Sage.
Lévi-Strauss, C. (1969) *The elementary structures of kinship* (No. 340), Boston: Beacon Press.
Lieberson, S. and E.O. Bell (1992) 'Children's first names: An empirical study of social taste', *American Journal of Sociology*, 98(3): 511–554.
Merton, R.K. (1973) *The sociology of science: Theoretical and empirical investigations*, Chicago: University of Chicago Press.
Mills, C.W. (1940) 'Situated actions and vocabularies of motive', *American Sociological Review*, 5(6): 904–913.
Padgett, J.F. and W.W. Powell (2012) *The emergence of organizations and markets*, Princeton, NJ: Princeton University Press.
Schultz, J. and R.L. Breiger (2010) 'The strength of weak culture', *Poetics*, 38(6): 610–624.
Van Doosselaere, Q. (2009) *Commercial agreements and social dynamics in medieval Genoa*, Cambridge: Cambridge University Press.
White, H.C. and C.A. White (1965) *Canvases and careers: Institutional change in the French painting world*, New York: Wiley.
Whitham, M.M. (2014) *Symbolic social network ties and cooperative collective action* (PhD dissertation, University of Arizona).

11
Getting beyond the surface
Using geometric data analysis in cultural sociology

Henk Roose

Introduction

Correspondence analysis is 'a relational technique of data analysis whose philosophy corresponds exactly to what, in my view, the reality of the social world is. It is a technique which "thinks" in terms of relation, as I try to do precisely with the notion of field' (Bourdieu and Wacquant 1992: 96). This quotation from the French sociologist Pierre Bourdieu is often invoked as an argument to veer away from traditional correlational techniques like multivariate regression analysis and to opt for Geometric Data Analysis (GDA) as statistical toolbox – away from 'general linear reality', which centres on dependent and independent variables with a focus on causality and usually assumes causal attributes to be independent from one another (see Abbott 1988). GDA refers to a group of techniques including for example Correspondence Analysis (CA) that use spatial measures like Euclidean distance and dispersion along principal axes to analyse, describe and visualise large datasets (for good technical introductions and more, see for example Benzécri 1992; Greenacre 2007; Le Roux and Rouanet 2004, 2010; Murtagh 2005; Tenenhaus and Young 1985). Outcomes of GDA are clouds of points in a geometric space – just like numbers are the outcome of standard regression procedures.

The aim of this article is to elaborate and think about GDA as a technique that 'thinks in terms of relations' and show what it can add to the use of traditional regression based techniques. I do not mean to downplay the importance of regression analysis – I am a happy user of regression techniques myself. Rather I want to highlight the potential of GDA and explain the way it can be linked to relational thinking. Hereto, I use an example I am fairly familiar with and which very much parallels the analyses presented by Bourdieu in *Distinction* (1984), i.e. an analysis of the social structuring of cultural practices. What is the relationship between class and taste as an attempt to re-think Weber's classical opposition between 'Klasse' and 'Stand'?

Multiple correspondence analysis

Basic ideas

The basic rationale in GDA is not to isolate 'independent' or 'dependent' variables, but to explore and visualize complex relations between variables and categories of variables – called 'modalities' – that are 'hidden' in the data. Correspondence Analysis (CA) is one of the most popular and powerful tools within the GDA toolbox and is used to detect latent structuring principles comparable to Principal Component Analysis, be it that CA deals with categorical variables. The basics of Multiple Correspondence Analysis (MCA), the multivariate variant of CA, can be linked to relational reasoning à la Bourdieu, as it tries to unravel and visualize the objective system of positions grounded in the distribution of resources and the subjective 'lived' social life of different actors framed by that system and their position within it (Mohr 1998, 2000). E.g. Bourdieu distinguishes a space of positions with aggregation points of capital and a space of position-takings, 'i.e., the structured system of practices and expressions of agents' (Bourdieu and Wacquant 1992: 105). Bourdieu assumes a relation of homology between these two spaces, in the sense that position-takings relate to each other in a way that is homologous to how positions relate to each other.

The nature of a field is inherently historical: the field and its dimensionality are the result of diachronic struggles which remain entrenched in any cross-sectional image of it – struggles over what is good/bad, over what practices are worthy/unworthy, etc. Conflicts are central. The field logic forces you to think in oppositions: certain practices for example do not have significance in and of their own, but in relation/contrast to other practices. The analysis evolves not so much about whether or not people attend an opera, for example, and what characteristics are related to opera attendance – like a regression analysis would do. In MCA, opera attendance is considered in relation to attending rock concerts, visiting museums or Chinese restaurants, doing sports for kicks, or liking Flemish Primitives paintings. Practices are seen in the context of other, (dis)similar practices. Thus, practices are determined not only by their attributes, but also by their position *vis-à-vis* each other in the field. So, MCA is a relational method à la De Saussure: cultural activities are not considered *per se*, but in relation to other cultural activities – within the field of cultural practices, objects and dispositions. And it is these patterns of activities that are linked up with the relative possession of a certain type of capital associated with privileges, power and success.

Next to the cloud of modalities, there is the cloud of individuals that projects each individual onto the same Euclidean space. This is one of the unique properties of MCA: it simultaneously visualizes variables as well as individuals. So, it generates both variable-centred as well as individual-centred analyses. It should be noted, however, that MCA creates a system of objective relations between individuals, no real interpersonal networks (cf. Bourdieu and Wacquant 1992: 97; De Nooij 2003). Individuals are dispersed within the Euclidean space, their distance reflecting dissimilarity with regard to mental, embodied structures, dispositions and practices as well as to the 'objective' power resources/restraints – not necessarily reflecting any real social connection/contact. This is what the 'magical eye' of GDA succeeds in (Rosenlund 1995): MCA bridges subjective meanings/consciousness of actors with 'hidden' objective power structures. In other words, it discloses the invisible power relationships to an untrained eye, because 'they are obscured by the realities of ordinary experience' (Bourdieu 1984: 22) and relates them to individuals' common everyday assumptions and ideas rooted in practicality of social life. Of course, regression analysis is also able to relate 'hidden' structural variables to practices, but the strength of GDA is situated in the comprehensive way it discloses latent patterns in the data, without relying all too heavily on the choice of specific manifest variables.

Illustration: Cultural practices/dispositions and social position

A social field in Bourdieusian terms is a snapshot of processes of contestation and redefinition about what activities are valuable or worthwhile endorsing, what cultural practices/

dispositions are superior and for whom. Within the social space you can see different and differing oppositions at work – in *Distinction* (1984) Bourdieu finds cultural lifestyle to be structured along capital volume and capital composition. Using data from the survey 'Cultural participation in Flanders 2003–2004', a large-scale survey conducted among a representative sample of the Flemish population ($N = 2,849$), I analyse how the field of cultural practices in Flanders *anno* 2000 is structured. What dimensions are central in making up the space of lifestyles? Hereto, I use 64 variables – no sparseness problems with MCA as any number of variables can be entered – that can be subdivided into two groups (for a more comprehensive description of the analysis, see Roose *et al.* 2012). Firstly, there are the participation variables that include cultural activities ranging from lowbrow to highbrow and situated both in the public as well as the private sphere, such as watching television, going to the movies, reading comics, going to a restaurant, traveling, doing sports, etc. Secondly, there is a group of variables that focus on the ways people do things, attempting to get at the dispositional aspects of cultural behaviour, like, for example, motives for traveling, expectations towards movies, attitudes towards what's good food, preferences in the fine arts, etc. Variables in the first group are dichotomous, in the second group they have three categories: 'like', 'neutral' and 'dislike' or 'agree', 'neither agree/nor disagree' and 'disagree' (see Table 11.A1 and Table 11.A2 in the appendix for an overview of the variables used in the global space).

Three axes or dimensions turn out to be essential in making up the global social space in Flanders – these axes are similar to comparable studies using MCA in the UK (Bennett *et al.* 2009), Denmark (Prieur *et al.* 2008) and Serbia (Cvetičanin and Popescu 2011). The first dimension is an engagement-disengagement axis contrasting an active, outward-oriented lifestyle with a more domestic and passive leisure pattern. This opposition in behaviour is related to attitudes opposing openness to new things versus an orientation favouring the familiar, things that have proven their use/quality. Dimension two opposes a preference for action, adventure and thrills versus a more contemplative, reflective lifestyle with a taste for consecrated or legitimate forms of culture. The third axis depicts again an openness to new things versus a neutral stance towards openness. This openness is a dispositional characteristic applicable to a variety of domains – for example, sport, movies, travel and food. Axis one and two are related to indicators of social position. Axis one is associated with educational credentials and cultural participation of the parents; dimension two is linked up with age, an indicator of life phase or birth cohort. Axis three is linked to a combination of characteristics, which I will return to.

Let me show in detail how exactly the sociological interpretation of the axes develops. The total variance of the contingency table, called inertia in GDA, is decomposed along principal axes using Singular Value Decomposition (SVD)[1]. Each variable/modality contributes to the principal inertia or the variation within each dimension – the variation of all dimensions sums up to the total inertia. Based on this SVD one decides on the number of axes to interpret – here: three, a decision corroborated by the modified rates (Benzécri 1992: 412). These rates are better indicators for the relative importance of the various dimensions than the raw inertia rates that tend to underestimate the relative importance of the first axes. Now, the relative contributions show what variables are responsible for the variation along an axis. So, higher contributions should be given more weight in explaining the 'sociological' meaning of a dimension. For example, Table 11.1 shows the contributions of all variables and modalities higher than the average contribution for the second axis (for variables this average contribution equals 1/64 (1.56 per cent) or the number of variables; for modalities this is 1/173 (0.57 per cent) or the number of active categories). As you can see in Table 11.1, the items

Table 11.1 Relative contributions of variables and modalities to the orientation of axis two (in per cent)

Variables	Contribution of variables (in %)	Modalities Lower side	Modalities Upper side	Contribution of modalities (in %) Lower side	Contribution of modalities (in %) Upper side
Arts: Flemish primitives	6.74	Dislike	Like	3.03	3.67
Arts: baroque portraits	6.64	Dislike	Like	3.18	3.27
Arts: renaissance	5.69	Dislike	Like	2.84	2.72
Listening to classical music	4.52	Never	Often	1.46	2.73
Arts: (post-)impressionism	4.25	Dislike	Like	1.67	2.51
Travel: party	3.91	Agree	Disagree	1.96	1.91
Listening to opera	3.83	Once/while	Often	2.03	1.13
Film: violent scenes	3.63	Like	Dislike	1.15	1.33
Travel: visit culture	3.10	Disagree	Agree	1.20	1.88
Travel: adventure	3.05	Agree	Disagree	1.20	1.79
Film: action and adventure	2.86	Like	Dislike	1.29	1.52
Listening to dance	2.70	Often	Never	1.44	1.25
Visiting museums of fine arts	2.64	—	Yes	—	2.23
Watching TV: VT4	2.47	Yes	—	2.23	—
Sport: kick	2.21	Agree	Disagree	0.99	0.45
Listening to pop/rock	2.20	Often	Never	0.76	1.44
Watching TV: MTV/TMF	2.05	Yes	—	1.94	—
Travel: sea and beach	2.02	Agree	Disagree	0.83	1.19
Film: special effects	1.96	Like	Dislike	0.90	0.91
Sport: limits	1.86	Agree	Disagree	0.89	0.59
Watching TV: KA2	1.83	Yes	—	1.68	—
Visiting museums cont. arts	1.79	—	Yes	—	1.55
Arts: nineteenth-century landscapes	1.78	Dislike	Like	0.79	0.94
Reading prose/poetry	1.59	No	Yes	0.59	1.00
Arts: surrealism	1.53	—	Like	—	1.08
Watching TV: Canvas	1.45	—	Yes	—	1.20
	78.30			34.05	38.29

Source: adapted from Roose et al. 2012.

are ordered from the highest to the lowest relative contribution (from 6.74 to 1.45 per cent). The variables shown are good for 78.30 per cent of the variation in the second axis. Indicators of taste in the fine arts are most distinctive: (dis)liking Flemish primitives (6.74 per cent), baroque portraits (6.64 per cent), renaissance paintings (5.69 per cent) and listening to classical music (4.52 per cent) are the four most important items differentiating the left from the right pole of the dimension (see Figure 11.1 on the left for the cloud of modalities contributing more than average to the second axis). The lower side of the graph depicts modalities showing a manifest dislike for the fine arts combined with a preference for partying; adventure when on holidays; liking movies with action, adventure and violent scenes and listening to dance music. The upper side shows items indicating a preference for highbrow arts, opera and classical music. The opposition between being disposed towards a preference for action and adventure versus contemplating the consecrated fine arts is corroborated by the other items, such as the type of television channel watched or the motives to do sports.

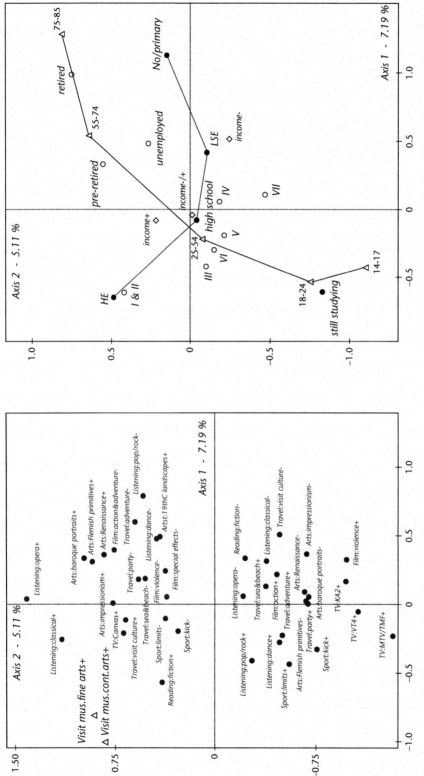

Figure 11.1 Modalities contributing more than average to axis two in plane 1–2 (left) and supplementary variables in plane 1–2 (right). Legend: No/primary: no or primary education; LSE: lower secondary education; HE: higher education (college or higher); EGP I: managerial occupations; II: professions; III: intermediate occupations; IV: small employers and own-account workers; V: lower supervisory and technical occupations; VI: semi-routine occupations; VII: routine occupations

Source: adapted from Roose et al. 2012.

Thus, the interpretation of the dimension is based on a whole series of indicators and so, has a tendency not to be biased too much by changes in manifested preferences or the use of specific items that may have changing meanings over time and undermine comparability. The same rationale holds for the interpretation of axis one and three. In that way, the active variables create a space of different global oppositions.

Of course, this space is mute on the power resources these oppositions are related to – they merely signal 'position-takings' and no 'positions' (Bourdieu and Wacquant 1992: 105). With MCA it is possible to include so-called supplementary variables that do not contribute to the construction of the space, but which can be added as illustrative points to see what variables the dimensions of the space are associated with. Usually characteristics like educational attainment, occupational category, gender, etc. are used and plotted into the space. This is a first step towards so-called 'structured analysis': by turning to the cloud of individuals, GDA uses the between- and within-variance of individuals' characteristics like age or gender for example, to explore their associations with the axes making up the space. Table 11.2 and the right graph on Figure 11.1 both show how age is related to the dimensions in the global space. This graph ignores the dispersion of the sub-clouds for age as it only shows the modality mean points of individuals belonging to a certain age group. In Table 11.2 the decomposition of variance of the individuals along the axes in terms of age is presented. The between-age variance divided by the total variance equals η^2. η^2 is comparable to R^2 in regression analysis: 29.0 per cent of the variance in the second dimension can be attributed to age, for axis one this amounts to some 20 per cent. Indeed, the age categories [14–17] and [18–24] are situated at the bottom on Figure 11.1 (right), while [55–74] and [75–85] are plotted at the top. This means that the contemplative, *Bildung*-oriented lifestyle is disproportionately situated among the higher age groups, while the active, adventurous and kicks-seeking disposition is relatively more common among youngsters.

The same graph also shows that – not surprisingly – higher education (HE) is associated with a preference for highbrow practices, while a high school degree or lower secondary education (LSE) is more common among the adventurous practices – be it that the last association is quite small considering the relatively small distance from the origin. I also plotted the EGP-class scheme as a supplementary variable in Figure 11.1, and it generates similar

Table 11.2 Coordinates of mean points and variances of age categories on the first three axes (breakdown of variance along axes and age)

Age	Weight	Mean point coordinates			Variances		
		Axis 1	Axis 2	Axis 3	Axis 1	Axis 2	Axis 3
14–17	209	−0.15	−0.33	−0.08	0.0682	0.0463	0.0875
18–24	323	−0.18	−0.22	−0.04	0.0729	0.0649	0.0689
25–54	1436	−0.07	−0.02	+0.01	0.0952	0.0684	0.0589
55–74	741	+0.19	+0.19	+0.01	0.1240	0.0597	0.0578
75–85	140	+0.45	+0.24	+0.05	0.0576	0.0372	0.0405
				within-Age	0.0962	0.0625	0.0608
				between-Age	0.0283	0.0260	0.0008
				total (λ_i)	0.1245	0.0885	0.0617

Legend: Used transition formula from coordinate of modality to modality mean point = coordinate * SQRT(λ_i); variances based on one-way ANOVA on coordinates (N.B.: Sum of Squares divided by n).
η^2 on axis 1 = 0.23, axis 2 = 0.29 and axis 3 = 0.01 (or between-variance divided by total-variance).

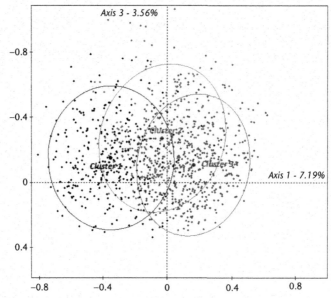

Figure 11.2 Three sub-clouds scoring high on axis three after hierarchical clustering in plane 1–3 (adapted from Roose *et al.* 2012)

findings: those in managerial occupations and professions are more prone to prefer legitimate cultural forms than people in routine occupations. This analysis underlines that the opposition between highbrow and lowbrow culture is still very relevant – the association with age may hint at an association with generation-based differentiation in manifestations of cultural capital (cf. Bellavance 2008).

It is clear that the idea of controlling for certain 'confounding' variables – and the assumption of linearity – central to multivariate regression analysis is absent in MCA. For some, this counts as a serious drawback. Yet, this reluctance to think in terms of independent and dependent variables, of having to control for 'confounding' characteristics, is founded on the 'illusion of constancy' (Bourdieu 1984: 18): it is not because the number of years of education are the same for men and women in 'statistical' terms, for city-dwellers versus people from the country, for members of the well-to-do bourgeoisie versus workers for example, that the sociological significance of these educational careers is similar. One runs the risk of 'lumping together' very different experiences – just for the sake of statistical metric. Usually, in regression analysis, the solution for incorporating these interrelations between different variables is the use of interaction-effects, but when three or more variables are involved in these interactions, an easy way of interpreting these interrelationships becomes improbable.

Clustering techniques: Hierarchical agglomerative clustering

Using the individual scores on the dimensions of the space, it is possible to try to find meaningful clusters within the space. This is what I have done to try to get at the type of individuals scoring high on axis three, the dimension that indicates openness to a variety of practices. At first sight, the third axis turns out to be somewhat enigmatic as it is related neither to educational attainment, age nor gender, but perhaps it is associated with a specific combination of values on these variables? This example shows how GDA can produce that 'network of structures' I mentioned above. Would it be possible to find a segment within the population scoring high on openness resembling the typical omnivore, who is supposed to be relatively young, be highly educated and belong to the (upper-)middle classes? Could also other segments be detected, scoring equally high on openness, but showing it in a totally different way than these 'traditional' omnivores?

Using the scores on all dimensions of the global space, I performed a hierarchical clustering using 'nearest neighbour' as criterion for segmentation. This generates an agglomeration tree which suggests a cut at seven segments. Three of these segments – each characterized by a specific combination of factors – score high on dimension three. Figure 11.2 plots them in plane 1 – 3: you can see they all score high on the third dimension (their modality mean points are situated above the origin) and differ along the first dimension, an indicator of overall possession of cultural capital. By comparing the relative frequencies of variables between segments and sample, it is possible to describe these clusters in terms of 'distinctive' variables. Briefly, they are (1) middle-aged managers and professionals with high schooling levels and a lot of cultural capital – they could be considered as prototypical examples of the omnivore: relatively young, highly educated and having a high social position (Peterson 1992); (2) Youngsters and students with less cultural capital but a strong predilection for amusement and action and (3) Older people (aged 65+) with relatively little cultural capital but a strong interest in classical, figurative art and cultural TV programs. So, openness – this is what the third dimension stands for – is manifested in totally different ways, the first being omnivorousness as it is usually conceived in the literature. The other two segments also score high on openness, but it manifests itself in different practices depending on generation – at least this is how the effect is interpreted in Roose et al. (2012). This is a clear illustration of how an underlying tendency may have behaviorally different manifestations according to someone's cultural capital – and/or the generation one belongs to – empirical findings that would not easily be discovered using correlational techniques only as they would be hampered by sparseness issues and difficulties in handling combinations of categorical variables.

Class-specific analysis

Whereas clustering techniques allow you to go beyond general linear reality in the global space – they focus on specific combinations of values on variables to account for the dimensions in cultural practices – Class-Specific Analysis goes one step further. The global dimensions disclosed by MCA may conceal logics and principles of distinction that are confined to certain localities within the social space, restricted for example to a certain social segment or occupational categories. Class-Specific Analysis (CSA) allows exploring these localised logics that may be traces of some of the contestations that have taken place over time within the field. With CSA it is possible to analyse if and to what extent oppositions and distinctions within specific subpopulations are similar to the dimensionality of the general population. For example, are the same kind of cultural activities as distinctive for the young as they are for older individuals (see Roose 2014)? When trying to get at what activities and dispositions generate distance between individuals within a specific sub-group or segment of the population, focus on the oppositions in the global space loses significance and relevance. It is the distances and the principal components making up the restricted sub-space that become of interest if you want to unravel the structuring dimensions of each cluster – be it with reference to the global cloud (Le Roux and Rouanet 2010: 61–69).

CSA looks for principal dimensions within a sub-cloud – say for example for the elderly, or managers or women – without 'extracting' it from the global space. CSA resonates with

Mohr's critique on linearity of axes reflecting capital. He argues – and perhaps rightly so – that within the concept of field only the global oppositions are taken into account to relate social positions to practices and that '[o]ther conflicts, other engagements and, especially, more localised struggles over resources and positions are not taken into account in this mode' (Mohr 2013: 124). It may give you an idea of the conflicts over what is worth struggling for.

As an illustration I will use CSA to explore the possibly different structuring principles for the young and the elderly as part of an investigation of so-called emerging cultural capital (Prieur and Savage 2013; Savage and Hanquinet, forthcoming). This new form of capital is considered to be the prerogative of the young, championing a screen-based, Anglo-cosmopolitan commercial culture that is appropriated with a certain ironical stance versus the Eurocentric, cerebral, ascetic and serious highbrow culture. There is growing evidence that the specific content of cultural capital is being contested. For example, working class respondents in the UK claim not to be 'in awe of legitimate culture and find no value in refinement' (Bennett *et al.* 2009: 205), neither is there 'a deference towards legitimate culture' (ibid.: 212). What is consecrated may not have universal legitimacy and different forms of 'capital' may be at work simultaneously. So, do you find traces of this 'emerging cultural capital' structuring the sub-cloud of the young?

Figure 11.3 shows the clouds of individuals of two sub-segments within the global space, the young (-25) on the left and the elderly (55+) on the right. You can see that both sub-clouds are situated in different parts of the global space: the young in the South-West quadrant, the older individuals positioned North-East – they are more disengaged and inclined to highbrow, legitimate cultural forms while shunning action and adventure. As for the dispersion of the individuals, the young are scattered along both axis one and two, the elderly more along axis two.

CSA starts off with a PCA of all global structuring dimensions obtained from the Specific MCA for the sub-clouds only.[2] When you compare the correlations of the dimensions

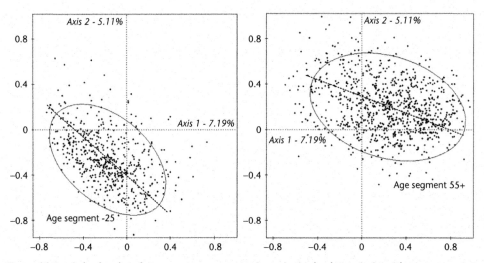

Figure 11.3 Sub-clouds of two age segments in principal plane 1–2 with mean points (grey asterisk) and concentration ellipses

Source: adapted from Roose 2014.

of the sub-clouds with the axes in the global space, you can see interesting differences. The sub-space of the 55+ is similarly structured as the global space: the correlation coefficients between their first axes are 0.97 ($p < 0.001$), for the second axes 0.72 ($p < 0.001$). This picture is somewhat different for the -24: the correlations are respectively 0.31 and 0.72, suggesting that the first dimension for the young is differently structured than the first axis in the global space. Figure 11.4 and Figure 11.5 together with Tables 11.3 and 11.4 contain the results of the two CSA's and allow for a thorough analysis of similarities and differences.

In Table 11.3 you can see the modalities that contribute more than average in the orientation of the first and second dimension for the young – these contributions are graphically represented in Figure 11.4. For axis one, it is especially a preference for screen-based action, fun and adventure and an outright rejection of the fine arts that stand opposed to a neutral attitude towards fine arts (e.g. Flemish primitives, renaissance paintings, baroque portraits, (post-impressionism) or other more contemplative things, like listening to chanson or classical music. Also watching musical and commercial television channels (MTV, TMF, VT4 and KA2) work as a distinguishing force. At the time, these channels aired music videos, reality shows like *Big Brother*, sitcoms like *Friends* and a lot of recent action movies. Axis two opposes a neutral attitude with a disposition towards an active lifestyle indicated by doing sport for the kick, wanting to change one's limits and to get a beautiful body and adventurous travel with backpack to meet new people or explore other cultures. Here, a sportive disposition is supplemented with some sort of openness towards new things, a sociable attitude towards the 'other' in terms of travel. This openness also seems to manifest itself through a preference for avant-garde art, like abstract expressionism, surrealism and Dada or listening to jazz – without a devotion for more consecrated forms of art which is the case in the global space. The love of art in the global space encompasses all genres with the older, canonised,

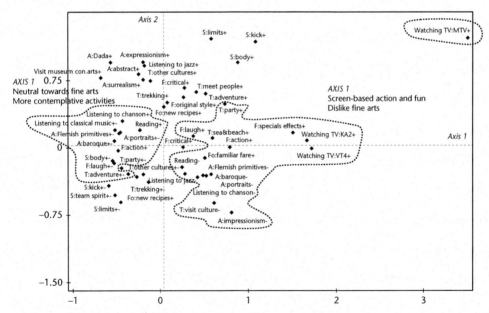

Figure 11.4 CSA of sub-cloud '14–25 years' with modalities contributing more than average to sub-plane 1–2

Source: adapted from Roose 2014.

Table 11.3 Contributions of modalities (in per cent) for first two axes in sub-cloud '14–25 years'

Age: –25 (n = 532)	Contribution of modalities				Contribution of modalities				
Axis 1	Left		Right		Axis 2	Left		Right	
Watching TV: music channel	—	—	Often	9.3	Sport: to change limits	Neutral	2.2	Agree	5.3
Film: contains violent scenes	—	—	Like	5.9	Travel: other cultures	Neutral	1.3	Agree	4.0
Watching TV: VT4	—	—	Often	4.0	Sport: kick	Neutral	0.9	Agree	3.0
Film: uses a lot of special effects	—	—	Like	3.6	Arts: abstract expressionism	—	—	Like	2.6
Watching TV: KA2	—	—	Often	3.4	Sport: a beautiful body	—	—	Agree	2.6
Film: contains action and adventure	Neutral	1.4	Like	2.6	Travel: meet new people	—	—	Agree	2.4
Arts: (post-) impressionism	—	—	Dislike	1.7	Travel: visit culture	Disagree	2.4	—	—
Travel: party and fun	Neutral	1.0	Agree	1.5	Arts: (post-) impressionism	Dislike	2.4	—	—
Arts: late-renaissance/ baroque	Neutral	1.3	Dislike	1.5	Arts: surrealism	—	—	Like	2.2
Reading	Yes	1.5	No	0.9	Listening to jazz/ blues/soul/funk	Never	1.0	Often	2.2
Travel: sea and beach	—	—	Agree	1.4	Travel: adventure	Neutral	0.8	Agree	2.1
Sport: kick	Neutral	1.1	Agree	1.4	Watching TV: music channel	—	—	Often	2.0
Film: makes you laugh	Neutral	1.3	Like	1.0	Film: original in form and style	—	—	Like	2.0
Travel: visit culture	—	—	Disagree	1.3	Travel: hiking and trekking	Neutral	1.3	Agree	1.9
Arts: baroque portraits	Neutral	1.1	Dislike	1.3	Food: try new recipes	Neutral	1.0	Agree	1.9
Sport: a beautiful body	Neutral	1.1	Agree	1.3	Visiting museum contemp. arts	—	—	Yes	1.7
Food: familiar fare	—	—	Agree	1.2	Sport: team spirit	Neutral	1.6	—	—
Arts: Flemish primitives	Neutral	1.0	Dislike	1.1	Arts: abstract art	—	—	Like	1.6
Listening to chanson	Once/ while	0.9	Never	1.1	Film: critical comment on society	—	—	Like	1.4
Listening to classical music	Once/ while	1.1	—	—	Arts: conceptual art/Dadaism	—	—	Like	1.3
Total contribution: 63%		17%		46%	Total contribution: 66%		17%		49%

Getting beyond the surface

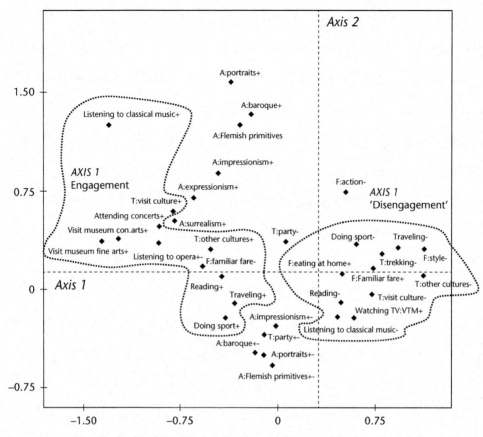

Figure 11.5 CSA of sub-cloud '55–85 years' with modalities contributing more than average to sub-plane 1–2

Source: adapted from Roose 2014.

figurative streams as being more important in the orientation of the second dimension than the more recent and more difficult 'abstract' forms.

Table 11.4 and Figure 11.5 show that, for the sub-space of the 55+ segment, axis one distinguishes an out-of-the-house, active lifestyle with concert attendance, museum visits, travel and sport activities with a more passive, home-bound disposition centred around watching commercial television and 'eating at home is the best there is'. With the elderly engagement is manifested through culture and traveling, less through going to the movies, shopping or going to a pub. The second axis for the 55+ contrasts a preference for consecrated art forms such as impressionism, baroque portraits as well as more contemporary streams (surrealism and abstract expressionism) with a neutral stance – while in the global space these aesthetic preferences are opposed to an outright rejection. Contrary to the younger age groups, consecrated, figurative art and more avant-garde art go hand in hand and co-exist as status marker. For the young, a preference for avant-garde art runs parallel with an active, adventurous way of living contrasted with a neutral attitude.

So, CSA shows empirically that the fine arts stand out as distinguishing practices both for the elderly and the young – be it in interestingly different ways. Preferences for people born before

Table 11.4 Contributions of modalities (in per cent) for first two axes in sub-cloud '55–85 years'

Age: 55–85 (n = 881)	Contribution of modalities				Contribution of modalities			
Axis 1	Left		Right		Axis 2	Left		Right	
Going to a restaurant	—	—	No	3.3	Arts: baroque portraits	Neutral	2.4	Like	10.2
Visiting museum fine arts	Yes	3.1	—	—	Arts: late-renaissance/baroque	Neutral	2.1	Like	8.4
Travel: other cultures	Agree	1.0	Disagree	2.5	Arts: Flemish primitives	Neutral	2.7	Like	8.2
Traveling	Yes	0.9	No	2.5	Arts: (post-)impressionism	Neutral	0.9	Like	4.0
Film: original in form and style	—	—	Dislike	2.5	Listening to classical music	—	—	Often	3.9
Food: try new recipes	—	—	Disagree	2.4	Arts: landscapes	Neutral	1.4	Like	2.3
Listening to classical music	Often	2.2	Never	1.3	Film: contains action and adventure	—	—	Dislike	1.7
Food: familiar fare	Disagree	0.9	Agree	2.2	Travel: visit culture	—	—	Agree	1.7
Visiting museum contemp. arts	Yes	2.1	—	—	Travel: party and fun	Neutral	1.1	Disagree	0.9
Shopping	—	—	No	1.8	Arts: abstract expressionism	—	—	Like	1.4
Travel: visit culture	Agree	1.7	Disagree	1.7	Arts: surrealism	—	—	Like	1.0
Travel: hiking and trekking	—	—	Disagree	1.7	Doing sport	—	—	No	1.0
Doing sport	Yes	1.1	No	1.6	Going to a restaurant	—	—	No	0.9
Watching TV: VTM	—	—	Often	1.2					
Food: eating at home is the best	—	—	Agree	1.4					
Listening to music: opera	Once/wh	1.4	—	—					
Reading	Yes	1.4	No	1.2					
Attending concerts	Yes	1.3	—	—					
Total contribution: 63%		25%		38%	Total contribution: 56%		12%		44%

1950 are very much characterised by a deference and no real dislike *vis-à-vis* legitimate culture. Liking legitimate culture signals openness, a wish to be confronted with new experiences. For people born after 1980 this is different: legitimate art is less central as a distinctive force – at least, if it turns out to be structuring the sub-cloud, it is as something that is disliked versus indifferent to (cf. the dislike for impressionism, late-renaissance/baroque, baroque portraits, Flemish primitives on dimension one). Apparently, younger people are not in awe for 'classical' fine arts – perhaps they consider them 'stained' or old-fashioned – while abstract expressionism, Dada, abstract art and surrealism are part of an underlying adventurous, open attitude.

Thus, CSA is able to show how legitimate culture means different things to different people, reminiscent of the different ways – the how – art works are appropriated. And likewise, the potential for social distinction of the same practices may differ depending on the social circles where they are deployed. So, it is not only other activities that form part of a possible change in the manifested preferences/dispositions/practices related to cultural capital (Prieur and Savage 2013), but also different ways of appropriating similar activities. This questions the idea of a societal and universally deployable symbolic meaning of cultural activities in terms of social distinction: e.g. the inter-generational difference of the meaning of the fine arts as indicator of openness for the elderly versus a sign of an old-fashioned nature or something *passé* for the young. I think that with the development of CSA, GDA allows researchers to get beyond the surface of things – and arrive at findings that add to insights grounded in correlational techniques.

Conclusion

In this contribution I wanted to highlight the potential and applicability of GDA within cultural sociology. The strengths of GDA can be found in its ability to include a lot of variables to produce a fine-grained detailed picture, its simultaneous handling of variables and individuals and its close connection with relational thinking. Using spatial measures and graphical representations, it provides attractive visual tools to summarize huge data-matrices in relatively easy-to-interpret graphs. With the illustrations I showed how MCA can disclose latent patterns from large datasets, how these patterns can be investigated through their associations with socio-economic and other variables, how also specific combinations of variables can be related to the dimensions via hierarchical cluster analysis and finally how different/differing principles of opposition can be at work simultaneously and disclosed by means of CSA.

Of course, GDA is not without its critics – and justly so. Tony Bennett for example (2007: 214), argues that the polarizing logic is 'partly a reflection of the ways in which multiple correspondence analysis converts cultural data into binary opposites which do not allow fine graded distinctions to be taken into account and which, if not guarded against, exaggerate differences at the expense of shared taste'. Indeed, the input for GDA is best served with dichotomous variables. Likert-scale items tend to produce the so-called horseshoe-effect or Guttman-effect, in which extreme answers ('strongly agree', strongly disagree') are opposed to the neutral categories ('neutral', 'somewhat agree') – from a substantial point of view quite uninteresting. Another standard critique takes charge with GDA's inability to do multivariate controls, which for some analytical purposes prove necessary. However, the strength of GDA is its ability to go beyond the surface of manifest categories and disclose hidden patterns in the data – paths hitherto unexplored by traditional regression analysis. It continues to have 'elective affinity' with the idea of social space/field and the recent developments within the GDA-framework – like hierarchical clustering and CSA – have considerably refined the toolbox making it even more attractive to deploy within cultural sociology.

Notes

1 SVD is similar to Eigenvalue decomposition, but SVD is used for rectangular matrices, and it reduces high dimensional data to less dimensions which capture the structures in the data from most to least variation.

2 I use a macro provided by Brigitte Le Roux, whom I want to thank for her willingness to share some of the intricacies of GDA with me. I am also grateful to my colleagues Frédéric Lebaron and Johs Hjellbrekke en Daan Vandenhaute who have been very helpful 'compagnons de route' in my explorations with GDA.

References

Abbott, A. (1988) 'Transcending general linear reality', *Sociological Theory*, 6(2): 169–186.
Bellavance, G. (2008) 'Where's high? Who's low? What's new? Classification and stratification inside cultural "repertoires"', *Poetics*, 36: 189–216.
Bennett, T. (2007) 'Habitus clivé: Aesthetics and politics in the work of Pierre Bourdieu', *New Literary History*, 38(1): 201–228.
Bennett, T., M. Savage, E. Silva, A. Warde, M. Gayo-Cal and D. Wright (2009) *Culture, Class, Distinction*, London: Routledge.
Benzécri, J.-P. (1992) *Correspondence Analysis Handbook*, New York: Dekker.
Bourdieu, P. (1984) *Distinction: A Social Critique of the Judgment of Taste*, Cambridge: Harvard University Press.
Bourdieu, P. and L. Wacquant (1992) *An Invitation to Reflexive Sociology*, Cambridge: Polity Press.
Cvetičanin, P. and M. Popescu (2011) 'The art of making classes in Serbia: Another particular case of the possible', *Poetics*, 39: 444–468.
De Nooij, W. (2003) 'Fields and networks: Correspondence analysis and social network analysis in the framework of field theory', *Poetics*, 31: 305–327.
Greenacre, M. (2007) *Correspondence Analysis in Practice*, London: Chapman and Hall/CRC.
Le Roux, B. and H. Rouanet (2004) *Geometric Data Analysis: From Correspondence Analysis to Structured Data Analysis*, Kluwer: Dordrecht.
—— (2010) *Multiple Correspondence Analysis* (Quantitative Applications in the Social Sciences), Thousand Oaks, CA: Sage.
Mohr, J. (1998) 'Measuring meaning structures', *Annual Review of Sociology*, 24: 345–370.
—— (2000) 'Introduction: Structures, institutions, and cultural analysis', *Poetics*, 27: 57–68.
—— (2013), 'Bourdieu's relational method in theory and in practice: From fields and capitals to networks and institutions (and back again)' in F. Dépelteau and C. Powell (eds.), *Relational Sociology: From Project to Paradigm*, New York: Palgrave, pp. 101–136.
Murtagh, F. (2005) *Correspondence Analysis and Data Coding with Java and R*, Boca Raton, FL: Chapman and Hall/CRC.
Peterson, R.A. (1992) 'Understanding audience segmentation: From elite and mass to omnivore and univore', *Poetics*, 21: 243–258.
Prieur, A., L. Rosenlund and J. Skjott-Larsen (2008) 'Cultural capital today: A case study from Denmark', *Poetics*, 36(1): 45–71.
Prieur, A. and M. Savage (2013) 'Emerging forms of cultural capital', *European Societies*, 15(2): 246–267.
Roose, H. (2014) 'Signs of 'emerging' cultural capital? Analysing symbolic struggles using class specific analysis', *Sociology*, online first doi: 10.1177/0038038514544492.
Roose, H., K. van Eijck and J. Lievens (2012) 'Culture of distinction or culture of openness: Using a social space approach to analyze the social structuring of lifestyles', *Poetics* 40(6): 491–513.
Rosenlund, L. (1995) 'Korrespondanseanalyse. Dataanalysens magiske øye', *Sosiologisk tidskrift*, 1: 55–78.
Savage, M. and L. Hanquinet (forthcoming) 'Emerging cultural capital in the city: Profiling London and Brussels', *International Journal of Urban and Regional Research* (volume edited by Loïc Wacquant).
Tenenhaus, M. and F.W. Young (1985) 'An analysis and synthesis of multiple correspondence analysis, optimal scaling, dual scaling, homogeneity analysis and other methods for quantifying categorical multivariate data', *Psychometrika*, 50(1): 91–119.

Table 11.A1 Relative frequencies for participation variables (*n* = 2,849)

	Yes	No		Often	Once in a while	Never
Going to the movies	.472	.528	Listening to pop/rock	.539	.174	.286
Watching movies at home	.819	.181	Listening to dance	.342	.272	.384
Reading	.535	.465	Listening to folk/traditional music	.104	.360	.535
Reading: prose/poetry	.373	.627	Listening to chanson	.124	.411	.463
Reading: comics	.291	.709	Listening to jazz/blues/soul/funk	.120	.352	.526
Attending concerts	.141	.859	Listening to classical music	.118	.331	.550
Visiting museum fine arts	.154	.846	Listening to opera	.032	.148	.818
Visiting museum contemporary arts	.130	.870				
Shopping	.833	.167		0–1 hrs	2–3 hrs	4+ hrs
Going to a pub	.775	.225	Frequency watching television	.181	.483	.330
Going to a restaurant	.854	.146				
Doing sport	.604	.396				
Traveling	.740	.260				
Watching TV: TV1	.485	.515				
Watching TV: Canvas	.148	.852				
Watching TV: commercial station VTM	.316	.684				
Watching TV: KA2	.099	.901				
Watching TV: VT4	.111	.889				
Watching TV: music channel	.062	.938				

Table 11.A2 Relative frequencies for dispositional variables (*n* = 2,849)

	A[1]	N	DA		A	N	DA
Film3: 'original in form and style'	.284	.529	.176	Food1: 'do not spend much money'	.259	.508	.229
Film4: 'makes you laugh'	.538	.399	.055	Food2: 'good food important in life'	.371	.483	.145
Film7: 'uses a lot of special effects'	.128	.473	.387	Food3: 'familiar fare'	.357	.403	.240
Film9: 'contains action and adventure'	.338	.502	.152	Food4: 'try new recipes'	.428	.409	.163
Film10: 'contains violent scenes'	.067	.330	.596	Food6: 'steak and French fries'	.306	.367	.326
Film15: 'is romantic'	.284	.542	.164	Food8: 'eating at home is the best'	.438	.413	.147
Film20: 'critical comment on society'	.146	.563	.280	Sport2: to change limits	.238	.403	.358
Arts1: (post-)impressionism[2]	.243	.551	.243	Sport4: team spirit	.326	.381	.293
Arts2: Flemish primitives	.249	.376	.372	Sport6: kick	.142	.335	.522
Arts3: surrealism	.178	.389	.432	Sport7: a beautiful body	.190	.461	.348
Arts4: baroque portraits	.193	.435	.368	Sport8: friendship	.426	.408	.166
Arts5: abstract expressionism	.133	.349	.516	Travel3: meet new people	.287	.513	.189
Arts6: landscapes	.325	.480	.193	Travel4: sea and beach	.319	.421	.251
Arts7: conceptual art/Dadaism	.067	.300	.630	Travel5: visit culture	.240	.466	.283
Arts8: late-renaissance/baroque	.223	.416	.359	Travel9: party and fun	.230	.429	.333
Arts9: abstract art	.108	.340	.459	Travel11: adventure	.264	.440	.287
Clothing2: 'new clothes every season'	.241	.361	.397	Travel14: other cultures	.339	.456	.196
Clothing4: 'clothes reflect personality'	.371	.473	.152	Travel15: hiking and trekking	.353	.406	.231
Clothing5: 'dressed properly'	.518	.351	.130				

Notes: 1 A=agree, N=neutral, DA=disagree or like, neutral, dislike; 2 For 'Arts: …' respondents are shown three works considered 'iconic' for each style.

Part II
The fabric of aesthetics

Introduction to Part II

This part, composed of two sections, reflects on how aesthetic criteria, norms and contents are created and diffused. We therefore explore the fabric of aesthetics, by focusing on the role of artists, cultural intermediaries and cultural institutions in the making of art and aesthetic principles, and the way these circulate within different networks. Such a detour through artistic production and mediation allows us to move beyond the separation between studies of audiences and producers which is characteristic of recent work. This move enables us to consider the broader dynamics of cultural hierarchies and classification and their interface with other agents within a global context.

As we explained in the introduction, we seek to build a bridge between what is traditionally defined as sociology of art and sociology of culture. In much work, the sociology of art takes interest more specifically in art processes – as 'the interaction and interdependence of the artist, the work of art and the public' (Silbermann 1968: 586) – and institutions[1], while the sociology of culture usually encompasses the broader study of cultural practices (including routine aspects of people's every day life). We seek to unravel the mechanisms that are constitutive and more distinctive of art compared to other areas of lifestyle and social relations more widely while acknowledging the links art also undertakes with the latter. In this sense a differentiation between the sociology of art and the sociology of culture can appear somewhat artificial given the dialectic relation between the two.

From the middle of the twentieth century, an interest in the art processes grew stronger. More specialized sub-disciplines emerged to de-construct what was once thought as completely 'a-social', art or arts. Placing art within its social context and social relations turned certainly to be a leitmotiv that led sociology of art to emerge as a separate discipline (Zolberg 1990). Classically the sociology of art became concerned with three main dimensions: the artists, the intermediaries and the audiences. In this part, we will primarily discuss the first two. The question of the public will be explored in greater depth in the next part on cultural classifications.

The first section will examine the production and mediation of aesthetics. It is useful to introduce the chapters by reviewing key developments that have affected the relations between art and the social. We will sketch some of the main transformations (which to be exhaustive should take into account the different national or regional contexts).

Introduction to Part II: The fabric of aesthetics

First, the establishment of the sociology of art and culture was marked by key studies of mythical artistic figures such as Mozart (Elias 1993), Beethoven (DeNora 1995) and van Gogh (Heinich 1991). The main idea behind these studies was to examine the social mechanisms by which some artists have become consecrated at a certain moment in time and to question the notions of genius and gift as unique reasons for the success and recognition successively among different strata of publics. These accounts, however, provide a sociological understanding of the socio-historical context that led to the emergence of the 'modern' artist at the end of the eighteenth century in Europe. This period was marked by the rise of a market system that freed the artist from rigid patronage and academy system (Harrington 2004; White and White 1965), although it provided other forms of constraints. In this context the artists could – and were encouraged to – follow their own artistic rules and principles, as originality and innovation were increasingly valued. Progressively the field of art was cutting itself from any extrinsic consideration in order to become more autonomous. Artists were deemed to be acting primarily for the sake of creation (as in 'art for art's sake') and progressively distanced themselves from the economic rationality of bourgeois society and its moral standards. Pursuing economic rewards wasn't perceived as legitimate for those who embraced a higher quest and artists were subject to poverty.

> Historically, at least since the late eighteenth century, autonomy in cultural production has been associated with freedom from the particular demands and constraints of the commercial world, and while self-determination can clearly be exercised by workers freely applying themselves to commercial activity and the accumulation of wealth, to speak of 'creative' or 'artistic autonomy' is to index a particular notion of freedom actively developed in the context of Romanticism. Here, the idea of autonomy was especially closely linked to the artist; that special, self-regulating being and 'free spirit' possessed of rare and precious gifts. Romanticism not only sought to separate art from the rational and instrumental demands of the new commercial society, but also its incipient bourgeois morality, and so artists' innate expressivity appeared to serve as a bulwark against the creeping incursions of the market, and quickly became a binding signifier of individual autonomy.
>
> *(Banks 2010: 252–253)*

However, there was a profound ambiguity in this growing tension between commerce and art: artists and people in their circles rejected commercial values as antagonistic to the purity of art, while it was precisely the market that gave to the artistic production the freedom essential to its autonomy. This liberty was one of the defining traits of the emerging paradigm of aesthetic modernism characterized by the transgression of canons and tradition. Of course, the autonomy of art could never be achieved and was itself an illusion that was required for the establishment of the myth of the starving and misunderstood artist who cared only about art. Yet this myth was also serving the market in many ways, starting by providing pools of creative ideas on which to draw inspiration for new products and cultural goods.

> Indeed, it soon became clear that the apparently separated worlds of art and commerce shared an intimate relationship. Not only did commercial growth lead to an increase in the production and commodification of art, but the emergence of art markets provided a means of liberating (rather than constraining) artists by exposing them to willing buyers, and of enabling the dissemination and popularisation of art works that would challenge the tastes and demands of erstwhile patrons and feudal elites.
>
> *(Banks 2010: 253)*

Introduction to Part II: The fabric of aesthetics

By relying on a principle of disinterestedness and in institutionalizing boundaries between art and everyday life the modernist paradigm also emphasized the importance of cultural knowledge and resources to grasp the meaning embedded in the art works while nourishing the illusion that art could touch anyone. This situation has helped maintain – over the years and up to the present–the division between experts and novices and between highbrow and lowbrow, which will be discussed in the next part.

The situation has now of course changed, and this for several reasons. Since the 1960s this paradigm has been under attack by different actors. Bourdieu and Darbel's *Love of Art* (1969) was one of the first attempts to deconstruct the alleged universality of art and to show the importance of cultural capital in art reception. Artists themselves were already challenging the role of the institutions of highbrow culture such as museums (Marcel Duchamp was a pioneer in this respect). New forms of sponsorship also emerged, notably from semi-autonomous state agencies (Moulin 1992). However, since the 1980s, successive economic crises have progressively decreased the public expenditures allocated to art, and artists turned themselves to commercial sponsorship and charitable organizations (Harrington 2004). During this period, there has also been some rapprochement between the logics of art and those of market and the associated techniques of management (Chiapello 1998). Artists have become less anxious about the idea of commercial involvement and more apprehensive of state art funding. Menger showed that we have moved beyond representations from the nineteenth century of the original and disobedient artist opposed to the rationalizing and calculating bourgeois (2002: 9). Artists now form an occupational group (although still weakly defined) characterized by some of the best traits of capitalist management: flexibility, high commitment to the job, high competition, self-employment, often rather small economic rewards, etc. (Menger 1999). Therefore the career patterns of prospective artists have radically changed over the last century. Much has been written on the historical changes they went through, but we know less about the figure of the contemporary artist in the twenty-first century. The contribution of Heinich in this handbook addresses this issue. Based on an empirical survey among former students of a French art school in the years 2000, she shows how young artists can enter the art world and how this process is quite different nowadays compared to previous periods of history.

Second, in defiance of the 'lone genius' stereotype, artists never produce art alone. This is why Becker conceived art as 'collective action'. 'It's the art world, rather than the individual artist, which makes the work' (Becker 2008: 194). In this sense the process of mediation between the artist and the audience is crucial in the art process and then for sociology which intends to study it. With the different changes successively affecting the art production, new actors emerged and played different roles as 'cultural intermediaries'. The notion has become common. It was first used in Bourdieu's work to describe new occupational groups involved in the provision of symbolic goods and services. The new cultural intermediaries, which belonged to the new class fraction, 'the new petite bourgeoisie', was supposed to act as 'taste makers' by pleading for a new ethics of experience and hence for an eclecticism in tastes. Featherstone (1991) endorsed that notion and expanded it, giving them more importance than Bourdieu did (on which see Hesmondhalgh 2006). He argued that these new cultural intermediaries had helped to democratize intellectual lifestyles (and institutions) and legitimize popular genres, contributing to the postmodernist blurring (but not the collapse) of cultural hierarchies and of life and art. Self-reflective, autodidactic and in search of new experiences, they were seen as receptive to some important principles of postmodernism, such as the challenging of conventions and social critique.

Since the mid-1990s, the more simple term 'cultural intermediaries'–its alleged *new* character has indeed been discussed (Nixon and du Gay 2002) – refers very generally to those

Introduction to Part II: The fabric of aesthetics

involved in linking production and consumption. An interest in intermediaries has opened up novel areas of research (Smith Maguire and Matthews 2014) which has come to encompass diverse categories of occupations, leading perhaps to the risk that it becomes a catch-all category. That is why Smith Maguire and Matthews (2012) have provided a list of three distinctive attributes of the cultural intermediaries. First, they have a framing activity, namely they identify what is worthy of interest and prescribe how others should engage with it. Second, they are characterized by a distinctive expertise: they have the necessary resources and knowledge to define (or frame) cultural goods and to make them valuable on different levels. Third, they have an impact on cultural hierarchies and classifications by prescribing the degree of legitimacy to be given to the various goods they promote.

In this handbook, we will focus on specific cultural intermediaries, those who are involved in the (re-) production of the art field, and explore how they perform their three roles portrayed here above. Using many examples of artists' careers, Peist provides an unusually insightful study of the historical development of the art field in the first and second halves of the last century. She explains how the field developed through interactions between artists and intermediaries but was also influenced by wider heteronomous socio-historic conditions. The artists' careers were dependent on the level of social and cultural capital and knowledge they had at disposal and the extent to which these resources matched the rules prescribed by the field. With Acord, we move on to the field of contemporary art. She provides an ethnographic research on the role of the curators, seeing them more as 'mediators' (inspired by the actor-network theory) than as 'intermediaries', to emphasize their active position in shaping artistic knowledge. Taking stock of now traditional approaches in the sociology of art (for instance, those of Bourdieu and Becker) and drawing on Bourriaud's 'relational aesthetics' (1998), she argues that sociology could develop an 'object relational aesthetic'. This would focus on 'the subjective relationships cultural producers sustain with art forms as aesthetic objects' rather than considering only art organizations, networks, conventions and values. Her approach is quite original given her focus on aesthetics but also her capacity to bring together theories from different traditions in a convincing account of the logics of contemporary art.

Although not concentrating on the art field alone, Kirchberg's chapter is also concerned with synthesizing different approaches of one specific object of research: museums. As Fyfe (2006) put it, museums have been for long considered as less worthy of interest for sociology, even though they are one of the constituents and also one of the consequences of the modern society (Bennett 1995). It is not surprising then that some of the greatest social theorists (e.g. Adorno) took an interest in them. These ambiguities and tensions inherent to their formation, their social ambitions and their expansion have made of them 'global social facts' (Fyfe 2006). These institutions, which frame and shape knowledge by their selections, embody the cultural logics that characterize our society and are essential to understand people's lifestyles (Hanquinet 2013). Even though some key works in sociology have emphasized their importance for the discipline (Bennett 1995; Macdonald and Fyfe 1996; Prior 2002) there is still much to be done, starting by undertaking a classification and definition of the sociology of museums. This is why Kirchberg's chapter is so welcome. He explores the relations between society, sociology and museums by providing an overview of the different dimensions that have structured the sociological perspectives on museums so far. In sharing his extensive knowledge, he lays the foundations of the discipline and sets an agenda for future research.

The second section underlines the necessity to consider the impact of national and transnational contexts on cultural evaluation. Bourdieu's theory of the field of art production has been essential for establishing the sociology of art. Yet it has its limitations, and especially when a Eurocentric account fails to apprehend logics which are only specific to particular national contexts. This doesn't challenge field theory *per se* – given its relational character – but underlines rather the need to revise it in order to grasp the position of international agents and the role of factors other than class, such as race and ethnicity. This is the essential insight of Bennett's chapter. Exploring the developments of the Australian art field and the place of Aboriginal art in it since the 1960s, he argues that Bourdieu's theory should be adjusted to account for the specificities of the Australian art field, shaped by old and more recent transnational art relations and practices by a late institutionalization of Australian art and by the presence of aboriginal art. Similarly, in considering this time the book market, Sapiro addresses the challenges raised by its globalization through the question of the flows of translations. She argues here that Bourdieu's theory is most useful when articulated with the core-periphery model to account for spatial relations between places. She shows that despite the intensification and expansion of the market, English has actually increased its domination and hindered cultural diversification.

Sassatelli also explores the effect of globalization through the case study of biennals. She analyzes the phenomenon of 'biennalization' as 'the proliferation and standardization of biennal exhibitions under a common (if rather loose) format'. Investigating the art world through that lens enables her to reflect upon the main debates that divide the cultural industries (e.g. celebration of diversity and cross-national dialogues or overriding standardization, commercialization or innovation, etc.). She thus shows that biennals do not operate simply to create global exchange but also create new tensions and ambivalences.

The last paper of this part focuses on embodied aesthetics and reminds us that aesthetics pervades all aspects of everyday life, starting by the way we look. Holla and Kuipers develop the notion of aesthetic capital as 'bodily styles, traits, preferences and tastes', which comes with different forms of social benefits. They show how in an economy increasingly based on services, appearance can become an asset for those who correspond to the dominant criteria and a source of exclusion for those who don't. The extreme case is of course the field of fashion modeling which, as they demonstrate, puts great constraints on the body of its workers and shapes beauty standards. Using cross-national comparison they also assess how ideas of beauty can vary in a globalizing world according to the intersections between socio-demographic and socio-economic factors, such as class, educational levels, gender, sexuality, age and metropolitanism. This chapter makes the link between the production of aesthetic standards on the one hand and the complexification of aesthetic classification and the related multiplication of symbolic boundaries on the other, which will be the topic of the next and last part of the handbook.

Note

1 See the description of the interests of the ESA Research Network on the Sociology of Arts: arts organizations, professionalization of the arts, production and mediation of the arts, etc.

References

Banks, M. (2010) 'Autonomy guaranteed? Cultural work and the "art–commerce relation"', *Journal for Cultural Research*, 14(3): 251–269.
Becker, H. (2008) *Art Worlds*, Berkeley: University of California Press, 25th anniversary edition.
Bennett, T. (1995) *The birth of the museum: History, theory, politics*, London: Routledge.
Bourdieu, P. and A. Darbel (1969) *L'amour de l'art. Les musées d'art européens et leur public*, Paris: Editions de Minuit.

Bourriaud, N. (1998) *L'esthétique relationnelle*, Dijon: Les Presses du réel.
Chiapello, E. (1998) *Artistes versus managers*, Paris: Editions Métaillé.
DeNora, T. (1995) *Beethoven and the construction of genius: Musical politics in Vienna, 1792–1803*, Berkeley and Los Angeles: University of California Press.
Elias, N. (1993) *Mozart: Portrait of a genius*, Berkeley and Los Angeles: University of California Press.
Featherstone, M. (1991) *Consumer culture and postmodernism*, London: Sage and *Theory, Culture and Society*.
Fyfe, G. (2006) 'Sociology and the social aspects of museums', in S. Macdonald (ed.), *A companion to museum studies*, Oxford: Wiley-Blackwell, pp. 33–49.
Hanquinet, L. (2013) 'Visitors to modern and contemporary art museums: Towards a new sociology of "cultural profiles"', *The Sociological Review*, 61(4): 790–813.
Harrington, A. (2004) *Art and social theory*, Cambridge: Polity Press.
Heinich, N. (1991) *La gloire de Van Gogh. Essai d'anthropologie de l'admiration*, Paris: Editions de Minuit.
Hesmondhalgh, D. (2006) 'Bourdieu, the media and cultural production', *Media, Culture and Society*, 28(2): 211–231.
Macdonald S. and G. Fyfe (eds.) (1996) *Theorizing museums: Representing identity and diversity in a changing world*, Oxford: Blackwell Publishers, pp. 1–18.
Menger, P. (1999) 'Artistic labor markets and careers', *Annual Review of Sociology*, 25: 541–574.
—— (2002) *Portrait de l'artiste en travailleur. Métamorphoses du capitalisme*, Paris: Editions du Seuil et La République des Idées.
Moulin, R. (1992) *L'Artiste, l'institution et le marché*, Paris: Flammarion.
Nixon, S. and P. du Gay (2002) 'Who needs cultural intermediaries?', *Cultural Studies*, 16(4): 495–500.
Prior, N. (2002) *Museums and modernity: Art galleries and the making of modern culture*, Oxford: Berg.
Silbermann, A. (1968) 'Introduction: A definition of the sociology of art', *International Social Science Journal*, 20(4): 567–588.
Smith Maguire, J. and J. Matthews (2012) 'Are we all cultural intermediaries now? An introduction to cultural intermediaries in context', *European Journal of Cultural Studies*, 15(5): 551–562.
—— (2014) *The cultural intermediaries reader*, London: Sage.
White, H.C. and C.A. White (1965) *Canvases and careers: Institutional change in the French painting world*. New York: John Wiley and Sons.
Zolberg, V. (1990) *Constructing a sociology of the arts*, Cambridge: Cambridge University Press.

12

From sociology of culture to sociology of artistic producers

How to become a contemporary artist

Nathalie Heinich

The term 'sociology of culture' is broad and ambiguous enough to elicit severe misunderstandings, so that its various uses need to be clarified. On the one hand, the English and the French meanings appear to be often quite different, as we shall see in the first part of this paper. And on the other hand, the sociology of consumption or reception tends to obscure the sociology of artistic producers, as we shall see in the second part. The last and main section will provide an illustration of how the focus on artistic production can be implemented regarding the issue of entering this world for a young artist, first according to an historical perspective, and then in the case of French contemporary visual arts.

'Sociology of culture' vs. 'sociologie de la culture'

The English 'culture' mostly refers to the mores and habits proper to a certain society, as in 'cultural sociology' (Alexander 2003; Lamont 1992), whereas in France it rather refers to artistic and learned education (Bourdieu 1979). Moreover, as for 'sociology' when associated to 'culture', it has long corresponded to what used to be called in French as either '*sociologie des pratiques culturelles*' or '*histoire culturelle*', understood as '*histoire des mentalités*' (Heinich 2010: 259).

Conversely, 'sociology of art' seems to be more often used in French humanities and social sciences than in it is in the Anglophone world. Moreover, the English 'sociology of art' (or 'sociology of arts') may still refer to what, some time ago, the French would have rather called '*histoire culturelle*', '*esthétique sociologique*' or '*histoire sociale de l'art*'. Those three trends mostly focus on art works, in a perspective grounded in 'humanities', whereas the French '*sociologie de l'art*' of the last fifty years mainly belongs to the 'social sciences', as long as it relies on empirical surveys, be they quantitative or qualitative (Heinich 2010: 258).

However, nowadays, one common crossroads between the Anglo-American and the French traditions is a focus on 'sociology of culture', or '*sociologie de la culture*', conceived as empirical surveys on practices and tastes related to arts or leisure: listening to music, attending concert halls or museums, reading books, going to the pictures, etc. This focus is sometimes so strong, as testified by the number of publications, either in English (e.g. Peterson 1992; Hills 2002; Bennett et al. 2009) or in French (e.g. Bourdieu and Darbel 1966; Bourdieu 1979;

Donnat 1994, 2003; Hennion and Maisonneuve 2001; Lahire 2004; Coulangeon and Lemel 2007; Coulangeon 2011; Glevarec and Pinet 2012) that some scholars seem quite astonished when one notices that the sociology of artistic producers is *also* part – and quite a prominent one – of the sociology of culture (or should we say the sociology of arts?).

From cultural consumption to artistic production

Why such a domination of cultural consumption studies over the sociology of artistic production? Two main reasons seem to be at stake here. The first reason is methodological: audiences can be counted and tastes can be measured through surveys, so that the statistical methods can be applied to 'cultural' (that is: art and leisure consumption) issues. The second reason is political: given the dramatic social inequalities evidenced by these surveys on cultural practices, and thus their high relevance in the eyes of 'critical sociology', discussions about their persistence or evolution remain at the top of social scientists' agenda.

The other possible targets of the sociological surveys related to arts seem to be less attractive, since neither polls nor critical discourse about inequalities are as easily at stake. They nonetheless offer rich topics for sociological investigation: be it the social history of recognition (Lang and Lang 1988; Bowness 1989; Heinich 1996a, 1999; Fauquet and Hennion 2000), artistic institutions, intermediaries and mediations (DiMaggio 1987; Moulin 1992; Hennion 1993; Heinich 2007), or the status of artistic professions, work and contexts (White and White 1965; Becker 1982; Moulin *et al.* 1985; Freidson 1986; Elias 1991; Bourdieu 1992; Heinich 1993, 1996b, 2000, 2005; Menger 2009).

Among the various issues offered to the sociology of artistic professions (morphological description, administrative and juridical status, social and economic positions, ways of behaving and creating, representations of what an artist is or should be, etc.), one is particularly interesting although rather under scrutinized, yet: that is, the ways to enter the artistic career. In other words, how to become an artist?

Becoming an artist in the past

Regarding the visual arts, Ernst Kris and Otto Kurz provided a very interesting insight on the representations of such a moment, mostly at the Renaissance, through painters' and sculptors' biographies (Kris and Kurz 1987). But what about the actual conditions under which one could become an artist? Reality?

In the case of the visual arts, these conditions varied according to time periods and to changes in the status of artistic activity. Until the Renaissance, things were rather simple: painting and sculpture were considered as crafts. Thus they obeyed the common rules of guilds: first, apprenticeship in a studio, then accessing the higher step of 'companion', and finally becoming a 'master', after having demonstrated one's skill through the production of a 'chef-d'oeuvre' in front of one's peers, and the payment of a certain amount of money.

During the times of academies, when artists happened to be considered not any more as mere craftsmen but rather as 'professionals', their training was dual: both in studios, where anyone could learn the basic skills against a fee, and in the academies, where a small number could receive more theoretical lessons. Then the career would develop either as an academician, provided one would be accepted in the institution, or outside: in the frame of a guild, as long as it still existed, or without any corporate frame once they had been suppressed (at the end of the eighteenth century in France). Clients and, sometimes, patrons thus became the major supports for artistic identity (Heinich 1993).

Things became more and more anomic in modern times, namely the nineteenth century, when the ever growing number of artists without any professional framing, and the difficulty to obtain the recognition of an extremely elitist and conservative 'Salon de peinture', elicited a kind of de-professionalization, with a lot of difficulties to enter the career (hence the '*vie de bohème*'); a lot of poor artists and also, probably, a lot of artists were forced to abandon art and find another occupation. Being a 'rentier' – which was a common condition for any 'bourgeois' – thus became a basic condition to remain an artist in spite of such a tough market situation, especially when one tried to develop innovate artistic paths, as Impressionists did (White and White 1965; Heinich 2005).

Becoming a French contemporary artist today

The situation remains roughly similar nowadays: a lot of aspiring artists, a very tight market, few collective professional frames except art schools. But one thing has dramatically changed during the last generation, at least in France: namely, the development of a strong institutional frame for artistic careers, through a complex system of state grants, and a number of regional institutions dedicated to purchasing contemporary art (FRAC: *Fonds Régionaux d'Art Contemporain*) or to exhibiting it (art centers). This particular context has opened up new ways of becoming an artist today. But to describe them, one cannot stand on a general level: what is at stake is not 'visual arts' but contemporary art, not 'modern artists' but present time artists, and not 'contemporary western artists' but French contemporary artists today. Once more, a close attention to historical and geographical contexts is the key condition for a genuine sociological approach.

To understand the specificity of this context, one has to take into account the very nature of contemporary art, in that it breaks not only with classical art but also – and even mostly – with modern art (Heinich 1998, 2014a). Classical art implements the traditional canons of representation, more or less idealized (historical paintings, mythological landscapes, official portraits) or realistic (scenes of daily life, still life, trompe-l'oeil). Modern art transgresses those canons, since its basic requirement is the expression of the artist's interiority or vision, as in impressionism, fauvism, cubism, surrealism, expressionism and even in abstract art, which transgresses the very imperative of figuration. Monet, Van Gogh, Picasso, Dalí, Soutine, Kandinsky, typically exemplify this rupture with the classical rules of figuration, legitimized by the capacity of their painting to fulfill the expectancy of a bond between the spectator's eye and the artist's interiority.

As for contemporary art, it also relies on transgression, but far beyond the canons of representation it transgresses the very boundaries of art such as it is commonly conceived – including the modern criteria of expressing the artist's interiority. In contemporary art, transgressing – or experiencing limits – is not anymore a technical matter ('Is this good art?'), but an ontological matter ('Is this art?'). Being mainly concerned to play with boundaries, contemporary art breaks both with classical and with modern art. An 'installation' or a 'performance' do not belong anymore to the classical or modern conception of an art work, that is, a painting in a frame or a sculpture on a plinth. They do not demonstrate anymore a bond between the art work and the artist's interiority or even body; and irony or play become more important than seriousness. Technical or social mediations are necessary, together with special devices, such as photographs or videos, in order to insure the durability of the work. Moreover, those devices are often foreign to museum rules, economic routines, transportation or insuring constraints, or else restoring techniques. This is why contemporary artworks are extrinsic to the classical and to the modern artistic paradigms not only through their aesthetic qualities, but first of all through their physical as well as their material, economic, legal, axiological properties (Heinich 2014b).

Belonging to contemporary art, and not to modern art, is a prior condition to enter the present art world: it is what the 'judges', i.e. the specialized cultural intermediaries (art critics, curators, conservators and gallery owners) evaluate before any consideration regarding the quality of the proposal. For example, in a municipal commission offering grants to artists, an application file proposing a series of figurative portraits painted in oil on canvas was violently rejected by the members of the jury as soon as it appeared that the artist did not provide a 'discourse' demonstrating some distance or irony towards the classical and modern traditions: the quality of the paintings was not even discussed, since the absence of a culture of contemporary art disqualified the entire artistic project as inauthentic or even fraudulent (Heinich 1998).

First step: Local institutions

Displaying one's mastery of the rules of contemporary art is thus a basic requirement to enter the art world. This is what the French economist Bénédicte Martin demonstrated in a survey on several cohorts of former students of an art school (Martin 2005). I will follow here the main points of her analysis, which offers a precise and empirically grounded contribution to the notion of 'recognition', not according to its theoretical definition and implications (Honneth 1995; Heinich 2009), but according to its pragmatic implementations.

According to her analysis, the 'first level of recognition' consists in identifying the aspiring artist as belonging to the world of contemporary art, before considering him/her as a 'professional' artist. This 'recognition test' (*épreuve de reconnaissance*) occurs through a series of steps, each corresponding to a 'market segment', obeying a relatively constant process from one case to another.

For the graduated student coming out of an art school, whose only links with the 'legitimizing institutions' is the school itself, the first step consists in making a contact with the local cultural institutions, mostly the DRAC (*Direction Régionale des Affaires Culturelles*, representing the central State): a grant obtained from the DRAC (be it for creating, for finding a studio or for a first exhibition) acts as a 'quality label'.

Second step: Central institutions and/or local exhibitions

After this first step in the 'recognition course' (*parcours de reconnaissance*), a second one, later in the career, consists in obtaining central State grants, such as an 'artist's residency' or a travelling support offered by 'Culture France', whose Parisian juries regularly examine young artists' applications. There, the criteria only partly rely on the quality of the work: artistic activity is a central criterion, such as having obtained a local grant, having participated in a collective exhibition or having helped to organize an event in a local art center. In other words, support for creation is grounded not so much on the artistic quality of the application than on the activity of its author, confirming his/her identity as an artist.

To establish the reality of this artistic activity, there is no other evidence than the portfolio and curriculum vitae of the candidate, demonstrating that he or she went through the common steps of the career. Thus the effective criteria tend to standardization, while the official criteria emphasize the search for originality. This is one of the fundamental problems of contemporary art, practiced according to common standards but praised according to the 'singularity realm' ('*régime de singularité*': Heinich 1996a).

Exhibiting in a local association or, better, in a regional center of art, or a FRAC, is an important moment in the verification of belonging to the world of contemporary art. Usually, this moment of the career begins with group exhibitions. It should be followed by an individual exhibition in a local place of art, and/or a collective exhibition in a Parisian place.

Once this second step completed, another test begins, with the opportunity to exhibit not anymore in the public but in the private sector of art galleries.

Third step: Prominent gallery exhibitions

The gallery exhibition can be seen as an important step, provided at least that the gallery in question is itself already recognized, inserted into the contemporary art world. In the French context, it means leaving the local (provincial) galleries to access the Parisian ones, often connected with the international market. Here begins the third step in the recognition process.

A contemporary artist rarely has his/her first exhibition in a Parisian gallery. In other words, after the collective exhibition in an art gallery or a provincial center, and an individual exhibition in a provincial gallery or a group exhibition in a Parisian gallery, the aim should be the solo exhibition in a Parisian gallery. This moment is decisive: the artist reaches another level of visibility, his/her identity as an artist is fully recognized, material resources become available out of his/her artistic activity. He or she is given access to private collectors as well as to specialized newspapers, art critics and curators, sometimes even art fairs or biennals. The career is eventually launched.

Note that in the Anglo-American world, such a journey from step to step is not fundamentally different, even if cultural institutions play a much less decisive role than in France, where the system of arts funding has been especially developed. According to anthropologist Sarah Thornton's analysis (2008), the first step in a contemporary artist's career is the 'Master of Fine Arts' (MFA); then obtaining a price or a grant by local institutions; then accessing to a first gallery, which opens up to critics in magazines and perhaps entries into prestigious private collections, individual or group exhibition in a museum, exhibiting in a major international biennal or fair and finally accessing to the 'secondary market' of auctions.

Our description of the steps leading from the outside to the core of the contemporary art world does not pretend to display the very criteria according to which the qualified judges allow an artist to become successful: such an issue – quite a relevant one indeed – would require specific modes of investigation. The restricted perspective of this paper only provides a view of the general frame inside which recognition or even fame may take place.

From recognition to fame

However, this actual level of 'recognition' of the artist as such is not yet 'notoriety' or 'fame'. While the former depends on both the private and the institutional art mediators, the latter requires an extension to a wider audience, beyond the world of contemporary art specialists: fame is an extended and cosmopolitan form of recognition. It is measured through the fact that the artist is known at a distance, within a framework of exchange he or she may not be aware of. This is an illustration of Alan Bowness's theory of the 'circles of recognition' (1989): first, recognition by other artists, who are competent but few; second, by institutional mediators (art critics, curators); third, by galleries and collectors; and finally, by the general public, numerous but far away from the artist, not always qualified, and whose confrontation with the work only occurs after some delay.

Now, how do sales contribute to this recognition process? Negligible at the beginning, they become really significant – and sometimes even spectacular – when recognition has given way to fame, with the entry into the private sector of prestigious galleries and major collectors, and then into the secondary market. According to Bénédicte Martin, young artists sell very little when entering the world of contemporary art. Hence, the importance of the 'second job' (teacher, cultural mediator, technical assistant for recognized artists etc.), which compensates for the lack of income out of artistic creation.

Hence, also, the high percentage of cases of abandonment, mostly ignored in a world that, by definition, tends to see only the most visible figures from those who might emerge: on a sample of 29 artists followed by Bénédicte Martin in 2003, only 19 remained in the course in 2005, that is to say, a drop-out rate of 35 per cent after two years of practicing artistic activity.

The age factor

This low relevance of the criterion of commercial success, at least at the stage of recognition, goes hand in hand with, symmetrically, the importance of recognition by institutions and specialized intermediaries, working in committees, art centers, FRACs, museums and biennals. Thus, an artist can reach a prominent position in the art world while selling very little, but obtaining various subsidies or payments for his/her projects.

This dependence of artistic recognition upon institutional intermediaries has important consequences. One of them is the strong interdependence of these intermediaries, placed in a very competitive position for power and influence in their world (Heinich 2005). Their competence is mostly measured by their ability to find promising future artists before their colleagues – which demonstrates the prevalence of the singularity realm in the whole artistic world and not only for artists. Consequently, young artists are likely to primarily attract their interest rather than artists already recognized by other intermediaries, more advanced in their careers and, therefore, older. This clear trend toward an early entry into the recognition process contrasts with what occurred when 'modern' art was dominant: art critics used to write about artists who were older than them (Bowness 1989).

Consequently, the trend toward conceptualism in contemporary art becomes stronger and stronger, since 'conceptual' artists are likely to emerge earlier than 'experimental' ones, as demonstrated by economist David Galenson in his study of the 'two cycles of artistic creativity' and their developments in various domains, including science (Galenson 2006). Thus, the bonus granted to young artists as a result of competition for innovation among institutional intermediaries mechanically leads to a premium paid to conceptual art.

How to remain a contemporary artist

Another effect of this premium paid to young people is that the main problem for a contemporary artist becomes not so much to enter into the art world than to keep on being visible and attracting attention once insertion and recognition have occurred. As soon as he or she no longer benefits of the novelty premium in the eyes of experts, how can he or she take the steps to succeed in obtaining still more critical, commercial and media attention? In other words, how can one not only become but remain a contemporary artist?

Sociological investigation tends to focus on visible artists, that is, those who succeeded in being recognized as artists, even sometimes as great artists. But what about those who remain obscure, or even those who could never reach the very status of artist? This issue is all the more interesting since it helps evidencing the very conditions which allow recognition as an artist, and their specificity regarding other kinds of professional activities. Contrary to art historians or art critics, who legitimately focus on great artists, sociologists should turn their eyes more often towards artists who have failed to attract useful attention: a close scrutiny and thorough analysis of their career, or of their efforts to enter a career, would no doubt provide a better understanding of the conditions of artistic success, compared with the conditions of success in non-artistic occupations.

References

Alexander, J. (2003) *The Meanings of Social Life: A Cultural Sociology*, Oxford: Oxford University Press.
Becker, H. (1982) *Art Worlds*, Berkeley, CA: University of California Press.
Bennett T., M. Savage, E.B. Silva, A. Warde, M. Gayo-Cal and D. Wright D (2009) *Culture, Class, Distinction*, London: Routledge.
Bourdieu, P. (1979) *La Distinction. Critique sociale du jugement*, Paris: Minuit.
—— (1992) *Les Règles de l'art. Genèse et structure du champ littéraire*, Paris: Seuil.
Bourdieu, P. and A. Darbel (1966) *L'Amour de l'art. Les Musées européens et leur public*, Paris: Minuit.
Bowness, A. (1989) *The Conditions of Success: How the Modern Artist Rises to Fame*, London: Thames and Hudson.
Coulangeon, P. (2011) *Les Métamorphoses de la distinction. Inégalités culturelles dans la France contemporaine*, Paris: Grasset.
Coulangeon, P. and Y. Lemel (2007) 'Is "distinction" really outdated? Questioning the meaning of the omnivorization of musical taste in contemporary France', *Poetics*, 35(2–3): 93–111.
DiMaggio, P. (1987) 'Classification in art', *American Sociological Review*, 52(4): 440–455.
Donnat, O. (1994) *Les Français face à la culture : de l'exclusion à l'éclectisme*, Paris: La Découverte.
Donnat, O. and P. Tolila (eds.) (2003) *Le(s) Public(s) de la culture, Politiques publiques et équipements culturel*, Paris: Presses de Sciences Po, vol. I.
Elias, N. (1991) *Mozart. Sociologie d'un génie*, Paris: Seuil.
Fauquet, J.-M. and A. Hennion (2000) *La Grandeur de Bach. L'amour de la musique en France au XIX° siècle*, Paris: Fayard.
Freidson, E. (1986) 'Les professions artistiques comme défi à l'analyse sociologique', *Revue française de sociologie*, 27(3): 431–443.
Galenson, D. (2006) *Old Masters and Young Geniuses. The Two Life Cycles of Artistic Creativity*, Princeton, NJ: Princeton University Press.
Glevarec, H. and M. Pinet (2012) 'Tablatures of musical tastes in contemporary France: Distinction without intolerance', *Cultural Trends*, 21(1): 67–88.
Heinich, N. (1993) *Du peintre à l'artiste. Artisans et académiciens à l'âge classique*, Paris: Minuit.
—— (1996a) *The Glory of Van Gogh. An Anthropology of Admiration*, Princeton, NJ: Princeton University Press.
—— (1996b) *Etre artiste. Les transformations du statut des peintres et des sculpteurs*, Paris: Klincksieck.
—— (1998) *Le Triple jeu de l'art contemporain. Sociologie des arts plastiques*, Paris: Minuit.
—— (1999) *L'Epreuve de la grandeur. Prix littéraires et reconnaissance*, Paris: La Découverte.
—— (2000) *Etre écrivain. Création et identité*, Paris: La Découverte.
—— (2005) *L'Elite artiste: Excellence et singularité en régime démocratique*, Paris: Gallimard.
—— (2007) *Faire voir. L'art à l'épreuve de ses médiations*, Paris: Les Impressions nouvelles.
—— (2009) 'The sociology of vocational prizes: Recognition as esteem', *Theory, Culture and Society*, 26(5): 85–107.
—— (2010) 'What does "sociology of culture" mean ? Notes on a few trans-cultural misunderstandings', *Cultural Sociology*, 4(2): 257–265.
—— (2014a) *Le Paradigme de l'art contemporain. Structures d'une révolution artistique*, Paris: Gallimard.
—— (2014b) 'Practices of contemporary art: A pragmatic approach to a new artistic paradigm', in T. Zembylas (ed.), *Artistic Practices. Social Interactions and Cultural Dynamics*, Oxford: Routledge, pp. 32–43.
Hennion, A. (1993) *La Passion musicale. Une sociologie de la médiation*, Paris: Métailié.
Hennion, A. and S. Maisonneuve (2001) *Figures de l'amateur*, Paris: La Documentation française.
Hills, M. (2002) *Fan Cultures*, London and New York: Routledge.
Honneth A. (1995) *The Struggle for Recognition. The Moral Grammar of Social Conflicts*, Cambridge: Polity Press.
Kris, E. and O. Kurz (1987) *L'Image de l'artiste - légende, mythe et image*, Marseille: Rivages.

Lahire, B. (2004) *La Culture des individus. Dissonances culturelles et distinction de soi*, Paris: La Découverte.
Lamont, M. (1992) *Money, Morals and Manners: The Culture of the French and the American Upper-Middle Class*, Chicago: University of Chicago Press.
Lang, G. and K. Lang (1988) 'Recognition and renown: The survival of artistic reputation', *American Journal of Sociology*, 94(1): 79–108.
Martin, B. (2005) *Evaluation de la qualité sur le marché de l'art contemporain. Le cas des jeunes artistes en voie d'insertion*, thèse d'économie sous la direction de François Eymard-Duvernay, Université de Paris X Nanterre.
Menger, P.-M. (2009) *Le Travail créateur. S'accomplir dans l'incertain*, Paris: Gallimard-Seuil.
Moulin, R. (1992) *L'Artiste, l'institution et le marché*, Paris: Flammarion.
Moulin, R., J.-C. Passeron, D. Pasquier and F. Porto-Vasquez (1985) *Les Artistes. Essai de morphologie sociale*, Paris: La Documentation française.
Peterson, R. (1992) 'Understanding audience segmentation: From elite and mass to omnivore and univore', *Poetics*, 21: 243–258.
Thornton, S. (2008) *Seven Days in the Art World*, London: Norton.
White H. and C. White (1965) *Canvases versus Careers. Institutional Change in the French Painting World*, Chicago: University of Chicago Press.

13
Avant-garde artworks, artists and mediators
A state of relationships

Nuria Peist

The relationship between individuals' material conditions of existence and their cultural production and consumption has been the focal point of a debate within the field of the sociology of art and culture in recent years. Many authors have analysed the relations between culture and its audience without assigning to the latter the ultimate meaning of production, or proposing a simple determination of the social over the cultural.[1] While the focus is usually on cultural reception and participation and especially of the correspondence between people's lifestyle and their socio-economic characteristics (work, social position, origin, etc.), in this article we shall instead concentrate on cultural production and investigate how key actors' relations to the arts in the first half of the twentieth century led to the constitution of the field of the artistic avant-garde.

There are two crucial necessities to studying the constitution of this field, which can be seen as a space from which the legitimate arts and culture of that period progressively emerge.[2] One is the possibility of studying the pioneer artists and intermediaries who formed part of the first autonomous field of art, as Pierre Bourdieu has suggested (1992). Studying the relationships these early agents established allows an examination of the logic of the constitution of the field itself and the roles played by artists, collectors, dealers, critics, museum directors and artworks at the moment of defining certain positions that would be maintained over time, with notable but never radical changes. Another advantage of analysing the art field at its beginnings is the opportunity it offers of observing how the relationships that were being generated impacted on artistic movements and how, in turn, the movements reconfigured the structure of the field.

The notion of the historical constitution of the art field will help us understand the possibility of initiating a career as an artist. This notion will enable us to analyse boundaries, particularly those that exist between consecrated and non-consecrated artists, or between amateurs and professionals (Mauger 2006a: 6) and, also, the 'gatekeepers' of those boundaries (Mauger 2006b: 5), that is to say, the intermediaries. The concept of cultural capital will serve here to analyse the correspondences between the cultural resources required by the space of the avant-garde and the capital that artists and intermediaries had to maintain or transform in order to participate in this space of relationships. It will be possible to understand what people needed to become artists and whether, and in what way, their social trajectory conditioned their entrance.

Our starting hypothesis is that cultural objects, in this case, artworks, are activated in different ways by contact with the spaces that receive them, although also with the spaces that produce them. In *La Passion musicale* (1993), Hennion shows that mediators (people, discourses, activities, etc.) give a value to the objects with which the recipient identifies.[3] The question of the correspondence between production and consumption has generated an intense debate centred on the diversity of spaces of consumption and on the relation between them.[4] From this debate we shall keep the idea that totally autonomous spaces of production and consumption do not exist because they all belong to a global social space in which exchanges of different degrees take place between each space and the global values of the legitimate culture. We believe, however, that cultural objects, in our case artworks, are also charged with aesthetic-social values associated with the type of relationships that are established in the field and that observing the realm of reception is not enough to understand their different meanings.

To Bourdieu's notion of the art field as a space of play historically constituted with its own institutions and laws, and based on a system of relations (1987: 108), we will offer here, in a complementary way, a more detailed study of the relationships between creators and intermediaries and the effects they produce, taking into account Erving Goffman's theories regarding interaction spaces as the basis of social order (2004). The importance of the degree of legitimizing power of intermediaries – highlighted by Nathalie Heinich (2002: 72–73) – will be especially significant, both in its synchronic dimension (the importance of each agent in the same time and place) and in its diachronic dimension (the accumulation of legitimation capital over time). Furthermore, we will look at how the constitution of the field was in constant contact with factors heteronomous to itself.

We will also discuss how the structure of the field formed by the relationship between its components had a specific impact on artworks and formal choices and how, in turn, the need for defining artistic movements influenced the establishment and success of artists and intermediaries alike. The objective of this paper is to highlight some of the factors that are important for a systematic study of the historical-artistic act, while attempting to avoid focusing solely on the historical-aesthetic analysis of the works or on artistic genius. However, we will not seek to demystify either aesthetics or the concept of genius. These are fundamental valuations for the constitution and upholding of the art world itself (Heinich 1998), valuations that are in constant dialogue with the material reality that sustains them.

In this chapter, we will focus on the encounters between a group of artists from the first half of the twentieth century and the mediating agents with whom they liaised in order to enter into the field of art and strengthen their positions. We will look at the transformations that occurred over the course of the century, when the world of avant-garde art reached a more stable state of organisation and relied on more defined positions and acquired a growing recognition in Western culture. The selected artists cover the first half of the twentieth century and the start of the second half. They are consecrated artists of Europe and the United States, the places where the world of legitimate modern painting gestated. The Impressionist movement will be studied as the first established style of modern art, and the artists who began to exhibit in the decade of the 1900s (Pablo Picasso, Kasimir Malevitch, Constantin Brancusi, Vassily Kandinsky and Marcel Duchamp), in the decade of the 1940s (Jackson Pollock, Jean Dubuffet, Antoni Tàpies and Louise Bourgeois) and the decade of the 1960s (David Hockney, James Rosenquist, Eva Hesse and Georg Baselitz).

Encounters of capitals

The space of modern art at the end of the nineteenth and early twentieth centuries was made up of subjects varying in the degrees to which they were established in the field: artists, collectors, dealers, critics, museum directors and specialists occupied positions that were being defined historically. The definition of the artists, their possibilities of forming part of the world of the avant-garde, depended on the type of relationships they established with other artists and mediating agents. Meanwhile, critics, collectors, dealers, etc., also had to look for a space in the field, linked to their relationships with the artists and other agents of the avant-garde.

An analysis of the careers of the artists of the first half of the twentieth century reveals two different types of artists accessing the space of the avant-garde: those who did and did not possess significant cultural capital, i.e. equivalent to that of the mediators who occupied the field's positions. Such a correspondence was not the obligatory condition for entry into the art world but rather differentiated those who could afford not to exhibit their work for immediate consecration and those who, lacking both the capital and the knowledge required by the field, could not refuse the success offered to them by the various agents.

Among the group of artists studied, Marcel Duchamp and Jackson Pollock embody these two ideal types (Peist 2012b). The former possessed the necessary social and cultural capital to gain access to the world of the French avant-garde of the period. His two older brothers, Raymond Duchamp-Villon and Jacques Villon (the pseudonyms of Raymond and Gaston Duchamp, respectively) were recognised artists in the Parisian circle and opened the door of the world of experimental art to him.[5] Even so, Duchamp had both the will and the means to lay down specific conditions for his entry in the space. Present in the most cultivated circles of avant-garde art of the time, he became one of the 'promoters of modernity' so to speak: he endorsed the work of Constantin Brancusi and organised the donation of the Queen Collection (Temkin 1995:64); he collaborated closely with Katherine Dreier, the painter and collector with whom he founded the *Societé Anonyme Inc., Museum of Modern Art*, a program of publications and exhibitions designed to make the most innovative artistic expressions known to the broader public, and he lent his services to numerous art lovers of the period. He sold his work regularly to the Arensberg, his most important collectors, but he didn't allow them to sell or exhibit it. He was written about by very important avant-garde artists, such as Guillaume Apollinaire, who included him in *Les peintres cubistes*, and André Breton, who, through his writings in the magazine *Littérature*, reinforced the legend around his person.[6] But nobody was familiar with the entirety of his work, which was skilfully 'guarded' by the Arensberg and other dispersed art lovers.

At the opposite pole, Jackson Pollock fought to belong to the American art world of the late 1940s. Coming from a rural family, his relationship with mediators was diverse, and his drive to become a recognised artist finally led to triumph as the most important artist of the American avant-garde after the Second World War.[7] In the space of exchange of two different sociocultural logics, the legitimate culture of the intermediaries – his wife, the painter Lee Krasner, the dealers Peggy Guggenheim and Betty Parsons, Sidney Janis, the critic Clement Greenberg, etc. – was essential to the artist's success (through contacts, sales, publications, exhibitions, etc.). Jackson Pollock's rustic culture provided an ideal image for the cultural propaganda American avant-garde circles were seeking to develop and to exploit: the ideal of the autochthonous man who, far from European refinement, could therefore build a typically American avant-garde.[8] Pollock became famous as the 'cowboy painter' for his pictorial technique (throwing lassos of paint across the open plains of the canvas), effective since legend had it that he had truly been a cowboy in his youth. The myth of the authentic savage echoed with the ambition of an avant-garde that aspired to be original in regard to the first avant-gardes of the old continent. The space of dialogue configured his work's aesthetics and his success as a painter.

The mediators who collaborated in elevating Pollock had considerable power of legitimation given that in most cases they were established figures within the world of the American avant-garde.[9] In the case of Eva Hesse, an American sculptor born in Germany who began to exhibit in the 1960s, some of the people responsible for promoting her managed to make a place for themselves in the art world alongside the establishment of her name. The case of the art critic and personal friend of Hesse's, Lucy Lippard, is illustrative in this respect. Both possessed significant cultural capital (Nixon 2002; Lippard 1976) and both entered the art world in unison. Along with her husband, the sculptor Tom Doyle, whom she had met in the circle of American galleries, Hesse established a space of relations with artists, critics and gallery-owners of the post-avant-garde art of the 60s. In her first individual exhibition at the Allan Stone Gallery, she met Lippard, who included Hesse in her first important show as a curator: *Eccentric Abstraction* at the Fischbach Gallery in New York in 1966. Lippard's exhibition was part of a series of exhibitions that emerged from a movement of reaction to the empire of Minimalism (Peist 2012a: 255–263). The famous exhibition *When Attitudes Become Form*, organised by Harald Szeemann in the city of Bern in 1969, was one of the most important shows of the new movement. The figure of Szeemann himself as the organizer of exhibitions makes it possible to evaluate, as Nathalie Heinich (1995) has done, the configuration of the mediator as a singular creator. The consecration capital of the artists grew along with that of the mediators in a space of exchange in which the positions co-constituted at the same time, within the framework of the gestation of a post-Abstract Expressionism and post-Minimalism movement. The force of gestation of the movement historically defined the space of the exchanges between production and mediation.

In the above-mentioned examples, we observe how the cultural capital of the artists becomes activated in contact with the agents of the field in three ways: by imposing the rules of the game, in the case of Duchamp and the Arensberg, by being nourished by the specific capital required, in the case of Pollock, Guggenheim and Greenberg; or by accumulating and mutually transmitting consecration capital, in the case of Hesse and Lippard. But along with the specific trajectory of artists and mediators and the types of interactions they establish, it is also necessary to consider history in a double sense: on the one hand, that of the field of modern art and on the other, that of the heteronomous factors that influence the trajectories and the agents' modes of relating.

The dialectic between heteronomous factors and the state of the field

In the case of the first styles of modernity (Impressionism, post-Impressionism and the first avant-gardes), artists and their mediators were in many cases in a peer-to-peer relationship given that the field – its limits, positions and general state – was in the process of being constructed. The collectors of the Impressionists – Hoschedé, Duret, Charpentier, De Bellio, Faure – (Distel 1989), their first dealer – Paul Durand-Ruel – the first critics – Chesneau, Mallarmé, Duranty, Zola, Duret, Fénéon – and the artists themselves, configured an informal network that defined the space of innovative art. The relationships of friendship maintained between these figures revealed a necessary physical proximity and a collective militancy devoted to the defense of the new state of the field.

The same occurred to the avant-garde artists of the first half of the twentieth century, although a fundamental difference exists compared to the late nineteenth century: the collectors and dealers of modern art increased in number, the first museums of modern art appeared, such as the MoMA (1929), the Whitney (1931) and the Guggenheim (1937) (Peist 2012a: 191–194), as did the first specialised monographs dedicated to innovative artists and movements. In this sense, the interactions of artists with mediators and institutions begin to be more distant. It is possible to speak of an ever more developed institutionalization of innovation that set a standard for the relationships existing between artists and intermediaries: despite often being very close, increasingly stable positions existed that demanded a greater degree of adaptation to what was required by the field.

As the twentieth century advanced, artists had to be part of a space with increasingly defined boundaries, and consecration required less time (Peist 2012a). Those who didn't enter into spaces of exchange had either to adapt their cultural capital to establish the necessary relationships or to use the cultural capital of nearby people as a launching platform. Otherwise they ran the risk of being excluded. Claude F. Poliak (2006) terms this the 'universes of consolation': spaces tangential to the world of big art with logics and organisations of their own which, with a much lower degree of recognition, perpetuate the belief in the existence of the field itself by keeping alive the hope of entering it. As Raymonde Moulin points out, 'when a "new wave" appears, artists who participate in an aesthetic trend without being either the first or the most famous, encounter such difficult access that many disappear from the art world'(1997: 339, author's translation). When the passage of time is not a sine qua non of success, as it was in the beginning of modernity, the chances that new artists will be included in established movements are thus lower. Many artists, however, don't 'disappear' but rather participate in the universes of consolation described by Poliak.

Historical conditions are another very important factor for understanding the quality and quantity of the established relationships. The careers of Kazimir Malevich and Vassily Kandinsky reveal that historical conditions are important for understanding the approach of artists to the art world. Both artists were born in pre-revolutionary Russia to well-off families of the period (Stachelhaus 1991; Allemand-Cosneau and Boissel 1998). They experimented with avant-garde solutions and their experiments defined the highest levels of modern art: Kandinsky was one of the first painters to experiment with abstraction and Malevich, at the height of Suprematism, painted his famous black on white painting, an ode to the disappearance of the artistic object. Whereas Malevich remained in the Soviet Union, Kandinsky decided to establish himself in Germany to teach at the Bauhaus school of design, homologous to the Vkuthemas workshops promoted by Lenin's revolutionary government.

The Bauhaus became a fundamental support to Kandinsky's career, but the rise of national-socialism truncated the school's pedagogical and productive project, and he had to emigrate to Paris. There, the opportunities to exhibit were very limited. With few contacts and in a city battered by the Great War, the person who is now considered to be the father of abstraction didn't enjoy much recognition while alive. The same occurred to Malevich. After various frustrated attempts to be accepted as a teacher at the Bauhaus, the artist ended his days with limited recognition from the revolutionary government and in conflict with the Constructivist artists (Stachelhaus 1991). Nevertheless, both artists belong to the pantheon of the European avant-garde. The key to understanding this lies in the action of Alfred Barr, the first director of the first museum of modern art, the MoMA of New York, inaugurated in 1929.

Barr's intention as director of the museum and art historian was to organise the most coherent possible history of the European avant-garde (Kantor 2002). He created the first important monographs related to the history of modern art (Barr 1966) and included Malevich and Kandinsky as fundamental artists. The meeting in this case was deferred.

Invested immediately with a very important power of legitimation, Barr was one of the figures responsible for the institutionalization and definitive enshrining of avant-garde art. He decided to travel around Europe in search of artists and artworks – often rescuing works from museum basements – which allowed him to complete his narrative of art (Peist 2012a: 185–188).

Once again, the space of interactions between artists and their works on the one hand and mediators on the other determines the way in which the artist is delivered to posterity. We see in this case that it is the intersections between unfavourable historical conditions and the configuration itself of the field of art. In its beginnings, this field needed to rescue and organise positions defined by the informal relationships that artists had established with agents and the space of mediation. The growing power of legitimation of mediators of the avant-garde also marked the quality of the relationships.

The power to legitimate

As we have seen, the social trajectory of artists influences the type of relationships they develop with mediating agents and the type of position they occupy in the field, more or less visible, more or less hasty at the start of their careers, according to the type and degree of cultural capital they possess. Also important is the degree of legitimising power possessed by intermediaries, which, as we have highlighted, grows as the twentieth century advances: the positions of the world of innovative art therefore become more defined and stable and can be 'inherited' or occupied more quickly. At the start of the twentieth century, avant-garde artists were in contact with figures of the art world holding different positions in the space. The agents' degree of legitimatising power determined how quickly the artist was established in a more or less stable position in the field.[10]

Pablo Picasso, the famous Cubist artist, was in contact with very important dealers, collectors and critics of the period, and Constantin Brancusi, considered the father of modern sculpture, enjoyed early market success among avant-garde American collectors. In this way, they occupied stable positions very early on in their careers as artists. After diverse experiences with French dealers and collectors such as Berthe Weill, Ambroise Vollard, Daniel-Henry Kahnweiler, Leon Rosenberg, Wilhelm Uhde and the Stein brothers (Gidel 2003: 134), Picasso was introduced (thanks to his previous contacts) to the famous Paul Rosenberg, associated with Georges Wildenstein. Rosenberg's position was privileged. A dealer of old masters, he could allow himself to gamble on an innovative artist without fear of jeopardizing his business. In addition to buying the artist's works and permitting him to live from his work, the dealer introduced him to a circle of art lovers that allowed Picasso to establish some lasting relationships with the world of European culture. The dealer's high level of legitimatizing power placed Picasso in one of the most stable positions of the avant-garde (Fitzgerald 1995; Peist 2012a).

While agents with legitimatizing power were apparent in the market, Picasso's first critics belonged to the avant-garde world, that is to say, they were also artists. This was a reality peculiar to experimental art. The Impressionists had established relationships with collectors and dealers, but also with numerous critics/literary figures, such as Émile Zola and Théodore Duret, who through their writings supported the literary and artistic avant-garde. Picasso was closely linked with various avant-garde writers who promoted his work, such as the surrealists Guillaume Apollinaire, Max Jacob and André Salmon. Later on, he developed close ties with André Breton. In this case, as often occurs with the avant-garde, the figures who were dealing commercially with the art or who were formulating discourses about it were themselves in a process of legitimatizing their own positions along with the artists. Picasso enjoyed two types of relationships: one with agents of the art market with defined and stable positions and another with figures of the avant-garde that allowed his work to retain an experimental value.[11]

In the case of Brancusi, the artist's relations with some art enthusiasts of his time, such as Walter Pach, Edward Steichen and Marcel Duchamp, and his participation in the famous Amory Show of New York in 1913, made it possible for him to establish contact with important American collectors of avant-garde art, such as the Meyers and John Queen (Temkin 1995). The visibility he gained was related to the immersion of his experimental sculpture in a market interested in the proposals of the European avant-garde. The strength enjoyed by the avant-garde collectors' market in the United States was corroborated over time. The process of the institutionalisation of modern art occurred in New York City, where European artists whose works circulated among the still narrow circle of American avant-garde art had greater possibilities of being included in the history of modern art. Here, Brancusi's informal relationships helped to launch his work in a market under a configuration keen on experimental art experiences, which were not as common in sculpture as in painting. When agents with a high degree of legitimatizing power because of the position they occupied, such as Alfred Barr, the director of the MoMA, started to look into these kinds of works, they also transmitted to the artists they selected and presented in their exhibitions, books and schemas a consecration capital that powerfully and stably made them a part of history.

For different reasons, Malevich, Kandinsky and Duchamp didn't enjoy the same success as Picasso and Brancusi early in their careers. Even so, all of them were delivered to posterity with the same force given that, as we saw in the previous section, the history of avant-garde art was in the process of constitution. In its process of formalization, which began more or less in the 1930s with the opening of the MoMA, when positions were less stable, different initial experiences were included. Not all of the artists, even some who are now very well-known, could find a place. The lack of visibility at the start of the careers is related to a low degree of legitimizing power of intermediaries, but that weakness didn't influence the long-term success of the artists of the first European avant-gardes examined here: In order to establish itself within a historical trajectory, modern art rescued artists with low visibility. The only condition necessary for these artists to be rescued was for them to belong to the initial, informal networks of interaction.

In respect to the artists who began to exhibit in the 1940s, we see an increase in the power of legitimatization of the intermediary agents. The cases of Jackson Pollock, Antoni Tàpies and Jean Dubuffet, the last two exponents of post-war European Informalism, are illustrative in this regard. From early on in their careers as artists, all of them were in very close contact with agents with stable positions in the field: Peggy Guggenheim and Clement Greenberg in the case of Pollock, Michel Tapié and Marta Jackson in the case of Tàpies, and Michel Tapiè and René Drouin in the case of Dubuffet. The art market and the associated discourse consolidated the reputations of the three artists. The difference, as we have noted, resides in Pollock's capitals of origin, although in no way do these imply a difference in the position occupied by the artist. Rather they influenced the type of relationship he established with intermediaries, which was intense and without the possibility of interruption. Conversely, Dubuffet refused to promote his work[12], although, unlike Marcel Duchamp, he didn't delay entry into the circuits of dissemination, but rather delegated to intermediaries that part of the job which appeared to him as purely promotional work (Peist 2012a: 138–140).

The artists analysed in this chapter who began to exhibit in the 1960s enjoyed a very profuse network of mediation. In the case of James Rosenquist, a representative of American Pop

Art, one can see that the force of the emergence of that movement led to the configuration of a potent space of relationships between different agents, which in turn provided a very important consecration of all of the artists involved in the movement.[13] David Hockney, an artist included in the ranks of British Pop, developed crucial professional relationships during his period of training at the Royal College (Webb 1989; Hockney 1976). Similarly, thirty years later mediators established stable relationships with the Young British Artists, most of who studied at the Goldsmith College of Arts, and their emblematic figure, Damien Hirst (Gallagher 2012). We thus see how new movements can emerge from agglomerations of artists and mediators in the space of the art colleges.

The presence of artworks in the relationships and the success of styles

Stylistic options or formal and discursive characteristics associated with works and styles also are part of the field of art production. The way in which Marcel Duchamp became one of the most important artists of his century allows us to observe how the work can contain the state of relationships. While the French artist maintained very close contacts with the art agents of his period, his work didn't circulate in the art world. At the start of his career, Duchamp didn't allow the Arensberg, his most important collectors, to sell or loan his work for exhibition (Tomkins 1996). Because his work was not immersed in the relationships of the period, it was not determined by the conditions of the field and could reach very high levels of formal experimentation.[14] In this way, the discourses of the art world from the 1960s onward could consider him a pre-cursor of contemporary art (Peist 2012b).

Pablo Picasso's changes of style can be seen partly as the result of the relationships he established with the different agents of the field of avant-garde art. Despite Picasso's refusal to be catalogued within the Cubist movement, the artist, alongside Braque, was at the centre of the movement's experiments. However, difficulties arising from the war, his relations with high society thanks to his participation in the ballet *Parade*, and his resulting relationship with a new dealer, Paul Rosenberg, led the artist to distance himself from bohemia: he considered his Cubist experience as one among many experiments, and he began to produce works in his 'classicism' style, accepted and encouraged by his dealer. On the other hand, the Cubist movement began to be seen as a dogmatic and academic style by critics and artists (Fitzgerald 1995). Picasso's neo-classicism can be seen as the renovation of an avant-garde that had begun to show signs of growing stale at the end of the 1910s. The first exhibitions organised by Rosenberg didn't include any of his Cubist works.

With the advent of Surrealism, the artist began a rapport with André Breton, who labelled him as a master of modernity. Picasso found in the surrealist proposals and in their interpretation a way to renovate his avant-garde experiments and to position himself once again within a setting of radical innovation, distancing himself from his dangerously bourgeois life in the eyes of modern criticism. When Cubism was again valued at the end of the 1920s, Picasso returned to his former stylistic approach, always promoted by Paul Rosenberg who, continuing in the vein he had been exploiting of exhibiting his client as an explorer of styles, asked the artist for new exhibition proposals (Peist 2012a: 154–157). We see how the artworks of the artist from Malaga quite notably revealed the state of his relationships with mediating agents.

Louise Bourgeois, a sculptress who began her career in the 1940s, acquired a significant reputation through a discourse related to a style posterior to the development of her work. The artist moved in the most important circles of American Abstract Expressionism of the 1950s, but the agents with whom she related (collectors, critics, dealers and artists) never included her within its boundaries. Her work didn't reach a high level of visibility until feminist and post-modern criticism of the 1970s and 1980s evaluated her as a precursor of feminine experiences in art (Mayayo 2002: 29). Such an inclusion allowed Bourgeois' works to acquire meaning through a new discourse and thereby begin to circulate and appear in the market and specialised circles. In a similar way to Duchamp, the artist was included in the space of the avant-garde art world of her time, but her work remained peripheral until it became more meaningful to the field then embedded into new discourses.

The same occurred to Georg Baselitz, who started to experiment in the 1960s with the beginnings of a new style different from that of the avant-garde (Crenzien 2006: 21). His work didn't move in specialised circles until the 1980s, when various German galleries and European museums organised different exhibitions – *A New Spirit in Painting*, in 1981 at the Royal Academy of Arts in London, and *Zeitgeist*, in 1982 in Berlin, being among the most important – in order to launch a new movement: Neo-Expressionism. The Venice Biennale of 1980 and the Documenta VII of 1982 ended up establishing a group of artists around the new trend (Peist 2012a: 252–254). In this case, as with Bourgeois, Baselitz' work acquired stylistic connotations in relation to later discourses that rescued the artists as precursors of styles in the process of configuration.

On many occasions, styles position artists within the field. Without the organisation of Neo-Expressionism, Baselitz' international consecration wouldn't have been possible. Without the feminist and post-modern discourse of the 70s and 80s, Bourgeois wouldn't have been considered a precursor of the importance of women in art. Without the force by which the discourse concerning the formal and symbolic principles of Pop Art was established among the artists, specialists and art market of the 1960s, the artists wouldn't have reached such high visibility. In addition, as we have seen, artworks receive the state of relations of the field and are created, in part and in combination with different factors, according to the action of people and positions.

Conclusions

In the debate on the relationship between society and culture, encounters, interactions and exchanges that often produce objects and specific states in social spaces are frequently ignored. The relationships between people confront different social logics and have an impact on cultural products. In other words, not only the mediator who gives value to the objects so that they may be absorbed by various consumer niches but also relationships have an impact on the products of culture, as the case of Picasso's changes of style illustrates. When examining an artist's entry into the art world, it is necessary to study not only her or his previous trajectory and the position to which he or she is acceding, but, above all, the quantity and quality of relationships she or he develops with established agents at the moment of entry and the way in which the artworks participate in the state of the relationships.

An examination of the different interactions between artists and cultural intermediaries reveals a range of variables that have an impact on how the spaces of production and dissemination of high culture are organised and the way in which those relationships influence and leave marks on the artworks. However, it is also necessary to consider the historical state of the field of art at the moment when the relationships occur, the historical state of heteronomous factors in the field and the dialectic with the art world, as the examples of Kandinsky and Malevich show, and the form in which movements, trends and styles are consecrated. These factors serve to contextualise the relationships as well as what they lead to.

We see that when the artist's trajectory and capitals don't match what is required by the field, inclusion can still happen but with some particularities, as in the case of Jackson Pollock.

Successful recognition might still happen but is achieved in a different way. Furthermore, the degree of legitimizing power possessed by the intermediary has a great deal of influence. That power, in the early twentieth century, could be accumulated along with the degree of consecration of the artist, but this situation began to change as the twentieth century advanced. Once the field of art passed through the process of institutionalization, the relationships began to be defined in the encounter between two different realities: that of the mediator who was positioned in the art world and that of the artists who wished to enter. Observing the state of the field at each historic moment makes it possible to understand the changes in the types of encounters and relationships.

On the other hand, the relationship of artists and intermediaries is significantly influenced by the different configurations of art movements but also can influence their gestation. Picasso was able to remain outside of the Cubist movement at the start of its configuration thanks to the number and power of mediating agents. Duchamp decided not to be a part of Dadaism through a more or less unconscious long-term inversion. But Tàpies and Dubuffet with Informalism, Pollock with American Abstract Expressionism, Bourgeois with postmodern feminist discourses, Rosenquist and Hockney with Pop Art, Hesse with Anti-form and Baselitz with Neo-Expressionism, were consecrated along with the movements.

As a final conclusion, the case of the artists who began their careers in the first half of the twentieth century offers interesting insights into the mechanisms that produce, structure and transform the field. For these artists, a lack of interactions with mediating agents and institutions didn't necessarily mean that they wouldn't reach recognition. On the contrary, at a time when institutionalisation of the field was just at its beginnings, some artists could be eventually rescued through an *a posteriori* labelling as precursors. Interestingly, this label was not merely due to their experimenting with innovative formal solutions but reflects some larger strategies that were aiming at consolidating the emergent field of art. If the artists had already been classified within a trend, they couldn't have been included in a trend to come. Definitively, it is still an ongoing question of taxonomy at the core of the field: what is not yet classified, can be classified, what hasn't entered into the space of relationships, has not been produced yet.

Notes

1. One of the most important contributions in this regard is the collective publication *Le(s) public(s) de la culture*, directed by Olivier Donnat and Paul Tolila (2003), the result of a Colloquium on the matter.
2. The time necessary for the consecration of the first artists of modern art, an experimental and innovative style not yet established in the cultural logic of the period, resulted in a deferred success (Peist 2012a).
3. Some manifestations can be valued and signify as much in the terrain of what is pejoratively considered commercial as in spaces of legitimation of high culture. Rap, hip-hop, commercial literature, musicals, Hollywood films, etc., can be referred to as mixed products. Other manifestations can be decontextualized and re-invested with new significations. Decontextualization can occur from low to high culture and often presents itself as kitsch: a melodic singer valued by high culture, religious images used in contemporary aesthetics, etc., or be re-assigned from high to low culture and designated as tourism: large museums, merchandising of artworks, artistic-historical monuments, the Russian Ballet in European capitals, etc. I have dealt with this subject in the Colloquium *Recognition and Consecration in the Arts* held at the University of Poitiers on November 7, 8 and 9, 2012, with the title 'Plastic artists, cultural mediators and commercial success. Historical cases for the analysis of a conflict'.
4. In the controversial debate over the degrees of cultural autonomy of the popular classes in the face of dominant models, Passeron argued that 'it is the forgetting of the domination and not resistance to it that conditions for the popular classes a privileged space in which the cultural activities least marked by the symbolic effects of domination take place' (Grignon and Passeron 1992: 97, author's translation).

Quoting the French sociologist, José Luis Moreno Pestaña posits in his research into eating disorders that 'that happy amnesia of domination' is hardly likely (2010:194).
5 Marcel Duchamp's biographical details are taken from the biography by Calvin Tomkins (1999).
6 'Breton's worship of Duchamp – observes Calvin Tomkins – was based to a certain degree on the slippery nature of his idol ... Breton might have seen two or three paintings by Duchamp when he dedicated this essay to him in 1922 (1999: 276).
7 Jackson Pollock's biographical details are taken from the biography by Steven Naifeh and Gregory White Smith (2001).
8 Serge Guilbaut, in the book with the significant title *How New York Stole the Idea of Modern Art* (1990), explains the conbohuration of the first American avant-garde in the years following the two world wars.
9 The presence in America of mediators of the avant-garde art world – collectors, specialists, museums, etc. – was very profuse. The Armory Show of 1913 was an unprecedented exhibition, collectors grew in number and the first museum of modern art, the MOMA, opened its doors in 1929 in New York City.
10 The art historian Allan Bowness (1990) suggests that different circles of recognition exist through which the artists make their way to consecration (peers, market, criticism and public). Nathalie Heinich (2002: 72–73) remarks that the importance of Bowness' proposal lies in a consideration of the passage of time necessary for achieving success and the slow distancing in time and space and the increasing degree of intermediaries' legitimatizing power. I borrow from the author the consideration of the accumulation of legitimatizing power. For an analysis of Bowness' circles, also see *El éxito en el arte moderno. Trayectorias artísticas y proceso de reconocimiento* (Peist 2012a). Regarding the subject of reputation in art, see *Arte y reputación. Estudios sobre el reconocimiento artístico* (Furió 2012).
11 After having turned to classicism upon contact with his dealers, and once that relationship was established, the ties with Breton allowed him to return to a more experimental style (Peist 2012: 152–157).
12 'My works found more and more buyers and their prices had risen.... I didn't derive from this situation, as would seem logical, a sense of success, but rather of torment, given the autistic attitude, so radically alien to aesthetic art, that I struggled to maintain. I was pleased that they had the character of unsalable productions' (Dubuffet 2004:74, author's translation).
13 The symposium on Pop Art held at the MoMA of New York on December 13, 1962, is a good indicator of the speed with which the movement triumphed within the contemporary American art scene and of the clear division into two groups, those in favour and those against it. Taking into consideration that most of the artists already considered Pop had only begun to exhibit that same year, the speed with which the world's most important museum of modern art held a symposium on the movement was unusual (Peist 2012: 299–300; Goldman 1985: 33–34; Dubreuil-Blondin 1980: 199–200).
14 Nathalie Heinich (2005) explains that the famous anecdote about the *Fountain: un urinoir* being rejected by the Society of Independent Artists for the Society's Exhibition in New York in 1917 was constructed a posteriori: the work was not rejected because there was no jury for that exhibition; instead it was relegated to a closet after not being identified or taken seriously as a work of art. Posterity constructed the anecdote of the rejection to give itself the mission of rescuing Duchamp's work from the incomprehension of his contemporaries, an inexistent incomprehension given that, as we have seen, it was the artist himself who refused to exhibit his work.

References

Allemand-Cosneau, C. and J. Boissel (eds.) (1998) *Kandinsky. Collections du Centre Georges Pompidou, Musée National d'Art Moderne*, Exhibition Catalog, Paris: Éditions du Centres Pompidou.
Barr, A. Jr. (1966) *Cubism and abstract art*, New York: The Museum of Modern Art.
Bourdieu, P. (1987) *Choses dites*, Paris: Éditions de Minuit.
—— (1992) *Les Règles de l'art. Genèse et structure du champ littéraire*, Paris: Seuil.
Bowness, A. (1990) *The condition of success: How the modern artist rises to fame*, New York: Thames and Hudson.
Crenzien, H. (2006) 'Painting that captivates and repels', in *G. Baselitz*, Exhibition catalog, Humlebæk: Louisiana Museum of Modern Art.
Distel, A. (1989) *Les collectioneurs des impressionnistes*, Paris: La Bibliothèque des Arts.
Donnat, O. and P. Tolila (eds.) (2003) *Le(s) public(s) de la culture. Politiques publiques et équipements culturels*, Paris: Presses de Sciencies Po.
Dubreuil-Blondin, N. (1980) *La Fonction critique dans le Pop Art américain*, Montréal: Les Presses de l'Université de Montréal.
Dubuffet, J. (2004) *Biografía a paso de carga*, Madrid: Editorial Síntesis.

Esquenazi, J-P. (2007) *Sociologie des oeuvres. De la production à l'interprétation*, Paris: Armand Collin.
Fitzgerald, M. (1995) *Making modernism. Picasso and the creation of the market for twentieth century art*, New York: Farrar, Straus and Giroux.
Furió, V. (2012) *Arte y reputación. Estudios sobre el reconocimiento artístico*, Barcelona: Memoria Artium.
Gallagher, A. (2012) *Damien Hirst*, Exhibition Catalog, London: Tate Publishing.
Gidel, H. (2003) *Picasso*, Barcelona: Plaza Janés, Barcelona.
Goffman, E. (2004) *La presentación de la persona en la vida cotidiana*, Buenos Aires: Amorrortu Editores.
Goldman, J. (1985) *James Rosenquist*, New York: Viking.
Grignon, C. and J.-C. Passeron (1991) *Lo culto y lo popular. Miserabilismo y populismo en sociología y en literature*, Buenos Aires: Nueva Visión.
Guilbaut, S. (1990) *De cómo Nueva York robó la idea de arte moderno*, Madrid: Mondadori.
Heinich, N. (1995) *Harald Szeeman, un cas singulier*, Paris: L'Échoppe.
—— (1998) *Ce que l'art fait à la sociologie*, Paris: Éditions de Minuit.
—— (2002) *La sociología del arte*, Buenos Aires: Ediciones Nueva Visión.
—— (2005) 'L'art du scandale: Indignation esthétique et sociologie des valeurs', *Politix*, 71:121–136.
Hennion, A. (1993) *La Passion musicale*, Paris: A.M. Métailié.
Hockney, D. (1976) *David Hockney par David Hockney*, Paris: Éditions du Chêne.
Kantor, S.G. (2002) *Alfred H. Barr, Jr. and the intellectual origins of the Museum of Modern Art*, Cambridge, MA: The MIT Press.
Kern R.M and R.A. Peterson (1996) 'Changing highbrow taste: From snob to omnivore', *American Sociological Review*, 61(5): 900–907.
Lippard, L. (1976) *Eva Hesse*, New York: New York University Press.
Mauger, G. (ed.) (2006a) *Droits d'entrée. Modalités et Conditions d'accès aux univers artistiques*, Paris: Éditions de la Maison des sciences de l'homme.
—— (ed.) (2006b) *L'accès a la vie d'artiste. Sélection et consécration artistiques*, Paris: Éditions du Croquant.
Mayayo, P. (2002) *Louise Bourgeois*, Hondarribia: Editorial Nerea.
Moreno Pestaña J.L. (2010) *Moral corporal, trastornos alimentarios y clase social*, Madrid: CIS.
Moulin, R. (1997) *L'artiste, l'institution et le marché*, Paris: Flammarion.
Naifeh, S. and G. White Smith (2001) *Jackson Pollock. Una saga estadounidense*, Barcelona: Circe Ediciones.
Nixon, M. (ed.) (2002) *Eva Hesse*, Cambridge, MA: Massachusetts Institute of Technology.
Peist, N. (2012a) *El éxito en el arte moderno. Trayectorias artísticas y proceso de reconocimiento*, Madrid: Ábada Editores.
—— (2012b) 'The heir and the cowboy: Social predisposition, mediation and artistic profession in Marcel Duchamp and Jackson Pollock', *Cultural Sociology*, 6(2): 233–250.
Poliak, C.F. (2006) 'Pratiques et univers de consolation. Les écrivains amateurs', in Mauger, G. (ed.), *Droits d'entrée. Modalités et Conditions d'accès aux univers artistiques*, Paris: Éditions de la Maison des sciences de l'homme.
Stachelhaus, H. (1991) *Kasimir Malewich. Un conflicto trágico*, Barcelona: Parsifal Ediciones.
Temkin, A. (1995) 'Brancusi et ses collectionneurs américains', in *Brancusi*, Exhibition catalog, Paris: Gallimard.
Tomkins, C. (1996) *Duchamp*, Barcelona: Editorial Anagrama.
Webb, P. (1989) *Portrait of David Hockney*, New York: E.P. Dutton.

14

Learning how to think, and feel, about contemporary art
An object relational aesthetic for sociology

Sophia Krzys Acord

All knowledge is sensorially embodied in some capacity. Knowledge may be mentally indexed through our physical learning experiences in the world, lodged in our muscle memory, or deeply felt in the sense of tacit knowledge or commonsense understandings that we come to expect in certain circumstances. And studying what (and how) individuals know in different situations is integral to developing a robust understanding of how culture works – or is put to work (Acord and DeNora 2008) – in our social worlds. As Emirbayer (1997) has argued in his manifesto on relational sociology, this idea that actors engage with cultural norms in dynamic, unfolding situations is a key part of illuminating action in society. As a tangible cultural form, visual art provides sociology with an excellent case study to examine these processes of knowing and sharing through close studies of artistic producers, mediators, and consumers. The dynamic terrain of contemporary art, in which the making and negotiation of artistic knowledge is visible, offers a particularly good opportunity to witness the formation and employment of knowledge as a cultural meaning system.

According to Zolberg (2005), the current state of contemporary art means that both art and sociology may need new paradigms for understanding and analysing the arts. Within the contemporary art world, many have embraced Bourriaud's (1998) relational aesthetics to describe and categorize contemporary artworks. This approach sees the aesthetic nature of an artwork not as a property of the artwork itself but, rather, as a dimension of one's behaviour in relation to the artwork, combined with other objects and events. In other words, as Witkin (2003) has described from a sociological agenda, the role of reception has become progressively greater in establishing the meaning and significance of contemporary artworks. As curators are often an artwork's first 'receivers', their judgements play an important role in shaping its meaning. This chapter examines curatorial judgments to see how Bourriaud's concept of relational aesthetics generated within the art world might also inform how sociology understands relationality in the study of culture.

Following Becker's (1982) landmark publication of *Art Worlds*, the role of curators and other mediators in the contemporary visual art world(s) has been a key area of sociological attention, as well as more popular interest (Millard 2001; Thornton 2008). In the uncertainty of aesthetic values that marks contemporary artistic creation (Crow 1996; Danto 1992), curators play an active role in evaluating artworks and shaping the institutional criteria for classification (Heinich 1998; Moulin 1987, 1992; Moulin and Quemin 1993, 2001; Quemin 2002; Tobelem 2005). Working independently or from a permanent position in a museum, exhibition curators play a dual role in the museum and market by choosing artists and artworks to feature in monographic or group exhibitions. The museum confirms these choices through immortalization in the exhibition catalogue (or purchase for its permanent collection), something which sends 'signals' to the rest of the field. While there may not be a unified consensus about the curator's choices, the dual machines of the institution and market support these decisions with enough capital (cultural and financial) to make them viable in the short-term (which, naturally, is the only state in contemporary art). A secondary effect of this process of cultural consecration is to enhance the curator's own reputation, in a cyclical manner.

Similar to the research on 'cultural intermediaries', curators operate as members of a larger creative team to assist the production of culture by linking products to groups, influencing the flow of information and establishing the practices for consuming products (Friedman and Miles 2006; Gardner 2012; Hesmondhalgh 2002). They define for others what art is. In the visual arts, the mediation work of curators includes selecting artists for exhibition and conducting associated promotional work, as well as working closely with artists as sounding boards and interpreters of their work for audiences. I choose to adopt the actor-network terminology of 'mediator' rather than that of 'cultural intermediary' (cf. Latour 2005) to emphasize that curators do not merely reproduce or pass on established artistic knowledge, but rather play a key role in shaping that knowledge through organizing framing devices for artworks in the form of exhibitions and their accompanying texts. These installations proceed in sometimes unexpected ways, creating unpredictable opportunities to understand artworks and their meanings (Acord 2014).

The research cited above has done the difficult work of demonstrating how contemporary art, as an organizational world, maintains its structures and forms a base of knowledge in the face of uncertainty. Yet, we still know little about how this knowledge is composed and enacted by the curators themselves: the relational aspects of art worlds. This is the question to which the current chapter is addressed. This chapter is based on ethnographic research with a snowball sample of over 30 international curators of contemporary art conducted between 2005 and 2008. I accompanied them on studio visits, exhibition installations, planning meetings, art fair trips, and other 'backstage' moments when they made decisions about the inclusion of particular artists/artworks in exhibitions. On these occasions, we used digital video or photography and subsequent video/photo-elicitation interviews to visually 'unpack' the moment of decision-making together (cf. Acord 2006). All quotations are presented in English, and any translations are my own. The gender and minor elements of speaking style for some speakers have been changed to protect their anonymity.

I will draw on this data to examine how curators, as experts of contemporary art, create and engage the criteria upon which their judgments are based. In particular, I will demonstrate how the artistic encounter is a critical moment that combines discourses of 'feeling' and 'thinking'. While the 'feeling discourse' reveals a curator's attraction to a particular work, the curator then turns to a more theoretical, 'thinking' discourse based in contemporary art world codes and conventions to 'explain' his/her decisions to fellow art world participants. I argue that this dual exercise of expertise may have more in common with Willis' (1990) relational 'grounded aesthetic' than Bourdieu's structured 'pure gaze'. Finally, I explore how the ways in which curators make meaning aesthetically offer groundwork for informing an *object relational aesthetic* approach for sociology. As the groundwork for this discussion, I first embark on a short literature review of the curatorial 'gaze', the elusive way we have sought to explain and transfer the mastery of contemporary artistic knowledge.

From the 'good eye' to the 'curious eye': Evolution of the expert gaze

Both art history and sociology have long sought to identify the way that expert aesthetic knowledge is learnt and manifested. Before modernism, an artwork was seen to have internal rules and art historians/critics had the special skills to 'decode' them in a more or less 'objective' manner (Witkin 2003). In the art world, elite mediators – particularly dealers, collectors, and curators – were described as possessing a 'good eye' (Rogoff 2002 [1998]) in their ability to quickly pick out the art historical 'codes' in a given artwork:

> When I was training as an art historian, we were instructed in staring at pictures. The assumption was that the harder we looked, the more would be revealed to us; that a rigorous, precise and historically informed looking would reveal a wealth of hidden meanings. This belief produced a new anatomical formation called 'the good eye'. Later, in teaching in art history departments, whenever I would complain about some student's lack of intellectual curiosity, about their overly literal perception of the field of study or of their narrow understanding of culture as a series of radiant objects, someone else on the faculty would always respond by saying 'Oh, but they have a good eye'.
>
> *(Rogoff 2002: 27)*

In this reflection by noted art historian Irit Rogoff, historical or curatorial expertise is traditionally defined as a mastery of symbolism, the knowledge of a set of symbols and the meanings that they signify. Similarly, as Bourdieu (1993) describes, the 'good eye' of art perception involves a conscious or unconscious deciphering option based upon a structuring 'code' which has been more or less completely mastered as a function of *artistic competence* (his italics). Repeated exposure to past works and their patterned meanings informs our ability to interpret correctly new works. For Bourdieu, speaking now of modern art, this artistic code privileges the search for symbols over more popular (emotional and literal) responses to the content of a painting, and thus acts as a form of social distinction – what is described as disinterestedness or the 'pure gaze' (cf. Bourdieu 1984, 1987; DiMaggio 1982). As art becomes more abstract, the importance of upbringing and education in creating the good eye intensifies. It is worth noting, for purposes of comparison, that the opposite of the good eye may be the 'good ear', or someone dependent on the opinions of others (Thornton 2004).

According to several prominent critics and historians of contemporary art, traditional criteria like the good eye no longer apply in the contemporary art world, where the production of a *new* intellectual discourse on a work of art is crucial to establishing its value. This discourse draws less on a textualist approach steeped in art history, and more on a theoretical discourse drawn from cultural studies, sociology, philosophy, and literary theory. This shift of interpretation leads Rogoff (2002) to dismiss the good eye of connoisseurship in lieu of the 'curious eye' of scholarship. Art historian/critic Arthur Danto follows this curious approach by observing that contemporary art concerns intellectual, not aesthetic, responses:

> Suppose it is a work of art? Then certain questions come into play – what's it about, what does it mean, why ... (and) ... when was it made and with respect to what social and artistic conversations does it make a contribution? If you get good answers to those questions, it's art.
>
> *(quoted in Wallach 1997: 36)*

The growth of the curious eye means that artistic expertise is now based less on the pure act of perception and the ingrained exercise of art historical knowledge and technical training, and more on the documentation or theory surrounding a work of art (Crow 1996; Marí and Schaeffer 1998). This is what Rosenberg (1972) terms the 'de-aestheticization of art', the total elimination of the art object in favour of a focus on the concept behind the object.

Bourdieu (1993) also acknowledges that contemporary art is in a 'period of continued rupture', in which the traditional codes of artistic perception (the good eye) lag behind the new instruments of art production (theoretical discourse). Of course, the need for expertise in these periods does not disappear. Rather, contemporary artistic expertise is exerted by a few 'virtuosi' or 'cultural prophets' who, by virtue of the position they occupy in the intellectual structure and artistic field, have an all-knowing understanding and awareness of past and present artistic and social codes:

> The fact is they demand a capacity for breaking with all the codes, beginning obviously with the code of everyday life, and that this capacity is acquired through association with works demanding different codes and through an experience of the history of art as a succession of ruptures with established codes. In short, an ability to hold all the available codes in abeyance so as to rely entirely on the work itself, and what at first sight is the most unusual quality in it, presupposes an accomplished mastery of the code of the codes, which governs adequate application of the different social codes objectively required for the available works as a whole at a given moment.
>
> *(Bourdieu 1993: 227)*

As Bourdieu describes here, the exercise of knowledge in contemporary art begins to give more agency to the 'work itself' and its 'most unusual quality', rather than residing purely in the application of an art historical framework. This accomplished mastery of all codes in contemporary art does not come from objective and collectively agreed-upon codes of artistic criticism for attributing value. Instead, a widespread and current familiarity of the international art context is the knowledge base for the expert of contemporary art; s/he is a permanent seeker and aggregator of information, a 'specialist of context' (Moulin and Quemin 1993: 1435). Expertise involves not a passive social exposure, but an active experience: an awareness of the history of modern art, empathy with the spirit of the times, regular contact and sustained relationships with artists, and influence in the art world. In her ethnographic study of a public art commission, Heinich (1997) confirms these characteristics, observing the way decision-makers drew on their familiarity with art-world actors, knowledge of market prices, and awareness of recent exhibitions. This curious eye of the contemporary curator takes them around the world to develop a deep and rich set of theoretical vocabularies for explaining their decision-making. And the multiple skill sets that this implies may mean that curators have more in common with Gardener's (2012) journalists than the traditional art historian or critic. The growth of the curious eye has also changed the nature of curatorial education.

Training curators: From art history to art networking

As I have discussed above, given the gradual formalization of artistic training over the second half of the twentieth century (cf. Singerman 1999), cultural studies and other analytical concepts have become increasingly important in the contemporary art world. As one curator said of his Ph.D. thesis on an avant-garde writer, 'This has been really helpful for me because it allowed me to develop all of these discourses that can cope with contemporary art'. Indeed, many members of the freelancing 'star' generation of curators had very little or no training in art history, something confirmed by Octobre (1999a), who found that over 60 per cent of those in her sample started out in another domain (although 68 per cent had university degrees, and, on the whole, curators of contemporary art had a higher level of education than other curators). Indeed, the curators in my sample have advanced degrees in a wide variety of fields, including artistic practice, literature, philosophy, economics, political science, sociology, classics, theatre, and even journalism and clinical psychology. For some curators, their cultivation of other fields provides important skills for writing, communication, and reflection. For others, their backgrounds provide precise analytical resources and tools, such as philosophy and critical cultural theory, that directly influence how they look at and frame works of art using the curious gaze. These analytical and transferable skills enable curators to invent and converse with theoretical discussions around artistic practice and artistic works.

As with the creation and growth of any profession, the contemporary curatorial world has recently witnessed an institutionalization of its role, prompted first and foremost by the immense, global growth of university-based curatorial programs, often founded by these same pioneering individuals in the 1990s. This return to an academic professionalization of curating has necessarily brought about a return to a dominant art-theoretical discourse in the field, as well as an emphasis on formal training and management (Tobelem 2005). Yet, I also heard repeatedly that the essence of curating 'cannot be taught', something which Octobre (1999b) describes as part of the curatorial rhetoric that describes expertise as a 'gift' rather than something learned. While these ways of thinking about curating bear a strong resemblance to our post-Van Gogh ways of attributing gifts to artists (cf. Heinich 1996), they also bear an important question: If star curators cannot 'teach' curating, then what do these curatorial programs do? Below, I share three answers to this question from different curators who have instructed in curatorial programs:

1. Curating cannot be taught. All that we can actually teach are things that may help people to become a curator, or to work as a curator. But ultimately the essence of this profession is something vague that has a lot to do with curiosity, inspiration, and the ambition to immerse yourself in a particular context.

2. Of course you can't teach curating. So, the way we've proceeded is to let the students develop a reading list that works for them. Obviously, this is very different than [another] curating course, which does it properly by teaching them about art history, theory, etc. Basically, my generation of curators is the very last generation of curators who can curate without having taken a course in curating. It's just like artists: they didn't need to go to school, but now they do. But, we are resisting any sort of orthodoxy or molding the students to be like us.... Instead, we've recently moved the curating program into the same space as the art students' studios. So, physically, we demonstrate the need for curators and artists to be constantly interacting, and that the role of the curator is to be around art and, more importantly, artists.

3. Curating, of course, can't be taught. Curating is something that is coming out of – let me think how you would say that – experience, or conditioning even, or listening, whatever that may be. But, you can definitely teach other aspects that may be useful for a curator. You could teach theory, reading, the history of exhibitions, analyzing a work of art.

As these curators emphasize above, curating is an experience or instinct. Training, then, takes a practical shape (spending time with artists or mounting an exhibition), as much as a theoretical shape (giving students conceptual tools derived from theory).

In speaking to recent graduates of these curatorial programs, however, another important part of cultivating curatorial knowledge is identified: writing. Writing is what one young curator termed a 'transferable art world skill', which complements the practical experience pursued through internships and on-the-job training. Two young curators weigh in below.

1. I abandoned my artistic practice, because it was weighing me down. I lost interest in it, I guess. But at the same time, I became more interested in the economy of culture. Plus, that allowed me to go to university and find the means – like writing – to understand and express all of the things that were interesting me. And, I found this to be increasingly more fruitful than the engagement I had with these ideas back in art school.

2. While I was [in school], I got a job working for [a gallery] part time.... I wasn't really doing any work, just things like opening the door. The job itself wasn't demanding, but just being exposed to how that system worked was really interesting.... So, I did that for a couple of years, and then I was beginning to consolidate what the idea of curating was much more, and how the practice of writing and bringing ideas together through writing might be manifested through an exhibition.

As illustrated in the quotes above, writing is described as an important way in which young curators learn to synthesize the 'code of the codes' and put into practice all of the ideas, theories, and interests that curators developed in their studies and life experiences. The analytic, discursive relationship to art accompanies the experiential, sensorial components of curatorial learning about art.

To summarize these varied tracks and orientations to curating contemporary art, there are a variety of learned activities that can make up the process of becoming a curator: networking, learning how to write about art, learning about the economy of the arts, and learning how to engage with artists. Although one cannot teach curating contemporary art, the informal learning that takes place through internships and curator-led training courses demonstrates that curatorial knowledge is not codified through abstract guidelines and principles, but rather, is suspended in the sphere of practical engagement that ultimately takes the form of exhibitions and written texts. As Henderson (1999: 8) notes in regards to design work, 'The knowledge used in everyday work is grounded in practice, the learning of practice, the history of a given practice, and the cultural, technical, and organizational constraints constructed around practice'. Similarly, the experiential engagement through social and material interaction plays an important role in learning the practice-based knowledge comprising curatorial work, as well as how to perform it successfully. The question remains, however, as to how curatorial knowledge manifested in physical exhibitions relates to that expressed through the written word.

Sensorial and theoretical discourses in curatorial decision-making

As art critic Rosenberg (1972) describes, the 'de-aestheticization of art' in favour of the ideas it produces does not mean that it does not have aesthetic properties. Indeed, the physical artwork remains a significant force in the contemporary art world. In the paragraphs that follow, I draw together quotes from curatorial interviews and observations to explore how formulating and applying the curious eye involves the sensorial relationship with object interactions as well as a theoretical discourse. The existence of this first kind of a relationship to artwork suggests that curation may involve not merely a vast store of theoretical experience, but also emotional and bodily experiences in the world.

The existence of a 'feeling'-based discourse in contemporary art mediation can be seen through ethnographic studies of curators at work. When curators see a work they like, they describe it in vague terms, often accompanied by dramatic flourishes of the hands or body. They say that the work 'struck them', or they 'liked it', or it 'excited them'. At the opening of one exhibition at a private foundation, the managing curator closed his eyes and recounted to me his first encounter with the artist's work three years prior at a gallery in a nearby city: 'I was completely taken aback.... And I said to myself, "Ah, really, this is ... this is...."' When he physically encountered the artist's work for a second time during the installation of the exhibition, he observed, 'I was struck again in the same manner, with the same emotion, the same sentiments, the same things that were sensuous and unclassifiable'. And, yet, when I asked this curator why he decided to invite this artist for a monographic exhibition at the foundation, he explained to me that the artist 'had a relation with politics' that excited him. There seems to be a distinction between the theoretical discourse on art ('a relation with politics') and the actual lived experience of consuming ('I was struck again in the same manner'). What is particularly interesting in this case, which parallels many other cases in my research, is that the actual emotional modality of artistic interest is translated into a more theoretical discourse to situate that experience within the expected logic of the art world.

Of course, artworks provoke feelings as well as intellectual reactions for experts; after all, art is an exercise in sensorial knowledge-making. And curators may draw on their sensory experience to elaborate their more intellectual curatorial concepts. To explain this, I turn to a thematic exhibition about racial and ethnic difference in a contemporary society. The central piece in this group exhibition was one of Afro-Caribbean artist Sonia Boyce's hairpieces (*Do you want to touch?* 1993), crafted by the artist from synthetic hair extensions. Reflecting on the inclusion of this piece in the exhibition in our interview, the curator Gilane Tawadros said:

> When I first conceived of the project and was writing the essay, I started off wanting to say something about the fact that the issue of race and representation is: (a) not something new, and (b) not something that has been resolved or gone away. And it is almost as if the [Tube bombing] events in July precipitated once again questions about race and belonging, definitions of Britishness, and the discomfort around difference. On some levels, the hairpieces are quite repellent. I tried to describe it to someone ... it's like finding somebody else's hair in the bath in a hotel room. It's like that. It's 'yucky' and uncomfortable. But, in a sense, that's what difference, incommensurate difference, feels like. That's what it feels like to encounter something to which you can't relate. It doesn't make sense to you. It feels foreign and alien. So, that's why those pieces are there.

In the reflection above, the curator describes how the visceral, immediate, 'feeling' experience with a work of art – the 'ewwgh' – is both shaping of and shaped by her discursive orientation to the theme of racial difference. The way the curator feels about the work is an important, constitutive part of what she thinks about it. Her ability to dialogue with and engage these feelings is an important element of her expertise and decision to include the work in the exhibition.

To digest what I have said so far, curators are drawn to particular art works for personal or situational reasons. They *feel* a connection to them and their judgment is embedded in the material circumstances of the work's reception. Yet, the only way they can say what they *think* about the work is to refer to a discourse following social or political discussions that exist outside of this object-relational moment. While sometimes the way a curator feels and thinks about a work of art goes hand in hand, as in the quote above, in other situations there can be more of an abrupt disjuncture between these two modalities. This is demonstrated by an additional interview quote below, by a curator of a monographic exhibition:

> It's quite a hard one to talk about, actually, what he [the artist] is doing. He's put together this stuff in his studio, visualizing the space, right, but, actually visualizing isn't quite right, but the thing is his own work is very much about the body, and these big lumpy objects which are kind of in relationship to your body.... So, what it looks like is almost irrelevant ... it's more like what it feels like, which sounds pretentious and arty, but it has this kind of physical presence. He has got a very particular aesthetic.... It's kind of garish, it's kind of like a child trying these things, but ... it really works. The only way I can say what I think about his work is to refer to something else.... Can I do that? [At this point the curator begins to tell me about Paul Valéry and his writings on the third body.]

As shown in the quote above, the theories of Paul Valéry become a way of verbally articulating the curator's feeling experience with a work. As the curator notes, the point of the work is 'what it feels like', but she turns to a published theorist to explain this. Here, 'thinking' becomes a way to try to access and explain 'feeling', a way of making the felt experience more accessible and less pretentious. In my interviews it was always clear that the experience of 'feeling' an artwork was never reducible to how one would speak or 'think' about it. Indeed, if a curator *can* easily and immediately speak about an artwork, it is perhaps a sign that the piece is not original because the curator could very easily draw upon existing verbal registers to describe it. Those artworks that curators identify as the most original make them first 'feel' and explore perhaps more novel and affectual ways of being.

Before moving on, I draw on one final curatorial interview quote that nicely summarizes this close relationship of thinking and feeling:

> I don't think you can respond to art in nice, neat ways. And, I think that it's very difficult to measure the balance between analysis and intuitive response, but we all have a mixture of the two in us. Some are more analytical, some are more intuitive, some are more 'feelers', some are more 'thinkers'. But, the big thing for me is not really caring where that balance is. It's all mixed up in there somewhere. A bit of you's thinking, a bit of you's feeling, it's kind of all working, stuff's ticking in your brain [sing-songy voice] ... it gets in your eyes, whatever it is, light gets in your eyes — this whole wacky existential notion — it's all kind of ticking over. And, you feel very much in the moment of experiencing it, as in, with the work, with the show, being there, it's all very much ... it's quite an experience, in the best exhibitions.

Curators' visual familiarity with an enormous range of artists and artworks allows them to perceive or create the social and artistic 'codes' found in contemporary artworks (such as similarities between artists and popular aesthetic themes or techniques). Identifying these codes helps curators to 'think' with artworks and place them in relations of value among others in the artistic field. This is what Bourdieu describes as a mastery of the 'code of the codes'. But, scholars taking an ethnomethodological approach warn that the use of language codes to bring object-interactions into shared meaning results in a loss of sorts (Sacks and Garfinkel 1970). As Bourque and Back (1971) demonstrate empirically, while these codes enable people to talk in depth about certain things, they also prevent them from exploring other facets of the ecstatic experience. It may be this fundamental relationship between feeling and thinking that undergirds expertise in contemporary art and the pursuit of originality (as works that break with the codes and cannot be easily identified by them). The state of curating contemporary art offers another sociological example of how knowledge – even that which assumes to be tightly codified and theoretical – involves more complex cognitive acts that involve sensorial experiences that emerge through and are suspended in object interactions.

Discussion: The grounded basis of relational aesthetics

I suggest that expert knowledge in contemporary art may be the result of successfully negotiating what one feels about a work of art with how one thinks about it. As masters of the 'code of codes', curators hold all of their knowledge about art in an intellectual repository when confronted with a new piece of art. They then have an aesthetic (sometimes emotive) encounter with the work – and a particular feature of it appeals to them – which spurs them to 'fix' their impressions of the work in existing discourses and codes that allow them to communicate about it in the art world. (They may also create new discourses to explain emerging trends). As demonstrated by Heinich (1997), this discursive mediation is a fundamental way in which experts convince others of the value of the art work and legitimate their own expertise as a function of accumulated knowledge about the field. But, it may not convey the totality of their experience. If the situational, felt encounter with art cannot be completely translated into a written form, a premise that this chapter aims to provide data to reinforce, how can sociology best account for the entire experience of artistic mediation? In this final discussion section, I seek to outline how sociology might draw on the concept of relational aesthetics from art – the idea that the aesthetic nature of an artwork is not pre-determined but shaped through our own behaviour and experiences in relation to it – to inform a sociological research program attuned to all aspects of cultural experience.

One established way of conceptualizing the relationship of feeling to thinking discourses is offered by work in expert studies. Experts have finely-tuned perceptual skills; they possess more tacit knowledge than novices and are able to notice more and make fine discriminations in any situation (Ross et al. 2006). As defined by Cianciolo et al. (2006: 615), tacit knowledge is 'a person-environment exchange that is not articulated and that arises without explicit attempt to link environmental stimulation to phenomenological experience'. It is an adaptive intellectual resource, in that the cognitive processes involved in the often unconscious manipulation of novel information learn from experience. In other words, experts are better equipped at translating their novel aesthetic experiences into art world discourses. It is because curators have both emotional and cognitive reactions to works of art that they are adept at recognizing how the former can inform the latter. This concept of tacit knowledge allows us to re-insert the sensorial aspects of expert judgment into a sociological analysis, but it falls short in its ability to explain the origins of new artistic codes.

Another way of understanding the presence of emotional and feeling discourses in relation to art is found in Willis's (1990) formulation of the 'grounded aesthetic'. In our original formulations of the 'good eye' or 'pure gaze' of cultivated mediators, emotion is only present insofar as curators take pleasure in a successful decoding operation. Indeed, the idea that one's emotional reactions to an artwork would inform his or her interpretation was identified by Bourdieu as a 'popular gaze' tied to lower social class. In complaining about the symbolic violence at the heart of this distinction, Willis (1990) rejected the popular gaze and instead defined the popular masses as engaging in a 'grounded aesthetic', a way of interpreting artworks by linking them to social relations of consumption in everyday life. Willis emphasizes that value is not intrinsic to a text or practice, but rather is always inscribed in the sensuous/emotive/cognitive act by which the good is used. For Willis, grounded aesthetics represent the creative ways in which symbols and practices are selected and highlighted so as to resonate with appropriate and specific meanings; these dynamics are emotional as well as cognitive.

Similarly, perhaps curators of contemporary art, in the absence of the fixed textual codes and display conventions that gave rise to the pure gaze, actually draw on a grounded aesthetic in their experiences with artworks. This approach gives artworks themselves significant agency to shape the discourses that surround them, as they engage in processes of interessement with their users. The notion of high cultural goods being consumed with distance and sobriety has already been broken by Benzecry's (2007) study of opera publics and other studies of contemporary art audiences (Farkhatdinov 2014; Hanquinet et al. 2014). And now here, we see that experts of contemporary art, while producers of artistic hierarchies, are also grounded, embodied, and feeling consumers of art. Most importantly, harkening back to our discussion of curatorial training programs, the experiences that feed artistic judgment are not tightly codified through an art historical discourse. Rather, they stem from a more decentralized, grounded network of curators' own readings, background, networking, and other experiences in the context of their use in their daily lives.

The sociological formulation of the grounded aesthetic for artistic reception works well to explain the social foundations for Bourriaud's concept of the relational aesthetic for contemporary art. In the foreword to his 2002 book (first published in French in 1998), Bourriaud suggests that contemporary artists break with other art movements by producing not works that are meant to 'represent' the world, but rather works that are meant to create an action or relation within it. Art is relational in that its form exists in the dynamic relationship that it enjoys with human interactions and social context. Art is a place that produces a specific sociability by 'keeping together' moments of subjectivity that only exist in this human-material-social encounter, and the exhibition is the 'arena of exchange' where this encounter occurs (Bourriaud 2002: 18–20). The relational aesthetic of contemporary art teaches us that the meaning of art is to be found in its encounter, and that this encounter has physical, material, and grounded elements that involve social informed perceptions as well as personal affects. Experts of contemporary art, then, are not 'disinterested', but rather, are highly interested in the grounded building blocks of their reactions to art and preoccupied with how to insert those into art world discourse.

Conclusion: Towards an object relational aesthetic for sociology

As I noted in the outset to this chapter, the current state of contemporary art means that both art and sociology may need new ways to understand how knowledge is produced in the arts. And, in the past decade, Nicolas Bourriaud's (2002) relational aesthetic has gained great notoriety in the contemporary art world as a new paradigm to describe and categorize many contemporary works. For Bourriaud, a relational aesthetic in art means that the knowledge of an artwork does not lie internally to it, but rather can be found in the multiple relationships that it establishes outside of itself in the world; art visitors activate and create this knowledge. Now, both Becker (1982) and Bourdieu (1983) describe their sociological approach to the arts as *relational*, in that they explain artistic works with reference to mediating activities external to the artwork. For Becker, artistic work is organized in relation to the tacit conventions permeating the art world, while for Bourdieu (1983: 312), the 'essential explanation of each work lies … in the objective relations which constitute this field'. These relations, then, are in the human social world. Further work by Emirbayer (1997) and Kirchner and Mohr (2010) has augmented this relational approach by demonstrating how the relations embedded in the structural dynamics of situations govern individual agency, and that language plays a central role in revealing this system of relations. This work reveals that one's building of relationships with others can be occasions for intrapsychic processes of self-reflection and agency, not only structural reproduction.

While these approaches are a vital part of understanding processes and practices in the contemporary art world, they do not capture the totality of experiences and interactions afforded by contemporary art. Indeed, the experiences of curators of contemporary art demonstrate that a relational approach in sociology must not only conceive of the relationships of actions to other practices and tastes for an individual; it must also conceive of the relationships individuals have to particular moments and situated aesthetic experiences with material forms. In demonstrating that expertise in contemporary art possesses a strong emotive component, embedded in the material environment and relationship between artwork and expert, I argue that sociology could follow Bourriaud and develop an *object relational aesthetic* as well. This object relational aesthetic for sociology would require basing analyses not only on organizational networks, cultural conventions, and values, but also on the subjective relationships cultural producers sustain with art forms as aesthetic objects, which can be functional, emotional, or completely serendipitous. As the discussions here of feeling and thinking demonstrate, the system of relations that define social life are not simply composed by language and discourse, but also by feelings. The meanings that contribute to our social relationships can be found, or worked out, outside of language as well as within it. And an object-relational aesthetic for sociology would examine not only collective emotions, but also the individual emotional encounters that may be the basic or breeding grounds for new acts or norms. Emirbayer (1997) has called for relational sociology to tackle the study of the dynamic, temporal, and unfolding processes that transform relations; I argue that the grounds for such a study are to be found in object relations and feeling experiences. This study, thus, connects to work that builds on Gibson's (1986) ecological approach to perception, in that it understandings how artworks, as aesthetic objects, provide affordances that act as the material building blocks of culture and cognition (cf. DeNora 1995; Hennion 1993).

Finally, it is my hope that such an approach would create new dialogues between art and sociology. Curators regularly spoke of feeling an affiliation between their work and sociology, because, as one curator explained, 'We both like to observe'. Moulin (1987: 127) notes that artists are 'experts in practical sociology', because they master organizational networks and reward systems and use them to their own benefit. Curators are experts in practical sociology in a different way. They have high emotional intelligence and are conscious, as Witkin (2003) would say, of 'sensing their own sensing'. Curators are experts in knowledge production, not only seen in the codification of knowledge in museum and art world texts, but also in understanding how to establish situations for knowledge production to take place, what I have earlier termed an 'environment for knowing' (Sutherland and Acord 2007). Yet, traditional sociology of the arts has examined curators as elite experts and viewed their ineffable experiences as examples of a symbolically violent 'pure gaze'. Instead of viewing the ineffable with suspicion, we might follow aesthetician Jean-Marie Schaeffer in trying to re-claim aesthetic experience as vital to a democratic relationship with art. 'Artworks are created not to be explained, but to be experienced; they are created not to be interpreted as signs of something else, but to be reactivated as virtual worlds' (Schaeffer in Marí and Schaeffer 1998:49).

Rather than seeing contemporary art as sense data to be decoded, a shared focus on the object relational aspects of the aesthetic experience might allow art world actors and sociologists to work together to see art as a vehicle for change rather than stasis. While past scholarship has explored intersections between contemporary art and science (cf. Galison and Thompson 1999) and contemporary art and anthropology (cf. Schneider and Wright

2005), there has been little research on the intersections of contemporary art and sociology as vehicles of knowledge production. An object relational aesthetic could create such an entree.

References

Acord, S.K. (2006) 'Beyond the code: New aesthetic methodologies for the sociology of the arts', *OPUS/Sociologie de l'Art*, 9–10: 69–86.
—— (2014) 'Art installation as knowledge assembly: Curating contemporary art', in T. Zembylas (ed.), *Knowledge and Artistic Practices*, London: Routledge.
Acord, S.K. and T. DeNora (2008) 'Culture and the arts: From art worlds to arts-in-action', *The Annals of the American Academy of Political and Social Science*, 619: 223–237.
Becker, H.S. (1982) *Art Worlds*, Berkeley, Los Angeles, and London: University of California Press.
Benzecry, C.E. (2007) 'Beauty at the gallery: Sentimental education and operatic community in contemporary Buenos Aires', in C. Calhoun and R. Sennett (eds.), *Practicing Culture*, London and New York: Routledge.
Bourdieu, P. (1983) 'The field of cultural production, or: The economic world reversed', *Poetics*, 12: 311–356.
—— (1984) *Distinction: A Social Critique of the Judgment of Taste*, Cambridge, MA: Harvard University Press.
—— (1987) 'The historical genesis of a pure aesthetic', *The Journal of Aesthetics and Art Criticism*, 46: 201–210.
—— (1993) *Outline of a sociological theory of art perception. The Field of Cultural Production: Essays on Art and Literature*, Cambridge: Polity Press.
Bourque, L.B. and K.W. Back (1971) 'Language, society and subjective experience', *Sociometry*, 34: 1–21.
Bourriaud, N. (2002 [1998]) *Relational aesthetics [Esthetique relationnelle]*, Dijon: Les Presses du réel.
Cianciolo, A.T., C. Matthew, R.J. Sternberg, and R.K. Wagner (2006) 'Tacit knowledge, practical intelligence, and expertise', in K.A. Ericsson, N. Charness, P.J. Feltovich, and R.R. Hoffman (eds.), *The Cambridge Handbook of Expertise and Expert Performance*, Cambridge: Cambridge University Press.
Crow, T. (1996) *Modernism and Mass Culture in the Visual Arts. Modern Art in the Common Culture*, New Haven, CT and London: Yale University Press.
Danto, A.C. (1992) *Beyond the Brillo Box: The Visual Arts in Post-Historical Perspective*, New York: Farrar Straus Giroux.
DeNora, T. (1995) 'The musical composition of social reality? Music, action and reflexivity', *The Sociological Review*, 43: 295–315.
DiMaggio, P. (1982) 'Cultural entrepreneurship in nineteenth-century Boston, part II: The classification and framing of American art', *Media, Culture and Society*, 4: 303–322.
Emirbayer, M. (1997) 'Manifesto for a relational sociology', *American Journal of Sociology*, 103(2): 281–317.
Farkhatdinov, N. (2014) 'Beyond decoding: Art installations and mediation of audiences', *Music and Arts in Action*, 4(2): 52–73.
Friedman, A.L. and S. Miles (2006) *Stakeholders: Theory and Practice*, Oxford: Oxford University Press.
Galison, P. and E. Thompson (eds.) (1999) *The Architecture of Science*, Cambridge, MA: MIT Press.
Gardner, D.H. (2012) *Abracadabra: Key Agents of Mediation that Define, Create, and Maintain TV Fandom*, thesis submitted to the Department of Communication: Paper 95, Georgia State University.
Gibson, J. (1986) *The Ecological Approach to Visual Perception*, Boston: Houghton Mifflin.
Hanquinet, L., H. Roose, and M. Savage (2014) 'The eyes of the beholder: Aesthetic preferences and the remaking of cultural capital', *Sociology*, 48: 111–132.
Heinich, N. (1996) *The Glory of Van Gogh: An Anthropology of Admiration*, Princeton, NJ: Princeton University Press.
—— (1997) 'Expertise et politique publique de l'art contemporain: Les critères d'achat dans un FRAC', *Sociologie du Travail*, 2: 189–209.
—— (1998) *Le Triple Jeu de l'Art Contemporain: Sociologie des Arts Plastiques*, Paris: Les Éditions de Minuit.
Henderson, K. (1999) *On Line and on Paper: Visual Representations, Visual Culture, and Computer Graphics in Design Engineering*, Cambridge, MA: MIT Press.
Hennion, A. (1993) *La Passion Musicale: Une Sociologie de la Médiation*, Paris: Édition Métailié.
Hesmondhalgh, D. (2002) *The Cultural Industries*, London: Sage.
Kirchner, C. and J.W. Mohr (2010) 'Meanings and relations: An introduction to the study of language, discourse and networks', *Poetics*, 38(6): 555–566.
Latour, B. (2005) *Reassembling the Social: An Introduction to Actor-Network Theory*, Oxford: Oxford University Press.

Marí, B. and J.-M. Schaeffer (eds.) (1998) *Think Art: Theory and Practice in the Art of Today: Symposium under the Direction of Jean-Marie Schaeffer*, Rotterdam: Witte de With.

Millard, R. (2001) *The Tastemakers: UK Art Now*, London: Thames and Hudson.

Moulin, R. (1987) *The French Art Market: A Sociological View* (Trans. by Arthur Goldhammer), New Brunswick, NJ and London: Rutgers University Press.

—— (1992) *L'Artiste, l'Institution et le Marché*, Paris: Flammarion.

Moulin, R. and A. Quemin (1993) 'La certification de la valeur de l'art: Experts et expertises', *Annals ESC*, 6: 1421–1445.

—— (2001) 'L'expertise artistique', in F. Aubert and J.-P. Sylvestre (eds.), *Confiance et Rationalité*, Paris: INRA.

Octobre, S. (1999a) 'Profession, segments professionnels et identité: L'évolution des conservateurs de musées', *Revue Française de Sociologie*, 60: 357–383.

—— (1999b) 'Rhétoriques de conservation, rhétoriques de conservateurs: Au sujet de quelques paradoxes de la médiation en art contemporain', *Publics et Musées*, 14: 89–111.

Quemin, A. (2002) *L'art Contemporain International: Entre les Institutions et le Marché (Le rapport disparu)*, Nîmes: Jacqueline Chambon.

Reza, Y. (1996) *Art* (Trans. by Christopher Hampton), London: Faber and Faber.

Rogoff, I. (2002) 'Studying visual culture', in N. Mirzoeff (ed.), *The Visual Culture Reader* (2nd edn), London: Routledge.

Rosenberg, H. (1972) *The De-definition of Art: Action Art to Pop to Earthworks*, New York: Horizon Press.

Ross, K.G., J.L. Shafer, and G. Klein (2006) 'Professional judgements and "naturalistic decision making"', in K.A. Ericsson, N. Charness, P.J. Feltovich, and R.R. Hoffman (eds.), *Cambridge Handbook of Expertise and Expert Performance*, Cambridge: Cambridge University Press.

Sacks, H. and H. Garfinkel (1970) 'On formal structures of practical action', in J.C. McKinney and E.A. Tiryakian (eds.), *Theoretical Sociology*, New York: Appleton-Century-Crofts.

Schneider, A. and C. Wright (eds.) (2005) *Contemporary Art and Anthropology*, Oxford: Bergh.

Singerman, H. (1999) *Art Subjects: Making Artists in the American University*, Berkeley, CA: University of California Press.

Sutherland, I. and S.K. Acord (2007) 'Thinking with art: From situated knowledge to experiential knowing', *Journal of Visual Arts Practice*, 6: 125–140.

Swidler, A. (2001) 'What anchors cultural practices?', in T.R. Schatzki, K. Knorr-Cetina, and E.V. Savigny (eds.), *The Practice Turn in Contemporary Theory*, London: Routledge.

Thornton, S. (2004) The rear view: What is a 'good eye?', *ArtReview*, 114.

—— (2008) *Seven Days in the Art World*, New York: WW. Norton and Company.

Tobelem, J.-M. (2005) *Le Nouvel Âge des Musées: Les Institutions Culturelles au Défi de la Gestion*, Paris: Armand Colin.

Wallach, A. (1997) 'ART; Is it art? Is it good? And who says so?', *The New York Times*, Available online at http://query.nytimes.com/gst/fullpage.html?res=9E03E1DE163CF931A25753C1A961958260 (accessed 10 October 2005).

Willis, P. (1990) *Common Culture: Symbolic Work at Play in the Everyday Cultures of the Young*, Buckingham: Open University Press.

Witkin, R.W. (2003) *Artful Agency: Studies in the Aesthetic Formation of Modernity*, Newbury Park: Sage.

Zolberg, V.L. (2005) 'Aesthetic uncertainty: The new canon?', in M.D. Jacobs and N.W. Hanrahan (eds.), *The Blackwell Companion to the Sociology of Culture*, Malden, MA: Blackwell Publishing Ltd.

15
Museum sociology
Volker Kirchberg

Introduction

The study of museums is not yet an established field of sociological research, or even an acknowledged sub-discipline of sociology of art in most countries. A Google search for the term 'museum sociology' yields 2,270 hits and 2,780 for 'sociology of museums'. The mentioning of museum sociologists in this search machine is also quite small, even world-wide: A Google search for 'museum sociologist/s' yields 1,200 hits, compared to, e.g. more than 20,000 hits for 'urban sociologist' (accessed 11 August 2014). However, sociological research in and of museums (even when it is not called as such) is often carried out under other headings, such as museum research, museology, museum management, or museum studies. This research is often motivated by practical reasons: typically to improve museum marketing, increase visitor appeal or advance market analysis, and only rarely to expand sociological knowledge about museums (e.g. about the latent or manifest social functions of museums in urban society), their organizational processes, and their audiences. Museum sociology is therefore rarely taught at universities under this title. The German Association of Museums lists 53 programs of study related to museums on its website,[1] only four of which however (Leipzig, Berlin, Heidelberg, and Würzburg) make use of explicit terms such as museology, museum studies, or museum in the titles of their programs of study.

The influence of society on museums and, vice versa, the influence of museums on society, do not necessarily have to be researched from a sociological perspective; museology is usually considered part of the field of museum philosophy. Nevertheless sociology can be considered a highly relevant approach to museum studies, since, as C. Wright Mills (1963) puts it, a sociological approach can theoretically and empirically relate the individual life circumstances of museum producers and recipients as well as the structures and processes of the museum as an institution. Since sociology is 'the science whose object is to interpret the meaning of social action and thereby give a causal explanation of the way in which the action proceeds and the effects which it produces' (Weber 1978: 7), it is able to make a sociological contribution to the analysis of museums because museums are a source and a result of social action. Museum sociology is located half-way between 'pure theory' and 'pure empiricism', which Merton (1995) calls a 'theory of the middle range'. This involves a rejection of comprehensive universal theories and large-scale historical approaches – grand theories – as well as of an empiricism that would use surveys only to further the objectives of market research or cultural policy-making. In Merton's understanding, museum sociology should produce neither far-reaching theories (valid for all societies and for all time) nor search for specific facts to solve practical problems found between museums and society. A museum sociology would avoid both the self-referentiality found in philosophy and the humanities as well as a purely practice-oriented orientation. As a discipline of the 'middle range', it would involve methods from social philosophy as well as results from empirical research. The major reason why sociological research into museums has, since the 1970s, been growing as a sub-discipline of sociology is the increasing self-doubt about the social legitimacy of museums (Harris 1990). In the mid-1990s Sharon Macdonald and Gordon Fyfe (1996) were pioneering figures in this new museum sociology, with their fundamental edited work *Theorizing Museums,* which initiated a genuine sociological discussion about museums.[2] Since then there has been an increase in sociological studies and publications on the structures and processes, the causes and consequences of the interrelationship between museum and society that make use of such sociological concepts as power, identity, memory, values, politics, economics, and organization. These studies are more or less equally divided between those that are empirical and those that are theoretical.

This chapter describes the state of the art of a sociology that analyses the interrelationships between museums and society. This will include studies on:

- the overall macro-social and individual micro-perspective;
- production, e.g. on the causes and development of exhibitions and collections;
- consumption and reception (e.g. on the causes and effects of museum visits and the visitors' perception and evaluation of exhibitions);
- the contextualization of museums in a space-time continuum (e.g. the consequences of globalization, historicity, and post-colonialism);
- the polarization of museums between change and affirmation;
- changes from a traditional (hegemonic and heterotopic) certitude to a postmodern (polysemic, polyvalent, and non-heterotopic) relativism;
- methodological categories of a museum sociology, with specific phenomenological, etymological, historiographical, and critical-rational approaches[3].

This chapter moves from the general to the specific. In the following part, I will describe the causes of an increasingly sociological view of museums. The third section of this article will be about cultural sociology's perspective on the museum. In the fourth section I will outline positions within museum sociology between structuralist and praxeological (i.e. agency-emphasizing) cultural sociologies. The fifth section will treat museum sociology as a post-structuralist cultural sociology. In the sixth section I will use the concept of heterotopy to discuss issues relevant to the space-time dependency of museums. Finally, I will locate the museum in a sociological space bifurcated in a textualistic and in a contextualistic area. This phenotypical dichotomization also characterizes museums as as part of a distinctive sociological sub-field[4].

Sociology and museum

For a very long time museums were neither interested in sociology, nor was sociology interested in museums (Fyfe 2006: 33). The first few contacts were through the sociology of art, especially regarding the consecration function of art museums (see Bourdieu, Darbel and

Schnapper 1990). Sociology once interpreted the museum as a pre-industrial institution of the aristocratic and haute bourgeois elite, while this discipline itself felt it was a child of the industrial revolution, the rise of capitalism as well as the social democracy and revolutionary movements of the nineteenth and twentieth centuries. In addition sociology had long relied on scientific textualization, statistics, and presentations and less on the methods of visualization and performance more typical in museums. It is only recently that – together with large-scale surveys, sophisticated analytical methodologies, theoretically grounded interpretations, and scientific presentations and publications on the interrelationships of society with museums – image analysis and artistic research were also accepted as methods by sociologists.

Only around the beginning of the 1980s did museums start to discover sociology because, at least in the small part of the museum field that was outward-facing, they faced a fundamental doubt regarding their social legitimation. There are doubts about their hegemonic disposition, about the unambiguousness of the information and identity they are disseminating, about the necessity of the museumification of many areas of society, and about the totality of their internal classifications. In a postmodern era, which has put the belief in linear progress *ad acta*, museums have been critically reflecting on their prior affirmative role and have been turning themselves into a 'contested terrain' (Macdonald 1996: 4). In this phase of existential self-criticism and with the concurrent rise of a politically minded and emancipatory new museology (de Varine 1986), museums have begun to realize that sociology as a science could have its uses – though at first they were more as a practical aid for cultural education, museum education, marketing, or visitor analysis.

In this second and advanced phase of self-analysis at the beginning of the 1990s, in the critical discussion of their hegemonic roles and their search for new, alternative, and emancipatory functions, museums have shown a greater interest in sociology. People in postmodern societies are going to museums in a search for security and for an emancipatory understanding of the world, and museums must then be prepared to interpret the world in all of its complexity. This is why museums increasingly look to sociology to support them in answering these questions, whether raised by actual visitors or by non-visitors interested in museums (cf. Fyfe 2006; Prior 2006).

Why has sociology discovered museums as an object of research? Possible answers to this question can be found in comparable domains in cultural sociology. Roy and Dowd (2010) ask 'What is sociological about music?' and many of their thoughts can be used to answer the question 'What is sociological about *museums*?' What are the sociological definitions of museum, who are the producers and recipients or consumers, and how do museums affect macro-social class, gender and educational structures (and vice versa)? The attempt to provide a sociological definition of the boundaries between the museum and the non-museum and between high and popular culture is an interesting one. Today, history museums and popular historical tourist installations (e.g. 'Colonial Williamsburg'), or technical museums and science centres converge to a certain extent, distinctive differences vanish in these types of 'postmodern museums' (see part four of this article). And the analysis of the political impact of museums and exhibitions is also sociologically interesting, whether it concerns urban society, individual groups in society or individual recipients. The latent functions of especially art museums as meeting places for the local elites outbalances their manifest functions as e.g. urban landmarks or major tourist attractions (Kirchberg 2003).

The importance of cultural sociology in museum research

The main reason for the recent uptake of sociological inputs by museums is their institutional self-doubt towards their anchoring in society. Harris (1990) describes this self-doubt as the phase of existential scrutiny, beginning at the end of the 1980s. According to him, this lasting phase of existential scrutiny is the result of a mutual opening of museums towards publics and of publics towards museums. However, this increasing consciousness of each other also amplifies a mutual scepticism: who are these publics and, if we have to, how can we reach them? Who are these museums which, probably in a gesture of 'popular deference' (Harris 1990: 51), feed some of the needs and wishes of certain publics? Many ambiguities emerge when museums become aware of their functions in society.

However, this institutional self-doubt is only rudimentarily developed in those major museums that claim to be independent of society and that have never been confronted by their societal stakeholders in this respect. After all, we have just seen that sociology took no noticeable interest in museums for a long time. In the past, the sub-discipline of sociology of art rarely made art museums a subject of investigation, with the mentionable exception of Vera Zolberg, who already in the 1970s and 1980s elaborated on the difficult relationship between art museums and society (Zolberg 1981, 1986). Back then, only critical sociology showed some interest in art museums to reveal how they were used as institutions of repression (see for example Adorno 1963). The recent cultural turn in sociology led Bourdieu, Darbel and Schnapper (1990) to critique the affirmative role art museums play in society as part of their institutional critique, demonstrating how workers – consciously or unconsciously – experienced art museums as places of symbolic power and hegemonic ideology. Interestingly it is only recently that people have been seen as active subjects and museums not simply as coercive institutions but as practical instruments in the hands of sovereign human beings (Fyfe 2006).

With the rise of a New Museology (Lavine 1992; Vergo 1997), an interest in understanding the role of museums in society and in theoretical reflection on their own activities has strengthened; with this new understanding of their own role, museums can no longer act autonomously and independently from the social contexts in which they are embedded. This new museology expects sociology to provide theoretical discourse and empirical findings on their contexts, e.g. ethnographic and phenomenological research on visitors, on the interaction of visitors and objects in an exhibition, on the legitimation and attribution of meaning to and in museums. Over the past years this interface between cultural sociology and the new museology has grown. The aesthetics of exhibitions and buildings, the symbolism of museums and the interactions between museums and their different publics have become justifications for reflection, not only in museums but also in cultural sociology and in the museum sociology that developed as a consequence. Earlier uses of statistical descriptions in visitor research (frequently in the form of univariate tables) were critically evaluated and as a result gained in complexity, and the traditional tasks of a museum (collection, storage, research, exhibition), which were taken for granted, were subjected to a critical review and were either re-evaluated or expanded with the aid of new concepts such as entertainment, memory, ecomuseum, and community, and even seen as instruments of social change (Fyfe 2006). The interest of cultural sociology is especially drawn to the functions of the preservation and communication of collective memory (Marontate 2005). Museums are understood as social institutions that preserve and also communicate socially relevant stores of knowledge. They preserve world-views and objects, and in doing so reinforce certain social values.

A further reason for the growing interest of museums in (cultural) sociology is the increasing visitor orientation of museums (Ross 2004). Postmodern theory in cultural sociology also encompasses insights from sociology of consumption (Schrage 2013). In addition a broader understanding of lifestyle research in cultural sociology includes an analysis of museum attendance (Kirchberg 2005). The user of museums as consumer is studied both as an object and as a subject of research, and so not only as a product but also as a creator of museums and exhibitions: 'it [is] important to avoid reifying museum visitors as though they were monads who arrive without any socially constructed compulsions to see or to know the world in their own manner and for their own reasons and purposes' (Fyfe 2006: 46). This quotation serves to illustrate the rejection of a behaviouristic-inspired research into museum attendance, as it was developed in particular by American psychologists beginning in the 1960s. Since then the development has moved towards a sociological action theory of visitor research (Hanquinet 2013).

Nevertheless museums occupy an uncomfortable position in the sociology of arts and culture. I do not agree with DiMaggio's (1996) rather optimistic appraisal that 'standards of social-scientific research have diffused more widely among museum workers and museums collaborate more actively with social scientists than they once did' (1996: 82). Firstly, there is evidence that this collaboration has occurred but in only a few instances, countries, and among enlightened institutions. Secondly, it is telling that a leading journal for social-scientific research in arts and culture, *Poetics*, has not published another special issue on sociological museum studies since 1996. And thirdly, if there is an emergence of academic museum studies it is not limited to sociology: it also encompasses museum psychology, museum philosophy, and museum administrative studies; the significance of sociological contributions should not be overestimated, especially in the realm of translating findings into museum practices.

The ambivalent position of museums in sociological research is a result of the tension between the elitist approach of some traditional museums on the one hand, and the increasing openness of some museums, especially of the more popular type like technology museums and natural history museums, to social publics on the other. For the former museum type, often epitomized by established art museums, there is a fear of social ingratiation that leads to popularization, commercialization, and ultimately a 'dumbing down' of a scholarly activity. For the latter museum type, openness to the public encompasses new marketing strategies and an educational outreach, especially to the socially deprived that make these museums socio-cultural institutions.

Museum sociology has neglected the difference between the inner-directed (enclosed, autopoietic) and the outer-directed (open, outreaching) museum as an object of research – both areas remain diffuse in their focus and scope (see the diagram in Figure 15.1). As a result, most museum sociological analysis of museum meanings and practices do not sufficiently distinguish in the investigation of structures and processes *within* the museum and on the *outside*, of the social context of the museum, the interrelationships between culture and society. Awareness of these two directions of museum sociological study is, however, necessary to explore major constructs such as meaning, status, representation, authenticity, authority, or time- and place-related contingencies (Marontate 2005).

Museum sociology as structuralist or as praxeological cultural sociology

There is a similar, constructive tension between a more structuralist and a more action-theory oriented museum sociology. An empirical and pragmatic cultural sociology, but also delineations of Foucault's theory of governmentality (2000), focuses on the affirmatively structuring functions of museums, reifying class, and other social groups. A structuralist cultural sociology derived from Foucault's governmentality concept is at work here, with museums seen as institutions with features of Jeremy Bentham's panopticon, where social self-regulation is practiced by visitors (Bennett 1995).

Over the last few years, since museums have become forming players in society, a praxeological, (i.e. agency-oriented) cultural sociology based on Bourdieu's theory of practice

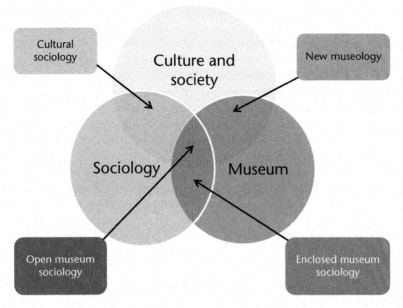

Figure 15.1 Museum sociology as an interface between culture, museum and sociology

(Bourdieu 1990) has become increasingly important in museum sociology (Kirchberg 2007). It questions the structuring function of museums as institutions of (state) hegemonic repression, because museums have become too diverse and now have too many different functions and objectives. Since the social movements of the 1960s, museums have taken a role in advancing social emancipation, in strengthening the participation and identity construction of weaker social groups and in communicating collective memories that further nonhegemonic interests. A praxeological cultural sociology provides museum sociology with the methodology to research the action level of the museum. Agent dispositions that influence the form and content of museums but also the possibility of the museum to have a progressive, emancipatory effect on social agents and institutions reveal a new perspective on communication between society and museum that invalidates the structuralist paradigm. The new curatorial qualities of museum work that shape societies were rediscovered as a field of research by an open museum sociology (Fyfe 2006).

A praxeological museum sociology corresponds to this politically progressive image of the museum that has been gaining importance over the past years (Marontate 2005). According to this view museums have become agents of civil society, acting as mediators in a society marked by social contrasts and conflicts (concerning both interests and resources), educating the public about intercultural differences in material and symbolic practices, mediating between different collectives, and taking on the political function of opposing hegemonic structures and of being an advocate for the powerless. The great variability in different types of museums enables them to address many different kinds of population groups and help them become advocates that are able to play a more active role in shaping their own social environment. The museum – with its evaluations and interpretations of exhibitions, texts, displays, and other objects – is becoming a catalyst for change and a contact zone where both visitors to the museum and more generally all those interested in the museum are able to communicate with each other and take constructive action (Mason 2006).

A differentiation of social forces in, from and to the museum into structural constraints and agency-producing effects is however a simplified dichotomy. These two poles are in fact dependent on each other and complementary. Structural factors such as individual socio-economic or demographic characteristics are still, and rightly, used to explain a variety of different interests in museums and their attendance. On the other hand, agent-specific factors are made use of in order to understand the rational voluntariness of the autonomous individual in museum attendance. An analysis using Bourdieu's theory of practice (1990), together with Giddens' theory of structuration (1992), argues that the autonomous and proactive museum visitor is more closely related to the socially determined and reactive museum visitor than an ideal-typical polarization would suggest. Individuals decide voluntarily ('agency') whether they visit a museum – their attendance pattern however gives rise to an expectation and behavioural framework that can become institutionalized and so determining ('structure'). These resulting structures are however not inevitable and unalterable; a constructive interaction in and with the museum is still possible, since changes in the practice of museum attendance can change for their part the museum as an institution and its structuring external impact (Kirchberg 2007).

Museum sociology as poststructuralist cultural sociology

Museums are at the intersection of a number of different dimensions in social space. Some of these dimensions can be described with the poles modern-postmodern, monosemic-polysemic, hegemonic-polyvalent, and colonial-postcolonial. These characteristics of museums and exhibitions are, generally speaking, located between the structuralist and poststructuralist poles. Similar concepts can be found in contemporary cultural sociology. Reinforcing poststructuralist characteristics in museum design and policy means a strengthening of an 'open', that is agency-orientated museum sociology (Fyfe 2006). A poststructuralist museum sociology understands museums as socially critical, self-reflexive and variously readable institutions that reject making the visitor solely an *object* of museum policy and instead sees him or her as the subject of his or her own actions and interpretations of what is being exhibited, or even as an independent agent constructing the museum and its exhibition (Meijer-van Mensch 2011). The emphasis of this critical 'recursivity' of social structures, attitudes, and behaviours is at the core of the kind of social science that Giddens (1992) advocated; there is an obvious parallelism of this sociology to the museums' own self-critical reflection. The postmodern relativism of sociology is also found in the contemporary self-doubt of museums. Originating in this relativism, both in the postmodern museum of a contingent world as well as in poststructuralist museum sociology of the agency-type, there is an emphasis on pluralist perspectives on content.

This pluralism of interpretations and meanings – the polysemy of museums, exhibitions, and objects – is at the core of the poststructuralist perspective on society, in which the monosemic political semantics of traditional or modern museums is also critically reflected upon and changed. Traditional or modern functions of museums, such as the unequivocal defining of meaning as a disposition of power, are replaced by an image of museums as differentiated and differentiating, reflexive and emancipatory, multiperspective, and mediatorial figures of a permanently changing society dependent on space and time (Macdonald 1996). This also involves institutionalizing flatter bureaucracies in museum organization, as mid-level museum professionals are now much more able to influence the content and design of new exhibitions than museum directors and curators, who traditionally were solely responsible for these tasks. Mid-level staff in museums are often more able to recognize what new goals are necessary for a museum, which can be implicitly or explicitly formulated in opposition to the agenda of the social elite – a function of change that the leadership of a museum institutionally rarely adopts (DiMaggio 1996).

Flatter museum bureaucracies are accompanied by greater variance in museum topics, which are now more than in the past characterized by so-called 'banal' and popular topics from everyday life. Only a poststructuralist museum sociology that recognizes the premises of polysemy can sufficiently interpret this more comprehensive range of the production and reception of the museum and the exhibition. In this respect such a polysemic, postcolonial, and polyvalent museum sociology corresponds to the current understanding of postmodern museums that with cross-over genres attempt to attract – hierarchy-flat, freely interpretable and culturally varied – the visitor as a cultural omnivore. With their polysemic exhibitions postmodern museums define themselves as places in which the visitor as recipient is called on to respond in unconventional and diverse ways to the museum's exhibitions. Traditional and modern museums make use of simple and predetermined categories to interpret their collections and thus choose to present them in a monosemic way. Moreover, this paradigmatic change of the museum is accompanied by a postcolonial museum sociology that expresses the old-style 'discomfort' in the museum (Kazeem *et al.* 2009) in an ideal-typical fashion,[5] or investigates the possible postcolonial role of museums with objects from non-Western regions in a diversifying society (Kamel and Gerbich 2014). This specific poststructuralism does not demand a relativisation of all classifications constructed by museums but it does require a careful and open interpretation of reality. Innovative forms of exhibition, open communication about the history of the exhibition, polyvalences such as feminism, civil rights, multiculturalism, and postcolonialism all have an increasing influence on the meaning and interpretation of museum objects (Mason 2006).

The mono- or polysemiousness of a museum is also dependent on both space and time. Old exhibitions are now investigated for their temporally dependent attribution of meaning, and the visitor may be informed that earlier exhibitions are now often considered to be distortions of their era. This objection to the past is also a more general critical examination of the aesthetic construct, the historical and material meaning, and the worthiness of objects to be displayed. In this context museum sociology treats questions of the value of exhibitions and storage, the legitimation of restoration and in general the physical presence of objects, which can also be allowed to visibly age and do not have to be exhibited as timeless (Marontate 2005).

Museums as heterotopic or non-heterotopic places

Similarly to the poles modern-postmodern, structuralist-poststructuralist, or monosemic-polysemic, museum sociology can also be localized on a heterotopic-non-heterotopic scale. Modern museums were long understood, according to Foucault (1993, 2005), as solely heterotopic places in which defined orders were promoted in hegemonic discourse; structural social constraints were reinforced by this traditional type of museum (Lord 2006). The museum was a place outside the normal areas of everyday life, whose autonomous boundaries placed its contents, times, and places in universal structures, which could not only expect general recognition but demand it. In the nineteenth century, museums were the kind of place where the audience expected well-established information on history and the social order. The traditional museum as heterotopic place allowed the Western visitor to interpret his world as a place of refuge for his or her exceptional 'civilized humanity'. This function of the traditional museum is revealed in particular in Bennett's concept of the 'disciplinary museum' (1995).

Following Foucault, Bennett interprets museums in general as disciplinary institutions that effectively contribute to self-regulation and self-control in society. As a means of governmentality, they contribute to regulate 'how the state indirectly and at a distance induces and solicits appropriate attitudes and forms of conduct from its citizens' (Hall 1999: 4) – and it is the task of a contemporary museum sociology to examine and expose the disciplinary function of the museum in society.

Today the non-heterotopic characteristics of the museum seem to predominate, with smooth transitions to other postmodern sites such as theme parks or other entertainment venues (Macdonald 2006). With their socially critical topics (e.g. the Holocaust, colonialism, war) and focus on specific target groups outside the social elite (immigrants, lower social classes, local communities), museums in particular justify their classification as non-heterotopic places, while museum sociology studies their corresponding social, historical, or geographical time-space dependencies (Roy and Dowd 2010). By understanding museums as non-heterotopic places, boundaries vanish between, for example, museum and non-museum, high-culture art museums and popular technology museums, traditional exhibition designs, and entertaining storytelling performances. If one agrees on museums as non-heterotopic places, all 'fixed' definitions of this institution become fluid, dependent on society, culture, time, and space.

A step further is taken by a postmodern museum sociology, which, in the turning away of the museum as a heterotopic place, interprets its offerings as commodities, that is, as legitimate elements of a culture industry and as a popular offering for the great variety of different social classes and customers. Since over the preceding decades museums have come to be accepted as everyday institutions, museum attendance can be seen as consumption and analysed from the perspective of sociology of consumption.

In her analysis of an everyday sociology of music, Tia DeNora (2000) demonstrates how music can be understood as building blocks in the social construction of scenes, routines, preferences, and everyday practices; music has always opened itself up to many different segments of the population and not just those knowledgeable about high-culture. I transfer her postmodern relativism of the uses of music to a pluralistic perspective on the multiple relationships in society between a diverse supply of museum exhibitions and a demand by different segments of population. Museum cultures focus on many cultural differences and tastes; in this non-heterotopic sense, I claim that museum cultures become everyday cultures; there is no longer a single museum culture with a single predetermined convention regarding taste or behaviour.

Rhiannon Mason (2006) links at this point Derrida's poststructuralism (2004) with a non-heterotopic museum sociology. This museum sociology, in which the signifier and the signified constantly vary (*différance*), is well aware of the spatial and temporal discontinuities of contents and images of the museum. While a social theory of heterotopy still postulates fixed structures, defines contents, and functions and interprets museums as a fundamental system of signification and social structuring (Pearce 1993), the opposing non-heterotopic approach postulates that both the meanings and the references of the signifier (content) to the signified (texts and media) in museums are subject to fundamental change over time and place. This is why it is a task for a correspondingly open, that is, an outer-directed museum sociology to recognize and analyse for museums their individual spatiality, historicity, and non-heterotopy. The knowledge of this epistemics of museums, its embeddedness in epochs and places, is important to deny museums their Foucauldian discursive power – for example, their 'arrogance of self-righteousness' – and thus strengthen their democratic and emancipatory function (Hooper-Greenhill 1992).

Museum sociology as textualistic or contextualistic analysis

In this article, the museum has until now been located in a sociological space made up of six dimensions: affirmative-progressive, structuralist-praxeological, heterotopic-non-heterotopic, modern-postmodern, monosemic-polysemic, and hegemonial-polyvalent[6] (see Figure 15.2). At this point these dimensions are ideal-typical circumlocutions; overlapping – e.g. between an unequivocally monosemic mission and the classification as modern or between a polysemic and a polyvalent orientation and the classification as postmodern – is possible and must in the future be empirically investigated. For this reason I am proposing, following the argumentation of Roy and Dowd (2010) and Mason (2006), an additional superordinate dichotomous classification. Museum sociology can either be categorized as belonging to the textualistic or to the contextualistic field. Since the introduction of these terms in cultural studies, textualistic analysis is understood as research in the light of the *poetics* and contextualistic analysis as research in light of the *politics* (Lidchi 1997). Broadly speaking, poetics includes the varieties and possibilities of (often qualitative and empirical) analysis of the design and reception of museums, exhibitions, objects, and curatorial activities – to an extent embedded in a hermeneutic sociology of knowledge. I call this approach *enclosed* museum sociology because its view is turned inwards. A focus on politics comprises the varieties and possibilities of what is often but not exclusively quantitative and empirical research into the context, production, consumption, and organization of museums, exhibitions, and their social and political environments. I call this orientation, following the organizational sociology by Scott (2003), *open* museum sociology, because his view tends to face outwards.

Textualistic museum sociology shows how museums and exhibitions are more than the sum of their manifest vitrines, information texts, design forms, marketing campaigns, etc. They are instead symbols, signifiers for a wide variety of meanings; as signifiers museums continue to communicate very different signified meanings. Poetics consists of the analysis

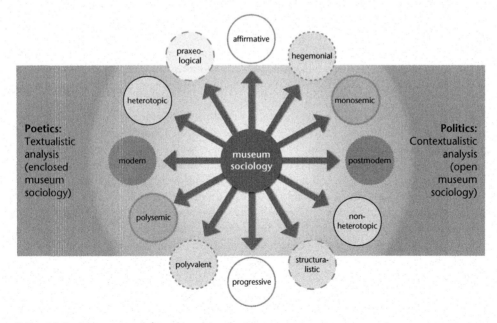

Figure 15.2 Museum sociology in epistemic space

of the inherent order of museums, such as the socially, spatially, and temporally changing perspectives and processes of signification (Mason 2006). The polysemic meaning of collected and especially exhibited objects, i.e. the ambivalent meaning of these objects in the eyes of different observers, is the *a priori* condition of textualistic museum sociology. Regarding cultural analysis as textualistic analysis, Bal (1992) argues that the narrative structures of texts and labels, the design of the room, lighting and sounds in the museum serve as factors behind different reception effects. Since a textualistic museum sociology stresses a widely changing narrative function of the museum between the storyteller of myths and the imitator of reality, it needs a curator who serves as a mediator that is able to critically and reflexively distinguish between myth and reality and also communicate that difference.

But a poetics of museum sociology investigates not only the capacity of the curator as educator or the comparable capacity of the visitor as interpreter, it also studies the reception of the visitor as he or she moves through the museum and exhibition rooms, being exposed to the stimuli of the museum. Interior architecture and exhibition design are not fixed structures, but become a production in motion not dissimilar to a film during the visitor's walk through the rooms of the museum (Kirshenblatt-Gimblett 1998). The museum thus allows the viewer to be able to read content 'against the grain', creating new meanings and thus in the tradition of cultural studies reading it subversively (Hall 1999). The visitor autonomously creates his or her own meanings of objects, exhibitions, and the museum (Hooper-Greenhill 1992). With this approach, museum sociology questions the power of the museum-maker to communicate unequivocal meanings. The text is at the same time product and producer of the surrounding social relations *and* its viewer, thus resolving the polarity between 'structure' and 'agency' (Kirchberg 2007).

The contextualistic counterpart to the *poetics* of an enclosed museum sociology is *politics* as an open museum sociology of the interrelationships between museum and culture and society – often, but not necessarily, embedded in an applied and pragmatic sociology. The functions, meanings, systemic qualities of museums, exhibitions, or objects are described and explained in their social contexts.[7] This contextualistic museum sociology has a broad interface with organizational sociology, especially with the 'production of culture' approach of the empirical American cultural sociology of the last decades (Peterson and Anand 2004) or the field theory of Bourdieu (1999). The approach of a politics-oriented museum sociology focuses on the question of organization (i.e. production, distribution, and consumption) of exhibitions and museums, which are socially (Bourdieu 1982; Kirchberg 2005) only collectively successful (Becker 1982), relevant to specified target groups (Peterson and Rossman 2007), and react flexibly to external influences (as outlined in the neo-institutionalism of Powell and DiMaggio 1991). Eva Reussner (2010), without curiously enough mentioning sociology, produced an insightful and detailed benchmarking analysis of politics-oriented research into museum attendance, evaluating the causes and effects of such research for museums.[8]

An exhibition is a product of a number of external influences on the museum. Du Gay (1997) describes these influences in his 'circuit of culture' with the phases of representation, identity, production, regulation, and consumption. The research of this reciprocal process of production and consumption has become a further important topic for contextualistic museum sociology. Political sensibilities, considerations of personal benefits and institutional path dependencies, result in a dovetailing of knowledge and practice, of theory and empiricism, which is analysed by an open museum sociology. A contextualistic museum sociology, which has its origins in organizational sociology theories, interprets the museum as a palimpsest of the influences of museum producers, museum consumers, and other social institutions influencing the museum from the outside. Museums, as all social agents today, are affected by the general commercialization, neoliberalization, and McDonaldization of society and culture (Ritzer 2012; applied to museums Kirchberg 2005). The investigation of the causes and effects of these macro-social processes, the analysis of the voluntary or imposed assumption of commercial rules in museums, and in general the submission to superordinate cultural, economic, and political powers are the objects researched in this contextual open museum sociology. Even a traditional function of museums, the collection and storage of collective memories, takes on an economic meaning in this perspective; authenticity becomes a commodity that is re-instrumentalized in the circulation of capital in the museum (Fyfe 2006). However, the museum also exercises influence on different groups in spatially adjacent areas to which not only users but also non-visitors – by different means (media presence, advertising campaigns, symbolic power) – belong.

The politics paradigm of contextualistic museum sociology is also accompanied by an analysis of: (a) the conflicts between museums and the environments in which they are involved, and (b) the dependencies of museums on their environments (Maronate 2005). These dependencies include public and private funding, for example, artworks from collectors (often on temporary loan), the disposition of the national idea, exclusion-inclusion mechanisms, and the expectations of users, to which not only visitors belong but also as part of a 'city crown' policy (Siebel 2013), city-marketing agencies, chambers of commerce, and government agencies concerned with promoting business, which would like to take advantage of the symbolic capital of a museum. Research into these objects, hegemonic and other typologies and functional systems, is at the core of a contextualistic and open politics museum sociology. This conflict analysis investigates the exercise of power and its effectiveness, for example by the consecration of objects, exhibitions, or museums by the provision of museum rooms as stages for the urban elite or by the instrumentalization of museums in the global competition of cities (Kirchberg 2003). Museums in this view are clearly political, as in a Foucauldian sense they are based on a conjunction of knowledge and power. In their perception of themselves and of others, they are clearly not outside space or time; from the perspective of a politics museum sociology they are not heterotopic places. As affirmative political institutions, museums not only preserve established power relations (distinction through consecration), they can also become progressive social agents of change (Macdonald 1996). The emancipatory and pro-social change function of museums is an important research topic for this contextualistic museum sociology (Kirchberg 2011). Stephen Weil's reflections on the legitimation of museums are a good example for this approach in museum sociology. In his article 'From being about something to being for somebody', Weil (2002) argues for the necessity of museums facing up to the fact of social power relations and work to change them for the better. In particular museums of the new museology (eco-museums, community museums, and technology museums) have a political intentionality and so are increasingly researched by this kind of museum sociology.

Museum sociology has at least as many different and also contradictory aspects as sociology itself and thus reflects the social diversity of the museum field as a whole. However that is exactly the reason to undertake a classification of this sub-discipline. The dichotomy proposed here between a textualistic, inner-oriented, and enclosed museum sociology and one that is contextualistic, outer-directed, and open seems to me to be also useful as it expresses both the different orientations of sociology and of museums. In sociology the interest in museums is often seen in a textualistic orientation, while the interest of museums in museum sociology tends to be shown in contextualistic expectations. The communication between both sides does not seem to be optimal yet as their interests in each other are not completely congruent. Nevertheless, the concept of museum sociology has since made progress both in the social sciences and in the museum landscape, and the term 'museum studies' now has a distinct sociological hue because museums take an interest in 'their' sociology. At the end of this chapter, it is thus important to quote Vera Zolberg, and in the museum sociologist's mind replacing 'art' with 'museum': 'the sociology of art cannot be insulated from art and art worlds.... Unlike specialists in esoteric fields, sociologists of art are not alone in the presence of the arts, nor can they lay claim to a monopoly of knowledge.... Admitting their interdependence is an important step' (Zolberg 1990: 215).

Notes

1 Available online at www.museumsbund.de/de/aus_und_weiterbildung/studiengaenge/museumsbezogene_studiengaenge (accessed 11 August 2014).
2 Special mention should be also made of the online journal *Museum and Society*, which is described as interdisciplinary, but since its beginning in 2003 has had a clear sociological orientation. It is associated with the School of Museum Studies at the University of Leicester and is mostly addressed to experts in the British Commonwealth (www2.le.ac.uk/departments/museumstudies/museumsociety).
3 Baur (2010: 15) defined these four coordinates of museum sociology. Certainly not all of these approaches to the museum as a research field can be considered to be sociological – but in each of these categories many sociological elements can be found.
4 I use the term 'museum sociology' instead of 'sociology of museums' in the course of Jeffrey Alexander's distinction of 'cultural sociology' ('museum' as a 'strong' independent concept impacting society) versus 'sociology of culture' ('museum' as a 'weak', dependent concept being impacted by society).
5 Clifford (1998) shows how in colonial museums (also in art museums) cultural artefacts of non-Western cultures were classified in order to make them works of art. The criteria were defined so as to evaluate the 'authenticity' of the museum pieces. African art, for example, was only considered 'authentic' if it was not yet 'debased' by contact with Western culture; postcolonial contact would have made then 'inauthentic'. The same holds for issues of repatriation and provenance research as well as the exhibition of sacred objects (cf. Marontate 2005).
6 Such phenotypical dichotomizations are used as an analytical instrument not only for characterizing museum sociology but also for analytical characterizations of museums. For instance, in his work on museum analysis, Baur (2010) distinguishes between museums that are large vs. small, old vs. young, public vs. private, local vs. global as well as disciplinary vs. interdisciplinary, focused vs. universal, professional vs. amateur, collecting vs. non-collecting, researching vs. educational, and form vs. function–oriented.
7 It is interestingly enough Jacques Derrida of all people was very positive about this open approach to museum research. Although the originator of the concept of the différance, he criticized the variability and flexibility of meanings and sign vehicles of a polysemic poetics because it advocates unverifiable, arbitrary, and uncritical norms. These postulates can only be examined by an empirical analysis of their contexts based on a politics-oriented science. Poetics and politics must be seen as complementary and not as opposites.
8 For Reussner (2010) the causes of successful research into museum attendance are integration, acceptance, leadership support, public orientation, practicality, research quality, communication, responsibility, willingness to change, participation, and resources. The effects of successful research into museum attendance are used for curatorial and other museum-internal application areas, for core tasks of exhibiting and educating, for management activities, for marketing tasks, for museum-external application areas such as publications and lectures, for additional museum tasks such as visitor service, and for museum services such as restaurants and shops.

References

Adorno, T.W. (1963) 'Valéry Proust Museum', *Prismen: Kulturkritik und Gesellschaft*, 159: 176–89.
Bal, M. (1992) 'Telling, showing, showing off', *Critical Inquiry*, 18: 556–94.
Baur, J. (ed.) (2010) Museumsanalyse. Methoden und Konturen eines neuen Forschungsfeldes, Bielefeld: Transcript.

Becker, H.S. (1982) *Art Worlds*, Berkeley, Los Angeles, and London: University of California Press.
Bennett, T. (1995) *The Birth of the Museum. History, Theory, Politics*, London, New York: Routledge.
Bourdieu, P. (1982) *Die feinen Unterschiede. Kritik der gesellschaftlichen Urteilskraft*, Frankfurt am Main: Suhrkamp.
—— (1990) *The Logic of Practice*, Stanford, CA: Stanford University Press.
—— (1999) *Die Regeln der Kunst. Genese und Struktur des literarischen Feldes*, Frankfurt am Main: Suhrkamp.
Bourdieu, P., Darbel, A. and Schnapper, D. (1990) *The Love of Art: European Art Museums and Their Public*, Cambridge: Polity Press.
Clifford, J. (1998) 'On collecting art and culture', in J. Clifford, *The Predicament of Culture: Twentieth-Century Ethnography, Literature, and Art*, Cambridge, MA: Harvard University Press.
DeNora, T. (2000) *Music in Everyday Life*, New York: Cambridge University Press.
Derrida, J. (2004) 'Die différance', in P. Engelmann (ed.), *Postmoderne und Dekonstruktion. Texte französischer Philosophen der Gegenwart*, Leipzig: Reclam.
De Varine, H. (1986) 'Rethinking the museum concept', in J.A. Gjestrum and M. Maure (eds.), *Økomuseumsboka – identitet, økologi, deltakelse. Ei arbeidsbok om ny museology*, Norsk ICOM, 1988.
DiMaggio, P. (1991) 'Constructing an organizational field as a professional project: U.S. art museums, 1920–1940', in W.P. Powell and P. DiMaggio (eds.), *The New Institutionalism in Organizational Analysis*, Chicago: University of Chicago Press.
—— (1996) 'Introduction, "special issue: museum research"', *Poetics – Journal of Empirical Research on Literature, the Media and Arts*, 24(2–4): 81–6.
Du Gay, P. (1997) *Production of Culture/ Cultures of Production*, London: Sage.
Foucault, M. (1993): 'Andere Räume', in K. Barck (ed.), *Aisthesis: Wahrnehmung heute oder Perspektiven einer anderen Ästhetik*, Leipzig: Reclam.
—— (2000) 'Die Gouvernementalität', pp. 41–67 in U. Bröckling, S. Krasmann, and T. Lemke (eds.), *Gouvernementalität der Gegenwart*, Frankfurt am Main: Suhrkamp.
—— (2005) *Die Heterotopien/Der utopische Körper*, Frankfurt am Main: Suhrkamp.
Fyfe, G. (2006) 'Sociology and the social aspects of museums', pp. 33–49, in S. Macdonald (ed.), *A Companion to Museum Studies*, Malden, Oxford, Carlton: Blackwell Publishing .
Giddens, A. (1992) *Die Konstitution der Gesellschaft. Grundzüge einer Theorie der Strukturierung*, Frankfurt am Main: Campus.
Hall, S. (1999) 'Un-settling "the heritage": Re-imagining the post-nation', in Arts Council of England (ed.), *Whose Heritage? The Impact of Cultural Diversity on Britain's Living Heritage*, London: Arts Council of England.
Hanquinet, L. (2013) 'Visitors to modern and contemporary art museums: Towards a new sociology of "cultural profiles"', *The Sociological Review*, 61(4): 790–813.
Harris, N. (1990) 'Polling for opinions', *Museum News*, 1990 (Sept./Oct.): 46–53.
Hooper-Greenhill, E. (1992) *Museums and the Shaping of Knowledge*, London: Routledge.
John, H. and A. Dauschek (2008) *Museen neu denken: Perspektiven der Kulturvermittlung und Zielgruppenarbeit*, Bielefeld: Transcript.
Kamel, S. and C. Gerbich (eds.) (2014) *Experimentierfeld Museum. Internationale Perspektiven auf Museum, Islam und Inklusion*, Bielefeld: Transcript.
Kazeem, B., C. Martinz-Turek, and N. Sternfeld (eds.) (2009) *Das Unbehagen im Museum. Postkoloniale Museologien*, Vienna: Turia + Kant.
Kirchberg, V. (2003) 'Categorizing urban tasks: Functions of museums in the post-industrial city', *Curator – The Museum Journal*, 46(1): 60–79.
—— (2005) *Gesellschaftliche Funktionen von Museen: Makro-, meso- und mikrosoziologische Perspektiven*, Wiesbaden: VS Verlag für Sozialwissenschaften.
—— (2007) 'Cultural consumption analysis: Beyond structure and agency', *Cultural Sociology*, 1(1): 115–135.
—— (2011) 'Gesellschaftliche Funktionen von Museen zwischen Assimilation und Akkommodation', *Museumskunde*, 76(2): 16–23.
Kirshenblatt-Gimblett, B. (1998) *Destination Culture: Tourism, Museums, and Heritage*, Berkeley, CA: University of California Press.
Lavine, S.D. (1992) 'Audience, ownership, and authority', in I. Karp, C. Mullen Kreamer, and S.D. Lavine (eds.), *Museums and Communities. The Politics of Public Culture*, Washington, DC: Smithsonian Institution Press, pp. 137–157.

Lidchi, H. (1997) 'The poetics and politics of exhibiting other cultures', in S. Hall (ed.), *Representations: Cultural Representations and Signifying Practices*, London: Sage.
Lord, B. (2006) 'Foucault's museum: Difference, representation, and genealogy', *Museum and Society*, 4(1): 11–14.
Macdonald, S. (1996) 'Introduction', in S. Macdonald and G. Fyfe (eds.), *Theorizing Museums. Representing Identity and Diversity in a Changing World*, Oxford, UK and Cambridge, MA: Blackwell Publishers.
—— (2006) Expanding Museum Studies, pp. 1–12 in Macdonald, S. (2006) (ed.), *A Companion to Museum Studies*, Oxford: Blackwell Publishing Ltd.
Macdonald, S. and G. Fyfe (eds.) (1996) *Theorizing Museums. Representing Identity and Diversity in a Changing World*, Oxford, UK and Cambridge, MA: Blackwell Publishers.
Marontate, J. (2005) 'Museums and the constitution of culture', in M.D. Jacobs and N. Weiss Hanrahan (eds.), *The Blackwell Companion to the Sociology of Culture*, Malden, MA and Oxford, UK: Blackwell Publishing.
Mason, R. (2006) 'Cultural theory and museum studies', pp. 17–32, in S. Macdonald (ed.), *A Companion to Museum Studies*, Malden, MA and Oxford, UK: Blackwell Publishing.
Meijer-van Mensch, L. (2011) 'Stadtmuseen und 'Social Inclusion': Die Positionierung des Stadtmuseums aus der "New Museology"', in C. Gemmeke and F. Nentwig (eds.), *Die Stadt und ihr Gedächtnis. Zur Zukunft der Stadtmuseen*, Bielefeld: Transcript.
Merton, R.K. (1995) *Soziologische Theorie und soziale Struktur*, Berlin: de Gruyter.
Mills, C.W. (1963) *Kritik der soziologischen Denkweise*, Neuwied and Berlin: Luchterhand.
Pearce, S. (1993) *Museums, Objects, and Collections: A Cultural Study*, Washington, DC: Smithsonian Institution Press.
—— (1994) 'Museum objects', in S. Pearce (ed.), *Interpreting Objects and Collection*, London: Routledge.
Peterson, R.A. and N. Anand (2004) 'The production of culture perspective', *Annual Review of Sociology*, 30: 311–34.
Peterson, R.A. and G. Rossman (2007) 'Changing arts audiences: Capitalizing on omnivorousness', in B. Ivey and S. Tepper (eds.), *Engaging Art: The Next Great Transformation of American's Cultural Life*, New York: Routledge, pp. 307–42.
Powell, W.W. and P.J. DiMaggio (eds.) (1991) *The New Institutionalism in Organizational Analysis*, Chicago: University of Chicago Press.
Prior, N. (2006) 'Postmodern restructurings', in S. Macdonald (ed.), *A Companion to Museum Studies*, Oxford: Blackwell.
Reussner, E.M. (2010) *Publikumsforschung für Museen. Internationale, Erfolgsbeispiele*, Bielefeld: Transcript.
Ritzer, G. (2012) *The McDonaldization of Society*, Thousand Oaks, CA: Sage.
Ross, M. (2004) 'Interpreting the new museology', *Museum and Society*, 2(2): 84–103.
Roy, W.G. and T.J. Dowd (2010) 'What is sociological about music?', *Annual Review of Sociology*, 36(9): 183–203.
Schrage, D. (2013) 'Vergesellschaftung durch Konsum', in H. Schmid and K. Gäbler (eds.), *Perspektiven sozialwissenschaftlicher Konsumforschung*, Stuttgart: Franz Steiner Verlag.
Scott, W.R. (2003) *Organizations. Rational, Natural, and Open Systems*, Upper Saddle River NJ: Prentice Hall.
Siebel, W. (2013) 'Stadtkronenpolitik', in Institut für Kulturpolitik der Kulturpolitischen Gesellschaft (ed.), *Jahrbuch für Kulturpolitik 2013*, Bonn, Essen: Institut für Kulturpolitik der Kulturpolitischen Gesellschaft, Klartext.
Vergo, P. (ed.) (1997) *New Museology*, Chicago: The University of Chicago Press.
Weber, M. (1978) 'The foundations of social theory', in W.G. Runciman W. (ed.), *Max Weber – Selections in Translation*, Cambridge: Cambridge University Press.
Weil, S. (2002) 'From being about something to being for somebody: The ongoing transformation of the American museum', in S. Weil (ed.), *Making Museums Matter*, Washington, DC: Smithsonian Institution Press, pp. 28–52.
Winter, R. (2003) 'Polysemie, Rezeption und Handlungsmächtigkeit. Zur Konstitution von Bedeutung im Rahmen von Cultural Studies', in F. Jannidis, G. Lauer, M. Martínez, and S. Winko (eds.), *Regeln der Bedeutung. Zur Theorie der Bedeutung historischer Texte*, Tübingen: de Gruyter.
Zolberg, V. (1981) 'Conflicting visions in American art museums', *Theory and Society*, 10: 103–125.
—— (1986) 'Tensions of mission in American art museums', in P.J. DiMaggio (ed.), *Nonprofit Enterprise in the Arts. Studies in Mission and Constraint*, New York and Oxford: Oxford University Press.
—— (1990) *Constructing a Sociology of the Arts*, Cambridge: Cambridge University Press.

16
Adjusting field theory
The dynamics of settler-colonial art fields

Tony Bennett

My primary contention in this chapter is that the dynamics that have characterized the development of the Australian art field over the last 30 to 40 years require that Bourdieu's formulations of field theory be qualified in three ways. First, such dynamics cannot be accounted for solely in terms of the struggles of successive generations of avant-gardes in their struggle for field-specific forms of capital; second, they cannot be accounted for in terms of the priority that Bourdieu accords to class relationships in structuring cultural fields; and third, they do not conform to the logic of a linear homogenous national time that characterizes Bourdieu's accounts of art fields. These contentions rest on an analysis of the longer-term dynamics governing the development of the Australian art field over the period from the mid- to late-nineteenth century and, more particularly, on the position that Aboriginal art has come to occupy in the Australian art field since the 1960s.

The controversies occasioned by the Royal Academy's 2013 exhibition *Australia* provide a useful point of entry into these questions. In reviewing this exhibition the art critic Peter Conrad complained that the first room outraged chronology by awarding priority to the indigenous artists whose work was exhibited there in spite of the fact that, apart from some bark paintings from the 1880s, that work had all been produced during the last 50 years. Dismissing the justification that was offered for this break with chronological logic – that indigenous artists belonged to 'the oldest unbroken art tradition in the world' – as a 'pious bluff that treats indigenous art as eternal not temporal' (Conrad 2013–14: 70), Conrad argued that more valid insights would have been generated by placing the art in its proper historical context. This, he argued, would have required a presentation of the role of Geoffrey Bardon, a teacher in the remote Aboriginal community of Papunya, in helping to shape the acrylic dot painting that became the signature of the Papunya Tula art collective. Established in the 1970s, this became the lead organization of the Western Desert Art Movement which, in the 1980s, was consecrated as a new form of Aboriginal high art with a significant presence in both national and international art markets and exhibition circuits.

Conrad is right to draw attention to this movement which, if it was partly shaped by Bardon and the Papunya Tula collective, was also shaped by the interactions of a wide range of other agents: the practices of the Aboriginal Arts Board of the Australia Council; the cultural policy bureaus of both the State and Federal levels of government; the New York art world; the anthropologists who mediated the relations between Papunya and international art circuits; and the agendas of the Australian government which gave birth to Papunya in the first place (Fisher 2012; Myers 2002, 2013).[1] The key factor that Conrad identifies, however, is the controversial purchase of Jackson Pollock's *Blue Poles* by the National Gallery of Australia in 1972.[2] For Bardon's significance, he argues, was that of encouraging the Papunya painters to become 'down-under analogies of Pollock' (Conrad 2013–14: 70), adapting his techniques for presenting 'the American landscape seen from above' (70) so as to lend a new inflection to their own traditions. *Blue Poles* is also a key point of reference for Nicholas Thomas's (1999) discussion of *The Myth of the Western Man (White Man's Burden)* (Figure 16.1) by Gordon Bennett – a visual artist of both Indigenous Australian and Scottish/English ancestry, whose work critically interrogates the relations between Western art histories and the category of Aboriginality. While clearly adapting Pollock's 'signature' abstract expressionist painting style of dripping and flicking paint onto canvas, *Myth of the Western Man (White Man's Burden)* is best interpreted, Thomas argues, as a critique of both white middle-class pretensions toward a cultural internationalism that were represented by the purchase of *Blue Poles* and of the foundational myths of Australian nationalism. The formalism of Pollock's poles is disrupted by the historical coordinates of Bennett's flag as it cuts a line between, at the bottom of the canvas, 1788, the date of white invasion, and at the top, 1992, the date of the High Court Mabo judgement which overturned the doctrine of *terra nullius* that had legitimized the colonial dispossession of Australia's Indigenous peoples. This north/south division of the canvas is accompanied, on either side, by a series of dated events referring to massacres and acts of Aboriginal resistance which throw the myths of Western settlement off course, rendered here pictorially in the central figure's inability to establish a secure footing.

However, *Myths* can also be interpreted, as much of Bennett's work (McLean 1999), as a commentary on the project of establishing an Australian art which has also always been thrown off course by the fraught relations between Western and Aboriginal art practices. This reading of Bennett's work provides a useful point of departure for my interrogation of Bourdieu's account of the temporal dynamics of Western art fields – dependent, largely, on modernist conceptions of the role of avant-gardes – in order to identify where and how it might need to be adjusted to accommodate the distinctive dynamics of art fields in settler-colonial societies. Thomas identifies the significance of indigenous art practices in this regard as consisting in a distinctive form of cultural autonomy, marked by a distinctive temporality, in the respect that it is neither entirely absorbed by nor excluded from the present:

> This culture belongs to the present, but also lies beyond it – beyond, that is, the space and time of colonial modernity and post-modernity. Maori art, for instance, is created out of genealogical time and tribal histories constituted by ancestral acts. It appears as a disturbing interruption in the modern colonial nation, but is not encompassed by that nation's homogeneous, linear modern time.
>
> *(Thomas 1999: 17)*

How the tensions between these different temporalities are worked through differs from one settler-colonial context to another. While I shall allude to these differences from time to time, my primary focus will be on the Australian case as the one I know best but also the one which, since Papunya, has most dramatically instanced the complex interrelations between the organization of national, transnational, and indigenous art practices. I look first, though, at the defining features of field theory in order to distinguish those of its underlying principles which seem generally applicable from those which need to be adjusted if they are to

Figure 16.1 Myth of the western man (white man's burden), Gordon Bennett, 1992

be extended beyond the European art fields Bourdieu was concerned with. I then return to the issues canvassed above regarding the distinctive temporalities of settler-colonial art fields. I conclude by reviewing the respects in which the relations between settler and indigenous populations complicate the organisation of art fields in settler-colonial contexts.

Reviewing field theory

Cyril Lemieux's (2011) assessment of field theory makes three main points that are relevant to my concerns here. First, he argues that the concept of field differs from the concepts of habitus and capital in its historical specificity; it is the competitive struggle for the stakes that are at issue in the 'jeu social' that is universal. The existence of an autonomous field as the setting for such struggles requires that there be specific forms of capital at stake, and that these are adjudicated and legitimated by specific authorities. The art and literary fields that preoccupied Bourdieu are, in this sense, largely the outcome of historical processes leading to their autonomisation (from the state, and from religion) that were associated with the development of new forms of intellectual authority, especially during the mid- to late-nineteenth century. Lemieux's second contention is that the concept of field came to occupy a more prominent place in Bourdieu's work as, from the 1970s, his attention shifted from the analysis of processes of cultural consumption to those of cultural production. He goes on to argue that the struggles within and between the cultural, scientific and political fields largely concern the relations between elites inasmuch as the popular classes lack any stake in the struggles between the different forms of field-specific capitals that are at issue. Lemieux argues, finally, that a universal characteristic of fields in societies where they occur is that their dynamics are the result of the partial revolutions produced by new entrants where such revolutions are also apprenticeships in the rules of the game.

Let me add to this four further principles focused more closely on Bourdieu's account of the dynamics of cultural fields as articulated in his classic studies (Bourdieu 1993, 1996).[3] The first comprises the complex relationality that Bourdieu attributes to fields of cultural production arising from the intersections of (i) the position takings of artists and of artistic movements – or of writers and literary movements, and so on – relative to one another; (ii) the actions of other agents – academies, art markets, museums, producers associations – relative to one another and to the position takings of artists, and (iii) the constantly mobile relations of inter-textuality that are generated by these relations.[4] Second, Bourdieu insists that the temporalities or 'historicities' of cultural fields that are the outcomes of such complex relations constitute a time that is specific to each field rather than the effect of a time that is pre-given to fields arising from an all-purpose chronology. Third, while cultural fields possess their own specific internal relations and dynamics, these are also shaped by their relations to the fields of power: that is, the economic and political fields. These relations generate a tension between autonomous and heteronomous principles of hierarchization, particularly in the case of fields of restricted cultural production. The relations between cultural fields and the field of power, finally, are structured by class relations. In his diagrammatic representations of these relations, Bourdieu thus accords the literary and artistic fields a dominated position within the field of power which he situates at 'the dominant pole of the field of class relations' (Bourdieu 1993: 38).

The first and second of these principles have proved to be the most generative and portable, shaping inquiries even where these have departed from Bourdieu's specific applications of them to the French literary and artistic fields. The aspects of Bourdieu's field theory which look more questionable are, first, the sharpness of the separation he posits between the field of restricted cultural production, in which artists produce work for one another and the educational system that legitimates their activities, and the demand-driven field of extended cultural production catering for middlebrow and popular tastes. The tide of current opinion and evidence acknowledges that while such divisions are still pertinent, their force is considerably diminished. The continued operation of an anti-economy organized in terms of the principle of 'loser wins' – that is, on a systematic inversion of the fundamental principles of all ordinary economies' (Bourdieu 1993: 39) – in what remains of the field of restricted production is also questionable as this looks increasingly like a niche market similar to other special-interest niche markets (Frow 1995; Davis 2007; English 2005). Finally, Bourdieu's account of the temporal dynamics of art fields is over reliant on a modernist conception of a succession of avant-gardes challenging earlier avant-gardes and, in the process, repositioning them as rear-guards. [5]

None of these criticisms calls field theory as such into question. Nor do they relate specifically to settler-colonial societies. The aspects of Bourdieu's approach that most obviously need to be adjusted to engage with cultural fields in such societies concern their inherently transnational characteristics. Bourdieu takes it for granted that, in the case of the art and literary fields of late-nineteenth-century France, these are national fields characterized by a high degree of hermetic closure except for their relations to European high art traditions. There are good reasons for this given the early establishment, in the case of the French art field, of national cultural institutions (Poulot 1997), and the strong Paris-centred focus of the national network of art galleries that had developed by the mid-nineteenth century (Sherman 1989). The consequence is that international agents scarcely figure in Bourdieu's accounts of these fields of cultural production.

The factors shaping cultural fields in settler-colonial societies are distinct in at least three ways. The first consists in the relatively late development of institutions articulating an ethos of artistic autonomy. This is a common feature in settler-colonial societies, albeit that its causes are variable. In the case of the United States, Barbara Novak (2007) attributes it to the subordination of the American landscape tradition to the idea of God's ruling presence in nature and thereby the belief in America's manifest destiny. Bernard Smith (1979), lamenting the lack of any interest prior to his own in the history of Australian art,[6] attributes the subordination of Australian art to religious and secular powers to a variety of causes – its enlistment as a utilitarian instrument for the visual description of Australian flora, fauna, atmosphere, and landscape; the influence of Methodism on Australia's early nineteenth-century free settlers; the reduction of artistic labour to the conditions of feudal servitude associated with the early employment of convict artists; and the conception of art as an agent of moral reform – prior to the influence of Australian impression in prompting a break with the (Royal) Art Society and the establishment of the Society of Artists in 1895.

The second tendency concerns the late development of the range of institutional actors that are needed to give a national art field a distinctive shape and definition. The location of Australia's early art and cultural institutions is relevant here, with the capital city of each colony – of New South Wales, Victoria, Queensland, Tasmania, South Australia, and West Australia – setting up its own art gallery in the mid- to late-nineteenth century. But the tempo of the development of national art institutions after the 1901 Act of Federation which brought the separate States into a system of federal government was also slow.[7] The establishment of a National Arts Acquisition Fund in 1910 and of the Commonwealth Art Advisory Board in 1912 stand pretty much on their own prior to the initiation, in the 1960s, of the debates leading to the establishment of the Australia Council for the Arts in 1967 and to the eventual opening of the National Gallery of Australia in 1982.[8] It was similarly largely only in the post-war period that a hitherto fledgling Australian art market became significantly articulated to international markets (Van den Bosch 2005), and that a distinctive art criticism concerned specifically with the Australianness of Australian art became significant.

However, as a key figure in announcing and shaping this project, Bernard Smith also argued that the general tendency of Australian art since 1788 had 'been toward an international fusion of many national styles' (Smith 1979: 30). To engage with the distinctive dynamics of art practices in Australia thus requires that account be taken of the ways in which these have been shaped by varied sets of transnational relations and institutions. The same is true, of course, of European art fields in view of the relative mobility of high art forms between European nations and the influence, through 'primitivism' for example, of the art practices of colonized peoples. It is, then, the distinctive quality of the transnational relations shaping the Australian art field that matter here. There is a range of approaches to these questions. I refer, for example, to Alison Inglis's (2011) account of how art practices in Australia were initially shaped by an imperial art system comprising the colonial art museum, an imperial art teaching system centred on South Kensington, and an international exhibition circuit also centred on London; to the accounts of the period from the late-nineteenth-century Heidelberg School, the most influential Australian champion of the *plein air* movement and of impressionism, through to the kinds of mid-century modernism represented by artists like Margaret Preston, Grace Cossington Smith, and Roy de Maistre, who were featured in the 2013 *Sydney Modern* exhibition at the Art Gallery of New South Wales (Edwards and Mimmocchi 2013), which stress the significance of the relations between Australian artists and European art fields, especially those centred on London and Paris, as 'a willed form of cultural interaction with a broad array of cultures beyond and within Australia' (White 2011: 109); to the significance of the American art field, and specifically of New York, in the post-war period (Gardner 2011) and, latterly, the repositioning of the Australian art field within an emerging Asian art field represented by initiatives such as the Asia-Pacific Triennium (Turner 2005); to the significance that has been accorded Oceania as a transnational context for Australian artistic exchanges from Bernard Smith's pioneering *European Vision and the South Pacific* (Smith 1960) to the more recent work of Nicholas Thomas and his colleagues (Brunt et al. 2012); and to Rex Butler's understanding of the ways in which, in appropriating art from other parts of the world, Australian artists have reinterpreted that art 'from the hitherto excluded subject position of Australia' (Butler 2005: 27).[9]

There are no intrinsic reasons why field theory cannot address dynamics shaped by the relations between transnational artistic practices. In analysing the contemporary British articulation of the field of modern art, Michael Grenfell and Cheryl Hardy (2007) thus adapt Bourdieu's scheme for representing the relations between artistic time and historical time (see Bourdieu 1996: 159) by plotting the relations between artists whose work has been consigned to the past by a succession of avant-garde practices in which European, American, and specifically British art practices intersect. If the consecrated avant-garde of late-nineteenth-century European modernists defined itself in opposition to classical painting, it was in turn assigned to the artistic past by post-war American abstract expressionists and minimalists who, in their turn, have been relegated to a superseded past by the practices of the British avant-garde (Figure 16.2).

But what would such a grid look like in the case of the contemporary Australian art field? It would require two intersecting axes of artistic age: one connecting a succession of post-invasion discontinuities in Australian art practices anchored in the longer and broader histories of Western art fields; and the other connecting tendencies in contemporary Australian art – both Aboriginal and non-Aboriginal – to the longer histories of both pre- and post-invasion

Adjusting field theory

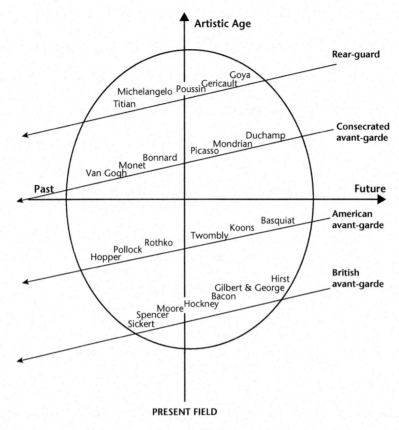

Figure 16.2 The field of modern art from art review 1990s

Aboriginal art practices. Account would also need to be taken of the respects in which the dynamics of the contemporary Australian art field have been shaped by art practices conducted at a remove from, and with no direct investment in, the position-taking of avant-gardes in relation to their predecessors. What is at issue in both of these considerations are the positions that Aboriginal art practices now occupy in relation to the Australian art field.

Conflicted temporalities of the Australian art field

At the 2011 Census, Aborigines and Torres Strait Islanders accounted for 2.5 per cent of the Australian population. The visitor to any major art gallery in Australia today would have the sense of a much larger indigenous population. Although they rarely collected it before the 1950s, all the major State galleries now have significant collections of Aboriginal art which are usually hung in separate exhibition spaces that account for a good proportion of the overall gallery floor space – certainly a good deal more than 2.5 per cent. Originally excluded from its definition of Australian art, the National Gallery of Australia accelerated its collection of Aboriginal art in the 1980s leading, in 1989, to a major exhibition as a prelude to the permanent installation of *The Aboriginal Memorial* – a protest against 200 years of colonial slaughter timed to coincide with Australia's Bicentenary in 1988 – which now occupies 'pride of place at the very entrance to the Gallery's exhibition space' (Caruana 2003; see also

McLean 2011: 33–38). These are very recent developments. For the greater part of the late nineteenth and early twentieth centuries, Aboriginal art practices were excluded from the category of art. Assigned to the culture pole of James Clifford's art-culture system (Clifford 1988), Aboriginal bark paintings had no place in Australia's initial array of State art galleries. They were consigned instead to natural history museums as illustrations of primitive cultures poised on the nature/culture divide. This division was complemented by a rigorous separation of the concerns of anthropology and art history: Aboriginal art practices were distinctly the province of the former alongside other (material, ritual) manifestations of Aboriginal culture, art history affording them no place whatsoever. While the anthropologist Baldwin Spencer compared the brushwork of Aboriginal artists to fine art traditions, the paintings he collected were housed in Victoria's National Museum rather than its National Gallery with the consequence that 'the art was lost in the ethnography' (Morphy 2007: 184).

That said, it was anthropologists rather than art historians who, following in the footsteps of those missionaries who initially brokered the relations between remote Aboriginal artists and metropolitan consumers, played the key role in the protracted processes through which Aboriginal paintings came to be classified as art (Fisher 2012; Jones 2011; McLean 2011). The first exhibition of Aboriginal art was held at the National Museum of Victoria in 1929, but as an illustration of 'primitive art' with its being mooted that the works displayed should be accompanied by the staged presence of Aborigines as 'living history' (Thomas 2011: 5). It was not until the 1940s that fine art categories began to be applied to the interpretation of Aboriginal art, again largely at the prompting of anthropologists – notably Ronald and Catherine Berndt and A.P. Elkin (McLean 2011: 22–26). Perhaps the most significant event, however, was the American-curated *Art of Australia 1788–1941* exhibition that toured the US (via MOMA) and Canada (via the National Gallery of Canada) as the first exhibition to propose a national framing of Aboriginal art while the 1943 Primitive Art Exhibition at the National Gallery of Victoria integrated it within a specifically aesthetic framing (Thomas 2011). These prompted, in the late 1940s and early 1950s, the first significant acquisitions of Aboriginal art collections on the part of State galleries following on the first such acquisition – an Albert Namatjira watercolour purchased for the Adelaide National Gallery by Daryl Lindsay, the art gallery curator/director who played the most significant initial role in shifting Aboriginal practices from the culture to the art pole of the art-culture system.

Anthropologists – Eric Michaels (1994), Howard Morphy (2007), and Fred Myers (2002), for example – also played leading roles in the later reappraisal of contemporary Aboriginal art practices alongside their valorisation as high art in international art fields in the 1980s and 1990s. Curators (Judith Ryan at the National Gallery of Victoria and Ron Radford at the Art Gallery of South Australia, for example) and collectors (Vivien and Tim Johnson) also played important roles here. However, these contributions formed part of a 'dance of agency' across a more complex and diverse range of actors. These have included, since the 1970s, perhaps the key watershed years, the role of new policy agencies in challenging the classification systems previously governing the allocation of government arts funding, particularly with the 1973 establishment of the Aboriginal Arts Board in the Australia Council; the revalorization of the art practices of remote Aboriginal communities that took place within the practices of Australian art institutions and art markets as a result of the legitimacy bestowed on them in international art fields – particularly, after the 1984 *Primitivism* at MOMA, those centred on New York; the role of postmodern critiques in undoing the values invested in Aboriginal art through its previous ethnographic framings; and, most importantly, the varied tactics deployed by Aboriginal artists, curators, and activists to develop Aboriginal art practices in pursuit of a variety of political and cultural ends. It has also included the activities of a range of museums – and not just art museums – as major participants in the reclassification of Aboriginal art practices in ways that have opened up the operations of the Australian art field to the influence of a range of knowledge practices alongside those of art history (Barrett and Milner 2014).

A comprehensive account of these matters cannot be attempted here. I shall instead, in a rough-and-ready periodization, focus on three different moments in the changing relations between Aboriginal art practices and the Australian art field. Ian McLean offers a succinct summary of the key difference between the first two periods in arguing that, between the late-nineteenth and early-twentieth centuries and the inter- and early post-war years, the place accorded Aborigines in settler discourse shifted from being 'in imperial texts ... the figure of exclusion or oblivion, the nothing or negative term from which an identity can be made' to becoming 'in Aboriginalist texts ...the very being of the place' (McLean 2011: 105): that is, the defining essence from which post-imperial, but still white representations of Australianness took their bearings. The third period – broadly from the 1960s – saw Aboriginal artists become significantly active in relation to the Australian art field in a plurality of ways which, while affecting the dynamics of that field, have also operated in accordance with principles which operate athwart its rules of the game or have inflected them along racial-political lines.

Nicholas Thomas highlights the distinctive qualities of the first two periods in his comments on how the dynamics of mid- to late-nineteenth century settler-colonialism led to the more or less total disappearance of Aborigines from Australian painting. He contrasts this to the later dynamics of settler primitivism which repopulated Australia with an imaginary Aboriginal presence that served as a point of identification for the 'white nativism' of Aboriginalist discourse: the work of Margaret Preston, for example, which, in bringing 'the bush right into the living room' provided a resource for 'the domestic routine of heroic self-fashioning' that resonated to an antipodean environment (Thomas 1999: 132). Whereas colonialisms based on overseas conquests typically led to appropriations of indigenous artistic traditions in creole forms of artistic production, settler-colonial art fields are more typically governed by narratives of succession which – as a complement to their removal from the land – situate indigenous peoples in the past.[10] While early colonial painting acknowledged indigenous presence in a variety of forms – from celebrations of the noble savage to depictions of Aborigines as a part of the landscape, often in association with scenes of wildness in contrast to scenes of settler pastoralism – Aborigines were subsequently 'painted out' of Australian visual culture.[11] This took a variety of forms: the removal of Aboriginal figures from popular reproductions of famous paintings, particularly in the lead up to and immediate aftermath of Federation, in anticipation of their removal from the nation that was to come; the significance of the Heidelberg school as the initial incubator of Australian modernism in eliding Aboriginal presence from Australian painting ('No major work by any Heidelberg artist featured any aspect of indigenous life', Thomas 1999: 90); and in the denial of Aboriginal creativity in the past (Aboriginal responsibility for certain kinds of rock paintings in the Kimberley region was denied as being beyond their level of cultural competence and was attributed instead to an imagined Sumatran influence). Progressively excluded from the public discourse of Australian art, Aborigines, who had 'already been consigned to oblivion by the politics of frontier life', were assigned to the field of anthropology where they figured as 'the other of history, progress and culture' (McLean 1998: 67).

'The central conceit of modernist primitivism,' Daniel Sherman has argued, 'holds that the artist ... can, through a valorisation of the primitive, advance a personal, inventive form of expression while at the same time critiquing the hypocrisy, soullessness, or sterility of the modern West' (Sherman 2011: 3–4). However, as Myers (2006) reminds us, 'primitivism' comes in many different forms depending on how the two terms 'primitive' and 'art' – each of which detached indigenous practices from their originating contexts – are interpreted and combined. Settler primitivism, Thomas argues, differed from its European variants along several dimensions: it was typically less a project of formal innovation stimulated by tribal art than an attempt to affirm a relationship to a new locality; it constituted an engagement with a particular 'primitive culture' rather than with a generic one; it usually supported settler nationalism rather than comprising an avant-garde critique of nationalism; and it was, as a consequence, usually supported by state and commercial art agencies rather than taking the form of an artistic revolt against these. This resulted initially, Ian McLean has argued, in a 'desert pastoralism' – initially represented by Hans Heysen – in which the Australian desert (largely neglected in the previous Australian landscape tradition), its inhabitants and their culture were depicted as emblems of Australianness. In what was a complex form of cultural cross-dressing in painterly form, the figure of the 'Caucasian Aboriginal' served, in the 1940s, as an important emblem for a new kind of national identity, providing a template for the self-fashioning of 'white blackfellows' as a prelude to the subsequent redefinition of Aboriginality in which the new Australian figures as a 'white Aborigine' sprung from the bush and shaped by an outback ethos of white nomadism. This in turn provided a focus for critical engagement by artists like Sydney Nolan and Russell Drysdale, whose transformations of outback scenes into ones of estrangement constituted a painterly critique of these earlier traditions.

The key questions in these first two periods largely concerned the places accorded Aborigines and 'traditional' Aboriginal art practices such as bark paintings in the practices of white Australian artists or the discourses and practices of anthropology and art history. These can, as the above account suggests, be accommodated within modernist accounts of the formal dynamics of art fields. The major exception here was the watercolourist Albert Namatjira (1902–1959), the leading figure of the Hermannsburg school, whose work effected a distinctive fusion of Aboriginal and Western landscape traditions. For later Aboriginal artists, like Lin Onus and Galarrwuy Yunupingu, Namatjira's art was pivotal to the development of the Aboriginal land ownership movement. For his white contemporaries, including Daryl Lindsay, it represented a troubling challenge to the temporalities of modernity. To be aestheticized as 'primitive art' in testimony to a universally shared human capacity for artistic creativity was one thing; to be included as a form of 'modern art' was quite a different matter which, had it been admitted, would have confounded the primitive/modern division which still governed the dominant cultural conceptions and the political arrangements governing the relations between white and Aboriginal Australians. The ideological perturbation this would have entailed was avoided by denying Namatjira's art any authenticating Aboriginality. Interpreted, instead, as largely a derivative application of contemporary European landscape traditions, his paintings were assessed as testifying to a capacity for mimicry. This was given a positive spin as heralding an assimilationist future in which even the 'full-blooded' Aborigine would be able to learn and master white traditions (for fuller discussions see: McLean 1998: 96–101; Thomas 1999: 166–173; and Thomas 2011).

Developments since the 1960s introduced two new tendencies: the entry into the art field of new forms of contemporary Aboriginal art practice and the development of new relations between the Australian art field and a range of transnational art relations and practices. These have not, however, been all of one piece. Ian McLean's (2011) documentation of the relations between Aboriginal art practices and the Australian and transnational art fields over this period includes four such entanglements I want to highlight here. The first concerns the impact, in the 1960s, of the black liberation movement and of emerging transnational indigenous movements on indigenous art practices in Australia. These led to a political questioning of the category of the Aborigine as a colonial and racist category and the development of an alternative discourse of Aboriginality that side-stepped the tribal or biological conceptions that had informed settler-colonialism by connecting indigenous art practices to the politics of land. I have already touched on the second tendency concerning the production of an Aboriginal high art through the new relationships that were developed, from the 1980s onwards, between indigenous desert artists in remote communities and both new agents in the Australian art field (the Australia Council, for example) and key players in the international art field (such as MOMA). The third tendency concerns the later influence of postmodern art practices and conceptions, particularly as represented by immigrant artists, in fuelling a renaissance of urban indigenous art – perhaps most famously represented by artists like Tracey Moffatt and Gordon Bennett – that interrogated earlier conceptions, both white and black, of Aboriginality through a critical deconstruction of settler and Western art practices.

Account has finally to be taken of the transformative effects of the new alignments between Western and indigenous knowledges brought about by archaeological confirmations of Aboriginal claims to a long history of Australian habitation in producing new timelines for the calibration and assessment of the pre-invasion history of Aboriginal art practices. The clear evidence that these have to be interpreted as dynamic, registering creative responses to changing circumstances and their influence on contemporary Australian art practice – both Aboriginal and non-Aboriginal – have produced a contemporary Australian art field with temporalities that now stretch back into, and effect a dialogue between, the longer histories of both Aboriginal and Western art.[12] We can see something of what is involved here in the contemporary valorisation of the traditional form of bark painting as a canonical art tradition. The 2013 exhibition *Bark Paintings – Old Masters* at the National Museum of Australia was a case in point in depicting the bark painters as 'quite literally, Australia's old masters' whose work 'constitutes a peerless artistic canon' (www.nma.gov.au/exhibitions/old_masters/home, downloaded June 2014). So is a current (2014) curation at the Art Gallery of New South Wales which brings together a diverse set practices presented as different aspects of Australian non-figurative traditions: grave posts decorated by Tiwi artists, presented as the first commission (1958) of Aboriginal art by a modern art gallery; a number of 1950s and 1960s bark paintings by Mithinari Gurruwiwi and Wandjuk Marika, for example; abstract landscapes from the same period by Ian Fairweather and Fred Williams; and abstract expressionist canvasses of the Egyptian immigrant painter Tony Tuckson.

Conclusions

Let me go back to Lemieux's contention that the dynamics of art fields are driven by the partial revolutions produced by new entrants serving their apprenticeship in the rules of the game. While many aspects of twentieth-century Australian arts practices can be accounted for in these terms, the interventions of indigenous artists do not conform entirely to this logic. It is true, as Laura Fisher (2012) argues, that for some urban Aboriginal artists the critique of Aboriginalism has been a way of sloughing off an imposed identity to take up the position of artist and, thereby, adopt the strategy of competitive struggle with other artists in accordance with the logic of partial revolutions and the quest for specific forms of artistic cultural capital. This is, though, less true for many painters from remote indigenous communities whose connections with both the Australian and international art fields have been indirect, mediated through complex networks of cultural intermediaries, and premised on either a disinterest in or an explicit eschewal of those forms of artistic creativity required for the competitive struggle for field-specific forms of capital. Howard Morphy has shown how the denial of any aspiration to original forms of creativity on the part of Yolngu painters reflects the significance they invest in continuity with past traditions in view of the associations that these establish between specific formal motifs and ancestral histories considered in terms of their relations to specific clans and their attachments to land (Morphy 2007: 148–159). These not only radically contradict the terms in which the relations between paintings are ordered in Western art markets; they also reflect the influence of community-specific forms of authority and cultural and political capital that are in tension with those of the art field. This dual orientation – of being in such markets but not of them – is further reinforced by the variety of mechanisms through which leading Aboriginal intellectuals, community organizations, and kin networks maintain an integrated identity for Aboriginal art practices, no matter what position they are accorded in Western art fields (Langton 1999). This affects a racial partitioning of the art field where race is understood not as a biological category but as an ancestral-cultural category that asserts a sense of a common heritage forged through the shared experience of discrimination and oppression.[13]

This is not to deny the pertinence of considerations of class to the dynamics of the Australian art field, particularly where matters of consumption are concerned. These are no less important than in other Western societies, and they are configured along roughly the same lines with participation in the art field being largely limited to the professional middle classes (Bennett, Bustamante, and Frow 2013). Engagement with the increasing presence of Aboriginal art in the Australian art field since the 1980s has exhibited a corresponding class logic. Myers, citing contemporary survey evidence, argues that its place in this regard has 'been sustained by the taste and hegemony not of the working class or the immigrant ethnic groups or the elite of the old squattocracy but of the historically distinctive class fraction of university-educated public servants and bureaucrats who took over the Australian Labor Party' (Myers 2002: 204–205). While this is perhaps too tight a specification, there is little doubt regarding the middle-class characteristics of non-Aboriginal engagement with Aboriginal art.[14] These – particularly when translated into state forms of arts patronage and funding – have also been factors at play in organising the field of artistic production. However, the increasing force and presence of Aboriginal art has sat athwart, complicated and in many respects overshadowed the influence of class so far as both the formal dynamics of the art field and their social and political articulations are concerned. It is, in particular, clear that the influence of the field of power on the Australian art field cannot be reduced to the singular axis of class relations at the expense of the complex entanglements of race that have informed the relations between its settler and indigenous populations. It is also clear that the temporal dynamics of the Australian art field cannot be reduced to a singular accumulating time of modernity. However, I would suggest that, in this regard, the Australian case identifies an adjustment that should be made in applying field theory more generally. For reasons that I have argued elsewhere (Bennett 2005), this aspect of Bourdieu's field theory is better interpreted as a side effect of his own commitment to the modernist project of the collective intellectual than to the properties of field theory.

Acknowledgements

I am grateful to Mike Savage and Laurie Hanquinet for their comments on earlier drafts of this chapter, and to Fred Myers and Tim Rowse for their advice regarding the relations between Aboriginal art practices and the Australian art field. I also thank Kathryne Genevieve Honey from the Sutton Gallery in Melbourne for her comments on Gordon Bennett's *Myth of the Western Man (White Man's Burden)*.

The research for this paper was made possible by a grant from the Australian Research Council (ARC) for the project 'Australian Cultural Fields: National and Transnational Dynamics' (DP140101970). I am grateful to the ARC for its support.

Notes

1 Papunya, located northwest of Alice Springs in the Northern Territory, was founded in the 1960s as part of a movement to return indigenous Australians to their traditional lands. These policies were subsequently lent a self-determination inflection under the Whitlam Labor government of the 1970s.
2 The use of public funds to purchase a work of international abstract art was controversial as a marker of an emerging division between a middle-class cosmopolitanism and a conservative national cultural populism that remains significant. See Van den Bosch (2005) for details.
3 See Savage and Silva (2013) for a more extended discussion of these questions.
4 Bourdieu applied these principles somewhat unevenly, however. Fabiani (1999) notes the undue attention that Bourdieu accords to the relations between authors at the expense of institutional actors in his account of the literary field. Fligstein and McAdam (2002) similarly note Bourdieu's tendency to focus on individual actors at the expense of collective ones.
5 See Hanquinet, Roose, and Savage (2014) for further discussion of this modernist framing.
6 His contentions here are polemically overstated, particularly in overlooking the role of Sydney Ure Smith and the inter-war journal *Art in Australia* (Carter 2013).
7 What was established in 1788 was not 'Australia' but New South Wales as a colony centred on Sydney and governed from London. This was followed by the establishment of a succession of colonies, each of which was independent of the others, with its own political institutions, and ruled, ultimately, from London. The first significant step in establishing a national governmental domain by redesignating the colonies as States and integrating them into a national structure came with the Act of Federation in 1901.
8 The development of art institutions with a specific interest in American art is also largely post-war with the exception of MOMA, the Whitney Museum of American Art, and the Carnegie Institute in Pittsburgh. Harris (1995) attributes this to the Eurocentric orientations of late-nineteenth and early-twentieth century American elites who accorded American art practices little place in their practices of distinction.
9 This has been a significant orientation of Australian art discourse since the publication, in 1959, of *The Antipodean Manifesto* by Bernard Smith and others, proposing the perspective of the antipodean as that of a strategic alterity that destabilizes Eurocentric art categories (see Beilharz 1997).
10 While following convention in describing Australia as a 'settler-colony', it should be stressed that the process of settlement involved the invasion of the Australian continent and a prolonged war of racial elimination directed against the indigenous population in order to secure its removal from the land (see Reynolds 2013).
11 For a discussion of the parallel elision of Native Americans from American painting and history, see Conn (2004).
12 Carroll (2014) offers an interesting re-reading of the longer history of Aboriginal art through the lens of contemporary Aboriginal art practices.
13 I draw here on Kamala Visweswaran (2010) who argues the importance of such early nineteenth century racio-cultural conceptions to the development of shared political identifications for Native Americans drawn from different tribal cultures.
14 Chris Healy (2008) suggests broader social patterns for white Australian engagement with other aspects of Aboriginal cultural presence.

References

Anderson, J. (2011) (ed.) *The Cambridge Companion to Australian Art*, Melbourne: Cambridge University Press.
Barrett, J. and J. Milner (2014) *Australian Artists in the Contemporary Museum*, Farnham: Ashgate.
Beilharz, P. (1997) *Imagining the Antipodes: Culture, Theory and the Visual in the Work of Bernard Smith*, Cambridge: Cambridge University Press.

Bennett, T. (2005) 'The historical universal: The role of cultural value in the historical sociology of Pierre Bourdieu', *British Journal of Sociology*, 56(1), 141–164.
Bennett, T., M. Bustamante, and J. Frow (2013) 'The Australian space of lifestyles in comparative perspective', *Journal of Sociology*, 49(2–3), 224–245.
Bourdieu, P. (1993) *The Field of Cultural Production*, New York: Columbia University Press.
—— (1996) *The Rules of Art*, Cambridge: Polity.
Brunt, P., N. Thomas, S. Mallon, L. Bolton, D. Brown, D. Skinner, and S. Küchler (2012) *Art in Oceania: A New History*, London: Thames and Hudson.
Butler, R. (2005) 'Introduction' to Butler (ed.), *Radical Revisionism: An Anthology of Writings on Australian Art*, Brisbane: Institute of Modern Art, 7–36.
Carroll, K. von Zinnenburg (2014) *Art in the Time of Colony*, Farnham: Ashgate.
Carter, D. (2013) 'Drawing the line: Art in Australia and the contemporary modern' in *Always Almost Modern: Australian Print Cultures and Modernity*, North Melbourne: Australian Scholarly Publishing, 45–66.
Caruana, W. (2003) 'The collection of Indigenous Australian art: Beginnings and some highlights' in P. Green (ed.), *Building the Collection*, Canberra: National Gallery of Australia.
Clifford, J. (1988) 'On collecting art and culture' in J. Clifford (1988), *The Predicament of Culture: Twentieth-Century Ethnography, Literature, and Art*, Cambridge, MA: Harvard University Press.
Conrad, P. (2013–14) 'Girt by picture frame: Australia at the Royal Academy London', *The Monthly*, December 2013–January 2014, 69–71.
Conn, S. (2004) *History's Shadow: Native Americans and Historical Consciousness in the Nineteenth Century*, Chicago and London: University of Chicago Press.
Davis, M. (2007) 'The decline of the literary paradigm in Australian publishing', in D. Carter and A. Galligan (eds.), *Making Books: Contemporary Australian Publishing*, St. Lucia, Queensland: University of Queensland Press.
Eagle, M. (2011) 'Expressions of social identity by settlers and indigenes in the first 80 years of British colonisation' in Anderson (ed.) (2011), *The Cambridge Companion to Australian Art*, Melbourne: Cambridge University Press, pp. 38–54.
Edwards, D. and D. Mimmocchi (2013) (eds.), *Sydney Moderns: Art for a New World*, Sydney: Art Gallery of New South Wales.
English, J. (2005) *The Economy of Prestige: Prizes, Awards, and the Circulation of Cultural Value*, Cambridge, MA: Harvard University Press.
Fabiani, J.-L. (2001) 'Les règles du champ' in B. Lahire (ed.), *Le travail sociologique de Pierre Bourdieu. Dettes et critiques*, Paris: La Découverte.
Fisher, L. (2012) 'The art/ethnography binary: Post-colonial tensions within the field of Australian Aboriginal art', *Cultural Sociology*, 6(2), 251–270.
Fligstein, N. and D. McAdam (2012) *A Theory of Fields*, Oxford: Oxford University Press.
Frow, J. (1995) *Cultural Studies and Cultural Value*, Oxford: Clarendon Press.
Gardner, A. (2011) 'Post-provincial, still peripheral. Australian art on the global stage 1980–2009' in Anderson (2011) (ed.), *The Cambridge Companion to Australian Art*, Melbourne: Cambridge University Press, pp. 231–247.
Grenfell, M. and C. Hardy (2007) *Pierre Bourdieu and the Visual Arts*, Oxford and New York: Berg.
Hanquinet, L., H. Roose, and M. Savage (2014) 'The eyes of the beholder: Aesthetic preferences and the remaking of cultural capital', *Sociology*, 48(1), 111–132.
Harris, J. (1995) *Federal Art and National Culture: The Politics of Identity in New Deal America*, Cambridge: Cambridge University Press.
Healy, C. (2008) *Forgetting Aborigines*, Sydney: University of New South Wales Press.
Inglis, A. (2011) 'Imperial perspectives on art in nineteenth-century Australia' in Anderson (2011) *The Cambridge Companion to Australian Art*, Melbourne: Cambridge University Press, pp. 55–70.
Jones, P. (2011) 'The art of contact: Encountering an Aboriginal aesthetic from the eighteenth to the twentieth centuries' in Anderson (ed.) (2011), *The Cambridge Companion to Australian Art*, Melbourne: Cambridge University Press, pp. 22–37.
Langton, M. (1999) 'Certainty and uncertainty: Aboriginal studies as the fulcrum of national self-consciousness' in Smith (1999), *First Peoples, Second Chance: The Humanities and Aboriginal Australia*, Canberra: Australian Academy of the Humanities, pp. 23–46.
Lemieux, C. (2011) 'Le crepuscule des champs. Limites d'un concept ou disparition d'une réalité historique?' in M. de Fornel and A. Ogien (eds.), *Bourdieu. Théoricien de la practique*, Paris: Éditions de L'École des Hautes Études en Sciences Sociales.

McLean, I. (1998) *White Aborigines: Identity Politics in Australian Art*, Melbourne: Cambridge University Press.

—— (1999) 'Being and nothing – figuring Aboriginality in Australian art history' in Smith T. (ed.) (1999), *First Peoples, Second Chance: The Humanities and Aboriginal Australia*, Canberra: Australian Academy of the Humanities, pp. 105–130.

—— (ed.) (2011) *How Aborigines Invented the Idea of Contemporary Art*, Sydney: Institute of Modern Art/Power Publications.

Michaels, E. (1994) *Bad Aboriginal Art: Tradition, Media and Technological Horizons*, St. Leonards, NSW: Allen and Unwin.

Morphy, H. (2007) *Becoming Art: Exploring Cross-Cultural Categories*, Oxford and New York: Berg.

Myers, F.R. (2002) *Painting Culture: The Making of an Aboriginal High Art*, Durham and London: Duke University Press.

—— (2006) '"Primitivism", anthropology and the category of "primitive art"' in C. Tilley, W. Keane, S. Kuechler, M. Rowlands, and P. Spyer (eds.), *Handbook of Material Culture*, London: Sage.

—— (2013) 'Disturbances in the field: Exhibiting Aboriginal art in the US', *Journal of Sociology*, 49(2–3): 151–172.

Novak, B. (2007) *Nature and Culture: American Landscape and Painting, 1825–1875*, New York: Oxford University Press.

Poulot, D. (1997) *Musée, nation, patrimoine, 1789–1815*, Paris: Gallimard.

Reynolds, H. (2013) *Forgotten War*, Sydney: New South Books.

Savage, M. and E.B. Silva (2013) 'Field analysis in cultural sociology', *Cultural Sociology*, 7(2): 111–126.

Sherman, D.J. (1989) *Worthy Monuments: Art Museums and the Politics of Culture in Nineteenth-Century France*, Cambridge, MA: Harvard University Press.

—— (2011) *French Primitivism and the Ends of Empire, 1945–1975*, Chicago: University of Chicago Press.

Smith, B. (1960) *European Vision and the South Pacific 1768–1850*, Oxford: Oxford University Press.

—— (1979) *Place, Taste and Tradition: A Study of Australian Art since 1788*, Melbourne: Oxford University Press.

Smith, T. (1999) (ed.) *First Peoples, Second Chance: The Humanities and Aboriginal Australia*, Canberra: Australian Academy of the Humanities.

Thomas, B. (2011) 'Daryl Lindsay and the appreciation of indigenous art at the National Gallery of Victoria, Melbourne in the 1940's: "No mere collection of interesting curiosities"', *Journal of Art Historiography*, 4, 1–32.

Thomas, N. (1999) *Possessions: Indigenous Art/Colonial Culture*, London: Thames and Hudson.

—— (2012) 'Introduction' in P. Brunt, N. Thomas, S. Mallon, L. Bolton, D. Brown, D. Skinner, and S. Küchler (2012), *Art in Oceania: A New History*, London: Thames and Hudson, 10–25.

Turner, C. (2005) (ed.) *Art and Social Change: Contemporary Art in Asia and the Pacific*, Canberra: Pandanus Books.

Van den Bosch, A. (2005) *The Australian Art World: Aesthetics in a Global Market*, Sydney: Allen and Unwin.

Visweswaran, K. (2010) *Un/common Cultures: Racism and the Rearticulation of Cultural Difference*, Durham and London: Duke University Press.

White, A. (2011) 'Foreign natives. Australian modernism 1915–1955' in J. Anderson (2011) (ed.), *The Cambridge Companion to Australian Art*, Melbourne: Cambridge University Press, pp. 109–121.

17

The world market of translation in the globalization era
Symbolic capital and cultural diversity in the publishing field

Gisèle Sapiro

Introduction

How do cultural products circulate accross cultures? In contradistinction to painting or music, written texts often require the mediation of translation in order to move between cross-cultural and national borders. The circulation of literary works thus constitutes an interesting case study for the sociology of culture, and more specifically for the empirical analysis of processes of intermediation, which has come to the fore in recent scholarship, with a growing focus on the agents acting as mediators between cultural goods and their consumers. A sociological approach to translation, considered as a social practice, needs to take into account the agents involved in this process: publishers, translators, authors, critics, scholars, state representatives. Among these agents, publishers have come to play a major role in the international circulation of books, in original language as well as in translation.

Despite some early significant studies (Bourdieu 1977; Coser et al. 1982), the sociology of publishing did not develop before the late 1990s, in contrast to the history of the book and, more recently, the economics of the book market, both of which have become specialized areas. Bourdieu's empirical study of the French field of publishing (Bourdieu 1999) provided a theoretical and methodological framework which fostered a series of sociological studies on publishing, but it was confined to specific nations. This paper proposes to rethink Bourdieu's economy of symbolic goods and field theory on a global scale, by demonstrating its heuristic value for the sociology of the international circulation of books, and more specifically for the sociology of translation[1]. Bourdieu's approach of the publishing field is presented in the first section. In the second section, I propose three theoretical and methodological directions for extending Bourdieu's model to a global sociological analysis of the circulation of books in translation: first, a displacement from the national to the global market of translation; second, a focus on publisher's strategy and list; third, a study of the reception processes.

While participating in the transnational approaches which have developed in the wake of the criticism against 'methodological nationalism' (Wimmer and Glick Schiller 2003), the proposed model does not reject comparativism: the nationalization of fields is a historical fact which started in the nineteenth century, with the attempt of nation-states to monopolize education and control the national markets, and it contributed to the differentiation of fields (Sapiro 2013). Whereas this fact should not overshadow, as it has until recently, the role of international organizations (like UNESCO), transnational processes (such as the expansion of markets) and intercultural exchanges (circulation of agents, models and goods), the nation-states are still active agents in the globalization era and a relevant unit of analysis for the fields of cultural production. The model proposed here combines three levels of analysis: macro, meso, and micro (Sapiro 2012). The concept of field helps moving from one level to the other: on one hand, national fields and markets are more or less embedded in transnational fields and markets (here the world market of translation), where they occupy a central (dominant) or peripheral (dominated) position, and which have an impact on their evolution (for instance the international circulation of models of publishing from the centers to the periphery); on the other, agents' strategies (for instance, a publisher's line) take place within a system of relations (competition, cooperation, alliances) and a space of possibilities (defined by constraints such as censorship but also by the history of the field) at the national and/or trans/international level.

The field of publishing and the economy of symbolic goods

In his seminal 1971 article on the market of symbolic goods, Bourdieu (1971) developed a theory of the production and circulation of such goods. The field of cultural production is structured around the opposition between small-scale and large-scale circulation. The law of the market rules the pole of large-scale circulation: the value of a work is measured according to its profitability, that is, in the case of books, sales. By contrast, at the pole of small-scale circulation, aesthetic, or intellectual criteria, emanating from the judgement of peers or specialists (writers, literary critics, scholars), prevail over economic considerations. This pole thus functions as an 'economic world reversed' (Bourdieu 1983). However, its functionning is not entirely devoid of economic rationality: symbolic recognition by the peers is likely to bring in the long run a larger consecration of the work and of its author. When a work is canonized as a classic and included in anthologies, academic programs and literary textbooks, it becomes a profitable product for its publisher. This conversion of symbolic capital into economic capital is a long-term process, as opposed to the search of short-term profit that is typical of the book industry's commercial pole. It distinguishes the economy of cultural industries, based on the production of prototypes (each product is unique), from that of other industrial production.

The publisher plays a major role in the process of legitimating literary works. In his 1977 article titled 'La production de la croyance' ('The production of belief'), Bourdieu analyzed this role as a transfer of symbolic capital from the publisher to the writer: to publish is to consecrate. Consequently, the publisher 'creates the creator'. Her or his own authority is based on the 'credit' she or he is awarded by all participants in the recognition chain, ranging from writers to members of literary juries and literary critics. This chain demarcates a space that Bourdieu theorized with the concept of field. However, fields cannot be reduced to networks (like in Howard Becker's *Art Worlds*, 1984). At odds with interactionist theory, the concept of field implies a structural approach of the power relations within a relatively autonomous social space, characterized by specific rules of the game and a specific type of capital. According to the amount of symbolic capital (based on recognition according to the field's specific criteria) they hold, agents occupy a different position in the field, wherein they compete to achieve recognition and impose their idea of cultural legitimacy. The structure of the field results from the unequal distribution of social properties and symbolic capital among the agents. Fields are generally organized around two main oppositions: dominant v. dominated (established agents and newcomers); autonomy v. heteronomy (small-scale v. large-scale circulation; see Bourdieu 1992, 1993; Sapiro 2003).

This theory of symbolic goods gave momentum and new directions to the sociology of literature which developed in the 1980s and the 1990s, while Bourdieu's insights on publishing were echoed by major historians of the book like Robert Darnton and Roger Chartier. Bourdieu's 1999 empirical survey on French contemporary publishing was the first extended sociological study on this object. Based on a statistical survey, it provided a theoretical and methodological framework for studying the field of publishing, opening up a new domain for sociological investigation (see, for instance, John Thompson's qualitative research on the Anglo-American trade publishing, 2010).

The main difference between Bourdieu's approach and economic surveys is that he takes into account symbolic capital and tries to build indicators to measure it. First, he argues, the selection process can be observed sociologically through a study of the chain of agents within it, from the series editor to the board and the publisher or manager, including writers and translators who recommend the manuscript. The editorial board, which gathers together people belonging to various networks in the media (literary juries), functions as a 'bank of social and symbolic capital' (Bourdieu 1999: 125). But this is not all. In order to understand the signification of a single publisher's selection principles, one has to reconstruct the whole space in which she or he acts and her/his relations with rivals. The perception of this space orients not only the publishers' practices, but also frames the writers' representations when they make the decision to send their work to a specific publisher (in France as in many other countries, publishers still play a major role in the selection process, contrary to the Anglophone world where literary agents have taken this function over). Alongside the publisher's role in the recognition process, this field approach is Bourdieu's main contribution to our understanding of the publishing world.

Bourdieu's survey focused on the field of French literary publishers, leaving aside publishers specialized in other domains. The first methodological question was: what is the relevant unit? A conglomerate composed of different publishers cannot be considered as a unit. Having a brand name is a minimal condition, yet not a sufficient one, because it is does not necessarily imply the existence of an autonomous publishing policy for a publisher who belongs to a group. Consequently, some other indicators of such autonomy were taken into account in order to determine the sample. Very small publishers who don't reach a certain level of production were also left aside. The sample was composed of 61 publishers of French or translated literature.

The second methodological question was the construction of relevant indicators of publishers' position in the field. Five groups of variables were defined: 1) juridical and financial status of the publishing house; 2) commercial dependency; 3) weight on the market; 4) symbolic capital; 5) share of translated literature in the list (percentage of the overall number of titles edited) and languages translated. The fourth group of variables is the most original compared to economic surveys, since it establishes indicators of symbolic capital on the basis of the age of the firm, the prestige of its backlist as measured by the Jurt index (number of citations of authors of the list in a corpus of 28 textbooks of literary history, dictionaries, or literary overviews published after World War II), and the number of Nobel Prize winners in the list. The fifth group, which is about translation, will be discussed below.

These groups of variables were submitted to Multiple Correspondence Analysis (MCA), a tool for exploring and representing geometrically the data: the higher the number of modalities individuals share, the closer they will appear on the graphic of individuals (here the publishing houses); by the same token, the higher the number of individuals sharing the same modalities, the closest these modalities will appear on the graphic of variables (Benzécri 1992; Rouanet and Le Roux 1993; Lebaron 2006; for an application to the literary field, see Sapiro 2002). The first (horizontal) axis of MCA distributed the publishing houses according to the overall amount of both economic and symbolic capital they hold. It thus opposed the oldest firms, founded before 1945, and endowed with a high symbolic capital as measured through their backlist, to small publishers born after the war, most of them since the 1970s. While the first ones are located in the heart of Paris and mainly ruled by male heirs, the second ones are more likely to be found in province and headed by women with high cultural capital. On the second (vertical) axis, publishers are mainly differentiated according to their being independent or not: big and small independent publishers are opposed to middle-size firms which have been integrated in a larger conglomerate.

The result of the analysis challenges the common opposition between conglomerates and independent publishers. It is often argued that the latter are innovative, whereas the former favor the standardization of literary products. This alleged relation between innovation and independence is put into question here. From Bourdieu's analysis, one can draw the conclusion that independence is not a sufficient condition to ensure innovation.

Bourdieu was especially interested in the big independent publishers. He argued that even those endowed with the highest symbolic capital, like Gallimard, rely on their past and tend to manage their assets, their prestigious backlist, to the detriment of innovation. They also contribute to standardization by preferring traditional novels to more original literary experiments. They praise the storytelling model, imitating the mainstream American novel, against the formalism of the French modern novel since the Nouveau Roman, which is denounced as abstract or self-centred. This argument, Bourdieu claimed, conceals commercial criteria underlying their choices and decisions.

Innovation in the field is mainly supplied by small publishers. Since they cannot afford to pay high advances on fees to well-known writers, they need to take risks and discover new authors in order to survive. This contribution to the renewal of the literary production gives new impetus to the dynamics of the field. However, as a result of this dynamics, these small publishers often cannot keep their authors when these achieve recognition: for instance, publisher Jacqueline Chambon was the discoverer of Elfriede Jelinek in France long before she won the Nobel Prize, but by the time the award came, she had already moved to the larger and older Éditions du Seuil. This is not an isolated case. The small Bostonian publisher David Godine told me in an interview (December 9, 2007) that when one of his authors gets a review in the *New York Times*, he knows that she or he will be immediately contacted by a literary agent who will take her or him to a larger firm, which offers high advances on fee.

What are the implications of Bourdieu's analysis for translation? Variables regarding translation were coded, as we noted above, in the fifth group. It included the percentage of translated literature in the publishers' list and the languages translated. These variables appeared to be significant in the MCA. The first variable opposed, on the first axis, large and small publishers: while translated literature represented less than 10 per cent of the big companies' production, the rate often climbed above 25 per cent in small publishers' list. Small publishers thus take more financial risks with translation, though the comparison is a little misleading since big firms publish a larger variety of books, including practical, youth, essays, along with literature, while small ones are often more specialized (in literature in the present case). And of all domains, literature has the highest rate of translation: it reaches between 35 to 43 per cent of new novels in France. Consequently, if we consider only the literary production of these publishers, the rate of translations must be higher than 10 per cent. For instance, translations were estimated to represent about 25 per cent of the novels published by Le Seuil in 1999. A more precise survey would be required in order to compare the actual share of translations in the literary production of these publishers.

Moreover, the rate of translations probably also varies as a function of the publisher's symbolic capital: idea-typical is the case of the very prestigious Éditions de Minuit, the publisher of Beckett and of the Nouveau Roman, who publishes no literary translations at all. This can be explained by the fact that publishers endowed with high symbolic capital have many French authors and receive numerous manuscripts in French, so that they are less motivated to search for new works abroad and invest in translation costs. By contrast, newcomers lacking literary prestige are not appealing to French writers; translation can therefore be a means for accumulating symbolic capital and building a credible list. Specializing in translation from rare languages like Chinese can also offer newcomers and small firms a 'niche', a term used by economists to designate specialized domains where competition is limited.

This leads us to the second variable of the fifth group of indicators described earlier: the languages translated. Big publishers translate from English and from Western European languages. They take part in the harsh competition around best-sellers, with specific means and specialized agents like scouts, foreign rights persons, and literary agents, whereas small ones seldom translate from English, since they cannot afford the expenses. This explains the role they play in discovering writers in peripheral or semi-peripheral languages, according to the 'niche' strategy.

Bourdieu's insightful analysis demonstrates the relevance of publishing to the sociology of translation and more broadly to the study of the social conditions of circulation of cultural products, as it helps explain how and why literary works (or other categories of books such as academic ones) travel. Moreover, the focus on the publishing industry, which is the oldest one, invites us to historicize, and thus relativize, the globalization process in the market of cultural goods (Sapiro 2010a). The research program he launched with this inquiry, that his sudden death prevented him from completing, was taken over by other scholars. It has developed in three main directions that will be presented in the next section.

From the national to the global book market

Studying books in translation requires changing the focus from the national to the international book market, in which the first one is increasingly embedded as the second becomes global. This international market has its own structure, one that partly determines the unequal flows of translations and the power relations in the process of buying or selling rights. These transactions must also be analyzed in the light of the publishers' strategies and of their list: what are their criteria for selecting books to be translated? What is the balance between economic and symbolic criteria? How are different languages represented in the lists? From a methodological standpoint, this implies analyzing databases of books, parallel to consulting archives and/or conducting interviews. The change of focus from the national to the international market does not mean that the national level is no more relevant: it is still decisive if we are to understand the importation and reception processes, as will be shown in the last subsection.

The global market of translation

The change of focus from a national to a global scale has been successfully experimented on various objects, ranging from political economy to literature. Translation is related to both these domains. On the one hand, the international circulation of literature depends mostly on translation. On the other, translation is not a disembodied activity but a social practice, which depends on intermediaries and, for a large part, on the book trade.

Various models for thinking this global space have been elaborated. The core-periphery systemic model is endowed with a powerful explanatory force. It has been insightfully applied by Wallerstein (1974, 1980, 1989) in his world-system analysis. Abram de Swaan (1993, 2001) used it to delineate the system of power relations between linguistic communities as assessed by the number of primary and secondary speakers. On the basis of de Swaan's model, Johan Heilbron (1999) described the functioning of the world system of translation. Using the Unesco *Index Translationum* database, he showed that translations flows move mainly from the core to the periphery. More than half of the translated books in the worlds are translated from English, the hyper-central language: the rate was around 45 per cent in the 1980s and reached 59 per cent in the 1990s. Translations from three central languages, French, German, and Russian, represented each 10 per cent to 12 per cent of this market until 1989, but the number of translations from Russian drastically decreased in the 1990s (it fell to 2.5 per cent), leaving only two central languages apart from English. In 1978, six languages (Italian, Spanish, Swedish, Danish, Polish, and Czeck) had a semi-peripheral position, with a share that varies from 1 to 3 per cent of the international market. There were only four semi-peripheral languages left in the 1990s (Italian, Spanish, Russian, and Swedish). The other languages all had a share of less than one per cent, and may thus be considered as peripheral. These rates clearly indicate that the intensification of exchanges in the globalization era – the number of translations in the world increased by 50 per cent between 1980 and 2000 – did not imply a diversification: on the contrary, English has reinforced its domination, while diversity has diminished, despite the rise of Asiatic languages on this market (Sapiro ed. 2008).

The core-periphery model was also applied to literature by Itamar Even-Zohar in his polysystem theory (Even-Zohar 1990; Toury 1995). Polysystem theory shares with field theory a relational approach, though it is more functionalist than structuralist. The second main difference is that it is more focused on texts than on social agents (individuals and institutions). Field theory was extended to an international scale by Pascale Casanova (1999), who used the dominant-dominated opposition and the notion of literary capital to describe the power relations between countries in the *World Republic of Letters*. The relation between core and periphery offers a spatial representation of the dominant-dominated opposition in Bourdieu's theory of social space, making possible its extension to the geo-political relations between countries and/or cultures (for a general theory of unequal spatial relations under global capitalism in a Marxist perspective, see Harvey 2006). The advantage of combining these two sets of notions is that the center-periphery opposition is a powerful descriptive model for spatial relations, including semi-central and semi-peripheral positions. Centrality is also a measure in network analysis, which is a useful tool for describing the relations between agents, for instance, in our case publishers from two countries linked by a common title that was translated by the foreign publisher. Grounded on the unequal distribution of capital (Bourdieu 1979), the dominant-dominated opposition provides an explanatory framework for the phenomenon of centrality. As we saw, Bourdieu's theory also differentiates symbolic capital – and thus symbolic domination – from economic and political one, a distinction which is highly relevant for understanding the patterns of international circulation of cultural products.

Combining the core-periphery model with field theory and the economy of symbolic goods allows us to describe the market of translation as embedded in both the international book market and the international relations between countries (Sapiro 2010a). On this market, different domains (like literature or the different disciplines in the social sciences and humanities) enjoy a relative autonomy and have their specific agents, stakes, and rules of functioning. They thus constitute more or less internationalized fields (Gingras 2002). At its most autonomous pole, the literary field has its specific agents: writers, literary translators, literary critics, and its specific aesthetic criteria.

The core-periphery model also allows us to denationalize the book history. The book market is structured by two different kinds of borders, which do not necessarily overlap and which can compete one with the other: linguistic borders and State borders (which circumscribe a legal space for laws on freedom of the press and customs duties, as well as for the implementation of public policies). Historically, the linguistic areas, such as the Anglophone, the Francophone, the Spanish- and Arab-speaking areas, were structured around centers located in central cities like London and Paris, and the periphery, which included the province and the countries under the hegemony of these centers (for instance the United States in the Anglophone area, or Latin-America for the Spanish-speaking one). The colonization extended the territories of circulation of books in the linguistic areas. The emergence of an international market of translation was strongly related to the cultural construction of national identities and to the development of the book trade (Anderson 1991; Thiesse 1998). While it had been until then defined by linguistic rather than by State borders, this market was increasingly embedded in the formal cultural exchanges between countries (Espagne and Werner 1990–1994), and it began to organize at the end of the nineteenth century, with the Berne international convention on literary property.

Since the 1970s, with the growth of the book market and its concentration around large conglomerates, some of which are transnational, this market has become more global and unified. It has its specific agents (literary agents, foreign right persons, translators), places (international bookfairs), and rules of functionning. The globalization of the book market thus entailed the professionalization of agents specialized in mediation between written cultures, a process which provides a framework of analysis to understand the evolution of the social condition of translators (Sapiro 2014a). If the states are still major agents in this market, it has become more autonomous from their control, and they have to adapt to its rules. Though still relatively autonomous, the national book markets are increasingly embedded in the international book market, which mediates between the globalization process and the changes in the publishing industry at the national level.

Combining the models by Wallerstein, De Swaan, and Heilbron, we can contrast the core countries of the Western world with the peripheral countries of the East and of the South. Rather than the number of speakers, it is the number of readers which is relevant here. A second parameter is the development of publishing, which occurred much later (if at all) in many countries where the elites were bilingual and there was no standardized national language, as in the former colonies and in the so-called Third World (Pym and Chrupala 2005). The globalization of the book market has fostered the development of publishing in many of these countries since the 1980s.

Furthermore, economic factors and the size of the book market are not sufficient to explain the translational power relation between countries (Heilbron and Sapiro 2007). Political factors must be taken into account (see Jacquemond 1992; Popa 2010; Sapiro 2002), as must cultural ones (Casanova 2002). As suggested by Casanova (1999), language and cultural traditions are endowed with symbolic capital, according to the number of world masterpieces they have provided. This symbolic capital can vary between domains: French literature and German philosophy are endowed with a high specific capital; this explains that there were still more translations of philosophical works from German than from English into French in the 1990s (see Sapiro and Popa 2008).

This brings us back to the economy of symbolic goods and field theory. The international book market can be considered as structured, like the national markets, around the opposition between large-scale and small-scale circulation. On one side are best-sellers and other commercial genres: romance, touristic guides, practical books – all short-sellers that are sold in tens to hundreds thousands of copies. On the other are scholarly works and upmarket literary works, including novels, short stories, poetry, drama, which only exceptionnally reach ten or twenty thousand copies in the first year after publication. These differences are reflected in literary agents' classifications, which distinguish commercial literature from literary up-market products. Some national book markets are divided into distinct segments: in the United-States, the nonprofit publishers (mainly the University presses, but also independent publishers like The New Press or Archipelago Books) have a different economic organization than the trade publishers, though some trade publishers do publish upmarket books. Other markets, like the French one, are much more unified. Another specificity of the French book market as opposed to that in the US is the existence of a dense network of independent bookstores. This is one of the conditions for maintaining a pole of small-scale circulation, since the economic constraints are in large part imposed through the distribution and the bookstores chains (Bourdieu 1999: 145; on the consequences of the concentration of the distribution in the Anglophone book market, see Thompson 2010). The survival of such independent bookstores is due to the French book policy (namely the law on the fixed book price). The French book policy supports the pole of small-scale circulation in other ways, notably by subsidizing translations of literary works as well as scholarly works in the social sciences and the humanities from French and into French. This public policy can be regarded as the structural equivalent of the role of Philanthropic foundations in supporting nonprofit publishing, despite their being private organizations. The objective is, in both cases, to encourage creative and intellectual projects credited with a cultural or pedagogic value. Translation is part of such a mission.

Bourdieu's analytical model has many advantages: it allows us to compare the structure of publishing in different countries in the light of structural homology, notwithstanding their differences and specificities regarding the juridical status of firms, the role of the state, or the division of labor between publishers, literary agents, and the chain of distribution. Moreover, it enables us to take into account the specific agents (individuals and institutions) as well as the international circulation of publishing models. For instance, the literary French publishing model was imported to the United States by agents such as Richard Seaver, a leading editor and publisher, who also introduced there writers like Beckett, Ionesco, Genêt, Duras (Sapiro 2010b). This has to do with publishers' strategies, which is the topic of the next section.

This model also helps to break with very simple oppositions between countries. Though it is certainly right to locate the impulse for the commercial development of publishing in England, the United States, and Germany (Schiffrin 2001; Thompson 2010), the national book markets, in France like in the US or elsewhere, are all structured around the same opposition between small-scale and large-scale circulation. This opposition is still in force, notwithstanding the siffenning of commercial constraints. A quantitative survey on the translations of foreign literature into French from 1980 to 2002 (Sapiro ed. 2008), has shown that the rise in the numbers of translations was largely due to commercial literature translated from English and to youth books (again mostly translated from English). However, although they have not increased as quickly, translations of upmarket literature have been stable, and genres like poetry or drama, far from disappearing, continue to hold a significant share in translations from other central or semi-peripheral languages (around 8 per cent of the literary translations from German or Italian and 15 per cent from Spanish are poetry, as opposed to 2 per cent from English).

Furthermore, while the pole of large-scale circulation has its international actors (scouts, foreign right persons, literary agents), publishers at the pole of small-scale circulation do, as already suggested, have their own networks in the specific relatively autonomous fields: writers, literary critics, translators for the literary field, scholars for the academic fields. These international networks embody the elective affinities between publishers in different countries, a factor often emphasized in the interviews I conducted with American, French, and Israeli publishers and editors, expressing a homology of position in different national publishing fields.

The change of focus from the national to the international book market also reveals the harsh competition between countries over territories. Contrary to the common idea that globalization entails a deterritorialization, the case of the book industry reveals the intensification of the competition and struggle over territories, especially within linguistic areas, as illustrated by this excerpt of an interview I conducted in October 2007 with the head of an American imprint in a large multinational conglomerate:

> We always have a list of territories appended to our contracts, and this has to do with the open market, so that we are very careful to try and get as many territories as we can. And the British publishers traditionally had all the territories that used to be in the old British Commonwealth when Britain was empire, and the United States has had to chip away very hard at that because there is no empire, and why should you automatically get the right to sell in India? India is not your colony anymore and neither is South Africa, neither is Singapore or Malaysia or Hong Kong. We face the Pacific from California actually; it is easier for us to market there. Why shouldn't we send our books there? Yes, you can have Europe because it is right across the channel. But why shouldn't we have Asia? We'll battle you for South America and Africa and Asia as well. So it is constantly a matter of contention. The thing that makes me laugh is that I bought a book from a British publisher, and I looked at their schedule of territories, it is arranged by continent. And they actually had Antarctica. Underneath, 'British Antarctica'. Antarctica is divided, so they had British Antarctica in their territories, which made me laugh out loud; I'd never seen anything like that. I count the days there might be a bookstore. I don't know when. There is more likely to be one on Mars or the Moon before there is one in Antarctica but they have it on their schedule of territories just so that we, Americans, don't think we can peddle a book into Antarctica. That was really funny.

For this reason, publishers try to get world rights for translations, instead of sharing it with publishers in other parts of the same linguistic area. This is all the more true with the rise of sales through internet, which put in competition different editions in the same language, for instance the British and American ones: the British books being more expensive, British publishers fear the competition with the American ones.

Publishers' strategies and the list

Studying publishers' strategies and their lists is another way of developing Bourdieu's sociological approach. This is not a new object of investigation: historians of the book have long been tracing the stories of single publishers and analyzing their strategies, some of which, as already stated, more or less inspired by Bourdieu's theory of field. But the history of book has not until recently identified translation as a specific object. Furthermore, very few studies on publishers are based on a quantitative analysis of their lists. Quantitative analysis is a rich source for confronting publishers' discourses (delivered in public settings, such as the media or memoirs, or in a private context, in correspondence which can be found in archives and in interviews) to their practice.

The focus on the publishers' lists, in turn, has been a tool for testing some of Bourdieu's insights. It obliges to rethink Bourdieu's dual economic model at the level of a single publishing house, since shortsellers often co-exist with longsellers in a same list (Simonin 2004). The investigation thus has to turn to the publisher's strategy and to the classification principles of the list, in particular the series, domains or genres.

Translations can play a role in the building of a list. Such was the case for les Éditions du Seuil, a newcomer in the field after World War II, which invested in German and Eastern European literatures at a time when Germany was a defeated country and Eastern Europe was being dominated by the USSR: Gunter Grass, Heinrich Böll entered Le Seuil's list at that time, long before they were awarded the Nobel prize (Serry 2002). Around 1975, Le Seuil had become a big literary publisher. The translations from English began to increase, rising beyond those from German, thus illustrating the unequal power relations between languages. Le Seuil's initial strategy cannot be reduced to an economic strategy but resulted also from cultural and political motives and was partly based on elective affinities – Catholic networks – with publishers from other countries. Such cultural and political motives explain also the choices of publishers who translated Eastern European literature during the Communist period (Popa 2010).

Focusing on series is a means to delineate the space of translated literature, especially in countries like France where 'foreign literature' ('*littérature étrangère*') is traditionally distinguished from literature in French and published in separate series. The space of translated literature in France is structured around the opposition between large-scale and small-scale circulation (Sapiro ed. 2008). On a first level, this opposition globally differentiates small publishers from big ones (Bourdieu 1999: 132). But on a second level, we should distinguish different series in the same publishing house: a series of foreign literature as opposed to a series of thrillers or of best-sellers, for instance. A series of foreign literature like Gallimard's '*Du monde entier*' has a very high symbolic capital: to be included in it is a real consecration for a foreign author. But it has a small-scale circulation, most of the books published in it being longsellers (Sapiro 2011). Gallimard has also a series of detective novels (the 'black' series), where translations – mainly from English – are not separate from novels in French, and where the sales figures are higher. The relative weight of these series in each publishing house could provide the grounds for a comparative study of the balance between symbolic and economic capital, but such a comparison requires a very large and thorough survey of their lists, including literature in French and other categories of books as well.

However, the source language variable, which is specific to translated literature, is a good indicator to compare series and to measure cultural diversity. It appears that whereas the pole of large-scale circulation is characterized by linguistic concentration on the hyper-central English language, there is a high linguistic diversity at the pole of small-scale circulation (Sapiro ed. 2008). The foreign literature series or domains of the big literary publishers like Gallimard, Le Seuil, or Fayard include novels and other literary works translated from twenty to thirty different languages (and up to forty countries), English representing only one-third (and the works translated from English coming from different English-speaking countries, including the former colonies and peripheral areas). By contrast, most of the thrillers and romance literature are translated from English. Some publishers like Harlequin specialize in romance. They represent the very commercial pole of the publishing field. Laffont is an example of a big publisher with a diversified list, what is called in France '*un éditeur de littérature générale*', but it does not have a high symbolic capital, and it does not have such an important series of foreign literature as Gallimard and Le Seuil; it can be located at the commercial pole of the field of literary publishing. In its series called 'best-sellers', 75 per cent of the titles are translated from English, most of the rest being written in French.

At the pole of small-scale circulation, the series of foreign literature in big publishing houses must be distinguished from that of small publishers. The degree of language diversity is of course much lower in the lists of small publishers whose strategy is, as already stated, to specialize in a few languages other than English. But as suggested by Bourdieu, they often – though not always and not for all languages – act as 'discoverer' for unknown authors who, when they gain recognition, enter the list of a bigger literary publisher like Gallimard or Le Seuil (as illustrated by the example of Jelinek).

If we combine the criteria of linguistic diversity of translated literary books with the percentage of translations from English, three clusters of foreign literature publishers or series can be distinguished: the small publishers, the big literary publishers' foreign literature series, and the commercial series. These can only partly be superimposed upon Bourdieu's three poles (notably the distinction between big and small publishers), and do not correspond exactly, mainly because of my focus on series and the different way I built my linguistic indicators (isolating English and counting the number of source languages represented).

While the focus on series as a unit of analysis is relevant to the study of the French publishing field, it is not in the Anglo-American publishing industry, where series have become a relatively rare classification principle. The structural equivalent for these countries would be the imprints in conglomerates, for instance, the former publishing houses which were acquired by a group in which they became an imprint, and where they enjoy more or less autonomy, some of them specializing in either upmarket or commercial products.

Databases of books in translation are also a rich source for exploring the circulation and exchanges between publishers in different countries. For instance, from research on the translation of French literary works in the United States between 1990 and 2003 (Sapiro forthcoming), it appears that Gallimard concentrates 29 per cent of the titles in translation, a measure of its centrality, which is here due to the symbolic capital rather than to the seize or business of the publisher. This is also proved by the fact that Gallimard is followed far behind by Le Seuil (7 per cent), Éditions de Minuit and Presses de la Cité (around 5 per cent each), Grasset and POL (around 4 per cent each); Éditions de Minuit and POL being two small publishers endowed with a great amount of symbolic capital, whose share is equivalent to that of larger and more profitable houses such as Grasset or Albin Michel. Most of the publishers who had literary works translated in the US during this period reside in Paris, which attests to the centrality of this city in the Francophone area. On the American side, the publishers appear to be more dispersed quantitatively and geographically, even if we focus on the sixty-nine publishers who published at least five titles during the period under study. We can split them in three groups: imprints in large conglomerates, small independent publishers, and university presses, the distribution of the translations among them being uneven. Though some prestigious imprints affiliated with large groups such as Knopf; Harcourt Brace Jovanovich (which has since then disappeared as an imprint); and Farrar Straus and Giroux, still continue to publish translations of French literature, they represent only one-third (23) of the sixty-nine publishers who published at least five titles during the period, whereas 40 per cent (27) are independent publishers, and 19 per cent (13) university presses. One quarter of these sixty-nine are nonprofit publishers. This reveals the investment of the non-profit sector in translation as the trade sector tends to abandon it because it is considered as not profitable enough. Moreover, the small publishers tend to take more risk in investing in contemporary literature, whereas the imprints in conglomerates prefer to manage their assets and publish classical works (Sapiro 2010a).

The focus on the publishers' strategies also opens up a whole domain of research for studying the norms of translations and connecting social factors to translation pratices. In his insightful article on 'The nature and role of norms in translation', Gideon Toury (1995: 53–69) emphasized the socio-dimensional aspects of the constraints that bear upon translators. These constraints are not only internalized by translators in their practice, but sometimes imposed upon them by the publisher in the process of revising the manuscript (Sapiro 2008a). Evidence for this process can be found in archives. The translation practices also depend on the habitus of translators, their social trajectory and education – a whole research domain that is still waiting to be explored (Simeoni 1998; Sapiro 2014b).

Reception

Reflection on norms of translation arose from a change of focus from the source to the target culture (Holmes *et al.* 1978; Even-Zohar 1990; Toury 1995). But while the reception process has been investigated for many years in literary studies (see for instance Molloy 1972), its rich potential for the sociology translation was not fully explored until the last two decades. Some recent socio-historical research on the reception of foreign works has combined Bourdieu's theory of the field of publishing and his reflections on the international circulation of ideas (Bourdieu 2002). These studies focused either on the reception of a single author through different periods or on the import and reception of literary works from some specific language or area and their evolution (see for instance Jurt 1999; Sapiro 2002; Popa 2010), or on the 'import' of foreign literature at a given historical moment (Wilfert 2002; Sapiro ed. 2008). They share a common interest in the role and social properties of importers (writers, translators, publishers), and in the literary and social uses of the translated work according to the specific stakes of the target field. This approach situates publisher's strategies and their choices within a broader cultural context.

This does not mean that 'export' is not relevant: states do have export policies for their national cultures which must be, and have been, encompass in these works. The notion of 'cultural transfer' was developed in order to encompass both the export and import processes (Espagne and Werner 1990–1994). But as the international market of translation becomes free and global, some state representatives begin to act as literary agents, promoting national authors to be translated by publishers in the target country. It is not the place here to discuss the various reasons for these policies (commercial, political, or cultural). All the more if we consider that the motives of the importers can differ.

As Bourdieu (2002) reminded us, citing Marx, texts circulate without their context; their signification is provided by the context of reception. The publisher, the series, sometimes the preface, the presentation of the text and of its author, along with the translation itself – all these elements contribute to assign a meaning to the translated text, even before the critical reception, which must also be taken into account. A common strategy used for introducing a foreign author is to ask a famous local author to write a preface. For instance, André Malraux was invited to introduce the French translation of Faulkner's *Sanctuary*, which was published by Gallimard in 1933: he defined it as 'the intrusion of Greek tragedy in the crime novel', thus presenting this work at once as innovative and universal. Translated works can be instrumentalized in the inner struggles of specific fields, such as the literary field or the academic field, in order to renew the space of possibilities: for instance, in his critical essays of the 1930s, Sartre used Faulkner and Dos Passos in order to subvert the classical norms of the French novel. They can also be used to strenghten cultural identities of minorities, or to reinforce more or less stereotypical representations of foreign cultures.

In this process, texts can be depoliticized, or on the contrary, highly politicized. Their political meaning might also be radically altered. In some cases, it is their universal aesthetic or intellectual value that will be emphasized; in others, it is their documentary ethnographic character. This is partly, though not entirely, independent of the texts themselves, and may have to do with the position of the original literary field in the World Republic of letters: texts imported from the center will tend to be presented as universal, according to the propension of the dominant to universalize their point of view, while those coming from the periphery will arise ethnographic interest. These two oppositions, politicized-depoliticized, universal-particular, structure the space of reception of translated works (Sapiro 2008b: 206).

Conclusion

The relevance for the sociology of translation of Bourdieu's approach to the field of publishing is demonstrated at the macro, meso, and micro levels. At the macro level, it can be combined with the core-periphery model to understand not only the flows of translation from one language to the other but the kind of works translated (commercial v. upmarket, genres or categories), according to the economic, political, and cultural power relations between countries or linguistic communities. At the meso level, publishers' strategies should be analyzed in the light of the relevant field (national or international markets like the francophone, anglophone, and germanophone) and of their elective affinities based on the homology between different national or linguistic publishing fields. Comparing lists and series, in addition to evidence from archives and interviews, offers an empirical ground for analyzing these strategies and for measuring cultural diversity in different areas of the field of publishing. Finally, at the micro level, the process of selecting and translating one peculiar book or the work of a single author can be thoroughly investigated, while taking into account the constraints imposed on the translator by the publisher and the specific stakes (economic, political, and/or cultural) that determine its importation and its reception. Translation and reception, in turn, impact upon the trajectory and strategies of authors, some of whom increasingly tend to adjust to the global market or to the relevant international field. This last point highlights the relevance of translation and of publishing to a broader understanding of literary and intellectual history.

Note

1 This paper is a revised and extended version of an article published in *Translation Studies*, 1(2), 2008: 154–166.

References

Anderson, B. (1991) *Imagined Communities: Reflections on the Origin and Spread of Nationalism*, London: Verso, first published in 1983.
Becker, H. (1984) *Art Worlds*, Los Angeles: University of California Press.
Benzécri, J.-P. (1992) *Handbook of Correspondence Analysis*, English transl., New York: Dekker.
Bourdieu, P. (1971) 'Le marché des biens symboliques', *L'Année sociologique*, 22: 49–126.
—— (1977) 'La production de la croyance: Contribution à une économie des biens symboliques', *Actes de la recherche en sciences sociales*, 13: 3–43.
—— (1979) *La Distinction. Critique sociale du jugement*, Paris: Minuit, English transl. (1984), *Distinction. A Social Critique of the Judgement of Taste*, English transl., R. Nice, Cambridge, MA: Harvard University Press.
—— (1983) 'The field of cultural production, or: The economic world reversed', *Poetics*, 12(4–5): 311–356.

—— (1992) *Les Règles de l'art. Genèse et structure du champ littéraire*, Paris: Seuil, English transl.: 1996, *The Rules of Art*, Cambridge: Polity Press.

—— (1993) *The Field of Cultural Production. Essays on Art and Literature*, R. Johnson (introd. and ed.), Cambridge: Polity Press.

—— (1999) 'Une révolution conservatrice dans l'édition', *Actes de la recherche en sciences sociales*, 126–127: 3–28, English transl., (2008) 'A conservative revolution in publishing', *Translation Studies*, 1(2): 123–153.

—— (2002) 'Les conditions sociales de la circulation international des idées', *Actes de la recherche en sciences sociales*, 145: 3–8, English transl., (1999), 'The social conditions of the international circulation of ideas', in *Bourdieu: A Critical Reader*, edited by R. Shusterman, Oxford: Blackwell, 222–228.

Casanova, P. (1999) *La République mondiale des lettres*, Paris: Seuil, English transl., (2004), *The World Republic of Letters*, Cambridge: Harvard University Press.

—— (2002) 'Consécration et accumulation de capital littéraire. La traduction comme échange inégal', *Actes de la recherche en sciences sociales*, 144: 7–20.

Coser, L.A., C. Kadushin, and W.W. Powell (1982) *Books. The Culture and Commerce of Publishing*, New York: Basic Books.

De Swaan, A. (1993) 'The Emergent World Language System', *International Political Science Review*, 14(3): 219–226.

—— (2001) *Words of the World: The Global Language System*, Cambridge: Polity Press.

Espagne, M. and M. Werner (eds.) (1990–1994) *Philologiques*, Paris: Editions de la MSH.

Even-Zohar, I. (1990) *Poetics Today* 11(1), Special Issue, 'Polysystem Studies'.

Gingras, Y. (2002) 'Les formes spécifiques de l'internationalité du champ scientifique', *Actes de la recherche en sciences sociales*, 141–142: 31–45.

Harvey, D. (2006) *Spaces of Global Capitalism: Towards a Theory of Uneven Geographical Development*, London: Verso.

Heilbron, J. (1999) 'Towards a sociology of translation: Book translations as a cultural world system', *European Journal of Social Theory*, 2(4): 429–444.

Heilbron, J. and G. Sapiro (2007) 'Outlines for a sociology of translation: Current issues and future prospects' in M. Wolf (ed.), *Constructing a Sociology of Translation*, Amsterdam/Philadelphia: John Benjamins Press, 93–107.

Holmes, J., J. Lambert, and A. Lefevere (ed.) (1978) *Literature and Translation: New Perspectives in Literary Studies*, Louvain: Université Catholique de Louvain.

Jacquemond, R. (1992) 'Translation and cultural hegemony: The case of France-Arabic translation', in L. Venuti (ed.), *Rethinking Translation. Discours, Subjectivity, Ideology*, London and New York: Routledge, 139–158.

Jurt, J. (1999) 'L' "introduction" de la littérature française en Allemagne', *Actes de la recherche en sciences sociales*, 130: 86–89.

Lebaron, F. (2006) *L'Enquête quantitative en sciences sociales*, Paris: Dunod.

Molloy, S. (1972) *La Diffusion de la littérature hispano-américaine en France au XXe siècle*, Paris: PUF.

Popa, I. (2010) *Traduire sous contraintes: Littérature et communisme (1947–1989)*, Paris: CNRS Editions.

Pym A. and Chrupala G. (2005) 'The quantitative analysis of translation flows in the age of an international language' in A. Branchadell and M. West Lovell (ed.), *Less Translated Languages*, Amsterdam/ Philadelphia: John Benjamins, 27–38.

Rouanet, H. and B. Le Roux (1993) *L'Analyse des données multidimensionnelles*, Paris: Dunod.

Sapiro, G. (2002) 'The structure of the French literary field during the German Occupation (1940–1944): A multiple correspondence analysis', *Poetics*, 31(5–6): 387–402.

—— (2003) 'The literary field between the state and the market', *Poetics, Journal of Empirical Research on Culture, the Media and the Arts*, 31(5–6): 441–461.

—— (2002) 'L'importation de la littérature hébraïque en France: Entre communautarisme et universalisme', *Actes de la recherche en sciences sociales*, 144: 80–98.

—— (ed.) (2008) *Translatio. Le marché de la traduction en France à l'heure de la mondialisation*, Paris: CNRS Editions.

—— (2008a) 'Normes de traduction et contraintes sociales' in A. Pym, M. Shlesinger, and D. Simeoni (eds.), *Beyond Descriptive Translation Studies*, Amsterdam: Benjamins Press, 199–208.

—— (2008b) 'Les collections de littérature étrangère', in G. Sapiro (ed.) (2008), *Translatio. Le marché de la traduction en France à l'heure de la mondialisation*, Paris: CNRS Editions, 175–205.

—— (2010a) 'Globalization and cultural diversity in the book market: The case of translations in the US and in France', *Poetics*, 38(4): 419–439.

—— (2010b) 'French Literature in the World System of Translation', in C. McDonald and S. Suleiman (eds.), *French Literary History: A Global Approach*, New York: Columbia University Press, 298–319.

—— (2011) 'À l'international', in A. Cerisier et P. Fouché (dir.), *Gallimard: Un siècle d'édition*, Paris, BNF/Gallimard, 124–147.

—— (2012) 'Comparaison et échanges culturels: Le cas des traductions', in Coll., *Faire des sciences sociales*, vol. 2, *Comparer*, Paris: Éditions de l'EHESS, 193–221.

—— (2013) 'Le champ est-il national? La théorie de la différenciation sociale au prisme de l'histoire globale', *Actes de la recherche en sciences sociales*, 200: 70–85. English transl., Forthcoming, 'Field theory in a transnational perspective', in T. Medvetz, and J. Sallaz (eds.), *Oxford Handbook of Pierre Bourdieu*, Oxford: Oxford University Press.

—— (2014a) 'The sociology of translation: A new research domain', in S. Berman and C. Porter (eds.), *Companion to Translation Studies*, Hoboken: Wiley-Blackwell, 82–94.

—— (2014b) 'Translation and identity: Social trajectories of the translators of Hebrew literature in French', *TTR*, 27(1).

—— (forthcoming) 'Translation and symbolic capital in the era of globalization: French literature in the United States', *Cultural Sociology*.

Sapiro, G. and I. Popa (2008) 'Traduire les sciences humaines et sociales: Logiques éditoriales et enjeux scientifiques' in G. Sapiro (dir.), *Translatio. Le marché de la traduction en France à l'heure de la mondialisation*, Paris: CNRS Editions, 107–143.

Schiffrin, A. (2001) *The Business of Books: How the International Conglomerates Took over Publishing and Changed the Way We Read*, London: Verso.

Serry, H. (2002) 'Constituer un catalogue littéraire', *Actes de la recherche en sciences sociales*, 144: 70–79.

Simeoni, D. (1998), 'The Pivotal Status of the Translator's Habitus,' *Target*, 10(1): 1–39.

Simonin, A. (2004) 'Le catalogue de l'éditeur: Un outil pour l'histoire. L'exemple des Éditions de Minuit', *XXe siècle. Revue d'histoire*, 81: 119–129.

Thiesse, A.-M. (1998) *La création des identités nationales: Europe XVIIe siècle-XXe siècle*, Paris: Seuil.

Thompson, J. (2010) *Merchants of Culture*, London: Polity Press.

Toury, G. (1995) *Descriptive Translation Studies and Beyond*, Amsterdam and Philadelphia: John Benjamins.

Wallerstein, I. (1974) *The Modern World-System*, vol. I: *Capitalist Agriculture and the Origins of the European World-Economy in the Sixteenth Century*, New York/London: Academic Press.

—— (1980) *The Modern World-System*, vol. II: *Mercantilism and the Consolidation of the European World-Economy, 1600-1750*, New York: Academic Press.

—— (1989) *The Modern World-System*, vol. III: *The Second Great Expansion of the Capitalist World-Economy, 1730-1840's*, San Diego: Academic Press.

Wilfert, B. (2002) 'Cosmopolis et l'homme invisible. Les importateurs de littérature étrangère en France, 1885–1914', *Actes de la recherche en sciences sociales*, 144: 33–46.

Wimmer A. and N. Glick Schiller (2003) 'Methodological nationalism, the social sciences and the study of migration: An essay in historical epistemology', *International Migration Review*, 37(3): 576–610.

18
The biennalization of art worlds
The culture of cultural events

Monica Sassatelli

Introduction

A culture of the event – biennals, triennials and more generally art festivals – has become in the last few decades quantitatively and qualitatively prominent. Whilst 'festivals' have ancient roots, it is only in recent years that they have become an almost ubiquitous fixture of cultural calendars in cities around the world. This current proliferation is even more striking for art biennals: arguably emanating from the single model of the first *Biennale* in Venice, and up to the 1980s only reproduced in a handful of examples, biennals and derivates as large-scale, international and recurrent exhibitions (Altshuler 2013: 18) have become key institutional nodes linking production, consumption and distribution of contemporary art, and are counted now in their hundreds.

If we are to understand the production of aesthetic dispositions whilst addressing the institutional settings involved in the production and consumption of art and culture today, biennals thus offer a privileged perspective. With now over 150 biennals around the world, we are increasingly likely to encounter contemporary art through their mediation, directly as visitors or more indirectly via the nebula of critical discourse and more generally media coverage they generate. The phenomenon attracting attention has become not just the biennals but more specifically the *biennalization* of the art world. And whilst its extent and features are fuzzy, given the flexible definition of its constituent parts, a consideration of what the myriad of exhibitionary complexes that fit into this category share is more relevant for its study than a taxonomic analysis of differences. The term *biennalization* is used within the art world itself as shorthand to refer to the proliferation and standardization of biennal exhibitions under a common (if rather loose) format; however, it is possible to construe it sociologically. Similarly to how the common-sense notion of art world can be made into an analytical sociological concept (Becker 1982), biennalization can thematize the shifting set of cultural classifications, practices and values that differentiate the contemporary art world, affecting both its content (now too also sometimes referred to as *biennal art*) and the type of rationale and experience it crystallizes.

As a phenomenon that increasingly represents itself 'on a global scale' (Vogel 2011), biennals are a unique vantage point to access what is often termed 'global culture', but remains rarely empirically studied in clearly defined contexts.[1] Reprising within the art world unsolved dilemmas in the analysis of cultural globalization, alleged optimists see in biennals the 'embracing of a democratic redistribution of cultural power', whilst 'pessimists' point rather to the 'recognition of a new form of cultural hegemony and re-colonization' (De Duve 2009: 45) While some see it as a truly global phenomenon opening up spaces for reflection and cross-fertilization in settings that promote innovation in art and self-reflexivity in forms of cultural display, others regard it as the ultimate proof of the standardizing and banalizing effect of a culture industry intensified by globalization and forfeiting culture's partial autonomy to rampant economic expediency.

This chapter proposes a sociological analysis of this debate and of the phenomenon that gave rise to it, which so far has rarely reached beyond the art world and art history. In what follows, I first look into the lineage with the first recurrent biennal, the Venice Biennale, in order to trace, from the beginning so to speak, the permutations of the 'global' and its representation in the art world (section 1). I then briefly map out the spread of the format and the art world's own (enthusiastic or, increasingly, worried) perception of such biennalization (section 2). The chapter proceeds taking into consideration how biennalization is seen to specifically affect the art, artists and cities involved (section 3). In so doing, the chapter problematizes too linear stories of biennals' apotheosis or degeneration, whilst addressing through them some of the contradictions and open issues at stake. Overall, this will show how, from the point of view of a sociology of biennals, the above dilemmas are less there to be solved, theoretically or empirically, once and for all, than as a critical measure against which to assess the cultural significance of biennalization.

A view from Venice: The making of the biennal as a cultural format

At a cursory look, one of the first features to stand out in an analysis of contemporary biennalization is the diversity of events that go under the name of biennal, *biennale* or similar. To understand biennalization as a phenomenon and the biennale as a genre means first of all to prise out commonalities and 'family resemblances'. Interestingly, and irrespective of how little some of the more recent biennals share with it, the lineage with the first biennal, founded in 1895 in Venice as a biennal exhibition of international art, soon to be known as the *Biennale*, is never forgotten.[2] Festivals, including contemporary 'professional', post-traditional festivals, tend to have founding myths (Giorgi and Sassatelli 2011). In the world of biennales, Venice is the origin myth for all of them, either to establish a continuum or to assume a more antagonistic relationship. It is thus worth looking at Venice, and at its own lineage, in some detail.

The Biennale coined the concept and format of the periodical large exhibition surveying current trends and developments in one or more contemporary art forms, usually independent from previously existing institutions (museum or gallery) and their permanent directorship and curatorial choices. It did so combining aspects from previous models of art and trade exhibitions. Since the Parisian *Salons* of the nineteenth century, independent art exhibitions had become a successful genre in themselves (Altshuler 2008). Similarly, the Universal Exhibitions or *Expo*, following the great success of the first London Expo in 1851, had become a recurrent, itinerant feature spreading not only throughout urban Europe, but also 'across southern Asia, Australia, and northern Africa as exercises in European power and "uplift"' (Rydell 2006: 135; see also Roche 2000). For curatorial aspects such as artists' selection and the role and composition of the selection committee, the Biennale took inspiration from other successful art exhibitions of the time, the Secession in Munich in particular (see Di Martino 2013). However the framework lending meaning and clout to the enterprise was borrowed from Expos and their organizing principle of individual exhibitions commissioned, managed and financed by participating nations.

Clearly smaller in scale, at least to begin with, the Biennale shared the Expos ambitious, agenda-setting rationale and the framework of national competition. Sharing with the Expo the universalist rhetoric of panoptic/panoramic representation (De Cauter 1993), the Biennale sought to put Venice and newly unified Italy on the map of contemporary art, by creating that very map in the microcosm of the exhibition park, as an allegedly representative, state-of-the-art survey. Historians of the early biennale always note how Italian and Venetian artists were clearly overrepresented (West 1995). However, more than the questionable empirical achievement of universal representation, it is the aspiration to it that is relevant to understand how these art exhibitions were framed at the time, and how they evolved. Indeed, even in new biennales national (or regional) competition and gatekeeping remain underlying features, regardless of exhibitions being actually organized around national pavilions, a pattern that few tend to reproduce today, probably as much as for economic and organizational reasons as for the conceptual qualms explicitly evoked.

Both Expos and the Biennale by the early twentieth century had progressively expanded from a central exhibition palace to a park composed of several national *pavilions*, thus providing a miniaturized world tour, under the expert guidance of curators (for Expos see Barth 2008, for the Venice Biennale see Donaggio 1998; Mulazzani 2004). Whilst it may be pointed out that world fairs themselves developed from the model of the old city fair, the profound difference in the shift to world fair lies in the coupling with modernity's rationalization and instrumental reason, the ambition of the world fair to be an exhaustive, representative, 'universal' exposition of 'progress', and its embeddedness in national, bourgeois cultures already enwrapped in emergent, globalizing phenomena (Lechner and Boli 2005). Like in the Expos, the Biennale aspired to illustrate progress, providing legitimation and order. In Venice, this was sanctioned by awards for outstanding achievement, the sought-after and diplomatic incident-causing *Leoni d'oro*, Golden Lions, after the city's historical emblem.[3] The prizes are the clearest indicator that 'spreading of knowledge and shaping of taste' of current art (Alloway 1968: 141), the professed objective of the Biennale, was not the only one. The prizes created, as they measured it, prestige as cultural value (English 2009) whilst also fulfilling an important role for international cultural diplomacy and commerce. In a cultural climate where increasingly the hardest and most significant recognition to get is the very label of 'art' (Bydler 2011), the Biennale became the ultimate consecration. The proliferation of the format would then fulfil the need for these platforms that were becoming key indicators of artistic careers (on the latter and their conventional paths, see Heinich, this volume).

By the late 1960s, reviewing the state of contemporary art ceased to be considered sufficient or acceptable as an explicit rationale. As well as questionable, it appeared redundant: 'Umbro Apollonio, an official of the Venice Biennale, suggested that by the late 1960s the function of reporting on contemporary art was being performed quite adequately by art dealers and by museums' (Altshuler 2013: 13). Combined with the effect of a much wider circulation of art publications and reproductions, novelty was not anymore a reason to travel to Venice. Apollonio also saw a solution: 'what was needed, however, was conceptual insight provided by some interpretive plan. In his view the Biennale should move to structuring the selection and display of works according to a unifying theme' (ibid.). The changing, and increasingly prominent, role of independent curators hired especially for a single biennal, is how these increasingly hypertrophic events have sought to remain relevant in an art world in rapid transformation. In the history of art exhibitions a 'curatorial turn' has gradually become more prominent (O'Neill 2007), with biennals often leading the way. Swiss curator Harald Szeeman's Documenta 5 in 1972 is often taken as starting point of the thematic exhibition away from national representation, held together by the vision of a curator-author instead (Heinich and Pollak 1996). Other Venice rivals looking for a new *raison d'être* also started to emerge based on this premise; Sydney Biennal notably adopted a thematic approach since its inception in 1973.

The shift from territorial review to thematic interpretation, which Venice itself partially incorporated, further supported the consolidation and diffusion of this flexible format. As the art world became or perceived itself as increasingly complex, making sense of it and establishing criteria of validation (rather than simply (re)presenting a sample of an undisputed canon) became increasingly critical. As we shall see, by the time they started to grow exponentially in the 1990s, it had become clear that biennals were not just *exhibiting* the art world, but acted as one of its constituent parts. Every new edition, every new biennale, inevitably augments the complexity it tries to reduce, biennalization becoming a self-propagating phenomenon.

Biennals and cultural globalization

For several decades, Venice was the only biennale. Some lists include other large recurrent shows that emerged shortly after, such as the Canergie Institute's Pittsburgh International established in 1896, or the Whitney Biennal in New York established in 1932, or even the smaller Corcoran Biennal in Washington in 1907. These tended to focus much more on American art only (Corcoran and Whitney exclusively) and were integral to the private museums that initiated them. Generally recognized as second biennal is São Paulo's in Brasil, funded in 1951 and which fully adopted Venice's original model. Others started to follow: Tokyo (1952), Alexandria (1955), Documenta in Kassel (1955), Paris (1959). The proliferation meant an expanding and increasingly elastic concept. Variation concerns temporality (Documenta happens every five years, but especially in the early decades inconsistencies abound everywhere), coverage (Alexandria is devoted to artists from the Mediterranean) and approach (only São Paulo fully adopted a national representation model), as well as dimensions. Success and relevance are also not constant, as variation in longevity suggests (many end up lasting just one or two shows, famously in recent years the much acclaimed Johannesburg Biennale).

Until the last decade or so of the twentieth century, even as the landscape was already becoming more complex, a mainstream view of a fairly clear and limited panorama was still possible: 'In the early sixties ... there were two biennals: the Venice Biennale and the Bienal de São Paulo – and every five years there was Documenta', writes influential curator René Block (2013: 104). He closes the passage, however, describing a completely different scenario: 'Since then, not even forty years have passed and today we are confronted with so many so-called biennals, triennials, and quadriennials that it's almost impossible to get an overall perspective on them' (ibid.). At a close look, one sees that until the 1980s the development had been slow, with just a handful of influential biennals and at most about 30, in inclusive lists counting also minor arts biennals and short-lived attempts (Vogel 2011). It is with the 1990s that the growth becomes exponential; it can no longer be ignored and starts being a matter for reflection. If smaller biennals were happily overlooked before, now hyperbolic metaphors on the 'hundreds of biennals active all over the world' (Seijdel 2009: 4) have become the norm in the self-representation of the art world, where the proliferation of art biennals is seen as an expression of its own globalization (De Duve 2009). Since 2009, a Biennal Foundation, and since 2014 an International Biennal Association strive to monitor them and organize their networking, further signs of institutionalization and worldwide reach. Taking the BF estimate as the most authoritative, there are over 150 biennals, of which 44 per cent are in Europe, 32 per cent in Asia, 21 per cent in the Americas, 9 per cent in Africa and 3 per cent in Oceania.[4] Even at a glance, the distribution is far from equal, but with biennals in over 50 countries across all the continents, claims of a 'global' status are confidently held (Vogel 2011); the above-mentioned IBA by statute aims at equal representation across all continents. That biennals constitute a cultural correlate of globalization in the contemporary art world has itself become a trope, with biennals addressing globalization and its corollaries (cultural exchange, hybridization, cosmopolitanism, neoliberal capitalism and so on) in their themes and selections, as well illustrated by the proceedings of the first World Biennals Forum organised by the BF in collaboration with Gwanju Biennal (Bauer and Hanru 2013) as well as many biennals catalogues.[5]

Venice remains a point of reference, even for the most distant replicas. Especially for recent ones it can work as a counter-model: the forerunner of this is the Havana biennal, founded in 1983 and explicitly claiming for itself the role of alternative, deliberately anti-western and representative of another modernity (Esche 2011; Papastergiadis and Martin 2011). The genealogy out of Venice certainly contains a degree of simplification – as an example among many, it has been noted with reference to the Dak'Art biennal that a 'biennale's sense of its own history is characterized by a strange trio of forces: continuity, amnesia and disruption. In Dakar frequent references to the first World festival of Black Arts (1966) ... introduce another variable to the mix.... As contrived as this claim of kinship may be, it at least allows Dak'Art to reflect on itself outside of the Venice Biennale, which scholarship on the subject takes to be the basis of all biennales' (Vincent 2014: 5). This is however precisely what makes the selective storyline significant as a genealogy that creates a shared imaginary of *the* biennal. Increasingly, recognizing the strength of a diffuse model, biennals compete with each other, but most of all they connect. After several attempts and some time-limited and regional experiences, such as the European Biennal Network supported by the EU in 2007–09, self-defined biennals are now connected worldwide, joining networks and sharing debates, as well as more implicitly being connected by the recurrence of the same curators and artists in biennals at opposite corners of the world. Regional co-identifications such as an Asian biennales cluster also emerge, and common marketing tools are devised, such as the 'Grand Tour' promoted by Venice, Documenta and Sculpture Projects Münster as well as art fair Basel (Tang 2007), later imitated by Gwangju, Shanghai and Guangzhou biennals. In Central Asia and the Middle East similar forms of collaboration are underway, overall promoting a 'host of new regional imaginations' (Rogoff 2009: 115). These sometimes explicitly aim at creating regional centres away from Western hegemony which, given the European lineage of the format, if not of contemporary art altogether, remains a major point of contention (Bydler 2011).

Regardless of how unevenly spread biennals are, with zones of concentration in Europe and Asia in particular, it is thus the very performativity of the biennal as map that makes it a global phenomenon. Biennials do not *reflect* the global in an easy and schematic way: it is not as if a biennale can be taken as a direct indicator of relevance in the art world or geopolitically more generally. What biennales show, however, is what counts today as 'being on the map' and how new places are inscribed. A biennal puts you on the map because, today, biennals *are* the map, a shifting and expanding one; that is the case for the art displayed as for the places that host the event. Every new show calling itself biennal and successfully grafting onto the global discourse of biennals (propagated and perpetuated via art magazines off and online and in formal and informal networks of artists, curators, collectors and the like), extends not only the list but also the very typology of biennals, increasing both standardization *and* differentiation. This is a useful rejoinder to some assumptions of early globalization theories, which still haunt the art world – the disappearance of place or place relevance, the interchangeability of locales and the assumption of standardization as dominant if not sole effect.

Contrary to this, the proliferation of biennales and their connection to the host cities is an indication that place continues to matter – understood as the cultural construct acquiring new meaning through the topography of biennals worldwide, meaningful just for insiders. As is the case with festivals and 'events' more generally, having 'been there' is part of belonging to an art world and playing its game: 'being there – not only in Venice, Basle, and Madrid but now in São Paolo, Dakar and Shanghai – has become another way to confirm social distinction on the viewer (as only slight exposure to art-world chatter, so often fluttering about the latest exotic jamboree, will confirm)' (Stallabrass 2004: 26–7). New biennales fulfil the role of providing new possibilities of acquiring such badges of distinction for artists, audiences and cities alike. If we conceive of these social settings as fields governed by specific sets of rules of the game and power differentials, or competitive struggles (Bourdieu 1993), we can see how a key point of contention is the very membership in the field and the ability to make a difference in it. As part of a field of 'restricted' production, contemporary (high) art strives for differentiation and (semi)autonomy, sitting in tension not only with fields of mass production but more pointedly with the fields of power. This is particularly the case of the economic field which both creates the conditions for biennals' diffusion and threatens their very autonomy, as perceived by the art world itself.

This is in fact where the critical tide starts to turn: the growth has been so obvious and the format so hegemonic that even within the art world biennalization is becoming more a source of concern than celebration. The stakes are well summarized at the start of the *Biennal Reader*:

> For some skeptics the word biennal has come to *signify nothing more than an overblown symptom of spectacular event culture* ... a Western typology whose proliferation has infiltrated even the most far-reaching parts of the world .... For others, the biennal is *a critical site of experimentation* in exhibition-making.
>
> *(Filipovic, Van Hal and Ovstebo 2010: 13; my emphasis)*

On the one hand, thus, there are positive views which see in the very fact of the reproduction of biennales a liberating process that displaces the long established cultural hegemony of the centre, where the plurality also ensures that what emerges is not a new centre but a more distributed or democratic constellation. Exemplary of this position is Arthur Danto's famous hyperbole of the Biennale as 'a glimpse of a transnational utopia' (quoted in Tang 2011: 79). Viewed from the other extreme, instead, biennales have become sites of an empty 'festivalism' driven by entertainment and spectacularization (Schjeldalh 1999). Diametrically opposed, the critical view also sees biennals as a quintessential form and perhaps final proof of cultural imperialism, with plurality and mobility just the surface, distracting impression of a 'space of flows' actually dominated by mobile elites controlling it from a few, largely unchanged, locales.

This polarized debate is made even more intractable by the fact that even those at the core of the art world struggle to interpret its biennalization:

> many of these events are simply not designed to be seen in their totality....Without a frame of reference to validate it, the kind of specific operation carried out by these shows in the field of art and culture, is barely, if all, perceptible through the opinions of a host of commentators.
>
> *(Basualdo 2003: 126)*

As we have seen, biennales have been reinventing themselves since the 1960s, away from representation and towards 'a platform for process-oriented aesthetics where there is freedom for experimental chaos and radical thought' (Lee 2013: 10). Whether or not a new order out of chaos emerges – between the usual catalogue hyperbole and exhibitions that insiders themselves find 'overgeneralized, innocuous, or cryptic' (Smith 2007: 261) – is another, more subtle dilemma occupying the art world debate. From an external point of view, the unsolvable dichotomies of that debate can become critical measures to understand how concerns around issues of hierarchy and (cultural) capital are entangled within the production of novel forms of art, their attending discourses and aesthetic dispositions. From this angle, biennals provide a privileged viewpoint on the struggles and growing pains of new rationales providing acceptable and shared meaning for the contemporary art world. They are illustrations of the cultural logics of globalization beyond the blueprint of national cultures and their strategies of representation.

Biennal art, biennal artists, biennal cities: Art festivals and the expediency of culture

> The real story of the art world in the 1990s lies in how it subtly embraced and then reversed this trend toward hypercommodification by using the machinations of 'marketing' to shift the focus of art patronage away from the artist and back toward the institution... [T]he 1990s did not show its unique aesthetic hand in the emergence of any identifiable period style in the visual arts; rather, it did so with a building boom in stylish museum buildings and a concomitant proliferation of international biennal exhibitions.
>
> *(Van Proyen 2006: 30)*

The history of art exhibitions, describing itself as having had a discursive turn (Altshuler 2013: 22), has produced several attempts at interpreting the growing and protean phenomenon of biennals. Typologies abound, classifying biennals on the basis of their curatorial approach, type of organization and contextual significance (Martini 2010). Most take the heterogeneity of biennals for granted but see homogenization as a risk of their overall shift from their Western origin as a 'capitalist – philanthropic entreprise', through to post-World War II 'bloc-politic' intervention, to the 'flexible production- and event-oriented variety of the 1990s and 2000s' (Bydler 2004: 388). More or less implicitly these typologies include a periodization which describes a rather linear 'rise and fall' narrative for biennals, where the biennal eventually is destroyed under its own gigantism, having lost its original function and becoming prey of neoliberal capitalism and its imperative of instrumentalization of culture. Finding a 'synecdoche between the globalization of the marketplace and the biennalization of the art world' (Papastergiadis and Martin 2011: 49), this is then taken as a thorough explanation of the biennal phenomenon. Biennalization becomes an expression of what has been termed the 'expediency of culture paradigm' (Yudice 2003): what once had artistic and political finalities is under globalization and after the end of the Cold War reduced to an encompassing economic rationality. It is in particular with regards to three key components of the art world that the effects of its biennalization within the expediency of culture can be usefully discussed in a little more detail, problematizing such linear narratives: the art itself, the artists and the host cities.

As the excerpt opening this section shows, biennalization is perceived to be such a dominant process that it comes to overshadow the art which it is supposed to showcase, so that a period is not characterized by an art movement or style but by this now hegemonic format.

This substitution of content by its container may indeed be the deeper meaning of recent discussions of the emergence of 'biennal art'. It is not just that being exhibited in one or more biennales adds *provenance* and thus value to contemporary art, fulfilling a function museums and art history fulfil for earlier periods. More substantially, the spread of biennals generates art suitable to its format and logic creating, as by-product if not intentionally, ad-hoc art, which by the same token is dismissed as more uniform, less challenging art (Stallabrass 2004: chapter 2 and 4). Perhaps not surprisingly, this is framed as corrupting and degenerative within the art world. For a sociology of art this is instead a constitutive process of a world or field based on shared conventions and rules. Yet, the contradiction between a contemporary art system based on a rationale of originality and singularity and material conditions promoting standardization, already observed by Heinich (2005), assumes here another incarnation.

The expression 'biennal art' emerged in the late 1990s with the mushrooming of biennales as a derogatory term, as art of 'bombastic proportions and hollow premises' (Filipovic 2005: 326), that some even dismiss as bland and commercial 'airport art' (Byrne 2006). The expression itself suggests its dismissive judgement, as art that can be easily framed and classified, notably as 'tokenistic representations of cultural diversity' (Verwoert 2010: 187). One point these critiques omit, however, is that all art, considered from the point of view of its institutional settings, is prey to these constraints, and 'biennal art' may not ultimately be more unequivocally affected by this than 'church art' or 'gallery art'. What is true for biennals was, and is, true also for museums, galleries and so on: they are under pressure 'for an aesthetic standard flexible enough to produce approximately the amount of work for which the organizations have room and, conversely, for the institutions to generate the amount of exhibition opportunity required by the works the aesthetic certifies as being of the appropriate quality' (Becker 1982: 142). Understanding these constraints may help recognising 'biennal art' as a phenomenon without the attending negative connotation, as ways to work within and make sense of the constraints are outlined but not deterministically foreclosed by this institutional analysis. This should first of all open up new ways of looking at biennals and biennal art, rather than provide another totalizing interpretation: looked in any detail, the art found in biennals is hardly easily understood as conveying a single message speaking within a single domain (see Latour 2011).

The art world's malaise about biennals emerges even more strongly in light of the issue of the artists invited (often again and again) at biennals. A useful lens here is their global representativity, which continues to trouble *biennalists*, often inspired by feminist, postmodernist and postcolonial critiques that have had so much influence on the art world. If the dominant view seems to be that

> [e]xhibitions delimited by nationality, continents and other geographical demarcations have been subject to vigorous critique over the last few years, for many of the right reasons. In a cosmopolitan art world, in which artists travel to make work and tale part in exhibitions, the fact that an artist is British, Brazilian or Chinese is of diminishing significance.
>
> *(Farquharson and Schlieker 2005: 12)*

This can be easily criticized as disingenuous, once correlations of place of birth or work and participation in prominent biennales are shown. This is what Chin Tao Wu did in her review of non-Western artists participating in Documenta exhibitions between 1968 and 2007, in an attempt to problematize the 'flat-world' representation of global cultural flows by way of probing into the directions of the latter. As a result she describes an art world in which a concentric and hierarchical structure still holds: until the late 1980s, even if claims of artists 'from around the world' were ubiquitous points of pride in catalogues, careers were almost invariably the consequence of a migration towards Western hubs of contemporary art, and even in more recent years, the dominant direction of the flow of artists has not changed. She concludes voicing a not surprising, but still relevant, recurring critique that

> for the majority outside the magic circle, real barriers still remain. The biennal has, despite its decolonizing and democratic claims, proved still to embody the traditional power structures of the contemporary Western art world; the only difference being that 'Western' has quietly been replaced by a new buzzword, 'global'.
>
> *(Wu 2009: 115)*

These data and their interpretation are confirmed by others, adopting a similar quantitative approach (in particular, on the international contemporary art scene more generally, concluding that globalization is to a large extent illusory, see Quemin 2006; a similar approach and similar conclusions, with a different set of indicators, including biennals, are found in Buchholz and Wuggenig 2005). To some extent, with regards to biennals, this is not surprising given the conditions of access, as the gatekeepers often remain the national institutes practically financing artists' participation, as biennales themselves sponsor very few artists, and private galleries are more important for art fairs. These claims are crucial (as are similar ones related to gender issues; see Smith 2007). However, they are a partial account which hardly touches upon the meaning of the art and artists actually finding a space in biennals, as well as of the aesthetic dispositions and contextual resonances (Gell 1996) that these exhibitions presuppose, rightly or wrongly, from the public.

Finally, we may reflect on 'biennal cities' as these raise similar issues – we have already come across the uneven yet not random distribution of biennales – whilst more clearly pointing to the macro or structural factors within which biennalization occurs, foregrounding the expediency debate. Biennals are almost always named after the host city, for which such an event is often a recognized key step in what has been called a 'wordling' process, as a 'practice of centering, of generating and harnessing global regimes of value' (Roy and Ong 2011: 312). No matter how far from the Western progenitor, the urban nature of biennals connects them even more clearly with the artistic temporality of the current 'global' avant-garde, excluding genres and artists belonging to local artistic fields less connected to this worldwide professional sphere (Bennett, this volume). Like other mega-events (Roche 2000), biennals now form part of strategies of place promotion, as such the paradox of producing standardization whilst promoting specificity has long been observed. More or less at the time of the biennals' diffusion, in the 1990s, this has also coincided with a shift from national to city promotion in cultural policies more generally, as part of a shift to entrepreneurialism in urban governance (Quinn 2005).

One issue here is that these concerns seem to be pitched against a nostalgic vision of traditional festivals premised on purer, more authentic rationales (Sassatelli 2011). That this should be so adds an important dimension to our understanding of the current debate's premises and the perceived lost battle against 'commercialization'. What this degeneration tale tends to omit is that biennals always were, as well, about what is called 'culture-led regeneration' today in cultural policy circles. Take Venice, the revered progenitor. The Biennale was from the very beginning also an operation to rescue a dying star in the European cultural firmament. The founders did declare they meant to pursue art as a way to promote 'fraternal association of all peoples' (Cit. in Vogel 2011: 14); however Biennale's historians from very early on saw that it was also geared towards tourism and prestige (Alloway 1968). This came to the fore when the Cinema section of the Biennale was established in the 1930s to prolong and salvage the seaside holiday season of the Venice Lido. True, in recently established biennales the rhetoric is more explicit and specific, such as is the case for instance of Liverpool Biennal, created in 1998 and invoking regeneration as its legitimizing rationale (Papastergiadis and Martin, 2011: 45–6). Expediency however, economic *and* political, was never absent. Intrinsic or cultural rationales always had to share ground with more instrumental or extrinsic ones, in never settled equilibriums. In this too, new biennales follow and specify the original model, rather than simply transform or distort it – and in that they open much more interesting windows on contemporary culture.

Concluding remarks

We have seen how *laissez-faire* the definition of biennal is in many respects; the exception to this flexibility is the highly contentious and contended distinction between art biennals and art fairs, equally grand, recurrent (usually annual) exhibitions where galleries display and directly sell work. In this case, to demarcate a clear-cut, qualitative solution of continuity seems crucial within the art world, to underline how biennals are *curated* exhibitions, and as such their themes, purpose and politics are a great deal of what they do. 'Unlike the fair, the primary product of a biennale is *symbolic* capital, with its necessary suppression of economic capital, to maintain a myth of neutral exhibition space objectively according value to a disinterested work of art' (Tang 2011: 78). Fairs attempting to include biennal-like elements and become relevant for aesthetics as well as for the market (as when philosopher Jacques Rancière was recently invited to speak at Frieze, London's major art fair) are regarded with equal suspicion as biennals getting too close to fairs. And yet, once again, we only need to look at Venice: in its early days and until 1968, when protests raging across Europe arrived at the Biennale threatening to block it, Venice was also a fair, if we take as main characterizing feature having a sales office for the artworks on display and taking a commission on deals. Today, as the economic expediency paradigm takes over the explicit legitimation of art and culture, substituting earlier, equally extra-artistic justifications, national expediency in particular, that delicate balance between symbolic and economic capital is exposed, and policing it becomes more crucial. More than a rise and fall narrative that describes rapid apotheosis and degeneration of the biennale, and loss of its specific rationale to that commercialization which allowed it to prosper, we need nuanced analysis able to both distinguish and see the interconnections of different rationales and agendas. A flat analysis where 'optimist' and 'pessimist' views are pitched against each other as black and white alternatives is bound to lead to unsolvable dilemmas.

As we have seen, biennalization offers an elaborated, reflexive updating of old dichotomies in the critique of culture industry: not only cultural imperialism *vs.* resistance but also standardization/commercialization *vs.* freedom/innovation and deterritorialization *vs.* identity politics. The argument of contemporary art becoming more similar and acritical, realizing Adorno's worst nightmare of the effects of commodity form as an increasingly exclusive context of art production and consumption (Adorno 2001; Steinert 2003) still resonates in this biennalization debate. Like the wider thesis in which it may be seen to have been incorporated – culture within globalization as suffering homogenizing cultural imperialism, commercialization and instrumentality – it can easily find supporting evidence. So do, however, opposite views emphasizing processes of heterogenization and/or hybridization, as spaces of freedom and resistance (Nederveen Pieterse 2003). It is in the very updating and transposition of such debates that resides biennals' sociological interest, not in a fit-for-all solution. These dichotomies are there not to be solved, but rather to let us see how the specific expression they take, and the tentative solutions biennals must find, reflect and shape the art world. This can help advance our analysis of the state of public culture more generally. The global and diverse, if also patchy and standardized, stage for art and art discourse biennals provide offers plenty new material for cultural sociologists to probe into what current dilemmas are, what they share with older, but still relevant ones, and what makes both the dilemmas and the always temporary solutions meaningful.

Notes

1 Sociological interest in biennals and other festivals as such has been limited (Giorgi, Sassatelli and Delanty 2011). Also art exhibition and fairs, although arguably a key node for 'production of culture' or 'art world' approaches have even in these received limited attention (but see Alexander 1996). There is however a considerable literature linked to different artistic genres and often influenced by recent cultural and social theory (for art biennals, art history, aesthetics and art criticism in particular, see Vogel 2011; Altshuler 2008, 2013; Byrne 2005) – so much so that in these neighbouring fields some are starting to talk of *biennale studies* (a good starting point is the reader edited by Filipovic, Van Hal and Ovstebo 2010). Also of relevance is literature on cultural displays, which although geared towards museums also covers festivals and other temporary displays with particular focus on their cultural politics (see the influential collections promoted by the Smithsonian Institution: Karp and Levine 1991; Karp *et al.* 2006).
2 In this chapter I follow the common usage of interchangeably referring to biennal or *biennale* (from the original Italian) to indicate a type of event and institution; I use the term Biennale, with a capital B, as a short form for the Venice Biennale.
3 A famous example, well illustrating recurring exhibitions' wider significance, is the diffuse European dissatisfaction and rumours of manipulations following US artist Robert Rauschenberg's Golden Lion award for best artist in a national pavilion in 1964: 'The contention surrounding Rauschenberg's prize at Venice reminds us that large, recurring international art exhibitions continued to perform important functions after the war, remaining sites of cultural and commercial competition among nations as they had been since their origins in nineteenth-century world's fairs' (Altshuler 2013:12).
4 www.biennalfoundation.org, last accessed July 2014, my calculation on their A-Z list. Another authoritative source, the voluminous recent reader of *biennal studies* advances a vaguer estimate: 'Over the years, the term has been used to refer to a vast landscape of different exhibition projects, with no source agreeing on their total number (currently thought to be somewhere between one hundred and two hundred around the world)' (Filipovic, Van Hal and Ovstebo 2010: 13).
5 A historical sociology of (what we may today call) global art exhibitions, from the lineage of the Expo through to ground-breaking shows that have changed the discourse and practice of the field – such as *Magiciens de la Terre* in Paris, *The Other Story* in London, and the third *Bienal de la Habana* in Cuba, all in 1989 (Esche 2011) – can also provide an unusual perspective on the still open discussion of the actual periodization, continuities and breaks of globalization. Another corollary debate is that concerning globalization's different manifestation in high and mass culture, which again can find a rich empirical terrain in a field which is both so clearly situated in the avant-garde, 'restricted production' end of the spectrum and entangled in global cultural and economic exchanges, as biennalization illustrates. For an overview discussion of both see Buchholz and Wuggenig (2005).

References

Adorno, T.W. (2001) *The Culture Industry: Selected Essays on Mass Culture*, London: Routledge.
Alexander, V. (1996) 'Pictures at an exhibition: Conflicting pressures in museums and the display of art', *American Journal of Sociology*, 101(4): 797–839.
Alloway, L. (1968) *The Venice Biennale: 1895–1968, From Salon to Goldfish Bowl*, Greenwich: New York Graphic Society.
Altshuler, B.J. (2008) *Salon to Biennal. Exhibitions That Made Art History: 1863–1959*, London: Phaidon.
—— (2013) *Biennals and Beyond. Exhibitions That Made Art History: 1962–2002*, London: Phaidon.
Barth, V. (2008) 'The micro-history of a world event: Intention, perception and imagination at the Exposition universelle de 1867', *Museum and Society*, 6(1): 22–37.
Basualdo, C. (2003) *The Unstable Institution*, reprinted in Filipovic, Van Hal and Ovstebo (eds.) (2010), pp. 124–135.

Bauer, U.M. and H. Hanru (eds.) (2013) *Shifting Gravity (World Biennal Fofum N. 1)*, Ostfildern: Hatje Cantz.
Becker, H.S. (1982) *Art Worlds*, Berkeley, CA: University of California Press.
Block, R. (2013) 'We hop on, we hop off: The ever-faster spinning carousel of biennals' in U.M. Bauer and U. Hanru (eds.), *Shifting Gravity (World Biennal Fofum N. 1)*, Ostfildern: Hatje Cantz, pp. 104–09.
Bourdieu, P. (1993) *The Field of Cultural Production Essays on Art and Literature*, Cambridge: Polity.
Buchholz, L. and U. Wuggenig (2005) 'Cultural globalization between myth and reality: The case of the contemporary visual arts', *ART-E-FACT*, issue n° 4, available online at artefact.mi2.hr/_a04/lang_en/theory_buchholz_en.htm (accessed July 2014).
Bydler, C. (2004) 'The Global Art World, Inc. on the globalization of contemporary art', abridged and reprinted in E. Filipovic, M. Van Hal and S. Ovstebo (eds.) (2010), *The Biennal Reader*, Bergen: Bergen Kunsthall, pp.378–405.
—— (2011) 'Global contemporary? The global horizon of art events', in J. Harris (ed.), *Globalization and Contemporary Art*, Oxford: Wiley-Blackwell, pp.464–478.
Byrne, J. (2005) 'Contemporary art and globalisation: Biennals and the emergence of the de-centred artist', *International Journal of the Humanities*, 3(1): 169–172.
—— (2006) 'Biennals and city-wide events: Airport art: New internationalism or global franchise?', *a-n Research Papers – Biennals and City Wide Events*, December.
De Cauter, L. (1993) 'The panoramic ecstasy: On world exhibitions and the disintegration of experience', *Theory, Culture and Society*, 10: 1–23.
De Duve, T. (2009) 'The glocal and the singuversal', *Open*, issue *The Art Biennal as a Global Phenomenon*, 16: 44–53.
Di Martino, E. (2013) *Storia della Biennale di Venezia 1895–2013*, Enna: Papiro Arte.
Donaggio, A. (1998), *Biennale di Venezia. Un secolo di storia*, Art Dossier series, Firenze: Giunti.
English, J. (2009) *The Economy of Prestige. Prizes, Awards, and the Circulation of Cultural Value*, Cambridge, MA: Harvard University Press.
Enwezor, O. (2002) *The Black Box. Documenta11_Platform 5: Exhibition*, Ostfildern: Hatje Cantz, pp. 42–55.
Esche, C. (2011) 'Making art global', in R. Weiss (ed.), *Making Art Global (Part 1): The Third Havana Biennal 1989*, London: Afterall Books.
Farquharson, A. and A. Schlieker (2005) 'Introduction', in *British Art Show 6*, London: Hayward Gallery.
Filipovic, E. (2005) *The Global White Cube*, reprinted in E. Filipovic, M. Van Hal and S. Ovstebo, S. (eds.) (2010) *The Biennal Reader*, Bergen: Bergen Kunsthall, pp. 322–345.
Filipovic, E., M. Van Hal and S. Ovstebo (eds.) (2010) *The Biennal Reader*, Bergen: Bergen Kunsthall.
Gell, A. (1996) 'Vogel's net. Traps as artworks and artworks as traps', *Journal of Material Culture*, 1(1):15–38.
Giorgi, L. and M. Sassatelli (2011) 'Introduction', in L. Giorgi, M. Sassatelli and G. Delanty (eds.) *Festivals and the Cultural Public Sphere*, London: Routledge, pp. 1–11.
Giorgi, L., M. Sassatelli and G. Delanty (eds.) (2011) *Festivals and the Cultural Public Sphere*, London: Routledge.
Heinich, N. (2005) *L'Elite artiste. Excellence et singularité en regime démocratique*. Paris: Gallimard.
Heinich, N. and M. Pollak (1996) 'From museum curator to exhibition auteur; inventing a singular position', in R. Greenberg, B.W. Ferguson and S. Nairne (eds.) *Thinking about Exhibitions*, London: Routledge, pp. 231–250.
Karp, I., C.A. Kratz, L. Szwaja and T. Ybarra-Frausto (2006) (eds.) *Museum Frictions. Public Cultures/Global Transformations*, Duke University Press.
Karp, I. and S.D. Levine (1991) (eds.) *Exhibiting Cultures*, Washington: Smithsonian Institution Press.
Latour, B. (2011) 'Some experiments in art and politics', *E-flux Magazine*, issue 23, available online at www.e-flux.com/journal/view/217 (accessed July 2014).
Lechner, F. and J. Boli (2005) *World Culture*, Oxford: Blackwell.
Lee, Y. (2013) 'The crisis and opportunity of biennals' in U.M. Bauer and U. Hanru (eds.), *Shifting Gravity (World Biennal Fofum N. 1)*, Ostfildern: Hatje Cantz, pp. 10–13.
Martini, F. (2010) 'Una Biennale, molte biennali. Dalla Grande esposizione universale alla mostra globale', *Studi Culturali*, 7(1):15–35.
Mulazzani, M. (2004) *I padiglioni della Biennale di Venezia*, Milano: Mondadori Electa.
Nederveen Pieterse, J. (2003) *Globalization and Culture: Global Mélange*, Lanham: Rowman and Littlefield.
O'Neill, P. (2007) 'The curatorial turn: From practice to discourse' in J. Rugg and M. Sedgwick (eds.), *Issues in Curating Contemporary Art and Performance*, Bristol: Intellect Books, pp. 13–28.

Papastergiadis, N. and M. Martin (2011) 'Art biennales and cities as platforms for global dialogue', in L. Giorgi, M. Sassatelli and G. Delanty (eds.), *Festivals and the Cultural Public Sphere*, London: Routledge, pp. 45–62.
Quemin, A. (2006) 'Globalization and mixing in the visual arts. An empirical survey of "high culture" and globalization', *International Sociology*, 21(4): 522–550.
Quinn, B. (2005) 'Arts festivals and the city', *Urban Studies*, 42(5/6): 927–943.
Roche, M. (2000) *Mega-Events and Modernity: Olympics and Expos in the Growth of Global Culture*, London: Routledge.
Rogoff, I. (2009) 'Geo-cultures circuits of arts and globalizations', *Open,* issue *The Art Biennal as a Global Phenomenon*, 16: 106–115.
Roy, A. and A. Ong (eds.) (2011) *Worlding Cities: Asian Experiments and the Art of Being Global*, Chichester: Wiley-Blackwell.
Rydell, R. (2006) 'World fairs and museums', in S. Macdonald (ed.) *A Companion to Museum Studies*, Oxford: Blackwell.
Sassatelli, M. (2011) 'Urban festivals and the cultural public sphere: Cosmopolitanism between ethics and aesthetics' in L. Giorgi, M. Sassatelli and G. Delanty (eds.), *Festivals and the Cultural Public Sphere*, London: Routledge, pp.12–28.
Schjeldahl, P. (1999) 'Festivalism: Oceans of fun at the Venice Biennale', *The New Yorker,* July 5, pp. 85–86.
Seijdel, J. (2009) 'Editorial', *Open,* issue *The Art Biennal as a Global Phenomenon*, 16: 4–5.
Smith, R.W. (2007) 'Cultural development? Cultural unilateralism? An analysis of contemporary festival and biennale programs', *Journal of Arts Managements, Law and Society*, 36(4): 259–272.
Stallabrass, J. (2004) *Art Incorporated. The Story of Contemporary Art*, Oxford: Oxford University Press.
Steinert, H. (2003) *Culture Industry*, Cambridge: Polity.
Tang, J. (2007) 'Of Biennials and Biennialists: Venice, Documenta, Munster', *Theory, Culture and Society*, 24(7–8): 247–260.
—— (2011) 'Biennalization and its discontents', in B. Moeran and J.S. Pedersen (eds.), *Negotiating Values in the Creative Industries. Fairs, Festivals and Competitive Events*, Cambridge: Cambridge University Press.
Van Proyen, M. (2006) 'Administrativism and its discontents', *Art Criticism*, 21(2): 9–194.
Verwoert, J. (2010) 'The curious case of biennal art', in E. Filipovic, M. Van Hal and S. Ovstebo (eds.), *The Biennal Reader*, Bergen: Bergen Kunsthall, pp. 184–197.
Vincent, C. (2014) 'A non-linear history of Dak'Art', *C&.Platform for international art from African perspectives*, online magazine (contemporaryand.com), special print edition Dak'Art,14, pp.4–5.
Vogel, S. (2011) *Biennals, Art on a Global Scale*, Vienna: Springer.
West, S. (1995) 'National desires and regional realities in the Venice Biennale, 1895–1914', *Art History*, 18(3): 404–434.
Wu, C.T. (2009) 'Biennals without borders?', *New Left Review*, 57: 107–115.
Yudice, G. (2003) *The Expediency of Culture: Uses of Culture in the Global Era*, Durham: Duke University Press.

19
Aesthetic capital

Sylvia Holla and Giselinde Kuipers[1]

Beauty comes with benefits. There are the obvious perks, such as sexual attractiveness and a desire on the part of others to seek out the company of good-looking people. But people are also inclined to associate 'good looks' with other positive qualities, from moral goodness to economic success. Social psychologists call this the 'halo effect': the assumption that persons with visible desirable traits also have other, maybe less visible, positive qualities (Nisbett and Wilson 1977; Kaplan 1978). The belief that beautiful people are better than others can be found around the world and in all eras. In present-day societies, research has shown that people who are deemed more attractive tend to have higher wages, more durable relationships, higher grades and better assessments (Andreoni and Petrie 2008). Thus, physical attractiveness comes with many rewards, also in fields that at first glance have nothing to do with physical appearance.

Sociologists have increasingly identified looks[2] as yet another form of capital: a convertible social resource that is unevenly divided across people which leads to advantages in many domains, also outside the direct field of appearance and sexuality (Anderson et al. 2010; Hakim 2010). Following Anderson et al. we refer to this as 'aesthetic capital'. Related concepts like 'erotic capital' (Hakim 2010) and 'sexual capital' (Martin and George 2006) point to similar mechanisms.

Compared with psychologists and economists, sociologists have been slow to take up this field of study. The societal impact of appearance may have become more evident in today's media-saturated culture, with its abundant showcasing of images of attractive people. Also, looks are becoming an increasingly important asset in post-industrial societies, where many people work in service jobs that require a representative appearance. The increasing multiplication of 'forms of capital' in sociological theorizing reflects the increasing fluidity and fragmentation of stratification systems in contemporary societies and could make this question of beauty and looks structurally quite complicated. There are indeed many sources of status and inequality, which interact with each other in increasingly complex ways (Bennett et al. 2009; Róbert 2010; Savage et al. 2013; Bellavance this volume).

This chapter gives an overview of sociological theory and research regarding 'good looks' as a convertible social resource in contemporary Western – mainly European – societies. It has a twofold aim. First, it presents three main theoretical perspectives in sociological thought, which highlight the meanings and importance of physical appearance in social life around the turn of the twenty-first century. Second, we present three case studies of the workings of aesthetic capital, which ground as well as contest (parts) of these theoretical frameworks. The first case is the rise of 'aesthetic labour' (Warhurst et al. 2000), which sheds light on the pivotal role of physical appearance for people's working selves, as various sectors of the labour market increasingly demand employees to look good on the job. The other two cases are based on our own research. They discuss, respectively, work in a field that is entirely organized around physical beauty, the modelling world, and the diversity of beauty standards of 'average' people in four European countries.

Approaches to aesthetic capital

We distinguish three research traditions that explore the social benefits of good looks. The first sees 'aesthetic capital as human capital'. The second approach focuses on 'aesthetic capital as cultural capital'. The third perspective is interested in the 'aesthetization of economy and society'.

Aesthetic capital as human capital

As many studies in psychology, economy and (to a lesser extent) sociology have shown, people found attractive are significantly more successful socially and economically than people with average or unattractive looks (cf. Hamermesh and Abrevaya 2013; Kwan and Trautner 2009; van Leeuwen and Maccrae 2004; Mobius and Rosenblat 2006). Sometimes, this is the result of the direct contribution of looks. In jobs like modelling and entertainment, being attractive is an intrinsic part of one's work, but in many other domains, the process is more indirect. The 'halo effect' is essentially a cognitive bias: it leads people to believe that desirable qualities often co-occur. Thus, most people – including teachers, HR personnel, employers and other people whose decisions have lasting and important consequences – are biased towards beauty. This then becomes a self-fulfilling prophecy: success breeds success.

An attractive appearance functions as 'human capital' (cf. Coleman 1988): it is part of each individual's package of skills, competencies and qualities that leads to benefits both in the economic marketplace and in everyday life. However, whereas typical forms of human capital, such as education, are rather meritocratic, in the sense that they concern qualities that can be invested in and accumulated, with aesthetic capital this is less the case. People are mostly born with a certain appearance, but they can perform aesthetic labour – practices that are geared at attaining or shaping specific corporeal dispositions – to accumulate parts of it.

A recent comprehensive review by Anderson et al. (2010) gives an overview of studies of the 'perks and penalties' of an attractive appearance, asking 'what sorts of value research has found to be associated with beauty and what forms of individual wealth it returns' (2010: 565). Out of a total of 196 studies, 88 studies reported benefits for beautiful people, while 18 reported penalties for unattractive persons. These 'perks' covered multiple areas: health, employment opportunities and outcomes, as well as status and self-esteem.

Interestingly, no less than 51 studies found penalties for attractiveness. However, these negative effects tend to be more psychological – low self-esteem, low self-acceptance – whereas the perks are usually more tangible. Moreover, a key distinction lies in *having* versus *pursuing* beauty: trying to increase aesthetic capital is likely to lower self-esteem, while being judged as attractive by others is often associated with increased self-esteem (2010: 571).

These studies often show gender effects. In an early study, Kaplan (1978) found that the 'beauty effect' worked for women, but not for men. Later studies as well, generally show that women benefit more from looking good than men do (cf. Anderson *et al.* 2010; Hakim 2010). However, this is context-dependent. A widely publicized Israeli study (Ruffle and Shtudiner 2014) sending in CVs with and without picture to recruiters found that attractive men received significantly more call-backs than men with no picture or plain looking men. Interestingly, attractive women did not enjoy such a 'beauty premium'. The authors speculate that this gender bias is the result of envy among the HR personnel responsible for the first screening, 90 per cent of which is female (2014: 14). The contrasting results show not only that the workings of aesthetic capital are moderated by gender, but also that shifting gender relations and contextual factors affect how possessing ample aesthetic capital works out in practice. In some cases, beauty can work against you – especially when you are female.

Recently, Hakim (2010, 2011) developed the concept of 'erotic capital', which is a considerable refinement of the 'beauty premium' perspective. She stresses how erotic capital can be used strategically, especially by women, but that they are prevented from doing so by conventional morality.

In the 'human capital' perspective, attractiveness is a resource with clear profits and unequal distribution that may also have downsides. Beauty standards are usually taken as given, or at least shared within a particular context. Most studies use ratings of attractiveness (usually by students) to establish which of their stimulus images can be deemed attractive, assuming a considerable consensus on what attractiveness entails. Other studies discuss levels of beauty or attractiveness in the light of evolutionary psychology, which hold that beauty standards are universal and linked with outward signs of fertility, health and sexual fitness (cf. Etcoff 2000). Thus, while this approach has been very successful in showing the *effects* of good looks, it has bypassed the question what good looks are, and how standards of beauty and attractiveness come into being. The next perspective is centrally concerned with this issue.

Aesthetic capital as cultural capital

The second perspective starts from the assumption that standards for attractiveness are socially constructed. Therefore, they are variable within and across societies. Moreover, they are shaped by power relations and therefore not neutral. While beauty certainly 'pays off', beauty standards also benefit those who are most effective in establishing them.

This perspective sees variations on both sides of the 'beauty equation': there is variation across individuals (and groups) in aesthetic capital, but also considerable diversity in what people consider beautiful. These standards function as cultural capital (Bourdieu 1984, 1986). Beauty standards of working and lower-middle classes often diverge considerably from dominant middle-upper class styles (Bourdieu 1984; Crane 2000; Tyler 2008; Vandebroeck 2012). In *Distinction* (1984) for example, Bourdieu shows that the highbrow 'aesthetic disposition' allows for the appreciation of a photograph portraying an old woman's gnarled hands. People with lower class background and less cultured tastes typically disliked this image and saw beauty in more conventional images of pretty young women.

For Bourdieu, aesthetic evaluations – also bodily ones – mark social divides, most importantly class divides. In addition, Bourdieu discusses the different bodily styles of higher and lower social classes, which reflect divergent understandings of how to make *oneself* look good[3]. Like all aesthetic judgments, evaluating looks is an embodied process: a sensorial experience that happens almost automatically. But importantly, beauty standards are not only applied to 'external objects', such as paintings, but also to one's own face and body.

The evaluation of appearance, therefore, is characterized by what we call a 'double embodiment': the appreciation of is an embodied taste that people aim to express also in one's own body.

In the extensive literature building on Bourdieu's work, little attention has been paid to either the evaluation of physical appearance, or the way cultural capital affects bodily styles. A notable exception is the recent Flemish study by Vandenbroeck (2012), showing that people of different class backgrounds by and large have the same norms for body size: they like thin bodies. However, people with higher status more often meet these standards: they are on average thinner and taller. Lower class people accept hegemonic standards for body size, but are less able to meet them. Being overweight, moreover, is increasingly stigmatized (Saguy 2013), implying that societal beauty standards do indeed privilege high-status groups.

The Bourdieusian approach highlights how aesthetic standards maintain the cultural dominance of higher classes. Like other forms of cultural capital, the appreciation of beauty requires cultural knowledge that is distributed unevenly across society. Standards of influential people and institutions have a wide social impact and can function as cultural capital in society as a whole, whereas the cultural standards of others are marginalized, limited to specific settings, or even discredited. However, although 'lowbrow' bodily styles may be penalized in society as a whole, they carry social worth in specific surroundings. Moreover, some modes of adornment entail a wilful denial of mainstream beauty standards and are designed to be liked by few people only. Think of subcultural styles like punk or gothic, but also the sometimes arcane styles of trendsetting 'fashion forwards', which have yet to become fashionable.

British researchers in cultural studies have shown how the physical styles cultivated in subcultures also challenge societal hierarchies. This approach calls into question the Bourdieusian opposition of highbrow dominance and lowbrow domination, presenting instead a more fragmented system in which aesthetics – including appearance – function as identity markers for groups with various social positions. Hebdige (1979), for example, analysed the aesthetics of youth culture, notably punk, conceptualizing these subcultural styles as 'counter-aesthetics' with their own logic. While these alternative aesthetics started out as a reversal (e.g. punk) or exaggeration (e.g. mod) of conventional styles, some elements eventually became part of 'legitimate' styles. This approach, now grown into a full-fledged field of subcultural studies (Gelder 2005), not only shows the possibility of diversity in aesthetic standards and styles, but also shifts the attention away from bodily beauty as a given, towards bodily grooming and styling as active, constructive body practice.

The most radical position in this perspective is based in feminist theory. Scholars like Bordo (2003) and Wolf (1990) have argued that beauty standards predominantly serve to uphold gender inequalities. Beauty standards are produced in a patriarchal society, and mainly applied to women who have traditionally had limited influence on them. While beauty may have benefits for individual women (and possibly men), in society as a whole the pursuit of beauty suppresses women. Feminists argue these standards privilege a 'male gaze' and lead to objectification of women, blocking their chances of success in other domains. Moreover, the 'beauty myth' is a disciplining instrument: women spend considerable time and energy trying to meet standards that, for most of them, are impossible to attain (Bartky 1990). Ultimately, female beauty standards are beneficial to men in maintaining their dominant position in society. Importantly, it is not just men who impose oppressive beauty standards: women also do this to each other.

These feminist and gender scholars believe in beauty as capital, but they are sceptical about the value of aesthetic capital for women in general. They argue that individual perks of beauty do not defeat the disadvantages related to 'beauty myths' that women collectively experience.

With their shared focus on the social construction of beauty standards, the studies discussed show that aesthetic capital indeed supports existing power dynamics, leading to the marginalization of, for instance, lower classes, women or ethnic minorities. This perspective highlights that beauty – and therefore aesthetic capital – is not simply a matter of appearance. It results from a combination of given traits, styling and grooming in accordance with one's (group-specific) taste and the resources available given one's social position that may facilitate or hamper the achievement of a certain look. Moreover, appearance can be used for the marking of symbolic boundaries – to confirm, but also oppose social hierarchies.

The aesthetization of economy and society

The third perspective holds that aesthetic capital has become increasingly important in contemporary society. Since the early 1990s, various social theorists signalled the 'aesthetization of everyday life' (Featherstone 1991) in the wake of a new era variously referred to as late, high, reflexive or postmodernity (Giddens 1991; Lash and Urry 1993; Beck 1994; Featherstone 1991). This new phase is characterized by the erosion of traditional institutions and identities as a result of increasing individualization and globalization. Consequently, identities become more fluid and changeable, and meaning making becomes gradually detached from traditions. Instead, people organize their selves around lifestyles, often anchored in consumption and aesthetic preferences.

As a result, looks and appearance have gained both importance and meaning as a 'performance of self'. Clothing, grooming and styling no longer are reflections of one's social standing, or other traditional sources of identity. Instead they are supposed to show one's authentic self (cf. Veenstra and Kuipers 2013). This insight has spawned a whole new field of fashion and wardrobe studies that analyse how people select clothes that match their lifestyle and identity (Entwistle 2000; Woodward 2007; for a critique see Van der Laan and Velthuis 2013).

Aesthetic capital in this perspective, therefore, results from a balance between individuality and conformity to dominant tastes. Compared with the other two perspectives, the focus lies on appearance as it is actively achieved through practices of styling and adornment. The pay-off for engaging in bodywork is large: through one's aesthetic self-presentation, everyone can and *should* show who they are.

Another group of scholars has also signalled the increasing importance of appearance due to a fundamental societal shift towards a post-industrial service economy (Sassen 2001; Lloyd 2006). Increasing segments of the workforce are employed in the service or 'aesthetic economy' (Entwistle 2002; Hakim 2010), setting higher standards for self-representation as a professional requirement. This is particularly important in jobs that directly involve consumer contact or selling aesthetic goods, but other sectors are also affected by the demand to look good on the job (even university lecturers now wear designer clothes). Beauty standards emerge here not only as an expression of self: in post-industrial economies, aesthetic capital is not only a personal asset, but a job qualification – an essential competence required to function in the labour market.

This final perspective adds a third element to the beauty equation: apart from the individual appearance and socially constructed beauty standards, the meaning and effect of aesthetic capital are shaped by the importance allotted to beauty and appearance in a given society. While the general claim that 'looking good' has become more important in contemporary Western societies sounds plausible enough, it is not easy to prove empirically. However, the observations that appearance has become very important for people in specific *professional contexts*, has given rise to a fertile area of empirical research: the study of aesthetic labour.

Aesthetic capital in contemporary societies: Three case studies

Aesthetic capital thus refers to bodily styles, traits, preferences and tastes. It comes with certain (dis)advantages and can function as human capital, but also marks social differences as it reflects different levels of cultural capital. Moreover, it is historically and culturally contingent. In the following cases, we discuss the mechanisms and aesthetic labour practices that lead to the shaping of aesthetic capital (case one and two), and how it is evaluated (case three), both inside and outside the field of fashion modelling.

Aesthetic labour: Looks as a resource at work

Aesthetic capital can be acquired through engaging in aesthetic labour (Anderson et al. 2010). According to Warhurst and Nickson (2001), who coined the term, aesthetic labour refers to particular 'embodied capacities and attributes' that enable employees to 'look good and sound right' for a certain job. From a Bourdieusian perspective, these aesthetic capacities and attributes, such as language, dress codes, manner, style, shape and size of the body, can be called 'dispositions' (Bourdieu 1984). Whereas aesthetic capital refers particularly to bodily styles and appearances as outcomes of certain cultural taste patterns, aesthetic labour refers particularly to the practices that are geared towards attaining or shaping specific corporeal dispositions in people.

In most studies, aesthetic labour refers to jobs for which appearance is an important asset to produce value. However, aesthetic labour can also be used to refer to the effort people make to work on their own appearance. These two ways of aesthetic labour tend to co-occur: people who work on their appearance are more likely to get hired and be successful in jobs that involve aesthetic labour. However, as mentioned in the discussion of aesthetic capital as human capital, aesthetic capital is to a considerable extent fixed and can only be altered partly through aesthetic labour practices. Hence, by no means it guarantees to result in an appearance desired by organizations involving aesthetic labour.

The theory of aesthetic labour originated from empirical observations of the 'style' labour market of designer retailers, boutique hotels, style bars, cafes and restaurants in the 'new' Glasgow economy (Warhurst et al. 2000). They demonstrated how the emergence of this style labour market has changed the nature of the qualities employers are looking for when hiring labourers. Due to the gradual shift from manufacturing to service industries, aesthetic labour has become increasingly importance in comparison with, for example, workers' technical skills. Especially in service providing sectors such as hospitality and retail, potential employees are increasingly demanded to be 'outgoing', 'attractive', 'trendy', 'well-spoken and of smart appearance' (Warhurst and Nickson 2001: 17).

Organizations can choose to appeal to any of the senses to improve customer experience. For example, while fashion retailers are concerned with the physical appearance of shop floor workers, call centre operatives are predominantly preoccupied with customers' aural experience, like the accent and vocal intonation of the call centre operatives (Warhurst et al. 2000: 7). Employers strategically commodify and mobilize people's aesthetic attributes to their advantage when competing with other organizations. These attributes are often trained and developed once an employee has been hired in a variety of ways: through extensive grooming, deportment training, encompassing haircuts, styling, 'acceptable' make-up, posture and more (Karlsson 2012: 54).

Studies of aesthetic labour show that the value of aesthetic capital can vary greatly, as it is often defined along the lines of 'corporate standards' within specific industries and organizations. Because aesthetic attributes resulting from aesthetic labour are likely to be differently appreciated from one organization or field to the next, the conversion of people's 'aesthetic efforts' into valued aesthetic capital is context-dependent.

Moreover, corporate aesthetic standards tend to intersect with cultural norms regarding gender, race, class and age. For example, in her research on the aesthetic labour of black models in New York (2012), Wissinger showed how the 'white gaze' and the 'corporate gaze' intersect in this field. Black models have to adhere to a narrower set of aesthetic standards than other models, and consequently experience their race ambivalently: as both an asset and a liability (2012: 140). In another study of fashion models, Mears (2010) showed how professional requirements for models intersect with classed beauty standards. The slender physique that is the basis of selection at the gate of the modelling field, and which models are expected to maintain through diets and exercise, signals economic status, self-restraint, middle and upper-class background, while overweight bodies signal lower class (2010: 24).Thus, via the standard of slenderness the category of class influences what is valued as aesthetic capital within the field of fashion modelling and beyond.

Aesthetic capital therefore marks clear symbolic boundaries. People are excluded from certain professions, regardless of the amount and form of aesthetic labour they engage in. Some physical attributes, such as skin colour, are unalterable, just as some personal capacities are impossible to (un)learn. In addition, people can fail in carrying out aesthetic labour: it can have unintended outcomes. The discriminatory effects of aesthetic capital and aesthetic labour are referred to by theorists as 'lookism' (Warhurst *et al.* 2012).

Research on aesthetic labour has provided valuable insights on the importance of appearance as a professional asset. However, viewing aesthetic labour as a form of work that only occurs within delineated organizations fails to take into consideration the increasing 'aestheticization' of late-modern service societies (Featherstone 1991; Welsh 1996). Moreover, even in a professional context, aesthetic labour is carried out not only in the context of organizations, but increasingly by freelance workers (Entwistle and Wissinger 2006). In the absence of a clear corporate aesthetic, these freelancers have to adapt to different clients, trends and more vaguely defined 'floating norms' existing in broader professional fields (Mears 2008).

Consequently, Entwistle and Wissinger (2006) have pleaded for more emphasis on the interlinking of emotional and aesthetic labour (cf. Hochschild 2003), and the relation between identity and the embodiment practices involved in aesthetic labour. Especially in the case of freelance work, aesthetic labour is not carried out solely on the work floor. The enduring nature of aesthetic labour requires workers to 'always be on' and to adapt their whole lifestyle – their entire embodied self – to professional aesthetic imperatives (2006: 783). They argue that aesthetic labour usually entails much more than superficial work on the body's surface: it involves people's entire body/self, as constantly keeping up appearances requires serious emotional effort (2006: 774). The following section on fashion modelling illustrates this.

Fashion modelling: Working in a field organized around aesthetic capital

In a society focused increasingly on appearance and aesthetics, the profession of fashion modelling is culturally prominent (Mears 2011). Although models are holders of aesthetic capital *par excellence* and generally appreciated as symbolic carriers of beauty ideals (Brenner and Cunningham 1992), they are also publicly critiqued for their work. In various media, models are simultaneously attributed positive and negative characteristics, such as natural, artificial, effortless, obsessed, beautiful, unhealthy, glamourous or superficial.[4] Existing research on the aesthetic labour of fashion models focused on its disciplining and arduous nature. Within the fashion industry, models are predominantly looked upon as a 'physical surfaces' to be improved and made into 'looks'. In her work on plus-size models, Czerniawski (2012) documented how they are intensively managed through self-surveillance and corporeal discipline. Likewise, Mears (2008) has shown how models are subjected to intense surveillance, uncertain judging criteria and a persistent norm of 'infantile femininity' (2008: 444). Finally, Mears and Finlay (2005) have demonstrated how aesthetic labour challenges models to engage in specific forms of emotional management, as their work is irregular, physical demands are great and competition is fierce. Correspondingly, our own ethnographic research on fashion models in Amsterdam, Paris and Warsaw (carried out from March 2011 until March 2013) shows that, although fashion modelling is generally depicted as glamorous and 'fabulous', it presupposes a great deal of commitment (Holla forthcoming). The modelling industry is a typical 'greedy institution' that seeks 'exclusive and undivided loyalty' of its workers (Coser 1974: 4).

Fashion is about constantly changing styles, causing models' guidelines to be in constant flux (Entwistle 2002; Mears 2011). Therefore, a strong claim is made on models to be 'fresh', flexible and able to adapt to changing trends, symbols and technologies to get new jobs and survive in the industry (Neff, Wissinger and Zukin 2005: 326–327). This demand for flexibility and full engagement forces models to function as 'chameleons', able to change into whatever the fashion of the moment happens to be (Soley-Beltran 2006: 34). At the same time, this malleability requires models to maintain their bodies as a neutral basis upon which other professionals from the industry can project their envisaged image. At castings especially, models experience pressure to present themselves as a 'clean state'. During an interview fashion model Chantal explained to us:

> You have to be pretty natural, you cannot show up at a casting wearing thick eyeliner and red lipstick, because then you are already too much of a character. You must always give the impression of a clean slate. That they can form you the way they want to…. Their lack of imagination is really unbelievable!
>
> *(Chantal, 22, Amsterdam)*

The average model is young, tall, slim and white. However, this overall aesthetic exists in varying forms, due to a 'high-low divide' existing in fashion modelling (Neff, Wissinger and Zukin 2005; Mears 2011). Whereas high-end modelling generates prestige, commercial fashion modelling is less 'legitimate' but more profitable. It uses idealized but still 'recognizable' notions of beauty that consumers can identify with, because this leads them to buy the products. In high-end fashion modelling, the process of aesthetic production is more autonomous and lacks an explicit commercial logic (Neff, Wissinger and Zukin 2005: 323; Bourdieu 1996:142). High-end fashion modelling is concerned with status, is primarily intended for field insiders instead of mass-consumption, is more experimental and takes aesthetic standards more to the extreme. Thus, there are high and lower forms of aesthetic capital produced in fashion modelling, analogous to high and lower forms of art that call for different levels of cultural capital to be able to appreciate and understand them.

This high-low divide is intersected by gender, sexuality and age: in commercial modelling, the value of aesthetic capital is largely based on heteronormative male and female attractiveness, while in high-end fashion, male and female aesthetic standards converge to a considerable extent, which challenges sexual stereotypes.

This intersection results in different outlooks (as well as in variable interpretations of them by consumers, as demonstrated in the third case study discussed hereafter). Female commercial models are generally more 'curvy' and male models relatively more muscular than high-end or editorial models, who in turn are usually thinner and taller. There are seemingly fewer differences between male and female high-end aesthetic standards; all high-end models are tall, skinny, straight and 'dried out' – no fat, no curves. Many of them describe themselves or are characterized by others as somewhat androgynous. And finally, while youthfulness plays an important role in the overall aesthetic of fashion modelling, especially in high-end modelling, the value of models' aesthetic capital regresses as they age (Neff, Wissinger and Zukin 2005: 326).

However, despite these variations, the 'aesthetic basis' of slenderness, whiteness, youthfulness and tallness strongly inspires all models' body-work. The bodily attainment of these standards is everything but an effortless endeavour. To keep up with the demands, models continuously carry out aesthetic labour, such as yoga, dieting, practicing poses and more. Models carry out most of their aesthetic labour 'off the job'. They are never 'not models' because their entire embodied self *is* the product (Entwistle and Wissinger 2006: 791).

The case of fashion modelling is an extreme form of aesthetic labour. Requiring intense forms of emotional and physical involvement and being continuous in nature, their aesthetic labour has strong repercussions for how models live their lives. Because their private lives are so strongly guided by professional imperatives, maintaining a coherent sense of self is challenging to many models. Although in many modern-day professions, the boundary between work and leisure has become increasingly porous (Maguire 2008), this issue is particularly important for fashion models. In our research we have found that models draw moral boundaries between 'good' and 'bad' ways of being a model, through which they attempt to justify the professional 'colonization' of their body/selves, towards themselves and others. This means that other than merely a new form of work, aesthetic labour is a potential source of identity construction: it determines to a considerable extent how people relate to their selves.

Diverse beauty standards and cultural capital in a globalizing world

Besides the creation of beauty standards within the field of modelling, our research also analyses how beauty standards vary across social groups in relation to shifting inequalities. As we saw, the 'aesthetic capital as cultural capital' makes many claims about the relation between social inequalities and beauty standards, but so far has produced little empirical research. In our current research project we investigate how people in four European countries – Italy, the Netherlands, Poland and the UK – evaluate physical beauty of men and women.

Given the shift in stratification systems and the 'multiplication of symbolic boundaries' in contemporary Western societies, we look at cultural capital and gender, as well as other social dividing lines: age, urbanity and engagement with global culture (cf. Prieur and Savage 2013; Savage *et al.* 2013)[5]. We analyse people's beauty standards and their implications in social life. How do people apply beauty standards to themselves and others? How are they related to social background? How do people attempt to produce and influence their own 'aesthetic capital'?

For this study we use Q methodology, a research method designed to combine the strengths of qualitative and quantitative research (Brown 1993). It uses a combination of semi-structured interviews and a sorting assignment[6]. In all four countries, we created a stratified sample structured by gender, educational level, age group and metropolitanism, interviewing a total of 106 persons. Respondents were asked to sort four sets of images of male and female faces and bodies according to beauty in a pre-set grid; and to comment on the images while sorting. The images were selected to be as diverse as possible, with people of different physical types, different styles of photography and a wide variety in grooming and styling. We used factor analysis to find underlying aesthetic standards or 'logics', and the interview materials to interpret these factors. In addition, we combined factors with information on informants' personal beauty practices, life history and social position, and the degree to which they draw symbolic boundaries on the basis of beauty. Finally, we used regression analysis to gauge whether the factors extracted from the Q analysis were related to social background.

We found that evaluations of facial images show the clearest relation with symbolic boundaries. There are clear 'repertoires of evaluation' (Lamont and Thévenot 2000) reflecting different aesthetic logics. These repertoires differ greatly within countries, and are related to specific social backgrounds. The Q-sorts for bodies showed considerably less variation – that is, greater consensus – within each country. Thus, standards for bodily beauty are more standardized and probably more hegemonic (thus confirming Vandebroeck's 2012 findings). In contrast with the standards for facial beauty, the evaluation of bodies appears to be more nationally specific and less influenced by international or global styles and standards.

The Q sorts of facial beauty show considerable variations in beauty standards. These vary systematically across social groups, suggesting that they are linked to the demarcation of symbolic boundaries. Moreover, we find considerable differences in evaluatory logics applied to male and female faces.

The judgments of female faces follow a 'Bourdieusian' logic akin to the evaluation of other aesthetic products. Across all the countries surveyed, less educated, older and non-metropolitan informants look for pleasing, appealing faces, whereas more educated, younger, metropolitan informants prefer a beauty that is 'interesting' or 'original', reflecting a Bourdieusian 'aesthetic disposition'. We found no significant differences between countries. This divide is more complex than the traditional highbrow/lowbrow division as it points to an intersection of education, age and urbanity within each of the four countries. This reflects a divide between cosmopolitan urban youth, in ample position of 'emerging cultural capital', and older, less cosmopolitan people who may be more oriented towards local culture.

Both the highbrow and the lowbrow repertoires come in 'subjectified' and 'objectified' versions. The objectifying gaze uses formal, standardisable or stylistic features to distinguish the beautiful from the less beautiful. In gender theory, this gaze is associated with the traditional objectification of female appearance (Kress and Van Leeuwen 2006). In the subjectifying view, the (perceived) personality of the models strongly impacts their attractiveness. Informants tend to speculate about the person, or imagine themselves interacting with them. Women and older people are more likely to take this subjectifying stance. This finding on the subjectifying gaze somewhat opposes the third theoretical perspective on 'the aesthetization of society', which holds that looks and appearance have gained importance and meaning as a reflection of identity. The subjective gaze reminds us that people also look beyond the surface of appearance, searching for clues about the character and personality of people portrayed.

Beauty 'logics', moreover, differ on gender normativity. In general the highbrow styles are less gender-normative: people with this taste prefer androgynous fashion models, or faces with unusual styling and make-up (reflecting the relatively gender-neutral highbrow standards within the modelling field). Less gender-normative faces are also liked better by the educated, younger metropolitans. Again, this repertoire of evaluation is not related to either gender or country of origin.

Male facial beauty is judged according to a less aestheticized, more gender-normative logic. In line with findings from gender studies, evaluations of men are less objectified and less easily measured by a strictly aesthetic yardstick. Instead, these evaluations are strongly informed by variations in gender norms and ideologies, leading to considerable cross-national variations. The appreciation of male looks is therefore less globalized than the judgment of female beauty and more shaped by nationally specific styles and gender relations.

The presence of distinct tastes based in social divides suggests that human appearance and beauty standards serve as a means of distinction: what people find beautiful provides information – consciously or unconsciously – about their social position. In the case of appearance, this information is quite literally embodied, for instance in styles of dress and grooming. However, we find that the politics of distinction are more complicated than a straightforward highbrow-lowbrow divide. The judgments of beauty intersect with other social background factors. Especially in the case of female beauty, standards are increasingly globalized, probably as a result of the growing impact of transnational visual culture. Moreover, we find that valuations of beauty are strongly gendered: both male and female respondents are more inclined to objectify and aestheticize women, reflecting an age-old tradition of viewing women as aesthetic objects. Male beauty, on the other hand, is less affected by global media culture or an aesthetic gaze. Instead, when people are explicitly requested to judge how beautiful a man is – something many informants found remarkably difficult – they were more likely to speculate what sort of person they were and how well they lived up to conventional standards of masculinity. Thus, they shied away from seeing male faces as purely aesthetic objects.

Conclusion

This chapter highlighted the meanings and importance of 'good looks'. We presented three main (cultural) sociological perspectives on the role of appearance in advanced Western societies around the turn of the twenty-first century. The first perspective, 'aesthetic capital as human capital', deals with the social advantages and drawbacks of being attractive. The second approach, 'aesthetic capital as cultural capital' sheds light on the variability of what is regarded as beautiful by whom, and shows how social and cultural constructions of aesthetic capital allows for new inequalities to arise. Finally, the third perspective depicts the overall importance of appearance in present-day societies – at work, but also in society at large, as a marker of identity. We empirically grounded and contested (parts) of these theoretical frameworks by presenting three case studies on the workings of aesthetic capital. The first case on 'aesthetic labour' demonstrates an increasing demand for good looks in various sectors of the labour market. The second case shows how the aesthetic labour of fashion models has considerable consequences for how models live their lives and relate to their selves. The third case about evaluations of facial images by broader publics in Europe, highlights that the politics of distinction are more complicated than a straightforward highbrow-lowbrow divide: both cultural constructions and appreciations of beauty intersect with a multitude of social background factors, such as gender, sexuality, age and metropolitanism.

The involvement of these intersecting variables is, at least partly, explained by the presence of a 'double embodiment'. While all tastes involve a sensorial experience in response to specific objects or persons, the judgment of physical appearance is dually embodied: beauty standards also apply to the self and to one's own face and body. Consequently, embodied attributes like gender, sexuality and age are particularly significant in shaping and evaluating aesthetic capital, compared to, for example, judgments of paintings or books.

Our analyses especially underscores the importance of gender for cultural sociologists, who have often been content to leave gender to feminist and gender theorists, preferring to focus on national differences and class-related dispositions instead. This chapter shows that gender plays a pivotal role in understanding constructions and valuations of appearance. It probably does for explaining other cultural processes of meaning making as well.

Finally, we argue for an intersectional and relational approach to aesthetic capital. 'Looking good', and appreciating looks of others respectively, can only be sufficiently understood by analysing how multiple variables intersect and by considering the social and cultural contexts within which people's aesthetic practices and tastes are shaped and expressed.

Notes

1 University of Amsterdam, the Netherlands.
2 The terms 'looks' and 'appearance' are used interchangeably throughout this chapter. 'Looks' is an expression that is often used within our field of study, the fashion modeling industry, to denote the appearance of, for example, fashion models.
3 This understanding of aesthetic capital as cultural capital mostly refers to consumption: to being able to recognize and talk about beauty in the right ways. Moreover, cultural capital is grounded in a relational framework that recognizes the contingency and power dynamics of the production of beauty norms. As such, it significantly differs from aesthetic capital as human capital – a term derived from economics rather than sociology – which looks at the productive effects of aesthetic capital and tends to assume that standards for beauty are stable and shared. However, in the Bourdieusian tradition as well, aesthetic capital can bring advantage and is convertible into other forms of capital. Thus, the distinction with human capital is strong in some respects, but also overlaps to an extent.
4 To illustrate, this is just a small selection of headlines from the web: *Skinny models 'send unhealthy message'*, available online at www.theguardian.com (31 May 2000, accessed 29 August 2014); *Smile and say 'No Photoshop'*, available online at www.nytimes.com (27 May 2009, accessed 29 August 2014); *Fashion week embraces grey hair and the rise of natural chic*, available online at www.theobserver.com (18 September 2011, accessed 29 August 2014); *Models' cotton balls diet: Bria Murphy describes unhealthy model habit*, available online at www.huffingtonpost.com (11 June 2013, accessed 29 August 2014).
5 We use educational level as a proxy for cultural capital, because occupational and class structures differ considerably across countries. Existing operationalizations of class position often fail to capture this. Therefore, cross-national comparative studies often employ educational level as an indicator of cultural capital. Across European countries, completion of tertiary education is a good predictor of job status and income levels (Eurostat 2012): it generally functions as a qualification for higher white-collar or middle-class jobs. Moreover, higher education is fairly comparable because of long-standing international connections and recent formal standardization (the Bologna treaty).
6 Q method studies usually combine semi-structured interviews with cards with statements that interviewees are asked to sort. Our study used images. The cards serve a several functions. First, they are used for elicitation. Second, they structure the interview. Third, and most importantly, they allow for quantification. Because all images are sorted along a pre-structured bell-shaped grid, all cards can be assigned a score from most to least beautiful. These scores can then be used as basis for a factor and a regression analysis. The interview material is then employed to interpret these factors. Thus, Q method allows for the 'measurement of subjectivity'.

References

Anderson, T.L., C. Grunert, A. Katz and S. Lovascio (2010) 'Aesthetic capital: A research review on beauty perks and penalties', *Sociology Compass*, 4(8):564–575.
Andreoni, J. and R. Petrie (2008) 'Beauty, gender and stereotypes: Evidence from laboratory experiments', *Journal of Economic Psychology*, 29(1): 73–93.
Bartky, S.L. (1990) *Femininity and Domination: Studies in the Phenomenology of Oppression*, London: Psychology Press.
Beck, U. (1994) *Reflexive Modernization*, Stanford: Stanford University Press.
Bennett, T., M. Savage, E. Silva, A. Warde, M. Gayo-Cal and D. Wright (2009) *Culture, Class, Distinction*, London: Routledge.
Bordo, S. (2003) *Unbearable Weight: Feminism, Western Culture, and the Body*, Berkeley: University of California Press.
Bourdieu, P. (1984) *Distinction: A Social Critique of the Judgement of Taste*, London: Routledge.
—— (1986) 'The forms of capital', in J. Richardson (ed.), *Handbook of Theory and Research for the Sociology of Education*, New York: Greenwood, 241–258.

—— (1996) *The Rules of Art: Genesis and Structure of the Literary Field*, Stanford: Stanford University Press.
Brenner, J.B. and Cunningham, J.G. (1992) 'Gender differences in eating attitudes, body concept, and self-esteem among models' *Sex Roles*, 27(7–8): 413–437.
Brown, S. (1993) 'A primer on Q methodology', *Operant Subjectivity*, 16: 91–138.
Coleman, J.S. (1988) 'Social capital in the creation of human capital', *The American Journal of Sociology*, 94: 95–120.
Coser, L.A. (1974) *Greedy Institutions: Patterns of Undivided Commitment*, New York: Free Press.
Crane, D. (2000) *Fashion and Its Social Agendas*, Chicago: University of Chicago Press.
Czerniawski, A.M. (2012) 'Disciplining corpulence: The case of plus-size fashion models', *Journal of Contemporary Ethnography*, 41(2): 127–153.
Entwistle, J. (2000) *The Fashioned Body: Fashion, Dress and Modern Social Theory*, Cambridge: Polity.
—— (2002) 'The aesthetic economy: The production of value in the field of fashion modelling', *Journal of Consumer Culture*, 2(3): 317–339.
Entwistle, J. and E. Wissinger (2006) 'Keeping up appearances: Aesthetic labour in the fashion modelling industries of London and New York', *The Sociological Review*, 54(4): 774–794.
Etcoff, N. (2000) *Survival of the Prettiest*, New York: Anchor Books.
Eurostat (2012) *Key Data on Education in Europe 2012*, Brussels: Education, Audiovisual and Culture Executive Agency.
Featherstone, M. (1991) *Consumer Culture and Postmodernism*, London: Sage.
Gelder, K. (2005) (ed.) *The Subcultures Reader*, London: Routledge.
Giddens, A. (1991) *Modernity and Self-identity*, Cambridge: Polity.
Gill, R. (2007) *Gender and the Media*, Cambridge: Polity.
Hakim, C. (2010) 'Erotic capital', *European Sociological Review*, 26(5): 449–518.
—— (2011) *Honey Money: The Power of Erotic Capital*, London: Penguin.
Hamermesh, D. and J. Abrevaya (2013) 'Beauty is the promise of happiness?', *European Economic Review*, 64: 351–368.
Hebdige, D. (1979) *Subculture: The Meaning of Style*, London: Routledge.
Hochschild, A.R. (2003) *The Managed Heart: Commercialization of Human Feeling*, California: University of California Press.
Holla, S. (2015) 'Justifying aesthetic labour. How fashion models enact coherent selves', *Journal of Contemporary Ethnography*. Published online ahead of print: doi:10.1177/0891241615575067
Kaplan, R. (1978) 'Is beauty talent? Sex interaction in the attractiveness halo effect', *Sex Roles*, 4(2): 195–204.
Karlsson, J.C. (2012) 'Looking good and sounding right: Aesthetic labour', *Economic and Industrial Democracy*, 33(1): 51–64.
Kress, G. and van Leeuwen, T. (2006) *Reading Images: The grammar of Visual Design*, New York: Routledge.
Kwan, S. and M. Trautner (2009) 'Beauty work: Individual and institutional rewards, the reproduction of gender, and questions of agency', *Sociology Compass*, 3(1): 49–71.
Lamont, M. and L. Thévenot (2000) *Rethinking Comparative Cultural Sociology. Repertoires of Evaluation in France and the United States*, Cambridge: Cambridge University Press.
Lash, C. and J. Urry (1993) *Economies of Signs and Space*, London: Sage.
Lloyd, R. (2006) *Neo-Bohemia. Art and commerce in the post-industrial city*, New York: Routledge.
Maguire, J.S. (2008) 'Leisure and the obligation of self-work: An examination of the fitness field', *Leisure Studies*, 27(1): 59–75.
Martin, J.L. and M. George (2006) 'Theories of sexual stratification: Toward an analytics of the sexual field and a theory of sexual capital', *Sociological Theory*, 24(2): 107–132.
Mears, A. (2008) 'Discipline of the catwalk: Gender, power and uncertainty in fashion modeling', *Ethnography*, 9(4): 429–456.
—— (2010) 'Size zero high-end ethnic: Cultural production and the reproduction of culture in fashion modeling', *Poetics*, 38(1): 21–46.
——(2011) *Pricing beauty: The making of a fashion model*, California: University of California Press.
Mears, A., and W. Finlay (2005) 'Not just a paper doll: How models manage bodily capital and why they perform emotional labour', *Journal of Contemporary Ethnography*, 34(3): 317–343.
Mobius, M. and T. Rosenblat (2006) 'Why beauty matters', *American Economic Review*, 96(1): 222–235.
Neff, G., E. Wissinger and S. Zukin (2005) 'Entrepreneurial labour among cultural producers: 'Cool' jobs in 'hot' industries', *Social Semiotics*, 15(3): 307–334.

Nisbett, R. and T. Wilson (1977) 'The halo effect: Evidence for unconscious alterations of judgments', *Journal of Personality and Social Psychology*, 35(4): 250–256.
Prieur, A. and M. Savage (2013) 'Emerging forms of cultural capital', *European Societies*, 15(2): 246–267.
Róbert, P. (2010) 'Stratification and social mobility', in S. Immerfall and G. Therborn (eds.), *Handbook of European Societies*, Berlin: Springer.
Ruffle, B. and Z. Shtudiner (2014) 'Are good-looking people more employable?', *Management Science*, published online in advance May 2014.
Saguy, A. (2013) *What's Wrong with Fat?*, New York: Oxford University Press.
Sassen, S. (2001) *The Global City: London, New York, Tokyo*, Princeton: Princeton University Press.
Savage, M., F. Devine, N. Cunningham, M. Taylor, Y. Li, J. Hjellbrekke, B. Le Roux, S. Friedman and A. Miles (2013) 'A new model of social class? Findings from the BBC's great British class survey experiment', *Sociology*, 47(2): 219–250.
Soley-Beltran, P. (2006) 'Fashion models as ideal embodiments of normative identity', *Trípodos.com: revista digital de comunicació*, (18).
Spiess, L. and P. Waring (2005) 'Aesthetic labour, cost minimisation and the labour process in the Asia Pacific airline industry', *Employee Relations*, 27(2): 193–207.
Tyler, I. (2008) 'Chav mum chav scum. Class disgust in contemporary Britain', *Feminist Media Studies*, 8: 17–24.
Van der Laan, E. and O. Velthuis (2013) 'Inconspicuous dressing: A critique of the construction-through-consumption paradigm in the sociology of clothing', *Journal of Consumer Culture*, online first. doi:10.1177/1469540513505609.
Van Leeuwen, M. and C. Maccrae (2004) 'Is beautiful always good? Implicit benefits of facial attractiveness', *Social Cognition*, 22(6): 637–649. Vandebroeck, D. (2012) *Harnessing the Flesh. Social Class and Reflexive Embodiment*, Brussels: Free University.
Veenstra, A. and G. Kuipers (2013) 'It is not old-fashioned, it is vintage. Vintage fashion and the complexities of 21st century consumption practices', *Sociology Compass*, 7(5): 355–365.
Warhurst, C. and D. Nickson (2001) *Looking good and sounding right: Style counselling and the aesthetics of the new economy*, London: The Industrial Society.
—— (2009) '"Who's got the look?" Emotional, aesthetic and sexualized labour in interactive services', *Gender, Work and Organization*, 16(3): 385–404.
Warhurst, C., D. Nickson, A. Witz and A. Marie Cullen (2000) 'Aesthetic labour in interactive service work: Some case study evidence from the "new" Glasgow', *Service Industries Journal*, 20(3): 1–18.
Welsch, W. (1996) 'Aestheticization processes: Phenomena, distinctions and prospects', *Theory Culture and Society*, 13: 25–50.
Wesely, J.K. (2003) 'Exotic dancing and the negotiation of identity: The multiple uses of body technologies', *Journal of Contemporary Ethnography*, 32(6): 643–669.
Wissinger, E. (2012) 'Managing the semiotics of skin tone: Race and aesthetic labour in the fashion modeling industry', *Economic and Industrial Democracy*, 33(1): 125–143.
Witz, A., C. Warhurst and D. Nickson (2003) 'The labour of aesthetics and the aesthetics of organization', *Organization*, 10(1): 33–54.
Wolf, N. (1990) *The Beauty Myth*, New York: William Morrow.
Woodward, S. (2007) *Why Women Wear What They Wear*, Oxford: Berg.

Part III
The complexity of cultural classifications

Introduction to Part III

The sociology of art and culture which we champion here does not believe in universals: cultural forms change, new mediums and innovative aesthetic paradigms emerge. All of this influences the type of cultural resources one can draw on, and the ways one relates to others and to one's environment. It also affects how people perceive themselves and build their identity. We therefore need to not only pursue new avenues of inquiry but to also revisit more established ones. This final part of the handbook focuses on three of these avenues that strike us as particularly promising for the development of the discipline.

The first section of this last part revisits one of the now classical tensions that underpin cultural classifications, namely that between high and low culture. For a long time, the boundaries between high and low culture were unquestioned; they were conceived as reflecting *only* intrinsic qualities of the art forms – alongside the characteristics of the audiences for such art forms (with snobbery hence directed at the kind of people who did not appreciate high culture). The work of sociologists, and especially of Bourdieu, was crucial to show that cultural classifications were not independent from social stratification processes and that such classifications embodied forms of 'symbolic violence'. As DiMaggio put it, classification systems order artistic genres which classify together art works 'on the basis of perceived similarities' (1987: 441) and constitute social constructions with very real consequences. It quickly became evident that the cultural resources one has at disposal – one's cultural capital – were essential for navigating through the cultural codes and classifications defining dominant and dominated cultural forms of a society but also possibly for creating new ones. Cultural capital is therefore clearly associated with the (re-)production of symbolic boundaries that '[…] are conceptual distinctions made by social actors to categorize objects, people, practices, and even time and space' (Lamont and Molnár 2002: 168). People's taste categorizes them and gives them symbolic value – either positive or negative – that influences the type of interactions they can develop in the everyday life (on this see Skeggs 2004).

The link between culture and stratification is amply evident in empirical research. Still the overarching power of this argument shouldn't hide the complexity of this link. It is important to avoid the reflex view that culture and art are simply a product of stratification; we need to have a more sensitive awareness of the possible disjunctures between these. Lahire provides an essential contribution to the debate. While recognizing the statistical correspondence between social hierarchy and cultural classifications, he argues that the boundary between high and low culture should not be only examined at the group level – important though this is for the study of social inequalities – but also at the level of individual tastes and dispositions. If we don't do this we can end up treating individual people as ciphers for social categories in much too simplistic a way. We also run the risk of simplifying the way cultural classifications and their legitimizing effects work and giving a monolithic vision of individuals who are much more 'dissonant' culturally speaking than a focus on the aggregated level could suggest. Lahire's target here is against Bourdieu's concept of habitus, which he thinks over-generalizes people's cultural profiles. Tensions between high and low differentiate the cultural practices and preferences not only between different classes but also within individuals themselves whatever their class. According to Lahire researchers should try to understand the reasons for these intra-individual variations.

Bellavance's chapter connects with Part I of this handbook by dissecting the apparent omnivorousness of art lovers and cultural consumers among the upper middle class in Quebec. To understand this eclecticism, Bellavance argues that we need to further complicate the relationship between taste on the one hand and social status and profession on the other. Even though taste is influenced by socio-professional milieu, this link is blurred by 1) the complexity of people's professional and life trajectories and 2) the multiplication of classificatory schemes, of which the opposition between high and low culture constitutes only one. The opposition between old and new would be another one. Omnivorousness would then go along with the multiplication of symbolic boundaries rather than their disappearance and takes different forms to the extent that it falls apart as a distinctive construct.

Friedman's exceptional study on British comedy taste sheds another light on the mechanisms of cultural classification. His focus on comedy, which he describes as 'the low-brow art *par excellence*', enables him to reconsider how boundaries between high and low are being redrawn in the light of 'emerging' forms of cultural capital. The precise way that cultural objects or performances are evaluated is crucial to his concerns. The latter questioning is especially important for reflecting upon the alleged rise of eclecticism in cultural taste. Indeed comedy is appreciated by people with a high cultural capital on more aesthetic and intellectual grounds than simply for its capacity to make people laugh.

The final chapter of this section reminds us that the opposition between high and low has often been approached in binary terms – and that we need to think about the role of middlebrow culture. Drawing on two quite separate bodies of literature, Carter traces back the history of the emergence of the word 'middlebrow' and its part in the classification of institutions, practices and tastes. He shows that despite Bourdieu's interest in *'la culture moyenne'*, cultural sociology has left this in-between category largely under-theorized. Reflecting upon the book culture and the new developments of its industry, he argues though that middlebrow constitutes a useful category able to capture particular cultural orientations that are not quite encapsulated either in high or in popular culture.

The second section reflects upon the rise of digital culture. The Internet, the World Wide Web and associated social networking sites, blogs, and groups have reconfigured the traditional triad in sociology of art and culture of production, mediation, and consumption. As Vincent Miller put it, 'the online sphere is no longer a realm separate from the offline "real world", but fully integrated into offline life' (2011: 1). This is even truer when we think about the pervasiveness of mobile and wireless technologies in our everyday life. We live now in a connected world and this has transformed our lifestyle, identities and sense of belongings. This is obviously a huge topic and this handbook doesn't seek to address all the issues posed, but nonetheless it is essential for us to consider its potential significance.

Introduction to Part III: Complexity of cultural classifications

Mackenzie and his colleagues provide a very interesting case study to illustrate the potentialities of digital sociology – focusing on the development of devices within these growing and complex media environments that are now embedded in many dimensions of our everyday life. They examine a social media platform, Github.com, which hosts many coding and software development activities with many concrete applications, such as algorithms (see Couldry's chapter). By doing so they show how a sociological analysis of the field of devices and of the practices of its players makes it possible to account for crucial changes in the making and the texture of culture.

Couldry's chapter highlights the importance of studying 'social analytics'. Social analytics refers to 'social actors' everyday use and reflections on "analytics", that is, any digital tools that measure them and their presence in a world of online presences'. Couldry recognizes the structuring force of the algorithmic measurements and classifications on everyday life given the pervasiveness of the digital culture. Yet he also argues that these algorithmic operations can be acted upon *reflexively* by individuals and shows how they can provide new opportunities for the active presentation of the self of individuals but also of groups and organizations. The online presence can, for instance, be monitored, measured and possibly enhanced by adjusted actions. New cultural practices here emerge and with them new symbolic hierarchies.

While the two latter contributions concentrate on digital objects and interactions with the digital world, the last contribution here discusses the position of digital practices among a wider set of cultural practices. Relying on the insights from the survey on cultural participation, *Les Pratiques culturelles des Français*, conducted since the 1970s, Donnat offers an exceptional overview of the changes that the rise of 'screen culture' has introduced in people's lifestyle. The screen culture has been implicated in two major steps since the emergence of television in the 1960s. First, the 1980s were marked by the expansion of television as a clearly dominant medium in the audio-visual landscape. Second, the end of last century was characterized by the rise of 'new screens' through the deployment of Internet and new mobile technologies (computer, smart phones, tablets, etc.). Both forms of screen culture have had different impacts on other practices. The decline of the print culture is particularly explored. Donnat concludes by reflecting on the significance of these shifts for understanding the relationship between cultural practices and stratification.

The last section explores the important link between place and culture, which is fundamentally important given the power of global forces. Research has pointed to the ambivalent role of culture in driving new urban dynamics (see Florida's disputed theory of 'creative' class 2002 and Peck's 2007 critique) in reshaping neighbourhoods as part of urban gentrification (Zukin 1995; Butler 2003; Jackson and Butler 2014) and regeneration (Bailey, Miles and Stark 2004), and in developing a sense of belonging in a globalized world (Jones and Jackson 2014; Savage, Bagnall and Longhurst 2005). Less focus has been placed on the complexity of cultural classifications and the intersection between social stratification and spatial divisions (though see Hanquinet, Savage and Callier 2012). This section provides pioneering examples of research that connects the sociology of art and culture with urban sociology through a special interest in cultural capital, resources, and lifestyles. It is worth noting that if it has become clear that culture influences place, then place also influences the very texture of culture. As we show elsewhere, cultural capital is structured by a diversity of aesthetic paradigms and there is a growing affinity between urban location and an emerging urban aesthetic (Savage and Hanquinet forthcoming).

Méndez provides an exceptionally refined account of the making of symbolic boundaries in Latin America. Although she values Bourdieu's work on *Distinction* (1984), she also shows that his theory should be adapted to the socio-political context of non-European countries.

Introduction to Part III: Complexity of cultural classifications

Drawing on many examples including from her own research, she describes the multiplicity of cultural referents at stake in the formation of new middle classes (ethnic, national and global). Her own research underlines the importance of the spatial aspect of symbolic boundaries which are inscribed in different territorial tensions and senses of belonging to the city.

Drawing on Bourdieu's insights as well, Pereira explores the space of lifestyles in Porto. Using a rich mixed-method approach, he shows how the relationships between social position, socio-demographics and lifestyle are deployed within the city. Pereira uses survey, ethnographic and social history material to dissect the volume of capital and the structure of the capital composition that underpin different class cultures and explores how these socio-historically situated cultures structure Porto as an illustration of a wider relational research programme.

Zhang provides a brilliant study of artistic production in a specific area – TZF – of Shanghai. She shows how it is possible to combine Bourdieu's field analysis with Becker's account of art worlds to unravel how particular urban locations become a magnet for potential artists. Although TZF was initiated by Chinese cultural policy, she demonstrates how these artistic zones are not simply receptacles for artists. These areas come to permit artistic innovation and encourage artists to take on new identities and practices. We can thus see how urban space and art can combine to allow the emergence of new modes of cultural production.

Finally Lloyd establishes a very fruitful link between urban sociology and sociology of culture through his concept of 'neo-bohemia'. He traces back its historical origins in order for us to better understand the properties of this new version of bohemia, which refers to 'the encounter between the traditions of "the artist in the city" birthed in nineteenth century Paris and the structural dynamism reshaping cities at the end of the twentieth century'. Using examples from his own research on Chicago's Wicker Park, he shows how specific lifestyles have been associated to urban restructurings but also progressively used in a neoliberal urban agenda in postindustrial cities by promoting new forms of work, of cultural consumption, and of urban gentrification.

References

Bailey, C., S. Miles and P. Stark (2004) 'Culture-Led Urban Regeneration and the Revitalisation of Identities in Newcastle, Gateshead and the North East of England', *International Journal of Cultural Policy*, 10(1): 47–65.
Bourdieu, P. (1984) *Distinction: A Social Critique of the Judgement of Taste*, translated by Richard Nice, Cambridge, MA: Harvard University Press.
Butler, T. (2003) 'Living in the Bubble: Gentrification and its "Others" in North London', *Urban Studies*, 40(12): 2469–2486.
DiMaggio P. (1987) 'Classification in Art', *American Sociological Review*, 52(4): 440–455.
Florida, R. (2002) *The Rise of the Creative Class ... and How It's Transforming Work, Leisure, Community, and Everyday Life*, New York: Basic Books.
Hanquinet, L., M. Savage and L. Callier (2012) 'Elaborating Bourdieu's Field Analysis in Urban Studies: Cultural Dynamics in Brussels', *Urban Geography*, 33(4): 508–529.
Jackson, E. and T. Butler (2014) 'Revisiting "Social Tectonics": The Middle Classes and Social Mix in Gentrifying Neighbourhoods' *Urban Studies*: 1–17.
Jones, H. and E. Jackson (2014) *Stories of Cosmopolitan Belonging*, London: Routledge.
Lamont, M., and V. Molnár (2002) 'The Study of Boundaries in the Social Sciences', *Annual Review of Sociology*, 28(1): 167–195.
Lloyd, R. (2010) *Neo-Bohemia: Art and Commerce in the Postindustrial City*, 2nd ed., New York: Routledge.
Miller V. (2011) *Understanding Digital Culture*, London: Sage.
Peck, J. (2007) 'The Creativity Fix', *Eurozine*: 1–12.

Savage, M., G. Bagnall and B.J. Longhurst (2005) *Globalization and Belonging*, London: Sage.
Savage, M. and L. Hanquinet (forthcoming) 'Emerging Cultural Capital in the City: Profiling London and Brussels', *International Journal of Urban and Regional Research*, volume edited by Loïc Wacquant.
Skeggs, B. (2004) *Class, Self, Culture*, London: Routledge.
Zukin, S. (1995) *The Cultures of Cities*, Cambridge: Blackwell Publishers.

20
Cultural dissonances
The social in the singular

Bernard Lahire

Since the mid-1960s sociologists have learned to understand 'culture' (the dominant cultural arbitrary that imposes itself and is recognized as the only 'legitimate culture') in relation to the social classes or class fractions; they then observe the social inequalities in access to 'Culture' (the frequent use of the capital letter indicating its greatness). They also emphasize the social functions of art and culture in a differentiated and hierarchised society. Social classes and their more or less great distance from culture, cultural hierarchies that rank individuals, objects and practices from the most legitimate to the least legitimate – these are the key elements of the sociological meaning assigned to culture in the last forty years. The great shaping moments of this scientific history were marked by the publication of the works of Pierre Bourdieu and his various collaborators – on students and their relation to culture (Bourdieu and Passeron 1964), photography (Bourdieu ed. 1965), museums and art galleries (Bourdieu and Darbel 1969), the educational system (Bourdieu and Passeron 1970), and class styles (Bourdieu 1979).

By cross-comparing the variables 'respondent's educational attainment' or 'respondent's socio-occupational category' with the various indicators of cultural activities (preference for a genre, frequency of a type of cultural visit, etc.), the sociology of cultural consumption fairly generally confirms the unequal probability of access to (i.e. taste for and interest in) a given category of cultural goods or institutions. It establishes the existence of a fairly strong *statistical correspondence* between the *hierarchy of the arts* and, within each art, the *hierarchy of genres*, and the *social (or cultural) hierarchy of the consumers (or audiences)*. Such a reading of the reality of cultural practices is clearly intrinsically unexceptionable. What is problematic is its routinization, which leads to the masking of other possible readings of the same survey data. But can one investigate cultural practices other than through these correlations of cultural (or socio-occupational) groups and cultural products – in a way that, without forgetting the groups and categories, would more respect the specificity of individual trajectories and profiles?

A study carried out in the early 2000s (Lahire 2004), based on wide and varied material (statistical data, interviews with over a hundred respondents with varied social properties, direct observation of behaviours, various written and audiovisual documents, etc.), did not aim to deny the existence of social inequalities in relation to legitimate culture and wipe out the picture of cultural reality painted by four decades of work on the social uses of culture.

It aimed nonetheless to put forward another, no less empirically grounded, picture, which would not have been conceivable without the work done by the painters of the past, but which does not show the same forms. This new picture, which composes the same reality in a different way, was made possible by a change in the scale of observation: it offers the image of the social world that can be produced by a gaze that starts by examining the differences internal to each individual (intra-individual variations) before changing the viewing angle and looking at the differences among social classes (inter-class variations).

By adopting this perspective, it brings to light a fundamental fact, namely that *the boundary between cultural legitimacy ('high culture') and cultural illegitimacy ('popular culture', 'mere entertainment') does not only separate the practices of the different classes, but divides the different cultural practices and preferences of the same individuals, in all classes of society*. On the scale of the individual, what first strikes the observer is the statistical frequency of individual cultural profiles made up of dissonant elements: they are in an absolute or relative majority in all social groups (although distinctly more probable in the middle and super classes than in the working class), at all levels of education (although much more probable among those who have at least the *baccalauréat*) and in all age groups (although decreasingly probable as one moves from the youngest to the oldest). What one next observes is the much greater probability for the individuals composing the sample population of having a homogeneous cultural profile 'at the bottom' (with weak legitimacy) than 'at the top' (with strong legitimacy). Finally, having constructed this series of new statistical facts concerning cultural dissonances and consonances on the individual scale, one can try to explain sociologically the intra-individual variations of cultural behaviours.

'Facts' never speak for themselves; they always presuppose a point of view that constitutes them. The gaze that is brought to bear in this research consisted in bringing to light the central character of the statistical margins and exceptions and shows that the most fundamental structures of the social world manifest themselves as much in individuals as in the groups they compose, as much in intra-individual and inter-individual variations as in inter-group variations.

The complex and nuanced pictured of socially differentiated relations to culture that can be built up from research conducted on the basis of an observation of the world on an individual scale first aims to renew our knowledge of the state of the relations of the 'cultural consumers' to the various cultural registers, from the most elaborate to the most accessible, from the most disinterested to the most commercial, from the most legitimate to the most illegitimate. It can also make actors who seek to implement policies of cultural democratisation and those who strive to impose their definition of what is culturally legitimate more aware of the subtleties of the cultural order of things.

The individual scale of cultural behaviours

Reprocessing of the data from the statistical survey on the 'cultural practices of the French 1997' (DEP/Ministère de la Culture; $N = 3000$) and analysis of a long series of interviews ($N = 111$)[1] make it possible to continue the work of empirically testing elements of a sociological reflection on the social world at the level of the individual (Lahire 2002, 2003, 2010). Rather than presupposing the systematic influence of a necessarily coherent incorporated past on present individual behaviours, rather than imagine that *all* our past, *en bloc* or as a homogeneous synthesis (in the form of a system of dispositions or values), weighs *at every moment* on *all* the situations we experience, the sociologist may examine the triggering or non-triggering, the implementation or suspension of incorporated dispositions and competences, by the different action contexts. The *plurality of dispositions and competences* on the one hand, and the *variety of the contexts of their actualisation* on the other, are what can sociologically explain the variation of the behaviours of a single individual, or a particular group of individuals, depending on the domain of practice, the properties of the action context or the more singular circumstances of practice.

With a smaller number of respondents and in a thoroughly experimental and intensive way, an earlier study[2] made it possible to begin to show the significant variation of the degree of legitimacy of the respondents' cultural practices. This variation becomes apparent on the one hand when one takes the trouble to sufficiently detail the individual practices and preferences within each cultural domain and, on the other hand, when instead of focusing all attention on a single domain or sub-domain, one follows the pattern of individual behaviours in different cultural domains. Each individual portrait, which was not designed to illustrate cultures of groups, classes or class fractions, showed clearly that, far from confining themselves to a single cultural register, the respondents manifested ambivalences, oscillations or alternations within each domain (e.g. classical music and popular variety shows or classic literature and airport novels or celebrity magazines) and/or from one domain to another (from reading to music, from television to cultural visits, etc.).

Moreover, in the various case studies, analysis already brought out a series of elements which, generally in combination, accounted for such variations in cultural behaviours. They include: heterogeneous socialising experiences in childhood or adolescence (in the family, school, peer group and cultural institutions frequented), major changes in material and/or cultural living conditions (e.g. cases of upward or downward social mobility), specific and localised effects of very specialised academic training (e.g. a high-level literary education set against a lack of competences in areas which could not be constituted in either early upbringing or schooling), an ambivalent relationship with the original family culture linked to the conditions of 'transmission' of the parental cultural capital, conjugal influences which modify the dispositions acquired within the family, friendships that favour practices distinct from those activated between spouses, extent and above all variety of friendships, which allows a heterogeneous distribution of practices according to the friends who are frequented, closely delimited contexts that are spatially and/or temporally particularly favourable (with least legitimate practices taking place during vacations or other holiday times, in periods of relaxation following a time of occupational pressure, etc.).

The same research approach was thus applied on a larger scale, with the main aim of showing that, far from being the interpretative product of the study of too atypical or too singular cases, these elements highlighted not only *a very general sociological problem*, but also *some central aspects of our highly differentiated social formations*. Intra-individual variations in cultural behaviours are the product of the interaction between, on the one hand, the plurality of incorporated cultural dispositions and competences (presupposing plurality of socialising experiences in cultural matters) and, on the other hand, the diversity of cultural contexts (cultural domain or sub-domain, relational contexts or circumstances of practice) in which individuals have to make choices, to practice, consume, etc. The origin and logic of such variations are thus fully social.

Measuring the singular

Before carrying out the necessary categorisations (socio-occupational category, educational attainment, sex, age, etc.) of the individuals surveyed by questionnaire, one can endeavour to take as much account as possible of the individual logics that mean that each individual is characterised by a *set of behaviours that are not necessarily homogeneous* in terms of the degree of legitimacy of cultural practices and preferences. Such a procedure does not lead the researcher towards a departure from sociological reasoning, but towards an endeavour at sociological reasoning that is attentive to social realities in their individualised form. Nor is it a matter of refusing to classify individuals into groups or categories on the grounds of a supposed "disappearance" of groups or classes (a well-known theme that is now regrettably part of the unscientific common sense on which some sociologists rely). And it is still less a matter of adding another voice to the already well-stocked choir that regularly intones the chant of contemporary individualism. To suppose that scientifically constructing a sociology of individual socialisations is incompatible with a theory of social classes would be as perverse as imagining that the study of atoms or molecules logically implies denying the existence of bodies or planets.

It is a matter of producing a sociological knowledge of cultural practices that retains a strong individual basis or, to put it another way, that takes account (as far as possible and within the limits of what can be interpreted) of the specifically individual scale of social life (it is the same individual who does this and that, who likes one thing and not another, who visits one type of cultural institution but also attends another venue, etc.). This would make it possible to advance, on the one hand, in apprehending the more or less homogeneous or heterogeneous *individual stocks of culturally incorporated dispositions and competences* and, on the other hand, the *properties of the various contexts of practice* that are more or less in harmony or in contradiction with these individual stocks of dispositions and competences. Just as one can investigate the accumulation (or non-accumulation) of cultural competences (Donnat 1994: 19), so can one examine the survey data on the basis of the question of the contextual variation of cultural legitimacy of individual preferences or activities.

The theory of cultural legitimacy lends itself fairly readily to actors who have a very sure and accurate sense of distinction, legitimacy or cultural dignity. A museum-goer's sense of dignity would prevent her, for example, from going to funfairs or watching blockbusters on television. Such an overinterpretation, which is not an inevitable outcome of the theory of cultural legitimacy, then leads one to suppose, by a purely imaginary intensification of cultural investments and knowledge, that all the culturally best endowed consumers are comparable to cultural critics, professionals of culture or committed enthusiasts. Whatever the context (with whom? at what times? for what purpose?), and whatever the cultural activity in question (cinema, television, literature, music, painting, etc.), the cultivated dispositions would be stronger than anything and would act like sorting machines, perpetually separating the cultural grain from the vulgar chaff.

The existence of many counter-examples that emerge from the case studies already justifies the fact that one is able to consider the intra-individual variations of cultural behaviours, and in particular aim to grasp *individual cultural 'colour charts'*, i.e. the variations of tastes and practices for each individual, according to the domain or type of practice in question, thus respecting more than is customary both the complexity of individual *stocks of cultural dispositions and competences* and the variety of the *contexts* in which individuals set their actions. Such questions have hardly been addressed except in relation to persons who have effected a radical change of class (strong upward mobility) through the educational system and who, depending on the domain of practice, may enact dispositions acquired in the family (in a working-class milieu) or dispositions acquired through education and/or occupation (Bourdieu 1989: 259–264). They may be 'working class' in some of their consumption (e.g. of food or clothing) but elsewhere may turn to certain very legitimate cultural products (e.g. in literature), while also making somewhat less 'pure' choices in other areas (e.g. in cinema or television). The closer one moves to areas where the educational system (and sometimes occupation and the accompanying social contacts) has exerted its influence (as is the case with literature, somewhat less with music or painting, etc.), the more these individuals reapply scholastic categories of perception and classification and with them a sense of cultural legitimacy. By contrast, the further one moves away from them, the more their activated social dispositions, tastes, categories of classification, etc., can become working class again.[3] The behaviours of these upwardly mobile individuals are statistically less predictable than those of immobile individuals who perpetuate the original social and cultural conditions in their adult lives. The fact that they make legitimate (or less legitimate) choices in one area of behaviour does not make it easy to predict how they will behave in other cultural domains (Van Eijck 1999).

The methodological approach applied to the data from the statistical survey has three main phases. First, the practices and products are ordered according to their degree of cultural legitimacy. In a second stage, one aims to reconstruct cultural profiles that are more or less chequered or homogeneous in terms of cultural legitimacy. By selecting a series of variables one can bring to light individuals who manifest cultural practices and preferences that are very dissonant (e.g. those who like the most legitimate literature and most often listen to light music, or those who enjoy classical music but watch the least legitimate products on television or at the cinema), moderately dissonant or mixed (with inflections of the degree of cultural legitimacy or mixtures of strong and weak legitimacies in certain areas of practice) or eminently consonant (those who commit no 'lapses' from legitimacy or, at the other extreme, being at a great distance from the most legitimate cultural institutions, consume only 'popular' products). Finally, looking anew at the social determinants classically highlighted, one investigates the probability of such profiles appearing according to sex, age, social class, educational attainment and social origin. In particular one aims to discover which categories provide the most coherent profiles and which provide the most contradictory or ambivalent ones.

One hypothesis that fairly rapidly proved pertinent is that the groups with the most homogeneous (least dissonant) cultural practices and preferences occupy totally opposite positions in social space: homogenisation may be the product of cultural and material deprivation; it may, by contrast result from a long-standing and 'naturalised' embedding in the most legitimate cultural frameworks. In *The Presentation of Self in Everyday Life*, Erving Goffman refers to the aristocratic style of certain social groups, which would be characterised by an attention, a self-control, applied at all times in all areas of existence, both public and private. Drawing on a text by Adam Smith, who declares that a gentleman, being aware that he lives constantly under the scrutiny of others, internalises this gaze in the form of a permanent disposition to behave according to the legitimate norms,[4] Goffman nonetheless seems to doubt the real social existence of 'such virtuosi' (Goffman 1959: 34). A study of intra-individual variations shows that he had good reason to do so.

Between the small intellectual fractions of the dominant classes – (at least) second-generation bourgeois who have the greatest statistical likelihood of combining a large number of the most legitimate cultural practices and preferences – and the (much larger) educationally most deprived members of the working class (with working-class parents), who are largely excluded from the legitimate cultural frameworks, a majority of members of the upper, middle and working classes have in common the heterogeneity of their never perfectly consonant cultural profiles.

By combining information on the practices or preferences of the same persons, one acquires the means of measuring the degrees of cultural asceticism or cultural demandingness, and more generally the degrees of coherence of the cultural commitment. In this case, it makes it possible to seriously relativise the proportion of people manifesting a demanding cultural orientation at all times, a high degree of cultural involvement, leading them to persistently refuse anything that might resemble a culpable 'cultural relaxation' and a vulgar, futile participation in ordinary leisure activities.

When the sociologist habitually cross-compares socio-occupational, gender or age categories with practices, preferences, tastes, etc., he privileges a logic of inter-category variations. When, by contrast, he constitutes individual cultural profiles (an individual who does this *and* that, likes this *but also* that, but *on the other hand* detests that, etc.), he then preserves the individual data of his survey, as he would in processing interviews, and grasps intra-individual variations. Proceeding in this way, someone who tries not to neglect too much the social logics that weigh on individual behaviours is not impelled by any rejection of the classic social determinants. But while cultural activities are pursued unequally according to the social group to which the respondents belong, this should not lead one to forget that the same person (assignable to a category) may have very different tastes and practices depending on the domain, the circumstances of 'consumption' or the types of cultural activity considered (cinema, music, literature, etc.) and that this kind of variation – statistically very widespread in the population – is nonetheless social.

In bringing to the fore these frequent phenomena of intra-individual variations with the aid of statistical surveys, one provides some particularly interesting evidence, in as much as survey by questionnaire can only favour the imposition of coherence on their answers by respondents who can better control each of them and (more or less consciously) 'keep watch' on the harmonisation of the whole. Survey by questionnaire does not benefit from the trust established in interviews, a relationship which enables the respondents to own up, as in a confessional – sometimes jokingly, as if trying to win the complicity or indulgence of the interviewer – to their cultural 'lapses' or 'sins' in certain areas and/or on certain occasions.

Self-distinction and struggles of self against self

Here a cultural 'demand for rigour', there a 'relaxation' experienced more or less in the mode of guilt or necessary entertainment; here a relative incompetence leading to choices 'intermediate' between 'high standards' and 'facility', there a greater cultural rigour adopted to please others; here a complete absence of cultural competences and dispositions, there a fierce demand for 'self-improvement', etc. – the heterogeneous character of the individual palette of practices and tastes can only be understood if one takes note of the plurality of the contextual and dispositional logics that guide cultural behaviours. One is thus led to hypothesise the relative specificity of each cultural domain (which calls for specific competences on the part of the 'cultural consumers'), the important role played by the general conditions or more singular circumstances of the 'consumption' of practice (alone, within the family, with a particular friend, in private or in public, etc.), and the no less important place of the plurality of socialising experiences in the formation of cultural competences and dispositions.

Intra-individual variations in cultural behaviours, the scale and importance of which are brought to light, are not necessarily made explicit, conscious and verbalised by the respondents, who may move from a legitimate practice to a much less legitimate one without necessarily giving a sense to this variation other than through the multiple excuses ordinarily invoked to justify less legitimate cultural practices (fatigue, curiosity, constraint, second-degree, etc.). But some professional producers of discourses (essayists, aesthetes, philosophers) have begun to theorise this cultural heterogeneity, which is more 'undergone' by the actors than asserted as a genuine style of behaviour or existence, and to give it a general meaning, whether positive or negative. In particular, the current state of affairs is seen through the singular (and singularly distorting) lens of *cultural eclecticism* or *cultural mingling*, which is of little or no help in explaining the reality of intra-individual variations in cultural practices and preferences.

Moreover, even if there has been a deliberate intention to privilege the point of view of the 'consumers' (their practices and their non-practices, their tastes, indifferences and distastes), if more attention is paid to the order of 'cultural consumption' than to the structuring of cultural supply, work on the cultural producers and on the transformations of the supply side (in terms of its differentiation and hierarchies) could also be useful for an understanding of the overall situation. A case in point is that of the cultural professionals who now conceive and produce their products on the basis of a generative formula such as the *mixing of genres*, a formula that is close to the one made explicit in discourses on eclecticism or hybridisation and which presents, stages and interprets, especially in televisual formats, the *heterogeneity of practices and preferences* characteristic of a great majority of individual cultural profiles[5].

Finally, the processing of quantitative survey data and the analysis of interviews put forward another social function of the dominant legitimate culture than the function hitherto evoked by the various sociological commentators. While social inequalities in relation to the dominant legitimate culture persist and while that culture does indeed play a central role in the processes of social distinction and legitimation of social differences in class societies, it also has a meaning from the point of view of the individual variations in cultural practices and preferences. For the boundary between the 'legitimate' and the 'illegitimate' does not only separate the groups or classes of society. As a *point of view* on the world, a *scheme of perception*, such an opposition (and the whole series of oppositions that come with it: high/low, worthy/unworthy, cultured/uncultured, intelligent/stupid, etc.) is also applied to the different members of the same group and – a crucial fact that is rarely noted – to the various practices and preferences of many individuals. There are indeed differences between classes, but also inter-individual differences (within groups or classes) and differences between self and self (between a present state of the self and a former state of the self, or between parallel states of the self), and the latter can even give rise to internal struggles of (legitimate) self against (less legitimate) self.

As a means of (collective or individual) legitimation, sophisticated culture and the cultural categories of perception and hierarchisation that accompany it provide a framework enabling individuals to give a *distinctive* meaning to their practices and tastes and feel themselves justified in existing as they do, to have the sense of leading a life worth living, i.e. more worthy of being lived than others. This is a psychological function of support and reassurance provided by culture as legitimate culture. But while the social world is a field of struggles, the individuals who compose it are often *themselves* the sites of a battle of classifications. And it is the struggle of the self against the self, the domination of a legitimate self over the illegitimate part of the self, control and mastery over what is illegitimate in oneself, that generates the sense of distinctive superiority over those who, one imagines, have no control or mastery over themselves. Only personal efforts (of education, training, selection and maintenance of a high level of culture, etc.) make the cultural ascetic (like any other ascetic) that different being who has the sense of being above ordinary mortals, who are seen as living in permanent facility and relaxation, and of being *worth* more than them. Self-domination and domination of others thus prove to be indissociable, and distinctions and symbolic struggles are as much individual (intra-individual and inter-individual) as collective (inter-class).

Conclusion: cultural transferability in question

The sociologist of North American culture Herbert J. Gans wrote in 1999 that individual cultural choices are 'not made randomly' but are 'related':

> People who read *Harper's* or the *New Yorker* are also likely to prefer foreign movies and public television, to listen to classical (but not chamber) music, play tennis, choose contemporary furniture, and eat gourmet foods. Subscribers to the *Reader's Digest,* on the other hand, probably go to the big Hollywood films if they go to the movies at all, watch the family comedies on commercial television, listen to popular ballads or old Broadway musicals, go bowling, choose traditional furniture and representational art, and eat American homestyle cooking. And the men who read *Argosy* will watch westerns and sports on television, attend boxing matches and horse races, and let their wives choose the furniture but prefer the overstuffed kind'.
>
> *(Gans 1999: 92)*

To support his argument, Gans tells us that 'these relationships between choices exist because the choices are based on similar values and aesthetic standards'. He acknowledges, however, in a note, that these are only 'hypothetical descriptions' since few academic studies have in fact been made of these 'interrelations of choices'. A wise precaution, since the statistical data profoundly challenge these cultural stereotypes. The natural interpretative slope of sociologists of culture, but perhaps more generally of ordinary actors, namely the idea of a transferability of tastes or attitudes from one area of practice to another, is contradicted by many survey data. More prudently than others, the sociologist will speak of 'statistical probability', but still tend towards the same caricatural typifications, such as Gans's 'hypothetical descriptions', and the same astonishment at readers of the *New Yorker* who go to boxing matches.

A concept is scientifically useful only if it enables one to observe elements in reality and to order one's observations in a specific way. It must make it possible (and even necessary) to carry out empirical investigations that could not have been imagined without it. Thus, the notion of the 'transfer' of incorporated dispositions or schemes leads one to look for the generative principles of behaviours in apparently unrelated domains of practice (food, culture, sport, politics, etc.) or in relatively autonomous sub-domains (music, literature, painting, cinema, theatre, etc.). To gain an idea of the statistical probability of the transfer of a sense of cultural legitimacy from one cultural sub-domain to another and to evaluate the importance of non-cumulations of 'weak' or 'strong' cultural legitimacy, one can thus begin by systematically cross-comparing the indicators of weak cultural legitimacy with the indicators of strong legitimacy.

One could state – and it is quite frequently confirmed – that weak (or strong) legitimacy in a given cultural domain statistically attracts weak (or strong) legitimacy in another cultural domain. Concretely, those who have a legitimate cultural practice in one domain (music, cinema, literature, etc.) *generally* have more statistical likelihood of being on the side of the legitimate cultural practices of another domain than on the side of non-legitimate practices. This information is not anodyne, since one might, for example, observe that having a legitimate practice in one cultural domain makes one no more predisposed to legitimate practices than to non-legitimate practices in a series of other domains. In terms of the *statistical tendencies* attached to *groups* or *categories,* one can partly (but only partly) agree with Pierre Bourdieu when he writes that:

> the clearest proof that the general principles of the transference of learning also apply to learning at school lies in the fact that the practices of the same individual or at least of

individuals of a certain social category or level of education tend to constitute a system, such that a certain type of practice in any given area of culture is associated, with a very strong degree of probability, with an equivalent kind of practice in all the other areas. Thus regular museum visiting is almost necessarily associated with regular trips to the theatre and, to a lesser extent, to concerts. In the same way, all the indications are that knowledge and tastes arrange themselves into constellations (strictly linked to level of education) such that a typical structure of preferences and knowledge in matters of painting is very likely to be linked to a similar structure of knowledge and tastes in classical music or even in jazz or cinema'.

(Bourdieu and Darbel 1969: 101)

Only in part, since, when one looks more closely, the *statistical* tendency towards transfer is not verifiable in a certain number of cases. Moreover, it is difficult to assert on the basis of the observation of *statistical* tendencies that one observes 'overall' a 'transfer' of the sense (practice) of cultural legitimacy from one domain to another, since this type of reasoning applies to categories of individuals. If one needs to stress the *statistical* character of the tendency towards transfer, this is in order to bear in mind the existence of a good proportion of respondents left outside the explanatory model. What one observes for the individuals composing the categories is that a proportion of them – sometimes a small minority, but not always a marginal one, and in some cases a majority – do not make choices of cultural dignity or nobility that are equivalent according to the domain of practice considered. Starting from the most elementary cultural profiles, with just two variables, it is clear that the number of those who combine weakly legitimate practices or tastes with highly legitimate practices or tastes is never negligible.

Adding a third cultural domain, then a fourth, a fifth, etc., reveals a progressive erosion of the consonances and brings out dissonances in some of those who had previously (on the basis of the first two cultural practices) shown a perfectly coherent profile. The more practices one adds, the greater the likelihood of bringing to light dissonances in cultural profiles and highlighting culturally hybrid or composite individuals, individuals with a variable cultural geometry (which does not mean culturally free of all determination). In any case, it is very difficult to concur with Bourdieu's assertion that 'the generative schemes of the habitus are applied, by simple transfer, to the most dissimilar areas of practice' (Bourdieu 1979: 196).

Broadly presupposing a general mechanism of cultural transferability at work, Bourdieu argued in *L'Amour de l'art*, discussing a paradox:

Even while the academic institution only gives a restricted role to strictly artistic teaching, and even while it provides neither specific encouragement of artistic practice nor a body of concepts specifically aimed at works of plastic art, it does tend to inspire a certain *familiarity* – part of the feeling of belonging to the cultivated world – with the universe of art, where one feels at home and among friends, as the accredited addressee of works which are not delivered to just anybody.

(Bourdieu and Darbel 1969: 99)

Two main reasons are put forward to support the idea of a transfer. Firstly, a kind of statutory assignment of the sense of cultural dignity and duty whereby, given his social position, his educational attainment, etc., the highly educated respondent cannot do other than apply all means to maintain his rank, whatever the domain in question (*ibid.*: 100). Secondly, a technical competence (a set of intellectual habits) which, initially constructed from the study of literary works ('an equally generalized and transferable aptitude for classification, by artist, genre, school or period' (*ibid.*: 100), indicates, by analogy, the direction to take in order to appropriate extra-literary works in a legitimate way.

Read rapidly, the argument may appear entirely satisfactory: if there is cultural transferability – broadly presupposed and empirically little verified in the work quoted, in *La Distinction* (1979) and in some earlier theoretical texts (Bourdieu 1966: 904) – it comes from (1) a sense of the rights and duties attached to a social position and (2) technical competence.

One may, however, nuance the weight of these two supposed factors. First, the strength of assignment by status may vary considerably depending on the respondents' trajectories (a lack of self-assurance can stem from a slightly declining family trajectory or, conversely, from a rising trajectory that has not been well assimilated) and depending on the degree of rarity of the status held (the opening up of a qualification or social position and its consequent devaluation may play a part in strongly reducing the personal sense of assurance). Secondly, even if the competence in relation to literature imparted by education may serve as a basis for more effectively appropriating other competences, the fact remains that if the legitimate appropriation of extra-curricular cultural domains has not been prepared for in the family, it presupposes a non-negligible time devoted to constituting new competences, which is not necessarily expended by those who nonetheless possess legitimate curricular competences. Faced with such a need to expend time in distinctly less favourable conditions (the times of childhood and adolescence, protected by family and school, are followed by the sometimes more demanding times of professional, conjugal and parental life), individuals may either narrow their cultural domain of predilection without losing their sense of cultural nobility or relax their demands in areas remote from those they learned to master in school. This second attitude is all the more likely given that individual lives are becoming (domestically, occupationally, etc.) more stressful and the degree of classically 'high' culture is tending to decline with the impact of competition from the new media – the age we live in no longer offers a general ambiance conducive to efforts towards cultural appropriation.

But one of the great taken-for-granted principles of the model of generalised transfer is that of the homogeneity of the multiple cultural situations experienced by the actors in terms of cultural legitimacy. To put it another way, the sociologist hypothesises that what is legitimate and enviable in one context (e.g. work, family, friends, etc.) continues to be so in another. Impelled by a cultural 'force stronger than me', the actor is assumed to have no sense of situations, their constraint and relative legitimacies and to apply the same cultural dispositions compulsively, whatever the context, whatever the persons with whom he interacts, whatever their social and cultural properties, whatever the nature of the situation – formal or informal, tense or relaxed, etc. While the sociologist acknowledges the potential diversity of situations, he nonetheless takes for granted that the probability of an actor encountering heterogeneous situations is so low (his habitus systematically steering him away from surprises, deviations and crises, through social homogamy, etc.) that there is no chance of the theoretical question of the variation of situations arising empirically. And yet it is precisely because actors have a sense of situations and adapt their behaviour to what they perceive of them that intra-individual variations in cultural practices and attitudes are observable. If they sense that a practice highly legitimate in one setting (conjugal or professional) or at one moment (in everyday life) might appear pretentious, fogeyish, absurd or inappropriate in another setting (friends or relatives) or at another moment (holidays), they adjust their behaviour.

Notes

1 The intention of bringing to light the intra-individual variations in cultural behaviours requires one to write individual portraits. Only in this way can one exemplify the modifications of cultural practices and preferences according to the domain, the sub-domain, the context or the circumstances of practice. Because these portraits make it possible, in addition, to bring out relatively singular configurations of general properties and relate all the information to specific family, educational, occupational or friendship contexts, they pull several strands together at once. They weave a fabric with singular patterns and situate practices and preferences in the complex networks of crossed constraints in which individuals are caught. For an argument concerning the value of studying relatively singular configurations, see Stouffer (1941) and Lahire (1995).
2 Six long interviews with each respondent, to cover domains of dimensions of existence that were sufficiently diversified to enter into the detail of intra-individual variations and call into question sociological self-evidences about the mechanisms of the transferability of dispositions (Lahire 2002).
3 Pierre Bourdieu observed that 'at equivalent levels of educational capital, the weight of social origin in the practice- and preference-explaining system increases as one moves away from the most legitimate areas of culture' (Bourdieu 1979: 12).
4 'As all his words, as all his motions are attended to, he learns an habitual regard to every circumstance of ordinary behaviour, and studies to perform all those small duties with the most exact propriety' (Smith 2002: 65).
5 I have developed elsewhere the difference between the model of omnivorous cultural consumption (Peterson 1992; Peterson and Simkus 1992; Peterson and Kern 1996) and the study of intra-individual behavioural variation (Lahire 2008: 180–185).

References

Bourdieu, P. (1966) 'Champ intellectuel et projet créateur', *Les Temps modernes*, 246: 865-906 [translated as 'Intellectual Field and Creative Project', in M.F. Young (1971) (ed.) *Knowledge and Control: New Directions for the Sociology of Education*, London: Collier Macmillan].
—— (1979) *La Distinction. Critique sociale du jugement*, Paris: Minuit [translated as *Distinction: A Social Critique of the Judgement of Taste*, London: Routledge, 1984].
—— (1989) *La Noblesse d'État. Grandes écoles et esprit de corps*, Paris: Minuit [translated as *The State Nobility: Elite schools in the Field of Power*, Cambridge: Polity, 1996].
Bourdieu, P. (ed.) (1965) *Un Art moyen, Essai sur les usages de la photographie*, Paris: Minuit [translated as *Photography: A Middle-Brow Art*, Cambridge: Polity, 1989].
Bourdieu, P. and A. Darbel (1969) *L'Amour de l'art. Les musées d'art européens et leur public*, Paris: Minuit [translated as *The Love of Art: European Museums and Their Public*, Cambridge: Polity Press, 1991].
Bourdieu, P. and J.-C. Passeron (1964) *Les Héritiers, les étudiants et la culture*, Paris: Minuit [translated as *The Inheritors: French Students and Their Relation to Culture*, Chicago: University of Chicago Press, 1979].
—— (1970) *La Reproduction. Éléments pour une théorie du système d'enseignement*, Paris: Minuit [translated as *Reproduction in Education, Society and Culture*, London: Sage Publications, 1970].
Donnat, O. (1994) *Les Français face à la culture, de l'exclusion à l'éclectisme*, Paris: La Découverte.
Gans, H.J. (1999) *Popular Culture and High Culture: An Analysis and Evaluation of Taste*, New York: Basic Books [Revised and updated edition (first ed. 1974)].
Goffman, E. (1959) *The Presentation of Self in Everyday Life*, New York: Doubleday.
Lahire, B. (1995) *Tableaux de familles. Heurs et malheurs scolaires en milieux populaires*, Paris: Gallimard/Seuil, Hautes Études.
—— (2002) *Portraits sociologiques. Dispositions et variations individuelles*. Paris: Nathan, Essais & Recherches.
—— (2003) 'From the Habitus to an Individual Heritage of Dispositions. Towards a Sociology at the Level of the Individual', *Poetics*, 31: 329–355.
—— (2004) *La Culture des individus. Dissonances culturelles et distinction de soi*, Paris: Éditions la Découverte, Laboratoire des sciences sociales.
—— (2008) 'The Individual and the Mixing of Genres: Cultural Dissonance and Self-Distinction', *Poetics*, 36: 166–188.
—— (2010) *The Plural Actor*, Polity Press: Cambridge.
Peterson, R. (1992) 'Understanding Audience Segmentation: From Elite and Mass to Omnivore and Univore', *Poetics*, 21: 243–258.

Peterson, R. and R.M. Kern (1996) 'Changing Highbrow Taste: From Snob to Omnivore', *American Sociological Review*, 61(5), 900–907.

Peterson, R. and A. Simkus (1992) 'How Musical Tastes Mark Occupational Status Groups', in M. Lamont and M. Fournier (eds), *Cultivating Differences: Symbolic Boundaries and the Making of Inequality*, Chicago and London: University of Chicago Press.

Smith, A. (2002) *The Theory of Moral Sentiments*, Cambridge: Cambridge University Press.

Stouffer, S. A. (1941) 'Notes on the Case-Study and the Unique Case', *Sociometry*, 4(4): 349–357.

Van Eijck, K. (1999) 'Socialization, Education, and Lifestyle: How Social Mobility Increases the Cultural Heterogeneity of Status Groups', *Poetics*, 26: 309–328.

21

The multiplicity of highbrow culture

Taste boundaries among the new upper middle class

Guy Bellavance

The relationship between cultural practices and social status has been, since Veblen, a constitutive question in sociology. In this regard, Pierre Bourdieu's work on the more or less intentional effects and uses of taste as a form of distinction represents a turning point. Taste is understood here as a central element in a symbolic struggle, the product of a class *habitus*, that allows elites to distinguish themselves and thereby recognize each other. His theories, primarily in *La distinction* (1979), are once again the source of much ongoing debate.[1] His writings notably gave rise to many critical responses and outcomes, from a variety of national perspectives, which have questioned to varying degrees the validity of his work. The most intriguing finding of recent decades without a doubt concerns the relatively widespread 'eclecticism' regarding the tastes and cultural practices among the higher social classes. This observation, recurring on an international scale, has destabilized the expected relation between social position and cultural practice. It has put into question the idea of a perfect concordance between social and cultural space, as well as the consistency and coherence commonly found in the cultural behaviours of different social classes. This finding is particularly interesting in that it primarily concerns those circles most likely to maintain a 'cultivated' relation with culture, namely highly educated elite professionals. The hybridization of so-called highbrow and lowbrow tastes among elites further suggests a weakening or softening of cultural hierarchies, a blurring of the symbolic boundaries among the classes, and even an effacement of inequalities with respect to culture.

The goal of this chapter is to question this observed eclecticism – or 'omnivorousness', in the expression popularized by R.A. Peterson – in light of the results of a study I conducted in Quebec (Canada) on art lovers and cultural consumers among the upper middle class.[2] One of the principal objectives of this inquiry was precisely to study the relation between professional and cultural worlds: In what ways does professional status determine one's cultural sphere? And up to what point do these two worlds cohere? Another equally important objective was to establish for this population the criteria considered relevant in matters of taste: Is the long-standing high/low distinction the most determining factor in the expression of taste, or do other classificatory schemes play a more significant role? This led to an exploration of a double complexity: that of the cultural universe of the elite, which is actually far more heterogeneous than one may assume *a priori*; and that of the multiplicity of symbolic markers that underlie the process of taste legitimization. In this chapter, I first turn to this question of eclecticism and omnivorousness among the new elite classes. Next, I present the principal variations from the cultural universe of the study's sample with regard to participants' affiliations with different professional spheres. Making a connection between taste and social status leads to an analysis of two difficulties that arise from this effort. The first relates to the interference surrounding the true social status of participants, given the complexity of their occupational and life trajectories; the second concerns the blurring of high/low distinction, based on the abundance of classificatory schemes used by the participants to define and justify their preferences for certain cultural 'items' inside their repertoires of taste. The analysis of this double complexity ultimately allows revealing the multiple meanings assumed by cultural eclecticism today.

Cultural activity and social status: The analysis of 'eclecticism'

Beginning in the 1990s, an international current of almost entirely quantitative research emerged that highlighted the hybridization of highbrow and lowbrow tastes among the upper classes.[3] This solid empirical analysis seems to hold for all developed countries, and contradicts the commonly assumed aversion among the elite classes towards popular forms of art; it also serves as the basis for a strong hypothesis on the evolution or transformation of the historical relation between social status and cultural behaviour. According to this hypothesis, initially posited by R.A. Peterson and his colleagues (Peterson and Simkus 1992; Peterson and Kern 1996), this hybridization of tastes and cultural practices reflects a rise of cultural eclecticism among the affluent and educated classes. In contradistinction to the assumed purity of taste among the traditional elite, the new eclecticism now represents, according to many, an alternative form of cultural legitimacy, 'from snob to omnivore' in the words of Peterson.

The eclecticism in question in these studies does not concern as much the number of different cultural domains (visual arts, music, etc.) appreciated or consumed by members of different social classes. Rather, it deals with the status of aesthetic variations within these activities: popular/cultivated, minor/major, hedonistic/ascetic, fun/serious, etc. The questions raised by these investigations are more qualitative than quantitative, and the definition of different kinds of art – which are also classes of taste – is central. For example, who implements and enforces the rankings, and according to what criteria are they classified? Where are the boundaries crossed? What are the most pertinent principles of distinction or differentiation, the most structuring or most discriminating in the sorting process?

Furthermore, the discussion does not focus on the eclecticism of taste in general, but rather on one of its particular forms, that of the distinction (or the indistinction) between high and low forms of art. One of its characteristics is to directly link types of items (high/low) with types of people (*highbrow/lowbrow*). In fact, the high/low distinction represents a particularly powerful and encompassing 'ritual' of symbolic classification, and is nearly universal in the West. In many ways, it intersects with the much older separation between the sacred and the profane. It simultaneously refers to cultural items and individuals' differentiated connections to them: serious or fun, ascetic or hedonistic, etc. In addition, this distinction finds a certain empirical basis nowadays in relation to the workings of institutions and the market: lowbrow genres correspond to commercialized and publicized artistic forms generated by large cultural markets; highbrow genres emerge from more long-term traditional cultural institutions. However, there remains a significant blurring: we are dealing not with discrete entities, but rather with continuously evolving and interactive processes, which still take place locally; certain forms of art considered lowbrow in particular contexts will be more associated with legitimate or elite culture elsewhere, and vice versa. The high/low distinction proves to be even more hazy when commercial and institutional concerns converge in the arts sector, as is the case today: on the one hand, standard advertising strategies have been increasingly adopted by traditional arts institutions; on the other, left to the workings of the market, forms of expression deemed until recently illegitimate have seen a rise in legitimacy among traditional institutions (cinema, rock 'n' roll, photography, TV series, the circus arts, humour, comics, etc.). As well, this is thoroughly demonstrated by the promotion of cultural (and creative) industries within cultural public policy, in addition to the continued rehabilitation of many forms of expression and investigation in the field of cultural studies.

In fact, the sociological debate focuses on the distinction between highbrow and lowbrow genres because it represents a principle not only of classification, but also, and most importantly, of hierarchization and legitimization (high/low). In this sense, this distinction tends to encompass several others. To begin with, its link with social status seems evident: lowbrow tastes and practices tend to correspond to lower classes; highbrow tastes and practices tend to correspond to affluent and educated classes. This distinction in effect offers a scale that, plotted on an axis or continuum 'from low to high', demonstrates the relationship between activities and status. In this respect, the primary motivation behind the analysis of high/low eclecticism is, without a doubt, the erosion, decline, or disappearance of traditional hierarchies in order to complicate (or even contest) the expected relationship between cultural activities and social status.

While this finding seems solid, its implications remain unclear. Interpretations range from the positive – the loosening up of cultural hierarchies, whether traditional or arbitrary – to the negative – the race to the bottom, the decline of culture, the rise of relativism, or the process of 'decivilization' (Elias 1991). These interpretations are equally able to attribute radically different historical meanings to cultural phenomena. Between the idea that classical European (even Western) culture has lost its legitimacy, and the idea that the social classes have disappeared, many others are also possible, such as the diversification of tastes following the historical 'process of individuation' (Lipovetsky 1983); omnivorousness as a new strategy of social distinction (Ollivier and Fridman 2004); and the cognitive dissonance found among the new upper classes, a consequence of social mobility (Lahire 2004). We can even refute the claims of novelty surrounding this phenomenon; perhaps the upper classes have always had lowbrow tastes to some degree, but today it is just easier – or even more profitable – to publically admit it (Bellavance, Valex and Ratté 2004).

These interpretations vary, moreover, according to national and local realities from which eclecticism is analysed. It is interesting to compare here the more optimistic North American perspective with the more pessimistic European one. In North America, following the above-mentioned work of Peterson and others, we regularly represent the rise of eclecticism as a tidal wave. We often also associate it with a rise of 'tolerance' and an 'openness' to the world; we have passed from the exclusive 'snobbery' of traditional elites, criticized by Bourdieu in *La distinction*, to the inclusive 'omnivorousness' of new cosmopolitan elites, who appear more tolerant and open. In France, on the contrary, the work of Donnat (1994) and Lahire (2004) tends to insist on the multiplication of taste boundaries and the maintenance of hierarchies. For Donnat, eclecticism remains a highly localized phenomenon, restricted to a few small groups who are highly endowed with cultural capital. For Lahire, eclecticism rather appears as a 'dissonance' affecting all social classes, but modulated according to more or less legitimate trends – and no less shameful on an individual level. Indeed, the gap between the North American and European perspectives is striking.

This discrepancy holds in part to structural and historical differences in the 'supply' of culture in the two countries: the relative importance of markets and cultural institutions being different, the repertoires from which consumers establish their preferences, and the cultural intermediaries and supports on which they base their tastes, diverge accordingly. Neither are the markers of cultural domination the same on both sides of the Atlantic: the fine arts enable cultural domination in Europe, while Hollywood, Broadway and even Las Vegas hold more power and status in North America. This disparity seems equally to come from different intellectual and political perspectives on culture. Broadly speaking, in France, investigations of cultural practices are overdetermined by issues surrounding the democratization of culture, often originating from data produced (and constructed) by a ministry or department that has made this work its central mission. In the United States, such investigations are less dependent on government purposes and more dependent on the logic of the market; yet they are no less marked by the 'politicization of the arts' related to multiculturalism. Indeed, bottom-up logics of cultural democracy differ radically from more classic top-down forms of democratization.

The Quebec study

This research on Quebec revisits such broad cultural and geo-political questions, as well as those of contextualization and data, within a specific place. Indeed, the locus of research is highly effective in examining the confrontation of the Anglo-American and Franco-European perspectives. Specifically, by giving voice to an ethnically hybrid group of primarily francophone North Americans, it allows for the exploration of the question of cultural domination in a more ambivalent context than those generally offered in the debate on omnivorousness: the centre of cultural authority is in effect more hotly contested and ambiguous in Quebec (a nation without a state) than in legally recognized nation-states like France, England, or the United States. French by language and certain cultural references, British in political institutions (e.g. parliamentary system and arts councils), and North American in their way of life, Quebecers occupy an interesting if sometimes uncomfortable position among various cultural models. In contrast to French cultural democratization and Anglo-American (and more specifically Canadian) multiculturalism, Quebec cultural policy remains overdetermined by issues of national affirmation and identity (centred around the promotion and defence of the French language and Quebec cultural heritage). Moreover, this cultural policy emerged more from third-world ideologies of decolonization than from French democratization or American multiculturalism. In such a context, the status of the cultural elite remains particularly problematic. Where, indeed, is the source of cultural dominance? A minority within Canada (and North America) but a majority within Quebec, francophone Quebecers are by turns able to be perceived as one or the other. In this respect, is the source of cultural legitimacy Anglo-American, Franco-European, Canadian, or strictly Quebecois? Can a dominant taste truly gain recognition here, and if so, at what level: local, national, or international?

The semi-structured qualitative interviews on which this research is based were conducted between 1999 and 2001 with nearly 100 participants active in artistic and cultural activities in Quebec. The strategy first consisted of diversifying the sample with regards to membership in five identified professional categories associated with the upper strata of society: upper management and business (n=19), general professional (n=14), science and technology (n=14), humanities and social science (n=14), and arts and culture (n=25).[4] In addition to belonging to one of the above categories, participants were asked to meet two additional criteria: hold a university degree (which is generally considered a marker of 'highbrow' cultural consumption), and have a pronounced interest in at least one form of artistic practice (the invitation explicitly called for 'strong consumers of art and culture', leaving it open to interpretation of what this means). This allowed identifying a part of the population whose level of belief, respect, and 'trust' with regard to arts and culture (in whatever form) was high or very high relative to the general population of Quebec.

A strong majority of the sample (8 out of 10) lived and worked in Montreal.[5] The presence of a large majority of French-Canadians was offset by a significant minority of people from other ethno-linguistic groups (25 per cent) by birth or by affiliation through parents or spouses: English Canadians, Hispanic Americans, Franco-Europeans – some multilingual, others unilingual.[6] In general, the group was associated with high or very high incomes, and was also characterized by a relatively high level of social mobility.[7] In explaining current artistic taste, however, early exposure to the arts appears to be more determining than socio-economic class: two out of three participants had some form of training in the arts during childhood (below 12 years of age). The sample mainly comprised male baby-boomers: the priority given to professionals at the time of the interview explains the survey's low proportion of women (who tend to hold lower positions in the labour market) and the high proportion of baby-boomers, those aged 40 to 55 (born between 1945 and 1960), who were most active in the labour market at the time of this interview. The recruitment of avid cultural consumers may also explain the high incidence of households without young children, a condition generally considered more favourable to participation in cultural life.

The interview was intended to study the homogeneity and coherence of cultural tastes and practices of the wealthy and educated members of the upper classes. First, it led interviewees to highlight the role different art forms and art works play in their lives (their repertoire)[8] and to state the reasons for their choices (their tastes). This allowed me to take into account all cultural items that were significant for each individual (rather than a single domain or some predetermined ones, music for example), and observe the possible combinations, in light of the educational history and professional lives of the participants. What follows are the main results of a cross-sectional analysis of socio-professional trajectories and repertoires of taste. First, emphasizing the relationship between cultural and professional spheres, I discuss two key observations that highlight the inherent difficulty in linking cultural status with social status: the first concerns the ambiguities surrounding the occupational status of the participants; the second relates to the multiplicity of classificatory schemes that they used.

The socio-professional attributes of taste

The repertoires of taste identified through this study display relatively distinct socio-professional attributes. Indeed, socio-professional styles stand out not only in participants' tastes and practices, but also in the motivation and legitimization of these practices and tastes. Thus socio-professional milieus seem to possess an undeniable structuring power. However, this relation only becomes clear through a reorganization of the sample. Initially built around the five professional groups mentioned above, the sample was restructured around three broader cultural/professional categories, which are fairly similar to those identified by Peterson and Simkus (1992): *higher managerial*, *higher technical*, and *higher cultural*.

The first group, *higher managerial* (n=28), includes not only most of the participants from the 'upper management and business' group, but also a good number from the 'general professional' one – those whose profession approaches the first category, e.g. lawyers and accountants – as well as a few cultural professionals whose activities are more commercial or entrepreneurial in nature. The tastes of this group may initially seem more popular and conservative, as well as less informed and cultivated. Their practices are also mainly focused on 'cultural outings' (shows, museums, cultural tourism, etc.). Despite these more lowbrow tastes, members of this group consider themselves somewhat 'rare birds' in their professional environments, which they see as offering few opportunities and prospects in terms of art. In this world, access to various highbrow art forms is frequently just part of 'business relations' or forms of corporate sponsorship and patronage. Indeed, such instrumental or social justifications for art (often placed in the foreground) seem to be a potentially inherent dimension of the managerial-entrepreneurial *habitus*.

The second group, *higher technical* (n=29), primarily includes members of the 'science and technology' group, including some members of the social science and humanities sector, as well as those general professionals whose training and work more or less relate to science, such as medical professionals. The members of this group are far more classical in their taste, and their cultural practices reveal a propensity for serious leisure and erudition. Their preferred items clearly belong to the more established and recognized forms of art in the Western cultural heritage. However, their tastes for the most popular and widespread forms of art are much more reserved, and they are more often critical of the most experimental forms of contemporary art. Members of this group also more regularly reported a serious amateur participation in art practices, primarily music and literature. From this perspective, the model of taste for this group reflects well Bourdieu's (and Passeron's) canonical idea of the *héritier* [inheritor]: endowed by their families with strong cultural capital, members of this group seem to share similar (highbrow) class (pre)dispositions. However, the classical trend declines sharply among younger generations, as well as those in newer careers in the applied sciences. These subgroups are more open to popular genres, and are generally not immune to the influence of various forms of popular music since the 1960s. Moreover, the overlap between the scientific-technical and management-entrepreneurial distorts the model: new career paths typical of the knowledge-based economy (Drucker 1969; Machlup 1962) have influenced or altered cultural repertoires that likely should have been far more conventional.

The third group, *higher cultural* (n=29), includes artists (mostly visual artists), but also professional mediators (such as gallery owners, curators, museum directors, art critics, cultural administrators), as well as intellectuals involved professionally (such as teachers, critics, activists) in these areas (generally as university professors in the humanities). The cultural practices of this artistic-cultural group are heavily determined by their professional relation to culture. Their tastes are usually well informed and up-to-date, in tune with current trends in their areas of expertise. The model of taste that emerges from this group is a form of connoisseurship that differs significantly from the traditional highbrow erudition typical of the previous group. In the third group, such learning, if it exists, seems more conditioned by the strategic role played in their careers by the acquisition of recent and pertinent cultural information. Also notable is that the share of cultural *inheritors* (who prefer traditional 'legitimate' culture) is far smaller in this third group than in the second group and only marginally higher than in the first; thus, the cultural sectors are not necessarily the best endowed with legitimate cultural capital. Several members of this group expressed regret over the 'extreme specialization' and 'lack of openness' of their milieu, both in terms of taste and practice. Many in this group are involved with culture out of a sense of professional duty; indeed, 'getting away from culture' also often represents for them a common form of leisure or relaxation. Offbeat practices – those ironic, critical, or even cynical toward established art worlds – are also more common here than in other categories.

Though the link between professional and cultural worlds does exist, it is not, however, as much a function of professional activity in a strict sense. On the contrary, the analysis suggests that the three domains correspond to more general professional socialization models (and patterns), and even possible cultural professional fields [*champs*] (in the Bourdieusian sense): business, science, culture. In this respect, the weak cultural coherence within the 'general professional' category, which primarily triggered the reorganization of the sample, is without a doubt one of the most striking results of this study. This group does not represent (or no longer represents) the regulatory umbrella body of current good taste. In effect, the tastes of members of these professions (lawyers, notaries, doctors, engineers, etc.) seems fragmented, scattered among the worlds of business, science, and culture, according to the proximity an individual has to these milieus: accountants and lawyers are more affiliated with the managerial profile; doctors and other health professionals with the scientific profile; and others, perhaps due to the influence of family or friends, will tend towards the cultural profile. To the extent the general professions have traditionally formed the social matrix of highbrow taste (which remains to be fully proven), the dissolution of this milieu could explain in part the differentiation of 'legitimate' tastes among the emerging elites.

The complexity and diversity of career paths

This mapping between the professional world and the world of taste remains no less complicated on two levels: that of the exact taste of the participants (see below), and that of their true professional status. In terms of the latter, taking fully into account the professional trajectories of each individual makes it difficult, or even impossible, to place them within one single professional category. Indeed, one's apparent status quite often masks the complexity of professional affiliations. The number of different degrees, abilities, and work experiences of the participants shows that almost everyone, either simultaneously or successively, belongs to several professional spheres. In many cases, the constructed profile tends to resemble an unexpected or hidden profile, which is often far more revealing in matters of taste. For example, several literature graduates, whose cultural repertory remains firmly marked by their educational training, occupy senior positions at companies that have nothing to do with culture. In addition, multiple or overlapping education histories – science and management, and social science and management being the most common – also blur the boundaries among categories. There is also a high occurrence of cultural professionals with training in management or the sciences, or who occupy managerial positions in cultural organizations. In many cases, multiple activities are conducted not only successively but also simultaneously: some participants in applied science combine their roles as researcher (or sometimes teacher) with that of shareholder or entrepreneur; others, in addition to their many activities, are patrons of the arts, even when not directly involved in cultural markets (as agents or cultural producers). The study of these entanglements in fact constitutes an area of research in itself.

The high degree of overlap and duplication between cultural and professional practices is thus not only limited to cultural professionals. Rather, the analysis suggests that non-professionals are also often strongly involved in cultural life – not parallel to their professional activities, but through them. In some cases, an individual's official professional status can be misleading.[9] For example, does an entrepreneur loaded with science degrees who is developing multilingual translation software belong to the world of business, science, or culture? What about a professor-entrepreneur in techno-science whose first career was as a rock musician and now has a parallel 'mini-career' composing neo-classical music for his Masonic lodge? Is the owner of an advertising and public relations agency, though primarily rooted in the realm of business and politics, not a full member of the art world because of the various corporate sponsorships and invaluable cultural financing he offers? Such entanglements are all the more inextricable when one takes into consideration not only an individual's current position (at the moment of the interview) but also his or her previous studies and career paths. The multiplicity of social, professional, and cultural affiliations is a general phenomenon that makes it quite difficult to assign individuals to a single professional universe. Such an abundance of experiences is thus the source of the great diversity, eclecticism, and/or apparent incoherence of the tastes found among many highbrow cultural omnivores.

Beyond this first form of professional 'heterogamy' exists that of conjugal relationships: for example, a business leader or politician is married to a prominent film critic. The influence of the spouse or partner is often significant in even the most remote areas of the cultural sphere, such as business. Other dominant figures can similarly be influenced by the tastes of members of the 'less established' categories: an entrepreneur father, for example, can take advice from his daughter, or a university professor can be influenced by his or her students. The various forms of socio-professional 'exogamy' or 'heterogamy'[10] and informal socialization encourages an analysis of the wider relationships between the formation of taste and the possible systems of 'multiple affiliation' (de Singly 2003; Lahire 2004), especially in comparing *exogamous* situations and simultaneous affiliations with conventional social determinations (based on education, social origin, professional status, and income). These affiliations, which can be quite open, discreet, or even secret, are greatly multiplied once you take into account all the social paths taken by a particular individual. From this perspective, the potential diversification of cultural repertoires is primarily a result of the diversification of social affiliations and bonds.

The classification and stratification of taste

The ambiguity of socio-professional status associated with the multiplicity of paths adds a symmetrical complexity tied to the status of cultural repertoires. At this level, the interference is twofold. The first relates to the number of art forms and cultural practices, obviously quite numerous in a study that focused on an audience deeply involved in culture, and where the number of forms and practices of art under consideration was left open. The second and more interesting concerns the types of items appreciated in terms of their degree of legitimacy. The establishment of a cultural item's status does not directly relate to its formal or thematic content: it is not a discrete entity, but the result of a process of evaluation established 'on the basis of *perceived similarities*' (DiMaggio 1987: 441). Classification is thus founded on a social pact built on perception, and consequently, it is comprised of a strong relation between the cognitive, the normative, and the affective: 'Taste classifies the classifier' (Bourdieu 1979). Classifying artworks is to classify oneself with respect to the other, and the other with respect to oneself, particularly on the highbrow/lowbrow continuum. Insofar as this distinction refers to a scale of legitimacy, the act of classification is inextricably coupled with the work of legitimization, hierarchization, and stratification.

The establishment of a 'genre of art' has become an increasingly complex procedure, marked both by progressive (or historical) and interactive (or social) factors. This act stands at the junction of at least three defining categories: the 'official' categories resulting from the combined action of both cultural institutions and the market; the 'scholarly' categories (including sociology); and the 'natural' categories, applied by individuals according to their own artistic experiences.[11] The pact is sealed when these three categories manage to accommodate each other, which is not very common in reality. Indeed, the natural categories are often at odds with the other two. Participants will thus speak of 'discovered' art, not necessarily indicating the avant-garde in the strict sense, but more that which is relatively unknown to them. 'Classic' art is considered by many not to be the heritage of high European culture, but the product of today's mediated world. 'Simple' art can also serve (for one interviewee in particular) as a summarization and critique of both minimalism and street art. These heterodox categories – superficially denoting a certain degree of incompetence among participants – remain significant. But the opposite problem is encountered when sociologists find themselves in a situation of incompetence with regards to the finely grained and subtle categories of this or that art form used by specialists.

While the distinction between high and low remains a standard classificatory scheme and the source of potential debate over legitimacy, other systems of distinction are increasingly becoming just as all-encompassing and determining. This is particularly the case with the distinction between old (classical, traditional, established, conformist, etc.) and new (current, modern, emerging, rebellious, etc.). Indeed, this distinction was particularly inescapable during the survey and is highly structuring in terms of symbolic demarcation. Rejection and frustration are often more openly expressed towards contemporary art forms than towards lowbrow ones; aversion and misunderstanding tend to lump together all experimental highbrow forms in an undifferentiated whole, which is not the case with more popular genres in which participants can more easily discern nuances. Irreducible to the former, the old/new distinction adheres less to socio-economic divergences than to generational ones; moreover, pointing directly at the cultural tensions between tradition and modernity, this distinction appears to be more general as well. The fact that its relationship with social status is less clear likely explains why it is not often taken into consideration in the debate at hand. Its interpretation in matters of legitimacy is more ambiguous: the traditional is not evidently superior to the new, and vice versa. More 'temporal' than 'social' in nature, this distinction is nevertheless crucial in understanding the evolution and transformation of the relationship between cultural tastes and social stratification.

Other general classificatory schemes can be considered equally pervasive on the ground. The distinction between masculine and feminine, for example, proves to be inescapable as well, while the polarization between local and global culture is particularly decisive in the context of the globalization of cultural markets. Generally speaking, this classificatory scheme includes a mix of widely different distinctions, marked by the divisions between the national and the international, the particular and the universal, the near and the far, among others. In fact, in terms of cultural legitimacy, it is unclear whether one is dealing with a single, pertinent, and unique principle of distinction 'in last instance'. On the contrary, many diverging principles seem to be competing and converging to create and establish a relatively fluid and contested measure of legitimacy.

A theoretical model of taste?

I initially attempted to theoretically identify the relative weight and role played by two of the major, above-mentioned systems of classification and legitimization: high/low, and old/new (Bellavance 2008: 195). Their combination and cross-analysis resulted in an overall 'theoretical space' of taste, with quadrants corresponding to four types of cultural objects and registers of taste. Assuming that highbrow items objects correspond to those defended by large cultural institutions and lowbrow items are those that circulate through the market or the mass media, we can distinguish four general types of items (rather than two): 'classical' items associated with high Western culture; 'contemporary' items connected to current international artistic practices; 'folk' items that come from local popular traditions; and 'pop' items, urban modern forms of art distributed through more recent and global cultural industries. We can also see that the local/global distinction transects this bi-dimensional space, introducing a third dimension that is more difficult to represent. Distributing individuals within this schema enables the identification of several trends in the specific roles played by the first two classification systems. The distinction between old and new spaces is thus primarily connected to age (combining generational differences and the life cycle): the average age of those in the sample was 46, and those classified in the 'classical' and 'folk' categories were considerably older than those in the classified 'contemporary' and 'pop' ones (54 and 46; 42 and 43 respectively). The distinction between lowbrow and highbrow space was primarily related to factors such as socio-economic status, education level, field of study, and social origin. The highbrow space tends to include those who maintain professional or quasi-professional relationships within the field of culture: professors, artists, mediators, cultural 'activists', or 'inheritors' who benefited from an early association with the arts. The lowbrow space does not exclude all forms of high art, but the practices here are more exclusively dependent on mass media.

It is also interesting to note how these two systems interact with the third (local/global). For example, the 'classical' category, which refers to a humanist symbolic universe and a form of universal cosmopolitanism, includes many multilingual scientists, as well as a large number of people of European descent or those who have spent significant amounts of time in Europe (usually as part of their university studies). The 'contemporary' category includes a large majority of artists and cultural intermediaries, and in this case a large majority of those connected to international networks of contemporary art, as well as those who frequently travel abroad (for professional reasons), though for shorter times than those in the previous category. The distinction between 'folk' and 'pop' that transects the lowbrow space suggests as much a spatial tension between city and country – *cityscape/countryside* – as a temporal tension between old and new.

However theoretically satisfactory, this first classification is much less successful on an empirical level. It remains difficult to associate each participant with one of the theoretical subgroups; indeed, most have combined tastes and thus shift from category to category. The highly variable levels of knowledge and competence among the participants only adds to this complexity: one can be a skilled amateur practitioner of one art (music, for example), but completely unfamiliar with others (literature, the fine arts, for example); one can also appreciate or consume many forms of art, but only understand them superficially. This issue, which exists even if we stick to one type of artistic practice, becomes much more complex when including a multiplicity of various genres, as in this study. In this respect, there is no pure type of consumer, either classical or contemporary, pop or folk; in fact, the more we expand the list of compiled items, the more we see the degree of eclecticism among participants rise.

Taking into account the degree of specialization and competence among individuals nevertheless serves to underline the relationship between forms of cultural capital and forms of eclecticism. Two major configurations emerge in this regard (the second of which involves sub-types). The first is that of an eclecticism limited to certain domains, primarily music (to which the majority of studies on cultural omnivorousness have been devoted), but also sometimes film. Many participants exhibited a relatively diverse array of musical and/or cinematic tastes, although ultimately in quite limited registers. This appears to highlight both the continued expansion of these two markets, as well as their segmentation. The majority of participants in the sample were eclectic in at least this respect. The second configuration is, on the contrary, marked by the co-existence of a primary artistic specialization in one cultural sphere (either lowbrow or highbrow), and a secondary one in another, which, according to the specific case, is either more or less low or highbrow, but also less specialized and less mastered. On the classical side, for example, a music-lover and art-collector only goes to the cinema to be entertained and is interested in new and emerging art forms practiced by young artists. This type of 'enlightened' eclecticism (Coulangeon 2003) can be compared to a different type of 'hip' and 'edgy' eclecticism (Donnat 1994) based on irony and a countercultural attitude: for example, a rising contemporary art star from the world of street art defends the music of Céline Dion, B-movies, and lowbrow culture, but is rather indifferent, even openly hostile, to classical forms of high culture. On the lowbrow side, in the folk category, there are many business people who, through either patronage or the influence of a spouse or the local milieu, have access to forms of culture quite different from those suggested by their initial tastes or professional background. On the modern (urban) side, in the 'pop' category there seem to be many anti-elitist cultural activists arguing strongly for the recognition of more mediatized forms of popular art (rock 'n' roll, comedy, TV series, etc.), and who defend cultural industries and criticize contemporary art institutions. This 'pop' version of cultural legitimacy, widespread among the new urban middle class, strongly indicates a form of legitimacy 'from below' quite different from traditional 'top-down' forms of legitimacy.

A final difficulty of the theoretical model relates to the ambiguity of classificatory schemes actually used by the participants; the first two systems of distinction tend to intersect and overlap. While not matching perfectly, they do sometimes fuse significantly. For example, for several participants, 'classical' overlaps with the category of mass media: bypassing the temporal axis (*old/new*) and social status axis (*high/low*), as identified above, they suggest that the mass media are increasingly setting the standards of cultural legitimacy. Other classification schemas are emerging, which is confusing the issue, such as the above-mentioned distinction between local and global: several participants appear to not only assimilate the traditional with the 'lowbrow', but also the 'lowbrow' with the local; others have equated the old with a universal (global) and highbrow style. The three scales do gradually tend towards alignment. Note that currently the lowest level of legitimacy is often not occupied by popular cultural items, but by those that are both local and out-of-date; however, because of their international reputation, certain popular local items can benefit from a high degree of legitimacy (for example, Céline Dion and Cirque du Soleil). More spatial than social (*high/low*) or temporal (*old/new*), this third classification schema (*local/global*), which allows individuals to distinguish local and global cultural items, introduces a de facto geopolitical dimension to the ritual of classification and legitimization of tastes. Indeed, cultural nationalism and cosmopolitanism are two powerful engines driving the justification and polarization of consumer choice in art, as well as overall participation in cultural life. As one participant said regarding his taste in popular music: 'I feel like I'm being patriotic when I consume culture from Quebec!'

Since several systems of distinction tend to overlap and entangle, it is difficult to tell with total accuracy which one dominates in terms of legitimacy. In addition, the same cultural item can be polarized around totally contradictory values, positive or negative, depending on the various biases – traditionalist or modernist, nationalist or cosmopolitan, populist or elitist – of the participant. It is also difficult to distinguish the descriptive from the normative, the type of thing from the type of taste, and the item from the person. Moreover, the same individual can combine many apparently contradictory cultural orientations.

All this eventually leads to questioning the relevance of research that focuses on only one system of distinction. One can be particularly open on the highbrow/lowbrow axis while remaining quite intolerant on the old/new axis, or particularly elitist on the local/global axis. Equally, one can be learned in one cultural sphere, and ignorant in many others. Numerous different configurations are possible, varying among circumstances and contexts. Yet, the relativity of the *highbrow/lowbrow* polarity with regard to other principles of distinction does not support the thesis of the disappearance of the boundaries of taste. Rather, the discovery of a multiplicity of relevant systems of distinction suggests the maintenance – and even the deepening – of such symbolic boundaries.

Conclusion

The results of this study demonstrate a lack of unity regarding the orientation of taste among the new professional classes; many forms of cultural legitimacy seem rather to compete with each other. The case of elites maybe is an illustration of the multiple tensions that subtend the relationship to culture among the general public. This leads one to wonder if, instead of a single system of distinction, there are several systems, all conflicting and overlapping, referring to irreducible orders of legitimacy, and essential for assessing the true measure of cultural openness and tolerance. Such results contradict or complicate many recent readings of contemporary eclecticism. The openness to diversity certainly has a number of filters and much resistance, even among the most tolerant cultural consumers; tolerance is certainly not synonymous with openness, and we will continue to make distinctions. Neither does the process of communication end the process of domination. The relational dimension of taste and the complexity of the processes of socialization rather imply the confrontation of forms of taste associated with constrained and contextualized schemas of distinction. Cultural boundaries still exist, and they can surely be traversed – but not in every way, in every place or at every time. Interpreting these results according to a theory of cultural legitimacy necessarily involves reformulating this theory in different terms: eclecticism represents a new form of highbrow 'disposition' (a good *habitus*), and hybridization a new generating principle of the cultural field.

Notes

1 The analysis of Bourdieu's work in this perspective required taking the evolution of his thought into consideration, from *L'amour de l'art* (1969) to his revisiting of *La distinction* proposed in 'Espace social et espace symbolique' (1994).
2 This study was made possible thanks to two grants from the Social Sciences and Humanities Research Council of Canada (SSHRC).
3 For a critical presentation of these studies, see Bellavance, Valex and De Verdalle (2006).
4 The detailed table of characteristics for the sample can be found in Bellavance (2004). For a discussion on the methodology, see Bellavance (2008).
5 The other participants live and work in Ottawa, Quebec City, Rimouski and Sherbrooke.
6 For the most part, the interviews were conducted in French, while a few were conducted in English.
7 The sample is roughly equally divided between those from the upper, middle and working classes.
8 The first part of the interview consisted of reviewing art forms that circulated through the market or through cultural institutions.
9 For a more detailed analysis of the following three cases, see Bellavance (2008).
10 'Exogamy' is a strict matrimonial rule requiring that one seek a spouse from outside their social group. 'Heterogamy' is similar, when one more or less consciously seeks a spouse from outside their social group.
11 I'm referring here to the three categories of Demazières and Dubar (2004).

References

Bellavance, G. (2004) 'Non public et publics cultivés: le répertoire culturel des élites', in P. Ancel, et A. Pessin (eds) *Les non publics* (Tome II), Paris: l'Harmattan.
—— (2008) 'Where's high? Who's low? What's new? Classification and stratification inside cultural "Repertoire"', *Poetics*, 36(2-3): 189–216.
Bellavance, G., M. Valex, and L. De Verdalle (2006) 'Distinction, omnivorisme et dissonance: La sociologie du goût entre démarches quantitative et qualitative', *OPuS-Sociologie de l'art*, 9: 125–143.

Bellavance G., M. Valex, and M. Ratté (2004) 'Le goût des autres: Une analyse des repertoires culturels de nouvelles élites omnivores', *Sociologie et Sociétés*, 36(1): 27–57.
Bourdieu, P. (1979) *La distinction: Critique sociale du jugement*, Paris: Minuit.
—— (1994) 'Espace social et espace symbolique' in P. Bourdieu *Raisons pratiques: Sur la théorie de l'action*, Paris: Éditions du Seuil.
Bourdieu, P. and A. Darbel (1969) *L'amour de l'art*, Paris: Minuit.
Coulangeon, P. (2003) 'La stratification sociale des goûts musicaux: Le modèle de la légitimité culturelle en question', *Revue Française de sociologie*, 44(1): 3–33.
Demazières, D. and C. Dubar (2004) *Analyser les entretiens biographiques: L'exemple de récits d'insertion*, Québec: Les Presses de l'Université Laval.
DiMaggio, P. (1987) 'Classification in art', *American Sociological Review*, 52: 440–455.
Donnat, O. (1994) *Les Français face à la culture: De l'exclusion à l'éclectisme*, Paris: La Découverte.
Drucker, P. (1969) *The age of discontinuity: Guidelines to our changing society*, New York: Harper and Row.
Elias, N. (1991) *La société des individus*, Paris: Fayard.
Lahire, B. (2004) *La culture des individus: Dissonances culturelles et distinctions de soi*, Paris: La Découverte.
Lipovetski, G. (1983) *L'ère du vide: Essais sur l'individualisme contemporain*, Paris: Gallimard.
Machlup, F. (1962) *The production and distribution of knowledge in the United States*, Princeton: Princeton University Press.
Ollivier, M. and V. Fridman (2004) 'Ouverture ostentatoire à la diversité et cosmopolitisme: Vers une nouvelle configuration discursive', *Sociologie et sociétés*, 36(1): 105–126.
Peterson, R.A. and R. Kern (1996) 'Changing highbrow taste: from snob to omnivore', *American Sociological Review*, 61(5): 900–907.
Peterson, R.A. and A. Simkus (1992) 'How musical tastes mark occupational status groups', in M. Lamont and M. Fournier (eds) *Cultivating differences: Symbolic boundaries and the making of inequality*, Chicago: University of Chicago Press.
Singly, F. de (2003) *Les uns avec les autres: Quand l'individualisme crée du lien*, Paris: Armand Colin.

22
'There's something fundamental about what makes you laugh.'
Comedy as an aesthetic experience

Sam Friedman

Introduction

In 2013 the English comedian Michael McIntyre became officially the most successful comedian in the world. His stand-up tour, *Showtime*, grossed £21 million in ticket sales and his three comedy DVDs sold more than three million copies (Price 2013). The secret of McIntyre's success, according to most commentators, is simple. He makes people laugh. As Britain's most respected comedy critic, Steve Bennett has repeatedly pointed out, McIntyre's 'laugh-rate' is simply unrivalled, his 'perfectly-honed' and 'precision-engineered' stand-up akin to a 'chuckle-factory running at maximum efficiency' (Bennett 2009; 2012). In many ways, this positive correlation between laughter and success is relatively uncontroversial in the world of comedy. After all, comedy is unique among art forms in the sense that its appreciation implies a specific bodily reflex. Most thus see laughs as the fundamental building block of comedy, and laughter-density the primary indicator of a comedian's quality and success.

Yet, as a comedy critic who has worked in the British comedy industry for the last decade, my own experiences of comedy audiences have always somewhat confounded these common-sense presumptions. Indeed, I have always been fascinated by the *diversity* of aesthetic experience at comedy gigs. Once people are engrossed in a comedy performance, many don't laugh at the same jokes, and even when they do they're not necessarily laughing at the same time, with the same voracity and enthusiasm, or with the same style or state of bodily contortion.

Such observations about comedy, and its vast interpretative diversity, acted as the main catalyst in my decision to start investigating comedy sociologically. Therefore, between 2008 and 2012, I carried out the first ever empirical study of British comedy taste, surveying 901 people at the Edinburgh Festival Fringe (the biggest comedy festival in the world) about their preferences for 16 stand-up comedians and 16 comedy TV shows. I then followed up with 24 in-depth interviews with a sub-sample of survey respondents. The aim of these qualitative interviews was to delve deeper into people's sense of humour, to understand precisely what does and doesn't make them laugh and why.[1]

The findings demonstrated that comic reception can be organised into distinct and relatively opposing *styles of appreciation* that correspond to people's resources of cultural capital.[2] I also found that the aesthetic preferences of those rich in cultural capital tend to be externally legitimated by comedy critics and other cultural intermediaries and, therefore, that demonstrating a 'good' sense of humour may now be a powerful contemporary marker of cultural distinction (Friedman 2014).

In this short chapter, however, I want to focus my attention on arguably the most central, and certainly the most contested, aspect of comic appreciation – laughter. The chapter is structured in three parts. First, I outline laughter's traditionally discredited position within the field of aesthetics and explain how this has shaped comedy's lowbrow status within the cultural hierarchy. I then move on to my empirical work on comedy taste, arguing that despite the somewhat invariant understandings of laughter in aesthetic theory the actual *experience* and *practice* of comic laughter is remarkably diverse. In particular, I illustrate how those with strong resources of cultural capital demonstrate their cultural distinction by distancing themselves from conventional understandings of laughter as instinctive and pleasurable, and instead consciously reserving their laughter for comedy that has first challenged them intellectually or which aligns with their political or moral views. Finally, I illustrate the wider significance of aesthetic battles surrounding laughter, demonstrating how these same culturally privileged respondents use different approaches to laughter to draw symbolic boundaries between themselves and others in social space.

These findings matter for the wider sociology of culture, I argue, because they are indicative of 'emerging' strategies that are being utilised by new generations of the culturally privileged to reassert their dominance in the contemporary era. Instead of relying on the consumption of traditionally legitimate 'high art' objects, the culturally advantaged are diversifying into fields of popular cultural consumption such as comedy, street art (Young 2014), salsa music (Bachmayer and Witerdink 2014) and 'bad' television (McCoy and Scarborough 2014). However, while many sociologists have interpreted these shifts as evidence of a new era of open and accepting cultural omnivorousness, my findings indicate such a picture may be misleading. In particular, I argue here that by delving beyond *what* culture people consume to the *way* they consume and, even more importantly, to how they *judge* the way *others consume*, it is possible to see how popular culture – including, but certainly not confined to, comedy – is increasingly being implicated in the pursuit of cultural distinction.

Comedy, the body and the cultural field

To understand connections between comedy taste and social stratification, it is first imperative to understand British comedy's traditionally discredited position within the wider cultural field. Academic deliberations concerning the place of comedy date back to ancient Greece and most significantly Aristotle's *Poetics* (335 BC), where comedy was first discussed as a form of drama. Notably, comedy was defined in relation to tragedy, a binary distinction that has proved remarkably persistent in the cultural field (Stott 2005). Indeed, for Aristotle, the opposition between comedy and tragedy symbolised the wider conflict between the two aesthetic capabilities of the human character, tragedy representing the transcendental goals of 'high-art' and comedy the 'low' counterpoint of vulgar entertainment (Stott 2005). Key to this vulgarity was comedy's relationship to the human body, both in terms of the themes in its production and the mode of its consumption. While I have discussed the role of the body in comic production elsewhere (Friedman 2014: 11–27), I want to focus here on the way the body is uniquely implicated in the aesthetic experience of comedy.

The classic starting point in this regard is Bakhtin's (1984) analysis of the early modern 'Carnival', where humour and comedy functioned to return the individual to the uncivilised body. For Bakhtin, the carnival operated according to a 'comic logic', where graphic and humorous descriptions of bodily functions and sexual activity represented a deliberate mocking of the dominant order (1984: 68–74). He celebrates these comic expressions as a form of 'grotesque realism', which reached beyond societal limits and interacted with audiences in a distinctly sensual way:

> Wherever men laugh and curse, their speech is filled with bodily images. The body copulates, defecates, overeats and men's speech is flooded with genitals, bellies, urine, disease, noses and dismembered parts.
>
> *(Bakhtin 1984: 319)*

The role of comedy in this direct inversion of social etiquette was also apparent in the holiday festivities of the Elizabethan era (1558–1603). Barber (1963) argues that the loosening of social controls and deliberate merrymaking experienced during holidays such as May Day and Shrove Tuesday both informed, and was reflected in, the comedy of the period. The best dramatic example of this was arguably the 'Saturnalian Comedy' of Shakespeare. In plays such as *Twelfth Night* (1601), the plot centres around the 'release' from social norms experienced by characters during the festive period, where 'the energy normally occupied in maintaining inhibitions is freed for celebration' (Barber 1963: 7).

Underpinning this subversive potential, and perhaps most central to comedy's enduring connection to the uncivilised body, is the issue of laughter. Indeed, for Bakhtin (1984: 92), laughter is a potentially revolutionary political tool. It is the extra-linguistic voice of 'the people' who are normally silenced by an official culture that consolidates its power through seriousness. However, while Bakhtin celebrates the subversive capabilities of laughter, the wider field of culture has historically been markedly less optimistic about its aesthetic potential. According to Stott (2005), this hostility can be traced back to early Christianity, where all sensual pleasure was considered suspicious and antithetical to the pursuit of pious abstinence. The more a person's body was closed to the world, the more it was considered open to God (2005: 129–131). Such ethical opposition to laughter remained strong in clerical circles throughout the early modern period and by the eighteenth century extended to exclude laughter more firmly from 'official' culture (Bremmer and Roodenburg 1997).

In Britain, Stott (2005) notes how this disapprobation of laughter even became incorporated into a distinct class consciousness that considered the act of laughing an 'enemy of social distinctions'. With its lack of self-restraint and implied loss of control, laughter threatened one of the key tenets of modern Bourgeois civilization – the governing of bodily manners (Elias 1993). An edict of the eighteenth century middle-class etiquette thus implored that 'men of quality' did not laugh on grounds of breeding (Stott 2005: 134). Laughter here was seen not as an enemy of God but an enemy of intellectual enlightenment – a 'vulgar expression of passion' (Congreve 1973: 7). As Addison claims: 'Laughter slackens and unbraces the Mind, weakens the Faculties and causes a kind of Remissness, and Dissolution in all the powers of the soul' (1979, vol. 2: 237–238).

There are indications that this aesthetic animosity towards comic laughter has continued in the contemporary era. The critical aesthetic theory of Adorno and Horkheimer (1944), for example, argued that comedy is one of the main art forms to be co-opted by the 'culture industry' in order to divert people from reflecting on their inauthentic existence. They argued that comedy, and the laughter it produces, are used as an infantilising placebo, a basic, fleeting and empty pleasure that obscures the pursuit of genuine pleasure and experience.

Perhaps even more significant than this, however, has been the work of Pierre Bourdieu (1984) on cultural taste. In *Distinction* (1984), Bourdieu argues that dominant social classes demonstrate their cultural distinction by drawing on a powerful and externally legitimated mode of aesthetic appreciation. The key component of this aesthetic is the Kantian (1987) idea of 'disinterestedness', which over time has disseminated into the public discourse on art (Ang 1985). This is premised on a refusal of taste that is easy, facile, or which activates immediate *bodily* sensations like laughter. Instead, the Kantian ideal denotes that true artistic beauty and transcendence can only be experienced if one separates oneself from any physical, emotional or functional investment in an art work. By employing this principle of detachment and distance, Bourdieu argues, the dominant classes are able to employ a 'pure gaze' in their appreciation of cultural objects, stressing the virtue of culture's formal properties rather than its function (Kant 1987: 234). Accordingly, this Kantian aesthetic firmly locates comedy – with its inseparable connection to the corporeal pleasure of laughter – at the very lowest reaches of the cultural hierarchy.

However, in Bourdieu's empirical work there is some – albeit limited – acknowledgement that the aesthetic reception of comedy and humour, as well as the type of laughter it elicits, is not simply uniform. In a telling passage, Bourdieu (1984: 191–192) illustrates how different *approaches* to laughter are key in distinguishing the 'deepest' aesthetic orientations of those from different social classes. Whereas the disinterested middle classes limit bodily reactions to comedy and humour by emitting only the 'wrinkled nose of repressed laughter', the working class 'belly laugh' foregrounds pleasure and physical sensation – 'as if to amplify to the utmost an experience which will not suffer containment, not least because it must be shared, and therefore clearly manifested for the benefit of others' (ibid.).

While Bourdieu's examination of laughter in *Distinction* is characteristically impressionistic, it does at least point toward a more textured and polysemic understanding of comic appreciation. In particular, it highlights how different approaches to laughter may be hierarchically ordered, with more spontaneous and communal forms of laughter – of letting oneself go in public and surrendering to the uncivilised body – less aesthetically legitimate than more restrained expressions of amusement. In this chapter, I aim to build on this fleeting suggestion by delving further into comedy as an aesthetic experience. In particular, my data problematises historical conceptions, such as that presented by Adorno and Horkheimer (1944), which reduce comic appreciation to the mechanical generation of laughter. Instead, I find that aesthetic experience of comedy, particularly the type, style, and volume of laughter it generates, varies greatly and particularly according to the cultural capital resources of the consumer.

Laughter as an aesthetic battleground

Among eight interviewees who all shared low levels of cultural capital (LCC), the commonsense link between comedy and laughter very much held true. For these respondents, the amount a comedian made them laugh was the principal indicator of the quality of their aesthetic experience. In fact, these respondents expressed a certain incredulity that anyone would not judge comedy based on laughter. 'You've got to laugh,' Hannah, an office manager, declared with a palpable sense of certainty in her voice. Others echoed her sentiment:

> I like my comedy to be comedy, I don't want some sort of Alan Bennett thing where it's drama with a wee comedy edge. If it's comedy make it bloody funny.
>
> *(Dave, events assistant)*

> My take on comedy is that it's got to make me laugh. It doesn't mean to say I need to think about it, except for that split-second in the punchline. I'm not looking for them to educate me.
>
> *(Laura, secretary)*

Notably, these respondents also laughed significantly more during interviews. The recollection of a particular joke, TV sketch or catchphrase thus invariably invoked the *memory* of laughter and respondents often laughed their way through these anecdotes, even if I – the interviewer – didn't necessarily know the comedian or share the joke. The importance of laughter was also indirectly underlined during discussions about favourite comedians. Here the respondent's affective response to the comedy was always foregrounded. Andy, for example, a picture framer, described how he was 'in-stitches' throughout a memorable 2005 John Bishop gig and Dan, a supermarket assistant, explained how he was 'literally crying with laughter' after seeing Michael McIntyre in 2008. Again, these physical reactions illustrated how laughter was fundamental to how these people recalled the aesthetic experience of comedy, with the *frequency* and *intensity* of laughter the key arbiters of value.

Moreover, expressions of ideal aesthetic experience not only rested on the *volume* of one's laughter, but also implied the superiority of a particular *type* of laughter. The best type of comedy was thus associated with involuntary eruptions of laughter, laughter that could not be controlled, that implied a temporary loss of physical control. For example, asked about his favourite experience of watching comedy, Finn, a tree surgeon, explained:

> I want to go and see comedy and be sore with laughter (laughs). I went to see Billy Connolly in Glasgow and I came out aching, y'know, tears streaming down my face. I was absolutely buzzing.

Strongly connected to this ideal affective response to comedy was its relationship to the feeling of pleasure, of 'buzzing' as Finn put it. Indeed the main function of comedy, these respondents told me, was 'to make you feel good' (Sophie, retired primary school teacher). 'Good' comedy was 'like a drug' (Finn), it guaranteed pleasure, and respondents thus described consuming comedy instrumentally as a means of improving, complementing or enhancing how they were feeling. Significantly, though, this pleasure was invariably contingent on the notion of enjoying comedy as a shared experience. As Andy, a small shop owner, noted: 'There's something great about a whole room just erupting [with laughter]. I love that.' This desire to share comedy and laughter was particularly striking in relation to live comedy, where memorable gigs invoked a sense of temporary, democratic community – 'everyone was just pissing themselves' (Dave); 'he had everyone eating out of his hand' (Laura). These findings parallel many conventional sociological understandings of humour as fundamentally shared (Bergson 1900) or as a tool to build social solidarity and cohesion (Coser 1960).

Yet while interviewees with low cultural capital largely echoed[3] conventional understandings of comedy as involved, pleasurable and above all physical, those with high cultural capital (HCC) reported very different orientations. In particular, these interviewees strongly challenged the notion that comedy is aesthetically bounded to the creation of laughter. Although most admitted that some laughter was needed to enjoy comedy, it was not seen as a legitimate basis for the judgement of quality. As Andrew, an IT consultant, declared, 'something can be funny without you needing to laugh'. Indeed, HCC respondents were sceptical of the way laughter is automatically connected to comedy, particularly through the use of 'canned laughter' in TV comedy. Canned laughter was considered fundamentally coercive and HCC respondents resented the implication that they were 'being played' (Marilyn, actress), their 'emotions manipulated', or that they were being 'told when to laugh' (Trever, TV writer). For some this ambivalence towards laughter went even further, with laughter seen as potentially contaminating the true experience of comedy:

> I don't think laughter is integral. It's really irrelevant for me personally. I know a lot of friends who go to a lot of gigs and say they don't really laugh at all. I mean they'll say that comedian was really funny but I suppose you're taking in the artistic value rather than just purely what makes you laugh.
>
> *(Steve, postgraduate student)*

It is interesting to note how this HCC disavowal of laughter mirrors similar aesthetic hostilities expressed by British elites in the seventeenth and eighteenth century or by Bourdieu's (1984) French elites in *Distinction*. Indeed, it is through these sentiments that we see a strong echo of Kantian disinterestedness in HCC comic styles. In an attempt to distinguish their appreciation from 'barbarous sensate pleasures' (Kant 1987: 121), many HCC respondents either distanced themselves from, or outright rejected, the supposedly 'natural' physiological reflex mechanism of comedy – laughter (Dunbar 2005).

It was also significant that, in contrast to LCC respondents, references to the actual affect of laughter were largely absent from HCC discussions of the comedy they liked. Funniness was clearly important, but this wasn't necessarily equated with spontaneous laughter. Instead, there was a sense that respondents wanted to 'work' for their laughter, to strive intellectually to 'get' the joke, with laughter a more calculated by-product of this aesthetic labour. In this way, laughing at comedy played a fundamentally different role for HCC respondents. It was less an involuntary physiological reflex to be enjoyed communally and more an autonomous and socially performative act which signalled to others that one had correctly decoded humour at the appropriate moment. Dale's (journalist) discussion of watching the live comedy of critically-acclaimed stand-up Stewart Lee illustrated this calculated comic consumption:

> To be perfectly honest he makes me feel like I'm in an in-crowd of *comedy nerds*. You need to see the pull back and reveal (laughs). You've got to see him delay the punchline ... the repetition. He's got all the tricks there. It is almost like *sitting an exam*. You go in and you know you're going to be challenged, you know a few people in the audience won't get him. Overall it makes you feel a bit smug, and it's an awful thing to say, but it *makes you look down on the people who don't get him* (emphasis added).

This analogy of comic appreciation functioning as an 'exam' neatly rendered visible the performative nature of HCC comic styles. For Dale, there was no communal or democratic pleasure from enjoying Stewart Lee. In contrast, there was something gratifyingly exclusive about 'getting' Lee's comedy[4]. Dale was able to successfully 'sit' the comedic exam set by Lee, and therefore profited from the 'smugness' of recognising, and being able to laugh at, the precise moments that Lee plays with formal conventions – the 'delay of the punchline', the constant 'comedy through repetition'.

Notably, HCC respondents also distanced themselves from the presumption that comedy is necessarily pleasurable. In fact, many seemed to see pleasure, particularly that which resulted from laughter, as somehow fleeting, temporary, and superficial. As Frank noted of his favourite comedians:

> One idea is sustainability. That you haven't just had a moment of *cheap pleasure*. But that in hundred years, or even in your tenth viewing, you will still be finding it funny or

good. For me that's an aspect of needing and wanting intelligence and sophistication in comedy.

(Frank, arts professional; emphasis added)

Most thus saw the function of comedy as ambiguous. 'Good' comedy provoked a wide range of emotions, and many respondents expressed preferences for 'dark' or 'black' comedy where disturbing subjects are probed for humorous effect. These respondents argued that by invoking negative as well as positive emotions, the comedian was better placed 'to challenge' them intellectually. Kira, for example, an environmental consultant, recounted a 'brilliant set' she saw at the 2009 Edinburgh Fringe performed by experimental comedian Kim Noble. She explained that Noble's show began by him explaining that he was going 'to kill himself at the end of the Fringe' and continued to follow him through the nervous breakdown he suffered in 2002. For Kira this performance was 'insane', but at the same time 'exactly what good comedy is all about'. She described leaving the gig crying and noted that Noble's comedy had 'really lodged itself in her mind'. For other respondents exploring negative emotions was not only acceptable in comedy, but often integral to achieving a satisfying aesthetic experience:

> I think with anything you go and see there needs to be highs and lows. Otherwise you don't really feel the highs. If you go and see Daniel Kitson, for instance, he'll take you on lovely passages where you'll feel very sensitive to him, but then there'll be sad bits, parts of his latest show, say, which were about dying, that are really sad and really dark. But I think that means you experience the funny bits more, almost like there's no pleasure without pain.
>
> *(Dale)*

What was striking about both Dale and Kira's comments here is how they resemble the critical aesthetic theory of Adorno and Horkheimer (1944). These theorists argued that 'light-hearted' laughter was one of the main aesthetic effects co-opted by the culture industry to assuage people's fears and attempt to help them escape the harshness of real life. They note: 'In the culture industry, jovial denial takes the place of pain, (1944: 141). Yet, for Adorno, experiencing pain through aesthetic experience was essential for understanding reality. It promotes a higher level of self-understanding. The shadow of this aesthetic doctrine is arguably evident in Andrew and Dale's style of comic appreciation, where comedy that is 'uncomfortable' is 'good' and where 'there is no pleasure without pain'.

Beyond disinterestedness

Although elements of HCC 'disinterestedness' appeared to challenge conventional understandings of comedy reception, it is important to note that this was often mixed with different and somewhat conflicting taste criteria. For example, many HCC respondents talked at length about the 'experience' of watching great comedy, revealing a distinct emotional 'interest' in their aesthetic experience. Marilyn recalled the intensity of seeing Monty Python at The Albert Hall. 'I was just completely blown away. At the end of the show I remember thinking that everything else that's going on in my life, I just didn't think about it at all. I was just taken away from anything else that matters.' Frank described a similar experience:

> I get a wee bit wanky when I talk about stand up. Because I think it can really make you think. And what I get from a very good gig is a certain feeling when you leave, y'know,

or goose bumps. The emotional response you get from within yourself, you're not just necessarily listening to a particular joke, it's more about the entire experience.

What was striking about such statements of aesthetic experience was the combination of the intellectual *and* the emotional. Whereas in many parts of their interviews both Frank and Marilyn foregrounded analytical approaches to comedy, their recollection of the most satisfying comic experiences was also distinctly emotional. Respondents therefore described fleeting moments where they were 'blown away', or which invoked a 'certain feeling', where comedy yielded what Hennion (2001: 14) describes as an 'indescribable "sublime" moment which words can only trivialise'. This is significant because it appeared, at first, to somewhat undermine Bourdieu's (1984) presumption that the culturally privileged mark their distinction through the disinterested rejection of emotion, laughter and pleasure.

Significantly, though, HCC accounts of comic pleasure still implied a hierarchical distinction between emotion and intellect. Thus while many respondents reported markedly passionate reactions, which were often accompanied by laughter, these only took hold after initially being thrilled intellectually. HCC respondents like Frank reported a distinctly emotional experience from comedy, a 'certain feeling … or goosebumps', but this was only achievable when mediated through an intellectual proxy that makes 'you think'. The implication of this, then, was that emotion or laughter that sidesteps intellect is normatively inferior. Disinterestedness, or at least the shadow of it, was still the driving force in achieving an emotionally satisfying comic experience. Indeed, in many ways such accounts are reminiscent of Csikszentmihalyi's (1988) account of the 'flow' experience. Csikszentmihalyi argues that it *is* possible to experience truly transcendent and emotionally gratifying aesthetic experiences, but only if one is willing to devote considerable psychic energy and intellectual focus.

However, although these supposedly 'higher' forms of laughter and emotional appreciation did not necessarily conflict with detached HCC taste criteria, frequent political and moral judgements were more questionable. In particular, most HCC respondents expressed a preference for 'alternative comedy', which was usually defined as a particular 'style' rooted in the work of a set of performers from the 1980s Alternative Comedy Boom. Although many elements of this preferred style were formalistic, the comedy was also undoubtedly bound up with an explicitly liberal, left-leaning and secular agenda (Stott 2005; Wilmut and Rosengard 1989). For many HCC respondents, then, it was important that at least some comedy carry an explicit social role and political message. Certain topics were thus ripe for being 'brilliantly deconstructed', as Andrew noted, whereas other topics of satire were 'bullying' and 'offensive'. For example, comedians who satirise those in positions of power, or who subvert areas of social life dominated by traditionally conservative values – such as religion and drugs – were applauded because they 'aren't afraid to deal with topics that might offend people' (Steve). However, when 'trad' comedians who satirise from a more conservative and reactionary position were discussed, such as Roy 'Chubby' Brown and Bernard Manning, HCC respondents were quick to distance themselves:

> What I feel from Manning and 'Chubby' Brown is that in a complex socio-economic situation where it's only too easy for people without opportunities to despise those who have limited use of language or different colour, they add fuel without love. A string of empty racist jokes. It's a way of saying fuck it I want to hold on to my disgust at, I want to hold on to my hatred of, I want to hold on to my lessening of, that I'm more of. It is just pitiful.
>
> *(Graham, a photographer)*

The crucial moral and political distinction here was that 'trad' comedy 'kicked' downwards rather than upwards, ridiculing groups that are already socially marginalised and subordinated. Thus while these comedians might 'push boundaries' in terms of challenging dominant norms, their subversion conflicted strongly with political and moral values supported by HCC respondents who strongly rejected racism, sexism and homophobia.

It is worth noting that my point here is not to normatively judge the validity of this moral/political standpoint, but simply to illustrate its centrality to the HCC sense of humour. For most of these respondents the way that humour relates to social inequalities and wider structures of power was clearly a powerful consideration. This is significant because it supports Hanquinet, Roose and Savage's (2014) argument that the dominant aesthetic may have altered in important ways. Unlike Bourdieu's vision of the aesthetic disposition, which Hanquinet et al. (2014) argue is rooted in a Modernist preoccupation with detachment and distance, the HCC style includes a clear valorisation of comedy that is *actively engaged in society*. Here the power of 'alternative comedy', in particular, lies in its postmodern emphasis on agit-prop and explicit social critique rather than solely aesthetic disinterest.

Laughter and boundary-drawing

While the differences in comic styles outlined so far illustrate the diversity of aesthetic experience I encountered among comedy consumers, a key question remains. What is the wider sociological significance of these different aesthetic approaches to laughter and comic pleasure? Drawing on Bourdieu, it is possible to argue that because HCC comic styles have been externally consecrated by comedy critics and other cultural intermediaries, as well as being frequently misrecognised to as legitimate by LCC respondents[5], they are automatically imbued with symbolic power. Simply possessing an HCC sense of humour thus acts as a potent signal of one's embodied cultural capital and their symbolic distance from those with less legitimate comedy tastes. For Bourdieu, such symbolic boundaries need not to be drawn explicitly as the cultural hierarchy ensures that aesthetic styles necessarily negate one another (Bourdieu 1984: 223).

However, in recent years many have questioned Bourdieu's formulation of 'implicit' symbolic boundaries. In particular, Lamont (1992) has argued that class-based differences in cultural taste do not always necessarily imply hierarchically-ordered boundaries. In Britain, this thesis has been bolstered by the recent work of Bennett et al. (2009: 194), who argue that cultural snobbery among the British middle classes has all but disappeared. Reflecting on this issue, Lamont and Molnar (2002) argue that if researchers wish to meaningfully link taste to processes of symbolic violence they must specifically interrogate taste *boundaries*. In other words, they point toward an empirical emphasis on what Martin and Merriman – writing in this volume – term 'second-order aesthetic judgments'. It is only through such direct analysis of the judgments some people make about other people's aesthetic judgments, they argue, that it is possible to see 'the lines that include and define some people, groups and things while excluding others' (Lamont and Molnar 2002: 168).

Significantly, my research revealed that British comedy taste marked very strong and overt symbolic boundaries. I found that sense of humour acted as a key resource in the policing of social class boundaries, with HCC respondents, especially, reinforcing their sense of self through an explicit comedy *snobbery* (Friedman, 2014). Central to this boundary-drawing were again contestations around laughter and pleasure. HCC respondents were particularly disparaging of comedy audiences who they felt were *only* interested in laughter, who, according to Fred, are looking for 'first-degree emotional reactions' to comedy. Asked to elaborate, Fred continued:

> Y'know, John Bishop, working men's club, I've had six pints, I'm here to laugh my fucking face off. Bosh. That's fine. But I'm not looking for that.

What was notable here was not just the classed nature of Fred's derision of 'working men's club' audiences but also his caricature of a particular affective response, of the desire to get intoxicated and laugh one's 'fucking face off'. His tone implies a sense that such a reaction is not just aesthetically limited but in its excessive physicality and hedonism implies a lack of restraint, a lack of self-control. This disdain for an explicitly instrumental orientation to comedy was frequently connected to audiences for particular 'popular' observational comedians such as Peter Kay, Russell Howard and, above all, Michael McIntyre. Steve outlined his objections to McIntyre's audiences:

> It's just lowest common denominator. With McIntyre it's just this thing where parents and their 12-year-old kid can sit around, over dinner, and watch one of the DVD's. Where they can say 'oh yeah, we do that, don't we'. But that's all it is. It's almost like you've fed something into a computer, like you've interviewed 5,000 people about lots of different things and you've worked out their laughter on graphs ... I just find it lazy.
>
> *(Steve)*

HCC respondents not only drew boundaries on the basis that some audiences had inferior aesthetic preferences for comedy, but they often went further, implying that some simply didn't have the capacity to 'get' comedy that went beyond the immediately pleasurable. Steve, for instance, mentioned a particularly 'dark' part of Jonny Sweet's 2008 Edinburgh Fringe Show (which won the Edinburgh Comedy Award for 'Best Newcomer'), where he was dismayed to see a number of audience members leave because 'they just didn't understand'. Another example mentioned repeatedly was the 'paedophilia' episode of *Brass Eye*, which large amounts of the population 'simply couldn't handle', according to Sarah. A conversation with Frank highlighted the pivotal role this 'black' style of comedy played in delineating aesthetic boundaries:

> FRANK: If you sat a *Daily Mail* reader or a *Sun* reader in front of *Brass Eye* ... well certainly I think there's something in people that is so scared of the badness that they can't come on the journey ...
>
> SF: Why do you think some people can't 'come on the journey'?
>
> FRANK: We have a brittle, animal reaction to stuff and to take us from there to a place where we think philosophically, and in a civilised way, as part of a civilisation about these things is a hard journey. So it's not a simple thing to view a complex and difficult issue with sensitivity and with a desire to get on top of all the complexities, to steer the best course through a very difficult issue. It's much fucking easier to say (puts on a faux Cockney accent) 'These paedos, they're getting our children, watch out, name and shame 'em, could be in the park, could be next door'.

What is striking about these comments is the way HCC respondents implied that audiences who do not perceive 'black' comedy as funny somehow lacked intelligence. Such audiences, according to Frank, were confined to 'animalistic' reactions. Such damning judgments illustrated the stark and sometimes aggressive aesthetic boundaries drawn by HCC respondents. They also showed how HCC respondents tended to envision such audiences as 'imagined communities' (Anderson 1984), with comedy taste straightforwardly connected to characteristics with strong class connotations such as newspaper readership, regional accent and linguistic choice.

What was also noticeable about HCC boundary-drawing was that comedy taste did not just mark aesthetic boundaries but was often used as a proxy for judging personhood, for evaluating individual worth. The possession of certain comedy tastes, then, frequently acted as an almost unbridgeable social barrier. 'I would probably think they were fucking idiots to be honest,' Dale told me when I asked his thoughts on those who liked Michael McIntyre, or as Kira noted of fans of Bernard Manning 'It's definitely that feeling where you would recoil from that person'. Indeed, there was a sense that comedy had a unique boundary-drawing power rooted in its connection to the social properties of humour:

> I definitely make judgments about people. It's about liking comedy that's in your realm. And I'm probably not going to be friends with someone who has different interests, where different things make them laugh.
>
> *(Marilyn)*

TREVER: I mean when you're meeting people you're analysing these things all the time. You're assessing them, can I be friends with you? Do we share the same views? And this can come out in a number of ways, and certainly in a conversation about comedy (laughs).

SF: Why do you think comedy would affect whether you could be friends with someone?

TREVER: Because I think there's something really personal about what makes you laugh. And unique about it. So maybe it goes deeper. If someone says something made them laugh, I think you can make quite a deep judgment about that person whereas I think theatre and film is more interpretative. There's something fundamental about what makes you laugh.

These informants point to the importance of comedy – as distinct from other cultural realms – in drawing boundaries. In particular, Trever suggested that comedy's abilities to mark such symbolic divides was somewhat unique. Whereas he noted that film and theatre 'are more interpretative', comedy taste implied more 'fundamental' and 'personal' elements of a person's personality – namely what 'makes you laugh'. Reaching beyond purely aesthetic judgements of certain comedians or comic styles, then, these quotes suggested that comedy's potency has more to do with the pivotal role played by humour in everyday life. In particular, they illustrated the importance of sharing laughter in shaping possibilities of friendship and other social interactions. As Collins (2004; cf. Kuipers 2009) has noted, humour and laughter play a crucial role in everyday 'interaction rituals'. In everyday life people gravitate towards, and form durable bonds with, others with whom they can create positive and energising emotional energy. Often, the successful exchange of laughter is central to this. One only has to think of the enduring popularity of the abbreviation GSOH (good sense of humour) in lonely hearts columns, for example, to see humour's importance as a tool for building closeness and intimacy. Yet, paradoxically, for this same reason scholars have long remarked on the exclusionary effect of laughter (Hobbes 1991; Billig 2005). The discovery of shared taste in humour may be taken as a sign of similarity; and similarity breeds emotional closeness, solidarity and trust. But, inversely, failure to share humour and laughter is often taken as a sign of not being 'on the same wavelength'. It may be precisely because comedy has this ability to create social bonds, through the proxy of humour and laughter, then, that it also has a heightened capacity to build and reveal strong symbolic boundaries.

Conclusion

Comedy has traditionally been regarded as low-brow art *par excellence*. Consistently denigrated by aestheticians as an art form implying one uniform, invariant aesthetic response – laughter – it has largely been confined to the bottom of the cultural hierarchy, doomed to forever emphasise function over form, body over mind. Yet my research illustrates that by empirically examining the way people actually *consume* comedy, it is possible to see that the aesthetic appreciation of comedy, in Britain at least, is much more complex. My findings reveal that respondents with different resources of cultural capital read and decode comedy in very different ways. In other words, they employ distinct and opposing comic styles. Indeed, in this short chapter, I have demonstrated that the key aesthetic battleground distinguishing different styles of comic appreciation is laughter. Far from an involuntary physiological reflex, I find laughter to be a much more uncertain, ambiguous and contested aesthetic practice.

While some respondents' comic preferences, notably those with low levels of cultural capital, do imply conventional understandings of laughter as the instinctive, pleasurable, *currency* of comedy, those from culturally privileged backgrounds are markedly more ambivalent. Indeed, for these respondents, comedy should never be *just funny*, it should never centre purely around the creation of laughter, or probe only what Frank referred to as 'first-degree' emotional reactions. Instead, 'good' comedy should have meaning – whether this be a political message, an intellectual suggestion *or* an experiment with form. Either way, the consumer should have to 'work' for his or her laughter, and through carrying out this aesthetic labour he or she will glean more enjoyment and reach a higher plain of comic appreciation. Indeed, the sense of aesthetic superiority that underpins HCC comic appreciation is remarkably strong, with respondents making a wide range of aggressive social judgements based on those who laugh too easily, laugh too much and laugh without thinking.

Sociologically, I also believe these findings may have important implications. In particular, such charged aesthetic contestations over laughter – a previously discredited aspect of aesthetic experience – may be illustrative of wider shifts in the way that dominant social classes are expressing cultural distinction in the contemporary era. Released from the once restricted consumption of 'high' cultural objects, there is strong evidence throughout cultural sociology that the privileged are now increasingly also enjoying 'emerging' popular cultural forms (Savage *et al.* 2013). However, if cultural sociologists are willing to dig further into the particular *mode* of this omnivorous orientation, and in particular to the different *ways* popular culture is being consumed, they are likely to find that distinction strategies prevail. In the case of British comedy, at least, this is certainly the case. By foregrounding a restrained, contemplative and even sometimes ambivalent relationship to laughter, the culturally privileged deploy their sense of humour as a key instrument in communicating contemporary cultural aptitude and competence.

Notes

1 More detailed info on the methodology used in this project can be found in (Friedman 2014: 176–191).
2 Following the example of Holt (1997), I operationalised my respondents' cultural capital resources via equally weighted measures of their social origin (parental occupation and education), their own occupation and own education (see Friedman 2014: 179 for further detail).

3 It is important to note that not all elements of aesthetic experience were coherent among, and different between, cultural capital groups. Contextual factors as well as age, gender and ethnicity all played a role in individual accounts of comedy taste (see Friedman 2014: 85–87 for further detail).
4 The excluding function of humour has been explored extensively by Billig (2005) and Powell and Paton (1988).
5 There was a diffuse *misrecognition* of the intrinsic value of HCC comedy tastes among LCC respondents. The main manifestation of this was 'self-elimination' (Bourdieu 1984: 379) where LCC respondents would deliberately opt out of consuming HCC comedy, noting it was 'beyond me' or 'just went over my head'. These short utterances implied a certain imagery – of humour so sophisticated it somehow passes over LCC intellectual capacity – which indicated a deeply rooted sense of inferiority and deference (for further detail see Friedman 2014: pp. 67–90).

References

Addison, J. (1979) *The Spectator*, ed. Gregory Smith, 4 vols., London: Dent.
Adorno, T and M. Horkheimer (1944) *The Dialectic of Enlightenment*, Thetford: Thetford Press.
Anderson, B. (1984) *Imagined Communities: Reflections on the Origin and Spread of Nationalism*, New York: Verso.
Ang, I. (1985) *Watching Dallas*, London: Routledge.
Aristotle (1996) *Poetics*, trans. Malcolm Heath, Harmondsworth, UK: Penguin.
Bachmayer, T. and N. Witerdink (2014) 'Taste Differentiation and Hierarchization within Popular Culture: The Case of Salsa Music', *Poetics*, 47: 60–82.
Bakhtin, M. (1984) *Rabelais and His World*. Trans. by H. Iswolsky, Bloomington, Indiana: Indiana University Press.
Barber, C.L. (1963) *Shakespeare's Festive Comedy: A Study of Dramatic Form and Its Relation to Social Custom*, Cleveland and New York: Meridan.
Bennett, S. (2009) Michael McIntyre: Live at Wembley Review, *Chortle*, Available online at http://www.chortle.co.uk/shows/tour/m/16839/michael_mcintyre_2009_tour?review=1750 (accessed 13 January 2015).
—— (2012) Michael McIntyre: Showtime Review, *Chortle*, Available online at http://www.chortle.co.uk/comics/m/43/michael_mcintyre?review=3205&type=1 (accessed 13 January 2015).
Bennett, T., M. Savage, E. Silva, A. Warde, M. Gayo-Cal and D. Wright (2009). *Class, Culture, Distinction*, London: Routledge.
Bergson, H. (1900) *Laughter: An Essay on the Meaning of the Comic*, London: Routledge.
Billig, M. (2005) *Laughter and Ridicule: Toward a Social Critique of Humour*, London: Sage.
Bourdieu, P. (1984) *Distinction: A Social Critique of the Judgement of Taste*, London: Routledge.
Bremmer, J. and H. Roodenburg (eds) (1977) *A Cultural History of Humour From Antiquity to the Present Day*, Cambridge and Oxford: Polity Press.
Collins, R. (2004) *Interaction Ritual Chains*, Princeton, New Jersey: Princeton University Press.
Congreve, W. (1973) *The Double Dealer*, London: Scolar.
Coser, R. (1960) 'Laughter among Colleagues', *Psychiatry: Journal for the Study of Interpersonal Processes*, 23: 81–89.
Csikszentmihalyi, M. (1988) *Optimal Experience: Psychological Studies of Flow in Consciousness*. Cambridge: Cambridge University Press.
Dunbar, R. (2005) 'Laughter as Social Lubricant: A Biosocial Hypobook about the Pro-Social Functions of Laughter and Humour', *Centre for the Study of Group Processes Working Papers*, University of Kent: 1–45.
Elias, N. (1993) *The Civilising Process*, Oxford: Blackwell.
Friedman, S. (2014) *Comedy and Distinction: The Cultural Currency of a 'Good' Sense of Humour*, London: Routledge.
Hanquinet, L., H. Roose and M. Savage (2014) 'The Eyes of the Beholder: Aesthetic Preferences and Museum Audiences', *Sociology*, 48(1): 111–132.
Hennion, A. (2001)'Music Lovers: Taste as Performance' *Theory, Culture and Society* 18(1): 1–22.
Hobbes, T. (1991) *Leviathon*, ed. Richard Tuck, Cambridge: Cambridge University Press.
Holt, D. (1997) 'Distinction in America? Recovering Bourdieu's Theory of Tastes from Its Critics', *Poetics* 25(2): 93–120.
Kant, I. (1987) *Critique of Judgment*, trans. Werner S. Pluhar, Indianapolis: Hackett Publishing Company.
Kuipers, G. (2009) 'Humour and Symbolic Boundaries', *Journal of Literary Theory*, 3(2) 219–239.

Lamont, M. (1992) *Money, Morals, Manners: The Culture of the French and American Upper-Middle Class*, Chicago: Chicago University Press.
Lamont, M. and V. Molnar (2002) 'The Study of Boundaries in the Social Sciences', *Annual Review of Sociology*, 28: 167–195.
McCoy, C. and R. Scarborough (2014) 'Watching "Bad" Television: Ironic Consumption, Camp, and Guilty Pleasures', *Poetics*, 47: 41–59.
Powell, C., and Paton, G. (1988) *Humour in Society: Resistance and Control*, London: Macmillan.
Price, R. (2013) '£21m Man Who Isn't Laughing All the Way to the Bank', *The Daily Mail*, 15 January 2015. Available online at http://www.dailymail.co.uk/news/article-2262517/Michael-McIntyre-Hes-worlds-earning-comic-terrified-losing-everything.html#ixzz2vCCxO9ss (accessed 13 January 2015).
Savage, M., F. Devine, N. Cunningham, M. Taylor, Y. Li, J. Hjellbrekke, B. Le Roux, S. Friedman, and A. Miles (2013) 'A New Model of Social Class? Findings from the BBC's Great British Class Survey Experiment', *Sociology*, 47(2): 219–250.
Stott, A. (2005) *Comedy*, London: Routledge.
Wilmut, R. and P. Rosengard (1989) *Didn't You Kill My Mother In-Law: The Story of Alternative Comedy in Britain*, London: Methuen.
Young, A. (2014) *Street Art, Public City: Law, Crime and the Urban Imagination*, Routledge: London.

23
Middlebrow book culture

David Carter

Given its provenance in popular journalism and the culture wars of the early to mid-twentieth century – and before that in the pseudoscience of phrenology – the language of brow-levels is surprisingly common in the sociology of culture. The terms 'highbrow' and 'lowbrow' emerged in public debates around the turn of the twentieth century as a way of identifying divergent cultural tastes and more intensely in debates over the decline of cultural values. While resisting the combative hierarchies embedded historically in the terms, sociological studies of cultural dispositions have continued to deploy them to indicate distinct cultural strata, often without acknowledgement of their contentious history. The term 'middlebrow', in particular, which entered Anglophone sociology largely through translations of Pierre Bourdieu's concepts of *la culture moyenne* and *l'art moyen* (1984, 1990), has been used in an under-theorised way simply to indicate a broad middle zone between high and low cultural preferences.

This chapter will consider two bodies of work concerned with the middlebrow: first, largely Anglo-American scholarship that has emerged since the early 1990s from historical and literary studies directed at reclaiming the institutional and aesthetic space of a distinct middlebrow culture, middlebrow *book* culture in particular; second, a sociological tradition, often deriving from Bourdieu, which attempts to map cultural capital against social indicators such as class, education, gender and age on a hierarchical model. While the two literatures make little reference to each other, the former has drawn on Bourdieu for the concepts of cultural capital and cultural field (Driscoll 2014; Pollentier 2012; Radway 1997) while there are some surprising parallels between Bourdieu's work and popular sociological writing from the USA. More recently, from a sociological perspective, Savage (2010: 67–92) has re-examined the context of mid-century debates over brow levels to argue for the emergence, post-war, of a new middle-class identity based on technical expertise rather than aspirations to culture or the arts.

The chapter begins by describing the emergence of the key terms and the mid-century 'battle of the brows' (Brown and Grover 2012) which gave them significance. It argues that however unsatisfactory the term 'middlebrow', because of its imprecision and long-standing pejorative associations, the concept remains useful as a way of indicating a distinct historical constellation of institutions, tastes and practices. The chapter then turns to Bourdieu's account of *la culture moyenne* in *Distinction* and subsequent work on taste hierarchies and cultural capital. It concludes with a consideration of recent arguments within cultural studies about new cultures of reading which have emerged in the digital age, and what these mean for the redistribution of cultural capital, at least in the Anglophone world.[1]

High, low, middle

'Middlebrow' first appeared in English in the early 1920s, joining 'highbrow' and 'lowbrow' in a three-step hierarchy of tastes, texts, persons and practices. Its deployment was polemical, yet it did speak to major transformations in the field of culture and struggles over cultural authority. The middlebrow was named most insistently in relation to books and reading, but the terminology was widely applied, to theatre, music, cinema (Napper 2009) and the new consumer technology of radio. Indeed, what was until recently the first known use of 'middlebrow', from *Punch*, referred to the BBC: 'The BBC claim to have discovered a new type, the "middlebrow". It consists of people who are hoping that some day they will get used to the stuff they ought to like' ('Charivaria' 1925: 673). *Punch* managed simultaneously to satirise the BBC's claims as an arbiter of taste and the middlebrow consumer's lack of natural discernment; but its rendering of the aspirational and disciplinary dimensions of middlebrow values was astute. In America, these same dimensions were captured in the 1926 appeal of the Book-of-the-Month Club (BOMC) to readers 'anxious' about missing the best new books: 'Why is it you disappoint yourself so frequently?' (Rubin 1992: 99).

As in class analysis, any modelling of cultural tastes on a scale of high to low calls forth a middle ground, but a middle ground typically less easily defined and socially-fixed than the extremes on either side. Like the middle classes, the middlebrow is likely to be divided further into higher and lower strata, 'Upper Middlebrows' and 'Lower Middlebrows' perhaps (Lynes 1949: 25). Despite working with hierarchies of just this kind, cultural sociology has been little interested in the history of the middlebrow as a concept or set of institutions. However, the vibrant field of contemporary middlebrow studies enables an assessment of whether the concept remains useful to cultural analysis.

The idea that culture(s) existed in a hierarchy ranging from high to low was already widespread by the 1870s. It gained its modern sense of crisis towards the end of the nineteenth century in response to the rapid expansion of new forms of commercial entertainment and their multiplying publics, not least reading publics. But the novel concept of a *middlebrow*, a distinct middle range between higher and lower taste cultures, depended more specifically on developments in the twentieth century: on the simultaneous presence of high modernism, on one side, and 'mass commercial culture', on the other, in the period between the wars when both found enduring institutional form. The middlebrow can thus be understood as a modern phenomenon, not merely residual; structured by and structuring in the reconceptualisation of the cultural field which became visible or, better, institutionalised across the first half of the twentieth century. With the progressive acceleration of book, newspaper and magazine publishing, the emergence of new technologies of culture and entertainment, and the consequent growth of new audiences, the field of culture appeared to many – not just the cultural elite but also journalists, 'bookmen' and ordinary consumers – to be increasingly segmented into different publics and distinct cultures. But alongside segmentation, many also perceived a new kind of promiscuous mingling: where cultural distinctions ought to be clear they appeared increasingly blurred and confused. The idea of the middlebrow emerged as a way of defining these dual effects. While the values and practices associated with the middlebrow can be discovered from the nineteenth century until the present, it is useful to adapt

Bürger's (1984) argument in relation to the avant-garde and to delimit an 'historical middlebrow' extending from the early 1920s to the mid-1960s, when the term's currency fades as institutional structures around modernism, popular culture and technical expertise (Savage 2010) were again transformed. I will return later to a contemporary resurgence in usage of the term.

The historical middlebrow

The word 'highbrow' emerged first, in the last quarter of the nineteenth century in America, connoting professional expertise, superior education, intellectual distinction or cultural refinement. Around the turn of the century, 'lowbrow' appeared as its necessary opposite, signifying more definitely a lack of cultivation (Rubin 1992: xii), and manifesting a progressive differentiation between 'sacralised' and 'vulgar' forms of culture (Levine 1988). While 'highbrow' always carried a sense of qualities outside or above those of ordinary people, its earlier uses were mostly neutral, often ludic, and if negative no more so than in populist attitudes favouring practical against abstract knowledge. Its distinctively modern pejorative connotations arose in the early decades of the twentieth century as the term became more narrowly attached to the equally novel concept of 'intellectuals' (Collini 2006: 110–11), and then, most potently, to modernism.

Over the same period, 'middlebrow' became a byword for the false standards and lack of discrimination in matters of culture taken to be symptomatic of a more general malaise in modern civilisation manifested in increasing commercialisation, standardisation, and instrumentalisation. What distinguished the middlebrow from the merely lowbrow, at least from an elite or avant-garde perspective, were the former's misplaced pretensions to culture and good taste. For Q.D. Leavis (1932: 36–7), the *faux bon* was 'now the staple reading of the middlebrow', the 'respected middling novelists' who dealt in 'soothing and not disturbing sentiments, yet with sufficient surface stimulus to be pleasing'. Their style was 'easily recognised by the uncritical as "literature"' and thus offered (uncritical) readers 'the agreeable sensation of having improved themselves without incurring fatigue'. Leavis's *Fiction and the Reading Public* has been described as 'the first serious work of literary sociology to be published in English' (Sutherland 2000: xi). Certainly it was the first to observe that 'middlebrow taste [had] been organised' (Leavis 1932: 24), a valid perception even if its motivation was paranoid.

Yet the middlebrow or 'broadbrow' in J.B. Priestley's (1926) definition always had its supporters: authors, intellectuals and entrepreneurs who defended the pleasures of ordinary readers, validated their aspirations, and sought means to broaden their access to culture. Many – like Priestley – were engaged in the new journals, book clubs, radio broadcasts and publishing series that emerged between the wars (Baxendale 2012; Rubin 1992; Shapcott 2012; Wild 2012). Of course distinctions were made, between discriminating and undiscriminating consumers, between the mass audience and the 'average alert-minded person' (Radway 1997: 185); middlebrow institutions were not simply 'popular' but were engaged precisely in the game of making distinctions.

Against the dominant negative (and gendered) sense of the term,[2] contemporary middlebrow studies have attempted to restore the space of the middlebrow to cultural history, as a spectrum of texts and authors, a distinctive domain of cultural values and tastes, and, most productively, a set of institutions (Bracco 1990; Brown and Grover 2012; Macdonald 2011; Radway 1997; Rubin 1992; Travis 2002). A wide range of sometimes overlapping, sometimes incommensurate artefacts and practices functioned as middlebrow in different contexts. What links them loosely under the term 'middlebrow' is the notion that culture should be *accessible*: first, culture should not be the sole preserve of specialists or highbrows; second, it should be readily available for consumption. In literary terms, the range extended from 'the better class of thrillers', say, to the works of established contemporaries such as John Galsworthy or Arnold Bennett, newer writers such as Priestley or Elizabeth Bowen, even certain works by a modernist author like Virginia Woolf. Middlebrow scholarship has engaged with the exclusions of the modernist canon, refocusing attention on *other* modern literature of the twentieth century and using the concept of the middlebrow non-pejoratively to reclaim neglected authors, especially female writers (Botshon and Goldsmith 2003; Humble 2001; Harker 2007). More broadly, we can usefully distinguish between two middlebrow dispositions, one oriented to mastering the established canon, the other oriented to the modern, to the 'best of the new books' or the sophisticated modernity offered by magazines such as *Vanity Fair* and *Vogue* (Buckridge 1999; Carter 2011; Hammill 2007).

The middlebrow is no more objective a concept than high or low culture – but also *no less*. Like them it had material effects and took institutional form. There is of course nothing inherently middlebrow about the classics, but repackaged as accessible modern commodities – purchased in a World's Greatest Books series – they participate in a new cultural economy, offered to consumers less as 'timeless classics' than as useful acquisitions for modern subjectivity and sociability. The very idea of brow levels created the possibility of writing, publishing and reading into a middle space 'neither highbrow nor lowbrow', in a common phrase of the period. In Parchesky's terms (2002: 229):

> Since the 1920s, the term middlebrow has designated the vast field of cultural production and consumption located between the most disparaged of mass entertainments and the elite ranks of avant-garde and 'high' culture, at the intersection of consumers' efforts to access 'culture' and the efforts of critics, educators, and entrepreneurs to make such culture more widely accessible.

The 'betweenness' of the middlebrow is critical, but to retain any analytical force the term must be used to indicate something more (or less) than *everything in between*. What defined the historical middlebrow, if not in any singular way, was its positioning in relation to high culture, and to modernism more specifically, and its role in processes of self-cultivation and class consolidation. Thus the second part of Parchesky's definition is also critical, highlighting the intersection of consumer aspiration and an institutional network brought into being to meet and multiply that desire.

As Rubin argues: 'In the three decades following the First World War, Americans created an unprecedented range of activities aimed at making literature and other forms of "high" culture available to a wide reading public' (xi). These included subscriber book clubs such as the BOMC; 'great books' discussion groups and the Great Books curriculum at Columbia; 'how-to-read' books and 'world's greatest books' selections – most famously the Harvard Classics; popular 'outlines' of history, science and philosophy; new kinds of book papers and magazines; and new books and talk shows for radio (Radway 1997; Rubin 1992). There were similar developments in the British sphere (Buckridge 1999; Carter 2013: 128–52; Wild 2012). Middlebrow institutions affirmed that 'good books' were not the province of highbrow culture alone (indeed highbrows were likely to mistake artifice or pretension for quality) but equally that good books could be distinguished from bad. They addressed neither professional readers nor 'mere' consumers, but 'ordinary' readers who read with a purpose, even if that purpose was primarily recreation. Such ordinary categories were themselves divided into more and less worthy forms (Carter 2013: 161–6).

This dual commitment to culture *and* to its wider diffusion leads Rubin to define the middleness of the middlebrow through a series of tensions between potentially contradictory imperatives: between culture's universal value and its use value for the purposes of sociability or 'personality'; between democratising access to culture and maintaining established standards; between valorising ordinary readers and promoting literary expertise; between resisting consumerism and deploying its techniques in the service of culture; and, more immediately, between a wide definition of 'good books' and a narrow definition of 'great books', between entertainment and cultivation, and between a broad and a more restrictive sense of taste – between *meeting* readers' tastes and *improving* them. Rubin traces these tensions through transformations in the 'genteel tradition' of self-culture which took new form in universities among 'generalists' resisting academic specialisation and in the higher journalism: 'genteel values survived and prospered, albeit in chastened and redirected form, throughout the 1920s, 1930s, and 1940s…. The terrain of middlebrow culture proved solid ground on which the genteel outlook could be reconstituted' as the United States shifted 'from a producer to a consumer society' (xvii–xviii).

In her study of the BOMC, Radway (1997) emphasises the class and ideological function of middlebrow culture in this 'characteristically modern cultural institution' (15). She identifies both cultural entrepreneurs and consumers as belonging to an emergent 'professional-managerial class' (250–2):

> [A] new middle-class profession of cultural entrepreneurship developed that was devoted to the business of commodifying and marketing taste. As it developed, its participants forged a new and distinct aesthetic constellation not so much out of simple deference to the tradition of high culture but out of a set of instrumental values connected more closely with their own economic self-interest.
>
> *(248)*

And with the social interests of their clients. Radway suggests that the club's membership was drawn not from the wealthiest but rather 'those whose social position was based on its command of cultural and intellectual capital, on a certain acquaintance with the cultural tradition and a measure of specialised knowledge and expertise' (295). For this newly-arrived or aspiring class of consumers, set apart from labour by their educational and professional qualifications, middlebrow institutions repeated the lesson that culture was linked to social and personal distinction and this could be acquired, not just through inherited or inherent cultural capital, but through discerning consumption of more or less interchangeable commodities (a book a month). This was one of the 'scandals' of the middlebrow, its frank acknowledgement of books and ideas as commodities and as capital. The club commodified 'the whole concept of Culture itself' (249) not just individual books. It offered an ethos, a habitus, that Radway calls 'middlebrow personalism': 'the club constructed a picture of the world that, for all its modern chaos, domination by abstract and incomprehensible forces, and worries about standardisation and massification, was still the home of individual, idiosyncratic selves' (283). The middlebrow offered to reunite what modernity had torn asunder.

The class register of middlebrow culture has generally been pitched lower in work on the British sphere, identified more with lower middle-class aspiration than professional-managerial class consolidation (Wild 2006 and 2012). If there is an historical difference it most likely derives from the much higher levels of tertiary education in the USA, where college attendance tripled between 1900 and 1930 (Radway 1997: 161). The English middlebrow shares more with an older tradition of working-class self-education, transformed by the new cultures of modernity, high and low (Rose 2002: 116–45, 393–438). In both societies, however, the middlebrow is associated with aspirations to cultural 'insidership' and processes of recalibrating the markers of middle-class belonging:

> The [English] feminine middlebrow had a significant role in the negotiation of new class and gender identities in the period from the 1920s to the 1950s. In the obsessive attention it paid to class markers and manners it was one of the spaces in which a new middle-class identity was forged, a site where the battle for hegemonic control of social modes and mores was closely fought out by different fractions of the newly-dominant middle class.
>
> *(Humble 2001: 5)*

The potency of imagining cultural divisions through the brow triad owed much to its apparent homologies with class divisions. The terms were 'shot through with class *ressentment*' (Collini 2006: 110), for they expressed a sense not just of superior and inferior but of *antagonistic* taste cultures. For F.R. Leavis (1930: 25), 'highbrow' was 'an ominous addition to the English language' because of the attitude to culture it implied: 'culture has always been in minority keeping. But the minority now is made conscious, not merely of an uncongenial, but of a hostile environment'. Such views were unlikely to lessen class resentment among those aspiring to legitimate taste. Even as they remained wary of highbrow earnestness and affirmed the right to pleasure in their cultural pursuits, middlebrow audiences took culture seriously, for they too were invested in distinguishing the legitimate and worthy from the vulgar or ephemeral. Middlebrow institutions were dedicated to discerning and helping consumers discern the *best* of the new books and other cultural forms. It was precisely in this aim that middlebrow appreciation was likely to clash with a more restrictive sense of quality associated with modern literature and criticism.

Middlebrow and the mass culture debate

In seeking more sophisticated models of popular culture, Cultural Studies has been preoccupied with the 'mass culture' debate from which it emerged. But this focus has obscured the degree to which, mid-century, cultural anxieties were driven by the middlebrow more than the frankly lowbrow. For the Leavises, the middlebrow's insidious pretensions to culture were more dangerous than popular entertainments with no pretensions at all. For Virginia Woolf, highbrow and lowbrow were natural allies against the middlebrow which she famously characterised as a 'mixture of geniality and sentiment stuck together with a sticky slime of calf's foot jelly … in pursuit of no single object, neither art itself nor life itself, but both mixed indistinguishably, and rather nastily, with money, fame, power and prestige' (1942: 182, 180). Woolf's excess is calculated, but it nonetheless indicates the intense negative charge attached to the middlebrow, matched only by the negativity attached to the highbrow by her adversaries (Baxendale 2012; Collini 2006: 117–19).

In America, the same apprehensions were expressed towards 'ultra-modernism' and highbrow condescension and towards middlebrow commercialisation and standardisation, but class antagonisms were less manifest until after the Second World War, in a new period of consumer affluence and expanded access to cultural goods (Greenberg 1948; Lynes 1949). The most influential American analysis of the middlebrow was late in the history of the term, Dwight Macdonald's famous *Partisan Review* essay 'Masscult and Midcult' (1960a, 1960b). Echoing Q.D. Leavis, Macdonald asserted that a 'whole middle culture has come into existence' (1960b: 592) defined again by its mixing of commerce and pretension:

> [Midcult] has the essential qualities of Masscult – the formula, the built-in reaction, the lack of any standard except popularity – but it decently covers them with a cultural fig leaf.... Midcult has it both ways: it pretends to respect the standards of High culture while in fact it waters them down and vulgarizes them.
>
> *(1960b: 592–93)*³

Earlier, in 1949, *Harper's* editor Russell Lynes had described a 'new social structure' organised around 'taste and intellectual pretension ... a sort of social stratification in which the highbrows are the elite, the middlebrows are the bourgeoisie, and the lowbrows are *hoi polloi*' (19). While largely satirical, Lynes is on firmer ground sociologically than Macdonald and not entirely remote from Bourdieu's analysis of the homologies between social class and cultural tastes. Like Bourdieu, Lynes (in his 1954 book) offers a chart of high, middle and lowbrow tastes, cleverly indicating, for example, how Whistler's 'Arrangement in Gray and Black, No. 1' for highbrows becomes 'Portrait of the Artist's Mother' and then 'Whistler's Mother' as we move down the scale – the same work understood according to three different 'aesthetics'. In April 1949, *Life* had presented an even more detailed chart listing highbrow, lowbrow, and upper and lower middlebrow tastes in clothes, furniture, entertainment, salads, sculpture, records, and more. In reading, tastes were distinguished in descending order: from little magazines, criticism of criticism, and avant-garde literature; to 'solid non-fiction', the better novels and quality magazines; then book club selections and mass circulation magazines; and, finally, pulps and comic books ('High-brow': 100–1).

What distinguished the highbrow for Lynes, again anticipating Bourdieu, was its 'association of culture with every aspect of daily life' (1949: 20). The highbrow's 'real enemy' was the middlebrow 'whom he regards as a pretentious and frivolous man or woman who uses culture to satisfy social or business ambitions'; and 'the fact that nowadays everyone has access to culture through schools and colleges, through the press, radio, and museums, disturbs him deeply; for it tends to blur the distinctions between those who are serious and those who are frivolous' (21). The lowbrow, by contrast, inhabits 'a world in which people do things and enjoy them without analysing why or worrying about their cultural implications.... He knows what he likes, and he doesn't care why he likes it' (23).

Upper middlebrows were the 'principal purveyors of highbrow ideas', cultural intermediaries such as publishers, educators, museum directors, movie producers, art dealers, and editors of serious magazines. *Lower middlebrows* were the 'principal consumers of what the upper middlebrows pass along to them' (25). Upper middlebrow *professionals* 'straddle the fence between highbrow and middlebrow and enjoy their equivocal position' (25), while the upper middlebrow *consumer* 'takes his culture seriously, as seriously as his job allows' (26). If uncertain of 'his' own tastes, he is 'firm in his belief that taste is extremely important' (27). The lower middlebrow, by contrast, 'ardently believes that he knows what he likes' and yet his taste is highly susceptible to fashion and influence: 'he is unsure about everything, especially about what he likes' (27). While the boundaries between brow levels were as fluid as those between classes, Lynes concluded that the brows were consolidating, 'finding their own levels and confining themselves more and more to the company of their own kind' (28).

Middlebrow and *la culture moyenne*

Turning from the historical literature to Bourdieu, the first point to make is that Bourdieu himself, of course, never uses the word 'middlebrow'. His translators do, and the question of translation needs attention especially if we seek to understand the middlebrow historically, for there is no ready equivalence between the French originals, *un art moyen* and *la culture moyenne*, and their translations, 'middlebrow art' and 'middlebrow culture' (Bourdieu 1984 and 1990).[4] The former are broader than the English phrases and less historically marked as neologistic, referring simply to a middling or, less helpfully, an 'average' culture (Pollentier 2012: 37–41). Bourdieu's interest in this respect is in the space of lifestyles and tastes located in the intermediate position in the class hierarchy, a space which his model both identifies and produces. Early in *Distinction*, he describes 'three zones of taste which roughly correspond to educational levels and social classes': legitimate taste; popular taste; and, in between, middlebrow taste (*le goût 'moyen'*) distinguished by its preference for the 'minor works of the major arts' and the 'major works of the minor arts' (1984: 16). Perhaps as a result of Bourdieu's own insistence on the fundamental binary between 'the aesthetic disposition' and 'the popular aesthetic', subsequent commentators have overlooked his extended analysis of this intermediate space, even though, precisely because of its in-betweenness, it might best illustrate his central argument about relations between class and the 'hierarchy of legitimacies' (Bourdieu 1990: 95).[5]

Given Bourdieu's insistence on relational structures, class trajectories, and the *habitus* linking art and lifestyles, his relatively neglected account of *la culture moyenne* can be read productively alongside Anglo-American middlebrow studies. Indeed, Bourdieu can sound remarkably like Lynes, Leavis or Woolf. The petite bourgeoisie, 'divided between the tastes they incline to and the tastes they inspire to', can 'make "middlebrow" whatever it touches'; but, Bourdieu insists, this is wholly an effect of its position in social space, not its 'nature'. Like middlebrow scholars, Bourdieu emphasises the role of cultural intermediaries or 'tastemakers' (he uses the English word) in meeting middle-class cultural aspirations. In 1970s France this meant the producers of cultural programs on TV and radio as well as critics in 'quality' newspapers and magazines who, like the journalists and broadcasters Rubin describes, generate 'a whole series of genres half-way between legitimate culture and mass production', mixing the accessible, the *déclassé*, the popularised and the not-quite legitimate 'with all the institutional signs of cultural authority' (325–6). But although certain works are designed specifically for petit-bourgeois consumers, it is the *relation to culture* that matters, for the 'same object which is today typically middlebrow – "average" (*moyen*) – may yesterday have figured in the most "refined" constellations of tastes and may be put back there at any moment' (327).

This relation to culture is characterised by 'cultural goodwill' (*la bonne volonté culturelle*); that is, by reverence for the legitimacy of the legitimate culture to which it aspires but for which its lacks the cultural capital to fully 'know' or be at home with.

> The petit bourgeois is filled with *reverence* for culture.... [This] undifferentiated reverence, in which avidity combines with anxiety, leads the petit bourgeois to take light opera for 'serious music', popularization for science, and 'imitation' for the genuine article, and to find in this at once worried and over-assured false recognition the source of a satisfaction which still owes something to the sense of distinction.
>
> This middlebrow culture owes some of its charm, in the eyes of the middle classes who are its main consumers, to the references to legitimate culture it contains and which encourage and justify confusion of the two – accessible versions of avant-garde experiments or accessible works which pass for avant-garde experiments, film 'adaptations' of classic drama and literature, 'popular arrangements' of classical music or 'orchestral versions' of popular tunes ... in short, everything that goes to make up 'quality' weeklies and 'quality' shows, which are entirely organised to give the impression of bringing

legitimate culture within the reach of all, by combining two normally exclusive characteristics, immediate accessibility and the outward signs of cultural legitimacy.

(1984: 323)

Dependent on degrees of autodidacticism and scholastic knowledge, the petit bourgeois is 'always liable to know too much or too little' where the trick of distinction is 'to know without ever having learnt' (329–30). Perhaps aware of how close to pop sociology this might sound, Bourdieu pauses in the midst of his argument (adding a footnote in the French edition) to differentiate his procedure from the 'class contempt' common in writing on the petite bourgeoisie. *His* work 'relates the properties of the habitus … most often picked on by class racism, such as "pretension" and "narrowness", to the objective conditions of which they are the product' (1984: 338).

Bourdieu's primary object is not to define middlebrow culture but rather to map the distribution of petit-bourgeois dispositions, both synchronically, through comparing its upper, middle and lower strata, and diachronically, through comparison of older and newer, rising and falling, class fractions. The logic of the model guarantees that it is in the middle of the middle classes that Bourdieu finds middlebrow taste in its 'purest' form, among 'technicians', with junior executives and primary teachers ranged closely on either side (1984: 58).[6] But while he asserts a distinct, unified petit-bourgeois ethos, Bourdieu's final insistence is upon the differentiating trajectories that define this class space, for its 'system of dispositions takes on as many modalities as there are ways of attaining, staying in or passing through a middle position in the social structure [that] may be steady, rising or declining' (339). Indeed, of all social spaces, this middle region is determined by its indeterminacy; it is a structure of 'mobile crossing-points' (343). Here all the variables of age, occupation, social origin, educational attainment and cultural capital (its early or late, familial or scholastic acquisition) come into play in a series of 'ordered yet partially disordering' (344) differences and correspondences.

Bourdieu also identifies a *new* petite bourgeoisie, located in the 'most indeterminate zone of an indeterminate region, that is, mainly towards the cultural pole of the middle class' (345). This fraction specialises in the provision of symbolic goods in new and relatively indeterminate occupations (design, promotion, marketing, fashion, counselling, TV presenters, etc.). *Their* investment in distinction is to 'stand aloof from the tastes and values most clearly associated with the established petite bourgeoisie and the working classes', and from the 'anxious pretension of the promoted petite bourgeoisie' (362; see du Bois 2013 for an analysis of cultural intermediaries in contemporary France). The point for the present is that although this recognisable group is still positioned 'in between', there is little that is middlebrow (and less *moyenne*) about their cultural dispositions. We cannot conclude with a simple homology between middlebrow and middle class.

This relational analysis offers a way of bringing Bourdieu to bear on Anglo-American accounts of the middlebrow: first, in rendering dynamic the middlebrow's role 'as a controversial category embedded in a struggle for legitimacy' (Pollentier 2012: 42); more specifically, in indicating why the *rising* fractions of the lower-middle and professional-managerial classes are especially engaged in middlebrow culture. For these were the groups within the middle class most invested in maintaining an upward trajectory and with most at stake in the processes of cultural distinction. But while acknowledging the force of Bourdieu's relational modelling, Pollentier (2012) has criticised his failure to reflect on the category *moyen(ne)* and the fact that *la culture moyenne* is defined only negatively in relation to legitimate culture. She contrasts Priestley's notion of the 'broadbrow' as an ethos based *not* on a dominated relation to legitimate culture but positively on an ethics of inclusion and balance (Pollentier

2012: 45–6). While such an ethos might itself be seen as typically petit-bourgeois, Pollentier's argument that Bourdieu 'encodes the perspective of legitimate culture' in his account of *la culture moyenne* is persuasive (Pollentier 2012: 40; Bennett 2007: 202). Pollentier (2012: 43) also notes how Bourdieu's later writings establish a binary model of the literary field which allows little place for any significant middle ground of the kind he had himself earlier explored in relation to photography. While middlebrow book culture might be defined by its in-between position in this binary between autonomous and commercial art, this remains a theoretical consequence of the model rather than an object of Bourdieu's interest in its own right.

Omnivores and middlebrows

Despite Bourdieu's lead, cultural sociology, as suggested above, has by and large used 'middlebrow' in an under-theorised, under-historicised way to indicate a middle zone between high and low cultural preferences. It thus begs the question of whether a distinct middle disposition exists, if only as an amalgam of higher and lower tendencies. The most productive work has been that on cultural omnivorousness – that is, the tendency for those in (certain) higher status groups to range widely across higher and lower cultural forms rather than having a restricted adherence to the most consecrated – and that most closely engaged with Bourdieu's work in *Distinction* (Bennett et al. 2009). While the precise nature of elite or middle-class cultures remains contested, there is a degree of consensus, first, that Bourdieu overstates the homologous nature of class dispositions, thus understating both dissonant tastes within classes and shared tastes across classes (Bennett 2007: 205-14; Lahire 2008), and, second, that cultural capital no longer operates on the single scale of legitimate culture, if it ever did so, for 'omnivorous' tastes are now more significant than cultural 'snobbery' in defining elite cultures (Bellavance 2008; Holt 1997; Peterson 2005; Peterson and Kern 1996; Prieur and Savage 2011). Both points have a bearing on the question of whether a contemporary middlebrow culture exists. If the legitimating role of legitimate culture and the opposition between exclusive and popular tastes have weakened – if, that is, the formative conditions of the historical middlebrow have largely disappeared – is 'middlebrow' still a useful concept?

The most extensive recent study of cultural tastes and participation is the UK work of Bennett et al. (2009). Their findings support a version of the omnivore thesis qualified by the recognition of quite different forms of omnivorousness, only some of which appear significant as cultural capital (181–90). Their survey indicates systematic patterns in cultural preferences and engagement, closely related to social cleavages in terms of education, class and occupational status, while class and education remain significant in determining preferences in certain fields. In short, cultural capital still works to reproduce privilege and distinction. However this does not equate to uniform or unified taste cultures clearly differentiated by class position. While the professional-executive class is likely to have higher levels of cultural participation and to act as if the 'command of legitimate culture is a worthwhile form of investment' (190), that culture remains a minority taste. There is little anxiety about expressing preferences for popular forms, many preferences are shared *across* the middle ground from higher to lower, and the claims of high culture receive only relatively weak assent elsewhere. While 'cultural goodwill' can be discerned among the middle class it appears to be determined as much by age as by a specific petit-bourgeois habitus: 'The older generation will probably go to its grave with the highbrow/middlebrow alignment based around an accommodation to legitimate culture, but the structure of the cultural order has changed' (254). Legitimate culture, in short, 'has rather less importance in the UK than Bourdieusian interpretations would expect' (253).

In terms of book culture specifically, the study indicates that although the stratification is less pronounced, reading and book ownership, along with music and the visual arts among fields surveyed, contribute 'most to the differentiation of contemporary cultural tastes' (97). Participation in book cultures is 'socially located within urban, educated and cosmopolitan populations' (110), while a preference for 'modern literature' is strongly associated with cultural capital, 'with graduates and professionals in "cultural" occupations' (100). Even then it remains a minority preference and, across all groups, the focus of 'relatively intense dislike' (98). Otherwise, and again contrary to Bourdieusian expectations, book reading does not reveal strong clusters of tastes, intense oppositions (except for gendered attitudes towards science fiction and romance), or 'snobbish or exclusionary' claims for the superiority of canonical literary texts (111). Rather, 'engagement with "the literary" in its canonical or modern incarnations may be one element of an omnivorous portfolio for the professional middle classes' (111). The survey, however, did not extensively investigate new modes of *participation* in book cultures, for example in literary festivals or reading groups.

How, then, might we locate middlebrow culture in this 'post-Bourdieusian' scenario? Surveys of cultural tastes and activities do not give a definitive answer even where they indicate a distinct intermediate cluster of preferences.[7] The fact that the antagonisms between high and popular, traditional and 'mass-commercial' cultures have weakened, alongside the emergence of a new 'technically-oriented' middle class (Savage 2010: 244), might indicate an *expanding middle*, such that tastes shared widely across class positions – such as those for landscape painting but not Impressionism, popular classics but not modern literature (Bennett *et al.* 2009: 98, 181) – could be defined as middlebrow. As such, these *déclassé* or no-longer-rare forms of culture, while dominant preferences, are relatively insignificant as cultural capital, although possibly the object of 'misplaced' goodwill. More interesting is a focus on the middlebrow as the site of distinction. Cultural omnivorousness has its limits, key boundaries which are rarely crossed, and *distastes* which are strongly expressed (Bennett *et al.* 2009: 254–5; Tampubolon 2008) – for specific forms of 'popular' culture, certainly, but *also* forms of legitimate or once-legitimate culture (mainstream theatre, perhaps, or movie adaptations of classic novels). Indeed, history suggests, such 'middlebrow' forms can be the *most likely* candidates for stigmatisation. 'Voracious' cultural consumers, for example, like modern art, world music, and horror films but not landscape paintings (Bennett *et al.*, 2009: 181). Such discriminating plurality will (again) seek to distinguish itself from less-knowing forms of 'promiscuous' taste, even more, perhaps, in a context where 'popular cultural objects become aestheticised' and 'elite objects become popularized' – where 'to consume in a "rare" distinguished manner requires that one consume the same categories in a manner inaccessible to those with less cultural capital' (Holt 1997: 103; Prieur and Savage 2011).

Indeed, it could be argued that culture has re-emerged as a mode of distinction in the digital age, where technical expertise is no longer a rare form of capital, at least in those societies where tertiary qualifications and digital competencies have become relatively widely distributed across the population. As discussed in the next section, new forms of market-oriented cultural consumption have arisen, disseminating high cultural styles and values through mass-market forms of distribution, with ambiguous reference to traditional forms of legitimation. Books and reading – perhaps surprisingly – have been prominent in these transformations (Collins 2010).

Neo- or post-middlebrow?

To approach the question differently we can turn to accounts of institutional change which address more explicitly the residual or resurgent presence of middlebrow formations.

The period since the 1990s has seen extraordinary shifts, not only in publishing and bookselling with the arrival of global media corporations and digital production and delivery systems (Striphas 2009; Thompson 2012), but also in reading and book culture, with the emergence of new literary institutions which at least superficially resemble aspects of the historical middlebrow. Collins refers to a 'massive transformation in the culture of reading' (2010: 16), Fuller and Rehberg Sedo to a new 'reading industry' (2013: 15–18). Alongside the remarkable growth of formal and informal reading groups, the Anglophone world has seen the rise of 'mass reading events' such as One City One Book programs; personality-driven television book clubs; new literary festivals and literary prizes with high media profiles; and a new wave of quality screen adaptations of literary novels (Collins 2010; English 2005; Fuller and Rehberg Sedo 2013; Ramone and Cousins 2011; Carter 2013: 149–52). These and related developments – the refashioning of bookstores, the boom in how-to-read books and reading memoirs, the rise of the 'literary bestseller' itself – represent a new 'popular literary culture' (Collins 2010: 3; Fuller and Rehberg Sedo 2013: 10). Its defining characteristic, however, is not the presence of popular genres within the literary domain but of high-end *literary fiction* within consumer culture.[8] For Collins, a traditional, restricted high-cultural sense of good taste now meshes seamlessly with a new, widely-accessible consumer culture *no less* committed to taste: 'the delivery systems for literary experiences become increasingly large-scale, but the mechanisms of taste distinction appear to grow ever more intimate as reading taste becomes ever more personalized' (2010: 33).

While there is agreement that something significantly new has emerged in contemporary book culture, its relation to the historical middlebrow remains contested. Driscoll (2014) posits the emergence of a 'new middlebrow' manifested in the contemporary institutions of reading and book talk but otherwise having much in common with the values and practices of middlebrow culture. Similarly, Fuller and Rehberg Sedo argue that the new book culture is 'shaped by middlebrow formulations of literary taste' (2013: 27). While 'produced as part of popular culture' it is 'consumed as an aspect of a reading culture in which residual meanings about 'quality' (or 'highbrow') fiction and canonical ideas about aesthetics linger on' (Fuller and Rehberg Sedo 2013: 48). Certainly the term 'middlebrow' has re-emerged strongly in media and book trade discourses.[9]

Contemporary reading groups are seen as paradigmatic of the new middlebrow and celebrated or criticised accordingly. A flourishing infrastructure of reading guides, cheap classics series, book lists, and monthly book selections has (again) arisen to support them. Reading group selections are typically 'good books', above all quality contemporary fiction and sometimes popular classics, but rarely downmarket genre fiction (Fuller and Rehberg Sedo 2013; Hartley 2001). Their modes of appreciation 'are particularly susceptible to characterization as middlebrow' (Driscoll 2011: 112) and recall the 'middlebrow personalism' Radway finds in the BOMC, privileging a deep affective relation to character or context but also the sense that something has been learned, with a civic as well as personal dimension (Middleton Meyer 2002). The many analyses of Oprah's Book Club (Aubry 2011; Rehberg Sedo 2011; Striphas 2009) have foregrounded its investment in discourses of self-transformation through 'passionate' reading, while its book selections again recall those of the BOMC.

The new middlebrow is thus as reader-oriented – and feminised – as the old. It is similarly located outside and sometimes expressly *against* the academy, and derives part of its meaning from contemporary culture wars (Guillory 1995). Finally, it can be linked still to forms of middle-class consolidation. Elizabeth Long argues that for book club members 'literature becomes a cultural marker of distinction' (2003: 61), but there are conflicting interpretations of literature's significance in this regard. 'Serious' book reading remains a restricted form of cultural engagement among a minority 'reading class' (Griswold, McDonnell and Wright 2005). And while 'cultural hierarchies of taste still adhere to reading materials ... possessing knowledge of books may only be a visible and valuable asset to other members of the reading class' (Fuller and Rehberg Sedo 2013: 48). Yet the newness and density of the new literary cultures suggest a social significance not captured in surveys of cultural preferences.

Collins insists that it is 'a serious mistake to conceive of the current popularization of elite cultural pleasures as simply the most recent incarnation of middlebrow aesthetics' (Collins 2002: 7); to do so is 'to fail to recognise just how fundamentally cultural life in the United States has changed' (2010: 19). While middlebrow culture persists, in the light classics, say, or 'tasteful' reproduction furniture, the new visibility, accessibility and desirability of quality fiction or 'designer auteurism' in the mass market is something fundamentally new: *high-pop* in Collins's earlier neologism (2002: 7–9). He distinguishes the new cultural formations from the historical middlebrow by defining the latter, narrowly, as having promoted a class of fiction *apart from* the canonical or 'high'. In the new popular literary culture, by contrast, it is precisely the *aesthetic* experience of literary reading (and its transcendence of mere consumerism) that is marketised. But while his account of the new 'consumability' of high-end fiction is persuasive, Collins underestimates the engagement of middlebrow institutions historically with canonical and modern(ist) literature, and the links, via discriminating consumption, between literature and lifestyle. His own discussion suggests more similarities between middlebrow and 'high-pop' than his thesis admits.

In drawing attention to these variable uses of culture, the 'middlebrow', properly historicised, remains a useful category for cultural analysis as the 'ambivalent mediation of high culture within the field of the mass cultural' (Guillory 1995: 87). Perhaps most useful is that it forces a disaggregation of habitual categories: of 'middle class' and the range of cultural attributes attached to that term, of the 'modern', the 'high', and especially the 'popular', where common usage is both too broad and too narrow to capture the distinctive nature of middlebrow formations. Books and reading belong both to the 'old' media and the new: as the latter they participate in forms of cultural distinction attached to the new and technologically emergent (Prieur and Savage 2011: 578); as the former, they stand for the continuity of cultural values and traditions. The most likely hypothesis is that 'old' and 'new' forms of attachment to literary reading and social distinction co-exist in the (undoubtedly new) institutions of contemporary reading cultures, different forms susceptible to analysis through the categories of education, occupational status, class, age and gender.

Notes

1 Middlebrow studies have been very largely focused on the Anglophone world, although a January 2014 conference on European Middlebrow Cultures, in Ghent, Belgium, was designed expressly to broaden the range (http://europeanmiddlebrow.wordpress.com/). The sociological work, by contrast, has included studies from Scandinavia, the Netherlands, France, Quebec, etc.
2 All three terms – highbrow, middlebrow and lowbrow – were routinely negatively-gendered female. Priestley's 'broadbrow', by contrast, is distinctly masculine (Carter 2011: 148).
3 Macdonald's immediate reference is to *Horizon* magazine. Other Midcult exemplars are the *Reader's Digest*, *Life*, the *Ladies' Home Journal*, the *Saturday Review*, and novelists such as John Steinbeck, Pearl Buck and Herman Wouk, contrasted to Zane Grey: thankfully, 'it seems never to have occurred to him that his books had anything to do with literature'.
4 Richard Nice, in his translation of *Distinction*, recognises this by frequently including the French terms in parentheses.
5 In *Distinction*, Bourdieu devotes as many pages to petit-bourgeois cultural dispositions as to the bourgeois sense of distinction; this is more than twice the number devoted to working-class dispositions.

6 For Bourdieu the petite bourgeoisie includes in ascending order craftsmen and shopkeepers, clerical and commercial employers, junior administrative executives (*cadres administratifs moyens*), junior commercial executives and secretaries, technicians, medical-social services, primary teachers, cultural intermediaries and art craftsmen. He is at pains to point out the 'difficulty and relative arbitrariness of defining the limits of the class' (259, 339). Much of the analysis of the petite bourgeoisie in *Distinction* is based on Bourdieu's earlier work on photography (French edition 1965).

7 Bennett *et al.*'s statistical analysis of cultural activities in relation to class categories reveals an 'intermediate class' located almost equidistant from both the professional-executive class and the working class on a wide range of activities: 'The intermediate class thus engages with legitimate culture more than the working class and is in general more active, but to a lesser extent than the professional-executive class' (181). Its reading habits are more like those of the professionals. This indicates the existence of a distinct 'intermediate' constellation of cultural activities, but not, of course, whether this should be called 'middlebrow'.

8 The term 'literary fiction' is problematic because of its legacy in evaluative criticism. However it is common in the book trade, identifying a specific kind of fiction and market segment. Collins suggests that literary fiction has itself become a kind of 'category fiction': 'Lit-lit' (2010: 225).

9 In the *New York Times*, for example, uses of 'middlebrow' rise from 76 in the 1960s to 262 in the 2000s.

References

Aubry, T. (2011) *Reading as Therapy: What Contemporary Fiction Does for Middle-Class Americans*, Iowa City: University of Iowa Press.
Baxendale, J. (2012) 'Priestley and the Highbrows', in Brown and Grover, *Middlebrow Literary Cultures*.
Bellavance, G. (2008) 'Where's High? Who's Low? What's New? Classification and Stratification inside Cultural "Repertoires"', *Poetics*, 36: 189–216.
Bennett, T. (2007) 'Habitus Clivé: Politics in the Work of Pierre Bourdieu', *New Literary History*, 38 (1): 201–28.
Bennett, T., M. Savage, E. Silva, A. Warde, M. Gayo-Cal and D. Wright (2009) *Class, Culture, Distinction*, London: Routledge.
Botshon, L. and M. Goldsmith (eds) (2003) *Middlebrow Moderns: Popular American Women Writers of the 1920s*, Boston, MA: Northeastern University Press.
Bourdieu, P. (ed.) (1965) *Un art moyen: essai sur les usages sociaux de la photographie*, Paris: Les Éditions de Minuit; trans. S. Whiteside (1990) *Photography: A Middlebrow Art*, Stanford, CA: Stanford University Press.
—— (1979) *La distinction: critique sociale du jugement*, Paris: Les Éditions de Minuit; trans. R. Nice (1984) *Distinction: A Social Critique of the Judgement of Taste*, Cambridge, MA: Harvard University Press.
Bracco, R.M. (1990) *'Betwixt and Between': Middlebrow Fiction and English Society in the Twenties and Thirties*, Melbourne: History Department, University of Melbourne.
Brown, E. and M. Grover (eds) (2012) *Middlebrow Literary Cultures: The Battle of the Brows, 1920–1960*, Basingstoke, UK: Palgrave Macmillan.
Buckridge, P. (1999) 'Reading the Classics in Australia: Great Books Anthologies, 1900–1960', *BSANZ Bulletin*, 23(1): 36–45.
Bürger, P. (1984) *Theory of the Avant-Garde*, Manchester: Manchester University Press.
Carter, D. (2011) 'Modernity and the Gendering of Middlebrow Book Culture in Australia', in Macdonald (ed.), *The Masculine Middlebrow*.
—— (2013) *Always Almost Modern: Australian Print Cultures and Modernity*, North Melbourne: Australian Scholarly Publishing.
'Charivaria' (1925) *Punch*, 23 December: 673.
Collins, J. (ed.) (2002) *High-Pop: Making Culture into Popular Entertainment*, Malden, MA: Blackwell.
—— (2010) *Bring on the Books for Everybody: How Literary Culture Became Popular Culture*, Durham, NC: Duke University Press.
Collini, S. (2006) *Absent Minds: Intellectuals in Britain*, Oxford: Oxford University Press.
Driscoll, B. (2011) '"Not the Normal Kind of Chicklit?" Richard and Judy and the Feminized Middlebrow', in Ramone and Cousins, *Richard and Judy Book Club*.
—— (2014) *The New Literary Middlebrow: Tastemakers and Reading in the Twenty-First Century*, Basingstoke, UK: Palgrave Macmillan.
du Bois, V. (2013) *La Culture comme vocation*, Paris: Éditions Raisons d'agir.

English, J. (2005) *The Economy of Prestige: Prizes, Awards, and the Circulation of Cultural Value*, Cambridge, MA: Harvard University Press.
Fuller, D. and D. Rehberg Sedo (2013) *Reading Beyond the Book: The Social Practices of Contemporary Literary Culture*, New York: Routledge.
Greenberg, C. (1948) 'The State of American Writing', *Partisan Review* 15, August: 876–83.
Griswold, W., T. McDonnell and N. Wright (2005) 'Reading and the Reading Class in the Twenty-First Century', *Annual Review of Sociology*, 31: 127–41.
Guillory, J. (1995) 'The Ordeal of Middlebrow Culture', *Transition* 67: 82–92.
Hammill, F. (2007) *Women, Celebrity and Literary Culture between the Wars*, Austin, TX: University of Texas Press.
Harker, J. (2007) *America the Middlebrow: Women's Novels, Progressivism, and Middlebrow Authorship between the Wars*, Amherst, MA: University of Massachusetts Press.
Hartley, J. (2001) *Reading Groups*, Oxford: Oxford University Press.
'High-Brow, Low-Brow, Middle-Brow' (1949) *Life*, 11 April: 99–102.
Holt, D.B. (1997) 'Distinction in America: Recovering Bourdieu's Theory of Tastes from its Critics', *Poetics*, 25: 93–120.
Humble, N. (2001) *The Feminine Middlebrow Novel, 1920s to 1950s: Class, Domesticity, and Bohemianism*, Oxford: Oxford University Press.
Lahire, B. (2008) 'The Individual and the Mixing of Genres: Cultural Dissonance and Self-Distinction', *Poetics* 36: 166–88.
Leavis, F.R. (1930) *Mass Civilisation and Minority Culture*, Cambridge: Minority Press.
Leavis, Q.D. (2000 [1932]) *Fiction and the Reading Public*, London: Pimlico.
Levine, L. (1988) *Highbrow/Lowbrow: The Emergence of Cultural Hierarchy in America*, Cambridge, MA: Harvard University Press.
Long, E. (2003) *Book Clubs: Women and the Uses of Reading in Everyday Life*, Chicago: University of Chicago Press.
Lynes, R. (1949) 'Highbrow, Lowbrow, Middlebrow', *Harper's Magazine*, February: 19–28.
—— (1954) *The Tastemakers*, New York: Harper and Brothers.
Macdonald, D. (1960a) 'Masscult and Midcult: I', *Partisan Review* 27, Spring: 203–33.
—— (1960b) 'Masscult and Midcult: II', *Partisan Review* 27, Fall: 589–631.
Macdonald, K. (ed.) (2011) *The Masculine Middlebrow, 1880-1950: What Mr Miniver Read*, Basingstoke, UK: Palgrave Macmillan.
Middleton Meyer, K. (2002) '"Tan"talizing Others: Multicultural Anxiety and the New Orientalism', in Collins (ed.), *High-Pop*.
Napper, L. (2009) *British Cinema and Middlebrow Culture in the Interwar Years*, Exeter: University of Exeter Press.
Parchesky, J. (2002) '"You Make Us Articulate": Reading, Education, and Community in Dorothy Canfield's Middlebrow America', in B. Ryan and A. Thomas (eds) *Reading Acts: US Readers' Interactions with Literature, 1800–1950*, Knoxville: University of Tennessee Press.
Peterson, R.A. (2005) 'Problems in Comparative Research: The Example of Omnivorousness', *Poetics* 33: 257–82.
Peterson, R.A. and R.M. Kern (1996) 'Changing Highbrow Taste: From Snob to Omnivore', *American Sociological Review*, 61(5): 900–907.
Pollentier, C. (2012) 'Configuring Middleness: Bourdieu, *L'Art Moyen* and the Broadbrow', in Brown and Grover, *Middlebrow Literary Cultures*.
Priestley, J.B. (1926) 'High, Low, Broad', *Saturday Review*, 20 February: 222–3; reprinted in *Open House: A Book of Essays* (1927), London: Heinemann, 162–7.
Prieur, A. and M. Savage (2011) 'Updating Cultural Capital Theory: A Discussion Based on Studies in Denmark and in Britain', *Poetics* 39: 566–80.
Radway, J. (1997) *A Feeling for Books: The Book-of-the-Month Club, Literary Taste, and Middle-Class Desire*, Chapel Hill: University of North Carolina Press.
Ramone, J. and H. Cousins (eds) (2011) *The Richard and Judy Book Club Reader: Popular Texts and the Practices of Reading*, Farnham, UK: Ashgate.
Rehberg Sedo, D. (ed.) (2011) *Reading Communities from Salons to Cyberspace*, Basingstoke, UK: Palgrave Macmillan.
Rose, J. (2002) *The Intellectual Life of the British Working Classes*, New Haven and London: Yale University Press.

Rubin, J.S. (1992) *The Making of Middlebrow Culture*, Chapel Hill: University of North Carolina Press.
Savage, M. (2010) *Identities and Social Change in Britain since 1940: The Politics of Method*, Oxford: Oxford University Press.
Shapcott, J. (2012) 'Aesthetics for Everyman: Arnold Bennett's *Evening Standard* Columns', in Brown and Grover, *Middlebrow Literary Cultures*: 82–97.
Striphas, T. (2009) *The Late Age of Print: Everyday Book Culture from Consumerism to Control*, New York: Columbia University Press.
Sutherland, J. (2000) 'Introduction', in Q.D. Leavis, *Fiction and the Reading Public*: v–xxv.
Tampubolon, G. (2008) 'Revisiting Omnivores in America circa 1990s: The Exclusiveness of Omnivores?', *Poetics* 36: 243–64.
Thompson, J.B. (2012) *Merchants of Culture: The Publishing Business in the Twenty-First Century*, second ed., New York: Plume.
Travis, T. (2002) 'Print and the Creation of Middlebrow Culture', in S. Casper, J. Chaison and J. Groves (eds), *Perspectives on American Book History: Artifacts and Commentary*, Amherst: University of Massachusetts Press.
Wild, J. (2006) *The Rise of the Office Clerk in Literary Culture, 1880–1939*, Basingstoke, UK: Palgrave Macmillan.
—— (2012) '"A Strongly Felt Need": Wilfred Whitten/John O'London and the Rise of the New Reading Public', in Brown and Grover, *Middlebrow Literary Cultures*.
Woolf, V. (1942) 'Middlebrow', in *The Death of the Moth and Other Essays*, London: Hogarth Press.

24
Digital sociology in the field of devices

Adrian Mackenzie, Richard Mills, Stuart Sharples,
Matthew Fuller and Andrew Goffey

Introduction

Digital sociology focuses on culture as it plays out in the vast, expanding, power-laden and complex media environments of the last few decades. In these media environments, feedback loops running between devices and social practices constantly re-define culture. Culture – that which is lived in places such as cities, cafes, airports, streets, shops, museums, parks, clinics, offices or living rooms – is rapidly rewoven by transient device-specific play of signals passing through news, entertainment, advertising and social networking platforms such as Twitter, Instagram, LiveJournal, YouTube, LinkedIn or Weibo. Digital sociology addresses the problem of how to make sense of the signals generated, captured, organised, shared, and constantly sorted in form of hyperlinks, messages, transactions, text, and images flowing across media platforms by people living with and through digital devices (Lupton 2012). Digital social researchers seek to learn about the coherence, modes of thought and value, practices, materials and forms of contemporary experience and social action as they are drawn into what recent observers have called 'a massive, culturally saturated feedback loop' (Schutt and O'Neil 2013: 5) interlacing what people do and what they experience. None of the devices, practices and subjects of this form of the social are coherent, well-understood or stable. Indeed, these feedback loops predicate constant processing, adjustment, realignment, transformation, variation and mutation in social worlds. Amidst this targeting of transformation, much hinges on interactions in what we might call, following Ruppert *et al.* (2013), the *field of devices*. The field of devices is a complex weave of technical elements, more or less connected to each other through relations of contact and contest, convergence and divergence, similarity, imitation and variation. It is inhabited by people who react to, who experience and are affected by durable and transient calls to order their actions with and through devices.

While digital sociology draws on well-established methods such as ethnography, rhetorical, discourse and visual analysis, in the analysis of device-specific transformations in culture new skills and digital tools, borrowed or copied from domains of statistics, software development, hacking, graphic design, audio, video and photographic recording and predictive modelling – that is, from the media-textual environments of contemporary culture themselves – must come into play, with lesser or greater relevance. Social research in such settings, as Noortje Marres notes, 'becomes noticeably a distributed accomplishment: online platforms, users, devices and informational practices actively contribute to the performance of digital social research' (Marres 2012: 139). Given that the sociology of contemporary culture relies on the field of devices, the critical question is: how it will participate?

Digital sociology overlaps with, borrows from and seeks to make sense of much more prestigious, well-financed and heavily equipped practices in marketing, in scientific research, in government administration and commerce that target the expanded media environments of contemporary culture by intensifying work on data (Cukier and Mayer-Schoenberger 2013). *Scale* and *pattern* are key concerns in many of these settings, and scale and pattern also allure social researchers. As danah boyd and Kate Crawford suggest, 'Big Data tempts some researchers to believe that they can see everything at a 30,000-foot view' (boyd and Crawford 2012).[1] But the mode of ordering – 'recurring patterns embodied within, witnessed by, generated in and reproduced as part of the ordering of human and non-human relations' (Law 1994: 83) – of digital sociology diverge greatly from contenders and analogues such as 'data science' (Schutt and O'Neil 2013) or 'predictive analytics' (Prediction Impact Inc. 2009) or digital humanities. Aiming to pay close attention to the ways in which the data-driven description of culture has become a key economic and social concern (Savage 2009; Thrift 2006), digital sociology might take shape less as a social science of digital culture than as the study of how device-specific events pattern lives, experience, power and value on various scales. This apparently limited ambition harbours some surprising expansive possibilities. It might cultivate 'a sociological sensibility not confined to the predominant lines of sight, the focal points of public concern' (Back and Puwar 2012: 12) but able to develop novel empirical techniques of inquiry and evaluate the unprecedented volume of information we encounter. Its device-specific emphasis might entail novel empirical practices and conceptions of the empirical (Adkins and Lury 2009).

As we will see, particularly through the examples we draw from one moderately large but critically relevant social networking platform, GitHub.com, the process of researching device-specific events on the various scales and amidst the intricate patterns of practice in contemporary media environments is not at all straightforward. Patterns and scales of action and interaction it turns out, entwine with devices in both contemporary culture and in its analysis. The case we draw on here – Github.com – is interesting precisely because what goes on there – coding and software development amongst other things– is both typical of the vast and somewhat incoherent work done on devices as part of contemporary culture, and at the same time plays an important practical role in re-formatting that work so that it becomes more publicly visible as a call to social order. Launched in late 2007, Github at the time of writing (2014) claims to host around 13 million different code repositories made by around 6 million users who are mostly software developers (see http://www.github.com/about). While these numbers, like all social media statistics, need to be disaggregated and analysed (for instance, Github 'users' include automated software processes that hourly commit new code to certain repositories; or many repositories are simply copies of other repositories, etc.), they position Github as a mid-ranking social media platform in terms of size. But regardless of size, Github certainly exemplifies the profuse work done on devices that texture increasingly large parts of people's lives. A panoply of practical implementations of algorithms (see Couldry this volume), of graphic interfaces, of power-laden protocols, standards and infrastructures (such as operating systems, databases, security systems) can be found there.

Code repositories might be seen as vectors that on varying scales comprise much of the contemporary field of devices. These vectors display field-specific characteristics – code repositories contain code written in programming languages, they are accompanied by descriptions, they relate to a finite range of domains (science, business, publishing, gaming, graphic design, etc.) – and they also affect each other, as can be seen in the many imitations, variations, copies, re-implementations and versions found there. Moreover, Github increasingly serves as a model of social action that attracts many other practices not directly related to software: how-to guides, metadata on the Tate's art collection, the White House's open data policy, legal documents, recipes, books, and blogs are just some of the diversifying use-cases now found in repositories on Github. As a recent article in *The Atlantic* suggests, Github is increasingly of interest to non-programmers because the de-centralised, distributed and trackable collaborative processes it offers for coding can be used for many kinds of work: designs, legal documents, maps, images, books, blogs or websites (Meyer 2013). In this respect, Github, we might say, is an 'indexical icon' (Lee and LiPuma 2002) of the scaling and patterning that characterise the contemporary metamorphoses of culture.

Scales, scaling and fields of devices

One problem for digital sociology is the question of where to stand in looking at such complex processes.[2] In some respects, platforms like Github could be seen as what Andrew Barry termed 'technological zones of circulation.' These are

> spaces formed when technical devices, practices, artefacts and experimental materials are made more or less comparable or connectable. They therefore link together different sites of scientific and technical practice. Such zones take different forms. The points of access to the zones may be more or less clearly marked, with more or less well-defined and functioning gateways.
>
> *(Barry 2001: 202–3)*

Github is a kind of gateway to the linkages between devices. It offers analytic and empirical descriptions and data streams as well as search functions that might help us engage with different scales and patterns of connection between technical configurations, platforms and practices. Wrangling these affordances in sociologically inventive ways entails much engagement with the practices and device specificities of the Github platform itself. As we craft ways of dealing with different scales, with wholes, with events and device-specific relations in Github, the allure of total or exhaustive description promised by the platform itself needs to be reckoned with.

Given the heavily accumulative dynamics of the field of devices, there is a temptation for digital sociologists in their own empirical work to emulate the descriptive practices – the analytics – that accompany the scaling-up of digital media platforms. If digital sociology was simply a theoretically sophisticated version of media analytics or business intelligence, it would miss the transformations in culture attested by the availability of this data. The real analytical promise of large-scale data for digital sociology instead concerns the possibility of studying how re-scaling processes actually cut across pre-formatted notions of the individual or culture as a whole. The smooth conceptual poles of individual and whole culture constrain analytical purchase on open-ended, heterogeneous device-specific contestation of contemporary cultural spaces. They are attached to more static concepts of agency and structure that have long been disputed (we are not re-visiting those debates here; see Latour *et al.* [2012] for a broader engagement with this problem, which arguably still thwarts 'social physics'). For instance, while 'users' or consumers remain the focus of much market research and advertising, their demographic attributes of race, age, ethnicity, income and educational level are perhaps becoming less important as 'postdemographic' concerns of profiling in terms of groups, tastes, interests, device usage, etc., take hold (see Rogers 2013: 153–4). Furthermore, the feedback loops between social lives running through the field of devices mean that cultural processes change scale in many different ways. Like all fields, the field of digital devices is tensioned by many different vectoral relations (see Martin and Merriman, this volume for a relevant description of Pierre Bourdieu's field theory). As Evelyn Ruppert, John Law and Mike Savage write, 'fields of devices [are] relational spaces where some devices survive and dominate in particular locations while others are eclipsed, at least for the moment' (Ruppert *et al*. 2013: 13).

We can glimpse some of these relational transients in Github as a platform. On the one hand, like many social media platforms, Github.com broadcasts data about what people are doing on the platform. At the time of writing (August 2014), around 220 million events are available on the so-called Github.com timeline since early 2012. The timeline is a comprehensive time-stamped series of user-generated events.[3] Many of these events are highly ephemeral. They have little afterlife. Someone creates a repository and puts something there, and then never returns. Millions of such events occur. On the other hand, the Github timeline data does not necessarily include events generated by Github itself as it develops the platform. Platform-level events – changes in architecture, modifications to interfaces, shifts in underlying design or management practice – are much harder to see from the data. Changes in the platform affect what people do. In the flow of events marked on the Github.com timeline, there are some surprising features. For instance, the 18 months of Github event data graphed in Figure 24.1 shows growth.

We might not be surprised to see a steadily increasing count of events on a social media platform. (Github is, after all, a social media platform for coding.) While growth curves are common to many digital media platforms, here we see something anomalous. The number of events per week in April 2012 and especially September 2012 exceed the number of events per week at the end of 2013. Two peaks appear earlier than they should. These peaks reflect something about the way Github as a platform stored data rather than a dramatic change in what people were doing on Github. These kinds of features in the data suggest that even platforms in the field of devices themselves suffer from device-specific forces.

Even if we manage to filter these platform-generated effects or archival anomalies (statisticians and scientists often have to clean data before they analyse it), the plot in Figure 24.1

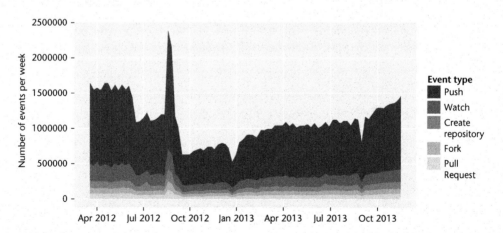

Figure 24.1 Events on the Github.com timeline

suggests other problems in analysing the field of devices. Events are not atomic social actions. 'Push' events, for instance, occur when software developers move code from a local repository to a Github repository. While there are some atomic events on the Github's timeline (for instance, a WatchEvent suggests that a person is interested in a particular code repository), other events such as PullRequest or PushEvents may wrap around complicated sequences and content 'payloads'. The payload complexity of events poses analytical problems. It steers analytical work into the depths of highly localised practices and highlights the importance of mapping local patches of action rather than general aggregates.

Yet the primary form of device-specific order in the vast textual fields of the Github data is the formatted events. Github as a device formats data on the field of devices in ways that encourage a focus on individuals and individual repositories. It affords little scope for examination of transverse flows or cross-cutting vectors in the field. The all-important APIs, the more or less real time data sources that GitHub exposes, effectively provide data about individual repositories and individual users or individual organisations. This formatting of data is typical of contemporary feedback loops: while device-specific data is readable by many, its formatting affords certain interested uses. Indeed, Github.com itself presents and encourages the production of various forms of visualisation and tabulation of what goes on in code repositories (and as mentioned above, the fact that we can access an archived version of the Github event timeline attests to this). GitHub ran a data competition in 2012 in which data analysts sought to do something with the timeline data (Doll, 2012). But what is most available from that data is the formatted events (as we saw in Figure 24.1) that more or less reinforce Github's conception of itself as first of all a *hub* and secondly as a *social* media platform. This means that we can easily, for instance, examine a most important or well-known repository on Github such as the Linux kernel, a much-vaunted, commercially, culturally and technically vital software device (https://www.github.com/torvalds/linux). Relatively quickly, individual developer contributions can be analysed, and we could begin to characterise the composition of the group of people who keep this important software object working and up-to-date. And indeed, this visualisation work is already supplied by Github.com itself (as the screenshot in Figure 24.2 shows).

It would even be possible through careful reconstruction to graph the changes in the network of relations that comprise the Linux kernel development teams, and perhaps to see how patterns of work on Linux kernel have changed over time as its economic and technical significance has extended through the popularity of the Android phones that rely on Linux and through the many corporate and industry users/producers invested in Linux. Issues, conversations, team and organisational changes could all be mapped. We could look further at the thousands of 'forks' and 'mirrors' (copies) of Linux to be found on Github, and characterise in fine-grained ways how processes of imitation generate flows of readers/writers, how meanings and practices are stabilised through repetition, and how invention might occur at intersections or overlaps between fields.

This leaves digital sociology in an interesting position. On the one hand, the Github data allows us to locate an important device – Linux – in the field of devices. The way certain devices attract work, imitations, and variations can be seen from the event data. And the incorporation of Linux into other devices – for instance, the Android platform – can also be gauged. These ongoing alignments and associations are important features of the field of devices. Yet other great patterns of practice on other scales do not immediately surface in the Github data. For instance, we know that particular code constructs are imitated or reinvented in thousands of different projects. We know too that same kinds of software device are re-implemented or imitated across different languages, or for different

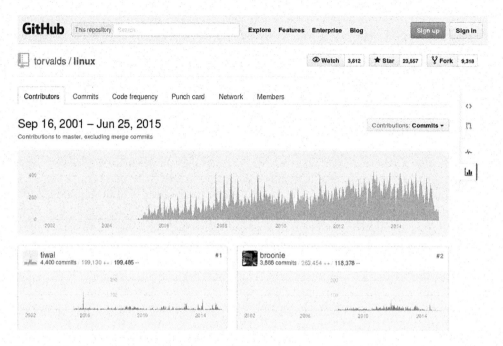

Figure 24.2 Top contributors to Linux on Github

platforms, often with only small variations. These common patterns striate the field of devices, but barely appear in the Github-formatted data. Those cross-cutting patterns span devices and weave them together in surprising conjunctions: the same code constructs might be found in projects focusing on an ecommerce platform, ecological models of rainforest species diversity, Mozilla Foundation's Firefox browser, the Linux kernel, a library to manipulate financial data, or a modified version of the Android operating system for smart phones. In short, despite the domain-spanning dynamics of the field of devices, the way in which code migrates across social fields cannot be readily analysed. In exploring the field of devices, digital sociology finds highly diverse domains of social action and transaction, linked by the common practices, formats and materials (code patterns, repository mechanisms).[4]

Although it might seem a purely technical or practical issue, the problem of traversing such data flows lies at the heart of digital sociology as well as many parts of contemporary culture. One response to the problem of traversing data flows is to make devices that capture, reduce or visualise data.

The scaling up of the information infrastructures needed to deal with diverse data flows, for instance, is a salient concern of the software projects on Github.com. Many Github repositories explicitly address problems of scale and data. For instance, over 1500 repositories relate to 'MapReduce,' a parallel-processing algorithm first developed at Google to improve web search engine response times (https://github.com/search?q=map+reduce); 3700 repositories engage with Hadoop, a widely used Java-language implementation of the MapReduce algorithm (https://github.com/search?q=hadoop;). This scaling attests to auratic effects propagating in the field of devices as patterns of imitation. That is, the infrastructures that increasingly bring people into various forms of relationality are difficult to concretely manage. One can gaze on somewhat sublime images of earth-spanning information flows or visualisations of networks of hundreds of millions of Facebook users, but it is the work on devices such as Hadoop that shows us how people concretely grapple with the auratic promise of data flows.

A second response, common in the field of devices, is to make judgements about what is happening to data. Why does Google make available via its 'BigQuery' service a massive public archive of all the data produced by Github since early 2012? While social researchers might find it enormously useful to have an aggregated, hourly-updated timeline of all Github actions, it is very unlikely that some group at Google marketing or engineering concerned with data architectures for cloud computing has social researchers particularly in mind. Much more likely, they seek to attract the attention of the millions of software developers who use Github.com for coding work. Trying to see themselves and others in this high volume datastream, software developers and programmers familiarise themselves with Google's BigQuery architecture, and perhaps use it more thereafter. On the one hand, work on the Github timeline data demonstrates the power of Google Inc.'s cloud computing services. On the other hand, it promotes those services to software developers by inviting them to explore an important aspect of their own work – coding – as a data flow, and to produce second order judgements on it, including many largely aesthetic judgements of taste (see Martin and Merriman, this volume). But the developers' interest in doing this presupposes that they have an interest or investment in making judgements about code, or finding patterns in coding work. For social researchers too working on Github.com, the Google BigQuery datasets enable a widely differing scale of exploration of practice in the field of devices, and constantly increase the risk of being drawn away from the singularity and variability of practices to produce large scale tabulations of results.

Against the flow: Anti-patterns in digital sociology

A final response to data flows – and this is one that we have pursued – asks: what work needs to be done against the data flows and against its inevitably device-specific formatting of data in order to apprehend forces tensioning the field of devices? One possibility here is to examine how people act in the field of devices to make sense of patterns in data. An interest in patterns lies at the heart of digital data flows. The problem of finding patterns in data is a chronic concern in science, business and government data practices. And certainly patterns and the seeing of patterns are the central pre-occupation in many contemporary sciences, in financial markets, in biomedicine and in business analytics (see for instance, the fields of 'pattern recognition' and 'machine learning', Hastie, Tibshirani and Friedman 2009). But a prior and crucial question here is how to think about the value of pattern, or pattern finding as aesthetics of the social. As we have seen, in sociological thought more generally, pattern is a long-standing concern. John Law speaks of 'recurring patterns of the social', Nick Couldry of 'patterns of flow', and Andrew Abbott suggests that 'if most things that could happen don't happen, then we are far better off trying first to find local patterns in data and only then looking for regularities among those patterns' (Abbott, 2001: 241). As Mike Savage suggests, we need to understand 'how pattern is derived and produced in social inscription devices' (Savage 2009: 171), whether these devices are objects of analysis or part of our own methods. A broader philosophical re-conceptualisation of patterns runs through some social and cultural theory (for instance, in recent work influenced by A.N. Whitehead, who writes 'beyond all questions of quantity, there lie questions of pattern' (Whitehead 1958: 195).

However it is conceptualised, the fact remains that concrete work on patterns largely takes a quite limited number of forms. This limitation in forms suggests that the device-specific formatting of data is hard to resist, and that the social aesthetics generated by the field of devices is a symptom of this. People craft many data visualisations. But the principal visible forms of pattern are rather limited. They include plots that show lines, curves, peaks and clusters of points, networks, trees, and maps. Drawing on the spectrum of plots, graphs and diagrams developed in the last few centuries (see http://www.datavis.ca/milestones/ for a catalogue; Edward Tufte's work [Tufte 2001] is a standard reference for quantitative digital data), contemporary visual displays of pattern abound in 'predictive analytics and the move back to visualisation in social statistics, the new cartography and associated Web 2.0 innovations, [and] visual montages designed to represent amalgams of "variables"' (Burrows 2012: 585). These patterns can take the form of plots (bar graphs, scatter plots, lines and curves drawn through clouds of data points, network diagrams), maps on many different scales (especially maps that superimpose different geo-located datasets), information visualisations (typically combining data graphics, text and typographic design elements), as well as tables and textual-graphic forms (word clouds), with varying degrees of animation and with many different forms of scale. Practices of data visualisation are routinised through the proliferation of certain visual forms (the network diagram, heat maps, bubble plots and chloropleth maps are widely found) in different places. They have field-specific attributes. Although network visualisations, tag clouds, stream graphs and the like have abounded in data visualisation on the web, especially with the growth of graphics libraries and packages such as Hadley Wickham's *ggplot2* (Wickham 2009), Mike Bostock's *d3.js*, or widely-used scientific plotting packages such as *matplotlib* (software projects all currently hosted on Github), we have little sense yet of the visual culture of these devices and their visual forms. While devices of various kinds may have been involved in producing them (for instance, many smoothing algorithms used to draw lines through points effectively fit a series of local linear models – splines – in building a smooth curve), the models themselves are not interpreted as such but act in the world more like things than thoughts. If pattern matching and pattern recognition are becoming mundane parts of contemporary culture in many different ways, it is partly because these forms of judgement or perception are endemic in the field of devices. (For instance, in the face recognition logic now built into many digital cameras, or the much-discussed recommendation systems typical of online commerce.) They are in any case widely distributed through various social fields where visual devices associated with displays, gauges, metrics, dashboards, graphs, and visualisations form part and parcel of social life, whether in the graphic displays that users of supply chain and inventory management systems or financial traders gaze at (Knorr Cetina and Bruegger 2004), or in the many news-related visualisations produced by data journalists for news sites such as *The Guardian* datablog (n.d.) or the *New York Times* (2012).

Some commentators suggest that the production and use of such visualisations is a key concern for contemporary sociology: 'the discipline . . . will have to take visualization methodologies far more seriously than we have hitherto' writes Roger Burrows because of the ways that they are being used and could be used to understand 'particular patterns of association that exist between persons, objects, symbols, technologies and so on' (Burrows 2012: 585). The renewed emphasis on visualisation in digital sociology differs somewhat from adjacent efforts such as computational social science (Giles 2012; Housley *et al.* 2013) where visualisation is usually close evaluation of statistical or predictive models. Sociological work on the transformations of data visualisation is still rather scarce. Scientific visualisation offers some leads here (Latour *et al.* 1990; Myers 2008) alongside work on visualisation in finance (Pryke 2010), but the visual culture of data as it moves out of scientific publication has received little attention. There is much scope for investigation of the seeing in data visualisation as forms of visual culture in which, as Gillian Rose writes, 'different ways of seeing are bound up into different, more-or-less conscious, more-or-less elaborate, more-or-less consistent practices' (Rose 2012: 549). This is a challenge to methodological practices precisely because the visual forms attest to a shift away from some traditional sociological concerns with abstractions, models and structures as deep explanations of social processes, and a lighter, perhaps more responsive descriptive attunement to patterns, groupings and flows.[5] What do they make visible? Both in the visual culture of data, and in its own visualisation of digital data, digital sociology faces the problem of describing how patterns are produced at the intersection of various concretisations and abstractions as reactions to certain aspects of experience. Digital sociology, we suggest, might take data graphics and the many judgements and discussions of data graphics seriously as a form of judgement endemic to the field of devices.

Patterns arise in very different ways. Many data visualisations seek to render perceptible something that occurs on spatio-temporal scales that are difficult to directly see, but they often struggle to distinguish something amidst the generic schematic formatting of the data. For instance, Figure 24.3 seeks to convey something of the patterns associated with different scales of activity in Github repositories by counting events that appear in the Github timeline over an interval of two years (2012–2013). The general pattern shown here is the somewhat ubiquitous 'power law' distribution of events, a distribution that often shows up in social media data. At the left hand end, the high point refers to the millions of Github repositories consisting of one or two events. At the low end on the right, where the curve approaches the x-axis, a small number of repositories receive many thousands of events. The power law distribution of events in social media often vexes data analysis and data visualisation. Many social media datasets yield heavy-tailed distributions when graphed. This common scaling of

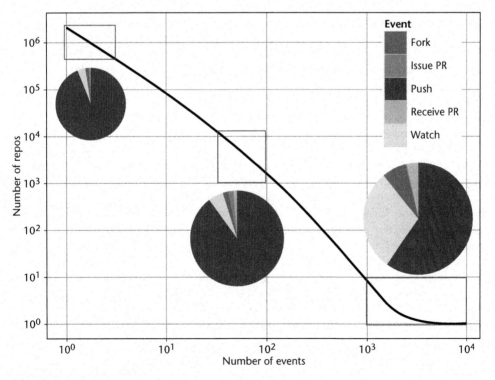

Figure 24.3 Patterns of repository events on Github

events across the 'many-some-rare' scales (Conte *et al.* 2012: 334) requires site-specific work. The visualisation of repository event counts begins to do this by showing something of the different composition of the repositories on the different scales. The many small repositories mainly consist of a few PushEvents. Mid-scale repositories show the presence of more social events such as Watch and Fork. The rarer very large repositories attract many more social events – Fork, Watch and PullRequest. But if this patterning across many-some-rare is so common as a reaction to something in the contemporary field of devices ('In recent years, due to ubiquitous computerization, networking and obsessive data collection, reports of heavy-tailed distributions have almost become a routine' [Muchnik *et al.* 2013: 1]), what does it say about the global organisation of the field of devices?

On the one hand, many data visualisations, whether in the form of networks, scatter plots or line graphs today present the power-law or scale-free pattern of digital media. If is often said that patterns are supplanting causes as modes of explanation in many places, and the growth of data visualisations might be understood in these terms. These descriptive visualisations might prompt some causal interpretation in their viewers but they are not premised on any such abstraction. Might they be seen perhaps more generally as an integral part of the cultural saturated feedback loop running through the field of devices? As technological concretisation binds practices, habits, emotions, and interactions through digital devices and infrastructures and devices, the derivation of patterns increasingly depends on abstractive devices that classify, cluster, calculate and predict events precisely in order to shape them. Predictive analytics, as demonstrated in Google Research's work on how users' searches foreshadow airline ticket bookings or car sales (Varian and Choi, 2009), derives patterns from data using a much more technical armature of machine learning techniques. This modelling is an increasingly dense force affecting the feedback loop between people and digital infrastructures (Pariser 2011). Algorithmic classificatory techniques such as k-means clustering, nearest neighbour classification, linear regression, logistic regression, principal component analysis, neural networks, decision trees, random forests, and support vector machines are rapidly becoming an integral part of every level and niche of digital assemblages, ranging from playful mundane devices such as 'kittydar', a neural network to detect cat photos (https://github.com/harthur/kittydar) through to thousands of projects implementing 'face detectors' or 'motion detectors' for smart phones, web browsers, and for different operating systems. Even a single technique like the popular random forest classifier (Breiman 2001) can be found hundreds of thousands of times in Gitbhub.com repositories, and tens of thousands of times in popular programming languages such as R (R Development Core Team n.d.). Again, the proliferation of these classificatory or pattern finding techniques is perhaps much less visible, and the ways in which they imprint or weave through flows of meaning and things is harder to analyse. They are somewhat withdrawn elements in the feedback loops of cultural space. These predictive models and classifiers sometimes operationally shape the experience and action (as in Netflix or Amazon recommendation systems, or in the classifiers that detect and classify body gestures in the Microsoft Kinect game controller), and sometimes they are analytic tools used by people working on platforms trying to make sense of emerging or divergent patterns in practice. As always, the feedback loops between knowing and acting are hard to disentangle precisely because they are becoming more tightly coupled. If decision trees were an analytic technique developed by statisticians in the late 1970s trying to make sense of air pollution measurements in Los Angeles (Breiman *et al.* 1984), in the Kinect game controller they become predictive devices that intensify the immediacy of computer game play. Online learning – the constant updating of predictive models in response to the flow of current events – is increasingly common in social network media and online transactions.

In the field of devices, patterns are generated, acted upon, altered and re-imprinted. Pattern recognition is no longer a practice conducted at leisure by expert interpreters or elite analysts. Patterns are operational components of device-specific zones of culture. The transformation of abstract analytic devices of many different kinds (linear regression models, clustering algorithms, Bayesian models, etc.) into things that either circulate much more widely in the world in gadgets and devices or into meta-things such as search engines that modulate flows on a large scale is a central component of the flow of texts, meanings, audiences, viewers, visitors, spectators, readers and players in many settings. These abstractions exercise an auratic effect akin to the data infrastructures we were discussing above. Journalists, social researchers and commentators on digital technology tend to attribute great potency to algorithms in general. The proliferation of algorithms is hard to deny, but digital sociology might play an important role in describing what happens as these algorithms shift shape and move into different settings ranging from pay day loans to computer game play, from web search engines or ecommerce recommendations to face recognition in digital cameras. The aura of algorithms as epistemic prime movers akin to steam power or electricity covers over their diverse provenance (they do not come just from computer science but also from statistics, psychology, cognitive science, ecology, archaeology or geology) and their diversity in practice. Perhaps more significantly the patterns that these algorithms produce or derive from data are neither obviously legible in descriptive devices, nor is their relation to existing structures, groupings, or classifications direct.

For digital sociology, recognising the effects of this pattern-making is a significant challenge. The imprinting of flows of meaning, media and practices is sometimes legible (for instance, in the 'induced viralities' seen in various social media platforms that identify trends using pattern recognition techniques and then shape flow of messages or network connections accordingly), but not always. Another difficulty is much more challenging. While descriptive devices can relatively easily slip into the analytical toolkit of social researchers – the spread of tag-clouds or Wordle graphics would be a typical instance of this – the appropriation and re-purposing of machine learning, pattern recognition or data mining approaches is more problematic. Many of these devices rely on formidable mathematical apparatus, ranging across linear algebra, probability theory, function analysis and numerical optimisation. The diverse provenance of the techniques means that, although they operate abstractly (that is, with little regard for the concrete specificities of a given situation), they handle notions of group, classification, difference and similarity heterogeneously. Nearly all of them bring to bear powerful scaling processes that reduce the high dimensions and volume of data to legible forms of variation and pattern.

Conclusion

While Bourdieu's comments on devices are not abundant, he wrote about traffic lights:

> The social world is full of calls to order which function as such only for individuals who are predisposed to notice them, and which, as a red light causes braking, trigger deep-rooted bodily dispositions without passing through consciousness and calculation.
>
> *(Bourdieu 2000: 176)*

Contemporary culture is deeply textured by device-specific calls to order. Reactions to these signals, for those who notice them, are often deep-rooted and bodily enacted. The repositories of Github.com, which we have only lightly explored here, illustrate something of the variety of signals flashing in contemporary social worlds. It points to forms of reactions that go well beyond braking or accelerating, yet remain for all that somewhat non-conscious or largely affective. The experience of spiralling in and out of device-specific feedback loops generates many forms of reaction and reactivity.

In the field of devices, relations between devices connect, disconnect, attract, configure, imitate, intensify and re-distribute signals for ordered social action. The case of Github shows too that attempts to configure social patterns of action have animated the growth of large-scale digital infrastructures and social media. The algorithmic elements of search engines such as Google Web Search's *PageRank* algorithm or Facebook's *Social Graph* are two better known instances of the ways in which the detection of social patterns and flows of meanings, texts and readers has been pivotal in the growth of digital culture. Devices devoted to pattern recognition or data visualisations themselves flash signals amidst a field of devices. In analysing the vectoral components of the field of devices or tracing the reactions to that field, digital sociology is not doing anything radically different to people who inhabit this field. Savage suggests that:

> a core concern [for social research] might be to scrutinise how pattern is derived and produced in social inscription devices, as a means of considering the robustness of such derivations, what may be left out or made invisible from them, and so forth. We need to develop an account which seeks to criticize notions of the descriptive insofar as this involves the simple generation of categories and groups, and instead focus on the fluid and intensive generation of potential.
>
> *(Savage 2009: 171)*

Patterns in cultural life today derive from social inscription devices assembled in wide-ranging feedback loops. Feedback runs between recording what people do, visualising or graphing what they do, finding/generating patterns in the recording, and shaping what they encounter next. If digital sociology attempts to describe what is happening in contemporary textual and media environments, it needs to map the paths of these feedback loops running across publics, infrastructures, techniques, textual and media forms, and diverse, expanding practices. At the same time, patterns themselves are increasingly heavily analysed and modelled inside the culturally saturated feedback loop between people and social inscription devices. Digital social research is not alone in its interest in these processes. Reputational, attentional and sentiment economies (Arvidsson 2011) directly act on that patterning.

Identifying events that animate this patterning and scaling is a key concern for digital sociology. The 'massive, culturally-saturated feedback loop' arises from device-saturated social action. As the case of Github shows, the process of making, configuring, arranging and aligning devices is itself a highly dynamic field of linkages, associations, and imitations, where social action is often concerned with problems of pattern and of scale. The 'simple generation of categories and groups' that Savage refers to can certainly be found there, replicating and propagating at scale.

We have suggested that social researchers in the field of devices react, like other participants, to calls to order in their own practice. Digital sociology and certainly social research more generally is not immune from the auratic imperatives to methodologically emulate and align themselves with the infrastructures and practices of the field of devices (such as 'big data'). It grapples with the reflexive-recursive problem of its own implication in methods, techniques and infrastructures for deriving pattern. Digital social researchers find ourselves lost in the labyrinth of technical possibilities opening up around platforms, tools, visual forms and data flows. The experience of being somewhat caught up in the entanglements of pattern and scale might for digital sociology be a necessary step towards sensing the fluid generative potentials in the field of devices. These entanglements between scale and pattern, and especially between the different ways in which pattern might be found could offer a way for sociology to deviate from the scaled-up homogeneity and uniformity of predictive analytics with their highly constrained commitment to increasing advertising revenue or sales.

Notes

1 We largely leave aside any further discussion, analysis or critique of these developments. They are extensive and multi-faceted, and can be seen at work in the digital humanities (Galloway 2014), in cultural analytics (Manovich 2011), in social physics and computational social science (Pentland 2014). The constant updating of events, the relatively frequent advent of new flows of data, the teeming and burgeoning ways of inhabiting the reefs of digital infrastructures, many of which are developed and publically available, confront digital sociology with challenges and alluring possibilities. Unlike the major social media platforms or even the legion of startup companies in London, New York, San Francisco, Shanghai, Berlin or Amsterdam who offer ways of packaging, summarising, monitoring or shaping flows of data in networks, digital sociologists do not have hundreds of developers to wrangle data, dozens of computers and disk-drives arrayed in racks to expedite the process of searching or exploring the data. Given the billions of events welling-up in diverse APIs, what can digital sociology do? Should it sample and filter according to the criteria of adequacy and representativeness? The expansive forms of textual environment we have just been describing are writ large at the moment under the broad banner of 'big data'. The proliferating discussions of 'big data' need to be analysed in their own right in terms of how they intensify desires to connect information flows, previously disparate infrastructures and systems (energy, telecommunications, entertainment, transport, retail and manufacturing), and how they actually reorganise work, domestic lives, forms of sociality and value in the name of flows of data. 'Big data' is certainly part of the feedback loop or accumulation strategy in which social practices recorded as data become the basis of new textualities that seek to enrol further readers or writers, to align reading, viewing and buying, writing and working, as well as other forms of value. The physical, life and environmental sciences offer both a lead and something distracting here. The term 'data' carries with it an aura of scientificity, objectivity or neutrality that digital sociology is still wrestling with. 'Big data' is an expansive grouping and its membership continues to grow: house prices, clicks on hyperlinks, vehicle detection loops on roads, mobile phone call details, satellite photos of crops, electronic payment, stellar images from orbiting telescopes, transactional data such as credit card authorisation or supermarket checkout scanners – these are just examples in a list that keeps growing. The listing of data sources is an interminable feature of most talk about big data (and digital sociology shares this habit). Scientific data, however, has a particular resonance and perhaps anchors some forms of referentiality in data talk. The standard reference to allude to transformations in scientific data is *The Fourth Paradigm: Data-Intensive Scientific Discovery* (Hey, Tansley and Tolle 2009), a book published by Microsoft Research Press (a publisher that probably lies quite close to the source of much business data practice). This book furnishes vignettes of a range of scientific enterprises ranging across physical, earth, environmental and life sciences in which flows of data have transformed knowledge-making practices. The data intensive sciences authorise data practices in specific ways. The auratic power of scientific instruments such as DNA sequences or infrared satellite photos differ, as Mike Savage observes, from the 'mundane descriptions,... ordinary transactions, websites, Tesco loyalty cards, CCTV cameras in your local shopping centre, etc., that are the stuff of the new social' (Savage, 2009: 171). It may be that this auratic/mundane difference, important though it is in differentiating certain practices, also usefully links different domains of the social. Auratic scientific instrument data, with its referential links to the diversity of life, the fate of the planet or the conundrums of missing matter in the universe, rivets data to things. The scientific examples allow data more generally in all its administrative, transactional or media-derived forms to carry universalising epistemic value. It suggests that the birth of stars in remote galaxies can be analysed in similar terms to the birth of stars in the media environments of Xfactor or reality TV shows. In this respect, the popularity of the term 'data *science*' suggests that the referential power of science matters to business, commerce, industry and government as they seek to commodify, extract or regulate contemporary cultural spaces.

2 The anthropologist Anna Tsing writes: 'Scale is the spatial dimensionality necessary for a particular kind of view, whether up close or from a distance, microscopic or planetary. I argue that scale is not just a neutral frame for viewing the world; scale must be brought into being: proposed, practiced and evaded, as well as taken for granted' (Tsing, 2005: 58). *Scale* refers to the relative dimensions of enlargement or reduction in a map, picture or model, as well as the marks or degrees used to measure intervals (as in the scale on the axes of a scatter plot), but it implicitly positions observers as well. *Scale*, however, is a verb as well as a noun. In digital culture, re-scaling or re-dimensioning is common. The *scaling-up* of databases, of transactions, of geographies (e.g. Amazon's data-centres divide the globe into eight regions), and capacities in many settings testifies to one aspect of this re-scaling.

3 While the textual environment for online code repositories such as Github includes the many forms of text and graphic visible on Github webpages, it also includes the flows of data that these platforms generate for use by others. As millions of people interact even with mid-level platforms such as Github, their actions generate large volumes of data that can be streamed as time-stamped events. So, like many other social media platforms, Github publishes all of these individual time-stamped events to anyone who wants to use them. (While some users may pay to have their repositories and working practices remain invisible, very many do not.) The events are available more or less as they happen (through the Github API – application programmer interface) or in bulk through various archives (https://www.githubarchive.org/; a mirror of the data is also published by Google as a demonstration of their 'BigQuery' cloud computing service). The data derived from what people do on social media is mixed in form. It includes when things were done (date-time), various free textual forms (descriptions, tags, titles, etc.), structured text (links or URLs of associated webpages; names of associated organisations and groups; names of user), categorical attributes (on Github these are limited: the event type and the programming languages used), and often a mathematically encoded summary of the result of actions that change the contents of the repository (in the case of Github, the *hash digest* of any new content or change to existing contents of the repository). Github events are categorised according to 18 different event types (PushEvent, CommitEvent, AddUserEvent, DeleteEvent). These event types are organic to Github.com, but as variables in any data analysis they are defined by the platform designers rather than by any questions that social researchers might bring to bear on what people do on Github. 'Source-defined variables' are a central concomitant of data analysis practice in digital sociology. We might say that in the new social fields, data has an 'organic' aura: it is generated and collected by virtue of the existence of the infrastructures and platforms that are part and parcel of the social field rather than from instruments or measuring devices introduced by market or social researchers. But even this relationship is becoming increasingly complicated by virtue of the intricate and shifting relations between 'organic data' and 'paid for data' (Google Inc. 2009). Even if this data is 'observational' rather than experimental, the fact that it is generated intrinsically as part of a social field has powerful referential attractions, and attracts much work.

4 In much social research, problems of scale largely related to scarcity. Where data was abundant, scale problems were handled by setting limits on data through sampling strategies, research methods and research designs that allowed social researchers to be more or less confident that their research covers the social field of interest (for instance, making sure that differences in age, gender, ethnicity, sexuality, nationality, education-level, or income are represented in the data; many of the chapters in a typical introductory statistics textbook for social science address these problems of scarcity and representativeness). Selecting and sampling strategies seem to work differently in digital sociology as it encounters expanding textual environments where data scarcity is rarely an issue. The much discussed problem is how to cope with the vast amount of material. What is worse, textual environments such as social media are explicitly expansive.

5 This contrast has been extensively debated in sociology (see Andrew Abbot's discussion of patterns versus causes; the 'empirical crisis in sociology' literature; as well as the explicit focus on digital devices in recent sociology [Abbott 2001; Ruppert 2013; Savage and Burrows 2007]) and we will not rehearse these debates in great detail here. They have been debated fairly widely elsewhere (see Burrows 2012 for an overview).

References

Abbott, A. (2001) *Time Matters: On Theory and Method*, Chicago: University of Chicago Press.
Adkins, L. and C. Lury (2009) 'Introduction: What Is the Empirical?' *European Journal of Social Theory*, 12(1): 5–20.

Arvidsson, A. (2011) 'General Sentiment: How Value and Affect Converge in the Information Economy', *The Sociological Review*, 59: 39–59.
Back, L. and N. Puwar (2012) *Live Methods*, Oxford: Wiley-Blackwell.
Barry, A. (2001) *Political Machines: Governing a Technological Society*, London: Athlone.
Bourdieu, P. (2000) *Pascalian Meditations*, Stanford: Stanford University Press.
Boyd, d. and K. Crawford (2012) 'Critical Questions for Big Data', *Information, Communication and Society*, 15(5): 662–79.
Breiman, L. (2001) 'Random Forests', *Machine Learning*, 45(1): 5–32.
Breiman, L., J. Friedman, R. Olshen and C.J. Stone (1984) *CART: Classification and Regression Trees*, Belmont, CA: Wadsworth, 156.
Burrows, R. (2012) 'Digitalization, Visualization and the "Descriptive Turn"', in Heywood, I., Sandywell, B. (eds), *The Handbook of Visual Culture*, London: Berg, 572–88.
Conte R., N. Gilbert, G. Bonelli, C. Cioffi-Revilla, G. Deffuant, J. Kertesz, V. Loreto, S. Moat, J.P. Nadal, A. Sanchez, A. Nowak, A. Flache, M. San Miguel, and D. Helbing (2012) 'Manifesto of Computational Social Science', *European Physical Journal-Special Topics*, 214(1): 325–46.
Couldry, N. (2000) *Inside Culture: Reimagining the Method of Cultural Studies*, London: SAGE.
Cukier, K.N. and V. Mayer-Schoenberger (2013) 'The Rise of Big Data. How It's Changing the Way We Think About the World', *Foreign Affairs*, Available online at http://www.foreignaffairs.com/articles/139104/kenneth-neil-cukier-and-viktor-mayer-schoenberger/the-rise-of-big-data (accessed 10 February 2014).
Doll, B. (2012) *Data at Github*, GitHub, Available online at https://github.com/blog/1112-data-at-github (accessed 3 March 2014).
Galloway, A.R. (2014) 'The Cybernetic Hypothesis', *differences*, 25(1): 107–131.
Giles, J. (2012) 'Computational Social Science: Making the Links', *Nature*, 488(7412): 448–50.
Hastie, T., R. Tibshirani and J.H. Friedman (2009) *The Elements of Statistical Learning: Data Mining, Inference, and Prediction*, New York: Springer.
Hey, T., S. Tansley, and K. Tolle (2009) 'The Fourth Paradigm: Data-Intensive Scientific Discovery', *Microsoft Research*.
Housley, W., M. Williams, M. Williams, and A. Edwards (2013) 'Computational Social Science: Research Strategies, Design and Methods Introduction' *International Journal of Social Research Methodology*, 16(3): 173–5.
Knorr Cetina, K.K. and U. Bruegger (2004) 'Traders' Engagement with Markets: A Postsocial Relationship', in Ash A. and Thrift N., *The Blackwell Cultural Economy Reader*, Oxford: Blackwell.
Latour, B., P. Jensen, T. Venturini, S. Grauwin, and D. Boullier (2012) 'The Whole is Always Smaller than its Parts. How Digital Navigation May Modify Social Theory', *British Journal of Sociology*, 63(4): 590–615.
Latour, B., M. Lynch, and S. Woolgar (1990) 'Drawing Things Together', in M. Lynch and S. Woolgar (eds), *Representation in Scientific Practice*, Cambridge, MA: MIT Press.
Law, J. (1994) *Organizing Modernity*, Oxford: Blackwell.
Lee, B. and E. LiPuma (2002) 'Cultures of Circulation: The Imaginations of Modernity', *Public Culture*, 14(1): 191–213.
Lupton, D. (2012) *Digital Sociology: An Introduction*, Sydney: University of Sydney, Available online at http://prijipati.library.usyd.edu.au/handle/2123/8621 (accessed 14 November 2013).
Manovich, L. (2011) 'Trending: The Promises and the Challenges of Big Social Data', *Debates in the Digital Humanities*, Available online at http://manovich.net/index.php/projects/trending-the-promises-and-the-challenges-of-big-social-data (accessed 15 April 2013).
Marres, N. (2012) 'The Redistribution of Methods: On Intervention in Digital Social Research, Broadly Conceived', *The Sociological Review*, 60(1): 139–65.
Meyer, R. (2013) 'Github, Object of Nerd Love, Makes Play for Non-Programmers', *The Atlantic*, Available online at http://www.theatlantic.com/technology/archive/2013/08/github-object-of-nerd-love-makes-play-for-non-programmers/278971/ (accessed 13 February 2014).
Muchnik, L., S. Pei, L.C. Parra, S.D.S. Reis, J.S. Andrade Jr., S. Havlin, and H.A. Makse (2013) 'Origins of Power-Law Degree Distribution in the Heterogeneity of Human Activity in Social Networks', *Scientific Reports*, 3, Available online at http://www.nature.com.ezproxy.lancs.ac.uk/srep/2013/130507/srep01783/full/srep01783.html (accessed 1 March 2014).
Myers, N. (2008) 'Molecular Embodiments and the Body-Work of Modeling in Protein Crystallography', *Social Studies of Science*, 38(2): 163–99.
Pariser, E. (2011) *The Filter Bubble: What the Internet is Hiding from You*, London: Penguin.

Pentland, A. (2014) *Social Physics: How Good Ideas Spread—The Lessons from a New Science*, New York: The Penguin Press.
Pryke, M. (2010) 'Money's Eyes: The Visual Preparation of Financial Markets', *Economy and Society*, 39(4): 427–59.
Rogers, R. (2013) *Digital Methods*, Cambridge, Massachusetts, London: The MIT Press.
Rose, G. (2012) 'The Question of Method: Practice, Reflexivity and Critique in Visual Culture Studies', in I. Heywood and B. Sandywell (eds) *The Handbook of Visual Culture*, London: Berg.
Ruppert, E. (2013) 'Rethinking Empirical Social Sciences', *Dialogues in Human Geography*, 3(3): 268–73.
Ruppert, E., J. Law and M. Savage (2013) 'Reassembling Social Science Methods: The Challenge of Digital Devices' *Theory, Culture and Society*, 30(4): 22–46.
Savage, M. (2009) 'Contemporary Sociology and the Challenge of Descriptive Assemblage', *European Journal of Social Theory*, 12(1): 155–74.
Savage, M. and R. Burrows (2007) 'The Coming Crisis of Empirical Sociology', *Sociology*, 41(5): 885–99.
Schutt, R. and O'Neil, C. (2013) *Doing Data Science*, Sebastopol, CA: O'Reilly & Associates Inc.
Thrift, N. (2006) 'Re-Inventing Invention: New Tendencies in Capitalist Commodification', *Economy and Society*, 35(2): 279–306.
Tsing, A.L. (2005) *Friction?: An Ethnography of Global Connection*, Princeton, NJ: Princeton University Press.
Tufte, E. (2001) *The Visual Display of Quantitative Informations*, second ed., Cheshire, CT.: Graphics Press.
Varian, H. and H. Choi (2009) 'Official Google Research Blog: Predicting the Present with Google Trends', Available online at http://googleresearch.blogspot.com/2009/04/predicting-present-with-google-trends.html (accessed 23 May 2011).
Whitehead, A.N. (1958) *Modes of Thought; Six Lectures Delivered in Wellesley College, Massachusetts, and Two Lectures in the University of Chicago*, New York: Capricorn Books.
Wickham, H. (2009) *ggplot2: Elegant Graphics for Data Analysis*, New York: Springer. Available online at http://ggplot2.org/.

Online sources

Google Inc. (2009) Back to Basics: Direct, Referral or Organic – Definitions Straight from the Source – Analytics Blog. *Google Analytics Blog*, Available online at http://analytics.blogspot.co.uk/2009/08/back-to-basics-direct-referral-or.html (accessed 7 February 2014).
The Guardian (n.d.) Data Journalism and Data Visualization from the Datablog. Available online at http://www.theguardian.com/news/datablog (accessed 30 January 2014).
New York Times (2012) *2012: The Year in Graphics*. Available online at http://www.nytimes.com/interactive/2012/12/30/multimedia/2012-the-year-in-graphics.html (accessed 30 January 2014).
Prediction Impact Inc. (2009) Predictive Analytics World Conference: Agenda. Available online at http://www.predictiveanalyticsworld.com/sanfrancisco/2009/agenda.php#usergroup (accessed 24 May 2011).
R Development Core Team (n.d.) The R Project for Statistical Computing. Available online at http://www.r-project.org/ (accessed 11 June 2010).

25
Researching social analytics
Cultural sociology in the face of algorithmic power

Nick Couldry

A new topic of research is opening up for cultural sociology: social actors' everyday use and reflections on 'analytics', that is, any digital tools that measure them and their presence in a world of online presences. I call this study 'social analytics'. This topic emerges at a moment when the longer histories of science and technology studies (STS) and phenomenology are intersecting in interesting ways in the digital age. Paradoxically some leading sociologists of culture fear that reflexive agency is no longer there to be studied, crushed out of existence by the all-encompassing force of 'algorithmic power' (Lash 2007). This premature fear of something like 'the end of cultural sociology' ignores the phenomenological richness of everyday struggles with and through the countless tools for measuring our digital presences, whose operations are now deeply embedded in routine action. It also turns its back on the contemporary potential for a 'sociology of social critique' focussed on the arbitrary operations of the institutional processes that shape and order our constructions of social reality (Boltanski 2010). This chapter, and the project it outlines, aim to reclaim that potential in a distinctive way.

Social analytics, as outlined here, defends, albeit in new form, a phenomenologically-influenced sociology of culture that is interested less in the reproduction of 'society' or in the measurement of society's macro-variables, and more in the changing material conditions for the presentation of the self: the 'self' not just of individuals, but also of groups and organizations. As such, it is less interested in the complexity of digital 'objects' (an important topic, however, for cultural sociology in its own right: see Mackenzie *et al.*, this volume), than in the richness of social actors' reflexive interactions with those objects, and particularly with the interfaces for interaction and digital presence built from those objects.

These recent topics for cultural sociology can be seen against a much longer and more partial history of incorporating media and communications infrastructures into sociology. The institutionally directed circulation of media products has been a routine feature of everyday life in rich countries for nearly two centuries. We know something about traditional media's broader consequences for the presentation of the self as originally conceived by Goffman (Meyrowitz 1985 on Goffman 1971), but less about its details. Indeed, in spite of the separate development of media and communications studies as a discipline, or interdisciplinary space, over the past 30 years, there has remained a lack of attention, even in specialist work on media consumption, to the *variety* of things people do with media. We have known for three decades that people interpret media texts in different ways (Morley and Brunsdon 1980; Ang 1986), but 'audience studies' became increasingly uncertain that it could map the diversity of things people do with media (Alasuutaari 1999), concentrating often on the *most* engaged members of the media audience. Meanwhile, people's individual trajectories through the rich and vast textual space of contemporary media remains surprisingly underexplored (see Couldry 2000: chapter 3). It has been in relation to taste, and mainly in France, where this problem has been best addressed: there, in explicit disagreement with Pierre Bourdieu's large-scale theory of the reproduction of class through taste, Bernard Lahire insisted on the complexity of individual consumption practice and the inability of general models to capture it (Lahire 2004; Lahire 2011).

The wider problem is how, in a sociology serious about addressing the 'complexity' of contemporary culture (Hannerz 1992), we can be adequate both to the open-ended *diversity* of individual adaptations of the cultural stuff around us *and* to the continuous work of power *through* such diversity. While Pierre Bourdieu's insight into the 'de facto division of labour of social production with regard to major varieties of experience' (Bourdieu 1992: 118) remains fundamental, the modes of 'social production' are changing radically, requiring attention to various forms of institutionalized symbolic violence (Boltanski 2010), not least how in a digital age social being is measured for competing institutional ends. In the digital world, where (at least in the global North) Internet access is available to most people most of the time, the 'textualization' of the world is taken to a more intense level, so the uncertainties about what people *do with* such textual excess are multiplied. A version of the same problem matters hugely to cultural producers too, since they no longer can be sure of reaching audiences most effectively through general modes of address (the mass advertisement). The resulting turn within advertising culture (Turow 2007; 2011) towards niche marketing and data-driven tracking of individuals (uniquely specified, even if their name has been stripped away) addresses this problem, but at a high social cost: the embedding of continuous surveillance and algorithmically-based data collection into the consumption process. Whenever we go online, we are lured into this surveillance space, where it is the aim of the software designers who shape our micro-access to the web to 'turn every customer touch point … into a point of sale' (quoted Turow 2007: 123). The infrastructure to deliver this new form of micro-advertising is based on algorithms: automated processes of counting, tracking and aggregating data and metadata. But measurement also takes broader forms in digital culture, one of which (via the use of analytics) is potentially open to intervention by social actors without special expertise, via actions at the 'front-end' of websites. It is this *everyday* embedding of algorithms in the stuff of culture (a deep textualization which often involves a codification) that generates the new opportunities for a sociology of culture which are this chapter's main focus.

Sociology of culture has always had to address the force of measurements of cultural performance. But the conflict that arises from today's embedding of measurement into the very texture of everyday experience is real, not trivial. José Van Dijck sums it up well when she writes: 'content and content *management* have become virtual synonyms in the ecosystem of connective media. Even when the aim of platforms is not to exploit content for monetary gain, as in the case of Wikipedia, content can only be made functional or valuable if it is managed through systems operating on the dual premise of "authentic" yet manipulated processing' (Van Dijck 2013: 162, added emphasis). Cultural sociology's task is to think and research *beyond* this conflict, registering how it is worked through in the everyday life of social actors. It can without doubt be argued that the automated measurements explicitly linked to social media platforms directly reproduce neoliberal norms of competitive subjectivity, in a replay of ealier Foucauldian arguments about disciplinary modernity (e.g. Marwick 2013). But a richer sociology of culture will want to go beyond such reproductive models to consider how social actors are *reflecting on* and/or *contesting* their relations to the measurement now routinized in our everyday use of platforms for the digital presentation of the self. I will explore this latter approach, first, from the perspective of theoretical debates about the consequences of algorithmic power, approaching the empirical details of social analytics later in the chapter.

Sociology of culture and the problem with algorithmic power

No one would disagree that algorithmic processes are now increasingly salient in the texture of everyday life (Halavais 2008, Lash 2007, Burrows 2009, Gillespie 2014). Some writers go further and argue that the deep embedding of algorithmic technology within everyday phenomena creates 'a collapse of ontology and epistemology' (Lash 2006: 581), installing a power-laden regime of 'facticity' (Lash 2007: 56) in which 'there is no time, nor space … for reflection' (Lash 2002: 18). If Lash is right, why pay close attention any more to what actors say when they 'reflect' on their position in the social world? But accepting Lash's line of argument means ignoring a key site of *tension* in a digital age when social actors are struggling to make effective use of analytics in particular social contexts. Such struggles are part of a much larger history of institutional symbolic violence (Bourdieu 1990), but we need to follow such struggles in their contemporary digital forms or miss an opportunity to build a richer sociological critique of the digital age.

If an earlier phenomenology advanced by grasping how 'we derive our sense of self from the image of our self that others reflect back to us in interaction' (Crossley 2001: 143, summarising Cooley 1902), a contemporary phenomenology must explore how today's social actors interact with the algorithmically generated versions of themselves that derive from the Internet's embedding in everyday life. Such a social analytics may also contribute to the wider and growing field of 'digital sociology' (Marres 2012; Mackenzie *et al.* this volume), although this is not a focus of this chapter.

There is no doubt of the sociological importance today of how 'categorization' – seen as a key process in the constitution of social order since Durkheim (Durkheim and Mauss 1970; Bowker and Star 2000) – has become automated and, as such, central to all consumption and information seeking online, as well as many aspects of government (Amoore 2011). 'Categorization' is no longer just something social individuals do within an open process of socialization: it is something done consistently *to them and their actions*. Yet it occurs not openly, but in the background, shaping (through advertisers' and sales entities' automated systems) what we can buy and at what price (Turow 2007), configuring (through the operations of their internal algorithms) what standard search engines reveal *to us* when we look for basic information (Paliser 2011), and shaping (through the operation of web analytics) how an organization appears in the world to the constituency of people who interact with it (funders, investors, supporters). Algorithms or, more broadly, the use of analytics in everyday life, shape fields of action in advance by shaping how things, people and organizations get counted, presented and seen. That is beyond doubt.

Lash however argues this form of algorithmic power, because based in the prearrangement of life's informational infrastructure (2007: 56), shifts the nature of power from a 'hegemony' that works externally on subjects through their minds to a generative 'force' that works within subjects and objects (2007: 56), a shift from 'normativity' to 'facticity', 'epistemology' to 'ontology'. A problem with Lash's dramatic account is that power based on norms, epistemology and authority has *always also* been condensed into *reified* forms that support such power. The idea that power has suddenly shifted its very nature to be more 'ontological' underestimates both the consistent role of reification (Honneth 2008) throughout history and people's opportunities from time to time to bring power's workings, *however* reified, to the surface, confronting ontological 'fact' with epistemological challenge. For sure, the workings of algorithmic power pose many challenges as its analysts note, not least through the hidden and highly technical nature of many of its operations (Halavais 2008, Gillespie 2014), but popular contestation, although it has taken a long time to emerge, is now emerging, and is far from trivial as a cultural process. A longer tradition of power analysis has always taken seriously the *difficulty* of challenging long-established power-blocs that rely on well-established symbols and, in the media age, on intense monopolies of symbolic power. Think of Alberto Melucci's (1996) work on 'symbolic power', resistance and 'naming' with its roots in Paolo Freire's conscientization theory which had proclaimed the importance of *renaming* the world, not just challenging the details of its explicit knowledge (Freire 1972). But Lash's generalized philosophical commentary misses these longer-term historical resonances of current battles over algorithmic power.

The historic shift Lash rightly registers is that 'power through naming' (or what we might call 'deep' categorization) is now embedded in a many-levelled technologically-established interface of unprecedented complexity that is not just generally opaque but technically very difficult to unbundle, let alone reverse. Recently US legal theorist Julie Cohen has captured this well when she writes that 'the configuration of networked space is increasingly opaque to its users' (2012: 202) and that its web of protocols, data requirements and data monitoring has created a 'system of governance that is authoritarian' because it is so difficult to challenge (2012: 188–189). This is a very important point, but it is not the same as saying that such power *cannot* in principle be challenged. Indeed Cohen's writing is just one element in a slowly building wave of challenge to the 'facticity' of the digital infrastructure: other examples come from information science (Mejias 2013), cultural studies (Van Dijck 2013), popular commentary (Lanier 2013, Paliser 2011), and social psychology (Turkle 2011). All of this writing takes us some way beyond the implications of Lash's original position.

However, it is worth going back to one element of that debate Lash generated, namely David Beer's (2009) commentary which insisted on the importance of some basic empirical questions about how algorithms are pervasively embedded in *culture*, that is, in the making of meaning and our experience of the world: questions concerning (1) 'the organizations that establish and cultivate Web 2.0 applications', (2) 'the actual operations and functionality of the software packages that organise our web experience', and (3) (most importantly for my argument here) how the outcomes of (1) and (2) 'play out in the lives of those that use (or do not use) participatory web applications' (Beer 2009: 998). We can broaden the implications of Beer's argument beyond interfaces that are formally participatory. Beer is rightly interested in people's ability to interact with the processes that are classifying them through what he calls a 'classificatory imagination' (2007: 998). Why not research the overall *phenomenology* of living *reflexively* in a world where algorithmic classification is embedded in multiple ways, even if often hidden from all but the most expert actor? The object of 'social analytics' research is to study how people act in, and in their everyday lives adapt to (Beer 2009: 997), this digitally-saturated, always-under-categorization world.

Tarleton Gillespie (2014) considers a complex form of reflexivity on the production side of algorithms: producers responsible for maintaining the public face of algorithm-driven platforms (like Twitter) must reflect constantly on the interplay between their 'technical' adjustments and the signals that their platform appears to send publicly to its users. Gillespie rightly insists that algorithms are not determining objects beyond human intervention; rather they are 'both obscured and malleable' (if they were wholly made public, the likelihood of people acting so as to manipulate their 'performance' would be too great). Gillespie is concerned with the role of algorithms on highly *public* platforms and interfaces such as Google and Twitter: such platforms he calls 'public relevance algorithms'. He insists that we need a sociology both of such algorithms' production and of how users react to, and act on the basis of, their background role. Such algorithms have broad consequences for the ontology of our public world. According to Gillespie, platform users strive to become 'algorithmically recognisable', gaming the logics of search engines and algorithm-based platforms such as Twitter (compare Beer 2009). That would certainly be part of 'social analytics', but a project of social analytics can look *even more broadly* at how actors draw on the basic workings of algorithms and analytics and seek to turn them consistently to their wider social ends. If so, social analytics can offer much more than an 'audience studies' of the digital world: it is concerned with the wider field of practice (Couldry 2012: chapter 2) focussed around the use and adaptation of algorithms and analytics, and all the further adjustments of action that flow from that. This might involve, to take a simple example, using customized analytics (that use algorithms as their basic mechanism) to heighten the clarity and intensity with which a particular website foregrounds and links up debate on a particular theme that matters to an organization.

In this sense, social analytics can contribute to our understanding of the 'culture' around analytics, and not only the algorithms on which large-scale commercial platforms are based; social analytics can also study the counting mechanisms that are, in part, conceived and devised by social actors to meet ends much closer to home. This picks up on the dimension of social construction that the best sociologists of software and code have always recognized (Mackenzie 2006). As Adrian Mackenzie puts it, 'Code, the material that lies at the core of software, is unstable because it is both expression and action, neither of which are materially or socially stable' (2006: 177). In other words, the production and use of algorithms is part of the making of the social today, but operating at a level whose consequences are yet to be fully understood.

Such consequences therefore need to be traced through a sociology of action. If 'taste classifies the classifier' in Bourdieu's famous phrase (Bourdieu 1984: 6), then the pervasive fact of background algorithmic measurement 'measures' the social actor, grounding new hierarchies of visibility (Marwick 2013), but also providing sites where such hierarchies can be contested and renegotiated. Social analytics is concerned with how analytics shape, in part, the ways in which such an actor can present herself or itself *as social*, and so the changing ground-rules of the actor's social and cultural presence. Such shaping is open to reflexivity, at least under some conditions, just as is the face-to-face presentation of the self (Goffman 1971). Boltanski and Chiapello (2007) have provided an important general framing of the new 'spirit of capitalism' in which individuals are inclined to compete in terms of their capacity as networked actors, and recent studies of practice around social networking sites show how this can be translated into forms of prestige based on connection and visibility (Banet-Weiser 2012; Marwick 2013). But there is considerably more scope for empirical research on how such technologically-extended processes allow also for reflexive agency. This is where the project of social analytics starts. The next section will explore in broad outline the possible topics for social analytics.

Doing social analytics

To appreciate this project's scope, it is necessary first to define the core problem for social actors today for which social analytics, as it were, tries to listen out. Sociology of culture has always been concerned with how social hierarchies are maintained through cultural means (for example, in the mechanisms of taste), but in the digital era the problem is that agency – and particularly the presentation of self and identity – is now consistently mediated by *calculative* mechanisms of *differentiation* that are *not* open – or at least not initially or obviously open except to actors with considerable technological literacy – to adjustment by actors themselves. The processes here are not analogous with how the physical infrastructure of an institutional setting mediates the presentation of self within that setting: notwithstanding some manifest inequalities of resource, such an infrastructure mediates the actions of *all actors equally*, even if their resources for acting within that setting may be unequal. That was the material context for the strategies and tactics for self-presentation in which Erving Goffman was interested. But algorithms configure the stage of self-presentation in ways that, from the start, actively and cumulatively *differentiate between* actors: in that sense, the interface of analytics is itself an actor in the process of self-presentation, what Lash calls vividly 'substance that thinks' (2007: 70). Worse, the algorithmic interface is an actor whose operations are generally hidden from the actor that is trying to present her- or itself. Clearly, this opacity is an *issue* for any project of self-presentation, but only becomes an object of action and reflection to degrees that *vary* sharply, depending on the self-presenting actor and her or its circumstances and resources.

The empirical work that social analytics involves thus can take many forms. I will discuss these in the following order: first, the tactics of individuals to *resist* what has been called the 'quantification of the self' (Gerlitz and Helmond 2013; Lupton 2012); second, group tactics to 'game' the workings of particular algorithmic platforms; and third, the longer-term practices of organizations to use analytics of various sorts as part of developing who they are. I will spend more time on the third case since it is the least studied.

Individual tactics

Since Goffman, sociology has been interested in individuals' practices for maintaining a certain presentation of the self in everyday life. It has been clear for some time that the digital world affords many new means for presenting the self: from diary or commentary blogs to social media platforms to microblogging platforms like Twitter. Studying their use is an extension of the study of the face-to-face presentation of self (Livingstone 2008; boyd 2008). Such research only becomes 'social analytics' (in my sense) when part of the *object on which* individuals act and reflect becomes the mechanisms for counting and measuring the self's presence online and its effects.

As David Beer noted, it is of sociological interest to follow how individuals begin to follow the relationship between the information they provide to calculative mechanisms (explicit or hidden) and how this starts to 'impact ... on the constitution of their life-worlds' (2009: 997) and, through this, begin, by modulating the information they themselves generate, to aim at having a different presentation of self through the algorithmic platform in question: 'the right profile' (2009: 997) for whatever algorithm they are interacting with. Some algorithmic platforms are relatively clear in their operations, for example the platform Last.fm, which counts up what users listen to and plays this back to them in the form of an available playlist. But many other algorithmic interfaces are much less open to be read and influenced, yet they may be crucial either to the presentation of self or to a person's interface with the world, for example their Facebook newsfeed.

There is now a large literature on how people's presentation of self and relationship to the everyday social world is being shaped by a reflexive relationship with the analytics that are embedded in everyday platforms of self-presentation. Gerlitz and Helmond (2013) examine the passage from a linking economy (connections between websites) to a Like economy, where

Researching social analytics

users gain social currency from the public articulation of connections on social networking sites. In locations such as online dating sites, for example, it is hardly surprising that users often choose to state that they are younger than they really are (Ellison, Heino, and Gibbs, 2006). Meanwhile teenagers take measures to protect their privacy online by making content meaningful only to those they wish to (boyd 2014). As Knapp (forthcoming) points out, the largely occluded operations of the algorithms which shape individuals' everyday interactional context constrain the degree of reflexivity possible, but certainly do not exclude it.

To the extent that individuals' aims (of self-promotion) are in tune with the *explicit purpose* of analytics-based platforms such as Twitter, there is no topic of social analytics, merely a conformity of actions to optimize the 'status' which those platforms precisely offer. Marwick (2013) argues exactly this for the uses of Twitter by the technological elite in San Francisco involved in IT development. But social analytics emerge where individuals' goals are more complex than simply promoting the self as a brand through analytics-based measures. At this point *reflexivity* comes into play as part of a more than purely instrumental approach to analytics and the platforms based upon them. Social analytics, however, emerges more clearly when we consider group and institutional actors, since there is no reason to assume that their goals can be reduced to fulfilling the expectations of visibility for its own sake, since those groups and institutions generally have more detailed reasons *why* they want to win visibility than just gaining higher visibility.

Group gaming

Because social analytics is concerned with interactions with calculative mechanisms that require data *volume*, groups, especially large distributed groups, have a major tactical advantage over the individual, because they can generate considerably more information and events for counting. They are therefore more likely to be able to see 'real time' results from their information inputs, and so start to 'aim' their further inputs accordingly. The result is what colloquially is called 'gaming' algorithmic interfaces, and this is one angle from which group actions can be of interest to social analytics.

As algorithmically-based social media interfaces have started to become part of the assumed infrastructure of political and civic action, so sociologists and anthropologists have started to observe evidence of such 'gaming' as an explicit tactic by social movements concerned to influence the course of collective action through moment-to-moment coordination through such interfaces. In their study of a range of Twitter uses in political action, Segerberg and Bennett (2011: 213) note the importance of tracking the 'user dynamics of hashtag use over time', suggesting the possibility of such tactical (de Certeau 1984) interactions with the algorithms on which Twitter is based. Thomas Poell (2014) in his study of the use of Twitter by Toronto G20 protesters in 2010 (Poell 2014) notes the possible longer-term tension between Twitter's concern to foreground topics that are trending (that is, attracting the largest volume of attention) versus protesters' interest in maintaining a fuller record of their collectively produced messages. Those first two studies investigate some effective preconditions for a social analytics study, but coordinated gaming of the Twitter platform starts to emerge more explicitly in Youmans and York's study of the Syrian Electronic Army, a group supporting the current Syrian regime which was determined to drown out the Syrian opposition's messages on Twitter through the use of automated Twitter accounts (Youmans and York 2012).

The anthropologist John Postill has observed the social use of analytics directly in the actions of the *indignados* (or 15M) movement in Barcelona, Spain that protested against

389

government cuts and economic injustice in 2011 (Postill 2013). The use of Twitter in this movement (including the linked platform Real Democracy Now – 'DRY', Democracía Real Ya) went beyond the basic use of the platform as a means of communication through appropriate hashtags, and so on. As Postill explains:

> A key part of DRY's strategy prior to the demonstrations was to make the campaign a regular occurrence on Twitter's "Trending topics". Knowing that Twitter's trending algorithm favours novelty over volume ... they succeeded by frequently changing the campaign keywords and encouraging followers to retweet the newly agreed hashtag so that it would 'trend', thereby reaching a much wider audience.

We can expect a huge variety of such 'gaming' practices to develop as familiarity with the logics of 'public relevance platforms' (Gillespie 2014) spreads. Some, as Postill notes, will depend on the particular literacy and foresight of an elite organizational group; other tactics will be more distributed, depending on the sheer volume of informational inputs that large numbers of informed participants can generate if at least minimally focussed on a particular end-result.

The examples so far suggest that social analytics involves the technological mediation of group action without any tensions or contradictions. But as Veronica Barassi's (forthcoming) work shows, a conflict may arise between *the time* needed to work on analytics (e.g. the data-inputting necessary for influencing analytics or managing communications dependent on multiple digital platforms) and *the time* needed for the core activity of political action itself. Without wanting here to get into the specific dynamics of political action, this illustrates a broader point about the tensions inherent in using 'measurement' to achieve broader social ends. We will consider this in more detail in the next subsection, which focusses on the social use of analytics within organizations.

Social analytics on an organizational scale

It was the use of measurement at an organizational level that first led to the idea of 'social analytics'. I was leading a participatory action project concerned to research the digital platforms and social conditions which support narrative exchange for purposes of encouraging voice and mutual recognition. The strand in question involved a reporter network (let's call them 'C Media') who trained community reporters and led a national network whose website presented the reports of those trained. Fieldwork within an action-research paradigm was conducted by myself, Luke Dickens and Aristea Fotopoulou with C Media for a period of 15 months between early 2012 and mid-2013.[1] When the fieldwork started, C Media's website was not generating the traffic they wanted: C Media sensed it needed better metadata to present the themes of its reporters' stories in a more effective way, but it did not know how to implement this. We quickly realized that, although our project was concerned with broader aims, to develop it in this strand there was no alternative but to become practically involved in acting and reflecting with C Media about how they used their website and its information architecture, to achieve their organizational purposes.

While doing this fieldwork (see Couldry, Fotopoulou and Dickens forthcoming for more details of the stages of our fieldwork), we realized that, in carrying out such 'technical' work, we were doing something more, something of wider sociological interest. We were tracking how real actors used and reflected on analytics not for the sake of measurement itself (that emphatically was not C Media's primary interest), but for the sake of meeting their broader *social* ends. We were tracking the process whereby a small civil society organization translated its ends as a social actor into a certain use of technical tools, that is, analytics, here understood as production process in which social actors (from individuals to institutions) work reflexively with analytics in order to adjust their digital presence. By 'analytics' here, I mean *both* the automated measurement and counting installed within the operation of digital platforms (and associated websites, apps and tools) *and* adjustments made by actors themselves to, or around, such measurement and counting operations. Since, quite clearly, the use of analytics in this sense is unavoidable in the everyday practice of all organizations today (except perhaps those that want to avoid a public presence and, even then, analytics of a sort is needed to ensure this is achieved!), we were tracking the technical mediation of an organizational self, the reflexive process inherent to dealing with the technological interface through which organizations in the digital age must *present themselves* to and in the world. We were, if you like, doing a phenomenology under digital conditions, and specifically at the level of organizations with social or civic ends. This insight was the birth of the project of social analytics (Couldry, Fotopoulou and Dickens forthcoming).

Implementing such a project is, however, more complex than it first appears. This is because the process of reflecting and acting on one's mode of 'self-presence' in an algorithmically-saturated world is complex. The primary means through which constituencies interact with an organization in most cases is its website, a particular multi-part presentation of its organizational 'self'. But, once conceived as an organization's means for presenting itself actively and cumulatively to the world, a website becomes a complex object of reflection. It depends on certain 'inputs' (information that *could* be presented), certain ways of presenting that information (which certainly *could* be otherwise), and certain ways of storing and then further presenting the cumulative force of how those visiting the site *interact* with the original presentation. Indeed the degree to which 'interactivity' with the site becomes thematized and made the object of active reflection is itself a key part of the translation process to be researched. All these levels, from the first (information inputs) to the last (the presentation of interactivity) involve the continuous accumulation and processing of information through basic counting, but also through coding (by which I mean here not initially the writing of computer code, but the systematic interpretation of, say, story contents or interactive events as belonging to a significant type or 'code'). But which types matter to the wider story that an organization wants to tell about itself (more technically, what metadata it needs to tell that story through its website) is also a key part of the reflections that must be made explicit. So too are the processes of data collection and data sorting in which the organization is at any one time involved, or might (depending on what it is trying to do through its web presence) *want to be involved in*. The apparently simple process of developing a website through which an organization presents itself to the wider world becomes a window for observing a recursive process of reflection and action.

In participating in such a process actively, sociologists need to monitor carefully the boundary between their practical involvement and the processes intrinsic to their own activity as sociologists, that is, the tracking of social actors as they act and reflect. This boundary-making requires an architecture of its own. In our project, it involved developing in explicit written form documents that gave an account of what the organization agreed it was setting out to do, and how it saw those aims being translated into digital form, including all the practical steps (such as information collection, metadata implementation, and the like), that such a translation involves.[2] Without such documentation, we and C Media would have had no explicit reference point against which to assess our collaboration, no statement of what it was we were jointly engaged in reflecting and acting upon. With that specified, however, our research team was able, in a more conventional sociological way, to track, through participant observation, interviews and documentary and website analysis, the process of translating C Media's digital presence into and through analytics as it was reflected upon by the actors involved. It is worth emphasising here that the project of social analytics does not depend on assuming any simple, unmediated 'intention' on the part of social actors: as the literature on the quantified self (and the social-networking-based 'culture of connectivity' generally: Van Dijck 2013) has taught us, actors living in a world saturated by practices of algorithmic measurement are, to some degree, already adjusting their ways of acting in the world in order to *anticipate* possible measurement, indeed to seek it as an explicit goal (Marwick 2013). That does not, however, as argued in relation to the original debate between Lash and Beer, rule out the possibility that social actors can, as in this case, develop specific aims in relation to the uses of analytics, which are then put into reflexive practice.

None of this fieldwork would have been possible, of course, without C Media's very active collaboration; since C Media was very busy making the most of its limited resources to achieve its immediate ends, that collaboration would, in turn, have been impossible if our interests and C Media's had not converged: C Media's aim of promoting community voice fitted with the wider interests of our research project. Both our and C Media's interests, in that sense, *looked past analytics*: for C Media to the translation of its social aims through analytics, and for us as sociologists to understanding how that translation got done. Implementing that in detail of course involved its tensions, but these were resolved over time, as with any project of participatory action research. One can certainly imagine now carrying out other projects of social analytics research in different circumstances where there was not the explicit convergence between the researched organizations' aims and those of the research project, but only because as sociologists of culture we will have started making social analytics an explicit part of what we do!

Admittedly, the involvement this project required in an organization's practical day-to-day life might seem a strange topic for the sociology of culture. Some of what we did could *appear* to be a banal matter of making a website work better. But things look different when one realizes that it is *here* – in how organizations gather data about their websites' workings and others' interactions with them, how they think about their websites' metadata and its uses, and their reflections on how, as organizations, they might change in response to such cumulative information – it is here, in raw form, that everyday battles to make sense of a data-saturated world in terms of social actors' *own goals* beyond just data production or metrics outcomes alone are conducted. Far from compromising the tools and aims of cultural sociology, such empirical research is a means whereby a sociology concerned with how actors reflexively modify their presence in the world (for whatever wider competitive or practical purposes) can address the irreducibly 'calculative' world in which social actors, such as civil society organizations, must today act and on which, if they want to act well, they must continually reflect. Any *less* engagement on the part of sociologists with the technological aspects of the 'presentation of the self' means *not* engaging with how actors now have presence in a digital world. If acting with and on analytics (in the extended sense in which I have used the term) is now part of actors' toolkit in everyday life, then cultural sociologists who want to study the changing forms of everyday life must research them.

Conclusion

In this chapter I have considered how a sociology of culture responds to the challenge of an algorithmically-saturated world. This involves not quarantining off the empirical domain in advance through generalized 'philosophical' argument about what power now 'is' or 'must work', but rather paying close attention to the types of technologically-mediated, often frustratingly constrained action in which social actors are now engaged, and on which they must constantly reflect.

I have sketched an outline of the project of 'social analytics' that emerges from such an approach, first, by reviewing the state of the debate in the sociology of culture about the consequences of the deep embedding in the texture of everyday life of calculative processes (performed through automatic measurement based on algorithms and other uses of analytics). If, as William Sewell, has eloquently argued, the 'social' is – and always has been – both 'language-game' and 'built environment' (2005: chapter 10), then so-called 'algorithmic power' (Lash 2007) is just the latest of the ways in which language-games get 'hardened' into the built environments for action with which actors must deal. Pursuing social analytics involves more possibilities than I have been able to outline here, including tracking social actors as they resist the imposition of analytics as the basis of management or other forms of organizational control, or as they use analytics to enhance broader strategies of implementing social change. In all such cases, including those considered in detail here, social actors can be tracked as they move reflexively from dealing with and reacting to mere measures of their being-in-the-world ('data' that as yet is only interpreted automatically without reference to wider matters of meaning *to them*) to treating those measures (and their automated impact on the operations of everyday reality) as themselves a topic for reflection and adaptive action, that is, a reworking of data back into meaning that, potentially, restores some element of meaning in an increasingly automatized and systematized world.[3]

The task of a sociology of culture, in response, is not to further reify the outcome by claiming, for example, that algorithmic power leaves no space for reflexivity or resistance to power, but, on the contrary, as Sewell says, to contribute to the '*de*-reification of social life' (2005: 369), and so to build possibilities of social critique based in how social reality is constructed by powerful institutional forces (Boltanski 2012: 51, referring to Berger and Luckmann 1966). Translated into practical terms, this means attending, through situated fieldwork, to social actors as they themselves struggle to de-reify the tools with which they must work in order to be present in the world as they want to be. While the challenge for social actors of translating their broader aims through techniques of measurement and audit (Power 1997) is not new in itself, the opacity of how calculation is embedded in everyday life poses special challenges for reflexive agency. Registering that site of agency is the purpose of *social* analytics, conceived as an empirical project of cultural sociology that addresses the constructed 'realities' of a digital age, while seeking to preserve the possibility of grounded critique.

Acknowledgement

Thanks to Kate Nash, Lilie Chouliaraki, Monika Krause and the volume's editors for their comments on an earlier draft of this chapter. Thanks also to Anthony Kelly of the London School of Economics for assistance with some references for this chapter. The research from which this paper draws was part of a wider, multi-strand action research project led by Goldsmiths, University of London (see http://www.storycircle.co.uk) within the Framework for Innovation and Research in MediaCity consortium (see http://www.firm-innovation.net), and funded by the UK's Engineering and Physical Research Sciences Council (grant number EP/H003738/1).

Notes

1 The Storycircle project conducted 2010–2013 at Goldsmiths, University of London (http://storycircle.co.uk) funded by the RCUK Digital Economy Programme as part of the FIRM consortium: http://www.firm-innovation.net/ (accessed 15 January 2015).

2 I want to thank here particularly Dr Luke Dickens, now based at the Open University, for his remarkable work in developing such documentation for the first time: for sample documents developed out of our specific fieldwork, see www.storycircle.co.uk. Many thanks also to Dr Aristea Fotopoulou (now at Sussex University) for her detailed work on, and Dr Richard Macdonald (Goldsmiths) for his overall contribution to managing, the research strand on which this chapter is based.
3 For the distinction between uninterpreted 'data' and interpreted 'information', see Kallinikos (2009).

References

Alasuutaari, P. (ed.) (1999) *Rethinking the Media Audience*, London: Sage.
Amoore, L. (2011) 'Data Derivatives: On the Emergence of a Security Risk Calculus for Our Times', *Theory Culture and Society*, 28(6): 24–43.
Ang, I. (1986) *Watching Dallas*, London: Routledge.
Banet-Weiser, S. (2012) *Authentic™*, New York: New York University Press.
Barassi, V. (forthcoming) *The Web and Everyday Critique: The Struggle Against Digital Capitalism*, London: Routledge.
Beer, D. (2009) 'Power through the Algorithm? Participatory Web Cultures and the Technological Unconscious', *New Media and Society*, 11: 985–1002.
Berger, P. and T. Luckmann (1966) *The Social Construction of Reality*, New York: Double and Company.
Boltanski, L. (2010) *On Critique*, Cambridge: Polity.
—— (2012) *Sociología o la Crítica Social*, Santiago: University of Diego Portales Press.
Boltanksi, L. and E. Chiapello (2007) *The New Spirit of Capitalism*, London/New York: Verso.
Bourdieu, P. (1984) *Distinction: A Social Critique of the Judgement of Taste*, Cambridge, MA: Harvard University Press.
—— (1990) *Language and Symbolic Power*. Cambridge: Polity.
Bourdieu, P. with T. Eagleton (1992) 'Doxa and Common Life', *New Left Review*. [old series] 191: 111–121.
Bowker, G.S. and S.L. Star (2000) *Sorting Things Out*. Classification and Its Consequences, Cambridge, MA: MIT Press.
boyd, d. (2008) 'Why Youth ♥ Social Network Sites: The Role of Networked Publics', in D. Buckingham (ed.) *Youth, Identity and Digital Media*, Cambridge, MA: MIT Press, 119–142.
—— (2014) *It's Complicated: The Social Lives of Networked Teens*, New Haven: Yale University Press.
Burrows, R. (2009) 'Afterword: Urban Informatics and Social Ontology' in M. Foth (ed.) *Handbook of Research on Urban Informatics*, Hershey, PA: Information Science Reference, 450–454.
de Certeau, M. (1984) *The Practice of Everyday Life*, Berkeley: University of California Press.
Cohen, J. (2012) *Configuring the Networked Self*, New Haven: Yale University Press.
Cooley, C. (1902) *Human Nature and the Social Order*, New York: Charles Scribner's Sons.
Couldry, N. (2000) *Inside Culture: Reimagining the Method of Cultural Studies*, London: Sage.
—— (2012) *Media Society World: Social Theory and Digital Media Practice*, Cambridge: Polity.
Couldry, Fotopoulou and Dickens 'Real Social Analytics' (resubmitted to BJS, July 2014, awaiting final decision).
Crossley, N. (2001) *The Social Body*, London: Sage.
Durkheim, E. and M. Mauss (1970) *Primitive Classification*, London: Cohen and West.
Ellison, N., R. Heino, and J. Gibbs (2006) 'Managing Impressions Online: Self Presentation Processes in the Online Dating Environment', *Journal of Computer Mediated Communication*, 11(2): 415–441.
Freire, P. (1972) *Pedagogy of the Oppressed*, Harmondsworth: Penguin.
Gerlitz, C. and A. Helmond (2013) 'The Like Economy: Social Buttons and the Data Intensive Web', *New Media and Society*. First published on February 4, 2013 doi: 10.1177/1461444812472322.
Gillespie, T. (2014) 'The Relevance of Algorithms', in T. Gillespie, P. Boczkowski, and K. Foot (eds) *Media Technologies*, Cambridge: MIT Press.
Goffman, E. (1971) *The Presentation of the Self in Everyday Life*, Harmondsworth: Penguin.
Halavais, A. (2008) *Search Engine Society*, Cambridge: Polity.
Hannerz, U. (1992) *Cultural Complexity*, New York: Columbia University Press.
Honneth, A. (2008) *Reification: A New Look at an Old Idea*, Oxford: Oxford University Press.
Kallinikos, J. (2009) 'The Making of Ephemeria: On the Shortening Life-Spans of Information', *International Journal of Interdisiciplinary Social Sciences*, 4(3): 227–236.
Knapp, D. (forthcoming 2015) 'Living with Algorithms: Reclaiming Agency under Conditions of Data-Driven Surveillance', PhD thesis undertaken at London School of Economics and Political Science.

Lahire, B. (2004) *Le Culture des Individus*, Paris: La Decouverte.
—— (2011) *The Plural Actor*, Cambridge: Polity.
Lanier, J. (2013) *Who Owns the Future?* London: Allen Lane.
Lash, S. (2002) *Critique of Information*, London: Sage.
—— (2006) 'Dialectic of Information'? A Response to Taylor', *Information Community and Society*, 9(5): 572–581.
—— (2007) 'Power after Hegemony: Cultural Studies in Mutation', *Theory Culture and Society*, 24(3): 55–78.
Livingstone, S. (2008) 'Taking Risky Opportunities in Youthful Content Creation: Teenagers' Use of Social Networking Sites for Intimacy, Privacy, and Self-Expression', *New Media and Society*, 10(3): 393–412.
Lupton, D. (2012) 'The Quantified Self Movement: Some Sociological Perpsectives'. Available online at https://simplysociology.wordpress.com/2012/11/04/the-quantitative-self-movement-some-sociological-perspectives/ (accessed 11 July 2014).
Mackenzie, A. (2006) *Cutting Code*, New York: Peter Lang.
Marres, N. (2012) 'The Redistribution of Methods: On Intervention in Digital Social Research, Broadly Conceived', *The Sociological Review*, 60(1): 139–165.
Marwick, A. (2013) *Status Update: Celebrity, Publicity and Branding in the Social Media Age*, New Haven: Yale University Press.
Mejias, U. (2013) *Off the Network*, Minneapolis: Minnesota University Press
Melucci, A. (1996) *Challenging Codes*, Cambridge: Cambridge University Press.
Meyrowitz, J. (1985) *No Sense of Place*, New York: Oxford University Press.
Morley, D. and C. Brunsdon (1980) *The Nationwide Audience*, London: Routledge.
Paliser, E. (2011) *The Filter Bubble*, New York: Basic Books.
Poell, T. (2014) 'Social Media and the Transformation of Activist Communication: Exploring the Social Media Ecology of the 2010 Toronto G20 Protests', *Information, Communication and Society*, 17(6): 716–731.
Postill, J. (2013) 'Democracy in an Age of Viral Reality: A Media Epidemiography of Spain's Indignados Movement', *Journal of Ethnography*, doi: 1466138113502513.
Power, M. (1997) *The Audit Society*, Basingstoke: Palgrave.
Segerberg, A., and Bennett, W.L. (2011) 'Social Media and the Organization of Collective Action: Using Twitter to Explore the Ecologies of Two Climate Change Protests', *The Communication Review*, 14(3): 197–215.
Sewell, W. (2005) *Logics of History: Social Theory and Social Transformation*, Chicago: University of Chicago Press.
Turkle, S. (2011) *Alone Together*, New York: Basic Books.
Turow, J. (2007) *Niche Envy*, Cambridge, MA: MIT Press.
—— (2011) *The Daily You*, New Haven: Yale University Press.
Van Dijck, J. (2013) *The Culture of Connectivity*, Oxford: Oxford University Press.
Youmans, W.L. and J.C. York (2012) 'Social Media and the Activist Toolkit: User Agreements, Corporate Interests, and the Information Infrastructure of Modern Social Movements', *Journal of Communication*, 62(2): 315–329.

26

The rising power of screens

Changing cultural practices in France, from 1973 to 2008

Olivier Donnat

An analysis of the results of the five editions of the French government survey on cultural practices, *Pratiques culturelles des Français*, conducted since the early 1970s[1], gives an overview of the major trends in media use and participation in cultural life. This medium-term perspective is particularly valuable at a time when it is tempting to present the effects of the 'digital revolution' as radical changes, while ignoring all the elements of continuity with the previous period.

In this chapter I will examine how this survey data shows that although the 'digital revolution' radically transformed the conditions of access to culture and destabilised the cultural industries and media, nonetheless it has not upset the overall pattern of cultural practices nor has it bent the main trends observed in previous decades.

Pratiques culturelles des Français *survey: The verdict*

On the basis of the questions included in the five successive versions of the questionnaire using an identical wording, four major evolutionary trends can be identified over the period 1973–2008. We will give a brief overview of them, drawing on the figures summarised in Table 26.A1 in the Appendix[2] before putting forward some general thoughts regarding the significance of screen culture.

Four major trends

The most remarkable change concerns the steady increase in audio-visual consumption: more and more French people are spending a considerable proportion of their spare time firstly listening to music and watching television and, secondly, with 'new screens' (computers, games consoles, smart phones, tablets, etc.).

The increasing range of devices in households and steady diversification of available television programmes, music and other audio-visual entertainments have led to a remarkable diversification in forms of consumption: over a period of thirty-five years, screens and music have gradually become absorbed into French people's everyday lives. Over the course of these successive technological transformations, at-home audio-visual practices have taken up a large proportion of the time freed through reductions in working hours and the lowering of the retirement age: television was the major beneficiary of this throughout the 1980s and 1990s, before the increasing time spent on the Internet and new screens curtailed this trend. For the first time since television appeared in homes, the amount of time spent in front of it has stabilised and has even fallen for young people.

For a long time, the focus of intellectual debate on the increasing power of television, which many saw as a threat to the literary world, led to the underestimation of another phenomenon connected to the expansion of household audio-visual resources: the massive increase in music listening practices. The shockwaves of the music boom, which originated in the 1970s with the spread of the home stereo system and the Walkman, continue to reverberate throughout French society, and all the more strongly now that digital formats are making music even more accessible: the new possibilities for storage, exchange and transfer from one format to another as well as the proliferation of playing/listening devices, from mobile phones and MP3 players to computers, mean that music is becoming increasingly integrated into everyday life, particularly life on the move.

At the same time, the reading of printed materials has seen a decline, reflecting a steady fall in daily newspaper readership and in the proportion of avid readers (20 books or more per year) in the population aged 15 and over. Books are nevertheless still to be found in the majority of homes, library usage has increased enormously despite having tailed off recently, and yet the reading of printed matter has continued to fall: (paid-for) newspapers have lost almost half of their daily readership and, although the proportion of French people who have never read a book outside of any academic or professional requirement remains the same as it was in the early 1970s, readers in 2008 read on average five books less than their counterparts in 1973, due to the steady fall in avid readers.

It would however be premature to conclude that reading is declining based on this fact alone, for at least two reasons: education and work-related reading has probably gone up and on-screen reading (particularly) has increased over the last decade. Moreover, it is likely that the fall in avid readers owes more to changes of a symbolic nature than any actual change in reading behaviour: although book reading has indubitably been subject to competition over the last few decades from various leisure activities connected with household audio-visual devices, it has also lost part of its symbolic power amongst young people, particularly males, who are now probably less likely to overestimate their reading practices than their parents might have at the same age, or perhaps even to underestimate them by 'forgetting' some of them (Baudelot, Cartier and Detrez 1999).

The third trend for the 1973–2008 period shows that the French proclivity to going out in the evening is now greater despite the boom in at-home audio-visual consumption. Home may have become a place for personal development and entertainment, but this doesn't signify either a withdrawal into the domestic arena: overall, more French people now visit cultural institutions than they did thirty-five years ago. However, this observation should be nuanced given that opposite trends also occur in certain fields and/or at certain points in the survey period: thus, although theatre, cinema and certain types of concert have been experienced by more people over the last decade, expanding the base of their occasional attendees, particularly older people, book-lending and multimedia libraries have experienced a slight drop in attendance over the last two years, after a marked increase in the 1980s and 1990s. In those cases where attendance rates have increased in line with the French population (e.g. visits to cinema, theatre, dance performance, museum or exhibition attendance) this is largely accounted for by occasional attendance (once or twice a year): no cultural visit or activity has seen a significant increase in their core attendees. But should we really find this surprising, given the considerable diversification of live entertainments and activities available during the survey period? The greater the range of choices available, the further the range of activities attended by the most culturally active extends; their frequency of attendance, on a per-activity basis, is thus beginning to diminish.

Finally, the last thirty-five years were also marked by the growth of amateur artistic practices. If we look simply at the practices undertaken before the arrival of computers and digital technology, the results of the 2008 survey might give the impression that this growth stopped abruptly: musical practices have in fact decreased since 1997, as have those of writing, the visual arts and design. But if we include the creative uses of computers in amateur practices, these quite clearly have continued to rise, extending the trend observed in the 1980s and 1990s. The trend has diversified with the spread of photography and video in this field, as well as music, writing and the visual and graphic arts, all new ways of producing content characterised by a relationship with culture based on self-expression and peer-to-peer sharing. Moreover, confirmation of this growing trend is seen in the fact that the proportion of French having attended amateur live entertainment has doubled since the early 1970s.

Social inertia and generational dynamics

If we now compare the relative significance of factors encouraging a high level of cultural participation, the overwhelming impression is that continuity, rather than change, prevails. In many respects, things have barely changed over the last twenty-five years, particularly when we take into account the rising number of people with academic qualifications during the period in question. The links between educational attainment and cultural participation have not been weakened by the rise of mass education because of the relative depreciation of qualifications. In short, the data reveals a picture of overwhelming inertia in the domain of cultural practices, particularly with the persistence of marked social (and territorial) inequalities in accessing culture in a context characterised by profound technological, economic and social changes.

Those social classes which are least socially engaged have, strictly speaking, never really caught up with the other classes, particularly with regard to visiting cultural institutions. In all cases, the hierarchy remains the same, with professionals and senior executives at the top ahead of the middle management, followed by non-manual workers, skilled workers and shopkeepers for whom results are often similar, and finally, always lagging behind, farmers and manual workers.[3] Today, just as in the past, regular and diversified cultural participation still does not occur equally across French society, for it requires the highest possible accumulation of advantages (a high level of educational attainment and income, proximity to available culture, a precocious familiarity with the world of art, a taste for leisure oriented outside of the home and towards socialising with friends (Donnat 1994), properties which are predominantly found within senior management and higher intellectual professions.

The second major lesson concerns the significance of generational differences in most of the transformations observed, whether this involves increased time for watching television, the music boom, the fall in the reading of printed matter, increasing amateur practices or changed behaviour with regard to live entertainment. Each time, change has been initiated by the older generation before being intensified by the following generations, who carry into their later years a large proportion of the habits acquired during their youth.

In many respects, French society could be seen as the sum of four generations 'produced' under very different conditions and closely coinciding with successive developments in new technologies which have appeared over the last thirty-five years.[4] The oldest generation, born before the Second World War, grew up in a world in which nothing emerged to rival the supremacy of print-based publishing. They discovered television at a mature age and have remained pretty much away from the musical boom and, *a fortiori*, from the digital revolution. The so-called baby boom generation was the first to benefit from the opening up of the education system and the development of cultural industries and still retains today some traces of the music-oriented teen culture which emerged in the 1960s.[5] The generation which is today aged between thirty and forty benefits from the intensification of these same phenomena (e.g. wide access to higher education and diversification of cultural arenas), and as children or teenagers they experienced the profound transformation of the audio-visual landscape which occurred at the turn of the 1980s. It is the generation of the second age of the media, that of the multiple ownership of, and continuous broadcasting on, private radios and televisions. This has enabled them to draw considerable benefit from the possibilities offered by digital culture. Finally the under-thirty generation has grown up in a screen-based environment characterised by the dematerialisation of content and widespread access to broadband Internet: it is the third media-age generation, and it is still evolving.

Moreover, the evolution of cultural practices must currently be assessed from two mutually fairly irreconcilable standpoints: the first one emphasises the persistence of intense social stratification within cultural practices, lending credibility to theories about cultural capital, whilst the second one puts emphasis on generational mutation. This reminds us that cultural domination, far from being set in stone, renews itself reflecting transformations in the social structure and in the conditions governing access to culture and modes of artistic expression.

Neither of these two perspectives should be privileged over the other. Pointing out (yet again, some might say) the persistence of profound social and territorial divisions, when it comes to the regular use of books or cultural facilities, may seem pointless or redundant. Yet, it is unavoidable at a point where plenty of observers (and sociologists) are approaching the question of contemporary life by 'forgetting' to socially situate the individuals whose behaviour they are analysing. Can we really simply assume that the process of individualisation is socially undifferentiated whereas in fact it is based on both material and cognitive resources and support systems which are unequally distributed in our society (Castel and Haroche 2001)? At the same time, a focus on generational differences should not make us forget that intergenerational continuities and intra-generational differences are connected to social status, as well as gender, place of residence, etc. Consequently, we must try to bring both perspectives together in the hope of differentiating the new from the old amidst the transformations which are taking place today.

A third perspective, partly linked to that of generational renewal, emerges from a retrospective analysis of the results: educational progress, of which women have been the prime beneficiaries, has been accompanied by a feminisation of cultural practices. This movement of course assumes different forms and levels of intensity in various cultural fields, social milieux or generations, but it is nonetheless real: the extent to which women are involved in cultural life has greatly increased since the baby-boom generation onwards, in areas such as book reading, amateur leisure and, to a lesser extent, cultural attendance. Over the course of the last thirty-five years, women have outstripped men in many areas; in some cases this was all the more easily achieved as men were at the same time starting to distance themselves from certain traditional forms of access to arts and culture.

Eventually, our analysis of the forces driving cultural participation in France does not strikingly differ from the findings in other countries. Thus, my own research on the concept of 'eclecticism' (Donnat 1994) shares many affinities with the Anglo-American concept of 'omnivorousness'.[6] The main result is the same: the statistical data do not invalidate the idea of structural homology, which is at the centre of the sociological research program on cultural legitimacy. Yet our findings also add nuance to this paradigm. Indeed, researchers now have to pay more attention to the heterogeneous nature of socialisation processes (Lahire 1998), as well as take into account variables such as age and gender, which both have an important influence on cultural taste and cultural participation.[7]

New screens and old ways of accessing culture

The digital expansion via connected screens in recent years illustrates this last point by showing the complex interaction of cross-cutting effects of social class, generational membership and gender. The expansion of news screens, in spite of their looming presence, do not in fact affect the whole population: quite a few French people continue to avoid digital practices, others associate them only with the world of literature and traditional forms of culture, and others simply with television or radio.

There are two key points to make in this regard. Firstly, the new screens, unlike television (which is particularly the domain of the elderly and those with low levels of academic achievement), is primarily the area of the young, urban and educated, those whose approach to leisure is most strongly oriented outside the home and with the highest involvement in cultural life. The time spent in front of the new screens being inversely proportional to the time spent watching television, the overall amount of screen time spent is nevertheless not influenced by the main socio-demographic variables: women and men, young and old, lower and upper classes all devote an average of between thirty and thirty-five hours of their spare time each week to screen time.

Secondly, an individual's overall amount of screen time is also relatively independent of their general level of involvement in cultural life. In this regard the situation is quite radically different from that of the 'television years', in which two clearly opposing camps within the French population emerged: one including those with the highest level of cultural involvement, particularly with regard to the use of formal cultural institutions, and the other, those who rarely went out and watched a lot of television. There is now a huge variety of potential combinations between the use of new screens, television and traditional methods of access to culture, whether it be book reading or visits to the theatre, concerts, museums and other cultural places (Donnat 2009).

If we view French society as the sum of four different generations, taking account of the differences in class or gender which may exist within each of these, the main means of connecting old and new methods of access to culture can be briefly summarised in the following table.

The under-45 generations are those who have most enthusiastically adopted the new screens, as reflected in the considerable overall increase in their screen time. This is particularly true for those from more disadvantaged backgrounds, where the level of television programme consumption often remains high, but also for those from middle social and cultural backgrounds, particularly men. Women have shown certain reluctance towards adopting new screens whilst maintaining more frequent connections with cultural institutions and particularly with books.

As for the privileged classes, there are below average numbers interested in television and they have largely integrated new screens into their cultural patterns without radically changing their habits and cultural activities. Their predilection for going out in the evening and their patronage of cultural venues remain entirely unaffected by any competition from the new screens. In other words, the cumulative principle, which posits that the most well-off sections of the population in general get the most out of technological (and also aesthetic) innovations, has, on the whole, worked out. Nevertheless, competition between screens and traditional

Table 26.1 Cultural participation by generation, social background and gender

	Young generations (under 30)	Intermediate young generations (aged 30–45)	Intermediate generations born after the war (aged 45–64)	Generations born before the war (aged 65+)
Lower social and cultural background	SCREEN CULTURE	Men SCREEN CULTURE Women PRINT-BASED, MAINSTREAM MEDIA	TELEVISION, HEGEMONIC MEDIA	TELEVISION, HEGEMONIC MEDIA
Middle social and cultural background	Men SCREEN CULTURE Women ALL ACCESS METHODS	Men SCREEN CULTURE Women PRINT-BASED, MAINSTREAM MEDIA	Men SCREEN CULTURE Women PRINT-BASED	PRINT-BASED, MAINSTREAM MEDIA
Upper social and cultural background	ALL ACCESS METHODS	ALL ACCESS METHODS	ALL ACCESS METHODS	PRINT-BASED, MAINSTREAM MEDIA

forms of access to culture has become far more acute than it was during the television-dominated era: time has become a more precious resource than ever for the privileged classes and the cumulative principle, which so often dominates the cultural field, has probably reached its limits, particularly in the case of such time-consuming activities as book reading, particularly novel-reading which requires both large amounts of time and a long attention span.

For the older generations, the use of new screens has grown, particularly among the privileged classes to whom the cumulative principle also applies, at least for the baby boom generation. This group now attends most forms of live entertainment (classical music concerts as well as certain forms of theatre) and reads lots of books whilst also having adopted the new screens. On the other hand, the generation born before the war has largely shied away from the digital revolution and has made few changes to the way it accesses culture: television remains the predominant medium in lower class households whereas those from privileged backgrounds continue to favour books and the press.

From print to screen culture

At the end of this brief retrospective analysis, it would seem that the recent spread of the Internet and the new screens should not be viewed in isolation, rather it should be placed within the context of a wider movement whose origins go back to the arrival of televisions in homes. It is part of the growing time spent on screens and the related decline of print-based reading.

For several decades now the generational trend has been towards a fall in print-based reading: since the 1980s, young adults have shown lower level of newspaper and book readership than previous generations, and this gap from one generation to another doesn't decrease with age. With screens, while the generational trend in the 1980s and 1990s showed an increased proclivity to watching television before supplementing this with online screens, the vast majority of current young people play video games fairly regularly, have frequent if not daily contacts with the Internet and show a greater diversity of digital practices. It is of course difficult, without hindsight, to say whether this is a generational phenomenon rather than an age-related one, but it is hard to imagine that these generations who have grown up with online screens are going to stop playing video games or communicate via social networks entirely as they progress into adult life, even though their family and work commitments will certainly oblige them to do so less often.

This twofold generational trend (downward in the case of newspaper and book reading and upward in the case of screen use) seems to suggest that the shift in the centre of gravity in cultural practices from print to screens is set to continue and perhaps even intensify as the new generations grow up, the 'television generations' and the 'Internet generations' get older and as the baby boom generation, (the currently most invested group in print-based reading) slowly disappears.

One could see in this gradual rise of the screen culture the confirmation of a hypothesis formulated by Ehrenberg and Chambat (1988) more than twenty years ago. Both authors had indeed perfectly anticipated the effects of technological convergence: in the mid-1980s they had already foreseen the decline of the 'classic' television model and especially the hegemony of print culture. For them, the merging of audio-visual, computing and telecommunications sectors and the multiplication of screens opened a new era that ended the five-century period of predominance of the print.

A two-phase movement

Let us broadly outline the main stages of this increase in the importance of the culture of the screen since the arrival of television in the early 1960s. It is characterised by two distinct phases. The first occurred in the 1980s with the widespread move towards multiple ownership of televisions, remote controls, video players, etc. and the astonishing diversification of audio-visual programs available. This period constitutes an important transformation for French society. At the ideological level, the new spirit of capitalism (Boltanski and Chiapello 1999) accompanied by more concrete transformations, such as the rise of unemployment, the explosion of higher education, and the growing importance of mass media and advertising, dramatically changed the landscape and the relative structure of the cultural industries, reorganizing them around a new dominant medium: television. Indeed, it is during this decade that the different domains of cultural life responded to the new demands of the media society, for example with the multiplication of cultural events (festivals, temporary exhibitions, etc.) and growing importance of marketing in order to rationalise the promotion and diffusion of cultural events, which resulted in many jobs being opened in the communication and marketing sectors of public and private cultural organisations. It is also during this decade that the role of television as a vector of socialisation was considerably strengthened, particularly through the increasingly intense broadcasting of programs aimed at children and teenagers.[8]

The second phase of acceleration coincides with the turn of the century and with the dematerialisation of content, the widespread use of broadband Internet, and the popular adoption of the new screens, radically changing the means of accessing culture. In less than 10 years, individual devices designed for a specific function (listening to records, watching television programmes, reading information, communicating with others, etc.) were largely supplanted or supplemented by devices, often portable, offering a wide range of functionalities from entertainment to interpersonal communication.

If the digital revolution was inscribed in the context of broader social change, it should also be clear that the current situation in fact appears to be entirely different from anything that has come before in a number of ways. First and foremost, the Internet is a medium completely unlike any of the numerous new means of expression and communication which sprang up in the twentieth century. It might be more appropriate to talk of a hypermedia with the potential of absorbing all the other media, its defining property being that it incorporates the mass media (e.g. press, radio, television) and the interpersonal communication media (e.g. telephone, postal service) which previously belonged to distinct technological groupings. As a kind of 'all-purpose media' it simultaneously enables access to works, cultural industry and media content, as well as the creation, broadcast and sharing of one's own images, texts or music, speaking or writing to others in real time and carrying out some of the most trivial daily tasks.

More crucially, technological convergence definitively ordains screens as the privileged medium for our relationship with culture whilst emphasising the permeability between culture and amusement, between the world of art and that of entertainment and communication. Nevertheless, with digitisation and the multipurpose terminals now available, the majority of cultural practices are converging towards screens, which of course includes viewing images and listening to music, but also covers text reading and amateur practices, not to mention the fact that screens are now present in libraries, exhibition spaces and sometimes even live entertainment venues. These days everything can potentially be displayed on a screen.

This rising power of the screen culture over more than half a century raises questions about the future of print culture that had built up over the centuries. The central position which it has enjoyed in our societies has come under serious threat since the very tight-knit relationships forged over time between materiality of printed artefacts, the ideas they contain and ways of reading have started to work loose with the rising power of the screens and the arrival of the digital era.

Withering of the print?

The issue of the status of print–based material in a society dominated by screens needs to be addressed without falling into commonplaces which all too often end up cluttering debates on the future of books and reading. A downturn in the written press or books market does not necessarily equate to a downturn in reading when we consider the increasing diversity of reading formats, a crisis in the printed word is not necessarily a crisis in the written word, which is in fact enjoying something of a renaissance with the boom in instant messaging and text messaging, etc. Three points need to be made here.

The first concerns the book itself as an object which has always elicited various levels of attachment, even amongst readers who are not bibliophiles. For a long time now, with the extension of education and their retail in superstores, books have started to become a commonplace ordinary object. They have lost their force of attraction for those who were not brought up with them, as well as some of their power as social marker amongst the younger generations, and before even the digital boom began its hegemony as a way of accessing information and knowledge and weakening its 'natural' link with text. If, as Roger Chartier would want us believe, we are embarking on a process of emancipating the text from the physical format of the book, we must effectively admit that, as he puts it, 'all intellectual technologies and all operations working to produce meaning become similarly modified' (Chartier 1992: 96, author's translation). This begs the question, amongst other things, of the relationship to the book in its material dimension. Is it going to become entirely obsolete, or on the contrary will it regain some of its lost symbolic power? What qualities does this centuries-old object retain in the digital era? For what kind of content does it remain an unbeatable format?[9]

The second aspect of enquiry examines reading as an activity. For several decades now there has been increased competition from emerging ways of occupying leisure time and the increasing power of screen culture. However, do not make the mistake of thinking that the screen is exclusively about images: it also transmits texts and has, in a certain way, encouraged a return to the written form (with text messaging, instant messaging and social messaging now taking precedence over telephone calls) as well as the emergence of new ways of reading. In fact, one does not read a text on a computer (or indeed on a mobile phone) in the same way: devices such as hypertext links and mouse clicks which benefit on-screen reading techniques enable readers to jump from one text to another, encouraging fragmented, discontinuous reading, focused on the rapid search for information, to the detriment of a linear reading of texts which requires sustained and uninterrupted attention.

The 'TV generations' who grew up in the 1980s and 1990s and particularly the 'Internet generations', who have been surrounded by screens from an early age, have developed different skills and knowledge compared to their elders (who have tended to rely on the printed realm): not only do they increasingly rely on formats other than the book for reading but they also have new relationships with texts, whether printed or not.

From these observations new issues arise, which might be summarised as follows: how do we now ensure that everyone has the opportunity to master the different levels of reading required, from quickly seeking out specific information to the uninterrupted reading required for complex narrative forms, or even 'skimming' a text in order to get the gist of the content? Let us not forget in all this that the wise reader, even at the peak of the print culture era, did not solely follow one mode of reading but rather possessed a perfect mastery of the various reading methods which might be required in accordance with text and context.

Finally, it would seem that some of the decline evidenced in the surveys relates to a fall in linear reading (i.e. that required by literature) over a long period, in favour of more fragmented forms of reading. This makes it impossible to ignore the issue of literature's future. The rising popularity of screen culture prompts the question not of the disappearance of the novel in the form in which we have known it since the 19th century, but of its reliance on an audience whose social and cultural resources and age are increasingly homogenous. We must face the fact that a love of literature is no longer a major feature of the self-image identification linked to the adolescent period and that the reading of literature, a solitary and time-consuming activity, has lost part of its symbolic power in the eyes of a huge proportion of the younger generations (Pasquier 2005).Young people may of course continue to show genuine interest in certain narrative forms (science fiction and fantasy books, graphic novels and manga, for example) but in the current landscape of cultural and technological convergence their references draw more on a trans-media register than a purely literary register. How can we think that the increasingly early immersion of the younger generations in an almost permanent flux of audio-visual narratives (films, television series, video games, etc.) does not affect the way they satisfy their desire for the fictional/fantastic and their ability to get inspired by words alone, and, ultimately, their relationship with novels?

Cultural legitimacy and media visibility

These brief comments about book reading and television have illustrated some of the many transformations associated with the growing importance of screen cultures. In many respects, it is the very idea of culture itself – its outlines, its divisions and its internal hierarchies, its social functions – which is undermined. In the digital era, images, music and text circulate and get mixed together, passing from one screen to another, without the constraints of the physical world. The physical or material supports for cultural and artistic products, or even the types of media which could spread them, now matter less and the differences built over the years between artistic genres, producers, mediators and consumers, as well as between amateurs and experts, are becoming blurred.

It is too early to clearly assess the significance of these changes. Yet, we would like to conclude this chapter by mentioning two important points. The first one refers to three important changes affecting cultural consumption in the digital age. First, most cultural participation taking place through screens occurs at home. This private setting favours a more 'relaxed management of emotions' as well as a preference for lighter, 'fun' cultural activities[10]. Secondly, screen users now rely on several technological devices (remote controls or mouse devices, for example) allowing them to control and decide in real-time what they are going to watch, which provides consumers with a new kind of independence. Thirdly, screens typically have many different functions: it is now possible to perform several activities at the same time, for example watching videos online and answering messages on social networks. The cultural consumer is now able to do several things at once: enjoying a leisure activity, looking for information, making amateur art, and communicating with friends. So, what was once an exception in print culture has now become the rule in screen culture. Those who read, listen to music or view images increasingly end up doing several things at the same time, dividing their attention between reading, listening, etc. and simultaneously respond to incoming messages. Given these different points, it makes sense to assume that screen cultures have played a significant role in the relative disinvestment of younger cohorts from legitimate culture, as well as in their disinterest for books and other printed cultural content.

The second important point concerns the different forms of recognition and evaluation taking place in the cultural domain. In summary, we argue that the transformation of the media infrastructure (Voirol 2005), first with the rise of television and second with the Internet, destabilised the traditional processes of evaluation and consecration based on judgements by experts, which had first appeared at the end of the nineteenth century (Bourdieu 1992). Indeed, one of the specificities of the Internet is that it relies on a horizontal crowdsourcing logic. The Internet largely ignores previous hierarchies. It values instead the participation of lay Internet users, regardless of their social or professional status (Cardon 2010). The new medium makes it possible to become famous very quickly. It also relies in an essential way on user reviews, which now play a major role in the valorisation of cultural content (Karpik 2007). In other words, the traditional cultural hierarchies based on traditional expert judgement have lost some of their importance in the current Internet culture, which draws instead on algorithms and other technological devices to rank artistic content online.

By privileging images and favouring media visibility as a new form of cultural excellence (Heinich 2012), the screen culture has changed the relationship between legitimacy and fame: the former often now stems from the latter, whereas it used to be the other way around and, above all, it challenges the authority of experts and traditional cultural mediators (journalists, librarians, curators, etc.) in favour of non-human mediators. Yet, constraints and the power dynamics are strong all the more because they are applied invisibly through technological devices and algorithms.

Given these profound transformations, it has become harder to rely exclusively on the traditional framework of cultural legitimacy in order to analyse the symbolic status of contemporary cultural goods and practices. So, it might be time to revise the division of labour that exists between the sociology of culture and media sociology, which is stronger in France than elsewhere[11], and to reconsider the initial 'grand partage légitimiste' (Macé 2007: 133). Moreover, couldn't reflections on television and more generally on the role of media in the diffusion of neoliberalism – as announced by Pierre Bourdieu in the last years of his life – be interpreted in such a way? Couldn't his remarks on the growing heteronomy of artistic and intellectual fields under the pressure of market forces, or those on the 'almost absolute power' of major communication groups blurring the distinction between economic power and symbolic power, be read as an invitation to get a grip on the question of media? This arguably remains one of the major undeveloped parts of the theoretical framework of *Distinction*.

Notes

1 See the overview of the survey *Pratiques culturelles des Français* in the Appendix I in this document.
2 Detailed statistical data as well as analytical documents are available at: www.pratiquesculturelles.culture.gouv.fr.
3 It is worth pointing out that this hierarchy remains unchanged, even when we are looking at supposedly less elitist activities such as street performance, the circus or sound and light shows.
4 About the general relevance of the generational approach, see Chauvel 2010.
5 Yonnet Paul was one of the first French sociologists to underline the importance of the rock and more widely the young culture (Yonnet 1985) in line with reflections of pioneer Edgar Morin conducted in the early 1960s (Morin 1962).
6 The issue of *Sociologie et sociétés* published in 2004 which brought together French and Anglo-Saxon researchers around the theme of changing cultural tastes reflects this convergence in analysis of both sides of the Atlantic (Fridman and Ollivier 2004).
7 As a consequence, it is surprising how little attention has been given to the variables of age, generation and life cycle in Pierre Bourdieu's *Distinction*, even though the effects of such variables emerge clearly from the data presented in the book (Bourdieu 1979: 296). Similarly, it is possible to mention 'the relative blindness' of Bourdieu's framework with respect to gender. Interestingly, a close collaborator of Pierre Bourdieu has confirmed this point in a recent contribution (Saint-Martin 2013: 42).
8 Such deep transformations shed light on an important point which is often forgotten in current analyses of Bourdieu's *Distinction* (Coulangeon 2011, Coulangeon and Duval 2013). Indeed, Bourdieu almost never mentioned television in his book, even though television was already playing an important role in French society at that point, most importantly in working class households. A reader of *Distinction* not familiar with the importance of French television in the 1970s would probably have missed this point just from reading the book.
9 In other words, to what extent do we agree with Umberto Eco when he says "The book is like the spoon, scissors, the hammer, the wheel. Once invented, it cannot be improved" (Carrière and Eco 2009: 19).
10 'La sphère privée est propice aux relâchements contrôlés des émotions, à l'expression des dispositions les moins formalistes et les plus hédonistes (moindre contrôle du regard d'autrui, moindre officialité et moindre formalité de la situation) et, du même coup, propice aux consommations culturelles les plus divertissantes' (Lahire 2004: 630).
11 The break between the sociology of culture and the sociology of media in France dates from the 1960s, particularly as a result of the article Bourdieu and Passeron directed against those they called "mass mediologues" (Bourdieu and Passeron 1963).

References

Baudelot, C., M. Cartier, and C. Detrez (1999) *Et pourtant ils lisent …*, Paris: Seuil.
Boltanski, L. and E. Chiapello (1999) *Le nouvel esprit du capitalisme*, Paris: Gallimard.
Bourdieu, P. (1979) *La distinction, critique sociale du jugement*, Paris: Minuit.
—— (1992) *Les Règles de l'art. Genèse et structure du champ littéraire*, Paris: Seuil.
Bourdieu, P. and J.C. Passeron (1963) 'Sociologie des mythologies et mythologie de sociologues', *Les temps modernes*, 211.
Cardon, D. (2010) *La démocratie internet. Promesses et limites*, Paris: Seuil.
Carrière, J.C. and U. Eco (2009) *N'espérez pas vous débarrasser des livres*, Paris: Grasset [*This is Not the End of the Book*, Harvill Secker, 2011].

Castel, R. and C. Haroche (2001) *Propriété privée, propriété sociale, propriété de soi. Entretiens sur la construction de l'individu moderne*, Paris: Fayard.
Chartier, R. (1992) *L'ordre des livres*, Paris: Alinéa. [*The Order of Books*, Stanford University Press, 1994]
Chauvel, L. (2010) *Le destin des générations. Structure sociale et cohortes en France du 20ème siècle aux années 2010*, Paris: PUF.
Coulangeon, P. (2011) *Les métamorphoses de la distinction. Inégalités culturelles dans la France d'aujourd'hui*, Paris: Grasset.
Coulangeon, P. and Duval, J. (eds) (2013) *Trente ans après la Distinction de Pierre Bourdieu*, Paris: La Découverte.
Donnat, O. (1994) *Les Français face à la culture. De l'exclusion à l'éclectisme*, Paris: La Découverte.
—— (2009), *Les pratiques culturelles des Français à l'ère numérique*, Paris: La Découverte/Ministère de la culture.
Ehrenberg, A. and P. Chambat (1988) 'De la télévision à la culture de l'écran', *Le Débat*, 52: 107–132.
Fridman, V. and M. Ollivier (eds) (2004) Special issue: 'Goûts, pratiques culturelles et inégalités sociales: branchés et exclus / Tastes, Cultural Practices and Social Inequalities: In Fashion and Out', *Sociologie et sociétés*, 36(1): 3–245.
Heinich, N. (2012) *De la visibilité. Excellence et singularité en régime médiatique*, Paris: Gallimard.
Karpik, L. (2007) *L'économie des singularités*, Paris: Gallimard.
Lahire, B. (1998) *L'homme pluriel: les ressorts de l'action*, Paris: Nathan.
—— (2004) *La culture des individus. Dissonances culturelles et distinction de soi*, Paris: La Découverte
Macé, E. (2007) *Les imaginaires médiatiques. Une sociologie post critique des médias*, Paris: Editions Amsterdam.
Morin, E. (1962) *L'esprit du temps. Essai sur la culture de masse*, Paris: Grasset.
Pasquier, D. (2005) *Cultures lycéennes, La tyrannie de la majorité*, Paris: Autrement.
Saint-Martin de, M. (2013) 'Les tentatives de construction de l'espace social, d'Anatomie du goût à la Distinction. Quelques repères pour l'histoire d'une recherche', in P. Coulangeon and J. Duval, *Société et sociologies*, Montréal: Presses universitaires de Montréal.
Voirol, O. (2005) 'Visibilité/invisibilité', *Réseaux*: 129–130.
Yonnet, P. (1985) *Jeux, modes et masses*, Paris: Gallimard.

Appendix I

Table 26.A1 Changing Cultural and Media Practices, 1973–2008*

Out of 100 French people aged 15 and over	1973	1981	1988	1997	2008
Listen to the radio	**89**	**90**	**85**	**88**	**87**
those who listen:					
Every day, or almost every day	72	72	66	69	67
Average listening period	17h	16h	18h	17h	15h
Watch television	**88**	**91**	**90**	**91**	**98**
those who watch:					
Every day, or almost every day	65	69	73	77	87
20 hours or more per week	29	35	39	42	43
Average listening period (1)	16h	16h	20h	22h	21h
Listen to music (excluding radio)	**66**	**75**	**73**	**76**	**81**
those who listen:					
Every day, or almost every day	9	19	21	27	34
Read a daily newspaper	**77**	**71**	**79**	**73**	**69**
those who read one:					
Every day, or almost every day	55	46	43	36	29
Have read at least one book	**70**	**74**	**75**	**74**	**70**
have read 1–9	24	28	32	35	38
10–19	17	18	18	17	15
20 or more	28	26	24	19	16
Don't know	1	2	1	2	1

(Continued)

Table 26.A1 Changing Cultural and Media Practices, 1973–2008* (Continued)

Out of 100 French people aged 15 and over	1973	1981	1988	1997	2008
Are members of and visitors to a library	**13**	**14**	**16**	**20**	**18**
Have engaged in amateur practice of ...					
A musical activity	**5**	**5**	**8**	**10**	**8**
An artistic activity other than musical (2)	**11**	**13**	**17**	**23**	**22**
Have been to the cinema	**52**	**50**	**49**	**49**	**57**
Once or twice	13	15	15	13	17
3-11 times	23	20	19	23	27
12 times or more	16	15	15	13	13
Have been to live entertainment events:					
Dance (1)	6	5	6	8	8
Professional theatre production	12	10	14	16	19
Classical music concert (1)	7	7	9	9	7
Rock or jazz concert (1)	6	10	13	13	14
% of which were rock concerts	*	*	10	9	10
% of which were jazz concerts	*	*	6	7	6
Music hall or variety performance	11	10	10	10	11
Circus performance	11	10	9	13	14
Amateur production	10	12	14	20	21
Have visited a museum or exhibition	**33**	**36**	**38**	**40**	**37**
% of which to a museum	27	30	30	33	30
% of which to a temporary painting or sculpture exhibition	19	21	23	25	24

* Results refer to practices over the last 12 months
(1) The wording of this question is not exactly the same in each of the 5 surveys
(2) Writing outside of a personal diary, painting or sculpture, other artistic craft activity, theatre, dance

Note: The Department of Studies at the French Ministry of Culture and Communication has conducted five surveys into *French Cultural Practices* (*Pratiques culturelles des Français*) in 1973, 1981, 1989, 1997 and 2008. The approach was identical each time: a survey was made of a sample group representative of the French population aged 15 and over, stratified by region and population density, using the quota method taking variables of interviewees' gender and age as well as the social class of the head of the household, holding face-to-face interviews in the home of person interviewed. The sample size was as follows: 2000 individuals in 1973, 3000 in 1981, 5000 in 1989, 4353 in 1997 and 5000 in 2008.
The five survey questionnaires as well as most of the publications relating to the analysis of the results are available online at: www.pratiquesculturelles.culture.gouv.fr

27
Contesting the highbrow and lowbrow distinction
How Latin American scholars engage in cross-cultural debates

María Luisa Méndez

Introduction

Research regarding change in social structure as a by-product of neoliberal macro structural transformations has been ongoing for the past two decades in Latin America. Although this field has been taking shape in a relatively slow way, its attention to the broad effects of neoliberalism has been sustained (Filgueira and Geneletti 1981; CEPAL/ECLAC 1989, 2000; Filgueira 2001; Torche and Wormald, 2004; Atria 2004; Franco et al. 2007, among others). Given the expansion of the service sector and the explosion of a so-called consumer society (García Canclini 1989), one major focus of interest has been the study of the new urban middle classes as – arguably – the group that epitomizes processes of social and cultural change (Méndez 2010). This chapter will comment on studies conducted in the region on these groups, which are connected to broader and more pressing questions of cultural differentiation and the reshaping of social hierarchies in Latin America.

These concerns have exposed the limitations of traditional research on social stratification when it comes to understanding processes of cultural differentiation such as identity formation, lifestyles, symbolic boundaries, cultural repertoires of belonging, among other aspects. This chapter will try to show how – in the face of these limitations – the field of social stratification in this region has interacted with a certain kind of sociology of culture to find new directions for the study of the middle classes using a cultural lens. Special emphasis will be placed on the involvement of cultural capital in the formation and reformulation of social hierarchies in societies where there have been noteworthy processes of upward social mobility and the development of new urban middle classes.

Bourdieu's general approach regarding the power of cultural capital and the role of cultural fields in the reproduction of inequality has been shown to be particularly relevant for these concerns. Indeed, his contribution to a complex understanding of the role of cultural capital in the reproduction of inequalities is beyond question. This chapter will show, however, that the specific nature of these processes in the South American context differs from Bourdieu's formulation in his work *Distinction* (1984), where his perspective can be seen as Eurocentric. This chapter will attempt to question the extent to which, in other parts of the world, European reference points might be challenged.

We should nonetheless recognize that Bourdieu himself stressed the importance of avoiding taking concepts out of their original context of production and putting them into fields where they are adapted without knowledge of their origins. In the well-known paper, 'On the Cunning of Imperialist Reason', Bourdieu expressly supported the need to avoid a particular way of understanding theorization as the 'neutralization of historical context and the further universalization' (Bourdieu and Wacquant 1999: 41). According to Warczok and Zarycki (2014), Bourdieu argued that the flow of conceptual apparatuses into new contexts is usually employed in completely new struggles where local gatekeepers play a key role in 'arbitrarily select[ing] ideas from their original fields and using them in new contexts' (Warczok and Zarycki 2014: 336).

In this sense, as also argued by Swartz and Zolberg (2004), the concept of cultural capital as equated to highbrow culture has a particular trajectory and can be limiting. According to these authors, a more general understanding of cultural capital can be found in Bourdieu's work as the capacity of dominant groups 'to impose advantageous standards of evaluation whatever their form' (Swartz and Zolberg 2004: 7). Thus, in its conceptual flow from France to North America, cultural capital possibly 'became associated with "highbrow" aesthetic culture and became analytically and causally distinguished from technical forms of knowledge or competence' (Swartz and Zolberg 2004: 7). As put by Lareau and Weininger, 'cultural capital was intended to reflect the peculiarities of the French context that was being analyzed. Thus, the question arises whether Bourdieu considered congruity between educational norms and status practices to be essential to the concept of cultural capital, and, if so, whether they necessarily take a "highbrow" aesthetic form' (2004: 117).

This chapter will attempt to think in the terms proposed by Lamont's 'heterodox' interpretation of Bourdieu's influence on the sociology of culture (Lamont 2012). For this reason, the studies discussed below will, on the one hand, display various concepts that derive from Bourdieu's *oeuvre* such as symbolic boundaries or cultural repertoires, to name a few. This chapter will also try to connect the specific socio-political contexts in various countries in Latin America and the academic production that aims at understanding processes of cultural differentiation. To this extent, therefore, many responses to Bourdieu's 'canonical' way of thinking will be put forward.

According to Bennett *et al.* (2013) the portability of Bourdieu's concepts beyond their context of original production, as well as the use of his work across American and European sociology, has been a 'long-standing matter of concern, particularly in the work of Michèle Lamont (1992) and Loïc Wacquant (2007), both of whom have raised significant, largely sympathetic, questions regarding the transatlantic travelling capacity of Bourdieu's methods' (Bennett *et al.* 2013: 130). Regarding the work of Michèle Lamont on symbolic boundaries (Lamont 2012; Lamont *et al.* 2015, Lamont and Fournier 1992), it is worth mentioning that to a great extent it departs from Bourdieu's expectations in terms of the relationship between European and American reference points. Not only in the book *Money, Morals and Manner* (Lamont 1992) but also in the book *Rethinking Comparative Cultural Sociology* (Lamont and Thevenot 2000), Lamont takes a step further from Bourdieu's work on cultural differentiation in order to broaden the understanding of the mechanisms of differentiation: from those based on the appreciation of highbrow culture to those based on symbolic and moral boundaries.

According to Lamont, Pendergrass and Pachucki (2015) symbolic boundaries denote the exercise of classification in itself, both temporally, physically and symbolically. These can be conceptualized as 'lines that include and define some people, groups and things while excluding others (Epstein 1992: 232). These distinctions can be expressed through normative interdictions (taboos), cultural attitudes and practices, and patterns of likes and dislikes'

(Lamont, Pendergrass and Pachucki 2015: 1). In her book *Money, Morals and Manners: The Culture of the French and the American Upper-Middle Class* (1992) Lamont refers to the ways in which symbolic boundaries are shaped and re-shaped through life. She argues that cultural capital theory is helpful to clarify the relation between the operation of symbolic boundaries, the exercise of power and the reproduction of inequalities. One of the main points of the book, however, is a critique of cultural capital theory. As Lamont indicates, this theory underestimates the importance of moral boundaries, while exaggerating the importance of cultural and socioeconomic boundaries. She suggests people orient themselves in social space establishing cultural boundaries (which appeal to highbrow dispositions such as manners), or economic boundaries such as money. However, people also orient themselves according to moral boundaries, and cultural capital theory tends to conflate moral boundaries with cultural boundaries. As such, Lamont argues that Bourdieu's trajectory effect should also acknowledge the ways in which symbolic boundaries are constantly being shaped and how, in particular, moral boundaries might affect the trajectory of an agent. For example, according to Lamont, the boundary drawing activities of the upper middle class varies with the degree of instrumentality of their occupation.

Thus, these forms of cultural capital and cultural differentiation do not translate exactly along the lines of highbrow European legitimate culture, but address more precisely to other and various forms of legitimation of privilege (or advantageous standards in the words of Lareau and Weininger 2004). This chapter echoes these concerns and attempts to enrich 'the "ethos of usage" of Bourdieu's analytical categories' (Bennett *et al.* 2013: 135) by exploring not only Latin American scholars that have used Bourdieu's work on cultural differentiation, but also by connecting these uses to socio-political contexts of production.

Similarly to the case described in the Antipodean uptake (Bennett *et al.* 2013), Bourdieu has been mostly known in Latin America by his work in the field of the sociology of education and to a certain extent by his reflexive sociology of the nineties, particularly his views towards a more engaged practice of the discipline. As argued by Baranger (2008) Bourdieu's first works circulating in Latin America were those produced with Passeron, particularly *Reproduction* (1977). Over the 1990s, however, Bourdieu's theory of the habitus and his ideas about an engaged sociology gained more visibility, particularly with the book *Distinction* (1984), among others. This came to be most evident after his death, with the robust reception received by the book *An Invitation to a Reflexive Sociology* (with Wacquant 1992), which was first published in Spanish in 2005. It is not the concern of this chapter, however, to describe the influence of Bourdieu's work on Latin America sociological field per se. Rather, in thinking about the take-up of Bourdieu in Latin American it becomes pertinent to reflect largely on the ways in which Latin American scholars discussed here engage in cross-cultural debates, both theoretically and methodologically. As mentioned earlier in this chapter, the transition to neoliberalism and its consequences in terms of socio-cultural change challenged mainstream social sciences in Latin America, in that traditional approaches, specifically in terms of social stratification, proved to be insufficient to deeply understand emergent processes of social and cultural differentiation within the 'new' middle classes.

This chapter is structured around two sections. The first section considers work that has drawn upon Bourdieu's notion of cultural capital and related concepts such as symbolic boundaries in order to address the ways in which new/old social classes redefine their positions, identities and lifestyles in societies that are undergoing continual change. Notwithstanding that, however, this work also contests some of the premises of Bourdieu's ideas on the production and reproduction of inequality. This is particularly clear in the ways in which ethnic boundaries interact with class, and also in the relevant role of the American suburban lifestyle as a highly valuable cultural referent among certain segments of the middle classes. In the second part of this chapter I offer my contribution to this field of research, providing a critical stance toward Bourdieu's concept of habitus. In doing so, I use the work of Michèle Lamont regarding processes of boundary making, and the salience of moral boundaries in socio-cultural differentiation to argue that authenticity claims within middle class interviewees show processes of moral boundary making, which appears as a particular form of sociocultural differentiation.

Socio political context: Neoliberalism, lifestyles and class identities in Latin America

This first section presents work developed in Latin America during the last two decades that focuses on lifestyles and consumption, tastes, and middle class identities. To a great extent, these studies have as a common backdrop the problematization of change in the social structure in some countries of the region and the impact of neoliberalism. Inspired by Pierre Bourdieu's *Distinction* (see Bennett et al. 2009 for a review of the field), Latin American notions of lifestyle and cultural resources have become central to understanding the making of social hierarchies. Notwithstanding this, however, the ways in which scholars have engaged in these debates has been highly variable: accounts in the 1990s were largely influenced by Bourdieu's contribution to the debate on structure and agency and the concept of habitus; others have more recently been influenced by his work on the experience of social mobility and the accumulation of various forms of capital. Various scholars have been interested in Bourdieu's ways of understanding cultural practices as forms of reproducing inequality (Gayo, Teitelboim and Méndez 2013; Wortman 2003); while others have focused on his ideas of taste, distinction, and inequality (Arizaga 2005).

However, this literature does not necessarily share the same concern in referring to processes of social change and cultural differentiation: in Argentinean sociology, there is a tendency to consider the middle class from the point of view of its crisis and downward social mobility; while in Chile[1] the growth and heterogenization of this sector is emphasized. In Peru, Ecuador and Bolivia questions related to class, gender and racial identity are stressed; and in Brazil, there is special focus on the processes of expanding consumption, among others.

At the end of the 1990s, a group of researchers in Peru met to reflect on the characteristics of a social group that was starting to differentiate themselves in a new way within a traditionally stratified country: the rural, regional and ethnic new middle classes. This research was compiled in the book *Las clases medias: entre la pretensión y la incertidumbre* [The Middle Classes: Between Pretention and Uncertainty] (Portocarrero 1998), which explores the formation and class identity of the new middle classes in Peru from the end of the 1970s. It is argued that processes of structural adjustment (Veltmeyer et al. 1997) as well as political violence provoked a crisis that strongly affected the petty bourgeoisie (Stein and Monge 1998), and offered social mobility routes for an emerging sector stemming from the peasant culture of the regions. This group did not share the values of the traditional salaried, professional and urban middle class of Lima, nor did they accumulate symbolic and cultural capital in the same way. Rather, they exposed an ethnic and regional identity linked to the Andean world. Thus, the authors argue that ethnic and regional boundaries which were traditionally key axes of social stratification were becoming weaker, and meritocratic principles based on education were gaining prominence. This transition especially impacted Lima's social structure and opened greater spaces for the new ethnic and regional urban middle classes.

As this ground breaking study shows, the axes of high and lowbrow culture do not necessarily work as described by Bourdieu in *Distinction*. Rather, in this case, ethnic boundaries play a particularly relevant role in cultural and social differentiation. '*Entre la pretensión y la incertidumbre*' exhibits binary oppositions between regional culture and the dominant culture of Lima, between urban and rural, etc., and shows cases of both the reproduction of, and resistance to traditional social hierarchies of class, gender, and race. The case of the middle class of Peru, particularly in Lima, shows how urban belonging is affirmed through alluding to these oppositions, but not exactly along the lines exposed by Bourdieu.

In a similar vein, the book *The Native Leisure Class* (Colloredo-Mansfeld 1999) shows processes of social mobility in the case of the ethnic group the Otavaleros, in Ecuador. These craftsmen joined a thriving economy linked to the handmade fabrics, and among them, new generations appropriated *modern* devices of material culture (such as televisions) while revitalizing and re-signifying traditional practices and tastes of their ancestral cultures. As Colleredo-Mansfeld notes, this group is seen as an emerging urban lower middle class who have embraced more firmly their Andean collective identities, and somehow have been able to reverse certain historical processes of domination, traditionally tied to populations of mestizo and European descent.

In the case of Bolivia, Himpele (2003) shows how since the 1980s, mestizo revolutionary ideologies of the middle class tried to install an idea of a mestizo nation, particularly linked to the development and consolidation of the neoliberal model. In this work, Himpele develops an ethnography of the religious procession *El Gran Poder* in La Paz, where thousands of lower middle class Aymara and mestizo residents participate in a religious activity that expresses a syncretic identity, and subverts the historical marginalization of ethnic cultures. The reaffirmation of indigenous cultural identity involves a worship to the *cholas* culture and particularly a gratitude to the patron of the church of the 'entrepreneur and the prosperous' (Himpele 2003). Thus, according to Himpele, the mestizo and Aymara middle class is able to reject not only the ideologies of a mestizo nation but also a certain Western middle class identity, in search of an identity authentic to their cultural roots.

Although these studies exhibit various theoretical approaches, they reflect a common attempt to show processes not only of cultural differentiation but mostly of distinction and rejection of dominant culture. This is particularly clear in terms of symbolic boundaries at work in cultural tastes, lifestyles, sexualities, ethnicities, among others. In a similar line as proposed by Meuleman and Savage (2013), it is possible to see how the interactions with cosmopolitan tastes 'do not simply erode national boundaries but may actually create new stakes which differentiate within nations' (Meuleman and Savage 2013: 231). In particular, the interaction between indigenous and mestizo identities as well as with global cultures does not necessarily imply a subordination of the former to the latter. Following Calhoun (2012) we can see a possible reconstruction of national forms of cultural differentiation where more referents are at play (ethnic, national and global).

In these studies, cultural differentiation and boundary making practices of the new rural/urban middle classes shows that there is no single and neat coupling with global cultural referents such as the 'refined' European identity or the 'modern' American one. This argument has resonances with the findings of Bennett *et al.* on the Antipodean take of Bourdieu's work in that the:

> increasing presence of indigenous culture within different cultural fields and, indeed, the development of connections between Indigenous cultural practices across these fields to an extent suggests the emergence of autonomous Indigenous cultural fields with their

own properties, agents and regimes of value that traverse, and trouble, mainstream fields in a number of ways.

(Bennett et al. 2013: 140)

In the case of Argentina, questions about the 'old' and the 'new' urban middle classes have had as a backdrop processes such as downward mobility in the midst of hyperinflation in the 1980s and unemployment in the 1990s. Here, the concepts of the 'new poor' (Minujin and Anguita 2004; Kessler and Di Virgilio, 2008); the 'new bourgeois' in Wortman (2003), the 'winners and losers' of Svampa (2001) were commonly used to account for these new segments: some in a situation of growing precariousness and others increasingly distant (socially and physically) from the rest of society.

The book *Desde Abajo: la transformación de las identidades sociales* [From Below: The Transformation of Social Identities] (Svampa 2000) draws on the work of Bourdieu to show the 'experience of transition' or, in other words, the way in which (downward) life trajectories are experienced and how these trajectories affect the perception of one's place in the world and one's personal identity. Following this line of research, in the book *Los que ganaron: la vida en los countries y barrios privados* [The Winners: Life in Gated Communities], Svampa (2001) studies the opposite case: the configuration of the upper middle classes in Argentina and processes of self-segregation in the suburbs of Buenos Aires. This text revolves around the idea of 'social fracture', and at the same time, it uses the concept of social boundaries to refer to how gated communities (*countries* in Spanish) symbolically and physically separate the upper middle classes from the rest of society, primarily by accumulating privileges, but above all, exacerbating a feeling of fear of the 'other'.[2] In fact, the use that Svampa makes of social boundaries has to do with the crystallization of new social and cultural repertoires which are ubiquitous elements of the neoliberal model imposed in the country. These encompass new ways of appreciating the 'other' and of acting in daily life, for example, 'winners and losers' or 'those who could make it and those who failed'. Such categories serve to socially and physically define an 'inside' and an 'outside'. The idea is that the Argentinian upper middle class finds itself in a:

> process of elaborating a whole new collective cultural frame (*marco de vida colectivo*) that aims at improving life quality, particularly for children, and that implies the enactment of physical boundaries that delineate a tangible separation between the inside and outside world and an indubitable register of 'us' and 'them': between those who are alike and those who are different. Thus, the categorisation of the difference appears as an intrinsic element of the model of social organisation of gated communities.
>
> (Svampa 2001: 254)

In this case, however, and similarly in the case of Chile, discussed later in this chapter, processes of cultural differentiation promote a suburban kind of lifestyle, in which the image of the 'winners' is the main character. Here, the cultural referent is not an established, traditional European referent, but an American one.

From a different angle, Ana Wortman has looked at the case of the 'new bourgeois' in Argentina, exploring their lifestyles (Wortman 2004) and cultural consumption (Wortman 2003). In the books *Pensar las clases medias: consumos culturales y estilos de vida urbanos en la Argentina de los noventa* [Considering the Middle Classes: Cultural Consumption and Urban Lifestyles in the Argentina of the Nineties] and *Imágenes publicitarias/nuevos burgueses* [Advertising Images/ New Bourgeois], Wortman delves into the interdisciplinary work of a group of researchers interested in understanding the role of culture in the formation of a 'new' social class. These books display less of a 'highbrow' notion of cultural capital, and instead show how a 'trendy' cultural capital is more relevant in processes of recent cultural differentiation within the urban middle classes:

> we can observe the presence of new social actors whose work dynamic differs from those of the old middle classes, for example, there are changes in everyday life and family morality, child raising, the use of time, the perception of domestic space, house design and decoration, etc.
>
> *(Wortman 2004: 20)*

Bourdieu's work is used extensively to account for the emergence of varying lifestyles among sections of the middle class whose cultural capital is in tension with the appropriation of urban spaces.[3]

The case of the Brazilian middle class has been examined by Maureen O'Dougherty in the book '*Consumption Intensified*' (O'Dougherty 2002), which shows how – after the economic crisis (inflation) of the late 1980s/early 1990s – the middle classes in São Paulo experienced a redefinition of class identity through daily practices and discourses aimed at reaffirming their class position. By owning a house and a car, as well as by accumulating educational credentials, or travelling abroad, O'Dougherty argues the upper, university trained middle classes in São Paulo developed a sense of cosmopolitanism, which was reinforced through their consumer lifestyles (Parker 2002). In this case, consumption of both traditional and modern means of distinction in neoliberal societies (travelling to Disney World, having a maid, having a debutante ball, attending private-elite schools) constituted a way out of economic crisis. This book is particularly interesting in terms of showing how cultural and social differentiation is mediated by local and global consumption.

This first section has shown how, in the face of the transition to neoliberalism in Latin America, the question of cultural and social differentiation has been addressed. Various authors have drawn upon Bourdieu's work on cultural capital and concepts such as symbolic boundaries in order to examine the ways in which new/old social classes redefine their positions, identities and lifestyles in societies undergoing change. Moreover, the work of these scholars shows how socio-political contexts interact with and contest some of the premises of Bourdieu's ideas on the production and reproduction of inequality. This is particularly clear in the way ethnic boundaries interact with class, the relevant role of the American suburban lifestyle as a highly valuable cultural referent among certain segments of the middle classes, and also in the role of consumption in redefining class positions.

Authenticity claims within the urban middle classes: Boundary making and the use of global cultural referents

In this section I offer my contribution to this field of research. I will outline my work on the practices of boundary making within the middle classes in Santiago. My argument is rather different than Bourdieu's, in that I found highbrow and lowbrow culture to work as opposite poles offering valid and legitimate taste hierarchies, both of which are actively appropriated and contested by middle class individuals.

Following Bourdieu's work on *Distinction* (Bourdieu 1984) and *Pascalian Meditations* (Bourdieu 2000), I use the idea of *malaise* or unease in order to reflect on the ways in which upward social mobility is experienced and how it entails a mismatch between habitus and field (particularly new residential fields) (Méndez and Gayo, 2007; Méndez, 2008). These ideas allow me to describe the tensions that exist between different fractions of the middle class in Chile (upwardly and downwardly mobile). Using life histories of middle class families residing in Santiago, I explore competing narratives of middle class identity and the tensions between various types of class habitus in Santiago: the 'intellectuals', the 'average people' and the 'emerging upper middle class'.[4] My argument is that the increasing heterogeneity or heterogenization of the urban middle classes entails processes of differentiation that are both vertical (hierarchical) and horizontal as described in Bourdieu's work on the lifestyles of the middle classes in *Distinction*.

In my work symbolic boundaries also act as spatial distinctions between different groups which are producing competing narratives of belonging to the city. Such horizontal differentiation involves tension between competing middle class identities. Bourdieu – in some sense – addresses this problematic in *The Logic of Practice* when he contends that:

> contrary to the physicalist self-evidence which assumes that, in the case of continuous distribution, difference diminishes as proximity in the distribution grows, perceived differences are not objective differences, and social neighborhood, the site of the last difference, has every chance of also being the point of greatest tension. Minimum objective distance in social space can coincide with maximum subjective distance. This is partly because what is 'closest' presents the greatest threat to social identity, that is, differences (and also because the adjustment of expectations to real chances tends to limit subjective pretensions to the immediate neighborhood). The logic of the symbolic makes absolute 'all or nothing' differences out of infinitesimal differences.
>
> *(Bourdieu 1990: 137)*

However, and similarly to the qualitative data collected by Bennett *et al.* (2009), I also affirm that in order to establish these boundaries, my middle class interviewees do not only relate to national culture, but exhibit a complex variety of cultural referents and repertoires (Méndez 2008), evoking 'referents and icons from diverse locations' (Bennett *et al.* 2009: 238), particularly American and European cultures. I argue that they refer to global kinds of tastes, associated to European ('intellectuals') and American ('emerging upper middle class') lifestyles, both of which are used to construct global cosmopolitan identities (Méndez, 2008). In my research I have also found that people tend to associate the former with a more mature, older and sophisticated taste and the latter with a more modern and consumerist one (also stated by Lamont (1992) and Meuleman and Savage (2013). In terms of the symbolic boundaries at work, my study shows that Santiago's city centre is associated with a European aura that is commonly stressed in opposition to 'empty' spaces such as those 'outside' of the city, including communes and suburban areas that are frequently associated with a US oriented culture (see Table 27.1).

In this sense, European taste would seem to be a 'safer' taste for people to refer to, as it is more established. However, there is a tension between being 'intellectual' or 'trendy' and being 'authentic' or true to one's origins. In other words, in my interviews, people were critical of the extent to which European or US oriented aesthetics are sometimes at odds with a '*distinctive Chilean culture*'.

In the case of American taste, on the other hand, whereas it seems to be associated with economic progress, modernization and the emergence of a new economic elite, it is also linked to the 'corruption' of national culture. However, and despite this critique, it is interesting to note that there is a neat appeal of US oriented culture within the privileged and upwardly mobile sections of the upper middle class in Santiago (those that live in the

Table 27.1 Santiago: European aura of the city centre versus American dream of suburbia

European aura of the city centre	American dream of suburbia
Public space	Private space
Place for strolling	Place to retreat
Full place	Empty place
In the city	Out of the city
Highbrow (based on canonical taste)	Emergent lowbrow (although different from folk or working class culture)
Pretentious	Consumerist
Intellectuals/trendy people	Families/average person
Legitimate/consecrated taste	Modern taste
Heritage	Affluence

suburban areas), particularly in terms of the ways in which this new and modern taste – mostly related to consumption – constitutes a legitimate emergent lowbrow culture. In other words, it also entails a certain sense of authenticity (in opposition to a highbrow taste that appears more canonical in terms of its patterns of appreciation).

These findings show how highbrow culture crystalized in European taste which is not the only taste hierarchy at play. As opposed to Bourdieu's axes of differentiation, which are 'implicitly premised on a Eurocentric, indeed more precisely Franco-centric, model of cultural hierarchy' (Meuleman and Savage 2013: 232), my work shows that both highbrow and lowbrow culture are under scrutiny, with some elements more celebrated than others. In this sense, my work resonates with Bennett *et al.* (2009) in terms of emphasizing the need to understand the implications of cultural capital in relation to social reproduction, beyond and not solely within the bounded national fields. As these authors suggest, 'different kinds of trans-national identifications are themselves key components of cultural capital. ... Cultural capital is not organized purely within a national frame of reference, but deploys a complex, though contested, cultural geography' (Bennett *et al.* 2009: 250).

At the same time, my work also resembles Lamont's (1992) argument in which she asserts there are times when cultural standards – which are at the core of the definition of taste – are questioned; not through the same lenses of that particular doxa, but by trying to subordinate them to moral ones. I argue that the distinction between authentic and artificial could be considered as an example of this. In fact, there are different ways of understanding what authenticity is. For some of my interviewees, *being authentic* has to do with avoiding 'posing' and being *too* different to the extent of denying the 'origins' (ethnic, class, national culture, etc.). This is mostly related to intellectualism and being 'trendy', but also to being a 'social climber'. For others, it has to do with being able to resist and fight homogenization and consumerism (Méndez 2008).

In this sense, as argued by Meuleman and Savage (2013),

> cultural capital may involve familiarity with cultural reference points from a wider variety of geographical areas, not just within a particular national culture or from the classical European tradition. Therefore, rather than national fields being simply eclipsed by transnational fields, they co-exist with differing degrees of salience for specific social groups and across various cultural domains.
>
> *(Meuleman and Savage 2013: 234)*

As my findings show, highbrow and lowbrow culture work as opposite poles but both of them offer valid and legitimate taste hierarchies, which are actively appropriated and contested by middle class individuals.

Conclusions

This chapter has described and commented on a number of recent studies that look at the current state of Latin American societies after two or more decades of social restructuring under the neoliberal umbrella. They draw upon a Bourdieusian framework and engage with theories of cultural differentiation and symbolic classification to explore the reshaping of social hierarchies at the level of urban life in societies characterized by new and noteworthy forms of upward social mobility. This body of research addresses questions regarding processes of production, contestation and reformulation of symbolic, moral and cultural boundaries. The various accounts exhibit a common concern: how to account for the supposedly distinctive and new character of the middle classes in Latin America, particularly in the context of economic, political and cultural change. Most of these studies also point to a process in which the middle classes have moved from being a rather homogeneous group (mainly salaried and professionals) to a group that is more heterogeneous and diverse in its social composition, with varied trajectories of social mobility and distinct ethnic and social identities, tastes, etc.

This chapter has engaged with the wide and diverse debate about the portability of Bourdieu's categories (Bennett *et al.* 2013), and specifically a common concern about processes of boundary making and inequality reproduction. The studies discussed above show how cultural oppositions are still crucial in the justification of social hierarchies, particularly in the residential field: there is a strong spatial angle involved in this process because residential claims of belonging increasingly account for class identity in societies that have recently experienced marked processes of social mobility and the development of new (urban) middle classes. Notwithstanding that, however, the specific nature of these processes in the South American context contests canonical Bourdieusian understandings. The South American evidence indicates that cultural differentiation does not translate exactly along the lines of highbrow European legitimate culture; ethnic boundaries play a particularly relevant role in cultural and social differentiation, and global cultural referents do not necessarily subordinate national and indigenous forms of cultural differentiation.

Funding

This chapter received support from the Center for Social and Cohesion Studies, COES (Centro CONICYT / FONDAP/15130009) an FONDECYT project 1140136.

Notes

1 In the case of Chile, most studies have agreed in noting that there was a growth in this segment that reached almost half the population of the country (approximately 45%). However, this figure contrasts with self-perceptions of class position as reported by those polled: more than 70% of respondents identify with the middle class. This 'contradiction' or discrepancy could reinforce arguments in favour of a transition from a period extending from the 1920s to the 1970s in which a homogeneous middle class predominated (Cerda 1998; Barozet 2002) to another period characterized by the heterogeneization of this segment.
2 This work resonates with the work of Teresa Caldeira (2000) *City of Walls*.

3 One of the authors that we might highlight in this area is Cecilia Arizaga, who develops Williams' concept of 'structure of sentiment' to account for processes of urbanization and stylization in the daily life of the middle classes in Buenos Aires. In her book, *El mito de comunidad en la sociedad global* [The Myth of Community in the Global Society] (Arizaga 2005), new globalized practices, such as the fashion for organic food, feng shui, and others, are presented.
4 Based on an ethnographic study, Stillerman (2010) also identifies three groups within the urban middle classes in Santiago: left-wing intelligentsia, successful professionals, and lower middle class. According to Stillerman these groups differentiate on four key aspects through which they claim a symbolically distinctive lifestyle: their patterns of consumption, child-rearing, education, and identity. Also inspired by the work of Lamont (1992), Stillerman asserts that these competing groups are permanently negotiating their boundaries.

References

Arizaga, M. C. (2005) *El Mito de Comunidad en la Ciudad Mundializada: Estilos de Vida y Nuevas Clases Medias en Urbanizaciones Cerradas*, Buenos Aires, Ediciones El Cielo por Asalto.
Atria, R. (2004) 'Estructura ocupacional, estructura social y clases sociales', *Serie Políticas Sociales*, 96, Santiago, Chile: CEPAL.
Baranger, D. (2008) 'The Reception of Bourdieu in Latin America and Argentina', *Sociologica*, No. 2.
Barozet, E. (2002). 'L'échange de faveurs au sein des couches moyennes chiliennes: de l'entraide informelle à la régulation sociale', *Paris, École des Hautes Études en Sciences Sociales*: 341.
Bennett, T., J. Frow, G. Hage and G. Noble (2013) 'Antipodean Fields: Working with Bourdieu', *Journal of Sociology*, 49 (2–3): 129–150.
Bennett T., M. Savage, E.B. Silva, A. Warde, M. Gayo-Cal and D. Wright (2009) *Culture, Class, Distinction*, New York: Routledge.
Bourdieu, P. (1984) *Distinction: A Social Critique of the Judgment of Taste*, London: Routledge and Kegan Paul.
—— (1990) *The Logic of Practice*, Stanford, California: Stanford University Press.
—— (2000) *Pascalian meditations*, Cambridge: Polity Press
Bourdieu, P. and J.C. Passeron (1977) *Reproduction in Education, Society and Culture*, London: Sage.
Bourdieu, P. and L. Wacquant (1992) *An Invitation to Reflexive Sociology*, Chicago: University of Chicago Press.
—— (1999) 'On the Cunning of Imperialist Reason', *Theory, Culture & Society*, 16 (1): 41–58.
Caldeira, T. (2000) City of Walls: Crime, Segregation, and Citizenship in São Paulo, Berkeley: University of California Press.
Calhoun, C. (2012) 'Cosmopolitan Liberalism and Its Limits', in A. S. Krossa and R. Robertson (eds.) *European Cosmopolitanism in Question. Europe in a Global Context*. Basingstoke: Palgrave Macmillan, Basingstoke.
CEPAL/ECLAC (1989) *Transformación ocupacional y crisis social en América Latina*, Santiago: Reporte Naciones Unidas (UN Report).
—— (2000) *Panorama social de América Latina. 1999–2000*. Santiago: Reporte Naciones Unidas (UN Report).
Cerda, C. (1998). *Historia y desarrollo de la clase media en Chile*, Santiago: UTEM.
Colloredo-Mansfeld, R. (1999) *The Native Leisure Class: Consumption and Cultural Creativity in the Andes*, Chicago: The University of Chicago Press.
Epstein, C. F. (1992) 'Tinker-Bells and Pinups: The Construction and Reconstruction of Gender Boundaries at Work', in Lamont M. and Fournier M. (eds.) *Cultivating Differences: Symbolic Boundaries and the Making of Inequality*. Chicago: University of Chicago Press.
Filgueira, C. (2001). 'La actualidad de viejas temáticas: sobre los estudios de clase, estratificación y movilidad social en América Latina', Santiago: CEPAL: 41.
Filgueira, C. and C. Geneletti (1981) 'Estratificación y Movilidad Ocupacional en America Latina', Santiago, Chile: CEPAL.
Franco, R., R. Atria and A. León (eds.) (2007) *Estratificación y movilidad social en América Latina. Transformaciones estructurales en un cuarto de siglo*, Santiago: LOM/CEPAL/GTZ.
García Canclini, N. (1989) *Culturas híbridas: Estrategias para entrar y salir de la modernidad*, México: Grijalbo.
Gayo, M., B. Teitelboim and M.L. Méndez (2013) 'Exclusividad y fragmentación: los perfiles culturales de la clase media en Chile', *Revista Universum*, 28 (1): 97–128.

Himpele, J. (2003) 'The Gran Poder Parade and the Social Movement of the Aymara Middle Class: A Video Essay', *Visual Anthropology*, 16: 207–243.

Kessler, G. and M. Di Virgilio (2008) 'La nueva pobreza urbana: dinámica global, regional y argentina en las últimas dos décadas', *Revista de la CEPAL*, N°95: 31–50.

Lamont, M. (1992) *Money, Morals, and Manners: The Culture of the French and American Upper-Middle Class*, Chicago; London: University of Chicago Press.

—— (2012) 'How Has Bourdieu Been Good to Think With? The Case of the United States', *Sociological Forum*, 27(1): 228–237.

Lamont, M. and M. Fournier, (eds.) (1992) *Cultivating Differences: Symbolic Boundaries and the Making of Inequality*, Chicago: University of Chicago Press.

Lamont, M., S. Pendergrass and M. Pachucki (2015) 'Symbolic Boundaries', in J. Wright (ed.) *International Encyclopedia of Social and Behavioral Sciences*, Oxford: Elsevier.

Lamont, M. and L. Thevenot, (eds.) (2000) *Rethinking Comparative Cultural Sociology: Repertoires of Evaluation in France and the United States*, London: Cambridge University Press and Paris: Presses de la Maison des sciences de l'homme.

Lareau, A. and E. B. Weininger (2004) 'Cultural Capital in Educational Research: A Critical Assessment, in Swartz, D. and V. Zolberg (eds.) *After Bourdieu. Influence, Critique, Elaboration*, New York: Klumer Academic Publishers.

Méndez, M. L. (2008) 'Middle Class Identities in a Neoliberal Age: Tensions between Contested Authenticities', *The Sociological Review*, 56 (2): 220–237.

—— (2010) 'Clases medias en Chile: Transformaciones, sentido de pertenencia y tensiones entre proyectos de movilidad' en *Las clases medias en América Latina: Retrospectiva y nuevas tendencias'*, Hopenhayn, M., R. Franco, and A. León (eds.), México; Buenos Aires: Editorial Siglo XXI.

Méndez, M. L. and Gayo, M. (2007) El perfil de un debate: movilidad y meritocracia. Contribución al estudio de las sociedades latinoamericanas, in *Estratificación y movilidad social en América Latina. Transformaciones estructurales en un cuarto de siglo*. R. Franco, León, León, Arturo, et al. Santiago: LOM/CEPAL/GTZ: 121–154.

Meuleman, R. and M. Savage (2013) A Field Analysis of Cosmopolitan Taste: Lessons from the Netherlands, *Cultural Sociology*, vol. 7 no. 2: 230–256.

Minujin, A. and E. Anguita (2004) *La clase media : Seducida y abandonada*, Buenos Aires: Editorial: Edhasa.

O'Dougherty, M. (2002) *Consumption Intensified: The Politics of Middle-Class Daily Life in. Brazil*. Durham: Duke University Press.

Parker, D.S. (2002) 'Consumption Intensified: The Politics of Middle-Class Daily Life in Brazil' (review), *The Devil in Latin America, The Americas*, 59 (2): 258–259.

Portocarrero, G. (1998) *Las clases medias: entre la pretensión y la incertidumbre*, Lima: Sur, Casa de Estudios del Socialismo.

Stein, S. and C. Monge (1998) *La crisis en el estado patrimonial en el Perú*, Lima: Instituto de Estudios Peruanos.

Stillerman, J. (2010) The Contested Spaces of Chile's Middle Classes, *Political Power and Social Theory* Vol. 21: 209–238.

Svampa, M. (ed.) (2000) *Desde abajo. La transformación de las identidades sociales*, Buenos Aires: Universidad de General Sarmiento/Biblos.

—— (2001) *Los que ganaron. Vida y sociabilidad en los barrios cerrados de Buenos Aires*, Buenos Aires: Biblos.

Swartz, D. and V. Zolberg (eds.) (2004) *After Bourdieu. Influence, Critique, Elaboration*, New York: Klumer Academic Publishers.

Torche, F. and G. Wormald (2004) *Estratificación y movilidad social en Chile: entre la adscripción y el logro*, Santiago: CEPAL.

Veltmeyer, H., J. Petras and S. Vieux (1997) *Neoliberalism and Class Conflict in Latin America: A Comparative Perspective on the Political Economy of Structural Adjustment* (International Political Economy Series), Basingstoke: Macmillan.

Wacquant, L. (2007) *Urban outcasts: a comparative sociology of advanced marginality*, Cambridge: Polity.

Warczok, T. and T. Zarycki, (2014) 'Bourdieu Recontextualized: Redefinitions of Western Critical Thought in the Periphery', *Current Sociology*, vol. 62 no. 3: 334–351

Wortman, A. (2003) 'Pensar las clases medias. Consumos culturales y estilos de vida urbanos en la Argentina de los 90', Editorial La Crujía Ediciones, Edición Buenos Aires.

—— (2004) 'Nuevos intermediaros culturales y la construcción de hegemonía' in Antonelli, M. (ed.) *Cartografías de la Argentina de los noventa. Cultura mediática, política y sociedad*. Buenos Aires: Ferreyra Editores.

28
The structuration of lifestyles in the city of Porto
A relational approach

Virgílio Borges Pereira

Introduction

Based on an interpretation of the sociological legacy of Pierre Bourdieu's work, with a particular focus on the reading of *Distinction*, this chapter shows the potential of this perspective to understand the configuration of the space of lifestyles in the city of Porto, Portugal. For this purpose, the paper includes the information from an 'extended case study' on the city between 1998 and 2001. Specifically, it proposes a relational reading of the cultural practices and of the preferences of social agents questioned during the course of the research in light of the analytical programme developed by Bourdieu, using the Multiple Correspondence Analysis technique. Following this exercise, the paper also intends to explore the social composition underlying the identified relational configuration. This approach is then linked with a reading of some of the results from sociological research works that have replicated and innovated studies on cultural practices and tastes, and, based on the ethnographies that completed the analysis of the case of Porto, gives us food for thought on the relevance of the input of Pierre Bourdieu's theory for the analysis of the configurations of relationships between culture and class in the contemporary city.

On *Distinction* and its relevance to the study of relationships between culture and society

Associated with the gradual preparation of the *theory of practice* and its core concepts – *habitus*, *capital* and *field* – Bourdieu significantly reformulated the sociological understanding of the notion of social class, providing a refreshing reading of the relationships built between culture and social classes (Wacquant 2013). This reformulation is prefigured in an extensive body of work that Bourdieu prepared since mid-1960s, on the social structure of time experiences in Algeria (Bourdieu et al. 1963; Bourdieu 1977a and 1977b) and on the social, educational and cultural contradictions underlying the development process of post-war French society (Bourdieu 1966). This reformulation, however, materialised only in the 1970s with the publication of 'L'anatomie du goût' (Bourdieu and Saint-Martin 1976) and especially *Distinction* (Bourdieu 1979).[1]

Distinction builds on the critique of the Kantian aesthetics and inspiration received from works such as those by Baxandall (1972), and looks into the social production of aesthetic taste and its insertion into everyday life. Taking advantage of the statistical technique of Multiple Correspondence Analysis (MCA) (Rouanet, Ackermann and Le Roux 2000) and aligned with different ethnographical approaches, Bourdieu develops a three-pronged theorization of the social space, in which the social divides are interpreted in a relational manner, first based on how the agents are distributed according to the *overall volume of capital* they hold. The second divide here is interpreted according to the *structure of the composition* of the agents' different *capitals*, in particular the relationship between economic capital and cultural capital. Finally, in a third moment, greater stress is put on the *trajectory in time* of the capital held by the agents (Bourdieu 1984: 114ff.). Building on Max Weber's concerns (1978), *lifestyles* are addressed by Bourdieu as one of the core dimensions of the class formation processes, and as an active element in the struggle for practical and symbolic legitimization of inequalities. Sustaining the relevance of a structural homology between the social space and the space of lifestyles, Bourdieu proposes a specific reading of the processes here in question:

> In cultural consumption, the main opposition, by overall capital value, is between the practices designated by their rarity as distinguished, those of the fractions richest in both economic and cultural capital, and the practices socially identified as vulgar because they are both easy and common, those of the fractions poorest in both these respects. In the intermediate position are the practices which are perceived as pretentious, because of the manifest discrepancy between ambition and possibilities.
>
> *(Bourdieu 1984: 176)*

Looking in detail at each of the three major regions in the social space – dominant, intermediate and subordinate – from the perspective of the relationships between classes and culture, Bourdieu pinpoints, among those who occupy the dominant positions in the space, the importance of the variations to which the *distinct* lifestyles are subject, and highlights the specific weight of the *bourgeois* and of *intellectual* taste (Bourdieu 1984: 283ff.). He emphasises, among those occupying intermediate positions, the variations around the principle of *sacrifice* that pervades the structure of cultural practices, lived *tensely* (pre-tensely and pretentious, in Bourdieu's words) and geared towards more *conventional* tastes or greater *cultural goodwill*, depending on the social composition of those responsible for them (Bourdieu 1984: 339ff.). He stresses the specific weight of endured domination and *necessity* among those who occupy subordinate regions of the social space, not without recognising the variation at the margins around this deprivation, which are the result of a differentiated composition of capitals held by the agents (Bourdieu 1984: 372ff.) and, obviously, of their social history.

In addition to coordinating objectivism and phenomenology (Bourdieu and Wacquant 1992), the analytical effort represented by *Distinction* takes a refreshing look at the social divides in contemporary societies, which opens doors to the development of an empirical research project on the processes of social and cultural structuring of social classes. Besides the specific works of Bourdieu and his team, who continued this research project (see, in particular, Bourdieu 1989), a significant number of studies have contributed to following the empirical path suggested, showing that Bourdieu's findings are not restricted to France in the 1960s and 1970s. Since we do not have the scope to thoroughly document this body of work,[2] we will focus on three recent studies.

In a study dedicated to the city of Aalborg, in Denmark, Prieur, Rosenlund and Skjott-Larsen (2008) showed the relevance of a relational approach to the city's social space, emphasizing the importance of volume and how the composition of agents' capital is structured. Among various implications, this reading is decisive, as the authors argue, in establishing directions for understanding the relationship to culture among the social agents of the city under study. In addition to providing sustained evidence of the importance of social divisions in the structuring of cultural tastes, thus not supporting the well-known theses of Beck and Giddens on the individualization and fragmentation of tastes, the authors emphazise the importance of a relational view of cultural capital and the fact that it is likely to be mobilized in the framework of material and symbolic relationships of domination which are socio-historically constructed: '(...) cultural capital should be seen as an entity embedded in social contexts, and also as an entity in perpetual change' (Prieur, Rosenlund and Skjott-Larsen 2008: 50). To this they add two other meaningful elements. One contributes to the debate around *omnivorousness* (Peterson) and *snobbery* and stresses the differences in taste of those with social positions in distinct regions of the social space. The other element highlights the meaning of the relationship between cosmopolitanism and the predominance of cultural capital (Prieur, Rosenlund and Skjott-Larsen 2008: 63–67).

Bennett and his colleagues (2009) developed a relational portrait of cultural practices in the UK, defining a significant set of regularities in the British space of lifestyles. In this space, the authors identify very strong differences between cultural involvement and cultural estrangement, between culturally established tastes and more commercial forms, between inward and outward dispositions, and moderate *versus* intense cultural involvements. The way the differences in the space of lifestyles fall in line with the social background also reveals well-defined characteristics. Although the authors' conclusions are not identical to Bourdieu's findings, their research shows that fundamental cultural divisions are based on class, and the remaining differences are, respectively, age and gender sensitive, and they are also sensitive to differences within the middle class groups (Bennett *et al.* 2009: 43–57).

From an approach wholly consistent with Prieur *et al.*'s study on Aalborg, Rosenlund (2009) examines the case of Stavanger, in Norway, showing the heuristic value of the volume and structure of capital composition to interpret how social inequalities and distances are (re)produced locally, and their contributions to the analysis of cultural practices and representations. Besides being a challenging analysis of the construction of local social space, Rosenlund's study also includes an additional exercise on the construction of a space of lifestyles. Taking as a reference information on the symbolic dimension in the fields of elective affinities and their representations, on the uses and representations of the domestic space, on the practiced cultural activities and on political representations, the author documents a framework of symbolic divisions clearly set around accumulated cultural capital and another driven by the accumulation of economic capital, thus giving heuristic suggestions about the homology between the space of lifestyles and the space of social positions (Rosenlund 2009: 164–177).

It is therefore clear that Bourdieu's ideas have proved productive in recent research in three nations. Let us now turn to consider whether this is also true in the results of a sociological study on the city of Porto, in Portugal.

On the space of lifestyles in Porto in the early 2000s

Usually considered as Portugal's second city, Porto (located in the north of the country) is the capital of a metropolitan region with about 1.2 million people. Following a period of significant economic and demographic growth, in the late twentieth century the city experienced a drop in population growth and a profound change in its productive fabric. Whereas demographic loss largely resulted from young adults moving to peripheral areas and population ageing, economic transformation was marked by an intensive process of de-industrialization, leading to precarious wage relationships and unemployment, much of which was structural. Even though all these processes are important, when comparing the city with the surrounding metropolitan region and the northern area of the country, we find that its working population is more qualified in terms of schooling, and it has maintained a significant role as an employment base, especially in the tertiary sector. The structure of the processes involved in this relatively small urban area, with about 16 sq. miles, originates a complex social arrangement marked by the social divisions set within the physical urban space: relevant oppositions between the historic centre, the central area, the inner city periphery and the Atlantic seafront structure the city's territory (Marques, Fernandes and Martins 1990). These oppositions operate within a framework of multiple differentiations; notwithstanding the social diversity of each of the contexts found here, the privileged districts of the Atlantic seafront, the private condominiums in the Western inner-city periphery, or some residential contexts in the central area, are advantageously differentiated from the city's Eastern periphery, or its historic centre, and involve the unbalanced presence of public and private facilities, social housing dwellings (more than twenty per cent of the city's population lives in this type of housing solution), as well as alternative profiles of residents (Pereira 2005, chapter 2).

Given the historical importance of the structuring processes of economic, social and cultural inequalities in Portuguese society (for recent research on the subject, see Ferreira 2008; Rodrigues 2010; Almeida 2013), and their specificities in contexts such as Porto, we sought to develop, over several years, a strategy to sociologically target the city's social structure inspired by Bourdieu's empirical and theoretical proposals. Based on the author's initial concerns with understanding the relationships between time structures and social practices and the analytical legacy from *Distinction*, among other references, we intended to connect these approaches with the main concerns of Portuguese sociological research on social classes and class cultures.[3] With this in mind, we prepared a survey strategy based on the development of an 'extended case study' (Burawoy 1998), meaning that by creating 18 socio-territorial observatories in the city (see Map 28.1), we were able to collect systematic data resulting from an extensive questionnaire survey to more than one thousand household groups (carried out in 2000) distributed by the mentioned observatories. The survey strategy was also based on a programme of ethnographical observation developed between 1998 and 2001 in seven of the observatories and covering all the major divisions of the city, resulting in more than one hundred semi-structured interviews initially split according to key respondents and, in a second stage, to social agents initially surveyed as part of the inquiry (cf. Pereira 2005: methodological annex).

By partially restoring the *objectivation* strategy[4] developed by Bourdieu in *Distinction*, aimed at gathering knowledge on the city of Porto in the early 2000s, we were able to organise a systematic wealth of information on the social, cultural and political divides that shape the city, pinpointing the relevance of relational processes on the arrangement of its social space. Specifically, with this relational approach to the city's social space and its class divisions, we documented the relevance of relationships between the volume of capital and the structure of the capital composition of the social agents surveyed. Furthermore, we gained insights into the importance of the social space as a 'predictive map' (Lebart *et al.* 1984: 100) of practices and representations, and to establish, in a theoretically meaningful way, the relevance of class divisions in the structuring of culture. A similar reasoning showed that the *appartenance* (belonging) to specific neighbourhoods in the city was not indifferent to specific features of the divisions of its social space (Pereira 2013; for additional elements, see also Pereira, 2005: chapter 3).

Based on the data obtained in the questionnaire survey, from which we initially recorded information on 1,043 individuals belonging to as many household groups, in this paper we

The structuration of lifestyles in Porto

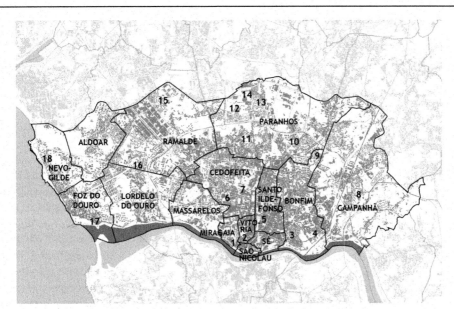

Legend: Correspondence between the major divisions of the city of Porto, the *PARISHES* and the approximate location of the observatories

Major divisions of the city	Parishes in 2001	Number and name of the approximate location of the observatories
Historic centre	Miragaia	(1) Miragaia: historic centre
	Sé	
	São Nicolau	
	Vitória	(2) Vitória: historic centre
Central area	Bonfim	(3) S. Vítor; (4) Bonfim and Campanhã; (9) Antas (Central area, in transition to East Periphery)
	Cedofeita	(6) Cedofeita; (7) Lapa and Constituição
	Massarelos	
	Santo Ildefonso	(5) Sto. Ildefonso
Inner-city periphery	Aldoar	
	Lordelo do Ouro	
	Paranhos	(10) Salgueiros; (11) Arca d'Água; (12) Amial; (13) S. Tomé; (14) Carriçal
	Ramalde	(15) Viso; (16) Foco and Boavista
Inner-city East Periphery	Campanhã	(8) Corujeira area and surrounding neighbourhoods
Atlantic seafront	Foz do Douro	(17) Foz do Douro (*Foz Velha*)
	Nevogilde	(18) Nevogilde

have revisited the research results obtained and provide an analysis on how the agents surveyed make use of their time, as well as some specific fields on how their representations and tastes are structured. The intention was to deliver a direct relational analysis of the agents' lifestyles; specifically, we intended to ascertain if it was possible to establish theoretically meaningful coordinates for the understanding of what we could call, adapting Weber's and Bourdieu's reasoning, the 'modalities of stylization of life' of the agents under scrutiny, questioning their lifestyles now and, unlike the aforementioned exercise about the social space, in an autonomous framework. In this regard, we are, thus, particularly interested in identifying the set of regularities to which the lifestyles may be subject, and to discuss, in particular, the patterns of their interrelation, which is especially important whenever the significance of phenomena such as the fragmentation and individualization (Beck et al. 1994; Beck and Beck-Gernsheim 2002) of social and cultural practices in contemporary societies is discussed.[5]

Provided with an inventory on time-use practices in domestic, local and urban contexts formed by about 100 variables, we recoded the information gathered by converting the modalities of the practices into three types of register, namely: very often (++), often (+) and rarely or absent (-). As mentioned previously, we also chose some domains to analyse the representations and tastes of the surveyed agents. In the latter case, we also recoded the information gathered using the open questions available in the survey to prepare adequate summaries. We kept information on 945 individuals (98 were considered supplementary) and 33 variables, distributed across five major fields of analysis, namely: television, reading, music, art and outdoor culture, sociability and sports, as shown in Table 28.1[6].

To further develop our research, we used the MCA technique (Lebart et al. 1984; Benzécri 1992; Lebart et al. 1998; Greenacre 1984; Le Roux and Rouanet 2004, 2010). Following an iterative procedure,[7] we developed a 'specific' MCA (Le Roux and Rouanet 2010: 61–64) on the information gathered, the original distribution regularities of which proved to be compatible with what we know about social and cultural practices in Portugal at the time: in general, these involve a strong domesticity, a relevant attachment to local interaction contexts and a selective development of outdoor cultural practices.[8]

As shown in Table 28.2, the first two axes correspond to more than 84 per cent of the explained variance (modified rates). For the purpose of interpretation, we focus on the first and second axes of the analysis, which explain, respectively, 74.6 per cent and 9.8 per cent of the variance. The two axes are defined by the importance of the contributing variables on the use of time, although the first axis stands out more in this respect. We may then assume that the configuration of lifestyles in the city is based on how regularly the practices are developed.

Table 28.1 Information used to elaborate the space of lifestyles based on MCA

Labels and variables used in the MCA (33 variables; 105 modalities)

Television: 1 question on time use, 8 questions on preferences = 9 questions; 31 modalities
Reading: 2 questions on time use, 1 question on preferences = 3 questions; 11 modalities
Music: 5 questions on time use, 1 question on preferences = 4 questions; 20 modalities
Arts and outdoor cultural activities: 6 questions on time use, 1 question on preferences = 7 questions; 18 modalities
Sociability and sports: 5 questions on time use, 3 questions on preferences = 8 questions; 26 modalities
20 questions on time use (51 modalities), 13 questions on preferences (54 modalities)

Table 28.2 Eigenvalues, percentage of explained variance, modified rates and cumulated modified rates

Number of axis	Eigenvalues	%	Modified %	Cumulated modified %
1	0.2134	9.73	74.6	74.6
2	0.0928	4.23	9.8	84.4
3	0.0683	3.11	4.0	88.4
		Total variance: 2.1938		

Whilst it is clear that these practices are not neutral, it should be noted that they are significantly associated to well-defined tastes, which is even more evident in the second axis.

As shown in Table 28.3, if we look more closely at the first axis we see that it is mostly shaped around the time-use variables dedicated to cultural and artistic activities, and listening to music. In turn, a closer look at the second axis shows that it is shaped mostly by the regularities of music consumption, along with specific contributions from musical taste, and, although less relevant in comparison, with sociability and sport and outdoor artistic and cultural activities.

Figure 28.1 shows the set of modalities that contributed the most to the first axis, enabling us to identify significant associations. Overall, we can see that this first axis separates the agents that participate the least socially and culturally from those whose daily lives are more intensely characterised by the different practices considered. Additionally, well-defined modalities of taste contribute quite significantly to the divides established. As such, the right side of the figure associates modalities with less regular practices. These include not spending holidays outside the home, reading newspapers, magazines, and books less intensely, and the same applies to listening to music at home, visiting museums, art exhibitions, going to the theatre or cinema. The rarity and absence of these practices is associated with the preference for specific television shows, such as soap operas, and to the choice of specific musical genres, such as lighter Portuguese popular music (*pimba* music, also dubbed 'tacky'), or Fado. The contrast between the right side and the left side of the first axis is, therefore, striking. In turn, the individuals on the left side of the axis are defined by more intense and regular engagement of the practices under analysis. So, holidays away from home are associated with very regular reading of books, frequent trips to art exhibitions, museums, the theatre, cinema and to various musical concerts (classical music, opera, jazz or rock concerts are significant modalities). Within these modalities of practice we also find specific choices in terms of holiday venues (holidays abroad), museums, e.g., the Contemporary Art Museum of Serralves, a

Table 28.3 Contributions of modalities from each domain of practice to the variations on each axis, multiple correspondence analysis

Labels (domains of practice)	Axis 1			Axis 2		
	Uses of time	Preferences	Total	Uses of time	Preferences	Total
TV	1	10	11	1	16	17
Reading	8	5	13	8	1	9
Music	21	5	26	22	13	34
Artistic and outdoor cultural activities	29	3	32	18	1	19
Sociability and sport	12	7	20	16	5	21
Total	70	30	100	64	36	100

Virgílio Borges Pereira

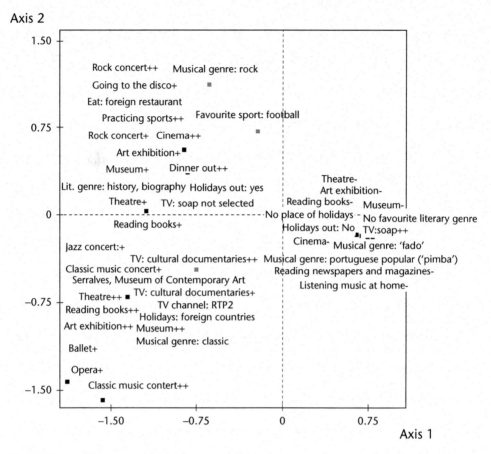

Figure 28.1 Porto's space of lifestyles. Multiple correspondence analysis: Axes 1 and 2, indicating variables contributing to axis 1.

preference for foreign cuisine restaurants, or specialised readings in the fields of history and biographies, and choosing RTP 2 as the preferred television channel (a public network that offers more cultural content), and also cultural documentaries. In short, the first axis clearly delimits alternative poles of social and cultural participation and a significant divide in terms of popular and selective tastes.

The second axis has a much smaller percentage of explained variance and a well-defined configuration. Some of the modalities with significant contributions to the first axis are replicated here, albeit with a different expression. Thus, as can be seen in Figure 28.2, the second axis associates, in its upper side, the individuals that listen to music at home, practice sports, go to the disco, to rock music concerts and to the cinema very regularly, whose favourite musical genre is rock music, and who also prefer foreign restaurants and like going to football games, in addition to the minor importance of religious practice and a preference for television programmes that offer films and football games. In its turn, the lower section of the second axis (see Figure 28.2) associates agents with strong cultural habits, who very frequently read books, go to museums, art exhibitions and classical music concerts, or who regularly go to the opera and ballet. Moreover, these practices are associated with specific preferences: besides electing classical music as a favourite

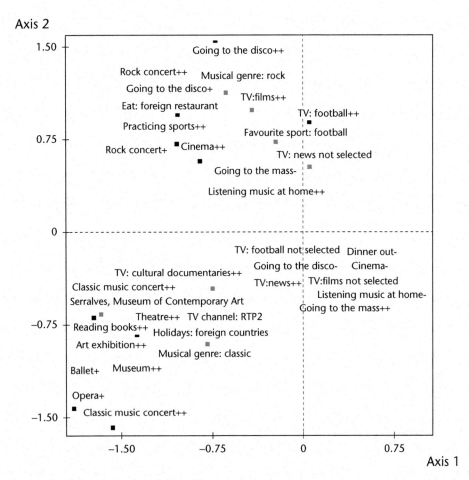

Figure 28.2 Porto's space of lifestyles. Multiple correspondence analysis: Axes 1 and 2, indicating variables contributing to axis 2.

musical genre, these individuals prefer foreign countries as holiday destinations, they choose the Contemporary Art Museum of Serralves as their favourite museum in the city, and the favourite TV programmes are news broadcasts or cultural documentaries. Listening to music at home, going to the cinema, dining out or going to the disco have a reduced expression in the everyday lives of the agents represented here. Equally significant in the axis is religious practice, translated as attending mass very regularly. Clear delimitations are therefore established in terms of regularities of practices and tastes of the individuals studied. This second axis conveys a significant divide between a pole marked by sociability and commercial urban culture, and another where classical culture and a more disciplined sociability are highly relevant.

In conjunction with the procedures developed, it is also quite significant that we are able to build a portrait of the social composition of the agents involved in the relational configurations considered. With the help of a small set of information, Figure 28.3 allows us to have a better notion of the *supplementary* variables underlying the production of such practices[9].

The first axis has a clearly outlined social composition. The framework of relationships shown on the right side of Figure 28.3, defined by lower levels of sociability and cultural

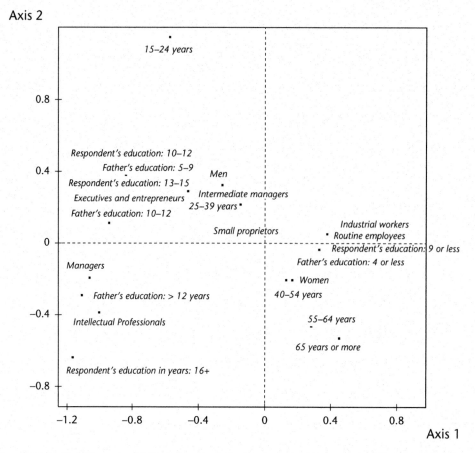

Figure 28.3 Porto's space of lifestyles. Supplementary variables: Respondent's gender, age, cultural capital (measured in years of education), individual class fraction, and father's cultural capital (measured in years of education), axes 1 and 2.

involvement, and by the presence of forms of popular taste, is characterised by specific social agents. In addition to being older, the individuals generally have weaker cultural capital (nine years of schooling or less). The class fractions of these individuals are also quite clear, particularly routine employees and industrial workers. In turn, the cultural capital of these individuals' fathers is also the lowest, never more than four years of schooling. In contrast, the individuals with a vaster, cumulative and selective range of practices and tastes, found on the left side of Figure 28.3, are young-adults with greater cultural capital. In terms of class, the individuals are notably executives and entrepreneurs, managers, professionals and intermediate managers. Their fathers' cultural capital is more extensive. It seems, therefore, that the framework of social properties identified can be interpreted as differences in overall volume of capital of the social agents here involved.

The second axis also conveys specific social properties. Divisions that are structured in terms of age and cultural capital are particularly relevant in this axis. However, the divisions structured in terms of the respondents' class fraction and cultural capital of the respondents' fathers are not negligible. A similar reasoning can be applied to gender. Thus, the pole structured around the largest sociability and commercial exposure is especially sensitive to the participants' youth, and is also marked by individuals with intermediate and high cultural capital (between 10 and 12 years of schooling; between 13 and 15 years of schooling), located on the top side of Figure 28.3. The pole structured around disciplined sociability and classical culture is related to the ageing of its social agents and to a very high cultural capital (16 years or more of schooling), as we can see on the lower side of Figure 28.3. It should be noted that the opposition between the poles of commercial and classical culture involves notable differences in terms of the respondents' class fractions, of the cultural capital of the respondents' fathers and their gender: entrepreneurs and intermediate managers differ from intellectual professionals; agents whose fathers have low-intermediate (5–9 years of school) cultural capital contrast with those who have higher cultural capital (more than 12 years of school); men differ from women. In view of the logic that shapes the axis, we can therefore consider that the social properties formed around the structure of capital of the agents analysed are not irrelevant.

The social (re)production of lifestyles in the city of Porto: A sociological interpretation

Taking Bourdieu's analytical concerns into the city of Porto, in the transition from the twentieth to the twenty-first century, gave us the possibility to design a systematic framework of questions on the relationships between culture and society. The relational reading of the inventory of time uses and of certain areas of preference enabled us to identify well-defined lifestyle configurations inscribed in an agonistic frame of relations of domination likely to be interpreted under the theoretical proposals inspired by Bourdieu's work on judgement and class.[10] The overall results of the research and the ethnographic work developed in specific neighbourhoods of the city complete and reinforce the reading that we made in this study.

As we have seen, the first configuration in the space of lifestyles that we identified involves a significant number of absences in participation and a limited, but not irrelevant, number of preferences, notably indulging in soap operas and a love for popular genres of music. Typical of older people and of agents with a lower volume of capital, this configuration is especially visible in working class social agents, but it is not unfamiliar to the world of non-manual routine employees (for recent convergent research results, see also Bennett *et al.* 2009: 48–49, 52). The ethnographic work provided a frame for the social and spatial positioning of this configuration and the relevance of the constraints imposed by necessity on everyday life (see also Bourdieu 1984: 386ff.). Impelled and magnified by the growth of socio-economic precariousness, deindustrialization and unemployment in the city (for further developments on the social forces herein, see Castel 1998; Beaud and Pialoux 2003), the structuring of popular lifestyles informed by the experience of domination could be identified in specific neighbourhoods. Notwithstanding its relevant status in the city, Porto's historic centre (see Map 28.1) is one of these contexts, where it was possible to document the effects of necessity in the structuring of popular lifestyles. In non-rehabilitated neighbourhoods such as Vitória or Miragaia (the contrast between rehabilitated and non-rehabilitated districts in Porto's historic centre is quite evident), the processes of obsolescence of physical spaces, the weakening of the social positions of local inhabitants, as well as the devitalization of local public and semi-public spaces, fed by meaningful processes of territorial stigmatization (Wacquant 2008), contribute to the reproduction of the domesticity of the social and cultural practices of old industrial workers and routine employees. Already suffering serious demographic loss by the early 2000s, the ancient part of the city revealed less social diversity than before, and saw its public space defined by the dilution of local community dynamics and progressively succumbing to the pressure of deviant practices (see also Pereira and Pinto 2012). In other neighbourhoods of the city, in the more impoverished and aged slums (*ilhas*, literally, *islands*) of central areas, or in certain council housing projects in the city's periphery (in neighbourhoods like Viso or in the parish of Campanhã, see Map 28.1), it was also possible to document analogous processes of sociability closure as constitutive elements of local everyday life (see also Schwartz 1990: 523). In a degree of structuring that varies according to the social history of the places in the city (non-favoured areas in the city have a history and are not necessarily socially and culturally homogeneous), the configuration of popular lifestyles, besides the aforementioned processes of reinforcing domesticity, also contemplated everyday practices structured in terms of social and cultural *autochthony* (from the French *'capital d'autochtonie'* generically meaning a set of resources provided by localized social networks) (Hoggart 1973 and 1975; Retière 1994; Renahy 2010). This autochthony was informed by the relevance of gender divisions and, although not as visible, by the formation of life projects guided by the accumulation of technical and cultural capital or by investment in economic capital (see also Rupp 1995; Mauger 2006). In specific cases, this social and cultural autochthony was also supported by the practice and, more frequently, by the memory of tenacity (*eigensinn*) (Lüdtke 1996) with clean-cut political outlines, primarily as a result of the social mobilization fostered by housing problems in some of these contexts before, and especially after the democratic revolution of 1974 (for further developments, see Downs, 1989: 15–33; Pereira and Queirós 2012a). Besides contributing to the production of a non-linear reading of the socio-history of popular lifestyles in the city, the ethnographic approach developed in this research, as well as the sequence of studies on the social structuring of specific places in the city developed later (Pereira and Queirós 2012b), clarified the meaning of domination in the production of popular lifestyles, enabling us to highlight the importance of the small, but nevertheless active, margins of variation that are established around the effects of necessity.

As opposed to this, an alternative configuration in the city's space of lifestyles was identified, structured around a cumulative and selective momentum of intense cultural participation, as well as around a choice of varied tastes, a characteristic of the agents that belong to the most favoured social positions of the city, as the left-hand side of Figures 33.1 and 33.3 showed (for recent convergent research results, see Coulangeon and Lemel 2009; Bennett *et al.* 2009: 48–54). The overall research results and the information gathered during the ethnographic work served as the basis for a detailed reading of the city's social and spatial contexts that prompted the production and, especially, the reproduction of the dispositions here involved, revealing the main distinctive traits of the dominant class habitus. Moreover, it was also possible to demonstrate the conditions under which *tension*, and the contradictory impact of the inadequacy between material and symbolic capacity to attain culture, emerged as an active element in the structuring of everyday life (between popular and distinctive forms of culture), a process that revealed special relevance in the agents that belonged to the intermediate social positions that we interviewed, for instance, in Porto's central area or in some neighbourhoods of the city's inner periphery (for further developments, see Pereira 2005: 781–793).

We also identified two other configurations in Porto's space of lifestyles, as Figure 28.2 showed, both of them defined by a diversity of practices and preferences and with a prosperous social genesis. As we have seen in Figure 28.3, the opposition between the commercial and the intellectual configurations of the space of the lifestyles is sustained by social differences in terms of age (young vs. old), cultural capital (high and intermediate vs. very high) and class (executives and intermediate managers vs. intellectual professionals), among other factors. The study of the fabric of everyday life in Porto's Atlantic seafront (see Map 28.1), an affluent, yet contradictory, neighbourhood of the city, showed how socially selective sociability, fashionable meeting clubs and restaurants, as well as the material and symbolic investments made in different forms of commercial urban culture, integrated the 'social closure' strategies (re)produced (Pinçon and Pinçon-Charlot 1998) by different generations of local affluent families. This is thus revealing of the significance of 'modes of appropriation' (Prieur and Savage 2011: 578) and 'manners', and not necessarily expertise (Zolberg 1992: 199), in the 'soft' capitalization of culture mediated by strong inter-acquaintance typical of bourgeois taste (Pereira 2005: chapter 9). On the other hand, evidence from alternative social positions in this same neighbourhood, as well as the ethnographic and sociological reading of the constitution of everyday life in the neighbourhood of Cedofeita, in Porto's central area (see Map 28.1), among other elements, revealed the prevalence of more ascetic classical cultural tastes in the formation of the habitus of the intellectual professionals (Pereira 2005, chapters 7 and 9), with similar properties to those we could identify at the bottom side of Figure 28.2.

Bourdieu's work highlighted the relevance of relational perspectives which proved vital in Porto too, in terms of theory and methodology, for the sociological understanding of the formation of symbolic divisions (Bourdieu 2013). He specifically highlighted the importance of the social inscription of these processes, showing how volume of capital and the structure of the capital composition could help us understand cultural practices and judgements of taste. Several authors, in different national contexts, have been pursuing this relational research programme[11], helping us to understand the general properties, but also the specificities, of the processes of boundaries (re)production and the socio-historic conditions that explain the constitution of capitals which are associated to it. With the help of an autonomous perspective about the space of the lifestyles in the city of Porto, the analytical exercise that we developed in this paper is a contribution to the development of that relational research programme.

Acknowledgements

We acknowledge the Fundação para a Ciência e a Tecnologia grant and the Institute of Sociology of the University of Porto (Project PEst-OE/SADG/UI0727/2014).

Notes

1. For further developments on the history of this research, see also M. de Saint Martin (2013).
2. For an assessment of the research here involved, see also Duval (2010).
3. See, for example, Pinto (1985, 1997) and Almeida (1986). For relevant research results about the relationships between social classes and values in Portugal and in Europe, see also Almeida, Machado and Costa (2006).
4. For a fruitful understanding of Bourdieu's sociological reasoning in methodological terms, see Bourdieu (1993; 2003), as well as his writings on this subject in *Distinction* (Bourdieu 1984: Appendix 1).
5. The original research design served to gather information on a wide set of practices, from free time routines to local sociability, religious practices or outdoor cultural activities. The preparation of the survey, besides Bourdieu's work, was made taking account of significant surveys on social and cultural practices. See Lalive d'Épinay et al. (1982), Elias and Dunning (1992), Donnat (1998), among others. See also Maget (1962: 59).
6. In all these cases, the head count considered in each of the modalities of the variables retained for the study (time-use practices and preferences) were always greater than 5% of the responses; modalities with a lower head count were considered *passive* or, if justified, gathered into more overarching and denser categories.
7. To this end, we used the SPAD software, version 7.4.

8 For reasons of space, the major trends of structuring practices and representations under study are not shown here in detail. For a full description of these trends, see, e.g., Pereira (2005: chapter 4) and the bibliography therein. As a result of an early concern in the research to capture, in great detail, the respondents' time-use practices, the relationship between variables and modalities could not be as homogeneous as intended regarding the distribution among variables in terms of time-use practices and preferences. Nevertheless, as regards the 105 active modalities in the analysis, such a distribution was more successful (see Table 28.1).

9 The supplementary variables represented in Figure 28.3 were not used in the active set of variables represented in Figures 33.1 and 33.2 and, thus, do not participate in the construction of the axes. For the identification of meaningful relations using supplementary variables in MCA, we follow the propositions of Le Roux and Rouanet: deviations between categories of supplementary variables will be considered as "notable" when greater than 0.5 and as "large" when higher than 1 (Le Roux and Rouanet 2010: 59).

10 According to Wacquant, "Pierre Bourdieu reformulated the classic problem of domination and inequality by *questioning the ontological status of groups* and by forging tools for disclosing how these come to be practically made and unmade in social life through the inculcation of shared schemata of perception and appreciation and their contested deployment to draw, patrol, or challenge social boundaries" (Wacquant 2013: 281).

11 For further developments and new analytical suggestions, see Prieur and Savage (2013).

References

Almeida, J. F. (1986) *Classes Sociais nos Campos*, Lisbon: ICS.
—— (2013) *Desigualdades e Perspectivas dos Cidadãos*, Lisbon: Mundos Sociais.
Almeida, J. F., F. L. Machado, and A. F. Costa (2006) 'Social Classes and Values in Europe', *Portuguese Journal of Social Science*, 5(2): 95–117.
Baxandall, M. (1972) *Painting and Experience in Fifteenth Century Italy. A Premier in the Social History of Pictorial Style*, Oxford: Oxford University Press.
Beaud, S. and M. Pialoux (2003) *Violences urbaines, violence sociale*, Paris: Fayard.
Beck, U. and E. Beck-Gernsheim (2002) *Individualization: Institutionalized Individualism and its Social and Political Consequences*, London/Thousand Oaks/New Delhi: Sage Publications.
Beck, U., A. Giddens, and S. Lash (1994) *Reflexive Modernization: Politics, Tradition and Aesthetics in the Modern Social Order*, Stanford: Stanford University Press.
Bennett, T., M. Savage, E. Silva, A. Warde, M. Gayo-Cal, and D. Wright (2009) *Culture, Class, Distinction*, London: Routledge.
Benzécri, J.-P. (1992) *Correspondence Analysis Handbook*, New York: Marcel Dekker.
Bourdieu, P. (1966) 'Différences et distinctions', in P. Bourdieu and A. Darbel (eds.) *Le Partage des bénéfices. Expansion et inégalités en France*, Paris: Minuit.
—— (1977a) *Algérie 60*, Paris: Minuit.
—— (1977b) *Outline of a Theory of Practice*, Cambridge: Cambridge University Press.
—— (1978) 'Capital symbolique et classes sociales', L'Arc 72: 13–19. English transl. (2013) 'Symbolic capital and social classes', *Journal of Classical Sociology*, 13, 2: 292–302.
—— (1979) *La Distinction. Critique sociale du jugement*, Paris: Minuit. English transl. (1984), *Distinction. A Social Critique of the Judgement of Taste*, transl., R. Nice, Cambridge, MA: Harvard University Press.
—— (1989) *La Noblesse d'État*, Paris: Minuit.
—— (1993) 'Comprendre', in P. Bourdieu (ed.) *La Misère du monde*, Paris: Seuil.
—— (2003) 'L'objectivation participante', *Actes de la recherche en sciences sociales*, 150: 43–58.
Bourdieu, P., and M. de Saint-Martin (1976) 'L'anatomie du goût', *Actes de la recherche en sciences sociales*, 2: 2–112.
Bourdieu, P. and L. Wacquant (1992) *Réponses*, Paris: Seuil.
Bourdieu, P., A. Darbel, J.-P. Rivet, and C. Seibel (1963) *Travail et travailleurs en Algérie*, Paris-La Haye: Mouton.
Burawoy, M. (1998) 'The Extended Case Method', *Sociological Theory*, 16: 4–33.
Castel, R. (1998) *As Metamorfoses da Questão Social*, Petrópolis: Editora Vozes.
Coulangeon, P. and Lemel, Y. (2009) 'Les pratiques culturelles et sportives: arbitrage, diversité et cumul', *Economie et statistique*, 423: 3–30.

De Saint Martin, M. (2013) 'Les tentatives de construction de l'espace social, d'«Anatomie du goût » à La Distinction. Quelques repères pour l'histoire d'une recherche', in P. Coulangeon and J. Duval (eds.), *Trente ans après La Distinction de Pierre Bourdieu*, Paris: La Découverte.

Donnat, O. (1998) *Les Pratiques culturelles des Français. Enquête 1997*, Paris: La Documentation Française.

Downs, C. (1989) *Revolution at the Grassroots: Community Organizations in the Portuguese Revolution*, Albany: State University of New York Press.

Duval, J. (2010) 'Distinction Studies', *Actes de la recherche en sciences sociales*, 181–182: 147–156.

Elias, N. and E. Dunning (1992) *A Busca da Excitação*, Lisbon: Difel.

Ferreira, L. V. (2008) 'Persistent Poverty: Portugal and the Southern European Welfare Regime', *European Societies*, 10 (1): 49–71.

Greenacre, M. J. (1984) *Theory and Applications of Correspondence Analysis*, London: Academic Press.

Hoggart, R. (1973) *As Utilizações da Cultura*, Vol. I, Lisbon: Presença.

—— (1975) *As Utilizações da Cultura*, Vol. II, Lisbon: Presença.

Lalive d'Épinay, C., M. Bassand, E. Christe, and D. Gros (1982) *Temps libre. Culture de masse et cultures de classes aujourd'hui*, Lausanne: Pierre-Marcel Favre.

Lebart, L., A. Morineau, A., and K. M. Warwick (1984) *Multivariate Descriptive Statistical Analysis. Correspondence Analysis and Related Techniques for Large Matrices*, New York: John Wiley & Sons.

Lebart, L., M. Piron, and A. Morineau (1998) *Statistique exploratoire multidimensionnelle*, Paris: Dunod.

Le Roux, B. and H. Rouanet (2004) *Geometric Data Analysis*, Dordrecht: Kluwer.

—— (2010) *Multiple Correspondence Analysis*, London: Sage.

Lüdtke, A. (1996) 'Ouvriers, eigensinn et politique dans l'Allemagne du XXe siècle', *Actes de la recherche en sciences sociales*, 113: 91–101.

Maget, M. (1962) *Guide d'étude directe des comportements culturels*, Paris: CNRS.

Marques, H., J. A. Fernandes, and L. P. Martins (1990) *Porto: Percursos nos Espaços e nas Memórias*, Porto: Afrontamento.

Mauger, G. (2006) *Les Bandes, le milieu et la bohême populaire. Études de sociologie de la déviance des jeunes des classes populaires (1975–2005)*, Paris: Belin.

Pereira, V. B. (2005) *Classes e Culturas de Classe das Famílias Portuenses*, Porto: Afrontamento.

—— (2013) 'L'espace social, les pratiques quotidiennes et la ville. Repères pour une sociologie des divisions sociales et symboliques dans la ville de Porto', in P. Coulangeon and J. Duval (eds.) *Trente ans après La Distinction de Pierre Bourdieu*, Paris: La Découverte.

Pereira, V. B. and J. M. Pinto (2012) 'Espace, relations sociales et culture populaire dans le coeur ancien de la ville de Porto', *Sociétés contemporaines*, 86: 115–134.

Pereira, V. B. and J. Queirós (2012a) 'State, Housing and the 'Social Question' in the City of Porto (1956–2006)', *Social Sciences*, 1: 203–214.

—— (2012b) *Na Modesta Cidadezinha: génese e estruturação de um bairro de casas económicas do Porto [Amial, 1938–2010]*, Porto, Afrontamento, Colecção O Estado, a Habitação e a Questão Social na Cidade do Porto, Vol. 1.

Pinçon, M., and M. Pinçon-Charlot (1998) *Grandes fortunes*, Paris: Payot.

Pinto, J. M. (1985) *Estruturas Sociais e Práticas Simbólico-Ideológicas nos Campos*, Porto: Afrontamento.

—— (1997) 'A sociedade urbana', *Colóquio 'A Política das Cidades'*, Lisbon: Conselho Económico e Social.

Prieur, A. and M. Savage (2011) 'Updating Cultural Theory: A Discussion Based in Studies in Denmark and in Britain', *Poetics – Journal of Empirical Research on Culture, the Media and the Arts*, 39: 566–580.

—— (2013) 'Les forms émergentes de capital culturel', in P. Coulangeon and J. Duval (eds.) *Trente ans après La Distinction de Pierre Bourdieu*, Paris: La Découverte.

Prieur, A., L. Rosenlund, and J. Skjott-Larsen (2008) 'Cultural Capital Today – A Case Study from Denmark', *Poetics – Journal of Empirical Research on Culture, the Media and the Arts*, 36: 45–70.

Renahy, N. (2010) 'Classes populaires et capital d'autochtonie', *Regards sociologiques*, 40: 9–26.

Retière, J.-N. (1994) *Identités ouvrières. Histoire d'un fief ouvrier en Bretagne, 1909–1990*, Paris: L'Harmattan.

Rodrigues, C. F. (2010) 'Algumas reflexões sobre a evolução recente da desigualdade e do bem-estar social em Portugal', in A. Teixeira, S. Silva, P. Teixeira (eds.), *O Que Sabemos Sobre a Pobreza em Portugal? Tributo à Professora Leonor Vasconcelos Ferreira*, Lisbon: Vida Económica.

Rosenlund, L. (2009) *Exploring the City with Bourdieu: Applying Pierre Bourdieu's Theories and Methods to Study the Community*, Saarbrücken: VDM Verlag.

Rouanet, H., W. Ackermann, and B. Le Roux (2000) 'The Geometric Analysis of Questionnaires: The Lesson of Bourdieu's *La Distinction*', *Bulletin de Méthodologie Sociologique*, 65: 5–15.

Rupp, J. C. (1995) 'Les classes populaires dans un espace à deux dimensions', *Actes de la recherche en sciences sociales*, 109: 93–98.
Schwartz, O. (1990) *Le Monde privé des ouvriers: hommes et femmes du nord*, Paris: PUF.
Wacquant, L. (2008) *Urban Outcasts: A Comparative Sociology of Urban Marginality*, Cambridge: Polity Press.
—— (2013) 'Symbolic Power and Group-Making: On Bourdieu's Reframing of Class', *Journal of Classical Sociology*, 13 (2): 274–291.
Weber, M. (1978) *Economy and Society*, Berkeley: University of California Press.
Zolberg, V. (1992) 'Barrier or Leveler? The Case of the Art Museum', in M. Lamont and M. Fournier (eds.) *Cultivating Differences: Symbolic Boundaries and the Making of Inequality*, Chicago: The University of Chicago Press.

29
When the artistic field meets the art worlds: Based on the case study of occupational painters in Shanghai

Chao Zhang

Introduction: Understanding urban art space

Art, with its thousands of faces, often remains mysterious in terms of its value. The Kantian aesthetic perceives the value of art as lying in itself and independent of any external judgement. Bourdieu's analysis, using 'the field of cultural production', however, considers that the value of art embodies the symbolic capital of producers and the relevant genres, schools – in a word, hierarchy of the social space of cultural production. Moreover, the field of cultural production, with its relatively autonomous existence, has homologies with the field of power rather than being its own enclosed domain (Bourdieu 1986, 1993). If the Kantian aesthetic places art in a pure and eternal state for human perception, then Bourdieusian analysis brings art to the social conditions and structure in which art is produced and consumed.

Over the past decades, the social embeddedness of art has received more examination. With the 'art world' approach (Becker 1982) and the recent development of the social network analysis of art (De Nooy 2002; Bottero and Crossley 2011), discussions are concerned with art as a profession of recurring networks and actions, and the conjunction of art with local scenes (Dubois and Méon 2012), which further demystifies the operation of art to the concrete level of everyday practice and social connections. While art possesses legendary features by virtue of its symbolic creation, the sociological analysis of art, on the other hand, tends to decipher how art is framed and related to practice, identity, social relations, and at the spatial level, cities. This article draws on an integrated perspective of field and world, and examines the operation of art at the local level. Through the case studies of occupational painters in a creative cluster in Shanghai, analysis will be focused on the painters' dual positioning in the artistic field and art worlds through the intermediary of the cluster. By revealing their strategies, struggles and networks, I explore symbolic capital and social capital for art, and how these forms of capital are transferred between field and worlds.

The clustering of painters in cities is not a contemporary phenomenon. The 'Bohemian Paris' reminds us of a period when artists' work and leisure activities were intimately bound with urban spaces, e.g. studios, cafes, theatres and streets, fostering an air of freedom and new aesthetics of urban cultural space (Seigel 1986). In Paris, Montmartre became the hub of impressionists during the 1870s–1910s and left a legacy of artistic ambience until today.

The more recent and influential case is the New York SoHo district after the Second World War. The clustering of artists and galleries in vacant factories and warehouses made SoHo an important site for contemporary art. Along with the shift of SoHo away from industrial remains to a cultural landmark, the pioneering practices of artists in urban renewal initiated the style of 'loft living' for the middle class, and a process of commercialisation was incubated. Zukin (1982) used the concept of the 'artistic mode of production' to reveal the nature of the process by which 'capital follows art' in SoHo's regeneration, and that artists, being trailblazers in reusing urban space and creating artistic milieu, were marginalised. Zukin's systematic analysis provides new insights into the process and dynamics of regeneration, and has influenced many studies on gentrification. However, the general critique of the logic of capital set in Marxist urban political economy tends to lead to a pre-established and overarching judgment following other studies of gentrification. Accordingly, 'pioneer but eventually sacrificed' is regarded as the conventional role that artists play in the urban chain of capital accumulation.

Therefore, what are the relations between artists and city? Indeed, gentrification has been a major component of urban image rather than a sideshow (Ley 2003), and the creative cluster studied in this article has also experienced gentrification over the past decades (Zhang 2012). Rather than the conventional interpretation of artists being sacrificed to gentrification or culture-led regeneration, I will consider what artists' strategies are to cope with social and cultural change. If the artistic field is a battlefield, abstract and strictly hierarchical, as Bourdieu defines it, then how can artists operate in the urban creative cluster? Is the cluster a concrete form of art worlds, and what does it mean for the artists? With these enquiries, I focus on a group of self-employed painters working and living in Shanghai. First, the two notions of art 'field' and 'world' will be respectively examined and how these two approaches could be complementary to each other will be discussed. Second, the background information about the cluster, named 'Tianzifang' (abbreviated as 'TZF'), in Chinese characters '田子坊', and the cases of the painters will be introduced. Thirdly, my analysis will focus on the painters' everyday practice, revealing their strategies, struggles and social networks. Located both in the abstract artistic field and concrete art worlds, their cultural practices can be found across these two, and the capital, mainly symbolic and social, is transferred between these two for higher field positions. Finally, the implications of the integrated analysis of artistic field and art worlds will be elucidated. Back to the urban context of the burgeoning creative clusters and the art market in China, I will also reflect on the dynamics of the cluster TZF together with the mobility of the painters.

An integrated perspective of artistic field and art worlds

In *The Field of Cultural Production* (1993), Bourdieu distinguishes two oppositional subfields: the field of restricted production and the field of large-scale production. The former is based on symbolic capital and the internal demands of the field, and leads to 'production for producers' and 'art for art's sake'. The latter subordinates art to economic capital and market demands, operating in large cultural industries and dependent on wide audiences. Between these two poles is defined the continuum of cultural production which combines symbolic capital and economic capital in different degrees. Symbolic capital is the highest form 'that one or another of three species of capital (economic, cultural and social) takes when it is grasped through categories of perception that recognize its specific logic or, if you prefer, misrecognize the arbitrariness of its possession and accumulation' (Bourdieu and Wacquant 1992: 119). For the artistic field located in the field of restricted cultural production, symbolic capital is essential, including prestige, reputation and consecration. The possession of symbolic capital means actualisation of the logic of the field, that is, to be recognised in terms of value of art works compared to other artists, art genres and art schools.

Following the definition of field as structured social space, the artistic field is also marked by hierarchies, field positions and struggles – all in all, those are applied to the field.

> In analytical terms, a field may be defined as a network, or a configuration, of objective relations between positions. These positions are objectively defined, in their existence and in the determinations they impose upon their occupants, agents or institutions, by their present and potential situation *(situs)* in the structure of the distribution of species of power (or capital) whose possession commands access to the specific profits that are at stake in the field, as well as by their objective relations to other positions (domination, subordination, homology, etc.).
>
> *(Bourdieu and Wacquant 1992: 97)*

The accounts above address the objectivity of positions and relations in the field. This emphasis is consistent with Bourdieu's refusal of the occasionalist illusion that 'what exist in the social world are relations – not interactions between agents or intersubjective ties between individuals, but objective relations which exist "independently of individual consciousness and will"' (Bourdieu and Wacquant 1992: 97). Compared to symbolic interactionism which places importance on context for meaning-making, Bourdieu sees the occasion as illusionary if it is without recognition of the objective power relations underlying the interactions. Interactions appear to be subordinate to objective relations, or as settings where the latter develop. For example, he wrote, 'the interaction itself owes its form to the objective structures which have produced the dispositions of the interacting agents and which allot them their relative positions in the interaction and elsewhere' (Bourdieu 1977: 81). Compared to interactions, objective structure is embodied in dispositions and gives a practical sense which 'operates at the preobjective, nonthetic level' and 'expresses the social sensitivity which guides us prior to our positing objects as such' (Bourdieu and Waquant 1992: 20). The guidance includes behavioural and mental structure, and as a result of habitus which is a *'structuring mechanism'* (Bourdieu and Wacquant, 1992: 18), and 'functions at every moment as a *matrix of perceptions, appreciations and actions* and makes possible the achievement of infinitely diversified tasks' (Bourdieu, 1977: 83). Thus Bourdieu brings habitus, field and practice into one logical analysis, and in this framework, interactions are the externalisation of objective power relations and 'defined by the *objective structure* of the relation between the groups they belong to, systems of dispositions ... structures which are active only when *embodied* in a competence acquired in the course of a particular history' (Bourdieu 1977: 81).

The approach associated with the concept of art worlds, however, views the social world in terms of collaborations, possibilities and openness. Compared to the metaphor of field emphasising hierarchies, classification and competition, art worlds ask how people get things done in their everyday context. Becker (1982) defines art as a social being created by networks of people acting together and mediated by accepted or newly developed conventions. Conventions, as tacit knowledge 'known to all well-socialised members of a society' (Becker 1982: 46), make cooperation easier and more efficient. Influenced by symbolic interactionism, the perspective of art worlds is concerned with the socio-interactive basis through which meanings are formed, negotiated and exchanged. The conventions and the recurring routines and networks, all together define the outer perimeter of an art world, and also become the foundation of activities. The social organisation of art, as empirically grounded in collective actions, thus reflects an art world as a miniature of a social world.

Field and social world are regarded as two very different perspectives, or even, opposites. Such an impression would be manifest at the first glance of their distinctive theoretical assumptions. As Becker and Pessin (2006: 285) put it: for world, the basic question is 'what is doing what with whom that affects the resulting work of art', and for field, the question is 'who dominates whom, using what strategies and resources, with what results'. Field is a space of closure, and world is featured by openness and possibilities.

However, neither field nor art world could provide sufficient explanations for art. It is meaningful to combine these two perspectives in art analysis. First, the emphasis of objective and structural relations by field is complementary to the emphasis of concrete ties, interactions and networks by world. While the structural sense of field presents a feel for the game between the dominant and dominated, and a map of power relations of positions, the mechanism about how everyday detailed relations and networks are contributed to objective relations and positions is under-discussed and neglected. The perspective of world, themed on the micro analysis of social organisation in art, liberates the subordinate and constitutive role of interactions as defined in field theory, but with a lack of structuring sense to approach various kinds of relations and networks, the social world analysis tends to anchor at the superficial level of actions and social phenomenon, or to present a one-sided social image of cooperation, compromise and harmony. In this aspect, the ideas of field are helpful to tease out the multiplicity of relations and decipher the power relations, asymmetries, conflicts and distances behind and beyond everyday perceived reality. The complementary status of field and world has already been recognised in social network analysis (De Nooy 2002, 2003; Powell et al. 2005; Botttero and Crossley 2011, 2014). The purpose here is to investigate how interactions mediate and transform objective relations, or to make the social network analysis sensitive to structures and evolving forces.

Second, combining field and social world perspective makes empirical urban case studies feasible. Defined as social space to a high level of abstraction, the geometrical space of field in correspondence analysis – used by Bourdieu – is abstracted from concrete location in cities. Though more interests in Bourdieu's theory in urban studies have been developed over the past few years (Savage et al. 2005; Parker et al. 2007; Savage 2010, 2011; Hanquinet et al. 2012), the reference of field as physical space is primarily in a general sense. Using field as a geographical term in researching a concrete place, and meanwhile not sacrificing the widely accepted potency of field as social space, would cause confusion. The use of field in a so-called physical sense might fall in the track of reducing space merely to be a container for what happens, thus losing the analytical depth which it was originally intended to achieve. By introducing and incorporating the idea of the art world, the painters' everyday practices can be defined and reached. In the next section I will introduce the fieldwork conducted in and around the art cluster and show in the next step that forms of socialising with painters are all characters of a social world.

Ethnography of the painters

The clustering of professional painters in urban cultural zones and art villages has become a spatial and cultural phenomenon in the mega cities of China. After the Reform and Opening-up Policy in 1978, the transition from the planned economy to the market economy gradually paved the way for the development of the cultural and art economy. First, the loosened control of culture from ideological moorings and from its functioning as 'political apparatus' propelled greater diversity of artistic styles and genres. Second, the success of a few Chinese artists in foreign art exhibitions and deals fuelled the formation of the art market in China. The presence of the Chinese artists in the contemporary art exhibitions such as Venice Biennale in the 1990s marked a significant shift after the silence of the Chinese modern art for decades. Along with a tremendous increase of foreigners working in international corporations after China's entry to the World Trade Organization, a rising demand for art space and exhibition took place. Thirdly, the computerised reform across the visual sectors since the 1990s brought the original labour that is specialised in drawing into a marginal status. As the young workers who were equipped with the skill of software-based design entered advertising and other image sectors, many older generation workers previously living on the skill of drawing by hand retired. The choice of becoming an occupational (or, self-employed) painter was an attempt to rediscover the value of drawing. Leaving their hometown, many of these painters went to big cities for new careers; art clusters appeared then, such as 798 and Songzhuang in Beijing, M50 in Shanghai and so on.

Besides, the systems of recognition within the artistic field have changed. In China, the academy system has been long dominant in establishing the canon. This systematic legitimacy is constructed on membership of state-founded art associations, relations to distinguished art colleges and institutions, and apprenticeship with renowned artists. For example, there is China Artists Committee, sponsored by the Communist Party, which organises national exhibitions. This bureaucratised form of membership recognises orthodox artists as well as framing art in the political belief of state. From the 1990s, however, the critic-dealer system arose as a new form of recognition separate from the canonical routes. Some Chinese painters first received fame in foreign art markets and then entered the public domain of mainland China. These are primarily avant-garde painters working on contemporary art with critical perspectives on consumer culture, globalisation and the Chinese political campaign. Under the intermediary of foreign art dealers and curators, a group of Chinese artists turn out to be flagship figures in this critic-dealer system. In an art cluster named M50 in Shanghai, the Swiss art entrepreneur Lorenz Helbing opened the first foreign art gallery in 1995 and successfully assisted its contracted artists[1] into the foreground of international exhibitions.

The cases of self-employed painters in TZF gains particular meaning in these sociocultural changes of art sectors and the formation of the critic-dealer system. Fundamentally, it is a market force, a new eye from audiences and consumers, collectors and patrons, to prompt the settlement of painters from provinces of China to Shanghai for a new expedition of art values. Being one of the earliest cultural and art clusters in inner Shanghai, TZF developed from vacant factories, warehouses and declined alleyway neighbourhoods. The settlement of artists in TZF can be traced back to the end of the 1990s when a few well-known visual artists first renovated the industrial spaces into their studios. Though the cluster has been experiencing commodification and gentrification over the past decades, Building 5 with the name of 'Painters' Building' maintains a relatively fixed total number of painters at different stages, which is around twenty. This article selects nine cases of painters who are in their emerging and rising stage. Such a selection aims to focus on self-employed painters and to provide micro exploration about their state of existence to make art as an occupation, which might better represent the point where the artistic field and art worlds meet in the forming critic-dealer system and art market. The painters selected all have close relations with TZF in Building 5. They all had their studios there, but some later left TZF, while some still remain. Most of the fieldwork was conducted between 2008 and 2010[2], and included semi-structured interviews, informal conversations, observations and taking part in social events with the painters. The ethnographical data collected from the field include images, words and texts, and cover the perspective of painters but also their networks, critics and patrons. Most of the painters and other artists mentioned in this article are anonymised[3], and the use of their paintings and relevant images, including mention of their life trajectories, has gained their consent. The active references to the painters' biographies and trajectories during ethnographic work is similar to Bourdieu's emphasis on trajectories and the historicity of field.

Among the nine painters, one was born in the 1940s, three in the 1950s, two in the 1960s and three in the 1970s. The majority of painters in TZF are male, though one is female. The average level of cultural capital of the painters is high. Seven of them received professional training in painting and art, four with bachelor's degrees, three with diplomas. Another two painters did not specialise in painting in their previous educational background, but studied design in their undergraduate programme. Before coming to TZF, the previous employment of the painters varied. Many of their jobs had loose connections with visual art or design, and generally their occupational trajectories from the 1980s epitomised the ebb and flow of art-related employment and the burgeoning of the art market in the past decades in China. Weiguang, one of the key informants who had his studio in Building 5 from 2002, regarded coming to TZF as marking a new phase in his life from his previous status of 'painting worker'. He was born in the 1960s and started painting as a child. After graduation from high school, he was recruited by the Institute of Crafts and Fine Arts in his hometown. His job was to draw oil paintings according to miniature pictures sent together with orders. Most customers were from Hong Kong and they wanted copies of Western masterpieces for interior decoration. After working there for seven years, with the advent of the marketisation reform of the collective-owned institute, he then shifted to the advertising company founded by the institute in 1986. In the early 1990s, he left the advertising company and decided to carve out his painting career in the metropolis. He took vocational training in Beijing for two years in the Central Academy of Fine Arts as he had previously failed the entrance exam for art colleges. In 1999, he went to Beijing again and tried to enter the art market. There, he painted a series of works depicting traditional manual workshops, such as the one making soybean sauce. However, the patron who supported him went bankrupt when the work was incomplete, and the originally planned exhibition lost financial support. After a year, he returned to his hometown as he could not sell his works to make a living in Beijing. Coming to Shanghai was the second expedition: again he left his wife and carried his savings in hope of new opportunities. TZF was the second stop. Before, he had stayed in the Pudong Painting Village,[4] located in the periphery of the city, for about a year.

The life and occupational trajectories of Weiguang revealed how he became a self-employed painter after doing other jobs which had side connections with crafts or fine arts. Over half of the painters made a similar occupational shift from working in peripheral areas of art to their current status of self-employed creators. Some worked in the design sector of a printing workshop, some worked in souvenirs by taking advantage of drawing, either applying the traditional craft of pyrography[5], or presenting the famous ancient painting – 'A City of Cathay' in the form of embossed brick. During the 1970s and 1980s when digital copying and printing had not yet been born, a good mastery of painting turned out to be a very valuable asset, and most of the painters were the backbone at the time for the visual sectors. Junyi, previously working as a graphic designer in cinema and theatre in his home city for nearly twenty years, painted over one thousand posters until 1993. When the transformation from the planned economy to the market economy brought many business opportunities in the end of 1980s and the early 1990s – the time when the computerised reform started in design and printing sectors, some left their original positions and set up their own business in interior decoration, fashion, etc.

The artistic field meets the art worlds

Figure 29.1 The view from inside Building 5 to the Lane 210 in TZF

Analysis of the cases

Settlement in Shanghai was regarded by the painters as a new stage of their life, a response to their love of art, a return to their long lasting passion for art after trying various kinds of jobs in their previous life trajectories. The following section will give a thick description of the painters' practices as well as analysing their strategies, struggles and social networks. Throughout their everyday practice permeated the matter of the value of art and the sense of positions. As the site where the painters' art studios were located, the creative cluster played a significant role in the dialogue between the artistic field and art worlds.

Locating strategy in TZF

Strategy and trajectory are two analytical concepts in Bourdieu's field theory. Strategy is the orientation towards practice, based on the current positions and accounts for the trajectories of the individuals in the field (Bourdieu 1977; Savage and Silva 2013). Reviewing the routes of the painters from various places to the destination – TZF – this spatial positioning is strategic with regards to the existing resources of TZF in art. The reputation of the place was composed of two levels: the prestige of several well-known artists who settled earlier and the titles of 'art street' and 'creative industries cluster' both of which were officially designated. This formed the symbolic capital of the place, which was understood by most of the painters as a resource they could draw on for their own art career. Weiguang (born in 1960), arriving in 2002 after the settlement of the famous visual artist Cheng Yifei, made explicit his intention of borrowing the reputation of the place established by Cheng Yifei:

> TZF has some fame. People come to Shanghai, besides Xin'tiandi[6], they will also come here. Above all it emerged (from an unknown place) because of Cheng Yifei. We borrow his glory, he is very renowned. Many people come here to see Mr Cheng and then stop

in our studios. They find our paintings are not sold at a high price and also not bad in quality. However, Mr Cheng died too early. When he was here, the people who settled in were all artists.

Weiguang's chance of being visited increased when people came to see Cheng Yifei and then might drop by at his studio. The benefits that he received were a 'spill over effect' as the core reputation of the place was built by Cheng Yifei but spread out in the vicinity where novice art workers settled. As their entry into the artistic field was experimental and their status was still low or relatively low, locating their studios amidst an artistic milieu was a strategy, serving as a passage to the professional context of production and exchange. Weiguang received the first order of a large painting only one week after his settlement in Building 5. The visibility of the place brought him confidence to meet patrons who might like his works.

Besides the fame of the place brought by several well-known artists as trailblazers in culture-led regeneration, official titles including 'art street' and 'creative industries cluster' were also considered as intangible assets. Fengbo (born in the 1960s), having been staying in TZF since 2006, talked about the importance of these titles for locating his studio in terms of publicity:

> Because someone is supporting this place. We don't have ability to tell others where we are. Since someone has already made TZF a 'creative industries cluster', there will be people coming to see your work and getting to know you. There is a lot of publicity for this place. Publications like traffic maps and tourist maps mark the place. Taikang Road (the road where TZF is located) is named 'Shanghai Art Street' and there has been a long-term promotion of it, for example through an adverting light box since 2003.

He considered that the titles implied official support and publicity. Since the job of being a self-employed artist remained insecure and outside the existing employment system, the titles granted by the government suggested special care and favourable policy, though this might be merely a one-sided judgement held by the artists. At least at the conceptual level, the identification of the place by using rhetorics of art and creative industries brought an impression of confirmation. Shizhe (born in the 1970s), arriving at the end of 2004, responded: 'it was planned as "art street" and then I came here for art'.

The reputation of the place was closely linked to the visibility of the place. By exposing to media and art consumers, some of the painters started their exchange in the art market. Weiguang made the point that visibility was essential:

> I feel as long as my work could be shown, it will certainly sell. When I was in the painting village, one customer bought over ten paintings from me just after discovering my work. If no one sees them, then they (my paintings) will die there.

He was confident about selling his work if shown. There were journalists who came to report TZF, both from China and abroad. His work was also introduced and published in some magazines. Positioned between the painters and the outside world, TZF became a platform, serving as a 'showcase' (Weiguang), or a 'starting environment' (Zhaosi), or a 'window' (Fanwen) for their entry to the artistic field and market. The eagerness for visibility implies the nature of the artistic field where value is based on recognition and credit. Jobs in art are precarious and there are two distinctive poles. On the one hand, there are consecrated (recognised) artists whose works are regarded to be invaluable. Assessment of their work does

The artistic field meets the art worlds

not abide by the conventional law of commodity exchange which is based on use value, but on symbolic value – the prestige of individual artists. On the other hand, doing art could be humble and analogous to a bread-and-butter job. Zhaosi, trying pyrography in depicting Shanghai's historical architecture, said in a slightly sad tone: 'I might be a poor painter for my whole life and my whole life might just pass in an anonymous state.'

By using the existing resources of publicity attached to TZF, new resources such as information flow and forms of capital were generated. There were various kinds of art magazines and leaflets delivered to the painters for free. These became a substantial source for self-learning and improvement in artistic skills and knowledge. Facing the dynamics of art creations from time to time, Fengmo got to keep track of the styles and the artists' portfolios from those free magazines. He was not sure about how he was known, 'I guess they came and noted down my information according to my name card on my studio's door'. Compared to his previous stay in the Painting Village even without a postal address, the function of TZF as a channel to the artistic field was acknowledged by the painters.

Figure 29.2 The first floor of Building 5 where Weiguang's studio was located

Manoeuvring between creative autonomy and the needs of projected consumers

Locating art studios in TZF is a spatial strategy by which the painters get more opportunities and are exposed to media, audiences and patrons. Strategy is an external aspect of field struggles, and for the painters both living for art and living by art, their struggles are more than that. In their everyday painting practices, their manoeuvres between creative autonomy and the needs of projected consumers are evident, implying their struggles between cultural capital and economic capital. On the one hand, the development of a certain art style is based on the judgement of its values in the artistic field; on the other hand, the artistic codes and subject matter are involved in compromises with the potential customers. Such a way of living is called 'walking on both feet' by the painters, suggesting the balance they need to make between artistic creativity and commercial needs. For example, Weiguang's adoption of urban impressionism is backed up by the legitimate status of impressionism in the modern history of art and accepted meanings of its art codes. Meanwhile, his style of representing cityscape embodies the aesthetic and emotional needs for a certain social group whom he identified as 'passing guests of the city'.

The first encounter of Weiguang's work with the city of Shanghai was in 2001 when the rapid development of Pudoing New District along the east bank of Huangpu River sharply contrasted with his previous impression when the place had been occupied by old dockyards in the 1980s. He painted *Clouds of the City* depicting the modernised view in the impressionist style that the clouds were moving between tower buildings in the New District. 'The clouds floating above the city are beautiful, but actually they are vagrant' (Weiguang). From his first painting about the urban landscape which subtly implied his status as migrant, unstable and mobile as the clouds, his later works then reveal his sentiment towards the changing city, and reflected how he adapted to the needs of projected art consumers – people who love Shanghai but passers-by of the city. He quoted a customer from Hong Kong explaining why he was buying his paintings:

> We are all passers-by of Shanghai. We saw the rapid economic development of China and Shanghai, so we came and settled here (to catch business opportunities). When we'll leave Shanghai one day in the future, we want to have something to remember. We will think of the days in Shanghai when looking at your paintings.

The orientation to the group 'passers-by of the city' is tacitly made through the accumulated exposure to the market and exchange, while the Chinese and foreign expatriates and sojourners as well as foreign tourists have become the primary buyers. Cherishing the need to 'impressionise' the city and potentially memorise it, Weiguang's painting style was a result of his pursuit of art conventions and innovations, and in other words, aimed at incorporating and improving symbolic capital and cultural capital. He sought a route between the Western Impressionist and traditional Chinese painting. On the one hand, he drew on the technique of colour use from Impressionism which remains sensitive to light and shadow, on the other hand, he tended to embody the spirit of Chinese ink and brush painting and transformed the artificial urban built environment into a feeling of natural landscapes. Such a combination of artistic codes creates his genre of urban expressions in both real and imaginary realms. The visual elements which are often presented are intentionally selected and symbolic. Among them, the area around the Huangpu River is highly visible, including the west bank named as 'Bund', a landmark of cosmopolitan Shanghai in the 1920s and 1930s characterised by the classical Western architecture built during the period of foreign settlement, and the east bank, known as a global trade and financial zone located in Pudong New District with the various modern and postmodern towers which were built from the 1990s on. Through repositioning

The artistic field meets the art worlds

Figure 29.3 Weiguang's painting of the city of Shanghai

of the buildings for geometrical aesthetics while maintaining a general resemblance to their layout, a trans-historical panorama of the city, which is strange but familiar, is presented. The works are like tales of the city, covering a wide spectrum of urban faces and sentiments – the mysterious, industrially polluted, green, foggy, nostalgic and so on.

These manoeuvring practices between creative autonomy, artistic codes and consumers' demands were also used by other painters. For example, Zhaosi appreciated the vicissitudes of historical architecture and perceived that potential customers of his paintings might be foreign visitors who liked heritage. He applied the conventional sepia tone for a nostalgic feel in painting the old part of the city while using the medium of wood and the skill of pyrography, which is relatively new for landscape painting. For Caoyin, the experiment of using mixed media, including the original ancient books and title deeds which she collected, showed her innovation in materials; while on the other hand, her painting of the lotus in yellow, pink or other bright colours for decorative effect was an adaptation to the conventions of 'beauty' for the female white-collar buyers. And Chengyun's paintings are themed on Taiji martial art painted in a single colour, such as red. The theme of the Taiji is favoured by foreign dealers, and his use of redness is also regarded as 'Chinese red' with the specified meaning of red in the Chinese culture. These conventions about the tacit codes in the symbolisation system of China are combined with his innovative method of painting in an abstract style by layer upon layer in order to create a three-dimensional effect. Such manoeuvres became a difficult tenet to get along with for many painters. It is like dancing with chains, and if one foot in market demands slips too far, then the painter will fall into the track of commercial production of art. Behind the scene of living for art and living by art, there were also mental struggles and depression. For example, Weiguang expressed his contradictory circumstances after painting the cityscape of Shanghai for many years:

> Now it is very difficult to make a different one – I have tried almost every way. In this case, I need to go out (to observe and gain urban experience) to collect fresh ideas. But Saturday and Sunday is the good time to meet visitors. I pay so much for the rent, if I shut the door and go out of the studio just for one day, it will cost me 200 RMB (10 RMB=1GBP) . Such pressure stops me taking a step away from my studio.

He further added:

> If I had been born in a rich family, I would not sell any paintings. I have to sell my paintings in order to live; I feed painting by selling them. ... If I really have money one day in

Figure 29.4 Weiguang's studio in TZF

The artistic field meets the art worlds

Figure 29.5 The label of a painting by Weiguang in his solo exhibition in 2014

the future, I want to go around the world, and paint every city one or two pictures from my perspective ... then hold an exhibition to show different cities.

In the past few years, there have been hundreds of painters coming to and leaving TZF; the shortest stay is only one month and the longest is over ten years. For the painters who remained in TZF for years, there was a distinctive sense of pride and self-achievement. Compared to the vast global art market, TZF was a miniature. During the time of economic crisis in 2008, many painters in Building 5 suffered – some without selling one piece of work during the latter half of 2008 – and had to leave. Developing a set of artistic codes and visual languages particular to each painter was conceived as essential for survival in TZF. This remained a challenging task for most painters. As their painting practices in previous jobs was more about imitating other images rather than free creation, to set up one's own languages in painting as well as catering to market demands was a difficult task.

Interactions and networks

Apart from these field struggles with their objective relations underneath, TZF is a concrete art world in and around which interactions, face-to-face ties and networks develop between the painters, art consumers, critics and other relevant sectors. Some of the interactions and networks lead to long-term patronage or a fixed source of support, turning to valuable social capital for higher field positions, while some remain at the level of friendship to provide mental support, apprenticeship or other forms of support.

Weiguang and Fengmo both met their 'important' buyers, who became their patrons. Sherry, a regular buyer of Weiguang, liked his works at first sight when she visited his open studio. Born in Shanghai but later moving to Hong Kong, Sherry finds memories of Shanghai in Weiguang's works. She named one painting which was bought from Weiguang 'I love chocolate', as the primary colour tone was brown and reminded her of the place where she had lived during her childhood in Shanghai. When knowing that Eastern Airline Magazine was making a column for Weiguang's paintings in 2004, Sherry wrote the commentary personally, 'city is often a reminder of pressure. When most people are ignoring the beauty of cityscape in their rush to work, Weiguang's paintbrush presents it by romantic layers of colour and vigorous rhythm, making people immersed into the cityscape without feeling the coldness'[7]. Having travelled in many cities abroad, she was surprised by his mastery of impressionism when she got to know that Weiguang did not have any experience of studying or living abroad. The ways of interaction between the painter and the patron were multiple. On the one hand, Sherry was learning painting with Weiguang and altogether collected over thirty pieces of his work. On the other hand, Sherry was actively involved in promoting his works through recommending the painter to art critics and galleries. Some comments were intentional, embedding the discussion of Weiguang's urban series in the context of impressionists and the rise of the middle class patrons in the West, thus posing the question about the Chinese middle class and their artistic taste which is of media and public interest. Nancy's Gallery, a private medium-sized gallery which is also located in Building 5, acts as partial agent of Weiguang's works. During Weiguang's stay in TZF for more than ten years, networks in art worlds were gradually built through the interactions with visitors, customers, friends and fellows from his home city. Some of these networks turned out to give substantial social capital in media, critic and art markets. In the opening reception of a recent solo exhibition of Weiguang held in a luxurious hotel by Nancy's Gallery, most of the attendees were from media and art relevant sectors. Some of them were the friends of Weiguang or the gallery's founder, and some were new and from newly emerged media and creative intermediaries looking for customer and network resources. In the private dinner after the opening reception for celebrating the painter's success and his gratitude to all his supporters, the number of attendees was smaller, primarily composed of his home city fellows living in Shanghai and those still living in the home city, and friends from art and design sectors including furniture design, landscape design, art collection, art training, antique trade and culture study in universities.

Fengmo also met his patrons in TZF. He considered the three years in TZF as a turning point for his career because it was during a most difficult time for him that a company boss from Taiwan came across his studio and then became his regular buyer. He recalled: 'TZF gave me a chance to meet a friend [the buyer from Taiwan]. He likes my paintings and appreciates me. He has an important position in my life. ... I had a pile of paintings in the studio and he came to recognise me. He is vital in my life.'

We can see, then, that there are various kinds of connections and relations centred on TZF. As well as the relations between painters and art consumers, and between painters and media, other relations include fellowship from the same hometown, friendship built on similar interests and common languages, teacher and students, and so on. For example, Weiguang, Yaxing and Fanwen became very good friends of mutual mental support, though they are from different places of China. Fanwen, who previously worked as a college teacher in fine arts before retirement, also took apprentices in his studio in TZF. Caoyin made many friends who were female white-collar workers of her age; though some of them had not bought anything yet, she chatted happily with them. Some of those who liked her works also had regular painting classes with her. There were non face-to-face relations as well, primarily embodied in information networks within cultural and art worlds. For example, salespeople from culture and art magazines went to note down the room number of the painters, and sent them free copies of magazines. The invisible interactions reveal the voluntary, collaborative and complex networks in the contemporary art world which has been more characteristic of an industry.

In Bourdieu's field analysis, interactions are placed in a subordinate position to objective relations. Such interpretative logic of interactions is reductive, regarding all forms of interactions as merely externalisation of structures, power relations and rankings. The examples of these painters show that the interactions and networks contribute to the accumulation of social resources which are needed for a better field position, and in this sense, the concrete relations with various parts of the art worlds in sum transform into social capital, which further have effect on the objective position and objective relations that the painters held in the artistic field. The surviving painters in TZF just develop their career from the multilevel and multifaceted social networks to the track of living for art and living by art. The increase of paintings' exchange value becomes an important signifier for their improved field positions. The price of Weiguang's paintings increased from 2,000RMB and 3,000RMB to 20,000RMB and 30,000RMB and more for the bigger sizes. Chengyun gained very fruitful performances in the art market, and opened his second studio in M50, the more famous art cluster in Shanghai charging much higher rents. Being located out of the canonical channel to recognition, i.e. from affiliations with the orthodox art authorities and institutions, these self-employed painters were involved into the art worlds through the multiplicity of networks, actual or virtual. The interactions provided means for achieving recognition and the individual identity as a painter or an artist; the social capital also transformed into symbolic capital which, in return, influenced the depth, spectrum, forms and efficacy of social networks.

Conclusion

The analysis of the painters reveals their dual existence in the artistic field and art worlds. Their everyday practices are actually a dialogue between these two realms. While this might remain a very subtle way to cope with their status of being self-employed painters, their strong sense of positioning and position takings – both in locating themselves in TZF and their choices of themes and styles – is evident. Interest is taken when sharing 'the belief in the value of what is dispute' (Savage and Silva 2013: 113), and for the artistic field, experiences of the painters reveal that symbolic capital is core. Their strategies and struggles are automatic embodiment for improving their symbolic capital which, in a practical expression, is read as 'being recognised in the art market and having good exchange value'. Such sense of the artistic field and feel for the game, however, at the mundane level, is incarnated in the concrete form of art worlds which is very closely linked to the painters' everyday life. TZF acts as an intermediary between the dialectics of the artistic field and art worlds. Centred on TZF, the social networks of the painters with consumers, critics, media and various parts of art worlds turn out to be important social capital for the painters' field positions. In this sense, although the artistic field and art worlds are very different from their respective theoretical assumptions; in reality forms of capital, mainly symbolic capital and social capital are transferred between these two realms, and interactions and social networks play an important role in transforming objective relations in the field through influencing the composition and volume of social capital.

Reviewing the burgeoning culture and art clusters in China over the past decades, the case of TZF presents a model of an art village – a combination of art and market, and of freelance artists and metropolis. By the comprehensive judgement of the painting level in TZF in comparison with other painting clusters and the entire artistic field of painting, production was located at the middle stratum. It is much better than Wending Road – a cluster producing paintings through colour printing followed by a few brushstrokes for a vivid look before completion, and also better than Dafen Oil Painting Village in Shenzhen in south China, which specialises in mass-production of copies of Western oil painting masterpieces through the stream-lined work of a team of painting workers. Besides, compared with many anonymous or less-known painting clusters in Shanghai, such as the painting village located out of the central districts including Nanhui and Minhang, the art space in TZF is more visible to media and the public and there are also some painters whose work is sold at relatively high prices. However, vis-à-vis legitimate and academic paintings, the position of the painting cluster in TZF remained modest. Wang and Qiang, two celebrated artists who were invited to settle their studios in TZF at its early stage and contributed to its reputation in art, both commented that artists should have an independent spirit and not be influenced by other people's opinions and the market demands.

No matter how the purely 'art for art's sake' would exert superiority over TZF – based on misrecognition of economic capital being nowhere – the existence of TZF as both a cultural and urban phenomenon is historic. It joins the global strand of culture and art-led urban regeneration from Shanghai, becoming a remarkable site for urban and cultural tourism. Its meaning for the city of Shanghai might not be that specific if judged from the global map linking many bohemian or artistic neighbourhoods in deindustrialised Western cities. However, TZF is a place under the critic-dealer system where possibly a professional painters' dream can come true and find its grasp from the rise of art consumers in China and the international art market of metropolitan Shanghai. It might be only a stop for the painters in their migrant journey for seeking the proper place to settle down, as the painter Yaxin used 'the particular kind of grass in the desert and being drifted here and there by the wind' to describe the trajectories of painters. When TZF has become more and more commercialised and gentrified, lamented as 'art finishing its role in making the place as creative industries cluster' and 'walking towards aging and grave from its infancy and adulthood' (Fengmo) in terms of the art cycle of the place, another 'TZF' under the trailbreaker of art is newly born in the city or elsewhere in China.

Notes

1 The artists who cooperated with Lorenz include Wang Guangyi, Zhouteihai, Xuesong, Dingyi and so on. Wang Guangyi (born in 1957) is in the vanguard of Chinese political pop art. His representative works are entitled 'Great Criticism' by which he uses the posters of the Cultural Revolution and develops them into criticism of influential global commodities in China. Zhou Tiehai (born in 1966) has been signed with Lorenz as his agent for over a decade. He regarded Lorenz as vital in introducing him to the world stage. In one work, he presented a lift which implied the role of Lorenz in his first entry to the Basel Exhibition. Besides Lorenz, there are two more important persons for his career: Harald Szeemann (the curator of the Venice Biennale) and Uli Sigg (the Swiss ex-ambassador in China who has a rich collection of contemporary Chinese art works including 1,200 pieces).
2 Study of the painters is a part of the PhD project 'Regeneration of Tianzifang and Social Relations' funded by the UK Department for Education, the University of Manchester, Universities' China Committee in London and China Scholarship Council. It aimed to better understand art-led regeneration in Shanghai as a new modality of urban renewal compared with previous local experiences, as well as to decipher the trajectories and social positions of the self-employed painters in the transitional period.
3 In this article, Cheng Yifei and Weiguang are not pseudonyms of the artists. Cheng Yifei died in 2005 a very famous artist and also significant contributor to TZF's art-led regeneration and artistic reputation; using his real name is showing this respect. Use of the real name Weiguang has gained the written consent from the painter. With the use of his painting and the relevant pictures, using his real name is also showing respect for his creation.

4 Pudong Painting Village was an apartment building of twenty-four storeys. It was located at Wulian Road in Pudong New District. It was originally built for commodity housing, but remained vacant for years owing to an ownership dispute over the land. It was rented to painters at a low rate under the plan of an art entrepreneur Chenggang. It had remained a 'painting village' since May 2001. As of September 2003, the painters were asked to move out as the building had been resold on the property market.
5 A traditional art form of decorating wood with burn marks by a heated poker.
6 Xin'tiandi is a well-known tourist site themed on Shikumen architecture located in the central part of Shanghai. It was completed in 2001 as a giant municipal flagship project of regeneration and was an investment of the developer Shui On Group from Hong Kong. By displacing all the original residents in this area, the project rebuilt Shikumen houses on the site where the old ones were torn down. The architecture of Tianzifang is similar to Xin'tiandi. In Tianzifang, there are also alleyways of Shikumen tenements. Apart from these, factory buildings compose the other architectural forms of Tianzifang.
7 This citation is translated from the copy of her commentary which is in the collection of Weiguang. The author got access to this commentary during the interview with Weiguang.

References

Banks, M. (2014) '"Being in the Zone" of Culture Work', *Culture Unbound*, 6: 241–262.
Becker, H.S. (1982) *Art Worlds*, Berkeley: University of California Press.
Becker, H. S. and A. Pessin (2006) 'A Dialogue on the Ideas of "World" and "Field"', *Sociological Forum*, 21(2): 275–286.
Bottero, W. and N. Crossley (2011) 'Worlds, Fields and Networks: Becker, Bourdieu and the Structures of Social Relations', *Cultural Sociology*, 5(1): 99–119.
—— (2014) 'Social Spaces of Music: Introduction', *Cultural Sociology*: 1–17.
Bourdieu, P. (1977) *Outline of a Theory of Practice*, New York: Cambridge University Press.
—— (1986) *Distinction*, Oxon, UK: Routledge.
—— (1993) *Field of Cultural Production*, Cambridge: Polity Press.
—— (1999) *The Weight of the World – Social Suffering in Contemporary Society*, Stanford, CA: Stanford University Press.
Bourdieu, P. and L. Wacquant (1992) *An Invitation to Reflexive Sociology*, Chicago: University of Chicago Press.
Caulfield, J. (1994) *City Form and Everyday Life: Toronto's Gentrification and Critical Social Practice*, Toronto: University of Toronto Press.
Caves, R. (2009) *Creative Industries: Contracts between Art and Commerce*, Cambridge, MA: Harvard University Press.
Chapain, C. and R. Comunian (2010) 'Enabling or Inhibiting the Creative Economy: The Role of the Local and Regional Dimension in England', *Regional Studies*, 44 (6): 717–734.
CURDS (2001) *Culture Cluster Mapping and Analysis*, prepared by CURDS, Centre for Urban and Regional Development Studies for One North East, Newcastle Upon Tyne.
Davies, C.A. (1999) *Reflexive Ethnography: A Guide to Researching Selves and Others*, London: Routledge.
De Nooy, W. (2002) 'The Dynamics of Artistic Prestige', *Poetics*, 30(2002): 147–167.
—— (2003) 'Fields and Networks: Correspondence Analysis and Social Network Analysis in the Framework of Field Theory', *Poetics*, 31(5): 305–327.
Dubois, V. and J. Méon (2012) 'The Social Conditions of Cultural Domination: Field, Sub-Field and Local Spaces of Wind Music in France', *Cultural Sociology*, 7(2): 127–144.
Fowler, B. (1997) *Pierre Bourdieu and Cultural Theory: Critical Investigations*, London: Sage.
Fox, E. (2014) 'Bourdieu's Relational View of Interactions: A Reply to Bottero and Crossley', *Cultural Sociology*, 8(2): 204–211.
Gill, R. and A. Pratt (2008) 'Precarity and Cultural Work in the Social Factory? – Immaterial Labour, Precariousness and Cultural Work', *Theory, Culture & Society*, 25(7-8): 1–30.
Grenfell, M. and Hardy, C. (2003) 'Field Manoeuvres – Bourdieu and the Young British Artists', *Space & Culture*, 6 (1): 19–34.
Hanquinet, L., M. Savage and L. Callier, (2012) 'Elaborating Bourdieu's Field Analysis in Urban Studies: Cultural Dynamics in Brussels', *Urban Geography*, 33(4): 508–529.
Hesmondhalgh. D. (2002) *The Cultural Industries*, London: Sage.

Hillier, B. and J. Hanson (1984) *The Social Logic of Space*, Cambridge: Cambridge University Press.
Ley, D. (2003). 'Artists, Aestheticisation and the Field of Gentrification', *Urban Studies*, 40(12), 2527–2544.
Lizardo, O. (2008) 'The Cognitive Origins of Bourdieu's Habitus', *Journal for the Theory of Social Behaviour*, 34: 375–401.
Madison, D.S. (2005) *Critical Ethnography – Method, Ethics and Performance*, London: Sage.
Mason, J. (2006) 'Mixing Methods in a Qualitative Driven Way', *Qualitative Research*, 6 (1): 9–25.
Oakley, K. (2009) 'The Disappearing Arts: Creativity and Innovation after the Creative Industries', *International Journal of Cultural Policy*, 15 (4): 403–413.
O'Connor, J. (2009) 'Creative Industries: A New Direction?', *International Journal of Cultural Policy*, 15 (4): 387–402.
Parker, S., E. Uprichard and R. Burrows (2007) 'Class Places and Place Classes – Geodemographics and the Spatialisation of Class', *Information, Communication & Society*, 10 (6): 902–921.
Powell, W.W., D.R. White, K.W. Koput and J. Owen-Smith (2005) 'Network Dynamics and Field Evolution: The Growth of Interorganizational Collaboration in the Life Sciences', *American Journal of Sociology*, 110(4): 1132–1205.
Santoro, M. (2011) 'From Bourdieu to Cultural Sociology', *Cultural Sociology*, 5(1):3–23.
Savage, M. (2010) 'The Politics of Elective Belonging', *Housing, Theory and Society*, 26 (1): 115–135.
—— (2011) 'The Lost Urban Sociology of Pierre Bourdieu', in G. Bridge and S. Watson (ed.) *Companion to the City*, Oxford: Blackwell. 511–520.
Savage, M., G. Bagnall and B. Longhurst (2005) *Globalisation and Belonging*, London: Sage.
Savage, M. and E.B. Silva (2013) 'Field Analysis in Cultural Sociology', *Cultural Sociology*, 7(2): 111–126.
Seigel, J. (1986) *Bohemian Paris: Culture, Politics, and the Boundaries of Bourgeois Life, 1830–1930*, New York: Viking Penguin.
Sullivan, M. (1999) 'Art in China since 1949', *The China Quarterly*, 159: 712–722.
Thrift, N. (1996) *Spatial Formations*, London: Sage.
Wacquant, L. (2008) 'Relocating Gentrification: The Working Class, Science and the State in Recent Urban Research', *International Journal of Urban and Regional Research*, 32(1): 198–205.
Zhang, C. (2012) *When an Aestheticised Space Meets Its Mundane Reality – a Case Study of Neighbourhood Change in Tianzifang Shanghai*, PhD dissertation, University of Manchester.
Zukin, S. (1982) *Loft Living: Culture and Capital in Urban Change*, Baltimore: Johns Hopkins University Press.

30
Institutionalizing neo-bohemia

Richard Lloyd

Neo-bohemia signals the encounter between the traditions of 'the artist in the city' birthed in nineteenth century Paris and the structural dynamism reshaping cities at the end of the twentieth century. The urban bohemia, linking distinct city districts with the lifestyle articulations of young artists, intellectuals and aesthetes, is among the most durable attributes of modernity. The traditions of bohemia powerfully shape the image of the modern artist and the normative artistic career, and also, to a disproportionate degree, the image of the city. Nonetheless, as a space of willed eccentricity, bohemia was largely neglected by urban sociologists and sociologists of culture through most of the twentieth century. While the classic bohemia was exotic, limited to a few cultural capitals in Europe and the US, neo-bohemia is today an increasingly ordinary feature of the urban landscape. Moreover, it engenders novel consequences, implicated in post-industrial urban trends including gentrification, the elevation of lifestyle amenities serving a changing city population, and the ascent of 'new economy' urban enterprises in tourism, technology, design and finance. These consequences are crucial to discerning the *new* in neo-bohemia. Long a tertiary concern, the arts have been elevated in both the social sciences and as a core concern of local policy makers. Gestating in the urban crisis of the 1970s, neo-bohemia is today an institutionalized space of the contemporary city.

Bohemia gained currency in nineteenth century Paris as a term depicting the real-and-symbolic niche carved out by growing numbers of young and underemployed artists, intellectuals and aesthetes. The conventions of bohemia took shape in response to the structural upheavals of the nineteenth century: large-scale urbanization, the extensions of the capitalist marketplace, and the formation of a dynamic class system including an overabundance of aspirants in a new cultural economy. The city, the capitalist economy, and the modern artistic field are simultaneously resilient and dynamic structuring contexts, stubbornly shaping the bohemian lifestyle ever since. Core bohemian conventions have proven correspondingly durable and transposable, repeated and updated across era and city contexts. They continue to animate the new bohemia.

The resilient conventions of bohemia, past and present, include fascination with the urban demimonde, both as a space of sociability and object of representation; artistic agglomeration in marginal and transitional city districts, for reasons both material and symbolic; the romance of the starving artist and 'art for art's sake', always in tension with veiled or not-so-veiled aspirations for fame and fortune; the exaltation of youth, with bohemia as a space of apprenticeship for cultural aspirants; and the propensity to transform everyday life into a work of art, via eccentricities of fashion and lifestyle. Cumulatively elaborated and broadly shared ideas about what living like an artist in the city *should* look like continue to impact what it *does* look like, even while, as we will see, important divergences exist between the ideal and the reality. Neo-bohemia addresses both the continuities of the bohemian lifestyle (bohemia) and the dynamism of the structuring field (neo).

Urban sociology and the sociology of art

The American tradition of urban sociology was rooted in Chicago in the early part of the twentieth century, depicting an industrial metropolis swelled by immigrants and black Northern migration. Centred on the blue collar 'city of broad shoulders', the Chicago School largely ignored the aesthetic dimensions of urban life beyond the repetition of folk culture in the urban 'mosaic of little worlds' (Park, *et al.* 1925: 40).[1] Subsequent Marxist challenges to the functionalist human ecology of the 'Chicago School' focused on industrial manufacture and class conflict, issues to which the arts appeared decidedly peripheral (Castells 1972; Harvey 1973; Lefebvre 1974). White flight and deindustrialization, culminating in the urban crisis of the 1970s, led sociologists to increasingly address pressing issues of racial segregation and concentrated poverty in the city (Anderson 2000; Massey and Denton 1993; Wilson 1987). As the 'inner city' became a racialized space in the popular imagination, urban studies correspondingly became coextensive with the sociology of racial and ethnic relations.

Still, even in the nadir of white flight and post-industrial urban decline, artists retained a stubborn commitment to a core city address and *la vie de bohème*, a commitment with surprising consequences for subsequent patterns of urban restructuring. Sharon Zukin (1982) broke new ground in *Loft Living*, recognizing how the informal artists' colony taking residence in SoHo lofts transformed former spaces of light industry into new opportunities for investment. In this and other works, Zukin was at the forefront of identifying a new urban trend, in which the arts and the bohemian lifestyle would figure prominently in emergent patterns of development, including residential gentrification, new retail and nightlife amenities, and new economy enterprises (Zukin 1991, 1995, 2010). Her work captures the origins of neo-bohemia, though without using the term, as a bridge between post-industrial urban decay and the reanimation of urban space driven by new economic, political and cultural principles, and by a changing urban population.

By the 1990s, urban sociologists were lurching towards new theories to account for the evident dynamism of some cities and city places in the wake of the urban crisis. Studies of gentrification proliferated, many taking glancing notice of the role that artists and aesthetes played as 'urban pioneers' (Abu Lughod 1995; Mele 2000; Smith 1996). These tended to largely neglect the motives and lifestyles of 'early gentrifies', and to focus disproportionately on consumption rather than the new styles of post-industrial production reshaping once-decaying neighbourhoods. Simultaneously, new theories of 'Disneyfied' downtowns and 'tourist bubbles' recognized the rising importance of culture and aesthetics to emergent patterns of development, while treating the new spaces of consumption – exemplified by New York's Times Square, LA's Bonaventure Hotel, or Baltimore's Inner Harbor – as strictly segregated from the residential life of the city (Eeckhout 2001; Harvey 1989; Jameson 1991; Judd and Fainstein 1999; Sorkin 1992). Along with ignoring actual city residents, they also ignored the new urban economy rising alongside the festival marketplaces.

This new economy was, according to Manuel Castells (1989), based on the processing of information rather than the making of things, and 'the informational city' in his account segregates its abstract 'space of flows' from 'the space of place' in which real people live. Saskia Sassen's influential *The Global City* (2001) similarly identified the new role of cities like New York, London, and Tokyo as 'strategic sites', or 'command and control' centres, in a *networked* global economy, and also as 'post-industrial production' sites with a catalogue of 'new economy' enterprises in which finance is dominant, but which also includes the aesthetic enterprises of fashion, design and new media. The vaunted 'LA School' of urban sociology meanwhile promoted a theory of 'postmodern' urbanism in which the Chicago-style focus on neighbourhood was deemed obsolete (Dear 2002; Scott and Soja 1996; Soja 1989). While Sassen stands nearly alone in considering a link between new urban enterprises, corresponding demographic change, and the rise of residential gentrification and new amenity provision, her work also led a trend of depicting a 'dual city' of glamour zones juxtaposed to spaces of devastation, lacking an account of interstitial districts and process in local transition (see Mollenkopf and Castells 1991).

Meanwhile, sociologists of culture, and particularly the 'production of culture' perspective, have considered virtually every contextual factor in the creation of art except for the geographic places where it occurs (Peterson 2004). Pierre Bourdieu's (1993) influential 'field of cultural production' is derived from a consideration of the nineteenth century Parisian literary field, but in his reach for generalizable principles he abstracts *La Ville Lumière* entirely out of the analysis. *The Rules of Art* (1992), based on Bourdieu's eccentric sociological reading of Flaubert's *Sentimental Education*, offers a detailed examination of bohemian conventions that likewise excludes the essential principle of urbanism as a way of life. Howard Becker's *Art Worlds* (1982) is an intricate account of the webs of social relations and the shared social conventions that inform the production of art, which also ignores how cities operate both materially and symbolically in the fostering of arts careers and the elaboration of arts enterprises. Bourdieu's conflict theory in *The Field of Cultural Production* and Becker's functionalist approach in *Art Worlds* have proven the most influential attempts to provide a holistic sociological theory of the production of culture. Both use spatial metaphors in analyses innocent of geographic considerations.

Neo-bohemia

Conceptually, neo-bohemia bridges urban sociology and the sociology of art, connecting the durable urban conventions of bohemia to trajectories of restructuring rooted in the urban crisis. As with Becker and Bourdieu, it belies modernist claims for artistic autonomy, identifying bohemia as a conventionalized space of artistic collaboration also embedded in broader social structures. Bohemia is impacted by shifts in the field of cultural production, in the nature of its host cities, and in the larger socio-economic system. Neo-bohemia further bridges theories of gentrification, aestheticized urban amenities, and the new urban economy associated with globalization and information technology. It is embedded in a wave of scholarship in the 2000s that connects the changing demographics of post-industrial cities – featuring an educated class that is also highly stratified economically – with new styles of work and new patterns of residence and consumption (Brown-Saracino 2010; Deener 2012; Centner 2008; Neff 2012; Hutton 2008; Indergaard 2009; Pratt 2008). Artists and committed lifestyle aesthetes (e.g. hipsters) – always a small if particularly ostentatious category of urban resident – contribute disproportionately to new place-making projects and new economic agendas.

Neo-bohemia illuminates the production of culture in an era when the conventional culture industries are compelled to seek ever greater flexibility, and digital media augurs both new opportunities and new forms of exploitation in the elaboration of artistic careers (Hesmondhalgh 1996; Kot 2010; Neff 2012; Scott 2000). It illustrates that, even with the rise of allegedly deracinating information technology, the space of place has not in fact given way to the space of flows. Moreover, it dissolves the problematic boundaries between spaces of production and spaces of consumption in scholarship surrounding the contemporary city. Traversing sociological fields, neo-bohemia theorizes both the production of culture, adding a long neglected spatial dimension to the sociology of art, and the production of urban space, adding a serious consideration of bohemian tradition to urban sociology.

Since 2000, the value of the arts to local development agendas and the attraction of high-human capital workers – described by Richard Florida as the 'creative class' – has increasingly captured the attention of both scholars and urban policy elites (Florida 2002a; Grodach and Silver 2015; Markusen and Gadwa 2010; Silver and Miller 2010). The tremendous popular success of Florida's work, which has also engendered substantial controversy in the scholarly community, contributes to the elevation of cultural concerns in policy agendas, a wave latched onto by arts advocates (Markusen 2006). If in the past bohemia has been regarded as a marginal and organic agglomeration of eccentrics, neo-bohemia in the 2000s has become an institutionalized feature of the urban landscape, part of a 'creative class' growth protocol dovetailing with neoliberal urban governance (Peck 2005). Still, while Florida floats the bohemian concept liberally in *Rise of the Creative Class*, his understanding of either its history or its contemporary articulation is shallow, and his claim that the 'sustainable economic base' of the creative industries has resolved once-seemingly intractable contradictions is off the mark. Neo-bohemia both supports elements of Florida's argument and challenges several of his conclusions.

The case study: Chicago's Wicker Park

The concept of neo-bohemia was elaborated via an extended case study of Chicago's Wicker Park neighbourhood from the early 1990s to the crash of the Internet equity bubble in 2001, ending what is now known as the Web 1.0 era (Lloyd 2010). Wicker Park, once a Polish ethnic enclave in the classic Chicago School style, had weathered post-industrial decay, with a population depleted by white flight. Population decline was partially arrested by the arrival of new immigrant groups, in this case Mexican and Puerto Rican. Advantageously located on the near West Side of the downtown Loop, along transportation arteries that tethered it to key sites including the La Salle Street financial corridor and the School at the Art Institute, the economically distressed neighbourhood boasted both rich-if-dilapidated housing stock and spaces of light industry ripe for adaptive reuse.

In the mid-1980's, artists increasingly joined immigrants in replenishing the local population, flying under the radar until the emergence of new or repurposed bars, restaurants, cafés and retail outlets, and the launching of the annual 'Around the Coyote' art festival in 1989, announcing their presence to a wider public. Identified in outlets including *Rolling Stone*, the *New York Times* and *Billboard* as a new 'indie rock' hot spot in 1993–95 – on the heels of the vaunted 'Seattle Scene' – Wicker Park's notoriety as Chicago's 'burst of bohemia' was accompanied by an exploding nightlife economy and advancing local gentrification.[2] As the millennium turned, the neighborhood became implicated in other emerging media trends, increasingly attracting boutique 'creative' enterprises in digital design, and in 2001 hosting the cast of MTV's pioneering reality television program *The Real World*.

In this trajectory, Wicker Park exemplifies the dynamic nature of neo-bohemia, implicated in the transition of low income and minority core city areas into new spaces of capital investment. As with Zukin's depiction of SoHo, artists are active agents in the adaptive reuse of dormant and/or derelict industrial spaces, providing both imagination and sweat equity to the process. Artists are also incorporated into the fabrication of new, 'hip' amenity economies, as both patrons and in flexible jobs as bartenders, baristas, and retail clerks, lending in either case the aura of their elevated subcultural capital (Lloyd 2010; Ocejo 2014).

The maturation of neo-bohemia includes the attraction of small-scale new economy enterprises in design and technology, also mining the aesthetic competencies of local residents. In early 2001, Wicker Park was identified by the now defunct digital trade publication *Industry Standard* as 'the best new place for media companies', identifying a number of boutique digital design enterprises including Buzzbait, housed in the neighbourhood's central northwest, 'Coyote' Tower, and Boom Cubed, with loft offices in a repurposed warehouse.[3] These enterprises exploited both the aura of local creativity and the surplus of local talent, though they faltered in the face of the Internet stock crash that same year. Nonetheless, as the major digital enterprises of suburban Silicon Valley recovered, so did the pattern of content-based web enterprises colonizing neo-bohemian districts, most spectacularly in San Francisco's Mission District (Centner 2008).

Gentrification and digital enterprises, with wealthier new residents and more highly capitalized businesses competing for local space, eventually price many committed bohemians out of the residential market, along with the typically non-white poor and working class residents of the earlier era. Following the brief recession of the early 2000s, the housing bubble prompted the accelerated infill of Wicker Park's remaining vacant lots, with home prices and rents soaring. The afterimage of 'hipness' and 'edginess' persists, deliberately nurtured as a key component of place value and ferried by enduring local institutions. If no longer able to live there, artists pushed to more marginal but still proximate districts continue to return to work, play and display in local galleries, cafés, performance venues, and bars. Like Wicker Park, New York's Lower East Side, San Francisco's Mission, and LA's Venice Beach continue to trade on a vaunted bohemian ethos long after the 'authentic' bohemian moment has past, provoking a familiar bohemian lament that amounts to what Renato Rosaldo (1993) calls 'imperialist nostalgia', where people mourn the loss of what they themselves have transformed (see also Brown-Saracino 2010; Deener 2012; Ocejo 2011).

The Parisian prototype

The theory of neo-bohemia charts this trajectory from its origins in the urban crisis through subsequent waves of political and economic restructuring. It also incorporates a longer historical consideration of bohemia as a fluid tradition of modernity, signalling both continuity and change. As such, it is a signature artefact of modernity, an epochal structure within which discontinuity and flux are paradoxically its most durable features (Berman 1982). Bohemian conventions are virtual, inscribed in works of aesthetic representation and mobilized by new generations that both make recourse to bohemia's authorizing aura while insisting on their own historical originality.[4] Bohemia, proto and neo, materializes in real city places, shaped and reshaped by distinct material contexts. Modern means *new* and bohemia in its Parisian origins named new conceptions of the artist in the city. Neo-bohemia is the *newest* new bohemia, and if neologisms inevitably reify dynamic social process, it is important to note that as such it remains a moving target. It gestated in the urban crisis of the 1970s, was implicated in subsequent processes of urban restructuring, and is today institutionalized as a standard and broadly diffused principle of contemporary urban identity. Its roots run even deeper, planted in the fertile soil of nineteenth century Paris.

Before becoming 'the kingdom of youth' in nineteenth century Paris, Bohemia named an actual kingdom in the present day Czech Republic which became a casualty of medieval internecine warfare. In pre-modern Europe, 'bohemian' became an epithet, synonymous with gypsy, expressing the low social standing and general mistrust of diasporic populations – those without a 'proper home'. The social cosmos of the Middle Ages was ordered by a fixed hierarchy and historic ties to the land; this was the era in which rural estate property stood for social wealth, worked by an immobile peasantry. The towns were the space of merchants, craftsmen and 'rootless cosmopolitans'. But modernity ushered in a generalized diaspora, with the waning of aristocratic and clerical privilege and the 'liberation' of the peasantry from the land (Polanyi 1957). Displaced from their ancestral homes and traditional caste locations, the poor and the privileged flooded the towns, looking for work, for fortune, or for fame. Paris and London duly swelled to great cities. Young students and artists poured into the cheap garrets of the Latin Quarter, calling themselves 'bohemians' to signify their vagrant status (Seigel 1986).

Like everything else in this era, art was exposed to the market to an unprecedented degree. The privatization of culture liberated aesthetic content from the yoke of patronage, and smashed the barriers to entry once regulated by craft guilds (Seigel 1986). Now *anyone* could claim to be an artist. Moreover, education was dramatically democratized, ferried by both expanding universities and a lumpen intelligentsia of docents and tutors. The new artistic field, premised on market exchange, is the beginning of the modern adage 'art for art's sake', initially contrasted to art for the sake of religious exaltation or the ratification of aristocratic privilege (Rookmaker 1970). But if the market opened up titillating new horizons of possibility, it was also ruthless in dispensing its rewards. In Paris, the 'dreamworlds' of modern capitalism, objectified in the Arcades and grand boulevards, were elaborated antecedent to teeming slums and gross penury (Benjamin 1999). Not incidentally, both became favoured objects of representation for modern artists, from the Impressionist painters to the literary giants Baudelaire, Balzac and Flaubert (Clark 1984; Harvey 2004).

By the mid-nineteenth century, the bohemian struggle had captured the public imagination, depicted by Balzac in *Un prince de bohème*, and, further down the literary food chain, by Henri Murger in a series of serialized stories in the penny papers that drew on his own experiences in the Latin Quarter. These popular tales were later combined into the novel *Scènes de la vie de bohème*, with a stage adaptation becoming a hit with bourgeois audiences of the Boulevard Theater. Murger's work is the foundation for Puccini's *La Bohème*, still among the most regularly produced operas. Bohemians may have been outcasts, 'without means and unrecognized' according to Seigel (1986: 4), but from its early stages, bohemia was also an object of popular fantasy (Wilson 2000). It is worth noting that despite routine associations between bohemia and the avant-garde, Murger's depiction, codifying durable features of the bohemian lifestyle, was aimed squarely at a popular audience, liberally employing the populist conventions of melodrama (Gluck 2010).

Murger's characters hatch grand plans while busily foraging for food and shelter, illustrating the durable juxtaposition of cultural aspiration and economic frustration. The bohemian pairing of extravagant imagination and harsh material circumstance dramatized the overweening contradictions of the modern metropolis. These pose distinctly modern challenges to the task of representation, and the reconciliation of ideal conceptions with the material realities of the artistic calling. The market untethers the imagination *and* introduces new modes of bondage; bohemia became a privileged ground for working out the contradictions inscribed in the modern field.

The terms of 'art for art's sake' duly shifted, making a virtue of necessity by ostentatiously refusing utilitarian calculation and bourgeois pandering (Bourdieu 1992). This refusal was inevitably shallow though. After all, Murger readily sold out, and in the last chapter of *Scènes de la vie de bohème* he depicts his bohemian heroes agreeing that they should sell out too. Similarly, Cesar Grana (1964: 4) observes that 'Balzac saw bohemia as a stimulating interlude before the chance for *real work* [emphasis added] arrives'. Benjamin takes that avatar of bohemia, Baudelaire, as his exemplary figure, archly noting the irony of bohemia's coy relation to the market. 'In the *flâneur,* the intelligentsia sets foot in the marketplace, ostensibly to look around, but in truth to find a buyer' (Benjamin 1999: 9).

Poverty, whether temporary or otherwise, consigned bohemians to the lived spaces of the dispossessed laboring classes, while education and pedigree aligned them with the bourgeoisie, buying them selective access to bourgeois privilege. 'Bohemians go everywhere and know everyone', wrote Murger (2004: xxxiii). In this liminal circumstance, bohemians made life itself an art, claiming the privilege, in the figure of the *flâneur,* to traverse all the spaces of the city, and to suture the fragments of Paris modernity into a grand mosaic. The 'starving artist' – at least while still in the full blush of youth – thus was codified as a hero of modernity, distinguished by noble refusal and intimations of imminence.

Aesthetic refinement was the key to plausibility in this role, and performing bohemian distinction on public stages preoccupied bohemians as much or more than the more solitary work of writing and painting. The bohemian aesthetic borrowed from and parodied proximate influences, exaggerating working class attire (the ragpicker) or bourgeois fashion (the dandy) in the creation of spectacular sartorial subcultures. This enduring feature of bohemia, making life into a work of art, has duly fed into the elaboration and marketing of fashions and fads, with bohemians as avatars of new modes of display and leisure activity (Clark 1984; Gottdeiner 1985; Hebdige 1979). Over time *la vie bohème* has inflected the modernist canon as well. The modernism of Baudelaire (*Fleurs du Mal* and *Paris Spleen*) and Manet (*Olympia* and *Bar at the Folies-Bergère*) codified an enduring bohemian fascination with the dark corners of the city and with the interstitial world of the demimonde. Perhaps sensing a special affinity – pricing the intimate self for the market – modern artists made prostitutes a favoured motif.

Bohemia in the early twentieth century

The model elaborated in Paris has proven both durable and transposable. In the next century, the vagrant artists of Greenwich Village were part of a larger diaspora, sharing space with European immigrant labourers and numbering expats like Marcel Duchamp and Mina Loy among its membership (Barnett 2004; Wetzsteon 2002). The nineteenth century prototype drew from the French provinces; in the nineteen teens and twenties, bohemia in both Paris and New York was considerably more cosmopolitan, circulating an international cast of artists and artist wannabes, with Paris hosting the Irishman Joyce, the American Hemingway, and the Spaniard Picasso (Franck 1998).

Meanwhile, in uptown New York, a Harlem bohemia took shape inscribed with the peculiarity of America's racial caste system and the Southern diaspora of African Americans. By the mid-twentieth century, the American urban bohemia drew more and more on black cultural styles, or fetishized understandings of them, as in the beat appropriations of jazz or Norman Mailer's hipster manifesto, 'The White Negro' (1959). The fantasy projections of Ivy educated writers like Mailer, Ginsberg and Kerouac onto the racially stigmatized repeats classic white bohemian privilege; 'bohemians go everywhere, and know everyone' (Murger 2004: xxxiii.) Thus they could visit Harlem juke joints without sacrificing a Harvard Yard pedigree beyond the reach of black hipster avatars like Dizzy Gillespie. And as with Murger's prototypical work, depictions like *On the Road* were rewarded with widespread popular success.

So, despite the routine anti-bourgeois posturing, bohemia was in its first one hundred years a by-product of bourgeois industry and the migration patterns that it ignited – peasants moving from province to city, Europeans crossing the Atlantic to America, and in the US, poor blacks migrating from the rural South to the urban North. Further, it was intimately bound up with the extensions of market exchange and the money economy, a development that both expanded the range of artistic expression and that offended artists by subjecting the ineffable qualities of their work to utilitarian calculation. 'Each epoch dreams the one to follow', Benjamin wrote, 'and in dreaming, precipitates its awakening'. The boulevards, arcades, back alleys, hovels, cabarets and cafés of nineteenth century Paris fostered the waking dream of the artist in the city, precipitating a host of heirs. 'It's an old romance, the boho dance', Joni Mitchell sang in the 1970s. 'It hasn't gone to sleep'.

Neo-bohemia and the urban crisis

The classic bohemia, elaborated in Paris and exported abroad, thus took shape against the backdrop of the industrial city. The United States passed England as the world's leading industrial power by the early twentieth century; spared the devastation of the blitz and occupation, it emerged from the dual traumas of Depression and War at mid-century as the undisputed leader of the international industrial economy. New York now towered as the world capital of both the capitalist economy and of modern art, positions for which it previously vied with London and Paris (Guilbaut 1983). The post-war New York bohemia, still centred on Greenwich Village, repeated the conventions of the classic bohemia, nourishing the literary movement of the beats and the fine art innovations of abstract impressionism and pop art. But change was coming, a change that would transform the dynamics of city growth and augur the coming of neo-bohemia.

The long post-war economic expansion, stretching to the early 1970s, glossed an incipient crisis in the American inner city. The automobile, the signature artefact of mass industrial production, opened up the suburban frontier. The suburbs inscribed a new image of domestic security and material prosperity for populations still smarting from the deprivations of the 1930s and 40s (Cohen 2003). Suburban houses were mass produced according to the same logic of product standardization that informed the industrial economy as a whole, and were stocked with the newly abundant and affordable appliances of industrial capitalism's 'golden age' (Aglietta 1979; Bensman and Vidich 1987). Not least among these was the television set, an emblem of the new culture industries and the onset of mass culture now infusing the space of domestic intimacy. The drama of the Civil Rights Movement in the US culminated with a new impetus to suburban expansion – white flight – and in the wake of 1960s urban uprisings by inner-city blacks, the popular perception of 'the race problem' in the US shifted from the Jim Crow South to the urban strongholds of the North (Sugrue 1997).

By the 1970s, these trends had culminated in a full-blown urban crisis throughout the United States. New York City nearly defaulted on its obligations, rescued by a reluctant federal bailout. In 1977 alone, New York suffered a massive blackout, race riots, and a terrifying serial killer, amplifying a general sense that the Big Apple had become 'Fear City' (Mahler 2006). The once-thriving theatre district in Times Square was billed as 'where the underworld meets the elite' in the popular 1933 film musical *42nd Street*, or at least where struggling showgirls met philandering executives. But the elite were staying home – or perhaps trading black tie and tails for trench coat anonymity – as Times Square decayed into a seedy milieu of street-walking prostitutes, flop houses, and pornographic entertainment (Traub 2004). All over the country, downtown commercial districts suffered a similar fate. Once multi-ethnic strongholds of the industrial working class, Brooklyn, the Bronx, and Manhattan's Lower East Side became overwhelmingly black and Latino, now deprived of the industrial jobs that once sustained local populations. Harlem's former lead position in a black cultural renaissance increasingly gave way to 'the tangle of pathologies' attributed to black inner-city populations (Vergara 2013). Similar developments took place in the once thriving black communities of Detroit and Chicago's South Side (Sugrue 1997; Wilson 1987).

The bohemian attachment to the city led artists and aesthetes to weather the urban crisis of the 1970s, even as capital and middle class residents largely abandoned older downtowns. Indeed artists of the era drew on the aesthetic of decay in the elaboration of new popular and high art forms, from punk rock to graffiti art and neo-expressionism (Hoban 1998; Taylor 2006). In a typical pattern, these spectacular subcultural innovations diffused into the domains of popular music, film and fashion, helping to sow the seeds of subsequent new development premised on a restored allure to urban living. Artists and cultural entrepreneurs actively engaged in the adaptive reuse of redundant built environment, transforming the seeming detritus of industrial capitalism into lofts, performance venues, galleries and night-clubs, and the banal artefacts of urban street life into spectacular lifestyle accessories.

Even when the bloom was still firmly on the suburban rose, bohemians never bought in. In Norman Mailer's (1959) formulation, the burbs stood for 'square' domestic security. Suburbanites were coddled by their mothers, they did not dig jazz or smoke reefer, their orgasms were pedestrian and not 'apocalyptic', they were, in sum, 'doomed not to swing'. In the late 1960's, Patti Smith's bohemian dream led her as naturally and as inevitably to New York as it had drawn Lucien to Paris in Balzac's *Lost Illusions*. There she communed with Allen Ginsberg and Andy Warhol, endured a stormy relationship with her bohemian soul-mate Robert Mapplethorpe, and helped to lead a musical revolution near the end of the seventies that illustrates the enduring link between bohemia and popular culture (Smith 2010). In short, commitment to urbanism as a way of life – bohemia's most fundamental attribute – sustained the New York bohemia (and others around the US) through the depths of urban decline.

The bohemian center of gravity in New York shifted from Greenwich Village to SoHo, as well as to the 'wild' Lower East Side. What happened in these downtown locales pre-figures the advent of neo-bohemia and its prominence in the transition to a new style of *post-industrial* urban renewal. 'Their everyday life was a work of genius' wrote Murger of the Latin Quarter pioneers (2004: xxvii), depicting the resourcefulness of (economically) under-resourced bohemians in Paris, while Baudelaire modelled the impulse to spin urban detritus into aesthetic gold. Repeating these conventions, New York's bohemians were masters of adaptive reuse, both materially and symbolically. Andy Warhol took over a loft in the 1960s and dubbed it (ironically) 'the Factory' (Bockris 2003). By the 70s, the leftover spaces of industrial capitalism were in ready supply, and SoHo's shift from light industry to artist colony modelled the unity of performance art, lifestyle innovations and practical necessity that has ever shaped bohemia (Simpson 1981). Adapting the spaces left vacant by industrial capital to their needs, artists contributed to an unprecedented degree their own 'sweat equity' in transforming the urban landscape, often under cover of darkness and flouting New York's zoning ordinances. And while the Parisian bourgeoisie would *never* have wanted to live in a bohemian garret, loft living (once appropriately codified with cultural cachet) would become a lifestyle trend for professionals as the city came back to life (Zukin 1982).

During the 1990s, the new bohemia became increasingly codified across city contexts as a space of post-industrial transition, as the case of Chicago's Wicker Park illustrates. The drama of 'living on the edge', codified in countless bohemian artworks dating to Parisian origins, led residents of Wicker Park and similar neighbourhoods to make a virtue of urban attributes others would deem liabilities, transforming post-industrial grit into a new form of 'edgy' urban glamor (Lloyd 2010: 75–100). 'There's an edge that you get when you're not sure of your personal safety', said one pioneering entrepreneur in Wicker Park. 'There's something exciting about having drug dealers up the street' (Ibid.: 81). But the success of the local art scene was accompanied by the increasing pacification of the neighbourhood's seedier elements, with new residents and new enterprises energizing the neighbourhood economy. A teeming bar scene was now nourished as much by young professionals aiming to take 'a walk on the wild side' as by artists and their ilk, though the artists added essential ambiance for other consumers. This helped to turn the neighbourhood into a nightlife destination, much like New York's Lower East Side, Washington DC's Adams Morgan, and San Francisco's Mission District during this era.

Artists as useful labour

Bohemia, proto or neo, is characterized by symbolic and material amenities specific to the realities of the artistic field in a given era. These amenities include a locally inscribed value system elevating artistic penury to heroic status; a heterogeneous urban environment stimulating artistic sensibilities across genre and expressive media, as well as across divides of class and status; and, on a more banal level, actual places to live, work and display within reach of aspirants long on specific cultural capital but short on hard currency (Lloyd 2004). The relationship between the material and the ideal is constitutive of the modern city, and is starkly dramatized in the spaces forged by those who make the imagination the object of their labour.

Neo-bohemia magnetizes artists and scene-affiliates, united by disposition and competence that align with the requirements of the new urban economy. Artists and young urban professionals share high levels of educational attainment and cultural capital, while encountering to various degrees a precarious occupational field characterized by flexible employment (Menger 1999). They are disposed towards relatively dense urban environments organizing diverse cultural and leisure amenities, from cafés to rock clubs. These are conceived not only as recreational outlets, but also as mechanisms for stimulating individual creativity. Artists must make a living somehow, but they also elevate the self-actualizing dimensions of paid employment, self-consciously trading remuneration for creative expression and/or the opportunity to be in the scene.

Both literally and figuratively, artists and aesthetes *make* the neo-bohemian scene composed of nightspots, cafés, and boutique retail. In many cases, young artists subsidize their aesthetic vocations with employment in the local service sector, as bartenders, waitstaff, baristas or shop clerks, prizing both the flexibility and the visibility these jobs afford. Taking once banal service sector jobs, neo-bohemian aesthetes add value not only via the routine discharge of mundane tasks but through their own honed aesthetic personae, along with the décor and wares imbuing local enterprises with an aura of hipness. As Harvey Molotch (1996) observes, 'artists do even ordinary work differently than others would', (p. 331) and that difference becomes a source of value for local entrepreneurs. Refined aesthetes with Oberlin degrees justify taking jobs once deemed working class by making recourse to 'real', if perhaps non-remunerative, work as a painter, poet, actor, or musician, while also earning high levels of scene visibility along with their tips. The appeal to bohemian legitimacy, with service labour adjunct to loftier ambitions, impacts the assessment of status attached to these jobs, and not only for actual artists. Just as non-union workers in unionized industries benefit from higher wages, non-artist workers in artified sectors enjoy improved status.

Beyond the service sector, artists take other jobs that also draw, to varying degrees, on their specific aesthetic competences and educational pedigree. As Carlo Rotella observes, many artists, from musicians to sculptors are 'good with their hands' (2004). As decades-old structures are rehabbed to meet new requirements in gentrifying districts, local artists find employment as labourers, painting, hanging cabinets, or running wires in new residences and commercial establishments. They sometimes embellish these manual labour activities with their distinct flourishes, as the industrial sculptor Alan Gugel did when he built the tables along the Urbus Orbis walls.

The technical competence acquired in pursuing their own creative ambitions are transposable to lower level positions in the conventional cultural industries, e.g. film, television, and popular music, with artists available as support personal, running wires and operating equipment on film sets, photo-shoots, concerts, and musical recordings. These competencies are particularly valuable in the context of culture 'industry towns' like New York, LA or Nashville (Lloyd 2014).

Moreover, neo-bohemia in both industry and 'off-centre' cities are spaces of apprenticeship, in which skills are honed that may eventually be mined by the higher stakes cultural enterprises, from the film studios of Hollywood to the prestige galleries of Manhattan. Outside of the leading centres of cultural production, artistic aspirants find themselves stopped out beyond a certain level of talent and ambition, with the most talented members of local neo-bohemias magnetized to the profit centres. In this sense, bohemia is like a farm league for the cultural industries, with artists scrambling to subsidize their apprenticeship free of charge to the potential industry beneficiaries (Lloyd 2004).

Frequently keen to mine the aesthetic potential in new technology, neo-bohemian denizens include many with exceptional savvy in digital technology. The Internet over two decades has proven a tool for not only the proliferation but also the aestheticization of information. The web requires constant infusions of arresting content, and designers who learned coding skills to promote their own work and that of their friends may now find themselves useful for more commercial applications. In contrast to the still dominant images of Microsoft millionaires and 'geek chic' Silicon Valley masters of the universe, many of these opportunities are contingent and project-based, earning only modest compensation but rewarding the preference for flexible and creative employment (Neff 2012; Ross 2004). Neo-bohemia attracts small shop enterprises in web design and other tech activities, organizing a thick labour market of skilled practitioners available to mobilize on a just-in-time basis. As with service sector employment, these workers rationalize their diminished earnings, lack of benefits, and job insecurity with recourse to their 'authentic' callings in the conventional art world.

Insofar as it sustains active creative scenes, relatively affordable housing, and adequate employment for artist class reproduction, neo-bohemia also serves as a significant resource for the large-scale culture industries, in publishing, film and television, and musical recording, and also in the restricted fields of the fine art market. When the guilds collapsed in the nineteenth century, bohemia became a space of de facto apprenticeship, where early career artists honed their talents. While university fine arts programs have been on the ascent, now filling this role to a greater degree, bohemia remains a key mechanism for filtering the excess of aspirants to both popular culture creation and fine arts recognition. Long periods of frustration are salved by recourse to the heroic status of starving artists, and by local compensations in the form of status regard and lifestyle perks that include sex, drugs and rock-n-roll.

Off-centre scenes in cities outside the handful of culture industry hubs contain minimal opportunities for compensation, but also correspondingly low barriers to entry. They routinely suffer from brain drain, as the most talented are siphoned off by coastal power centres New York and Los Angeles.

Conclusion: Instutionalizing the new bohemia

The classic bohemia made indelible contributions to both the history of art and the making of the modern city. Still, it received minimal notice in either the sociology of art or in urban studies, and was largely ignored by city planners and policy elites. By the 2000s, the new bohemia was suddenly an object of intense scrutiny, institutionalized as a locus of value in what is now called the 'creative city' (Florida 2004). The creative city discourse promotes an urban economy predicated on 'postmaterialist' enterprises in technology and design, demanding a steady supply of educated, high human capital workers. Theorists like Richard Florida (2002a) and Terry Nichols Clark et al. (2002) argue that local amenities, rather than the capital intensive infrastructure of the industrial economy, now 'drive urban growth', by attracting mobile members of the 'creative class' who prioritize lifestyle in determining where to take their coveted skills. As we saw above, neo-bohemia organizes lifestyle amenities that rise in appeal corresponding to a changing urban demographic. Florida (2002b) goes so far as to depict artists as animate amenities in their own right, constructing a 'bohemian index' to demonstrate that the presence of artists in a region correlates to high tech enterprise and the presence of non-arts, creative workers. He theorizes that artists provide the pull for other creative sorts. Whether this causal ordering prevails at the regional level, in neo-bohemian neighbourhoods the presence of artistically inclined 'early gentrifiers' clearly precedes the arrival of more affluent professionals and intensified investment in entertainment and design enterprises.

Arts advocates, having been routed in the 1990s culture wars attacking the NEA and other funding outlets, sensed an opportunity and have increasingly built appeals for support around the presumptive economic value that artists add to local economies. Chicago's Mayor Richard M. Daly proved far-sighted in the 1990s when he invested resources in promotion of an aesthetic agenda, pining to bring the cultural cachet of Chicago's sister city Paris to the erstwhile gritty industrial metropolis. Today city leaders all over the country have followed his lead, promoting local arts districts and subsidizing artist residence. These trends have produced sporadic benefits for working artists who have suffered from declines in both federal subsidy and private philanthropy, but they also represent a perhaps costly shift from arguments for the arts as a social value in their own right to the arts as an economic catalyst, part of an overall trend in urban governance in which market mechanisms trump other kinds of social framings or policy solutions (Markusen 2006).

The neo-bohemian neighbourhood has today become thoroughly banal, an essential part of any aspiring 'creative city' (essentially, every city, even Detroit). The recipe of adaptive reuse, art galleries, quirky new wave restaurants and boutiques, craft butchers and breweries, etc. is recognizable in cities as regionally diverse as Portland, Austin, Chattanooga, Paducah, Providence and beyond. Moreover, the neo-bohemian aesthetic is now associated with a widely derided social category that also – despite claims to the contrary (Greif et al. 2010) – does not appear to be going anywhere. It is perhaps hard to remember that *hipster* once attached to iconic figures like Dizzy Gilespie, Charlie Parker and Jack Kerouac, and was a term of esteem at least for some. Today it is applied to the expansive class of urban aesthetes who sport a routinized if revolving array of lifestyle signifiers, from American Spirit cigarettes to bushy beards. In the transition from the urban crisis through the maturation phase of the 90s, neo-bohemia still made claims on the tragic heroism of the classic bohemia; in its fully institutionalized phase, pathos has given way to parody in popular representation. The 1999 film *High Fidelity* was filmed in Wicker Park, depicting the new bohemia in its still-transitional phase. Today the satirical television programs *Portlandia* and *Girls*, attracting relatively negligible audiences in the broader national picture but wildly popular with young urban tastemakers, exemplify the full institutionalization of the model.

The mirth disguises the darker side of neo-bohemia. While some fine artists, now trained in elite university settings, have found unprecedented income opportunities providing rarefied interior décor for dot.com millionaires and Wall Street investment bankers, other cultural workers contend with both the standard deprivations of artistic aspiration and the new challenges associated with the digital revolution (Sholette 2011). Moreover, large numbers of educated urbanites find themselves saddled with crushing debt attached to pricey degrees that fail to return hoped-for compensation. In this case, the lifestyle compensations of neo-bohemia become ever more important as salve for economic hardship, providing the opportunity to trade on specific forms of cultural capital – hence the proliferation of hipsters. But as rents and housing prices rebound after the trauma of 2008, the institutionalized neo-bohemia is priced out of their reach, pushing the pioneers to ever more marginal districts and unlikely urban locales. Even formerly hipster-proof cities like Oakland, Philadelphia, or Nashville (a culture industry town associated with the uncoolest cultural products known to mankind) now promote the model.

Neo-bohemia was birthed in the urban crisis of the 1970s, with the lifestyle conventions of the classic bohemia auguring new city spaces that would be increasingly implicated in wide-scale urban restructuring. *Neo-Bohemia*, researched in the 1990s and early 2000s, depicts the generalization of the neo-bohemian model as a site of post-industrial production and new wave consumption, showing the way these dimensions interpenetrate in new place-making projects. In the 2000s, the status of neo-bohemia as an artefact of the neoliberal urban landscape becomes ever more transparent. Widening inequality in the US is inscribed in a precarious city environment, with neo-bohemia an emblem of the new urban class system. This not only divides the educated residents of the city from the increasingly redundant workforce lacking such codified symbolic and cultural capital (as is widely noted), but also stratifies the so-called 'creative class', a point largely neglected in Florida's mostly celebratory account. Far from resolving the classic tensions of bohemian life, as Florida claims, neo-bohemia remains animated by the contradictions of the capitalist economy, today in its globalized and post-materialist variant.

Notes

1 For an exception, see Harvey Warren Zorbaugh's discussion of Towertown in *The Gold Coast and Slum* (Chicago: University of Chicago Press, 1929). The Chicago School method of human ecology, depicting a functionally differentiated city in which discrete community areas form 'a mosaic of little worlds' (p. 40) largely defined by ethnic identity, is outlined in Robert Park, Ernest Burgess and Roderick McKenzie *The City* (Chicago: University of Chicago Press, 1925). The crowning work of the 'first Chicago School', St. Clair Drake and Horace Cayton's *Black Metropolis* (Chicago: University of Chicago Press, 1945), showed the durability of racial segregation against human ecology's 'natural history' of ethnic assimilation and spatial diffusion (invasion/succession). Gerald Suttles' *The Social Order of the Slum* (Chicago: University of Chicago Press 1968) and *The Social Construction of Community* (Chicago: University of Chicago Press 1973), Albert Hunter's *Symbolic Communities* (Chicago: University of Chicago Press, 1974) and William Kornblum's *Blue-Collar Community* (Chicago: University of Chicago Press, 1974) show the durability of the community area approach and the focus on ethnic identity to Chicago

sociology in the postwar decades. For a non-Chicago treatment of the 'urban village' as an insular space of ethnic solidarity (but political ineffectuality) see Herbert Gans, *The Urban Villagers* (New York: Free Press, 1962).
2 Eric Boehlert, 'Chicago, Cutting Edge's New Capital', *Billboard*, August 1993; Margy Rochlin's 'Edgy in Chicago: The Music World Discovers Wicker Park', *New York Times*, March 14, 1993; Jerry Shriver, 'The Windy City's Burst of Bohemia', *USA Today*, Aug 9, 2002.
3 Matthew Jaffe's 'The Best New Place for Media Companies', *Industry Standard*, January 2001.
4 For discussion of modern social structure as virtual, see Anthony Giddens' *The Constitution of Society* (Berkeley: University of California Press, 1984); William H. Sewell (1992) 'A Theory of Structure: Duality, Agency and Transformation', *American Journal of Sociology*, 98 (1):1–29.

References

Abu Lughod, J. (1995) *From Urban Village to East Village*, New York: Wiley-Blackwell.
Aglietta, M. (1979) *A Theory of Capitalist Regulation: The US Experience*, New York: Verso.
Anderson, E. (2000) *The Code of the Street*, New York: Norton.
Barnett, A. (2004) *All-Night Party: The Women of Bohemian Greenwich Village and Harlem*, Chapel Hill, NC: Algonquin Press.
Becker, H. (1982). *Art Worlds*, Berkeley, CA: University of California Press.
Benjamin, W. (1999) 'Paris: Capital of the 19th Century' in *The Arcades Project*, Cambridge MA: Harvard University Press.
Bensman J. and A. Vidich (1987) *American Society: The Welfare State and Beyond*, South Hadley, MA: Bergin and Garvey.
Berman, M. (1982) *All that is Solid Melts into Air: The Experience of Modernity*, New York: Penguin.
Bockris, V. (2003) *Andy Warhol*, New York: DiCapo.
Bourdieu, P. (1992) *Rules of Art*, Palo Alto, CA: Stanford University Press.
—— (1993) *The Field of Cultural Production*, New York: Columbia University Press.
Brown-Saracino, J. (2000) *A Neighborhood That Never Changes*, Chicago: University of Chicago Press.
Castells, M. (1972) *The Urban Question*, Cambridge MA: The MIT Press.
—— (1989) *The Informational City*, Cambridge UK: Blackwell.
Centner, R. (2008) 'Places of Privileged Consumption Practices: Spatial Capital, the Dot-Com Habitus and San Francisco's Internet Boom', *City and Community*, 7(3): 193–223
Clark, T.J. (1984) *The Painting of Modern Life*, New York: Princeton University Press.
Clark, T.N., R. Lloyd, K. Wong and P. Jain (2002) 'Amenities Drive Urban Growth', *Journal of Urban Affairs*, 24(5): 493–515.
Cohen, L. (2003) *A Consumer's Republic: The Politics of Mass Consumption in Postwar America*, New York: Vintage.
Dear, M. (2002) *From Chicago to LA*, Thousand Oaks, CA: Sage.
Deener, A. (2012) *Venice: A Contested Bohemia in Los Angeles*, Berkeley, CA: University of California Press.
Eeckhout, B. (2001) 'The Disneyfication of Times Square: Back to the Future?', *Research in Urban Sociology*, 6: 379–348
Florida, R. (2002a) *The Rise of the Creative Class*, New York: Basic Books.
—— (2002b) 'Bohemia and Economic Geography', *Journal of Economic Geography* 2(1): 55–71.
—— (2004) *Cities and the Creative Class*, New York: Routledge.
Franck, D. (1998) *Bohemian Paris*, New York: Grove Press.
Gluck, M. (2010) *Popular Bohemia*, Cambridge, MA: Harvard University Press.
Gottdeiner, M. (1985) 'Hegemony and Mass Culture: A Semiotic Approach', *American Journal of Sociology*, 80: 1319–1341.
Grana, C. (1964) *Bohemian vs. Bourgeois*, New York: Basic Books.
Greif, M., K. Ross and D. Tortorici (2010) *What Was the Hipster?*, New York: N+1 Inc.
Grodach C. and D. Silver (eds.) (2015) *The Politics of Urban Cultural Policy*, New York: Routledge.
Guilbaut, S. (1983) *How New York Stole the Idea of Modern Art*, Chicago: University of Chicago Press.
Harvey, D. (1973) *Social Justice and the City*, Oxford, UK: Blackwell.
—— (1989) *The Condition of Postmodernity*, Cambridge, UK: Blackwell.
—— (2004) *Paris: Capital of Modernity*, New York: Routledge.
Hebdige, D. (1979) *Subculture: The Meaning of Style*, London: Routledge.

Hesmondhalgh, D. (1996) 'Flexibility, Post-Fordism and the Music Industries', *Media, Culture and Society*, 18(3): 469–488.
Hoban, P. (1998) *Basquait*, New York: Bantam.
Hutton, T. (2008) *The New Economy of the Inner City*, New York: Routledge.
Indergaard, M. (2009) 'What to Make of New York's New Economy? The Politics of a Creative Field', *Urban Studies* 46(5/6): 1063–1093.
Jameson, F. (1991). *Postmodernism, or the Cultural Logic of Late Capitalism*, Durham, NC: Duke University Press.
Judd, D. and S. Fainstein (eds.) (1999) *The Tourist City*, New Haven, CT: Yale University Press.
Kot, G. (2010) *Ripped: How the Wired Generation Revolutionized Music*, New York: Scribner's.
Lefebvre, H. (1974) *The Production of Space*, Cambridge, UK: Blackwell.
Lloyd, R. (2004) 'The Neighborhood in Cultural Production: Material and Symbolic Resources in the New Bohemia', *City and Community*, 3(4): 343–372.
—— (2010) *Neo-Bohemia: Art and Commerce in the Postindustrial City*, New York: Routledge.
—— (2014) 'Differentiating Music City: Legacy, Industry and Scene in Nashville', in A. Barber-Kersoven, V. Kirchberg and R. Kuchar (eds.) *Music City*, Bielefeld, Germany: Transcript Verlag.
Mahler, J. (2006) *Ladies and Gentlemen, the Bronx is Burning: 1977, Baseball, Politics and the Battle for the Soul of a City*, New York: Picador.
Mailer, N. (1959) 'The White Negro', in *Advertisements for Myself*, New York: Putnam.
Markusen, A. (2006) 'Urban Development and the Politics of a Creative Class', *Environment and Planning A*, 38(10): 1921–1940.
Markusen A. and A. Gadwa (2010) 'Arts and Culture in Urban or Regional Planning', *Journal of Planning Education and Research*, 29(3): 379–391.
Massey, D. and M. Denton (1993) *American Apartheid*, Cambridge, MA: Harvard University Press.
Mele, C. (2000) *Selling the Lower East Side*, Minneapolis, MN: University of Minnesota Press.
Menger, P.M. (1999) 'Artistic Labor Markets and Careers', *Annual Review of Sociology*, 25: 541–574.
Mollenkopf, J. and M. Castells (eds.) (1991) *Dual City: Restructuring New York*, Thousand Oaks, CA: Sage.
Molotch, H. (1996) 'LA as Design Product: How Art Works in a Regional Economy', in A. Scott and E. Soja (eds.) *The City: Los Angeles and Urban Theory at the End of the Twentieth Century*, Berkeley, CA: University of California Press
Murger, H. (2004) *The Bohemians of the Latin Quarter*, Philadelphia: University of Pennsylvania Press.
Neff, G. (2012) *Venture Labor*, Cambridge, MA: MIT Press.
Ocejo, R. (2011) 'The Early Gentrifier: Weaving a Nostalgia Narrative on the Lower East Side', *City and Community*, 10 (3): 285–310.
—— (2014) *Upscaling Downtown: From Bowery Saloons to Cocktail Bars in New York City*, New York: Princeton University Press
Park, R., E. Burgess and R. McKenzie (1925) *The City*, Chicago: University of Chicago Press.
Peck, J. (2005) 'Struggling with the Creative Class', *International Journal of Urban and Regional Research*, 29 (4): 740–770.
Peterson, R.A. (2004) 'The Production of Culture Perspective', *Annual Review of Sociology*, 30: 311–334.
Polanyi, K. (1957) *The Great Transformation*, New York: Beacon Press.
Pratt, A. (2008) 'Creative Cities: The Cultural Industries and the Creative Class', *Geografiska Annaler*, 90 (2): 107–117.
Rookmaaker, H.R. (1970) *Modern Art and the Death of a Culture*, London: Intervarsity Press.
Rosaldo, R. (1993) *Culture and Truth*, Boston: Beacon.
Ross, A. (2004) *No-Collar: The Humane Workplace and Its Hidden Costs*, New York: Basic.
Rotella, C. (2004) *Good with Their Hands*, Chicago: University of Chicago Press.
Sassen, S. (2001) *The Global City*, New York: Princeton University Press.
Seigel, J. (1986) *Bohemian Paris*, Baltimore, MD: Johns Hopkins University Press.
Silver, D. and D. Miller (2010) 'Contextualizing the Artistic Dividend', Journal of Urban Affairs, 35 (5): 591–606.
Smith, N. (1996) *The New Urban Frontier*, New York: Routledge.
Scott, A. (2000) *The Cultural Geography of Cities*, Thousand Oaks, CA: Sage.
Scott, A. and E. Soja (eds.) (1996) *The City: Los Angeles and Urban Theory at the End of the Twentieth Century*, Berkeley, CA: University of California Press.
Sholette, G. (2011) *Dark Matter: Art and Politics in the Age of Enterprise Culture*, New York: Pluto Press.
Simpson, C. (1981) *SoHo: The Artist in the City*, Chicago: University of Chicago Press.

Smith, P. (2010) *Just Kids*, New York: Ecco.
Soja, E. (1989) *Postmodern Geographies*, New York: Verso.
Sorkin, M. (ed.) (1992) *Variations on a Theme Park*, New York: Hill and Wang.
Sugrue, T. (1997) *The Origins of the Urban Crisis*, Princeton, NJ: Princeton University Press.
Taylor, M. (ed.) (2006) *The Downtown Book: The New York Art Scene, 1974-1984*, Princeton, NJ: Princeton University Press.
Traub, J. (2004) *The Devil's Playground: A Century of Pleasure and Profit in Times Square*, New York: Random House.
Vergara, C.J. (2013) *Harlem: The Unmaking of a Ghetto*, Chicago: University of Chicago Press.
Wetzsteon, R. (2002) *Republic of Dreams: Greenwich Village, the American Bohemia, 1910-1960*, New York: Simon and Schuster.
Wilson, E. (2000) *Bohemians: The Glamorous Outcasts*, New Brunswick, NJ: Rutgers University Press.
Wilson, W.J. (1987) *The Truly Disadvantaged*, Chicago: University of Chicago Press.
Zukin, S. (1982) *Loft Living*, Baltimore, MD: Johns Hopkins University Press.
—— (1991) *Landscapes of Power*, Berkeley, CA: University of California Press.
—— (1995) *The Cultures of Cities*, London: Blackwell.
—— (2010) *Naked City*, New York: Oxford University Press.

Index

Page numbers in *italics* refer to figures. Page numbers in **bold** refer to tables.

Abbott, Andrew 62, 373
Aboriginal art 247, 252–3, 255
Aboriginal Arts Board of the Australia Council 247
Acord, Sophia Krzys 196, 219–31
acritical reconstruction in strong program 54–62
Act of Federation (1901) 251
actor-network-theory 42–3
Adelaide National Gallery 254
aesthetic capital: approaches to 291–4; in contemporary societies 295–8; as cultural capital 292–4; economy and society 294; fashion modelling field 296–8; globalization and 298–300; as human capital 291–2; introduction 193–7; overview 290–1; at work 295–6
aesthetic disposition and omnivore debate 99–101
aestheticisation of everyday life 12
aesthetic qualities in artwork 163–4, 166, 168
aesthetic refinement 5, 460
aesthetic 'stylization of life' 93
age and omnivores 126–7
agenda in omnivore debate 86–8
age-period-cohort (APC) effects: conceptualising of 121, *123*, 123–4; debate over 121–3, *122*; habitus 116–17, 119–20, *120*; identification problem 119–21, *120*; implications of omnivore debate 125–9; interpretation of the habitus 119–25, *120, 122, 123*; introduction 116–17; theorizing of 121
Album Top 100 charts 151
Alexander, Jeffrey: civil sphere 64–6; iconicity and 61–2; introduction 1; overview 22; performance and strong program 59–61; *see also* strong program (SP) in cultural sociology
algorithmic classificatory techniques 376
algorithmic power and social analytics 385–7
alternative lifestyle choices 94
American Abstract Expressionism 214, 216
Americanisation 80
analytical autonomization of culture 54–5
analytical bracketing 56–7

anti-Bourdieusians 107, 108
anti-Kantian aesthetic 95
anti-patterns in digital sociology 373–7, *375*
Apollinaire, Guillaume 209
appartenance (belonging) 425
appreciation, as key to cultural capital 100, 337–8
Arab Spring 59
Architecture Gothique et Pensée Scolastique (Panofsky) 61–2
Aristotle (Greek philosopher) 338
Arnold, Matthew 5
art criticism 136, 252
art festivals and biennalization 283–6
'art for money' logic 40
artistic autonomy 40, 194, 251, 456
artistic field in TZF: analysis of 442–50; creative autonomy and 445–8, *446, 447, 448*; ethnography of painters 439–41, *442*; integrated perspective 437–9; interactions and networks 448–50; introduction 436–7; locating strategy in 442–4, *444*; useful labour 463–5
artist's lifestyle 93
art world networks 162–5
Art Worlds (Becker) 13, 219, 263
attachment theory 14, 43
attractiveness *see* aesthetic capital
Australian art field 197, 253–7
autochthony 432
autodidacticism 359
autonomy of the cultural field 56, 436
avant-garde art: cultural capital and 209–10; heteronomous factors 210–12; legitimising power in 212–14; overview 207–8; relationships and success of styles 214–15
axes of differentiation 98–9, 417

baby boomers 328, 399
The Bachelor's Ball (Bourdieu) 170–1
Barassi, Veronica 390
Bardon, Geoffrey 247–8

Index

Barnes, Barry 50
Barr, Alfred 211–12, 213
Barry, Andrew 369
Baselitz, Georg 215
Bauhaus school of design 211
'beautiful photographs' quasi-experimental survey 94–6
'beauty effect' 292
beauty myths 293–4
Bearman, Peter 25, 161–73
beauty standards 292–3
Becker, Howard 1, 13, 164–5, 170–1, 195
Beer, David 386
Beljean, Stefan 23, 38–48
Bellavance, Guy 308, 324–36
Benjamin, Walter 7, 13
Bennett, Andy 156
Bennett, Arnold 354
Bennett, Gordon 248, 257
Bennett, Tony 9–10, 21, 25, 197, 247–61
Bentham, Jeremy 236
Benzécri, Jean-Paul 27
bi-dimensional space 97
biennalization of art worlds: art festivals 283–6; as cultural format 278–80; cultural globalization 280–3; globalization and 197; introduction 277–8
Biennial Foundation 280–1
'bildung' process 5, 179
binary codes 57
Birmingham Centre for Contemporary Cultural Studies 7, 10, 13
'bloc-politic' intervention 283
Bloor, David 50, 53
Blue Poles (Pollock) 248
the body and cultural field 338–40
Book-of-the-Month Club (BOMC) 352, 362
Born, Georgina 1
boundary defining 152
boundary making 150, 415–18, **417**
Bourdieu, Pierre: aesthetic disposition 299; axes of differentiation 417; 'beautiful photographs' quasi-experimental survey 94–6; contemporary art 222; cultural capital concept 9, 11, 13; cultural divisions and mass culture 34; cultural engagement and 117–19; cultural sociology 22–3, 30–3, 132–3; disinterestedness 344; domination networks 170–1; dual economic model 271; high/low distinction 409–10; high-status exclusiveness 92–4; 'homology' thesis and 96–9; insights on publishing 264; introduction 1, 3–4, 21–2; *la culture moyenne* concept 351–2, 357–60; lasting influence of 26–7; mastery of the 'code of the codes' 226; omnivore debate 23–4; practice theory 238; relational reasoning 175; reproduction of class through taste theory 384; science and art 163–4; social change theory 117–18; social critique of culture 8–10; studying pioneer artists 207; taste cultures 79; taste theory 91–6, 99–100; transference of learning 319–21; use of quantitative relational methods 25; *see also* cultural sociology; field of cultural production theory; field theory; habitus; omnivore debate; sociology of valuation and evaluation; strong program in cultural sociology
Bourdieusian sociology 104
Bourgeois, Louise 214–15
bourgeois lifestyle 93
Bourriaud, Nicolas 228
Bowness, Alan 203
Boyce, Sonia 225
boyd, danah 368
Brancusi, Constantin 209, 212–13
Breton, André 209
British Cultural Studies (BCS) 3, 7, 51
Brown, Roy 'Chubby' 344
Burrows, Roger 374

calculative mechanisms of differentiation 388
Camic, Charles 39
Canclini, García 109
Canergie Institute's Pittsburgh International 280
capitalism: 'dreamworlds' of modern capitalism 459; 'economic' relations on the eve of 161; fatal isolation inherent in 169; industrial capitalism 461, 462; introduction 3, 4, 6; neoliberal capitalism 281, 283; new spirit of 387, 402; Protestantism *vs.* 144; rise of 169, 234; spatial relations under 267
career paths of highbrow culture 330–1
Carter, David 308, 351–66
Casanova, Pascale 267, 268
Castells, Manuel 456
categorization, defined 385
Central Academy of Fine Arts 441
central art institutions 202–3
Chambon, Jacqueline 265
Chartier, Roger 403
Cheng Yifei 442–3
Chicago School pragmatism 25
China 439–40
China Artists Committee 440
Chin Tao Wu 284
Chong, Phillipa 23, 38–48
circles of recognition theory 203
cityscape/countryside, as a temporal tension 333
Civil Rights Movement 461
civil sphere 64–6
Clark, Terry Nichols 465
Clark, T.J. 10
'Classic' art 332
Class-Specific Analysis (CSA) 181–7, *182*, *183*, **184**, *185*, *186*
Clifford, James 254
Clouds of the City (Weiguang) 445

Club Tenco 67
C Media 390–2
Cobain, Kurt 68
codes and narratives in strong program 56–8
Cohen, Julie 386
cohort and omnivores 128–9
collective conscience 57
comedy/laughter as aesthetic experience: the body and cultural field 338–40; boundary-drawing 345–8; disinterestedness 343–5; introduction 337–8; laughter, as aesthetic battleground 340–3
Commonwealth Art Advisory Board 251
Communist Party 440
comparative research of valuation and evaluation 39
complexity theory 15
conflicted temporalities in Australian art field 253–7
conscientization theory 386
consecrated *vs.* non-consecrated artists 207
constitutivism 55
constructivist structuralism 62, 63
contemporary art: curatorial decision-making 224–7; expert gaze in 221–2; overview 219–20; relational aesthetics in 227–8; training curators 222–4
contemporary artists, how to become: age factor 204; central institutions 202–3; cultural consumption 200; current methods 201–3; gallery exhibitions 203; historical methods 200–1; how to remain 204–5; local institutions 202; recognition and fame 203–4; sociology of culture 199–200
'Contempo-Trad' group 167
contextualistic museum sociology *241*, 241–4
core-periphery model 267–9
corporate aesthetic standards 295–6
Correspondence Analysis (CA) 174–5
cosmopolitanism 34, 85, 90, 281, 333–4, 423
Coulangeon, Philippe 21–2, 26–37
Couldry, Nick 309, 383–95
Crawford, Kate 368
critical sociological thinking 112
Critique of Judgement (Kant) 139
Cubism/Cubist movement 201, 214–16
cultural capital: aesthetic capital as 292–4; appreciation as key to 100, 337–8; appropriation of urban spaces 415; in art reception 195; avant-garde art and 209–10; cosmopolitanism and 423; introduction 9, 11, 13, 21; privilege and distinction in 360; social hierarchies 409
cultural classifications 307–10
cultural consumption 200
cultural democracy 10, 31–2
cultural dissonance: cultural transferability 319–21; individual scale of cultural behaviors 313–14; measuring the singular 314–17; overview 312–13; self-distinction 317–18
cultural divisions and mass culture 34
cultural eclecticism/mingling 318

cultural engagement 117–19, 123
cultural field *see* field of cultural production theory
cultural globalization 280–3
cultural goodwill 358, 422
cultural intermediaries 220
cultural legitimacy 98
cultural legitimacy theory 315
cultural omnivorousness 107
cultural practices in GDA 175–80, **177**, *177*, *178*, **179**, *180*
cultural pragmatics 59–60
cultural production/producers 10, 27, 93; *see also* field of cultural production theory
cultural relativism 32, 92
cultural sociology: Bourdieu, Pierre, and 22–3, 30–3, 132–3; to cultural policies 30–2; field of judgements 139–41, 143–6; field of power 134–5; field theory 135–9, 143; French cultural divisions in 32–3; introduction 132–3; judgement and 139–41; museum sociology as 236–8, *237*; overview 199–200; perception, judgement, and action 141–6; postmodern theory formation in 235–6; post-structuralist cultural sociology 238–9; restricted application 133–4; social aesthetics and 132–3; *see also* sociology of art and culture; strong program (SP) in cultural sociology
cultural trauma 66–8
culture as '*Bildung*' 5
curatorial decision-making 224–7
curator training in contemporary art 222–4
Czech Republic 459

Daly, Richard M. 465
Danto, Arthur 161–5, 168, 221
data visualisations 374–6, 378
Davis, James 153
decivilization process 326
de-colonization 8, 327
deep antinomies in cultural theory **52**
Denmark, omnivorousness 128–9
DeNora, Tia 1, 13–14, 240
deterritorialization 270, 286
Dickens, Luke 390
dieting in aesthetic labour 298
differential highbrow exclusiveness thesis 95
differentiation theory 64
digital sociology: anti-patterns 373–7, *375*; conclusion 377–9; fields of devices 369–73, *370*, *372*; introduction 367–9
digital technology 122
Dijck, José Van 384
DiMaggio, Paul 11, 55
Direction Régionale des Affaires Culturelles (DRAC) 202
'disciplinary museum' concept 239–40
discriminatory effects of aesthetic capital 296

473

Index

disinterestedness idea 340, 343–5
Distinction (Bourdieu): aesthetic disposition in 100, 292; analytical legacy from 424; class culture in 94; cultural lifestyles 176; cultural sociology of 133, 135; dominant social classes 339; examination of laughter in 340, 342; field theory in 139, 141; French cultural sociology after 27–30, 34; high-status consumption patterns and 92–3, 96; introduction 8, 21–2; *la culture moyenne* concept in 351–2; malaise idea in 415–16; objectivation strategy in 425; overview 26–7; personal taste 165–6; relevance for contemporary theory 101; social hierarchies in Latin America 412; study of relationships in 421–3; weakness in 64
domesticity reinforcement 431–2
Donnat, Olivier 12, 309, 396–408
Dreier, Katherine 209
Drysdale, Russell 256
Dubuffet, Jean 213
Duchamp, Marcel 209, 213, 214, 215
Duchamp-Villon, Raymond 209

eclecticism: in highbrow culture 325–7, 333–4; in omnivore debate 77, 82, 84, 87, 399
economic sociology perspectives 43–5
economy of symbolic goods 263–6
Edinburgh Festival Fringe 337
Éditions de Minuit 272
educational attainment: agglomerative clustering 180; cross-comparing variables in 312, 359; cultural capital and 97, 101; cultural participation link with 398; dimensions of space 179; levels of 463; measuring the singular 314, 316; social position as 320
Elias, Norbert 55
Elizabethan era (1558–1603) 339
ELIZA program 142
English feminine middlebrow 356
'enlightened' eclecticism 334
erotic capital 290
Eurocentrism 83, 197
European avant-garde 211
Even-Zohar, Itamar 267
exclusionism 126
exclusive highbows 101
expert gaze in contemporary art 221–2
expressionism 183, 187, 201, 214–16, 462

Facebook's *Social Graph* 378
Fashionable Mind (Fraser) 168
fashion modelling field 296–8
fauvism 201
Featherstone, Mike 22
'feeling'-based discourse in contemporary art 220, 225
feminist theory 293–4
field dynamics 15, 65

The Field of Cultural Production (Bourdieu) 437
field of cultural production theory: civil sphere and 64–6; cultural trauma and 66–8; economic sociology 43–4; iconic power and 68–9; introduction 15, 16; post-structuralism 70
field of judgements 139–41, 143–6
field of power in cultural sociology 134–5
field theory: conflicted temporalities 253–7; core-periphery model with 267–9; modern art field 253; museum sociology 242; overview 135–9, 247–50, *249*; renewal of 250–3, *253*
Fisher, Laura 257–8
Fonds Régionaux d'Art Contemporain (FRAC) 201, 204
formal organization role 44
Fotopoulou, Aristea 390
Foucaultian social theory 51
fractalization of cultural studies 62–4, *63*
France, cultural practices: accessing culture 400–1, **401**; media visibility 404–6, **407–8**; overview 396; print-based material 403; from print to screen culture 401–4; social inertia and generational dynamics 398–400; trends in 396–8; two-phase movement 402–3
Franco-Europeans 328
Frankfurt School 3, 6, 13
Fraser, Kennedy 168–9
Freire, Paolo 386
French-Canadians 328
French cultural sociology 27–30
French homology thesis 111
French literary publishers 264–5
Friedman, Sam 25, 308, 337–50
Fuller, Matthew 367–82
Fyfe, Gordon 233

Galenson, David 204
gallery exhibitions 203
Gans, Herbert J. 319
Gayo, Modesto 23, 25, 104–15
Geertzian thick description 51–2
gender-normative faces 299
General Social Survey (1993) 12, 167
generational dynamics in French cultural practices 398–400
Genovese feudal society 169
geography of contemporary art 165
Geometric Data Analysis (GDA): basic ideas 174–5; Class-Specific Analysis 181–7, *182, 183,* **184, 185, 186**; cultural practices/dispositions and social position 175–80, **177,** *178,* **179,** *180*; hierarchical agglomerative clustering 180–1; introduction 174; Multiple Correspondence Analysis 174–80, **177,** *178,* **179,** *180*
German Association of Museums 232
Gestalt theorists 136–7, 141
Giddens, Anthony 55, 238

474

Gillespie, Tarleton 386–7
Gilroy, Paul 1
Girard, Augustin 30
Github.com 368–73, *370, 372,* 375, *375,* 377–8
globalization: aesthetic capital and 298–300; biennalization of art worlds 197, 280–3; biennalization of art worlds and 197; cultural globalization 280–3; influence of 109; publishing field in globalization era 263–6; *see also* translation in globalization era
global social space 176
Godine, David 265
Goffey, Andrew 367–82
Goffman, Erving 208, 316
Goldberg, Amir 167
Goodenough, Ward 153
'good looks' *see* aesthetic capital
Google Inc. 373, 376
Grana, Cesar 460
Greenberg, Clement 209, 210
Grenfell, Michael 252
Grignon, Claude 28
Gross, Neil 39
GSOH (good sense of humour) 347
Gugel, Alan 464
Guggenheim, Peggy 209, 210

habitus: age-period-cohort (APC) effects 116–17, 119–20, *120*; as class-based cohort effect 124–5; cultural classifications 308; defined 117–18; interpretation of 119–25, *120, 122, 123*; overview 29; petit-bourgeois habitus 360; study of relationships and 421
Hall, Stuart 7
Hardy, Cheryl 252
Heilbron, Johan 267
Heinich, Nathalie 2, 195, 199–206
Helbing, Lorenz 440
Hennion, Antoine 13–14, 29, 43, 208
hermeneutics 3, 6, 57, 62
Hesse, Eva 210
heterogeneity of practices and preferences 318
heteronomous factors in avant-garde art 210–12
Heysen, Hans 256
hierarchical agglomerative clustering 180–1
highbrow culture: as artificially rigidified 28; beauty standards of 293; career paths of 330–1; classification and stratification 331–2; cultural appreciation 86; defined 5; differential highbrow exclusiveness thesis 95; eclecticism in 325–7, 333–4; exclusive highbrows 101; high-status exclusiveness 92–4, 96–8, 109; introduction 4–6, 14; middlebrow culture *vs.* 23, 251, 351; overview 324–5; Quebec study 327–8; snobbish exclusiveness 91, 325, 326, 423; snobbishness thesis 94–5; in sociology of culture 32–3; socio-professional trajectories 328–30; symbolic boundaries by 91; theoretical model of taste 332–5; upper-middle-class individuals 105, 109, 357
high cultural capital (HCC) 341–3, 345–8
higher cultural group 329
higher education (HE) 179
higher managerial group 328–9
higher technical group 329
High Fidelity (film) 466
high/low distinction: boundary making within the middle classes 415–18, **417**; eclecticism and 325–6; introduction 409–12; principles of distinction 334–5; socio-political context 412–15; *see also* highbrow culture; lowbrow culture
high-status exclusiveness 92–4, 96–8, 109
Hoggart, Richard 7
Holla, Sylvia 197, 290–303
Homo Academicus (Bourdieu) 52
homogeneity of multiple cultural situations 321
human capital as aesthetic capital 291–2
Hutter, Michael 40
hybridity idea 109, 114

iconic consciousness/power theory 68–9
iconicity (iconic turn) and strong program 61–2
identification problem in APC effects 119–21, *120*
impressionism 201, 208, 212
Indigenous cultural practices 413
individual cultural 'colour charts' 315
individualization theory 110
individual scale of cultural behaviors 313–14
industrial capitalism 461, 462
infantile femininity 297
Inglis, Alison 252
Institute of Crafts and Fine Arts 441
institutionalization: Biennial Foundation 281; in contemporary curatorial world 223; cultural field/trauma 66; highbrow arts 5; of innovation 211–12; principles of vision and division 56; process of 216; social sciences 109, 111; sociology of art 12; transnational art relations 197; urban tastemakers 466
institutional self-doubt 234–5
instrumentalization of museums 243
Internet culture 405
intra-individual variations in cultural behaviours 317

Janis, Sidney 209
Jelinek, Elfriede 265
judgement and cultural sociology 139–41
Jurt index 264

Kandinsky, Vassily 211, 215
Kantian purity 133
Karademir Hazır, Irmak 23, 25, 77–89
kinship grammar 163
Kirchberg, Volker 196, 232–46

Index

Knorr-Cetina, Karin 39
Knowing Capitalism (Thrift) 10
Kris, Ernst 200
Kuhnian model of the paradigm 53
Kuipers, Giselinde 197, 290–303
'*Kultur*' 5
Kurz, Otto 200

la culture moyenne concept 351–2, 357–60
Lahire, Bernard 22, 307–8, 312–323
Lamont, Michèle 23, 25, 38–48
L'Amour de l'art (Bourdieu) 320
language of variable 52–3
La Passion musicale (Hennion) 208
l'art moyen concept 351, 359
'l'art pour l'art' logic 40
Lash, Scott 22
Latin America 109–12, 113–14, 412–18
laughter 340–3; *see also* comedy/laughter as aesthetic experience
Law, John 370, 373
Lazarsfeldian language of variable 52–3
Leavis, F.R. 10, 356
Leavis, Q.D. 356
Lee, Stewart 342
legitimising power in avant-garde art 212–14
Lemieux, Cyril 250, 257
Lena, Jennifer C. 24–5, 149–60
levels of cultural capital (LCC) 340, 345
lifestyles in the city of Porto, Portugal: in early 2000s 423–31, *424*, **425, 426, 427, 428, 429, 430**; introduction 421; social reproduction of 431–3; study of relationships 421–3
Lindsay, Daryl 254
linearity in multivariate regression models 180
Linux on Github.com 371–2, *372*
Lippard, Lucy 210
Lizardo, Omar 24, 29, 90–103
Lloyd, Richard 310, 454–69
local art institutions 202
Loft Living (Zukin) 455
The Logic of Practice (Bourdieu) 416
'lone genius' stereotype 195
Long, Elizabeth 362
Love, Courtney 68
Love of Art (Bourdieu, Darbel) 195
The Love of Art (Bourdieu, Darbel, Schnapper) 30
lowbrow culture: as artificially rigidified 28; beauty standards of 293; eclecticism 82; in sociology of culture 32–3; symbolic boundaries by 91
lower-middle-class individuals 357
lower secondary education (LSE) 179
Lynes, Russell 357

Macdonald, Dwight 356
Macdonald, Sharon 233
McDonaldisation of society 11, 243

McIntyre, Michael 337, 341, 346
Mackenzie, Adrian 309, 367–82
McLean, Ian 256
Mafias as systems 55
Mailer, Norman 462
Maistre, Roy de 252
malaise idea 415–16
male facial beauty 299–300
Malevich, Kazimir 211, 215
Malraux, André 273
Manning, Bernard 344, 347
Mapplethorpe, Robert 462
Marres, Noortje 368
M50 art cluster 440
Martin, Bénédicte 204
Martin, John Levi 14, 15, 24, 25, 132–48
Marx, Karl 13, 134
Marxism 8–9, 138, 437
Mary-Douglas-Filter of sameness 142
Mason, Rhiannon 240
mass culture: consumption of 105; cultural norms and 28; debate over quality 78, 79; domestic intimacy and 461; increased consumption of 105; middle class link to 110–11, 356–7; sociology of culture 32, 34
Mbuti people 153
meanings and relations in culture 168–70
Melucci, Alberto 386
members of formal organizations 44–5
Méndez, María Luisa 309, 409–20
Menger, Pierre-Michel 38
mental structures 64
Merriman, Ben 24, 132–48
Mertonian sociology of science 51, 53–4
meso-level theory of social organization 65
methodological nationalism 262–3
Michaels, Eric 254
Microsoft Kinect game controller 376
middlebrow culture: cultural distinctions 352–3; highbrow culture *vs.* 23, 251, 351; historical middlebrow 353–6; *la culture moyenne* concept 351–2, 357–60; link mass culture 110–11; mass cultural debate 356–7; new/old middlebrow 361–3; omnivores and 360–1; overview 351–2; personalism 355; *see also* working class cultures
Mills, C. Wright 172, 232
Mills, Richard 367–82
modalities in data 175, *178*
modernism 353
Moffatt, Tracey 257
Molotch, Harvey 463
Money, Morals and Manners: The Culture of the French and the American Upper-Middle Class (Lamont) 410, 411
Morphy, Howard 254, 257–8
Moulin, Raymonde 211
multilingual translation software 330

476

Multiple Correspondence Analysis (MCA): in Geometric Data Analysis 174–80, **177, *178, 179, 180*;** publishing variables 264–5; space of lifestyles based on **426,** 426–7, 426–9, **427,** *428, 429*; statistical technique of 422
multivariate regression models 119, 127, 180
Murakami, Takashi 41
Murger, Henri 459–60
museum sociology: as cultural sociology 236–8, *237*; importance of 234–6; introduction 232–3; museums as heterotopic/non-heterotopic 239–40; overview 233–4; as post-structuralist cultural sociology 238–9; praxeological museum sociology 237; textualistic/contextualistic analysis *241*, 241–4
musical genre: concluding thoughts 157; genre, overview 149–50; overview 149; relational methods in sociological approach 152–6; in sociological research 151–2; study of categorization 156–7
music in omnivore debate 82–3, 85, 118, 127
Myers, Fred 254, 258
Myth of the Western Man (White Man's Burden) (Pollock) 248, *249*

National Arts Acquisition Fund 251
National Gallery of Australia 248, 251, 253
National Gallery of Victoria 254
nation-states 87, 262, 327
The Native Leisure Class (Colloredo-Mansfeld) 413
neo-bohemia: Chicago's Wicker Park case study 457–8; early twentieth century 460–1; institutionalizing 465–6; introduction 454–5; overview 456–7; urban crisis 461–3; urban sociology and sociology of art 455–6
Neo-Expressionism 215
neoliberal capitalism 281, 283
neoliberalism 406, 409, 411, 412, 415
neo-positivist perspective in omnivore debate 27–8
networks and culture: art world 162–5; introduction 161–2; meanings and relations 168–70; summary 172; taste and differentiation 165–7; transformations in 170–2
New Museology 235
new screen culture 309, 401–4
The New Spirit of Capitalism (Boltanski, Chiapello) 10
Noble, Kim 343
Nolan, Sydney 256
non-arbitrary intuition 138
Norfolk's 'old' families 171–2
Novak, Barbara 251

Obama, Barack 59
objectivism 62, 422
object-relational aesthetic for sociology 229
O'Dougherty, Maureen 415

omnivore debate: aesthetic disposition and 99–101; agenda in 86–8; age-period-cohort implications of 125–9; Bourdieu's 'homology' thesis and 96–9; Bourdieu's theory of taste 91–6; conclusion 101; as dominant paradigm 90–1; eclecticism in 77, 82, 84, 87; introduction 77–8; measurement issues 80–5, **81, 82, 84**; music in 82–3, 85, 167; neo-positivist perspective in 27–8; omnivorousness, defined 80; overview 23–4, 78–80; shifts in emphasis over 85–6; snobbish exclusiveness 91, 325, 326, 423
omnivorousness: conclusions 113–14; critiques of 108–9; eclecticism and 399; empirical tools and methodology 107–8; evaluation of research outcomes 112–13; growth in 122–3; Latin American experience 109–12, 113–14; middlebrow book culture 360–1; as strategy of social distinction 326; theory of 106–7; understanding of 104–5
One City One Book programs 362
Onus, Lin 256
operationalization of openness 84
'ordinariness' of culture 1–2
organizational research perspectives 43–5

PageRank algorithm 378
Panofsky, Erwin 61–2
Papunya Tula collective 247
Parisian gallery exhibitions 203
Parisian prototype 458–60
Parsons, Betty 209
Pascalian Meditations (Bourdieu) 31
Passeron, Jean-Claude 28
Peist, Nuria 196, 207–18
perceived similarities basis 331
Pereira, Virgílio Borges 310, 421–35
performance and strong program 59–61
period effects and omnivores 127–8
Peterson, Richard: omnivore debate 77, 82, 104, 108, 324, 325; overview 12, 23; social and cultural reality 55
petit-bourgeois habitus 360
phenomenological reduction 56–7
Piaget's notion of genetic structures 125
Picasso, Pablo 212, 214
plurality of dispositions and competences 313–14
plus-size models 297
Poell, Thomas 389
Poetics (Aristotle) 338
Poliak, Claude F. 211
Pollock, Jackson 209–10, 213, 215–16, 248
polysystem theory 267
pop-rock music 150–1
Postill, John 389–90
postmodern theory formation in cultural sociology 235–6
post-retina perception 142

Index

post-structuralism 57, 70, 238–9
poverty of bohemians 460
practice theory 238, 421
praxeological museum sociology 237
The Presentation of Self in Everyday Life (Goffman) 316
Presses de la Cité (POL) 272
Preston, Margaret 252, 255
primary artistic specialization 333
Principal Component Analysis (PCA) 175, 182
publisher strategies 270–3
publishing field in globalization era 263–6
PullRequest 371, 376
punk music 155
PushEvents 371, 376

Q methodology model 298–9
quantitative analysis of omnivore debate 83–4

Real Democracy Now 390
Reform and Opening-up Policy (1978) 439
relational aesthetics in contemporary art 227–8
Relational Class Analysis (RCA) 167
relational 'grounded aesthetic' 220
relational methods in sociological approach 152–6
relational sociology 14–15
Relations into Rhetorics (Bearman) 171
relative autonomy of culture 54–6
relative frequencies for dispositional variables **189–90**
the Renaissance 200
Reproduction (Bourdieu) 411
reproduction of class through taste theory 384
Rethinking Comparative Cultural Sociology (Lamont, Thevenot) 410
Reussner, Eva 242
Rogoff, Irit 221
Romanticism 194
Roose, Henk 14, 25, 174–90
Rose, Gillian 374–5
Rosenberg, Paul 212, 214
Rosenquist, James 213–14
Rotella, Carlo 464
Rule, Alix 25, 161–73
Ruppert, Evelyn 370

Santoro, Marco 22–3, 49–76
Sapiro, Gisèle 197, 262–76
Sassatelli, Monica 197, 277–89
Savage, Mike 370, 373
Schaeffer, Jean-Marie 229
scheme of perception 318
Schweitzer, Thomas 153
science and technology studies (STS) 383
scientific visualisation 374–5
Seaver, Richard 269
second-order aesthetic judgments 140–1, 345

self-concepts in evaluation 41–2
self-distinction in cultural dissonance 317–18
self-fulfilling prophecy 291
self-segregation process 414
semiotic theory 56, 57
sense-making by social groups 152
September 11, 2001, attacks 59
settler-colonial societies 251
Sewell, William 393
sexual attractiveness 290
Sharples, Stuart 367–82
short-term material gains 44
Simmel, Georg 1, 6
'simple' art 332
Singular Value Decomposition (SVD) 176
Skiles, Sara 24, 90–103
Smith, Adam 316
Smith, Grace Cossington 252
snobbish exclusiveness 91, 325, 326, 423
social analytics 309; algorithmic power and 385–7; core problems 387–92; group gaming 389–90; importance of studying 309; individual tactics 388–9; organizational scale of 390–2; overview 383–5
social change, theory 117–18
social inertia in French cultural practices 398–400
social position in GDA 175–80, **177**, *178*, *179*, *180*
social space and judgement 139–40
Society of Artists 251
sociocultural classification 149
sociology of art and culture: Bourdieu's lasting influence on 8–10, 26–7, 132–3; formalization of contextual critique 11–12; high culture 4–6; introduction 193–7; overview 1–4; relational and aesthetic understanding of 12–15; relational approaches to 24–5; romantic-inspired critique 6–8; *see also* cultural sociology
sociology of cultural production 39
sociology of perception 141–2
sociology of science 50–1, 53–4
sociology of valuation and evaluation (SVE): classical model of 39–40; criticisms and revisions 40–2; introduction 38–9; new perspectives on 43–5; self-concepts in evaluation 41–2; subject-object relation 42–3
socio-occupational category 312
socio-professional trajectories 328–30
Solaroli, Marco 22–3, 49–76
Sonnett, John 151
strong program (SP) in cultural sociology: acritical reconstruction 54–62; codes and narratives 56–8; field of cultural production theory 64–70; fractalization of cultural studies 62–4, *63*; iconicity and 61–2; introduction 1, 49–50; naming of 50–4, **52**; performance and 59–61; relative autonomy of culture 54–6

structural hermeneutics 62, 63
structuralism: constructivist structuralism 62, 63; French structuralism 56; genetic structuralism 58; literary studies on 10; post-structuralism 57, 70, 238–9; Saussurean structuralism 58; social network structuralism 25
structuration theory 238
sub-clouds in CSAs *182,* 182–3, *183,* **184,** *185,* 185–7, **186**
subject-object relation 42–3
suicide 66–8
surrealism 183, 185, 187, 201, 214
Survey of Public Participation in the Arts (SPPA) 151
Swaan, Abram de 267
symbolic interactionism 438
symbolic revolution in sociology 50
Szeemann, Harald 210, 280

Tàpies, Antoni 213
taste: cultures of 78–80, 165–7; theory of 91–6, 99–100
Tawadros, Gilane 225
Taylor, Charles 5
'temporally dominant' occupations 97
Tenco, Luigi 67
textualistic museum sociology *241,* 241–4
theoretical model of taste 332–5
Theorizing Museums (Macdonald, Fyfe) 233
theory of *habitus see* habitus
Theory of the Leisure Class (Veblen) 165
thick descriptions 51–2
Thomas, Nicholas 248, 252, 255
Thompson, John 264
tolerance and omnivorousness 106, 126
totemism 61
training curators in contemporary art 222–4
transference of learning 319–21
transgression in art 99, 194, 201
translation in globalization era: deterritorialization and 270; introduction 262–3; national to global book market 266–74; publisher strategies 270–3; publishing field 263–6; reflection and 273–4
Tufte, Edward 374
Twelfth Night (Shakespeare) 339
Twitter platform 389
two-fold generational trend 402

Universal Exhibitions (Expo) 278, 279
upper-middle-class individuals 105, 109, 357

urban crisis and neo-bohemia 461–3
urban spaces and cultural capital 415
Urry, John 22

Valéry, Paul 226
Van Doosselaere, Quentin 169
variables and categories of variables 174–7, **177,** 179
Venice Biennale 278–86
Venice Lido 285
Villon, Jacques 209

Warde, Alan 21, 23–4, 25, 28–9, 77–89
Warhol, Andy 161
Weber, Max 1, 422
Weiguang (painter) 441–5, *444, 446, 447, 448*
Western Desert Art Movement 247
White, Harrison 55
Whitehead, A.N. 373
Wicker Park case study 457–8
Wickham, Hadley 374
Wildenstein, Georges 212
Williams, Raymond 4–6
Wolff, Janet 1
Woolf, Virginia 356
working class cultures: anti-Kantian working class aesthetic 100; binary oppositions linked to 139; bodily reactions of 340; bohemian aesthetic 460; consumption of popular culture 91, 105; dissonant elements in 313, 315–16; education of 355; gentrification and 458; high status *vs.* 92, 94–5; introduction 7; legitimate culture awareness 182; lifestyles of 431; as mass culture 157; as new petite bourgeoisie 359; omnivorousness of 109, 110; racial demographics 462; refined aesthetics of 463; taste and hegemony of 258; TV watching in 33, 87
World festival of Black Arts (1966) 281
World Trade Organisation 440
World War I 170
World War II 106, 125, 271, 283, 399
Wortman, Ana 414–15

yoga in aesthetic labour 298
Yunupingu, Galarrwuy 256

Zhang, Chao 310, 436–53
Zolberg, Vera 235, 244
Zukin, Sharon 455